PD 12-17-86

WITHDRAWAL

DICTIONARY OF
DATA COMMUNICATIONS

Second Edition

DICTIONARY OF
DATA COMMUNICATIONS

Second Edition

CHARLES J. SIPPL

A HALSTED PRESS BOOK

JOHN WILEY & SONS
NEW YORK   TORONTO

First published in Great Britain 1985 by The Macmillan Press Ltd.

Published in the U.S.A. by Halsted Press,
a Division of John Wiley & Sons Inc., New York

First edition published 1976

ISBN 0-470-20182-7

Printed in Great Britain

A

A AND NOT B gate: A binary logic coincidence (twoinput) circuit used to complete the logic operations of A AND NOT B, i.e., result is true only if statement A is true and statement B is false.

abend: Contraction for abnormal end. An unexpected halt in a program due to a logical error, data that the program cannot process (such as division by zero, or the addition of a number and a letter), or other similar bugs. Abend, also referred to as "bomb," is used as both a noun and a verb.

abnormal end: See abend.

abnormal statement: An element of FORTRAN IV which specifies that certain function subroutines must be called every time they are referred to. Abnormal declarations enable the compiler to optimize the calling of other (nonabnormal) function subroutines.

abort: A procedure to terminate execution of a program when an irrecoverable error, mistake, or malfunction occurs.

absolute alarm: An audio or visual alarm set off by the detection of a variable which has exceeded high or low limit conditions.

absolute coding: Coding in the numeric language form acceptable to the computer arithmetic and control unit.

absolute delay: The real-time interval from the transmission to reception of a signal over a circuit. Also called transmission time or circuit delay.

absolute instruction: A particular computer instruction which specifies completely a specific computer operation and is capable of absolute instruction causing the execution of that operation.

absolute loader: A routine that uses absolute coding to load a program into memory at fixed numerical addresses.

absolute-value device: A transducer that produces an output signal equal in magnitude to the input signal but always of one polarity.

absolute-value sign: A sign using the symbol as follows @abv indicating that the absolute value of a number is to be taken, i.e., the value of the number irrespective of the sign.

abstract symbol: 1. (ISO) A symbol whose meaning and use have not been determined by a general agreement but have to be defined for each application of the symbol. 2. In optical character recognition, a symbol whose form does not suggest its meaning and use. These should be defined for each specific set of applications.

ac bias (magnetic tape) : The alternating current, usually of a frequency several times higher than the highest signal frequency, that is fed to a record head in addition to the signal current. AC bias serves to linearize the recording process and is used universally in analog recording. Generally, a large ac bias is necessary to achieve maximum long-wavelength output and linearity, but a lower value of bias is required to obtain maximum short-wavelength output.

ac communication: Light, radio waves, sound, and data-transmission signals in alternating-current (ac) form are all described in terms of frequencies. In these various transmission forms the instantaneous amplitude of the signal at a given point in time varies rapidly, in a manner similar to the displacement of a string on a musical instrument. The rate of this fluctuation is referred to as the frequency and

1

is expressed in terms of cycles per second or hertz. The term "hertz" (abbreviated Hz) has by international agreement replaced the earlier term "cycles per second," thus honoring one of the early pioneers in the field of electrical transmission, Heinrich Hertz.

ac coupled flip-flop: A flip-flop made up of electronic circuits in which the active elements, either tubes or transistors, are coupled with capacitors.

accelerating anode: An electrode given a high positive potential to speed up the moving electrons in the beam of a writing tube.

acceleration time: The time between the interpretation of instructions to read or write on tape and the transfer of information to or from the tape into storage, or from storage into tape, as the case may be.

accentuation: A technique for emphasizing particular bands in an audio-amplifier.

accept ion: An atom in a doped semiconductor crystal which accepts an electron or gives up a hole.

acceptance cone: The imaginary cone at the end of an optic fibre whose half-angle is the angle of incidence of the core/cladding interface. Any beam of light entering the fibre that is inside this cone (at an angle less than the half-angle) will reflect and be propagated inside the fibre to the other end.

accepted signal call: Using data channel signalling transmission, a signal sent in a backward direction indicating a specific call can be completed.

acceptor circuit: Tuned circuit responding to a signal of one specific frequency.

access arm: A part of a disc storage unit that is used to hold one or more reading and writing heads.

access mode: Used in COBOL programming, the name of a technique used to obtain a record from, or to place a recording in a file contained in a storage device.

access scan: A procedure for receiving data from files by searching each data item until the desired one is obtained.

access time: 1. The time interval between the instant at which a control unit initiates a call for data and the instant delivery of the data is completed. Access time equals latency plus transfer time. 2. The time interval between the instant at which data are requested to be stored and the instant at which storage is started.

accounting checks: Refers to accuracy controls on input data that are based on such accounting principles as control totals, cross totals, or hash totals.

accounting function: The system of keeping track of machine usage and recording it.

accounting machine: 1. A machine that prepares accounting records. 2. A machine that reads data from external storage media, such as cards or tapes, and automatically produces accounting records or tabulations, usually on continuous forms.

accumulator register: The part of the arithmetic unit in which the results of an operation remain, and into which numbers are brought to and from storage.

accumulator shift instruction: A comter instruction which causes the contents of an accumulator register to shift to the left or right.

accuracy: 1. (ISO) A qualitative assessment of freedom from error, a high assessment corresponding to a small error. 3. (ISO) A quantitative measure of the magnitude of error, preferably expressed as a function of the relative error, a high value of this measure corresponding to a small error. Contrast with precision.

accuracy control character: A specific character designed with a function to control a given block of data, to indicate if the data.are in error, to indicate if they are to be disregarded or whether they can or cannot be represented on a particular device.

ACH: See automated clearinghouse.

ACK: See acknowledgment.

ACK (ARPANET): A short transmission between interface message processors (IMP) to indicate the successful reception of a message segment (referred to as a packet).

ACK0, ACK1, Affirmative, Acknowledgment: These replies indicate the previous block was accepted without error and the receiver is ready to accept the next block. Alternating these replies assists in the error-recovery procedures ACK1 is the response to the first transmission and successive odd blocks. ACK0 is the response to the second block and all even-numbered blocks, and is the positive response to selection (multipoint) or line bid (point-to-point) (BSC).

acknowledgment (ACK): In data transmission, data are usually grouped into fixed-length blocks. After transmitting a data block, the transmitting terminal sends a check character, calculated from the content of the data block. The receiving terminal compares this character with its own computation of the check character. If the values agree, then no transmission error has occurred and the receiving terminal sends the control character ACK to the transmitter to signify that no error occurred. The transmitting terminal then continues transmission of another data block. If the check characters differ, then an error occurred and the receiver sends a NAK (negative acknowledgment) character to indicate an error to the transmitter. The transmitter then repeats transmission of the same data block and the process repeats. Same as acknowledge character.

acknowledgment character (AKC): A specific character for communications control transmitted in an affirmative response from a message-receiving program. Most often used as an accuracy control character transmitted after a string of characters has been received with proper vertical and longitudinal redundancy check characters.

acoustic coupler: A device which provides the facility to transmit and receive messages using the standard telephone handset as the coupling to the line.

acoustic delay line: A device used to store digital information cyclically in the form of sound pulses. It consists of (1) a piezoelectric transmitter which converts normal digital information into an acoustic wave, (2) the acoustic transmission path, and (3) a piezoelectric receiving unit which converts the acoustic data back into its original form.

acoustic-sonic storage: Sonic delay line storage types and techniques.

acquisition time: The interval time a sample-hold circuit needs to acquire the input signal to within the stated accuracy. In conservative specifications, it includes the settling time of the output amplifier. In some cases a signal can be acquired fully (and the circuit switched into hold) before the output has settled. The output of the sample-hold is not meaningful until it has settled.

action line: When a cathode ray storage tube is operating in a serial mode, it refers to that line of the raster which is used during the active period.

action spot: The spot of the raster on the face of an electrostatic storage tube which stores the digits and holds a charge.

activate key (button): A primary switch on various control panels which when pressed or initiated will cause the first part or step of a program cycle or a procedure to begin. Same as start key (button or switch) and initiate button.

active element: 1. An element in use or in its excited state, i.e., a tube, transistor or device which is on or alive rather than off, dead or in a ground state. 2. A file, record, or routine which is being used contacted, or referred to. Computing components are active when they are directed by the control unit.

active file: A file which is being used in which entries or references are made on a current basis.

active intruder: An intruder who can record messages to hear later, send his own messages on the desired communication channel, or alter legitimate messages before they reach the intended receiver.

active master file: A specific master file that contains items relatively active or frequently used as contrasted to static or reference items.

active master item: The most active items on a master file by usage data.

active network: A electronic network which contains any sources of power other than signal inputs.

active state: The state of an interrupt level that is the result of the central processor starting to process an interrupt condition.

active transducer: Any transducer in which the applied power controls or modulates locally supplied power, which becomes the transmitted signal, as in a modulator, radio transmitter.

activity level: The value taken by a structural variable in an intermediate or final solution to a programming problem.

actuating signal: A particular input pulse in the control circuitry of computers.

ADAPSO: An association of U.S. and Canadian data processing service organizations.

add-on: Hardware attached to a computer to increase performance or memory.

add/subtract time: The time required to perform an addition or subtraction, exclusive of the time required to obtain the quantities from storage and put the sum or difference back into storage.

adaptive tree walk protocol: A limited contention protocol with stations organized in a binary tree.

add time (in microseconds): The time required to acquire from memory and execute one fixed-point add instruction using all features such as overlapped memory banks, instruction look-ahead and parallel execution.

add-to-storage concept: The process in which the sum of two numbers is calculated by adding the first number to the second and the results replace the second number (all in one operation).

adder-subtracter: (ISO) A device that acts as an adder or subtracter depending upon the control signal received. The adder-subtracter may be constructed so as to yield the sum and the difference at the same time.

addition without carry: A logical operation applied to two operands that produce a result relying on the bit patterns of the operands and according to rules for each bit position.

additional character: A character which is neither a letter nor a number, but which is usually a punctuation mark, %, —, #; i.e., a member of a specialized alphabet. A specific meaning is assigned to this character to use it to convey special information.

additional label processing: The use of the input/output label system to verify or create a standard label and then, by user's routines, verify or insert additional information in the optional field of the standard label.

address: 1. A character or group of characters that identifies a register, a particular part of storage, or some other data source or destination. 2. To refer to a device or an item of data by its address.

address, control data, and checksum fields: Four kinds of fields in bit oriented protocol frames.

address comparator: A device used to verify that the correct address is being read. The comparison is made between the address being read and the specified address.

address conversion: The translation of the relative or symbolic addresses into absolute addresses by use of a computer, or manually.

address field: The portion of an instruction word that contains the operand address.

address format: 1. The arrangement of the address parts of an instruction. The expression "plus-one" is frequently used to indicate that one of the addresses specifies the location of the next instruction to be executed. Such as one-plus-one, two-plus-one, threeplus-one, four-plus-one. 2. The arrangement of the parts of a single address such as those required for identifying channel, module, track, etc. in a disk system.

address generation: A number or symbol generated by instructions in a program and used as an address part, i.e., a generated address.

address immediate instruction: Specific instructions designed to contain the value of the operand in its address part rather than the address of the operand. It is used most often for incrementing a count by a fixed amount or masking a partial-word field of data, or for testing a special character for identical characteristics with the immediate character in the instruction.

address register: A register in a computer where an address is stored.

addressing level: A determination of the number of steps of indirect address which have been applied to a particular program. First level is direct addressing, i.e., the address part of the instruction word has the address of the operand in storage. In second level addressing (indirect), the address part of the instruction word gives the storage location where the address of the operand may be found.

adjacent channel: The channel whose frequency band is adjacent to that of the reference channel.

adjacent channel interference: The presence of undesirable energy in a channel caused by one or both sidebands of modulated carrier channels in close frequency proximity extending from one into another through electrostatic or electromagnetic coupling.

adjoint system: A method of computation based on the reciprocal relation between a system of ordinary linear differential equations and its adjoint.

administrative data processing: An expression usually meaning business data processing such as the recording, classifying, or summarizing of transactions, activities, events, etc. Usually of a financial nature, or the collection, retrieval, or control of such items.

admissible mark: Specific rules or conventions determine which marks, symbols, and numerals or characters are permitted in various areas of computing for all installations and for various languages.

advanced data communication control procedure (ADCCP): A version of synchronous data link control (SDLC) modified by the American National Standards Institute (ANSI).

Advanced Research Project Agency Network (ARPANET): The long-haul communications network maintained by an agency (ARPA) of the United States Federal Government. ARPANET is one of America's most important networks because it links not only government computers, but research computers at virtually every major American university as well.

AFIPS: An organization of computer related societies. Its members include: The Association for Computer Machinery; The

Institute of Electrical and Electronic Engineers Computer Group; Simulation Councils, Inc.; American Society for Information Science. Its affiliates include: American Institute of Certified Public Accountants; American Statistical Association; Association for Computational Linguistics; Society for Industrial and Applied Mathematics; Society for Information Display. Headquarters-Montvale, N.J.

agenda: The set of control-language statements used to prescribe a solution path or run procedures; an ordered list of the major operations constituting a procedure for a solution or computer run. (This usage corresponds roughly to the ordinary "agenda" for a meeting.)

agent: A process whose job is to provide a uniform interface to all hosts in a network operating system.

air movement data: Data presented most often with digital displays relating to flight plan information such as present position, future position, estimated time of arrival, etc.

alertor: A device which consists of a small box connected to a large floor pad laced with with wires. It sounds an alarm when the operator has not operated the pad for a specific period of time.

algebraic language: An algorithmic language many of whose statements are structured to resemble the structure of algebraic expression, e.g., ALGOL, FORTRAN.

ALGOL (ALGOrithmic Language): An international algebraic procedural language for a computer programming system.

ALGOL-Dartmouth: The Dartmouth ALGOL is essentially ALGOL-60 with only a few restrictions and extensions made to allow operation within the BASIC system timesharing framework.

algoristic: A step-by-step methodology; an exact answer; a systematic computation guaranteeing accurate solution.

algorithm: A prescribed set of well-defined rules or processes for the solution of a problem in a finite number of steps, for example, a full statement of an arithmetic procedure for evaluating sin x to a stated precision. Contrast with heuristic.

algorithm translation: A specific, effective, essentially computational method for obtaining a translation from one language to another.

algorithmic language (computer): An arithmetic language by which numerical procedures may be precisely presented to a computer in a standard form. The language is intended not only as a means of directly presenting any numerical procedure to any suitable computer for which a compiler exists, but also as a means of communicating numerical procedures among individuals. The language itself is the result of international cooperation to obtain a standardized algorithmic language. The International Algebraic Language is the forerunner of ALGOL.

algorithmic routine: That specific routine which directs the computer in a program to solve a problem in a finite or specified number of steps, but not rely on a trial and error procedure. The solution and solution method are exact and must always reach the specific answer.

alias: 1. An alternate label. For example, a label and one or more aliases may be used to refer to the same data element or point in a computer program. 2. An alternate name for a member of a partitioned data set. 3. In pulse code modulation telecommunication links, a spurious signal resulting from beats between the signal frequencies and the sampling frequency.

alien tones: Frequencies, harmonics and other products introduced in sound reproduction because of nonlinearity in some part of the transmission path.

alignment: See boundary alignment.

allocate storage: To assign storage locations or areas of storage for specific routines, portions of routines, constants, working storage, data, etc.

allocation: 1. The allotment, apportionment, or placement of data, items, storage, subjects, etc. See storage allocation, dynamic storage allocation. 2. The assignments of frequencies by the FCC for various communications uses (e.g., television, radio, land-mobile defense, microwave, etc.) to achieve a fair division of the available spectrum and to minimize interference among users.

allocation hardware resources (time-sharing): User and system programs and data reside in auxiliary random access storage devices with possible back up copies on a slower serial access medium such as magnetic tape. The system executive decides where information is to be stored and maintains necessary directories to permit retrieval. Programs and data must be brought into main memory for execution or modification. The executive assigns and transfers information between auxiliary and main memory as needed. The executive must also manage the assignment of serial access devices and peripheral devices to prevent conflict between concurrent user programs seeking use of peripheral devices. For example, a line printer cannot be used concurrently by several users.

allocation of data sets: The process of assigning auxiliary storage space to a data set. See also dynamic data set definition.

alphabet: 1. An ordered set of all the letters and associated marks used in a language. 2. An ordered set of symbols used in a language, for example, the Morse code alphabet, the 128 characters of the ASCII alphabet.

alphabetic code: A code according to which data is represented using an alphabetic character set.

alphabetic shift: A control for selecting the alphbetic character set in an alphameric keyboard printer.

alphabetic string: A character string consisting solely of letters from the same alphabet.

alphabetic word: 1. A word consisting solely of letters. 2. A word consisting of characters from the same alphabet.

alphameric: See alphanumeric.

alphanumeric: 1. A contraction of alphabetic-numeric. 2. Pertaining to a character set that contains letters, numerals, and special characters.

alphanumeric character: A single graphic selected from the coded character set consisting of the 26 letters of the English alphabet, the decimal digits 0 through 9, and other selected symbols up to a total of 64, which can be represented by a 6-bit binary code.

alphanumeric code: The code of the set of characters used, i.e., both letters and digits. See alphanumeric characters.

alphanumeric instruction: The name given to instructions which can be used equally well with alphabetic or numeric kinds of fields of data.

alterable memory: A user-accessible storage medium.

alteration: Any change involving an erasure or rewriting of a check.

alteration gate: Same as gate, OR.

alteration switch: A manual switch on the computer console or a program-simulated switch that can be set on or off to control coded machine instructions.

alternate buffering: A system of double buffering where the control words of input/output instructions are altered by program to direct data to a buffer area other than the buffer area currently being used for processing.

alternate path retry (APR): A facility that allows an input/output (I/O) operation that has developed to be retried on another channel assigned to the device peerforming the I/O operation. It also provides the capability to establish other paths to an on-line or offline device.

alternate route: A secondary communication path used to reach a destination if the primary path is unavailable.

Alternate Standard (AS) keyboard: See DVORAK keyboard.

alternate unit: A symbolic unit that is substituted for another symbolic mission unit as a result of programmer direction.

alternating current (AC):   An electric current which is constantly varying in amplitude and periodically reversing direction.

alternating mode: Applications programs where the program writes to the terminal, the program reads from the terminal, the program writes to the terminal, and so forth; as in half-duplex lines operation.

alternation: A technique which uses two or more input/output units in an attempt to speed up input and output operations. Examples might be: two to four card readers which serve the same control or input buffer, accepting data from each reader in sequence. Double feed hoppers and duo reading stations are examples of this type of alternation which is designed for increased reading volume.

alternative box: An element in a flow chart to signify where a decision is made. There is one entry and two or more exits. Synonymous with decision box, comparison box.

alternative denial: A logical operation which is applied to at least two operands and will produce a result according to the bit pattern of the operand.

ALU: Arithmetic and logic unit. See arithmetic unit.

AM: See amplitude modulation.

ambient conditions: The conditions of the surrounding medium (pressure, noise, etc.).

ambient noise: Acoustic noise existing in a room or other location.

ambiguity: Inherent error caused by multiple bit changes at code transition positions, which is eliminated by various scanning techniques.

ambiguity error: A gross error, usually transient, occurring in the reading of digits of numbers and imprecise synchronism which causes changes in different digit positions, such as in analog-to-digital conversion. Guard signals can aid in avoiding such errors.

Amble's method: An analog computer term relating to a connection devised by O. Amble, such that the output of an integrator contributes through an adder to its own input to solve differential equations of a specific form.

AMD: Abbreviation for Air Movement Data. Data presented most often with digital displays relating to flight-plan information, such as, present position, future position, estimated time of arrival, etc.

amendment file: To update a master file, this pertains to a collection of change records used in batch processing.

amendment record: A record whose function is to change information in a corresponding master record.

amendment tape: A length of paper tape or magnetic tape containing a transaction file.

American National Standard control characters: Control characters defined by American National Standard FORTRAN, ANSI X3.9-1966. Synonymous with ASCII control character, FORTRAN control character.

American National Standard labels: Magnetic tape labels that conform to the conventions established by the American

National Standards Institute. Synonymous with ASCII label. Abbreviated ANL.

American National Standards Institute (ANSI): Organizes committees formed of computer users, manufacturers, etc., in order to develop and publish industry standards, e.g., ANSI FORTRAN, ANSI Standard Code for Periodical Identification, etc. Formerly American Standards Association (ASA) and, prior to that, United States of America Standards Institute (USASI).

American Standards Association: The former name of the American National Standards Institute.

ammeter: A device for measuring the intensity of electrical currents.

amortization: The periodic allocation or charge of the costs of computer equipment over its useful life. The amortization period is a particularly important issue in the computer field because of the high cost of comuputer equipment and the rapid rate of technological change.

ampere-hour (AH) capacity: A measurement of a storage battery's ability to furnish a steady current for a specified period. Battery capacity is usually specified on an 8-hour rate or a 10-hour rate, e.g., a 1000 AH battery can be expected to supply a steady 100 amps for 10 hours.

amplification: 1. The strengthening of a weak signal. Contrasts with attenuation. 2. The ratio between the output signal power and the input signal power of a device. 3. Gain.

amplifier: A device that, by enabling a received wave to control a local source of power, is capable of delivering an enlarged reproduction of the essential characteristics of the wave. amplifier (CATV): A device used to boost the strength of an electronic signal. Amplifiers are spaced at intervals throughout a cable system to rebuild the strength of television signals which weaken as they pass through the cable network.

amplifier servo: An amplifier, used as part of a servomechanism, that supplies power to the electrical input terminals of a mechanical actuator.

amplitude: The size or magnitude of a voltage or current waveform.

amplitude distortion: Distortion in which the peaks of signal are altered.

amplitude modulation (AM): 1. Variation of a carrier signal's strength (amplitude), as a function of an information signal. 2. Specific modulation during which the amplitude of the carrier wave is varied in accordance with the instant value of the modulating signal.

amplitude ratio: The ratio of peak height of an output signal to the peak height of a related input signal.

amplitude selection: A summation of one or more variables and a constant resulting in a sudden change in rate or level at the output of a computing element as the sum changes sign.

amplitude vs frequency distortion: That distortion in a transmission system caused by the non-uniform attenuation or gain of the system with respect to frequency under specified conditions.

analog assignment of variables: Consists of deciding which quantities on the computer will represent which variables in the problem. The user must know the mathematical laws controlling the variables in the problem, as well as the laws controlling the currents, voltages, and reactances in the computer. He then matches those quantities which are analogous to each other; i.e., quantities which obey the same mathematical laws. For example, water pressure can be analogous to voltage, while flow rate can be analogous to current.

analog channel: A channel on which the information transmitted can take any value between the limits defined by the channel. Voice-grade channels are analog channels.

analog computer: 1. A computer that represents variables by physical analogies. It is any computer that solves problems by translating physical conditions (flow, temperature, pressure, angular position, or voltage) into related mechanical or electrical quantities and uses mechanical or electrical-equivalent circuits as an analog for the physical phenomenon being investigated. Generally, it is a computer that uses an analog for each variable and produces analogs as output. Thus, an analog computer measures continuously, whereas a digital computer counts discretely. 2. A computer where electrical signals are amplitude modulated suppressed carrier signals and where the absolute value of a computer variable is represented by the amplitude of the carrier. The sign of a computer variable is represented by the phase (0 to 180 degrees) of the carrier, relative to the reference ac signal.

analog computer dc: An analog computer in which computer variables are represented by the instantaneous values of voltages.

analog conditioning/equalization: The analog signal loses strength as it travels along the transmission circuit. The loss is proportional to frequency. Likewise phase shift occurs also as a function of frequency. Attenuation and phase shift are components of distortion which can be compensated for by adding complementary filters. When the filters are added to the physical plant, the process is called conditioning. When provided within the modem enclosure, it is called equalization. For leased lines fixed or manually adjustable conditioning or equalization suffices. When switched circuits are employed, automatic equalization is a convenience.

analog control reset: The reset control shorts all of the integrating capacitors, and sets all of the motordriven controls to the selected starting values or restores all values so that another run may be made.

analog data: Data represented in a continuous form, as contrasted with digital data represented in a discrete (discontinuous) form. Analog data are usually represented by means of physical variables, such as voltage, resistance, and rotation.

analog data channel: A one-way path for data signals which includes a voice-frequency channel and an associated data modulator and demodulator.

analog differentiation: It is possible to solve problems involving differentiation without being able to perform this operation explicitly. The answer is contained in the mathematical properties of integraldifferential equations. If a certain equation is true, then it remains true if all terms are differentiated, or if all terms are integrated. Furthermore, solutions developed from the differentiated or integrated equation may be used to solve the original equation. One procedure, then, is to perform successive integrations on the equation to be solved until there are no more derivatives present.

analog differentiation implicit: A procedure, which is frequently utilized with the analog computer, and performs a function implicitly. For example, if the output of a circuit is equal to twice the input, then the input must be one-half of the output. Or, if the output is the square of the input, then the input must be the square root of the output. Similarly, if the output of a circuit is the integral of the input, then the input must be the derivative of the output.

analog/digital adapters: When circuits designed for voice communication are used for data transmission, there must be a transformation between the domains. The adapter between the terminal and the transmission line provides modulation and demodulation. The name "modem" is a contraction of this functional description.

analog-digital-analog converter system: This is a system that performs fast, real-time data conversions between analog and digital computers.

analog feedback: Obtained by means of a resistor from output to input. An important property of this type of amplifier is that if a suitable capacitor is used in the feedback path instead of a resistor, the output will be the integral of the input. Conversely, the input will be the derivative of the output. Hence, the operations of the calculus can be performed, giving the machine great computational power.

analog function generator: A network of biased diodes which can produce a non-linear relationship between the input and output voltages of the network. Nonlinear functions can also be generated by means of potentiometers with specially built resistance elements. Another class of function generator uses an electro-mechanical device which consists of a motor-driven pointer that follows an arbitrary curve prepared in the form of a graph. A servo motor causes the pointer to move back and forth across the curve in accordance with the value of the independent variable (the "X" coordinate).

analog hold button: Causes the solution to be temporarily suspended, permitting the user to study the various quantities. The integrating capacitors are disconnected during hold so that they will neither charge nor discharge.

analog hold mode: The computing ac action is stopped and all variables are held at the value they had when the computation was interrupted. Same as freeze or interrupt mode.

analog-input expander: A unit which permits an analog input system to be configured around the data adapter unit.

analog-input module: In some systems, devices which convert analog input signals from process instrumentation into a digit code for transmission to the computer.

analog-input scanner: A device which upon command will connect a sensor to measuring equipment and cause the generation of a digit count value which can be read by the computer.

analog integration: Performed by means

of an operational amplifier with a capacitor instead of a resistor in the feedback loop. Analog integration is considerably faster than digital integration and is one of the principal justifications for selection of analog computing for reasons of speed.

analog line driver (ALD): Analog computers that use a power amplifier to permit the driving of several or many loads to thus develop an output channel which drives many more input channels.

analog multiplexer: Concerns a specific relay multiplexer designed to provide low-level differential switching of analog input signals to allow use of a common amplifier and analog-to-digital converter. High-level signals can be handled also. Typically, up to 100,000 points-per-second switching rate can be attained, with a maximum 50,000 point-per-second repetition rate (per point).

analog multiplexer/R: A device used to provide low level differential switching of analog input signals. High level signals can also be handled.

analog multiplexer/S: A solid state, high level single-ended (HLSE) multiplexer.

analog multiplier unit: A specific unit with two input variables and one output variable which is proportional to the product of the input variables. If the unit can perform more than one multiplication it is called a servo multiplier.

analog network: A circuit or circuits that represent(s) physical variables in such a manner as to permit the expression and solution of mathematical relationships between the variables, or to permit the solution directly by electric or electronic means.

analog recording: A method of recording in which some characteristics of the record current, such as amplitude or frequency, are varied continuously in a manner analogous to the time variations of the original signal.

analog representation: A representation that has discrete values but is continuously variable.

analog servomultiplier: An analog computer device or unit which has a position control and a capability of multiplying each of several different variables by a single variable, represented by analog voltages. The multiplier is used as an input signal to a mechanism that turns shafts.

analog start control: Pressing the start control begins the problem and is equivalent to the instant of $t = 0$.

analog stop control: The stop control terminates the solution, enabling the final values to be observed.

analog-to-digital conversion (ADC):   The conversion of analog signals from a voltage level to digital information by an analog-to-digital converter (ADC). Such converters are complex enough so that if multiple sources of analog signals are to be converted, they share the use of one ADC. The switching is accomplished by a multiplexer.

analog-to-digital converter: A coder; a sampling device which produces a digital output from an analog input conveying the same information.

analog-to-digital sensing: Physical measurements must be monitored and quantified with greater speed and accuracy than ever before. The collection of analog data and its conversion for presentation to the digital processor-controller is the function of the analog input features.

analog transmission: Transmission of a continuously variable signal as opposed to a discretely variable signal, such as digital data. Examples of analog signals are voice calls over the telephone network, facsimile transmission, and electrocardiogram information. See digital signal.

analysis block: A relocatable part of the computer storage in which program testing or statistical data are stored which can later utilized to analyze the performance of the system. During program testing there be may be an analysis block for each transaction in the system, and when the trans-

action leaves the system this block is dumped into a file or tape.

analysis mode: A mode of operation in which special programs monitor the performance of the system for subsequent analysis. Program testing data or statistical data may be recording automatically when the system is running in the analysis mode.

analysis, queuing: The study of the nature and time concerning the discrete units necessary to move through channels; e.g., the time and length of queues at service centers of grocery check-out stands, harbors, airports, etc. Queuing analysis is employed to determine lengths of lines and order, time, discipline of service.

analyst: An individual who defines problems and develops algorithms and procedures for their solution.

analytic relationship: The relationship which exists between concepts and their corresponding terms, by their definition and inherent scope of meaing.

analytical engine: An early edition of a generalpurpose mechanical digital computer.

analytical statistics: Enable one to draw statistical inferences about the characteristics of the entire statistical population of data from a small sample.

analyzer: A computer routine whose purpose is to analyze a program written for the same or a different computer. This analysis may consist of summarizing instruction references to storage and tracing sequence of jumps.

analyzer, digital differential: An incremental differential analyzer, usually electronic. Synonymous with DDA.

AND: A logical operator which has the property such that if X and Y are two logic variables, then the function "X AND Y" is defined by the following table: The AND operator is usually represented in electrical notation by a centered dot "·", and in FORTRAN programming notation by an asterisk "—" within a Boolean expression.

X	Y	X *AND* Y
0	0	0
0	1	0
1	0	0
1	1	1

AND element: One of the basic logic elements (gates or operators) which has at least two binary input signals and a single binary output signal. The answer or variable which represents the output signal is the conjunction (set theory) of the variables represented by the input signals. In set theory, the output is 1 only when all input signals represent 1.

AND negative gate: Same as gate, NAND. See gates.

AND operation: A logical operation applied to two operands which will produce an outcome depending on the bit patterns of the operands and according to rules for each bit position. For example, p = 110110, q = 011010, then r = 010010.

AND operator: 1. A logical operator that has the property that if P is a statement and Q is a statement, then P AND Q are true if both statements are true, false if either is false or both are false. Truth is normally expressed by the value 1, falsity by 0. The AND operator is often represented by a centered dot (P · Q), by no sign (PQ), by an inverted "u" or logical product symbol (P ∩ Q), or by the letter "X" or multiplication symbol (P × Q). Note that the letters AND are capitalized to differentiate between the logical operator and the word and in common usage. 2. The logical operation that makes use of the AND operator or logical product.

AND gate: A signal circuit with two or more input wires; the output wire gives a signal only if all input wires receive coincident signals.

angle modulation: Specific modulation in which the phase angle of the sine wave carrier is varied according to the intelligence-bearing signal.

angstrom (Å): A specific measurement of length equal to 10^{-8} centimeters, most often used to express wavelengths of visible light, for example, 7500 angstroms for the color red.

annunciator: A visual or audible signaling device, operated by relays, that indicates conditions of associated circuits.

ANSI: See American National Standards Institute.

answer lamp: Telephone switchboard lamp that lights when a connecting plug is inserted into a calling jack, goes out when the called telephone answers, and lights when the call is completed.

answerback: Terminal response to remote control signals.

answerback, voice (VAB): This refers to an audio response unit which can link a computer system to a telephone network to provide voice responses to inquiries made from telephone-type terminals. The audio response is composed from a vocabulary prerecorded in a digital-coded voice or a disk-storage device.

answering: A procedure by which a called party completes a connection (for switched lines).

answering time: The time which elapses between the appearance of a signal and the response made to it.

antenna: A metal structure or wire which picks up or transmits electromagnetic energy through space.

antenna farm: An area of land occupied by or reserved for transmitting and receiving antennae.

antenna feed: The transmission line which delivers power to an antenna.

antenna loop: A flat coil of wire which serves both as antenna and as part of the input resonant circuit of a receiver.

anticipated carry adder: A parallel adder

in which each stage is capable of looking back at all addend and augend bits of less significant stages and deciding whether the less significant bits provide a "0" or "1" carry-in. Having determined the carry-in it combines with its own addend and augend to give the sum for that bit or stage. Also called fast adder or look ahead carry adder.

anticipation mode: A specific type of reading of binary bits visually on various cathode-ray tubes. Usually one binary digit is represented by a line while the other binary digit is represented by the absence of a line.

anticoincidence circuit: A specific logic element which operates with binary digits and is designed to provide input signals according to specific rules; i.e., one digit is obtained as output only if two different input signals are received.

anticoincidence operation: A logical operator which has the property that if P and Q are two statements, then the statement P—Q, where the — is the exclusive OR operator, is true if either P or Q, but not both are true, and false if P and Q are both false or both true, according to the following table, wherein the figure 1 signifies a binary digit or truth. Note that the exclusive OR is the same as the inclusive OR, except that in the case with both inputs true it yields no output; i.e., P—Q is true if P or Q are true, but not both. Primarily used in compare operations.

P	Q	PQ	
0	0	0	(even)
0	0	0	(odd)
1	0	1	(odd)
1	1	0	(even)

anticoincidence unit: A binary logic coincidence circuit for completing the logic operation of Ex exclusive-OR, i.e., the result is true when A is true and B is false or when A is false and B is true and the result is false when A and B are both true or when A and B are both false. Same as difference gate, nonequivalence, gate, distance gate, diversity gate, addwithout carry gate, exjunction gate, non-equality gate, symmetric difference gate, partial sum gate, and modulo-two sum gate.

anti-siphoning: FCC rules which prevent cable systems from "siphoning off" programming for pay cable channels that otherwise would be seen on conventional broadcast TV. "Anti-siphoning" rules state that only movies no older than three years and sports events not ordinarily seen on television can be cablecast.

aperture: 1. (ISO) One or more adjacent characters in a mask that cause retention of the corresponding characters in the controlled pattern. 2. An opening in a data medium or device such as a card or magnetic core: e.g., the aperture in an aperture card combining a microfilm with a punched card or a multiple aperture core. 3. A part of a mask that permits retention of the corresponding portions of data.

aperture core, multiple: A specific magnetic core with multiple holes through which wires can pass to thus create more than one magnetic closed path, i.e., used in nondestructive reading.

aperture plate: A small region of perforated ferromagnetic material with the magnetic properties of a storage core.

APL: A programming language. A problem solving language designed for use at remote terminals; it offers special capabilities for handling arrays and for performing mathematical functions.

apparent power: The product of the root-mean-square value of the current and the root-mean-square value of the voltage.

application: The system or problem to which a computer is applied. Reference is often made to an application as being either of the computational type, wherein arithmetic computations predominate, or of the data processing type, wherein data handling operations predominate.

application-oriented language: A problem-oriented language whose statements contain or resemble the terminology of the user, e.g., a report program generator.

applications programs: A program written to accomplish a specific user task (such as payroll) as opposed to a supervisory, general purpose, or utility program.

approver: A program for protocol verification which mechanically generates all states reachable from a given initial state and checks the validity of user defined conditions in each state.

approximation, successive: 1. Relates to an analogto-digital conversion procedure in which increasingly larger or smaller known voltages are compared with the unknown voltage and an equality decision made in each interaction alternately forms the binary representation of the analog value. 2. A computational methodology utilized for solving individual or sets of equations or inequalities which are resistant to simple solution because of complexity. A trial value is assigned and the equation solved; the result is used to make a better "guess" of the unknown value until a trial value matches its solved value within a predetermined tolerance level.

arbitrary sequence computer: A computer in which each instruction determines explicitly the location of the next instruction to be executed.

archival standards: Standards set by the U.S. Bureau of Standards to assure permanence of microfilm images.

area: A specific section of storage set aside for some particular purpose or use in data processing.

area exchange: A defined area, served by a communications common carrier, within which the carrier furnishes service at the exchange rate and under the regulations applicable in the area as prescribed in the carrier's filed tariffs.

area numbering plan (ANP):   The unique scheme of uniform numbers (area codes) assigned to geographical locations served by the national switched telephone network.

area search: The examination of a large group of documents to select those which pertain to one group or category.

argument: An independent variable, e.g., in looking up a quantity in a table, the number, or any of the numbers, that identifies the location of the desired value.

argument error: The error caused when there is a difference between the true and actual value of an argument and the value used for the computation.

arithmetical instruction: Specifies an arithmetic operation upon data, e.g., addition or multiplication. Arithmetical instructions form a subset of the machine instruction set to be considered separately from logical instructions.

arithmetical operation, binary: An arithmetical operation with operands and results represented in binary notation.

arithmetic and logic unit: A phrase often used to describe the central processor in which basic arithmetic and logic operations are developed.

arithmetic check: An operation performed by the computer to reveal any failure in an arithmetic operation. Can also be used to ascertain whether the capacity of a register has been exceeded after an operation.

arithmetic expression: A conditional assembly expression that is a combination of arithmetic terms, arithmetic operators, and paired parentheses.

arithmetic operation: Any of the fundamental operations of arithmetic, for example, the binary operations of addition, subtraction, multiplication, and division, and the monadic operations of negation and absolute value.

arithmetic operator: 1. In assembler programming, an operator that can be used in an absolute or relocatable expression, or in an arithmetic expression to indicate the actions to be performed on the terms in the expression. The arithmetic operators allowed are: +, -, —, *.

arithmetic overflow: 1. With respect to an arithmetic operation, the generation of a quantity beyond the capacity of the register or location which is to receive the result; overcapacity; the information contained in an item of information which is in excess of a given amount. 2. The portion of data that exceeds the capacity of the allocated unit of storage. 3. Overflow occurs when attempts are made to write longer fields into a field location of a specific length; a 12digit product will overflow a 10-digit accumulator.

arithmetic point: The point is a true character in positional notation and can be expressed or implied. It separates the integral part of the number or expression from the fractional part using a decimal or binary point. The position of the point is programmed in the logic section of the computer usually falling between the zero and the minus-one power of the base and/or is implied to be at the right end of the integer. Same as base point or radix point.

arithmetic register: The particular register in a computer that holds operands for certain operations.

arithmetic relation: Two arithmetic expressions separated by a relational operator.

arithmetic shift: 1. A shift that does not affect the sign position. 2. A shift that is equivalent to the multiplication of a number by positive or negative integral power of the radix.

arithmetic statement, FORTRAN: Arithmetic statements are of the form $Y = E$, where Y is a variable of any allowed form and E is a meaningful sequence of variables, functions, and arithmetic operators; e.g., $Y = R + SIN(T) + Q/Z$. The equals sign denotes that Y is to be put equal to the result of the arithmetic operations and function evaluations. The character of the variable to the left of the equals sign determines whether the result is stored in fixed- or floating-point form. However, mixing of fixed- and floating-point variables is not permissible except as arguments of functions. However, floating-point expressions may contain subscripts (always fixed) and

fixed-point exponents. Floating-point exponents should not be appended to a fixed-point variable.

arithmetic subroutines: (FORTRAN) Includes subroutines such as sine, cosine, log, $\log_{10}$, exponent, tangent, arc tangent, and square root .

arithmetic term: A term that can be used only in an arithmetic expression.

arithmetic trap mask: The bit, in the program status doubleword, that indicates whether (if 1) or not (if 0) the fixed-point arithmetic trap is in effect.

arithmetic unit: That portion of the hardware of an automatic computer where arithmetic and logical operations are performed.

armed interrupt: Interrupts may be armed or disarmed. An armed interrupt accepts and holds the interruption signal. A disarmed interrupt ignores the signal. An armed interrupt may be enabled or disabled. An interrupt signal for an enabled condition causes certain hardware processing to occur. A disabled interrupt is held waiting for enablement.

armed state: The state of an interrupt level wherein it can accept and remember an interrupt input signal.

Armstrong oscillator: An oscillator in which feedback is achieved through coupled plate and grid circuit coils.

ARPA: Advanced Research Project Agency.

ARPA network (ARPANET) operation: The communications network or communications subnet is composed of interface message processors (IMP) and terminal IMPS (TIP) connected in a distributed fashion by 50,000 baud synchronous wide band circuits. The IMPS are Honeywell DDP 516s with 16,000 words of memory which act as interfaces for host computer systems and as store-andforward nodes in the network. A host is connected to an IMP and thus to the communications subnet by a channel, and if the host is very distant from the IMP, it can connect via a synchronous communications line using block control procedures. The latter method is appealing in that it eliminates the requirement of locating the IMP, a component of the communications subnet beside the host computer that wishes to connect to it. Presently each IMP can interface from one to four host computers to the network.

ARPA network control program (NCP): The software interface between host and IMP. It is responsible for initiating connections, regulating traffic flow, and realizing network protocols between all communicating processes. The NCP resides in the host computer, thus making the host an integral part of the communications network for communications to and from the host. The NCP is closely related to the supervisor of the host system and is difficult and time consuming to implement for even first rate systems personnel.

ARPA network elements and operation: Each of the netted computers (hosts) is connected to an Interface Message Processor (IMP) which transmits messages between its own host(s) and other hosts. There is frequently no direct communication circuit between two hosts that wish to communicate; in these cases intermediate IMPs act as store-and-forward message switches. The IMPs regularly exchange information that allows each IMP to adapt its message routing to the conditions of its local section of the network and to report network performance and malfunctions to a Network Control Center. This also permits message tracing so that network operation can be studied in detail, and allows network reconfiguration without reprogramming each IMP. Terminal IMPs (TIPs), each of which consists of an IMP and a Multi-Line Controller, permit the direct attachment to the network (without an intervening host) of up to 63 dissimilar terminal devices per TIP.

ARPA network messages: User messages of up to 8000 bits are sent through the network between destination sites within 1/2 second (including the time for acknowledgement signaling back from the destination to the originating host). Although traffic levels have been increasing dramatically in the ARPA network as of late, the aggregate utilization of the network's communication bandwidth is still nowhere near its maximum capacity.

ARPA packet switching: Host-to-host messages are passed from the sending host to its IMP, where they are broken into packets (thus the term "packet switching" used in describing the ARPANET) and relayed to their destination by the network of IMPs using store-andforward techniques. Packet routing is adaptive to the conditions of the network considering failures and loading characteristics and, in general, the several packets of a single message may follow different routes. The destination IMP will reassemble the message and deliver it to the proper host. The overhead of dynamic routing should be compared to the advantages gained over techniques where a route is chosen for communicating between two processes on the basis of communication facilities loading and then not dynamically altered for the duration of the connection.

array: 1. An arrangement of elements in one or more dimensions. 2. In assembler programming, a series of one or more values represented by a SET symbol.

arrival rate: An average number of jobs requested per time unit.

artificial cognition: The optical sensing of a displayed character in which the machine or equipment selects from its memory the shape of the character that is closest to the character being displayed.

artificial intelligence: 1. Research and study in methods for the development of a machine that can improve its own operations. The development or capability of a machine that can proceed or perform functions that are concerned with human intelligence as learning, adapting, reasoning, self-correction, automatic improvement. 2. The study of computer and related techniques to supplement the intellectual capabilities of man. As man has invented and used tools to increase his physical powers, he now is beginning to use artificial intelligence to increase his mental powers. In a more restricted sense, the study of techniques for more effective use of digital computers by improved programming techniques.

artificial language: A language based on a set of prescribed rules that are established prior to its usage.

artificial line: Repeated network units which have collectively some or all of the transmission properties of a line.

artificial load: 1. A device (e.g., a resistor) in which the output power can be absorbed. An artificial load is used for simulating conditions of operation for test purposes. 2. To effect the finding, and transfer to storage of a program or set of programs without execution to determine that all relevant specifications and components exist in the proper form in the library.

ASA control characters: See American National Standard control characters.

ASCII: A contraction for "American Standard Code for Information Interchange." This proposed standard defines the codes for a character set to be used for information interchange between equipments of different manufacturers and is the standard for digital communications over telephone lines.

aspect ratio: The 4:3 ratio of picture width to height in CRT.

assemble: To perform some or all of the following functions. 1. Translation of symbolic operation codes into machine codes. 2. Allocation of storage to the extent at least of assigning storage locations to successive instructions. 3. Computation of absolute or relocatable addresses from symbolic

addresses. 4. Insertion of library routines. 5. Generation of sequences of symbolic instructions by the insertion of specific parameters into macro instructions.

assemble-and-go: An operation technique in which there are no stops between the assembling, loading, and execution of a computer program.

assembler: A computer program which operates on symbolic input data to produce data machine instructions by carrying out functions such as translation of symbolic operation codes into computer operating instructions, assigning locations in storage for successive instructions, or computation of absolute addresses from symbolic addresses. An assembler generally translates input symbolic codes into machine instructions item for item, and produces as output the same number of instructions or constants which were defined in the input symbolic codes.

assembler directive command: A command that provides the programmer with the ability to generate data words and values based on specific conditions at assembly time. The instruction operation codes are assigned mnemonics which describe the hardware function of each instruction.

assembler directives: The symbolic assembler directives control or direct the assembly processor just as operation codes control or direct the central computer. These directives are represented by mnemonics.

assembler language: A source language that includes symbolic machine language statements in which there is a one-to-one correspondence with the instruction formats and data formats of the computer.

assembly: The output of an assembler.

assembly time: The time at which an assembler translates the symbolic machine language statements into their object code form (machine instructions).

assembly language coding: Assembly languages are used to avoid coding directly into machine code; mnemonics are used for both the command instructions and the operands, and it is usually not necessary to label the address for every instruction. In an instruction such as, ADD Y, Y is a mnemonic for a location. Assembly programs generate in a one-to-one fashion a set of machine-coded instructions as contrasted to a compiler, or macro language wherein one compiler instruction can generate many machine instructions, such as FORTRAN, COBOL, etc.

assembly language listing: A binary output program of the compiler that is optional at compile time. The listing contains the symbolic instructions equivalent to the binary code output of the compiler. This assembly language output listing is useful as a debugging aid. By including certain pseudo operation codes in "in-line" assembly language, the assembly language output can be assembled by the assembler if output is obtained on either cards, paper tape, or magnetic tape. This will allow modification of programs at the assembly-language level.

assembly language processor: A language processor that accepts words, statements, and phrases to produce machine instructions. It is more than an assembly program because it has compiler powers. The macro-assembler permits segmentation of a large program so that positions may be tested separately. It also provides extensive program analysis to aid in debugging.

assembly line balancing: A specialized program allowing production control management to plan the most efficient and profitable man-work element relationship in an assembly-line operation.

assembly list: A printed list which is the by-product of an assembly procedure. It lists in logical instruction sequence all details of a routine showing the coded and symbolic notation next to the actual notation established by the assembly procedure. This listing is useful in the debugging of a routine.

assembly output language: A symbolic assembly language listing of the binary object program; output of the compiler is optional at compile time. The listing contains the symbolic instructions equivalent to the binary code output from the compiler. This assembly language output listing is useful as a debugging aid. By including certain pseudo-assembly-language, output can be assembled by the assembler. This will allow modification of programs at the assembly language level.

assembly program: A program to translate a program written in pseudo-language (symbolic language) to a corresponding program in machine language. Principally designed to relieve the programmer of the problem of assigning actual storage locations to instructions and data when coding a program and to permit use of mnemonic operation codes rather than numeric operation codes. The address scheme used may be either numeric or mnemonic. The numerical systems utilize small blocks of code written in a numbering system allowing easy insertions, deletions, and amendments to the program. The mnemonic system uses alphanumeric names in referring to locations in storage. In both cases, the pseudo-addresses are converted to machine-coded addresses by the assembly program before the program is finalized for computer use.

assembly system: 1. An automatic system (software) that includes a language and machine-language programs. Such supplementary programs perform such programming functions as checkout, updating, and others. 2. An assembly system comprises two elements, a symbolic language and an assembly program, that translate source programs written in the symbolic language into machine language.

assembly testing: The testing of a group of functionally related programs to determine whether or not the group operates according to specifications. The programs may be related in that they have access to common data, occupy high-speed storage simultaneously, operate under common program control, or perform an integrated task.

assembly unit: 1. A device which performs the function of associating and joining several parts of piecing together a program. 2. A portion of a program which is capable of being assembled into a larger whole program.

assign: The particular action which reserves portions of computing systems (usually memory units) for specific purposes. Reservations of space, locations, etc. are often permanent for the duration of specific programs.

assigned symbol: A symbol given a specific value by the programmer, using a symbol definition pseudooperation.

Association for Computer Machinery (ACM): A prestigious professional and technical society whose publications, conferences and activities are designed to help advance the art, specifically as regards machinery and system design, language and program development, and other related activities. It is a member of AFIPS, American Federation of Information Processing Societies.

associative memory: A high speed search of computer memory based on the content rather than computer addresses.

associative storage: A storage device in which storage locations are identified by their contents, not by names or positions.

associative storage registers: Registers which are not identified by their name or position but which are known and addressed by their contents.

assumed decimal point: The point within a numeric item at which the decimal point is assumed to be located. When a numeric item is to be used within a computer, the location of the assumed decimal point is considered to be at the right unless otherwise specified in the appropriate record description entry. It will not occupy an actual space in storage, but it will be used by the computer to align the value properly for calculation.

astable circuit: A circuit which continuously alternates between its two unstable states. It can be synchronized by applying a repetitive input signal of slightly higher frequency.

asterisk protection: The insertion of a series of asterisks on the left of the most significant digit. This scheme is used in check protection systems.

asymmetrical distortion: A distortion affecting a two-condition (or binary) modulation (or restitution) in which all the significant intervals corresponding to one of the two significant conditions have longer or shorter durations than the corresponding theoretical durations of the excitation. If this particular requirement is not met, distortion is present.

asymmetry: The lack of symmetry between parts of a magnitude.

asynchronous: Having a variable time interval between successive bits, characters, or events. In data transmission, this is limited to a variable time interval between characters and is often known as start-stop transmission.

asynchronous data transmission: In this type of data transmission, each character consists of information bits 5, 6, 7, or 8 – depending on the code structure – preceded by a start bit (zero condition) and followed by a stop bit (one condition). Each bit in a data character is of equal time duration, with the exception of the stop bit which may be one, one and one-half, or two times as long as the other bits in the data character. An asynchronous input communication line terminal (CLT) recognizes the initial change of state from the one condition as the start of a data character. it then looks at the condition of the line facilities at time intervals corresponding to the middle of each of the following information bits in order to transfer a complete data-character into the assembly register.

asynchronous line driver: Interfaces a remote data terminal with a multiplexer, etc., or computer via 4wire metallic transmission facility. One type of line driver supports full-duplex, 9,600-baud asynchronous data transmission over 4-wire facilities for distances up to 2 miles, or longer distances at lower baud rates. The device derives balanced differential transmit/- receive signals via its internal line driver circuitry at one end, and accepts an Electronic Industries Association (EIA) RS-232-C compatible interface at the other end. The typical device can be switchoptioned for either end users or networks.

asynchronous   machine: Various machines which have operating speeds not related to any fixed or specific frequency of the system. Therefore, since no fixed period or interval signals the next event, it may begin at the end of a prior one, regardless of the time involved.

asynchronous   mode: In asynchronous mode one character is sent at a time, preceded by a "start" signal and terminated by a "stop" signal. FSK modulation is usually employed; there the BPS and baud are equal. Since the transmission rate is determined by the digital signal, it may vary up to the maximum supported. The existing conventional rates are 110, 134, 150, and 300 BPS. Provision may exist in the character code (i.e., ASCII) for error detection in the form of character parity.

asynchronous operator: 1. Pertaining to a lack of time coincidence in a set of repeated events where this term is applied to a computer to indicate that the execution of one operation is dependent on a signal that the previous operation is completed. 2. A mode of computer operation in which performance of the next command is started by a signal that the previous command has been completed. Contrast synchronous, characterized by a fixed time cycle for the execution of operations.

asynchronous   serial   transmission: The technique used by most electromechanical serial devices such as teletypewriters. With this technique, each character consists of three parts: a start bit, the data bits and a stop bit.

asynchronous signalling: Codes used in signalling, in which characters provide their own start and stop indicators.

asynchronous system: A system in which the speed (or frequency) of operation is not related to the frequency of the system to which it is connected. The performance of any operation starts as a result of a signal that indicates that the previous operation has been completed (e.g., teletypewriter signals). Also, selfclocking, in that event times are based on elapsed duration from some earlier event, not on an independent clocking signal.

asynchronous   time   division   multiplex (ATDM) advantages: The fundamental notion behind ATDM is to exploit the fact that in synchronous time division multiplex (STDM) systems, many of the time slots in the fixed-format frames are wasted since a typical remote terminal will be transmitting data less than 10 percent of the time it is on line. ATDM dynamically allocates the time slots in a frame of data to the currently active users, reducing the fraction of wasted time slots and thereby increasing overall line utilization and throughput.

asynchronous transmission output: Timing on asynchronous output-data transfers is not time critical. Since each output-data character is preceded by a start bit and followed by a stop bit, the time interval between characters will appear to the transmission facilities as nothing more than an extra-long stop bit. Although no information is lost if a data character is not transferred from the central processor to the asynchronous output communication line terminal (CLT) within the "character availability interval", a failure to do so may result in a reduced transmission rate.

async mini modem: A piece of equipment that plugs into a user's data terminal equipment to provide cost effective local data transmission. Its operating range extends to 4 miles at 50 to 9600 bits per second (bps).

asyndetic: 1. Omitting conjunctions or connectives. 2. Pertaining to a catalog without cross references.

Atlantic Merchant Vessel Report (AMVER): A system that keeps track of ships and airplanes that cross the Atlantic. When a craft is in distress, the system is activated. The SOS signal is picked up, its location fed into the computer, and almost instantly the machine indicates the ships traveling the Atlantic that are near enough to effect rescue operations.

atomic actions: Actions which are either carried to completion or not carried out at all. These actions are required by many algorithms for maintaining the integrity of a database system.

attach: 1. To create a task and present it to the supervisor. 2. A macro instruction that causes the control program to create a new task and indicates the entry point in the program to be given control when the new task becomes active.

attended operation: A communications data set application in which individuals are required at both stations to establish the connection and transfer the data sets from talk (voice) mode to data mode.

attended time: Concerns that specific time during which the computer is in serviceable operation and is being attended to, or is out of service for maintenance or engineering work.

attention interruption: An interruption of instruction execution caused by a remote terminal user hitting the attention key. See also simulated attention.

attention key: A function key on terminals that causes an interruption of execution by the central processing unit.

attenuation: A decrease in magnitude of current, voltage, or power of a signal in transmission between points. It may be expressed in decibels or nepers.

attenuation compensation: The use of networks to correct for varying attenuation, i.e., in transmission lines.

attenuation distortion: Distortion due to variation of loss or gain within a frequency.

attenuation equalizer: A modem or peripheral device designed to compensate for undesired levels of signal strength.

attenuator: A device, fixed or adjustable, which reduces the amplitude of an electrical signal with minimum or no distortion, such as the volume control on a radio.

attributes: In a relational database system, the fields of a tuple.

A-type address constant: In the assembler language, an address constant used for branching within a module or for retrieving data. See also V-type address constant.

auctioneering device: A specific device designed to automatically select either the highest or the lowest input signal from among two or more input signals. This is often referred to as a high or low signal selector.

audio amplifier: An electronic device to strengthen an audio signal.

audio communication line: A line attached to an audio response unit. An audio communication line is always a switched line.

audio frequencies: Frequencies that can be heard by the human ear (usually 15 cycles to 20,000 cycles per second).

audio response unit (ARU): An output device, that provides a spoken response to digital inquiries from a telephone or other device. The response is composed from a prerecorded vocabulary of words and can be transmitted over communication lines to the location from which the inquiry originated.

audio system: Various types of special equipment which have capabilities of storing and processing data obtained from voice sources, either recorded or transmitted.

audio terminal: A device associated with an audio response unit (ARU), at which keyed or dialed data is entered for transmission to the computer; an audio response is produced by the ARU.

audit programming: Use of a program designed to enable use of the computer as an auditing tool.

audit trail: An auditing concept that provides, in a step-by-step fashion, the history of an account by carrying in the account master file the date and serial number of the last previous transaction. This allows the auditor to trace back all transactions affecting the account.

augmentation: The operations that add one item to another.

augmented operation code: A particular code which is further defined or limited by information found in another position of an instruction, i.e., an instruction word but one which has addresses considered as the operation code.

authorized state: A condition in which a problem program has access to resources that would otherwise not be available.

auto-abstract: 1. The material abstracted from a document by machine methods. 2. To select keywords from a document by machine methods.

auto-answer: A machine feature that allows a transmission control unit or a station to respond to a call automatically that it receives over a switched line.

auto call: A machine feature that allows a transmission control unit or a station to initiate a call over a switched line automatically.

auto call sequencer (call manager): A unit – customized to serve from 2 to 64 incoming lines – that answers calls with a prerecorded messge, puts callers on hold, and indicates the next priority call. This type of microprocessor system has a broad application base, and improved private automatic branch exchange (PABX) switchboard console operations, providing a cost effective means to handle incoming messages. The typical telephone management information system (TMIS) is a dynamic reporting system that assists in daily evaluation of both telephone personnel and equipment performance. A TMIS may be installed in front of or behind an ACD/UCD, Centrex, 1A2-key system, PABS, EKTS, or hybrid phone system. Some systems are designed to work specifically with 1A2-key systems. Some offer interfaces with single-line telephones, modems, or trunks and are suited for the growing ACD/UCD environment. Reports are either hard copied or CRT displayed. The number of calls kept on hold, the average ringing and holding times, and the average duration of calls are among other management data provided.

autochart: A type of documentor used for the automatic production and maintenance of charts, principally flowcharts.

autocode: Use of the computer itself to develop the machine-coded program from macro codes; i.e., the conversion of symbolic codes for operations and addresses. Mnemacrocodes; i.e., the conversion of symbolics simplify programs for more efficient use by the computer and programmer.

auto-indexed addressing: A particular utilization of specified core memory locations for address incrementing operations; when referenced indirectly, the contents of the auto-index locations(s) is incremented by one and used as an effective address.

auto-indexing: An automatic means to prepare an index.

automata theory: The theory development which relates the study of principles of operation and application of automatic devices to various behavioral concepts and theories.

automated clearinghouse (ACH): An automated facility operated for the convenience of the banks in a region. ACHs electronically process interbank payments of funds, and may also handle the electronic transfer of government securities.

automated inventory control system: A systems approach to inventory control, involving attempts to maintain stocks at the minimal level necessary to meet expected demand with an adequate margin of safety. As a standalone application, it has value for critical supplies having limited "shelf-life" (e.g., short-lived radio isotopes, blood banking) and has broader application when it exists as a phase of an integrated supply/-requisition/order system.

automated management: All types of management completed with the aid of data processing equipment but usually depicted in more specialized terms as automated production management, etc.

automated production management: The management with the assistance or under the control of data processing equipment which relates to production planning scheduling, design or change, and control (reporting) of output.

automated tellers: Unmanned equipment activated by a bank customer to obtain banking services. This equipment is activated by a plastic card, pushbuttons, and a memorized code for each user. Such a device may be merely a cash dispenser or may accept deposits and transfer funds between a customer's accounts. Such a banking station might be located on bank premises or at a separate location. Also, such a device may or may not be linked directly to a computer at the controlling bank.

automatic-abstracting: See auto-abstract.

automatically programmed tools (APT): A language for programming numerically controlled machine tools, flame cutters, drafting machines, and similar equipment. It was written to minimize the effort, time, and money needed to take full advantage of numerically controlled techniques in engineering and manufacturing. In addition to providing machine-tool programming capabilities that are virtually impossible by manual methods, APT enhances most of the usual advantages found in numerical control—reduced lead time, greater design freedom and flexibility, lower direct costs, greater accuracy, improved production forecasting, lower tooling costs, better engineering control of the manufacturing process, and simplified introduction of changes. The APT III program represents over one hundred years of development and testing.

automatic branch exchange: A dial exchange offering private telephone service for a company of organization for transmitting calls to and from the public network facilities. The subscriber's office usually has a switching station often called a private automatic branch exchange (PABX).

automatic brightness control: Circuit used in some television receivers to keep average brightness level of screen constant.

automatic built-in check: A provision constructed in hardware for verifying the accuracy of information transmitted, manipulated, or stored by any unit or device in a computer.

automatic call device: System of relays responsive to a prearranged set of signals, connected to an unattended receiver so that an alarm is sounded on operation.

automatic call distributor: Equipment to distribute large volumes of incoming calls to attendant; (or computer line terminations) not already working on calls, or equipment to store calls until attendants or computer ports become available.

automatic calling: See auto call.

automatic calling unit (ACU): A dialing device supplied by the communications common carrier, that permits a business machine to dial calls automatically over the communication networks.

automatic camp-on: Service feature by which a switch observes that the wanted line is busy, waits until it is free, then automatically and immediately connects the calling line which has been waiting.

automatic carriage: A control mechanism for a typewriter or other listing device that can control the feeding, spacing, skipping, and ejecting of paper or preprinted forms automatically.

automatic check: A provision constructed in hardware for verifying the correctness of information transmitted, manipulated, or stored by any unit or device in a computer. Numerous internal checks continually monitor the accuracy of the system and guard against incipient malfunction. Typical are the parity and inadmissible-character check, automatic readback of magnetic tape and magnetic cards as the information is being recorded, the electronic tests which precede each use of magnetic tape or magnetic cards to ensure that the operator has not inadvertently set switches improperly. These internal automatic tests are supplemented by the instructions which may be programmed to ensure proper setup of certain units prior to their use. Console switches are designed to protect against inadvertent or improper use, and interlocks are provided on peripheral units to guard against operator error.

automatic check interrupt: Input/output interrupt occurs upon successful completion of an input/output operation, if a programmer has specified an input/output operation incorrectly, or if a machine malfunction (such as a parity error) occurs in the path to or from the input/output device. These interrupts permit an automatic check of the status of the operation and of any errors that may have occurred, and initiation of an error-recovery procedure when practical. In the event of intermittent errors, statistics can be kept and logged out between jobs.

automatic control: 1. Switching system which operates control switches in correct sequence and at correct intervals automatically. 2. Control system incorporating a servomechanism or similar device so that feedback signals from outputs of systems are used to adjust the control and maintain optimum operating conditions.

automatic control alarm: A specific audible or visible signal designed to indicate an abnormal or out-of-limits condition in the plant or control system.

automatic control engineering: A unique designated branch of technology related to the design and use of automatic control devices and systems.

automatic controlling system: A specific automatic control system without feedback; i.e., a specific portion of the control system which manipulates the controlled system.

automatic control panel: A panel of lights and switches used by a computer operator.

automatic crosstell: An American Air Defense term relating to the transmission of air surveillance information and data from one sector to another and usually performed with the aid of computers to determine target coordinates relative to the receiving station.

automatic data processing: Data processing performed by system of electronic or electrical machines so interconnected and interacting as to reduce to a minimum the need for human assistance or intervention.

automatic data switching center: See automatic message switching center.

automatic dialing: Provided to manage a pool or group of switched (dialed) telephone lines, and to perform the allocation of telephone numbers (terminals) to the lines. Additional features are validation that the desired terminal was reached (Terminal Answerback), computer identification (Processor Answerback) and terminal control. Another capability is to answer calls originating from the terminals automatically.

automatic dictionary: The component of a language translating machine which will provide a word-for-word substitution from one language to another. In automatic searching systems, the automatic dictionary is the component which substitutes codes for words or phrases during the encoding operation.

automatic digital network (AUTODIN): The data-handling portion of the military communications system.

automatic electronic-switching center: See automatic message switching center.

automatic error detection: A program itself, or a program embedded in a more complicated system, which is designed to detect its own errors, print them out with the cause, and take steps to correct them.

automatic exchange: An exchange between subscribers without the intervention of operators, it is completed by means of devices and equipment set in operation by the originating subscriber's instrument.

automatic-feed punch: A card punch that has a hopper, a card track, and a stacker. The movement of cards through the punch is automatic.

automatic frequency control (AFC): Electronic or mechanical means for automatically compensating (in a receiver) frequency drifts in transmission carrier.

automatic gain control (AGC): An electronic system in radar and the visual section of television receivers which controls the amplification of forward end tubes.

automatic hold: In an analog computer, automatic attainment of the hold condition through amplitude comparison of a problem variable, or through an overload condition.

automatic intercept center: A facility that processes intercepted calls automatically and connects to a vacant number announcement or to an announcement machine that gives the correct number, or transfers the call to an intercept operator for handling.

automatic interrupt: An automatic program-controlled interrupt system that causes a hardware jump to a predetermined location. There are five types of interrupts. 1. input/output, 2. programmer error, 3. machine error, 4. supervisor call, and 5, external (for example, timer turned to negative value, alert button on console, external lines from another processor). There is further subdivision under the five types. Unwanted interrupts, such as an anticipated overflow, can be masked out.

automatic/manual operator station (A/M station): In process control, a device designed to enable the process operator to position one or more values manually. A single-loop station enables manual positioning of a single valve; a shared station enables control of multiple valves; and a cascade station provides control of paired loops.

automatic message-switching center: A center in which messages are automatically routed according to information in them.

automatic modification: Various types of information systems which do not provide for and are not designed, as in many closed loops, for correction of data.

automatic monitor: Apparatus which compares the quality of transmission at different parts of a system, and raises an alarm if there is appreciable variation.

automatic paper tape punch: Refers to various tapes, mylar plastic or paper, upon which data may be sorted in the form of punched holes. Hole locations are arranged in rows across the width of the tape. There are usually 50 or 8 channels per row, with data represented by a binary-coded decimal system. All holes in the column are sensed simultaneously in a manner similar to that for punch cards. (synonymous with perforated tape.)

automatic polling: See auto poll.

automatic priority group: OS/VS2 is an example of a group of tasks at a single priority level that are dispatched according to a special algorithm that attempts to provide optimum use of CPU and I/O resources by these tasks. See also dynamic dispatching.

automatic programming: The process of using a computer to perform some stages of the work involved in preparing a computer program.

automatic recovery: Permits restart of the switched message flow after a fatal system failure. The recovery process is started by an operator response when the system is reloaded, and works from special records saved in the communications data base.

automatic repeat request (ARQ):   A system employing an error-detecting code and arranged so that a signal detected as being in error automatically initiates a request for retransmission.

automatic restart: A restart that takes place during the current run, that is, without resubmitting the job. An automatic restart can occur within a job step or at the beginning of a job step.

automatic routine: A routine that is executed independently of manual operations, but only if certain conditions occur within a program or record, or during some other process.

automatic segmentation and control: The computer can handle programs which exceed the core memory capacity of a particular system configuration. Without reprogramming, the computer automatically adapts its operational procedures to allow processing of any program on any system configuration. The user is not forced to install a system of maximum-memory capacity to accommodate one long program; he need not purchase more equipment than he normally needs for efficient operation. Segments of all programs concurrently being executed are "fitted" into available memory space for execution. (avaiable on some computers.)

automatic send-and-receive set (ASR):   A teletypewriter apparatus used for originating, transmitting or receiving messages. It consists of a page printer or a tape printer , a keyboard, a tape punch, and a tape reader. It can be used for 1. Off-line preparation of punched tape; 2. Keyboard transmission; 3. Simultaneous keyboard transmission and punched-tape generation; 4. Automatic tape transmission; 5. Page printing or tape printing; and 6. On-line control of associated devices and apparatus.

automatic sequencing: The ability of equipment to put information in order or in a connected series without human intervention.

automatic stop: An automatic halting of a computer processing operation as the result of an error.

automatic switchcover: An operating system which has a stand-by machine that is capable of detecting when the on-line machine is faulty and once this determination is made, to switch to itself this operation.

automatic tape transmitter: A device which senses data on tapes, such as paper tape or plastic and metallic magnetic tape. It includes mechanisms for holding, feeding, controlling, and reeling up the tape, as well as sensing the data on the tape. Usually used as computer input devices; to drive printers, plotters, card punches, or to send information over a communications line.

automatic volume recognition: The ability of an operating system to identify the physical address of a backing store file given only the file name. The operating system also directs operators where to load particular files.

automatic write: The facility on buffered line printers allowing more than one line to be printed as the result of only one print request from the central processor. This allows complete pages to be composed in core.

automation: 1. The implementation of process by automatic means. 2. The theory, art, or technique of making a process automatic. 3. The investigation, design, development, and application of methods of rendering processes automatic, self-moving, or selfcontrolling. 4. The conversion of a procedure, a process, or equipment to automatic operation.

automation simulation: A machine designed to simulate the operations of living things, or to respond automatically to predesigned programs, stimuli, or signals. An automatic or self-acting or reacting system, often with capability to form logic decisions on the basis of programmed criteria, guides, or rules of its designers. Some automatons mimic living organisms and are responsive to environmental conditions.

autonomous devices: Processors, memories, and input/output devices. Since each device is autonomous (no device is dependent upon another for its timing), a system configuration can include memory modules of different speeds, processors of different types sharing the same memory modules, and standard unique input/output devices (available on some systems).

autonomous packet switching: A packet switching mode where each packet is sent individually within the network according to the attached routing information.

autonomous working: 1. A specific type of concurrent or simultaneous working; i.e., the carrying out of multiple instructions at the same time. 2. The initiation and execution of a part of a computer or automation system independent of a computer, or automation system independent and separate

from other operations being performed on other parts of the system. The independent set of operations on various data are themselves often only monitored.

auto poll: A machine feature of a transmission control unit that permits it to handle negative responses to polling without interrupting the central processing unit.

auto-restart: A specific capability of a computer system designed to perform automatically various initialization functions usually required to resume operation following various equipment or power failures.

auxiliary access storage: Storage of relatively larger capacity and slower access than normal internal storage.

auxiliary console: As contrasted to main consoles, some computers or units have additional banks of controls, displays, switches, and other devices for operator manipulation or visual access to operations.

auxiliary data: That data which is associated with other data, but is not a part of it, such as comment data, back-up data, etc.

auxiliary equipment: Equipment not under direct control of the central processing unit.

auxiliary operation: An off-line operation performed by equipment not under control of the central processing unit.

auxiliary routine: A routine designed to assist in the operation of the computer and in debugging other routines.

auxiliary-second general processor: A specialized processor that is used to speed through concurrent operation; e.g., array processor, fast fourier transform (FFT) processor, or input/output processors (IOP).

auxiliary storage: A storage device in addition to the main storage of a computer, e.g. magnetic tape, disk or magnetic drum. Auxiliary storage usually holds much larger amounts of information than the main storage, and the information is accessible less rapidly.

availability: The degree to which a system or resource is ready when needed to process data.

availability, cyclic: That specific time period during which stored information can be read.

availability ratio: The ratio of total service time to the total time minus the sum total of fault time, regular maintenance time, supplementary time and serviceable time (hardware) or to the time avaiable to users (user availability) as opposed to non-user activities.

available frame count: A count of page frames that are ready for assignment.

available machine time: The elapsed time when a computer is in operating condition, whether or not it is in use.

available page queue: A queue of the pages whose real storage is available for allocation currently to any task.

available unit queue: Under telecommunications access method (TCAM), a queue in main storage to which all buffer units are assigned initially (that is, prior to assignment to TCAM lines and application programs requiring buffers).

AVC (automatic volume control):   An electronic system in radio receivers which controls the amplification forward end tubes.

average calculating operation time: The average time required to complete the computation or processing of a simple addition, multiplication as a measurement of machine speed or capability.

average data transfer rate: A particular rate of data transmission through a channel over a relatively long period of time to include gaps between blocks, words, or records. Also included in this time are regeneration time and other items not subject to program control. Starting, stopping, rewinding, searching or other programmed control items are not included.

average delay: The total waiting time of all bids divided by the total number of bids, including those not delayed. The mean waiting time.

average effectiveness level: A percentage figure determined by subtracting the total computer down time from the total performance period hours, and dividing the difference by the total performance period hours. For this computation, equipment down time can be measured by those intervals during the performance period between the time that the contractor or other person having maintenance responsibility is notified of equipment failure, and the time the equipment is returned to the user in proper operating condition.

average information content: The average of the information content per symbol emitted from a source. Note: The terms entropy and negentropy are sometimes used to designate average information content.

average transinformation: Transinformation averaged over the ensemble of pairs of transmitted and received symbols.

B

babble: The aggregate crosstalk from a large number of interfering channels.

background: 1. In multiprogramming, the environment in which low-priority programs are executed. 2. Under time-sharing option (TSO), the environment in which jobs submitted through the SUBMIT or SYSIN commands are executed. One job step at a time is assigned to a region of main storage, and remains in main storage to completion.

backgrounding: Performing background processing which is not on-line or directly connected to the computer for on-line operations. High priority programs take precedence over specific background jobs.

background or bias-induced noise: 1. Those extra bits or words that must be ignored or removed from the data at the time the data is used. 2. Errors introduced into data in a system, especially in communication channels. 3. Random variations of one or more characteristics of any entity such as voltage, current, and data. 4. Loosely, any disturbance tending to interfere with the normal operation of a device or system.

background processing: The automatic execution of lower priority computer programs when higher priority programs are not using the system resources.

background program: 1. In multiprogramming, the program with the lowest priority. Background programs execute from batched or stacked job input. 2. Under time-sharing option (TSO), a program executed in a region of main storage that is not swapped. Contrast with foreground program.

background programming: Programming which may be preempted by a program with a higher priority.

background reader: A system task started by the operator to process foreground-initiated background jobs.

backing region: A region to which a background job is assigned.

backing storage: A memory with a large capacity and slow access used to hold data and programs until they are needed in an internal storage.

backlash: See hysteresis.

backspace: To move one unit in the reverse or backward direction as opposed to moving one unit in the forward direction; e.g., to move back one record or file on an I/O device.

backspace character (BS): A format effector that causes the location of the printing or display position to be moved backward one printing or display space.

backspace key (shift key): Shifts all digits one place to the right, dropping the last digit on the right.

backspace tape: A procedure to return a magnetic tape to the beginning of the preceeding record.

backup copy: A copy of a file or data set that is kept for reference in case the original file or data set is destroyed.

backup operation: A particular provision of designed alternate means of operation in case of failure of the primary means of operation.

backup system: Combines several sophisticated error detection and correction techniques which spot and correct equipment and transmission errors.

backward learning: An isolated adaptive algorithm where data is gathered solely by communication with incoming packets.

backward reference: See backup system.

B address: The higher order position of the instruction code indicating the location of data to be processed.

badge reader: A data collection device, e.g., used in in-plant data communications systems, having the ability of reading data recorded as holes in prepunched cards or magnetics in plastic badges. Sometimes these are also fitted with keys so data can be entered manually.

balanced: Electrical or electronic symmetry concerning ground, or to some specific characteristic, i.e., the loads of two parallel-operating generators are in balance when each is loaded equally or if they are identical, similarly applied to tubes, transmission lines, etc.

balanced circuits: Circuits that are terminated by a network whose impedance balances the impedance of the line so that the return losses are infinite.

balanced error (range of):   1. A range of error in which the maximum and minimum possible errors are opposite in sign and equal in magnitude. 2. A range of error in which the average value is zero.

balanced line: A grounded transmission line composed of two conductors in which the voltage of the two conductors are equal in magnitude and opposite in polarity and the currents are equal in magnitude but opposite in direction.

balanced system: One in which the impedances to earth of the two conductors are made to be equal.

balancing error: A specific error which in effect balances or offsets another error, i.e., two offsetting errors of equal values or same numbers of opposite signs could exist and would be most difficult to detect or correct because the various check totals would agree or compare favorably.

balancing network: Lumped circuit elements (inductances, capacitances, and resistances) connected so as to simulate the impedance of a uniform cable or openwire circuit over a band of frequencies.

balancing of an operational amplifier: The act of adjusting the output level of an operational amplifier to coincide with its input reference level, usually ground or zero voltage.

ball resolver: A specific resolver using a ball that rotates about an axis through its center (zero), and which is tangentially in contact with three mutually perpendicular wheels at points X, Y, and Z. The ball is driven at a particular speed by the wheel with reference to a point, the ball thus driving two wheels.

band: 1. A group of tracks on a magnetic disc or on a magnetic drum. 2. In communications, the frequency spectrum between two defined limits.

band-elimination filter: See band rejection filter.

band expansion factor: Ratio of bandwidth to highest modulation frequency for an FM transmission. Equal to twice the deviation ratio.

bandpass: A measurement of the difference in cycles/sec between the limiting frequencies of a band in which the attenuation of any frequency, with respect to the central frequency, is less than a specified value (usually half power or three db).

bandpass filter: A filter that allows free passage to frequencies within its designed range and effectively bars passage to all outside that range. A filter having a single transmission band.

band rejection filter: A filter having a single attenuation band, with neither of the cutoff frequencies being zero or infinite.

bandsplitting: A technique of audio scrambling. The audio channel is divided into two or more sub-bands (usually five) and transposed in frequency.

band-stop filter: See band rejection filter.

bandwidth: 1. A group of consecutive frequencies constituting a band which exists between limits of stated frequency attenuation. A band is defined as more than 3.0 decibels greater than the mean attenuation across the band. 2. A group of consecutive frequencies constituting a band which exists between limits of stated frequency delay. 3. The difference, expressed in the number of cycles per second, between the two limiting frequencies of a band.

bank on-line teller system: Handles savings account and mortgage loan transactions. Teller consoles at each window at each office may be linked to the computer and the on-line central file.

bank wire: A private, computerized message system administered for and by participating banks, through the facilities of Western Union. The system links about 250 banks in about 75 cities. Managing banks include nine New York City banks and five Chicago banks which are the system's heavy users. The Bank Wire transmits funds transfer information as does the Fed Wire, but also transmits a variety of other information, on loan participations, bond closings, payment for securities, borrowing of Federal funds, and balanced in company accounts.

bar code: A two-digit binary coded number placed on the new customer ledger with the name and address. The binary coded number is read optically.

barrage reception: One in which interference of radio signals from any particular direction is minimized by selecting the appropriate directional aerial to give maximum signal/interference ratio.

barrel printer: A specific type of printer in which all characters are designed on a cylindrical surface (barrel). The entire character set is placed around the cylinder at each print position with print hammers located opposite each print position to be activated by the computer for bringing them in contact with a continuous ink ribbon between the printer and surface of the barrel.

barrier layer: To make certain that the Fermi levels in two materials are the same and to more absolutely influence semiconductor and contact conductivity, electrical double layers are formed at the contact surface between a metal and a semiconductor or between two metals.

base address: A given address from which an absolute address is derived by combination with a relative address.

base address relocation: The ability to augment memory references by the contents of a specific base register.

baseband: In the process of modulation, the frequency band occupied by the aggregate of the transmitted signals which first used to modulate a carrier. The term is commonly applied to cases where the ratio of the upper to the lower limit of the frequency band is large compared to unity. Examples are bands employed for the transmission of picture and synchronizing signals in television, and that for multichannel pulse telephone systems.

base displacement addressing system: A system that uses a displacement-base to designate all core storage locations and provides abilities to 1. easily relocate a program at load time, 2. address very large amounts of storage with relatively few address bits in each instruction, and 3.

conveniently address threedimensional arrays. See effective address.

base group: A number of carrier channels forming a channel bank which will be further modulated to a final frequency band.

base-minus-one complement: A number representation in a computer that is obtained by subtracting each digit of a number from one less than the base (of the numbering system that is used).

base (radix):   A number base, a quantity used implicitly to define some system of representing numbers by positional notation.

base register: A register in a computer whose constants are used to modify a computer instruction prior to its execution.

base time: A designed and precisely controlled function of time by which some particular process or exercise is controlled or measured.

BASIC: Beginner's All-purpose Instruction Code. A common high-level time-sharing computer programming language. It is learned easily and is used for direct communication between teletype units and remotely located computer centers. The language is similar to FORTRAN II and was developed by Dartmouth College for a General Electric 225 computer system.

basic access method: Any access method in which each input/output statement causes a corresponding machine input/output operation to occur.

basic coding: Computer instructions written in the computer's own language. Same as machine language.

basic direct access method (BDAM):   An access method used to directly retrieve or update particular blocks of a data set on a direct access device.

basic indexed sequential access method (BISAM):   An access method used in one form to retrieve directly or update particular blocks of a data set on a direct access device, using an index to locate the data set. The index is stored in direct access storage along with the data set. Other forms of this method can be used to store or retrieve, in a continuous sequence, blocks of the same data set.

basic language: A term used to indicate the lowest level computer language used.

basic linkage: A linkage which is used repeatedly in one routine, program or system and which follows the same set of rules each time.

Basic Operating System (BOS):   One of many operating systems; (see operating system).

basic partitioned access method (BPAM):   An access method that can be applied to create program libraries, in direct access storage, for convenient storage and retrieval of programs.

basic sequential access method (BSAM):   An access method for storing or retrieving data blocks in a continuous sequence, using either a sequential access or a direct access device.

basic telecommunications access method (BTAM):   An access method that permits read/write communications with remote devices.

basic transmission unit: In systems network architecture (SNA), a group of unrelated packets queued for the same transmission group which are blocked together to increase transmission efficiency.

batch: A group of deposits, incoming clearings, or other items assembled for proving purposes and for facilitating balancing. Normally, a batch contains about 150 items, which is approximately the pocket capacity of a proof machine. However, there is no minimum or maximum limitation to a batch size.

batch data processing: Computer processing in which similar input data items or problems are put in groups or "batches" for manipulating in single machine runs with the same program for economy and efficiency and as restricted by the particular computer's capability.

batched job: 1. A job that is grouped with other jobs as input to a computing system. 2. A job whose job control statements are grouped with job control statements of other jobs as input to a computing system.

batching: The methods used during batch processing operations in which transactions are collected and prepared for input to a computer for processing a single unit.

batch number: The number assigned to a batch of items being processed through the proof department. It is placed in the account number field of the batch ticket and on the back of the remainder of the items in the batch.

batch ticket: When used in an magnetic ink character recognition (MICR) system, a control document that is encoded with the total amount of a batch and identified by a special transaction code. The batch ticket can also contain such encoded information as batch number, source number, and/or proof machine number. This ticket accompanies the items from the proof department to the document processing center.

batch transaction file: Transactions accumulated as a batch ready for processing against the master file.

Batten system: A method for coordinating single words to identify a document, and developed by W.E. Batten.

battery: In communications, a source of direct current or the current itself. The source is not necessarily a storage device.

baud: 1. A unit of signalling speed equal to the number of discrete conditions of signal events per second. For example, one baud equals one-half dot cycle per second in Morse Code, one bit per second in a train of binary signals, and one 3-bit value per second in a train of signals each of which can assume one of eight different states. 2. In asynchronous transmission, the unit of modulation rate corresponding to one unit interval per second, i.e., if the duration of the units interval is 20 milliseconds, the modulation rate is 50 baud.

baudot code: A 5-level code used only for telegraphs, keyboards, printers, punches and readers. Although 5 bits can accommodate only 32 unique codes, two of the codes are figures (FIGS) and letters (LTRS). Prefixing the FIGS or LTRS code before other bit combinations permits dual definition of the remaining codes. This means that when a baudot terminal is interfaced to a computer, the software must maintain proper FIGS-LTRS status in order to interpret the necessary data properly.

baud rate: The number of information bits that can be transmitted in one second. In communication, a fixed amount of time is devoted to sending a pulse, known as a binary digit or "bit," (which can be either a positive pulse, as a telegraph dot, or a blank, as a telegraph pause). By definition, a baud is the reciprocal of time in seconds occupied by the shortest element of the code being transmitted. If one has a code, for example, with its shortest signal element 20 milliseconds long, the modulation rate of the code would be 50 bauds (per second).

Bayesian statistics: A branch of statistics that concerns estimates of (prior) probability distributions, as subsequently revised (posterior distribution) in order to incorporate new data by means of Bayes' equation. Often used in medical diagnostic programs as an alternative to analytical, sequential, or programmed diagnostic procedures.

b-box: A special counter constructed of hardware and contained in the control unit. See also counter.

BCD: See binary coded decimal.

beam deflection: On a cathode-ray tube (CRT) display device, the process of changing the orientation of the electron beam.

beam diversity: Essentially a way of transmitting a band of frequencies twice; when a satellite is orbiting over the Atlantic Ocean, for example, one frequency can be used for different transmissions to both the United States and Europe simultaneously.

Beam Frequency Oscillator (BFO): The oscillator in a CW receiver which heterdynes with the i-f signal to produce an audio note.

beam storage cells: An increasingly popular storage type in which one or more beams (of electrons) are used to gain access to the individual storage cells and to operate on them; i.e., cathode-ray tubes, etc.

beam switching tube: A vacuum or gas-filled tube constructed so that the cathode electron beam can be directed to any one of two or more anodes, i.e., most common are ten position tubes.

beat: 1. One of the fundamental states of the control unit of a computer or the duration of such a state. A beat might be designed to set up a correct circuit to perform a function, and execution of it might be the next beat. The duration might be a single word period. 2. A time measurement for a given computer word to pass a given point as in serial storage delay-lines. All of the bits of a word must pass through the input control gate; the beat is then the sum of all the bit times.

beat frequency: The difference in frequency between two heterodyned signals.

beginning end: The first or original end of a tape which has data recorded on it, except for those tapes which have data recorded in the reverse order.

beginning file label: A label in the beginning of a file that describes the contents of the file (on magnetic tape and disk, etc.).

beginning of magnetic tape (BMT): The point on a reel of magnetic tape that indicates the beginning of usable tape for recording purposes.

beginning-of-tape marker: A marker on a magnetic tape used to indicate the beginning of the permissible recording area, for example, a photo-reflective strip, or transparent section of tape.

begit: See bit.

Behind the Tape Reader (BTR): A means of inputting data directly into a machine control unit, other than a tape reader, from an external source.

bell character (BEL): A control character that is used when there is a need to call for human attention and may activate alarm or other attention devices.

Bell idles: Special code group (1000) sent during periods of nonactivity between AT&T 301 B data sets to maintain synchronism.

Bell Laboratories: Generally recognized as the largest industrial laboratory in the world. AT & T and Western Electric together own the Bell Telephone Laboratories. It has done a great deal of the research and development work that has made today's telecomunications possible. In 1948, the transistor was produced by the Bell Labs; other achievements include the solar battery and the first communications satellite (Telstar). It was here that Claude Shannon did his important work on information theory.

benchmark: 1. A problem used to evaluate the performance of hardware or software or both. 2. A problem used to evaluate the performance of several computers relative to each other, or a single computer relative to system specifications.

benchmark problem: A routine used to determine the speed performance of a computer. One method is to use one-tenth of the time required to perform nine complete additions and one complete multiplication. A complete addition or a complete multiplication time includes the time required to procure two operands from storage, perform the operation and store the result, and the time required to select and execute the required number of instructions to do this.

BH loop tracer: See BH meter.

BH meter: As related to magnetic tape, a device for measuring the intrinsic hysteresis loop as a sample of magnetic material. Usually the sample is magnetized in a 60 c field supplied by a solenoid and the intrinsic flux is detected by integrating the emf produced in an oposing pair of search coils, one of which surrounds the sample. The hyteresis loop may be displayed on an oscilloscope by feeding the X and Y plates with voltages proportional to the magnetizing coil current and the integrated search coil emf respectively.

bias: 1. The amount by which the average of a set of values departs from a reference value. 2. See ordering bias. 3. In teletypewriter applications, the uniform shifting of the beginning of all marking pulses from their proper positions in relation to the beginning of the start pulse.

bias distortion: Distortion affecting a two-condition (or binary) modulation (or restitution) in which all the significant intervals corresponding to one of the two significant conditions have different durations than the corresponding theoretical durations. Also called asymmetrical distortion.

biased data: A distribution of records in a file which is nonrandom with respect to the sequencing or sorting criteria. Biased data affects sorting time, depending on the technique used during the first pass on the data.

bias-induced noise: See background or bias-induced noise

bias sample: A sample selected by a method that is not random.

bias test: A form of test, usually as part of preventive maintenance or as a fault-finding or correcting operation, to test against safety margins for faults.

bidding: A type of scheduling algorithm where, when a new process is to be initiated, the parent processor broadcasts a bid request. Pool processors who wish to bid for the work send messages to the requesting processor, which then chooses a processor to carry out the work.

bidirectional operation: An operation in which reading, writing, and searching may be conducted in either direction, thus saving time and providing easy access to stored information.

bifurcation: A condition where two outcomes can occur – such as on or off, 0 or 1.

big: In the contention form of invitation or selection, an attempt by the computer or a station to seize control of a line so that it can transmit data.

billi: A specific prefix which designates the quantity one billion (10^9 power); i.e., synonymous with kilomega. Billibits mean one billion bits; one billion cycles per second.

bill payment: There are two basic electronic bill payment plans to reduce or eliminate items written to pay routine bills: 1. Preauthorized debit; a consumer authorizes a company to debit his account for periodic bills. For each billing period, the company prepares a magnetic tape of all such preauthorized debits, containing amounts account numbers and banks. The tape is processed through the company's bank and the local automated clearinghouse (ACH). 2. Combined bills and authorization stubs are an integral part. The consumer indicates on the stub the amount for which the company may debit his account and returns the stub to the company. The company then prepares the processes a magnetic tape as above. The Atlanta Project's bill check is such an instrument.

bimag core: A magnetic storage core which has two sets of magnetism.

BIMED programs: A package of FOR-TRAN computer programs for biomedical statistics.

binary: A characteristic, property, or condition in which there are but two possible alternatives, e.g., the binary number system using 2 as its base and using only the digits zero (0) and one (1).

binary card: A card containing data in column binary or row binary form.

binary cell: A storage cell of one binary digit capacity, for example, a single bit register.

binary chop: A search in which the series of items is divided into two parts, one of which is rejected. The process is repeated on the unrejected part until the item with the desired property is found. This process usually depends upon the presence of a known sequence in the series.

binary code: 1. A coding system in which the encoding of any data is done through the use of bits, i.e., 0 or 1. 2. A code for the ten decimal digits, 0, 1, ..., 9 in which each is represented by its binary, radix 2, equivalent, i.e., straight binary.

binary coded character: One element of a notation system for representing alpha-numeric characters such as decimal digits, alpabetic letters, punctutation marks, etc., by a fixed number of consecutive binary digits.

binary coded decimal (BCD) character code.: A set of 64 characters, each represented by six bits.

binary coded decimal (BCD) notation: A positional notation in which the individual decimal digits expressing a number in deci-mal notation are each represented by a binary numeral, for example, the number twentythree is represented by 0010011 in

the 8-4-2-1 type of binary-coded decimal notation and by 10111 in binary notation.

binary coded decimal (BCD) (Place Value): The 8421 system represents each digit by 4 binary digits with each place value equal to $8_2, 4_2, 2_2$, and 1_2, reading from left to right. A conversion of the decimal number 2471 to the 8421 BCD equivalent under the place-value concept would be as follows:

binary coded decimal (BCD) system: Since a group of 4 binary bits (a tetrad) can represent 16 states or conditions, such a group can be so arranged as to represent the 10 states (numbers) in the decimal system. The specific arrangement chosen from the variety of possible 4-bit (or even 5-bit or 7-bit) combinations depends on several factors. Three of these factors are 1. ease of arithmetic operations, 2. ease of comple-menting and 3. facility for error checking.

binary coded format: Represents dif-rent symbols only by allowing sufficient binary elements for each symbol. If one thinks of one binary digit (or "bit") repre-senting each symbol, there are only two choices: one symbol represented by the "on" state, the other represented by the "off" state. With such an arrangement, one could let the "on" or one-state represent "no" and the "off" or zero-state represent "yes".

binary countdown: A protocol where, in order to signal that is wants to send, a station writes its address into the header as a binary number.

binary counter: 1. A counter which counts according to the binary number system. 2. A counter capable of assuming one of two stable states.

binary digit (bit): 1. A numeral in the binary scale of notation. This digit may be zero (0), or one (1). It may be equivalent to an on or off condition, a yes, or a no. Often abbreviated to (bit). 2. The kind of number that computers use internally. There are only two binary digits, 1 and 0, otherwise known as "on" and "off." Follow the table below by progessing geometrically per column right to left, and add the column values where one appears, i.e.,; 7 is 1,2,4,0, right to left.

COLUMN VALUES			
8	4	2	1
0 is 0	0	0	0
1 is 0	0	0	1
2 is 0	0	1	0
3 is 0	0	1	1
4 is 0	1	0	0
5 is 0	1	0	1
6 is 0	1	1	0
7 is 0	1	1	1
8 is 1	0	0	0
9 is 1	0	0	1

binary dump: A printout of the contents of a memory unit in binary form onto some external medium such as paper tape or printout forms.

binary element: (ISO) A constituent element of data that takes either of two values or states. The term "bit", originally the abbreviation for the term "binary digit," is misused in the sense of binary element or in the sense of shannon.

binary equivalent: See equivalent binary digits.

binary image: An exact representation in storage of each hole in punched cards or paper tapes as distinct and contrasted from character representation or a combination of both.

binary incremental representation: Incremental representation in which the value of an increment is rounded to one of the two values of plus or minus one quantum and is represented by one binary digit.

binary logic: Digital logic elements functionaing with two distinct states. The two states are variously called true and false, high and low, on and off, or 1 and 0. In computers they are represented by two different voltage levels. The more positive level (or less negative) than the other is called the high level. The opposite level is called the low level. If the true (1) level is the most positive voltage, this logic is called positive true or positive logic.

binary lookup: Various techniques designed for finding a particular item in an ordered (sequence) set of items by repeatedly dividing in half the portion of the ordered set containing the sought-for item until only the sought-for item remains. Binary searching is several times more efficient than sequential searching, even when the number of items is relatively small. Same as dichotomizing search.

binary mode: Operations using basic machine arithmetic may use binary mode, i.e., the number system with a base 2 allowing only the digits 0 and 1, in contrast to the decimal system of base 10 with 0, 1, 2...9.

binary numeral: A binary representation of a number. For example, "101" is a binary numeral and "V" is the equivalent Roman numeral.

binary one: One of the two possible binary digits which has the value of unity assigned to it (the other digit being binary zero).

binary operator: An arithmetic operator having two terms. The binary operators that can be used in absolute or relocatable expressions and arithmetic expressions are: addition (+), subtraction (–), multiplication(*), and division (/).

binary pair: An electronic circuit having two stable states, two input lines, and two corresponding output lines such that a signal exists on either one of the output lines if, and only if, the last pulse received by the flip-flop is on the corresponding input line. A flip-flop or binary pair can store one binary digit (bit) of information, i.e., it is a bistable device.

binary point: That point in a binary number which separates the integral from the fractional part. It is analogous to the decimal point for a decimal number.

binary representation: A number system written to the base two notation.

binary row: A method of representing

binary numbers on a card where successive bits are represented by the presence or absence of punches in a successive position in a row as opposed to a series of columns.

binary scale: A numeration system in which only two symbols are allowed (0 and 1).

binary search: See binary look-up.

binary signalling: A communications mode in which information is passed by the presence and absence, or plus and minus variations of one parameter of the signalling medium only.

binary-state variable: A variable that can assume either one of two values (e.g., true or false, yes or no).

binary storage cell: A magnetic storage cell in which the two values of one binary digit are represented by different patterns of magnetism, and in which means of setting and sensing the contents are stationary with respect to the magnetic material.

binary synchronous communication protocol (BISYNC): Developed by IBM and used in the computer industry for polling remote terminals. BISYNC is intended for half-duplex lines, either point-to-point or multidrop. BISYNC operates with three character sets: ASCII, EBCDIC, and 6-bit transcode.

binary synchronous transmission: Data transmission in which synchronization of characters is controlled by timing signals generated at the sending and receiving stations.

binary to decimal conversion: Refers to the process designed to convert a number written to the base of two to the equivalent number written to the base of ten.

binary unit: See binary digit (bit).

binary word: A related grouping of one's and zero's having meaning assigned by definition, or weighted numerical value in the natural binary system of numbers.

bind: To assign as value to a symbol, parameter, or variable.

Biomedical (BIMED) program: A comprehensive set of FORTRAN packaged programs for biomedical statistics, developed at the UCLA Health Sciences Computing Facility under Dr. W. J. Dixon. These programs have relatively complete documentation and directions for use.

biometrics: A class of activity having to do with the measurement and systematic evaluation (especially statistical) of biological phenomena.

bionics: A branch of technology relating the functions, characteristics, and phenomena of living systems to the development of hardware systems.

biosensor: A mechanism for detecting and transmitting biological data from an organism in a way that permits display or storage of results.

bipolar transmission: See polar transmission.

bipolar (unipolar): A logical "true" input represented by an electrical voltage polarity opposite to that representing a logical "false" input. If both "true" and "false" inputs are represented by the same electrical voltage polarity, the signal is defined as unipolar.

biquinary code: A mixed radix notation in which each decimal digit represented is considered as a sum of two digits of which the first is zero or one with significance five and the second is 0, 1, 2, 3 or 4 with significance one.

BISAM: See basic indexed sequential access method.

bistable: Pertaining to a device capable of assuming either one of two stable states.

bistable trigger: Circuits which have two stable states require excitation triggers to cause transition from one state to the other. The excitation may be caused by one first and then the other of two inputs or by alternating two signals or excitations of a single input. Same as: binary pair, trigger pair, bistable circuit and flip-flop.

bit: 1. An abbreviation of binary digit. 2. A single character in a binary number. 3. A single pulse in a group of pulses. 4. A unit of information capacity of a storage device. The capacity in bits is the logarithm to the base two of the number of possible states of the device.

bit and symbol timing: Generated by a digital countdown chain driven by a crystal oscillator. By adding or deleting count pulses at a higher frequency point in the chain, the phase of the timing can be adjusted in steps of a small fraction of thee symbol interval. The symbol timing can thus be phase-locked to some property of the received symbols. If the demodulated symbols occur as a baseband wave, the instants of transition through the decision thresholds can be used for the phase lock.

bit bucket: A receptacle on a card punch to hold the chips that are punched out when a hole is made.

bit density: A measure of the number of bits recorded per unit of length or area.

bit drop-out: The loss of data bits from magnetic tape, disc, or drum.

bit location: A storage position on a record capable of storing one bit.

bit map protocol: A collision-free protocol where, since all stations agree on which is to transmit next, there are no collisions.

bit packing density: The number of bits of information per unit consisting of a single row serially recorded.

bit pattern: A combination of n bits to represent 2^n possible choices, e.g., a 3-bit pattern represents 8 possible combinations, an 8-bit pattern represents 256 possible combinations, etc.

bit position: A specific location in memory, space, or time at which a binary digit occurs or is located.

bit rate: The rate at which binary digits or pulses representing them pass a given point on a communications line or channel. QB rate, baud--the number of signal elements that pass through a channel or device in a second.

bit significance: The bit presence or absence in a specific location of an instruction word which distinguishes the instruction to be of certain type, for example, zero vs. one-address instruction.

bits per inch (BPI):   Used for measuring density of data on a recording medium.

bits per second (bps):   In serial transmission, the instantaneous bit speed with which a device or channel transmits a character.

bit stream: A binary signal without regard to groupings by character, word, or other unit. A line signal.

bit stream transmission: The method of transmitting characters at fixed time intervals. No stop and start elements are used and the bits making up the characters follow each other without pause.

bit string: A string of binary digits in which the position of each binary digit is considered as an independent unit.

bit stuffing: A data transparency method used by all the most recent protocols, in which each frame starts and ends with a special bit pattern. Whenever the transmitting hardware finds five consecutive ones in the data, it stuffs a 0 bit into the transmitted bit stream.

bit width: The angular increment of input position defined by either the true-1 or false-0 value of a bit. For example: the bit width of the least significant digit of a gray code comprises two quanta.

bivariant function generator: A function generator having two input variables.

black box: A device, module, type of processor, or communications linkage whose internal make-up, design, or operation is not pertinent or distinct to the output function it performs. The process special effect or action is known, but usually not its internal components and their relationships.

black screen: A television picture tube in which the screen is covered with a light-absorbing neutral filter, or the phosphor is a dark gray color. This increases contrast by reduction of ambient illumination reflected from the face of the tube.

blank: 1. The character which results in memory when an input record such as a card column which contains no punches is read. 2. The character-code which results from the printing of nothing in a given position. 3. A section of paper tape which has only the sprocket hole punched.

blank character: See space character.

blank deleter: A device that eliminates the receiving of blanks in perforated paper tape.

blanking: Cutting off the electron beam in a writing tube.

blanking pulse: The negative pulse that cuts off the kinescope electron beam.

blank medium: Various types of blank forms or media on which data has been recorded to establish a frame of reference to enable the medium to be used as a data carrier, such as, paper tape punched only with feed holes, etc.

blank paper tape coil: A coil of paper tape that has to be punched with the feed holes and can be punched with a pattern or holes that represent data.

blank-transmission test: A test that allows the checking of any data field for all blank positions. As a computer control, it can be used to prevent the destruction of existing records in storage, indicate when the last item from a spread card has been processed, skip calculation if a rate or factor field is blank, etc.

bleed: The capillary flow of ink beyond the original edges of a printed character.

B light: A control panel light which monitors the B register and signals parity check errors.

blind: To make a device nonreceptive to unwanted data, through recognition of field definition characters in the received data.

blind spot: The point, within normal range of a transmitter, at which field strength is abnormally small. Usually results from interference patterns produced by surrounding objects, or geographical features; e.g., valleys.

block analysis: A relocatable part of the computer storage in which program testing or statistical data are stored which can later be used to analyze the performance of the system. During program testing there maybe an analysis block for each transaction in the system, and when the transaction leaves the system this block is dumped into a file or tape.

block chaining: Associating a block of data in core with another block, in order to allow an item or queue of items to occupy more than one block. The blocks may be linked by programming, but some machines do it automatically.

block check character (BCC): In longitudinal redundancy checking and cyclic redundancy checking a character that is transmitted by the sender afer each message block and is compared with a block check character computed by the receiver to determine if the transmission was successful.

block cipher: Ciphers which accept a fixed-length block of input and produce a fixed-length block of output.

block delete: In punched tape programs, a code placed on the tape that tells the control to ignore the next block of information.

block diagram: A diagram of a system, instrument, or computer in which the principal parts are represented by suitably annotated geometrical figures to show both basic functions and functional relationships between the parts.

blockette: A subdivision of a group of consecutive machine words transferred as a unit, particularly with reference to input and output.

block format: The order of appearance of words or information within a block of data.

block gap: An area on a data medium used to indicate the end of a block or record.

blocking: Records are blocked, or grouped together in a buffer, in order to increase the average length of the physical records being written, thus reducing the process time per record, and increasing the total number of records that can be written on one unit.

blocking capacitor: A capacitor, the function of which is to block the flow of direct current; it allows alternating current to pass.

blocking factor: The number of logical records combined into one physical record or block.

blocking oscillator: A relaxation oscillator used in sync circuits of a television receiver.

block length: The number of characters or bytes contained within a block of data. Generally, the block length is a fixed value for a particular system or protocol. For example, under the Digital Research CP/M operating system for microcomputers, the block length is 128 bytes for all information written on floppy disks. Some systems allow for a variable block length, in which the value of the block length is appended to the front of the block when transferring data, so that the receiving terminal will know how many bytes to expect.

block loading: Bringing the control sections of a load module into adjoining positions of main storage.

blockmark: A storage-indicator mark that indicates the end of a block of data that would be written on tape for a processor that handles variable-length blocks on tape.

block multiplexer: A device that receives blocks of data from various sources, combines them into a single transmission path, and distributes them to various destinations. Generally, block multiplexers are most often used in large, multi-user systems as channels to provide communications between the computer and its peripheral devices.

block multiplexer channel: A multiplexer channel that interleaves blocks of data.

block prefix: An optional, variable length field that may precede unblocked records or blocks of records in ASCII on magnetic tapes.

block (records): 1. To group records for the purpose of conserving storage space or increasing the efficiency of access of processing. 2. A physical record so constituted, or a portion of a telecommunications message defined to be a unit of data transmission.

block sort: A sort of one or more of the most significant characters of a key to serve as a means of making workable sized groups from a large volume of records to be sorted.

block structure: A technique allowing program segmentation into blocks of information or subroutines of a total program.

block task control: The accumulation of control data relating to a particular task.

block transfer: The process of transmitting one or more blocks of data where the data are organized in such blocks.

block v-scan: A combination of u-scan and v-scan required for binary coded decimal (BCD) codes other than unit-distance. Binary code words are v-scanned in blocks of four bits each or less.

blue-ribbon program: An independently designed program that contains no mistakes or bugs. Same as star program.

BO: See output blocking factor.

bode diagram: A unique plot of log amplitude ratios and phase angle values on a log frequency base for a transfer function. This maybe an element, output or loop transfer function.

bomb: See abend.

book: A group of source statements written in the assembler or COBOL language.

book message: A message that will be sent to two or more destinations.

Boolean ADD: See OR.

Boolean algebra: A process of reasoning, or a deductive system of theorems using a symbolic logic and dealing with classes, propositions, or on-off circuit elements. It employs symbols to represent operators such as and, or, not, except, if...then, etc., to permit mathematical calculation. Named after George Boole (1815-1864), a famous English mathematician.

Boolean complementation: An operation performed upon a single operand in which the outcome produced has reverse significance in each digit position; e.g., a bit pattern p: 010110 would appear as r: 101001. This is contrasted with complementing which is a method for obtaining the negative of a number, whereas negation does not have this effect, merely reversing the bit value of each bit position in a word. Also called negation.

Boolean expression: In FORTRAN, a quantity expressed as the result of Boolean operations and, or, and not upon Boolean variables.

Boolean operator: An operator (gate) used in Boolean algebra as applied to logic units of computer architecture, i.e., the result of any operation is restricted to one of two values, generally represented as a 1 or 0.

bootstrap: 1. (ISO) An existing version, perhaps a primitive version, of a computer program that is used to establish another version of the program. 2. A technique or device designed to bring itself into a desired state. 3. To use a bootstrap. 4. That part of a computer program used to establish another version of the computer program.

bootstrap loader: A subroutine that is automatic and built into the hardware of the computer. It is capable of initiating the reading of another subroutine whose first instructions are designed to bring in the rest of the subroutine and initiate the total program schedule.

bootstrap loader (microprocessor): Enables users to enter data or a program into the RAM's from a teletypewriter, paper tape, or keyboard, and execute the program from the RAM's. Consists of several PROM's that plug into the prototyping board.

bootstrap program: A routine used to start the reading of a computer program (into the computer) by means of its own action.

B OR NOT A gate: A binary (two-input) logic coincidence circuit for completing the logic operation of B OR NOT A. The reverse of A OR NOT B, i.e., the result is false only when A is true and B is false.

bottom-up method: A compiling technique which identifies the statement type by examination of the syntactical relationship of each atom with its neighbor. Reverse of top-down method.

bound: To be limited in speed by a particular component of a system. A system that is linebound, for example, is limited in performance by the speed at which information can be transmitted over the communications line. A printer-bound system has a printer as its slowest component under the specified circumstances.

boundary: See character boundary.

boundary alignment: The positioning in main storage of a fixed-length field, such as a halfword or doubleword, on an integral boundary for that unit of information.

boundary error: An error condition that occurs when processing arrives at a limit, division, etc. This is a common type of error occurring in incompletely tested programs (sometimes after extended periods of successful use) when untested overflow procedures are exercised for the first time due to specification or file size growth, or when unanticipated concurrent conditions complicate an overflow or boundary handling procedure tested for a simple case.

boundary register: In a multi-programmed system, a register that designates the upper and lower addresses of each user's memory block.

BPAM: See basic partitioned access method.

BPF: See bandpass filter.

BPS FORTRAN tape compiler: A computer program which translates computer programs written in IBM System/-360 FORTRAN.

bracket: A facility provided by dialog control in Systems Network Architecture (SNA). A unit composed of a series of requests and responses in both directions.

branch: 1. To depart from the normal sequence of executing instructions in a computer. Synonymous with jump. 2. A machine instruction that can cause a departure as in (1). Synonymous with transfer. 3. A sequence of instructions that is executed as a result of a decision instruction.

branch cable: A cable that diverges from a main cable to reach some secondary point.

branching: 1. A computer operation, similar to switching, where a selection is made between two or more possible courses of action depending upon some related fact or condition. 2. Method of selecting the next operation for the computer to execute, while the program is in progress, based on the computer results.

branch instruction: An instruction which when executed may cause the arithmetic and control unit to obtain the next instruction from some location other than the next sequential location. A branch is one of two types: conditional, unconditional.

branch-on indicator: Branching takes place when appropriate indicators (switches, keys, buttons, etc.), or conditions, have been set to point to a particular group of registers, i.e., a branch may occur if the magnetic tape units are ready to receive a new block of data.

branch-on switch setting: Branching is often designed by the use of certain memory locations or index registers to set the value of the switches. The presetting of a switch may cause the program to branch to the appropriate one of N points, where N is the number.

branch on zero instruction: A test that determines the arithmetic account is zero and which will then proceed to either one of two locations, depending on the zero or nonzero state in the accumulator, i.e. a combined type of branch, causing the program to jump over to the first, or second, etc. next instruction in sequence.

branch operation: An operation that replaces the updated instruction address portion of the program status doubleword with a new instruction address, either unconditionally or only if specified criteria are satisfied.

branchpoint: A place in a routine where a branch is selected.

BRAP: A prototol where each station delays its attempt to seize the channel, with the delay period being proportional to the difference between the station and the number of the last successful transmission, modulo. Due to staggered delays, there are no collisions.

breach: Any successful and repeatable defeat of a computer's security controls which, could result in a penetration of the system.

breadboard: An experimental or rough construction model of a process, device, or construction.

break: 1. To interrupt the sending end and take control of the circuit at the receiving end. 2. See receive interruption.

break (communications): The receiving operator or listening subscriber interrupts the sending operator or talking subscriber and takes control of the circuit. The term is used especially in connection with halfduplex telegraph circuits and two-way telephone circuits equipped with voice-operated devices.

break feature: A provision in a communications system that permits the receiving station to interrupt the sending station and take control of the circuit. It is often used in connection with half-duplex telegraph circuits.

break-make ratio: The ratio of the break period to the make period.

breakpoint: A place in a routine specified by an instruction, instruction digit, or other condition, where the routine may be interrupted by external intervention or by a monitor routine.

breakpoint instruction: An instruction which, if some specified switch is set, will cause the computer to stop.

breakpoint switch: A manually operated switch which controls conditional operation at breakpoints, used primarily in debugging.

breakpoint symbol: A symbol which may be operationally included in an instruction, as an indication, tag or flag, to designate it as a breakpoint.

b-register: 1. Same as index register. 2. A register used as an extension of the accumulator during multiply and divide processes.

bridge-duplex system: A duplex system based on the Wheatstone-bridge principle, in which a substantial neutrality of the receiving apparatus to the send currents is obtained by an impedance balance.

bridge limiter: A diode bridge used as a limiter.

bridge tap: An undetermined length of line attached somewhere between the extremities of a communications line. Bridge taps are undesirable. Contrast with teminated line.

British Standards Institution (BSI): A British institution corresponding somewhat to the American National Standards Institute. It publishes various standards including a glossary of terms used in data processing.

broadband: Wide bandwidth greater than a voice-grade channel (4 kHz), equipment or systems which can carry a large proportion of the electromagnetic spectrum. A broadband communications system can accommodate broadcast and other services. Transmission using a bandwidth greater than a voice-grade channel (4 kHz) and therefore capable of higher-speed data transmission. Sometimes referred to as "wideband."

broadband demultiplexer: Device which accepts as input a broadband carrier signal and produces as output a group of separate audio frequency channels.

broadband exchange (BEX): A public switched communication system of Western Union, featuring various bandwidth full duplex connections.

broadband noise: Thermal noise which is distributed uniformly across the frequency spectrum at a wide range of energy levels.

broadcast data set: Under time-sharing option (TSO), a system data set containing messages and notices from the system operator, administrators, and other users. Its contents are displayed to each terminal user when he logs on the system, unless suppressed by the user.

broadcasting: Sending a packet to all destinations simultaneously.

broadcast message: A message that is transmitted simultaneously to all stations on a multipoint circuit.

broadcast recognition access method (BRAM):   A version of broadcast recognition with alternating priorities (BRAP).

brush reader: A card reading device that uses brushes rather than an optical reader.

brute-force approach: To try to undertake with existing equipment the mass of problems that do not use precise computation or logical manipulations (as accounting problems and scientific problems do).

BS: See backspace character.

BSX: See broadband exchange (BEX).

bucket: A slang expression used to indicate some portion of storage specifically reserved for accumulating data, or totals. Commonly used in initial planning.

buffer: 1. A storage device in which data are assembled temporarily during data transfers. It is used to compensate for a difference in the rate of flow of information or the time occurrence of events when transferring information from one device to another. For example, the IBM 2821 control unit (a control and buffer storage unit for card readers, card punches, and printers

in a System/360). 2. A portion of main storage used for an input or output area.

buffered keyboard (open keyboard): Allows entry of numbers while calculator is executing previous calculations.

buffered keyboard printer: Two main types (a) those that include some type of buffering from the line and (b) those that transmit directly to the line when a key is depressed. The buffering allows several transactions or messages to be batched. Editing and corrections are performed off-line to ensure accuracy. In addition, buffering makes better use of the transmitting facility because of a higher transmission speed; that is, more terminals can share a dedicated (private) line for a given response time than if nonbuffered terminals are multipointed on a line. Less time is also required for a dial-up connection where charges are based on time and distance. Buffering also allows fixed or repetitive information to be added to a transaction without the need for manual entry during each occurrence.

buffered line printer: These printers often have 120-character wide print drums with a 64 character circumference around the drum. They can be operated on line as well as off-line in five different modes.

buffering exchange: A technique for input/output buffering which prevents or avoids the internal movement of data. Buffers are either filled, empty, or in use, by an input/output device. Exchange buffering relates to distinct areas set aside for work and for buffering.

buffering simple: A technique for obtaining simultaneous performance of intput/-output operations and computing. This method involves associating a buffer with only one input or output file (or data set) for the entire duration of the activity on that file (or data set).

buffering system: A set of routines to block and deblock data records and to perform buffer switching operations.

buffer-memory register: A register in which a word is stored as it comes from memory (reading) or just prior to its entering memory (writing).

buffer offset: The first field within a physical ASCII record; it precedes the first logical record. For Dformat variable-length records, the buffer offset may contain information about the data in the logical records.

buffer pool: 1. An area of storage in which all buffers of a program are kept. 2. Under telecommunications access method (TCAM), a group of buffers having the same size. A buffer pool is established as initialization time in the message control program; the buffers are built in extents chained together.

buffer preallocation: Permanently allocating buffers to each virtual circuit in each interface message processor (IMP), so that a place will always be available for any incoming packet until it can be forwarded.

buffer prefix: Under telecommunications access method (TCAM), a control area contained within each TCAM buffer. TCAM fills the prefix area with buffer control information.

buffer size: Buffers may be of the chained fixed sized, chained variable sized, or large circular types.

buffer storage: 1. A synchronizing element between two different forms of storage, usually between internal and external. 2. An input device in which information is assembled from external or secondary storage and stored ready for transfer to internal storage. 3. An output device into which information is copied from internal storage and held for transfer to secondary or external storage. Computation continues while transfers between buffer storage and secondary or internal storage or vice versa take place. 4. Any device which stores information temporarily during data transfers.

buffer unit pool: Under telecommunications access method (TCAM), all of the buffer units for that system.

bug: 1. An error in a program which causes improper operation. 2. A mistake or malfunction. 3. An integrated circuit.

building block principle: A system that permits the addition of other equipment units to form a larger system. Also called modularity.

built-in check: See automatic check.

built-in controls: Various error-checking techniques built into EDP equipment by the manufacturer.

bulk erased noise: 1. Those extra bits or words that must be ignored or removed from the data at the time the data is used. 2. Errors introduced into data in a system, especially in communication channels. 3. Random variations of one or more characteristics of any entity such as voltage, current data. 4. Loosely, any disturbance tending to interfere with the normal operation of a device or system.

bulk memory: One of various types of auxiliary memory devices with storage capacity greatly in excess of working (core) memory; e.g., disk file, drums, cells, etc.

bulk message testing: The testing of a program by pushing through a great many messages to find errors that happen infrequently. Also called message testing, saturation.

buried coaxial cable telecommunications union: The system involves a pair of coaxial cables buried a few feet apart in shallow earth. The cables leak current through holes in their metallic sheaths. A remote processor controls the timing of pulses transmitted by one cable and returned by the second. Objects passing through the field cause a change in the signal returning to the processor, which computes the location of the disturbance. The information is fed to a display, pinpointing the intruder's location.

buried layer: A heavily doped (N+) region directly under the N-doped exitaxial collector region of transistors in a monolithic integraged circuit used to lower the series collector resistance.

burn-in: In this screening test, devices are operated at high temperature for an extended period of time to accelerate failure mechanisms. Normal burn-in consists of operation at +125°C and is designed eliminate what appear to be electrically good devices but are marginal that would probably result in early lifetime failures under normal conditions. Power-on burn-in testing will uncover metallization defects such as intermittent shorts or opens, pin holes in the passivation layers beneath metallization, and corrosion or contamination defects. This test will also locate circuits that have crystal dislocations, diffusion anomalies, contamination in or on the oxide, improper doping levels, and cracked dice. The burn-in screen is also used to evaluate the quality of a lot. If more than a prescribed number of circuits fail the subsequent electrical testing, the entire lot can be rejected.

burst: 1. To separate continuous-form paper into discrete sheets. 2. In data transmission, a sequence of signals counted as one unit in accordance with some specific criterion or measure. 3. See error burst.

burster: A device used off-line or peripherally in a computer system which is designed to separate individual forms as produced by printer output.

burst mode: A means of transferring data as a continuous block to or from a particular input/output (I/O) device on either the multiplexer or selector channel. All channel controls are monopolized for the duration of data transfer.

burst-oriented data transmission: The nature of data transmission is typically burst-oriented, where the communicating computers or terminals have need for a specific data rate for a short time period and then have no need for transmission for a more extended time period.

bus: 1. A circuit over which data or power is transmitted. Often one which acts as a common connection among a number of locations. (Synonymous with trunk.) 2. A path over which information is transferred, from any of several sources to any of several destinations. 3. One or more conductors used for transmitting signals or power.

bus driver: A power amplifier used as a driver for many points such as inputs or devices, by way of a conductor, usually a low-impedance bus in a digital computer.

Business and Engineering Enriched FORTRAN (BEEF): Sets of additional subroutines added to the capability of the FORTRAN programming language.

business data processing: 1. Data processing for business purposes, e.g., recording and summarizing the financial transactions of a business. 2. Same as administrative data processing.

business EDP system technique (BEST): A concept developed by the National Cash Register Company for programming business problem solutions on NCR computers.

business machine: 1. A machine designed to facilitate clerical operations in commercial or scientific activities. 2. In data communications, customer-provided equipment that connects to common carriers' communications services for the purpose of data movement.

business machine clocking: A time base oscillator supplied by the business machine for regulating the bit rate of transmission,. Synonymous with non-data set clocking.

business statistics: A concept which relates to the evelution of risks of wrong decisions due to the partial rather than total data availability. The statistical techniques of inductive inference concern bodies of precisely stated and empirically tested rules and laws for (a) securing information, (b) manipulating and formulating such data in mathematically or diagrammatically meaningful expressions, and (c) preparing the bases for effective action and control.

bus input/output (I/O) channels: Central processor communication paths consist of a high-speed data bus, a high-speed input/-output bus for computer peripheral equipment, and a low-speed bus buffer channel for slower process equipment (in some systems).

bussback: The connection, by a common carrier, of the output portion of a circuit back to the input portion of a circuit.

bustback: A Western Union term similar in meaning to bussback.

busy hour: The peak 60-minute period during a business day when the largest volume of communications traffic is handled.

busy test: In telephony, a test to find out whether certain facilities which may be desired, such as subscriber line or trunk, are available for use.

b-wind: The method of winding tape on a reel in which the oxide surface of the tape faces away from the hub.

bypass capacitor: A capacitor required to provide a low-impedance path around resistors or similar circuit elements for high frequency alternating currents.

by-product: Data in some form developed without additional effort from an operation whose basic purpose is to produce other data.

byte: 1. A sequence of adjacent binary digits operated upon as a unit and usually shorter than a computer word. 2. The representation of a character. 3. In System/360 and System/370, a sequence of eight adjacent binary digits that are operated upon as a unit and that constitute the smallest addressable unit in the system.

byte count storage: A way of storing records in which each record contains a byte count telling how long it is.

byte manipulation: The ability to manipulate, as individual instructions, groups of bits such as characters. A byte is considered to be eight bits in most cases, and forms either one character or two numerals.

byte mode: The movement of one byte at a time between devices, separated by an interrupt and release of channel control. Used in multiplexing, the byte mode permits the handling of data from several low-speed devices simultaneously.

byte multiplexer: A device that receives several bytes of data from various sources, combines them into a single transmission path, and distributes them to various destinations. Generally, byte multiplexers are used in large, multi-user computer systems as channels to provide communication between the computer and its peripheral devices. A byte multiplexer is similar to a block multiplexer except that it handles data on a byte-by-byte basis instead of in entire blocks.

byte multiplexer channel: A multiplexer channel that interleaves bytes of data. See also block multiplexer channel.

byte multiplexing: A procedure in which time slots on a channel are assigned to individual slow input/output devices so that bytes from one after another can be interlaced on the channel to or from main memory. Such a procedure is used on several IBM 360 and 370 systems.

C

cable: An assembly of one or more conductors, usually within an enveloping protective sheath, with such structural arrangement of the individual conductors as will permit their use separately or in groups.

cablecasting: Original programming over a cable system. Includes public access programming.

cable noise: When digital equipment is cabled together, care must be taken to minimize crosstalk between the individual conductors in the cables. Because of the fast rise and fall times characteristic of digital signals, these individual conductors can often generate significant amounts of noise.

Cable TV: Previously called Community Antenna Television (CATV), a communications system which distributes broadcast programs and original programs and services by means of coaxial cable.

cache memory: A set of registers addressable conventionally and heavily used for data or instructions.

CAI: Computer assisted instruction.

calculated address: An address generated or developed by machine instructions contained in the program which uses the address. This address may be determined as a result of some program or process and it may depend upon some set of criteria or conditions.

calculating operation average: A common or typical calculating operation longer than an addition and shorter than a multiplication.

calculating terminal: A system for providing basic arithmetic functions.

calculator: 1. A data processor especially suitable for performing arithmetical operations that require frequent intervention by a human operator. 2. Generally and historically, a device for carrying out logic and arithmetic digital operations of any kind.

calibration accuracy: The limit of error in the finite degree to which a device can be calibrated. (Influenced by sensitivity, resolution, and repeatability of the device itself and the calbrating equipment.) Usually it is expressed in percent of full scale.

calibre error measurement: A procedure to ascertain the error in the output of a device by checking it against a standard.

call: 1. To transfer control to a specified closed subroutine. 2. In communications, the action performed by the calling party, or the operations necessary in making a call, or the effective use made of a connection between two stations. 3. See subroutine call.

call barred facility: A facility that permits a data terminal to either make outgoing calls or to receive incoming calls, but not both.

call barring: A technique to prevent all or certain calls to or from a telephone line.

call card agendum: 1. A single agendum name and its parameters punched on one card in a stylized form; one item of the agenda. 2. A control language statement calling for the execution of the named agendum. 3. A set of agendum call cards is used to control a linearprogramming system, thus forming an agenda.

call collision: Refers to contention that occurs when data circuit or data terminal equipment simultaneously transfer a call request packet and incoming call packets specifying the same channel. Unless otherwise programmed, the data circuit terminating equipment (DCE) will proceed with the call request and cancel the incoming call.

call control character: Concerning data operations, a character that is used to control calls; used in conjunction with defined signal conditions on various interchange circuits.

call delay: The delay in obtaining access to an item of common equipment in a central office.

call detail recording (CDR): The computer-controlled collection, processing and reporting of all calling activity. This supports system performance and cost control.

call-directing code (CDC): Bell System term for an identifying call, which is transmitted on an outlying telegraph receiver and automatically turns on its printer.

called station: In communications switching, receives the request from a calling station.

call error: Indicates that too many subroutines have been called by the program. A maximum of 50 subroutines may be called by an object program on some computers.

call forwarding: A service feature available in some switching systems where calls can be rerouted automatically from one line to another or to an attendant.

call in: To transfer control of a digital computer temporarily from a main routine to a subroutine, which is inserted in the sequence of calculating operations to fulfil a subsidiary purpose.

calling: In communications, a procedure by which a first party attempts to establish a connection with a second party through a central exchange.

calling device: The dial or keypad which generates the pulses or tones to signal the customer's requirements to the central office.

calling sequence: A sequence of instructions, parameters and parameter addresses. The calling sequence specifies the entry to the subroutine and uniquely determines by its parameters the action to be performed. A minimum calling sequence consists of an entry specification only.

calling sequence subroutine: A designed arrangement of instructions and data necessary to set up and call a given subroutine.

calling station: In communications switching, the calling station directs the operations of selecting, polling, etc.

call instruction: A transfer instruction to a subprogram which may have no or multiple arguments and which may result in no or multiple variable values returned to the mainline program.

call-number: A set of characters identifying a subroutine and containing information concerning parameters to be inserted in the subroutine, information to be used in generating the subroutine, or information related to the operands.

call progress signals: Call progress signals are sent by the data circuit terminating equipment (DCE) to inform the data terminal equipment (DTE) of the result of the call. The signals consist of two digit numbers. The first number gives the general class of the result, (for example, call put through, try again, short- or longterm network congestion), and the second the details.

call-word: A call-number which fills exactly one word.

camp-on: A method of holding a call for a line that is in use and of signaling when it becomes free. Synonymous with clamp-on.

cancel character: A specific control character designed to indicate that the data with which it is associated are erroneous or to be disregarded.

CANCEL status word: Indicates that the remote computing system has deleted some information.

CANTRAN: CANcel TRANmission.

capability: Permission which the user process must possess for the object in order to carry out an operation on the object (i.e., to retrieve a file).

capacitance: The property of a system of conductors and dielectrics that permits the storage of electrically separated charges when potential differences exist between the conductors.

capacitance-coupled flip-flop: Same as ac coupled flip-flop.

capacitor: An electronic component consisting of two metal plates separated by a nonconductor.

capacitor, storage: A device which stores a digital bit or an analog voltage by charging a capacitor.

capacity (calculator): The capacity of a calculator is the maximum number of digits that can be entered or obtained in a result. In most machines, the capacity is equivalent to the number of digits in the display. In a few machines, it is larger than the number of digits in the display and a flip-flop key is used to show the full result. Where this is the case, it is noted in the table.

capacity, channel: 1. The maximum number of binary digits or elementary digits to other bases which can be handled in a particular channel per unit time. 2. The maximum possible information transmission rate through a channel at a specified error rate. The channel capacity may be measured in bits per sec. or bauds.

capacity display: A de facto standard for screen capacity might be 80 characters per line and 24 lines for a total of 1,920 characters displayed at one time. For some special applications in word or text processing it may be worthwhile to expand the number of characters per line to 100; however, if additional lines were required, additional memory would be added to the terminal and the additional lines can be displayed in the window or display screen by page flipping or rolling up and rolling down.

capstan: A rotating device in tape recorder which assists the movement of the tape.

capture effect: An effect where FM receivers are able to extract the stronger of two overlapping packets without error.

card: 1. A machine-processable information storage medium of special quality paper stock, generally $7\frac{3}{8} \times 3\frac{1}{4}$ inches. 2. An internal pluggable unit for printed-circuits wiring and components.

cardiology automation: 1. Electrocardiograms (EKG) processing: represents the single most widely used automated analysis procedure currently in use in medicine. Rigid certification procedures are available, and programs operating in over six different types of computers have passed the test with several more scheduled for trials. The analog EKG signal is converted to digital form and voltage, duration, and interval measurements tables are listed; interpretive messages are selected by reference to decision tables. Special digital and analog magnetic tape recorders and telephone transmission devices are available from several companies. 2. Cardiac catheterization on-line acquisition and analysis of blood pressures, dye curves, and other parameters simplify report preparation and allow more effective procedural decisions during the tests to maximize diagnostic yield . 3. Cardiac intensive care monitoring: post myocardial infarction monitoring concentrates mostly on arrythmia detection, offering generally better noise immunity than entirely analog systems. Continuous monitoring in the critical first 2-4 days significantly decreases early mortality.

card jam: A pile-up of cards in a machine.

card-programmed calculator: A unit in a group of conventional electronic accounting machines (EAM), often associated with a tabulator to read punched cards.

card punch: A machine which punches cards in designated locations to store data which can be conveyed to other machines or devices by reading or sensing the holes.

card routine loader: A routine generated automatically according to a programmer's specification and included in an object program to perform, respectively, program-loading operations and a printout of memory content upon request.

card stacker: A receptacle that accumulates cards after they have passed through a machine.

card-terminal transmission: A machine that transmits data from punched cards over telephone lines to a receiving machine.

card-to-tape program: Transfers binary or EBCDIC data from cards to magnetic tape.

card-unit type: Indicates the unit's function; reader only (RD) punch only (PN), or reader-punch combination (RP).

carriage: 1. A cable system's procedure of carrying the signals of television stations on its various channels. FCC rules determine which signals cable systems must or may carry. 2. See automatic carriage.

carriage control character: A character used in a specific coding sequence (e.g., the first character in a FORTRAN WRITE format statement) which indicates desired printer carriage action, such as skip to next page, double line skip, suppress skip, etc.

carriage return: In a character-by-character printing mechanism, the operation that causes the next character to be printed at the left margin.

carriage return character: A specific control character designed to cause a carriage return to be performed.

carriage tape: A paper or plastic tape used to control carriage operation of some printing output devices. It is also called control tape.

carriage space key: A push button which advances the hard copy one or more lines in various type printers.

carrier circuit: A transmission path used in a carrier system.

carrier, data: A single frequency or tone that is modulated by voice or data to communicate information.

carrier frequency: 1. The frequency of a carrier wave. 2. A frequency capable of being modulated or impressed with a second (information carrying) signal. In frequency modulation, the carrier frequency also is referred to as the center frequency.

carrier noise: Often referred to as residual modulation, carrier noise is noise produced by undesired variations of a radio-frequency signal in the absence of any intended modulation.

carrier power output rating: The unmodulated power nominally available at the output terminals of the transmitter when connected to its normal antenna, or to a circuit equivalent thereof. Unless otherwise stated, this is the normal rating of the transmitter.

carrier's carrier: Same as interconnection network, because the latter's only subscribers are the carrier's who run the individual networks.

carrier sense network: A type of local network. Its most common transmission medias are coaxial cables, twisted pairs, and fiber optics. Among its cable topologies are the segmented, linear, spine, and tree types.

carrier sense protocols: Network protocols in which stations listen for a carrier, or transmission, and act accordingly.

carrier shift: This is the difference between the steady-state mark and space frequencies in a datacarrier system using frequency shift modulation.

carrier-suppressed transmission: A method of communication in which the carrier frequency is suppressed either partially or to the maximum degree possible. One or both of the sidebands may be transmitted.

carrier system: A means of obtaining a number of channels over a single path by modulating each channel on a different carrier frequency and demodulating at the receiving point to restore the signals to their original form. Some typical carrier systems are:

AT & T Carrier System Type		Number of FDC Circuits Derived	Transmission Facility
J	(telephone)	12 FD	4-wire, open-wire
N	(telephone or program)	12 FD	Nonloaded toll or
ON	(telephone)	20-24 FD	Cable
TD2	(microwave)	500 FD	Radio
L3	(telephone or program)	1860 FD	Paired coax

carrier-to-noise ratio: The ratio, in decibels, of the value of the carrier to that of the noise in the receiver intermediate frequency (IF) bandwidth before any non-linear process such as amplitude limiting and detection.

carrier transmission: Transmission in which the transmitted electric wave results from the modulation of a single-frequency wave by a modulating (information-carrying) wave.

carrier wave: The basic frequency or pulse-repetition rate of a signal bearing no intrinsic intelligence until it is modulated by another signal which does bear intelligence. A carrier may be amplitude, phase, or frequency modulated; e.g., in a typical mercury delayline storage of a digital computer, the 8-mcs soundwave carrier is amplitude or pulse modulated by a 1mcs code signal, the presence or absence of a pulse determining whether or not a one or a zero is present in the binary number being represented.

carry: 1. A signal, or expression, produced as a result of an arithmetic operation on one digit place of two or more numbers expressed in positional notation and transferred to the next higher place for processing there. 2. A signal or expression as defined in 1 above which arises in adding, when the sum of two digits in the same digit place equals or exceeds the base of the number system in use. If a carry into a digit place will result in a carry out of the same digit place, and if the normal adding circuit is bypassed when generating this new carry, it is called a high speed carry, or standing on nines carry. If the normal adding circuit is used in such a case, the carry is called a cascaded carry. If a carry resulting from the addition of carries is not allowed to propagate, e.g., when forming the partial product in one step of a multiplication process, it is called a partial carry. If it is allowed to propagate, the process is called a complete carry. If a carry generated in the most significant digit place is sent directly to the least significant place, e.g., when adding two negative numbers using nine complements, that carry is called an end around carry. 3. A signal or expression in direct subtraction, as defined in 1 above which arises when the difference between the digits is less than zero. Such a carry is frequently called a borrow. Related to borrow. 4. The action of forwarding a carry. 5. The command directing a carry to be forwarded.

carry-complete signal: A signal generated by a digital parallel adder, indicating that all carries from an adding operation have been generated and propagated and the addition operation is completed.

carry condition: 1. A condition occurring during addition when the sum of two digits in the same column equal or exceeds the number base; 2. The digit to be added to the next higher column; 3. The process of forwarding the carry digit.

carry time: 1. The time required for transferring a carry digit to the higher column and there adding it. 2. The time required for transferring all the carry digits to higher columns and adding them for all digits in the number.

Carterfone Decision: In 1968, this dexision allowed customers to connect their own equipment to the telephone network. The explosive growth of data communications has attracted large numbers of manufacturers to the modem market, and to hundreds of other devices as well. "Manufacturers and sellers of such devices would then have the responsiblity of offering for sale or use only such equipment as would be in compliance with such revised standards. An owner or user of a device which failed to meet reasonable revised standards for such devices, would either have to comply with the revised standards or discontinue its use. Such is the risk inherent in the private ownership of any equipment to be used in connection with the telephone system."

cartridge: 1. Container for recorded programming designed to be shown on a television receiver. The cartridge contains a reel of motion picture film, videotape or electronically embossed vinyl tape, blank or recorded, and uses an external take-up reel. 2. Cassette-like container for computer tape, frequently used to record data input in data entry terminals and systems.

cascade: A succession of amplifying stages.

cascade control: An automatic control system in which various control units are linked in sequence, each control unit regulating the operation of the next control unit in line.

cascade control action: A specific type of control action in which the output of one controller is the set point for another controller.

cascaded carry: In parallel addition, a carry process in which the addition of two numerals results in a partial sum numeral and a carry numeral which are in turn added together, this process being repeated until no new carries are generated.

cascade merging: A method designed for a sort porgram to merge strings of sequenced data.

cassette: A self-contained package of reel-to-reel blank or recorded film, videotape, or electronically embossable vinyl tape for recording of sound or computer input signals, which is continuous and selfrewinding. Similar to a cartridge, but of slightly different design.

catalog: 1. An ordered compilation of item descriptions and sufficient information to afford access to the items. 2. The collection of all data set indexes that are used by the control program to locate a volume containing a specific data set. 3. To include the volume identification of a data set in the catalog. 4. Under DOS and TOS, to enter a phase, module, or book into one of the system libraries.

cataloged data set: A specific data set, usually contatenated, which is included in an index or a hierarchy of indices.

cataloged procedure: A set of job control statements that has been placed in a partitioned data set called the procedure library, and can be retrieved by naming it in an execute (EXEC) statement or started by the START command.

catalog, split: A catalog with sets of entries by subject, author and title.

catastrophic errors: When enough errors

have occurred so that no more useful diagnostic information can be produced, the compilation is terminated.

catastrophic failure: A failure which is total or nearly so, such as: breakdown of the power supply, making all circuits inoperative. Any type of failure which renders the useful performance of the computer to zero.

cathode: 1. Electron tube: the electrode through which a primary stream of electrons enters the interelectrode space. 2. Electrolytic; the electrode where positive ions are discharged or negative ions are formed or where other reducing reactions occur.

cathode follower: A vacuum tube circuit developing an input signal to the grid while the load is in the cathode circuit and the output signal is taken off of the cathode, i.e., the voltage follows that of the grid, the voltage gain always being less than unity. See emitter-follower.

cathode   ray: Stream   of   negatively-charged   particles   (electrons)   emitted normally from the surface of the cathode in a rarefied gas.

cathode-ray storage: See CRT storage.

cathode-ray tube (CRT):   An electronic vacuum tube containing a screen on which alphanumeric or graphic information may be displayed.

cathode-ray   tube   (CRT)   function keys: When depressed transmits a signal to the computer which can be equated to a prestored   typewriter   message   of   many strokes. Function keys by thus saving user actions provide convenience and ease of operation and increased response rate of the user. Special consoles of various types have been developed for a particular user. Examples are: airline agent's sets, badge readers, stock broker's inquiry consoles and many others.

cathode-ray   tube   deflection   beam: A distinct optic terminal and storage device. A vacuum tube with a controlled beam of electrons used as either a display or storage device, with a deflection of the beam of electrons in two dimensions on their way to the screen. Programmed control provides graphic display and digital storage capabilities. An electron gun, deflection plates, and the screen are the three major components of the storage display. Other CRT displays are: TV tubes, oscilloscopes, radar displays and remote station display tubes.

cathode-ray tube point mode: A mode of operation in which points may be established and plotted on the display.

CATV: See   community   antenna television.

CATV directional coupler: 1. A matched tapping device for insertion in a CATV cable, which introduces a loss of only 1 dB in the through transmission and provides a spur outlet. 2. A transmission coupling device for sampling separately either the forward (incident) or the backward (reflected) wave in a transmission line.

CATV line extender: Amplifier used in line to provide CATV service to remote subscribers.

CATV   penetration: The ratio of the number of subscribers to the total number of households passed by the cable system. Penetration is the basis of a system's profitability.

CAX, community automatic exchange: A small dial telephone office servicing an individual community.

CC: Closed circuit (transmission).

CCD: See charge-coupled device.

CCH: See channel-check handler.

CCW: See channel command word.

CDC: See call-directing code.

Ceefax: Digital data "Teletext" broadcasting service associated with TV signals transmitted by the British Broadcasting Corporation.

cell: 1. The storage for one unit of information, usually one character or one word. 2. A location specified by whole or part of the address and possessed of the faculty of store. Specific terms such as column, field, location, and block, are preferable when appropriate. 3. See binary cell, storage cell.

cell, photovoltaic: A specific cell which can produce electric potential when it is exposed to electromagnetic radiation, i.e., most often visible light.

cellar: A storage which works as though it comprised a number of registers arranged in a column, with only the register at the top of the column connected to the rest of the storage. Each word in turn enters the top register and is then "pushed down" the column from register to register to make room for the next words to arrive. As the words are transferred out of the storage units, from the top register, other data in storage moves back up the column from register to reg ister to fill the space vacated.

cellular telephone system: Various cellular communications systems for mobile and portable telephone service offer users such features as call forwarding, call waiting, and speed dialing. The typical system includes switch, processor, cell site and cell site equipment, antennas, and tower plus cellular terminals. Some systems serve smaller metropolitan areas, and other systems serve up to 100,000 mobile telephone users.

center feed tape: A type of perforated paper tape which has feed holes centered directly in line with the centers of the intelligence holes.

central communications controller: Provides simultaneous communications and processing where multiple sending and receiving units may share the same communications lines. Several hundred remote units may be online and up to 100 messages may be flowing in and out of memory simultaneously; the central controller ensures that all data is routed to its proper destination.

centralization: The concentration of decision making in an organizational structure. Centralization frequently takes place to make optimum use of a computerbased information system. Computers encourage centralization because centralized management can consider all the relevant data, whereas a fragmented system cannot.

centralized adaptive routing algorithms: Algorithms similar to static directory routing in that each interface message processor (IMP) maintains a table telling how to forward packets, and in that the table may or may not contain alternate routes. However, the routing tables inside the IMPs are constructed differently, and centralized routing uses an routing control center (RCC).

centralized configuration: A simple timesharing system, with channels radiating from a central computer system, and perhaps, multiplexers or concentrators serving to fan in still other radial communication channels, is an example of a centralized configuration. This organization can be applied on a local, national, or even international scale.

centralized data processing: Data processing performed at a single, central location on data obtained from several geographical locations or managerial levels. Decentralized data processing involves processing at various managerial levels or geographical points throughout the organization.

centralized network functions: In the centralized network, all the communications functions of message routing, speed conversion, code/protocol conversion, and error checking are performed in a common location. Network control functions relating to network job scheduling and the allocation of host resources to users are similarly monitored from a common location. The processor performing network control may be either dedicated to the control function or may alternate between the control mode and background processing of local jobs.

central office bridge: Supplied and installed by the local telephone company, like the data sets and lines, a bridge, located in the telephone company central office, connects lines from several offices into one circuit-line to provide optimum transaction loads for each line going to the processing center.

central office exchange: The place where a communication common carrier locates the equipment which interconnects subscribers and circuits.

central office plant: In communication practice, that part of the plant within a central office, intermediate station or subscriber's premises that is on the office or station side of the point of connection with the outside plant. The plant in a central office is commonly referred to as central office plant, and the plant on the station premises is referred to as station plant.

central processing element (microprocessor): The major compound of the bipolar microcomputer.

central processing unit (CPU): A unit of a computer that includes the circuits controlling the interpretation and execution of instructions. Synonymous with main frame.

central processor organization: Can be divided into three main sections: arithmetic and control, input/output, and memory. The arithmetic and control section carries out the directives of the program. The calculations, routing of information, and control of the other sections occur in this part of the central processor. All information going in and coming out of the central processor is handled by the input/output section. It also controls the operation of all peripheral equipment. The memory section is the heart of the central processor; it

provides temporary storge for data and instructions. Because of its importance, the total cycle time of the memory is the main determining factor in the overall speed of the processor. the processor.

central scanning loop: A loop of instructions which determines which task is to be performed next. After each item of work is completed, control is transferred to the central scanning loop which searches for processing requests in order to determine the next item to be processed. The computer may cycle idly in the central scanning loop if no item requires its attention, or it may go into a wait state which is interrupted if the need arises. The central scanning loop is the nucleus of a set of supervisory programs.

central terminal unit (CTU): This unit supervises communication between remote point-of-transaction terminals and the processing center. It receives incoming messages at random intervals, stores them until the central processor is ready to process them, and returns the processed replies to the terminals which originated the transactions.

Central Tumor Registry (CTR): An information processing procedure (nearly always computer-based) which collects, stores, selects, and reports case-wise information regarding patients with malignant neoplasms for the purpose of patient follow-up and hospital and regional tumor program planning and evaluation. Some CTR's print case reports to physicians as well as to hospitals (physician-oriented). Early CTR's primarily were used for statistical and epidemiologic studies and provided less assistance in hospital program management and practically none in patient-management (follow-up, etc.).

centrex: Central office telephone equipment serving subscribers at one location on a private automatic branch exchange basis. The system allows such services as direct inward dialing, direct distance dialing, and console switchboards.

certificate of conformance (C of C): A supplier's or contractor's written statement certifying that supplies or services comply with contract requirements. For screened microcircuits, the C of C confirms that all screening was performed and it usually indicates the date of each test.

certified tape: Computer tape that is checked on all tracks throughout each and every roll and is certified by the supplier to have less than a certain number of errors or, more usually, to have zero errors.

CESD: See composite external symbol dictionary.

chad: The circular piece of paper removed from tape where a hole is punched.

chad tape: Tapes which have been completely perforated.

chain: 1. Any set of records or items linked together either physically or logically in a specified sequence. 2. Pertaining to a routine consisting of segments which are run through the computer in tandem, only one being within the computer main-frame at any one time and each having access to the output from previously executed segments. The order in which the segments are executed may be data dependent.

chain code: An arrangement in a cyclic sequence of some or all of the possible different n-bit words, in which adjacent words are related such that each is derivable from its neighbor by displacing the bits one digit position to the left, or right, dropping the leading bit, and inserting a bit at the end. The value of the inserted bit needs only to meet the requirement that a word must not recur before the cycle is complete, for example, 000 001 010 101 011 111 110 100 000 etc.

chained list codifier: A specific list of items, each of which has a coded identifier for locating the next item to be used or considered, though they maybe scattered spatially.

chaining: A system of storing records in which each record belongs to a list or group of records and has a linking field for tracing the chain.

chaining, command: The execution of a sequence of I/O commands in a command list, under control of an IOP, on one or more logical records.

chaining overflow: On a direct access storage device, the writing of overflow records on the next higher available track; each track contains a record that provides a link between the home track and the overflow track. Contrast with progressive overflow.

chaining search: A search technique in which each item contains an identifier for locating the next item to be considered.

chain printer: A printer in which the type slugs are carried by the links of a revolving chain.

chain reaction: A programming technique for automatic initiation of multiple levels of address modification and indirect addressing without addressing instructions.

chains: A facility provided by dialog control. Messages are grouped into chains for error recovery and other purposes. In Systems Network Architecture (SNA).

change control procedures: Administrative procedures used to evaluate all suggested changes to a system and to oversee the implementation of approved change requests. Such procedures are necessary for coordination between users, system analysts, and programmers, for preventing undesirable or unexpected impacts upon supposedly unaffected parts of the system, and to control the scheduling of change implementation for the sake of efficiency.

change dump: A selective dump of those storage locations whose contents have changed.

change record: A record which results in

changing some of the information in the corresponding master file record.

change, step: A finite value of input change made in theoretically zero time. A very rapid change of level.

change tape: A paper tape or magnetic tape carrying information that is to update filed information. This filed information is often on a master tape.

channel: 1. That part of a communication system that connects the message source with the message sink. In the information theory in the sense of shannon the channel can be characterized by the set of conditional probabilities of occurrence of all the messages possible to receive at the message sink when a given message emanates from the message source. 2. A path along which signals can be sent, e.g., a data channel, output channel. 3. The portion of a storage medium that is accessible to a given reading or writing station, e.g., track, band. 4. In communication, a means of one-way transmission. Several channels may share common equipment. For example, in frequency multiplexing carrier systems, each channel uses a particular frequency band that is reserved for it. 5. Contrast with circuit.

channel adapter: A device which permits the connection between data channels of differing equipment. The device allows data transfer at the rate of the slower channel.

channel address word (CAW):   A word in main storage that specifies the location in main storage at which a channel program begins.

channel allocation: The allocation of channels for data transmission is performed in several different ways. If a large amount of traffic is expected from one point to another, the entire channel may be dedicated indefinitely to that transmission. Otherwise, most networks provide a mechanism for efficient sharing of each channel. This is especially important for data communications, since few data trans-

mission requirements exactly match the capacity of available channels.

channel bus, input/output: Central processor communication paths consist of a high-speed data bus, a highspeed input/-output bus for computer peripheral equipment, and a low-speed bus buffer channel for slower process equipment.

channel check handler (CCH):   In System/-370 and under OS/360, a feature that records, when a channel error occurs, information about the error and issues a message to the operator. Under DOS on System/360, a similar function is performed by machine check recording and recovery (MCRR).

channel, Class-E: Capable of transmission rates up to 1200 baud. The channel will also accept polar-pulse input conforming to EIA standards, and will deliver signals at the destination having the same characteristics.

channel command: An instruction that directs a channel, control unit, or device to perform an operation or set of operations.

channel command word (CCW):   A doubleword at the location in main storage specified by the channel address word. One or more CCWs make up the channel program that directs channel operations.

channel (communications):   An electrical transmission path among two or more stations or channel terminations in telephone or telegraph company offices furnished by wire, radio, or a combination of both. Also called link, circuit, line, data path, etc.

channel conditioning: The electrical balancing of a channel to reduce attenuation distortion, delay distortion, and the effects of noise.

channel connector: Available for every channel or just one of the channels. A channel connector provides a variety of uses that magnify the flexibility of the system.

One use is to connect a selector channel on one system to a selector channel on another system, thereby providing intersystem communications. When this is done, each system appears like input/output (I/O) equipment to the other.

channel controller: A device which provides an independent data path to storage and assures multiprocessor systems maximum availability, allowing each processing unit to have access to every channel in the system.

channel distortion: The amount of channel distortion is a function of channel length and complexity. The telephone company will ask for a customer's speed and code format so that regenerative repeaters can be used to ensure reliable operation. These repeaters will be located in the telephone-company central offices at different locations along the circuit path. Here the distorted signal is regenerated, that is, reshaped. However, if a machine uses different signaling rates or codes, standard regenerative repeaters cannot be provided and the distortion of the channel is not specified. A teletype machine is expected to deliver no more than 5 percent distortion at the transmitting location and can tolerate approximately 40 percent distortion at the receiving end of the circuit.

channel grade: The grades of channels are wideband, voiceband, and narrowband.

channel input/output switching: By linking certain input or output units to more than one channel, a variety of ways are open to reach the device, even if other units are occupying one or more of the available channels. A single unit can be linked through channel switching to one channel at the start of processing on a job, and then to another.

channelize: To subdivide a channel into multiple channels of lesser bandwidth.

channel packing: A technique for maximizing the utilization of voice frequency channels used for data transmission by multiplexing a number of lower speed data signals into a single higher speed data stream for transmission on a single voice frequency channel.

channel program: One or more channel command words that control a specific sequence of channel operations. Execution of the specific sequence is initiated by a single start input/output (I/O) instruction.

channel program block (CPB): Under telecommunications access method (TCAM), a control block used in the transfer of data between buffer units and message queues maintained on disk.

channel pulse: A pulse representing intelligence on a channel by virtue of its time or modulation characteristic.

channel reliability: The percentage of time the channels meet the arbitrary standards established by the user.

channel speeds: Available channels begin at the low end with those that provide a 60 to 100 bits per second (bps) data rate, sufficient to support a slow speed teletypewriter terminal. A "voice grade" channel, suitably conditioned, now supports 2000-9600 bps. Error rates experienced at these data rates are of the order of one in 10^5, but more meaningful block-oriented error rates vary considerably depending on how the channel is used and controlled. Higher bandwidth channels can be supplied, such as the 50 Kbps channels employed in the advanced research project agency (ARPA) network. A voice capacity channel is now in operation through the Pacific Intelsat IV satellite supporting 60 Kbps for a link of the ARPA network. If needed, much greater channel capacity can be made available using conventional telephone plant or new waveguide or laser technologies.

channel status table (CST): Used by input/output (I/O) drivers to wait until a specific channel is available prior to using it. CST is composed of separate entries for each channel available to the system. Each entry corresponds in order to the address of the channel. That is, entry 0 corresponds to channel 0, entry 1 to channel 1, etc. The size of the table varies according to the number of channels. Each CST entry is one 24bit word of the following format: CS is the channel status. If CS is zero, the channel is busy.

channel synchronizer: Housed with the peripheral control unit in a single cabinet, provides the proper interface between the central computer and the peripheral equipment. Other control functions of the channel synchronizer include: primary interpreting of the function words; searching, by comparison of an identifier with data read from a peripheral unit; and providing the central computer with peripheral-unit status information.

channel terminal device: A part of the equipment in a communication channel that may be used for either input or output to the channel.

channel-to-channel adapter: A hardware device that can be used to connect two channels on the same computing system or on different systems.

channel-to-channel connection: A device for rapid data transfer between two computers. A channel adapter is available that permits the connection between any two channels on any two systems. Data are transferred at the rate of the slower channel. See direct control connection.

channel utilization index: The ratio of the information rate (per second) through a channel to the channel capacity (per second).

channel, voice-grade service: A service provided by the common carriers that included a circuit capable of carrying a voice transmission. Now, when used in reference to the transmission of data, it also refers to a circuit of sufficient bandwidth to permit a datatransfer rate up to 3000 bits per second. Primarily the term distinguishes this service from teleprintergrade service in reference to regulatory agencies' tariffs.

channel width: Frequency band allocated to service or transmission.

character: One of a set of elements which may be arranged in ordered groups to express information. Each character has two forms: (a) a man-intelligible form, the graphic, including the decimal digits 0-9, the letters A-Z, punctuation marks, and other formatting and control symbols. (b) a computer-intelligible form, the code, consisting of a group of binary bits. Codes have been defined using 5, 6, 7 and 8 bit groups.

character-at-a-time printer: A printer which produces each line of print by consecutively printing each character from left to right along the line, e.g., a teleprinter or electric typewriter.

character boundary: 1. A real or imaginary rectangle which serves as a boundary, in character recognition, between consecutive characters or successive lines on a source document. 2. A character recognition term indicating the largest rectangle with a side parallel to the reference edge of the document. Each of the sides of this rectangle is tangential to the printed outline of a particular character.

character delete: A distinct operational character used to obliterate erroneous or undesired characters.

character-deletion character: A character within a line of terminal input specifying that it and the immediately preceding character are to be removed from the line. See line-deletion character.

character density: A measure of the number of characters recorded per unit of length or area.

character duration: The time required for all of the pulses which are associated with a specific character to pass a given point on a communication channel.

character element: 1. A basic information element as transmitted, printed, displayed, etc. or used to control communications, when used as a code. 2. Groups of bits, pulses, etc. occurring in a time period normally representing that for a character or symbolic representation.

character emitter: An electromechanical device which emits a timed pulse or group of pulses to form a character in some code.

character field: Bit positions 1 through 7 of a floating-point word or doubleword, which contain the base or exponent of a floating-point number (some computers).

character file separator: A specific control character which indicates or establishes logical boundaries between files.

character fill (to):   To replace all data in a storage location or group of locations with the repeated representation of a specific character, usually zeros or Xs.

characteristic distortion: Distortion caused by transients which, as a result of the modulation, are present in the transmission channel and depend on its transmission qualities.

characteristic impedance: 1. The ratio of voltage to current at every point along a transmission line on which there are no standing waves. 2. The square root of the product of the open- and short-circuit impedance of the line. When a transmission line is terminated in its characteristic impedance, energy is not reflected, but is absorbed fully in the terminating impedance.

character mode: The method of operation in which the basic unit of information is a character. One computer word may contain a maximum of 8 characters composed of 6 bits each. When transferred, a character is transferred usually as 7 bits (6 bits plus 1 bit for parity check).

character negative acknowledge: A communications character for control or for accuracy checking which is transmitted by a receiver back to a sender as a negative response.

character outline: The graphic pattern established by the stroke edges of a character.

character parity check (communications):   During transmission as the core storage readout is being converted from parallel to serial bit form, the data line terminal at the transmitting end functions to add a parity bit, where necessary, to make each data character odd or even parity. As the data characters are being received, the data line terminal makes a parity check as the conversion from serial to parallel bit form takes place for the storage entry. The parity and synchronizing bits are dropped off at this time. If the wrong parity is detected, an error is signalled by the receiving computer.

character printer: A device that prints a single character at a time. Contast with line printer.

character reader: A specialized device which can convert data represented in one of the type fonts or scripts read by a user directly into machine language.

character recognition: Two primary methods used for machine recognition of characters: (a) Optical character recognition (OCR) — cheap to produce but prone to error. (b) Magnetic ink character recognition (MICR) — needs special print fonts, but is more trustworthy.

character repertoire: The characters available in a particular code.

character row: See display line.

character set: 1. (ISO) An agreed upon finite set of different character. 2. An ordered set of unique representations.

character size: The number of bit positions used to represent a character.

character space: A special operating and graphic character designed to prevent a print.

character spacing reference line: In character recognition, a vertical line that is used to evaluate the horizontal spacing of characters. It may be a line that equally divides the distance between the sides of a character boundary or that coincides with the centerline of a vertical stroke.

characters-per-frame display: The maximum number of whole characters capable of being drawn flicker-free at the manufacturer's recommended refresher rate.

character string: 1. A group of characters in a one dimensional array in an order due to the reference of relations between adjacent numbers. 2. A sequence or group of connected characters, connected by codes, key words, or other programming or associative techniques.

character stuffing: A method for achieving data transparency in which the hardware automatically inserts an extra data link escape (DLE) in front of any DLE in the text. This is so that the receiver will not be confused by any DLE end of text (ETX) sequence in the data.

character style: In optical character recognition, a distinctive construction with no restriction as to size, that is common to a group of characters. Different sizes of a given character style are proportional in all respects.

character subset: A selection of characters from a character set, comprising all characters which have a specified common feature, for example, in the definition of character set, digits 0 through 9 constitute a character subset.

character tape: Information composed of bits stored across the several longitudinal channels of a tape.

character transfer rate: The speed that data may be read or written, i.e., characters per second.

character validating: Checking a character that has been accumulated for parity by

the communications interface or modem control unit to remove that job from the processor.

charge-coupled device (CCD):   Nickel-size silicon chip containing over 120,000 electronic elements. When an image is focused on the CCD, the sensor's electronic elements transform the picture into individual electrical charge paackets. These packets then are read out very rapidly by charge transfer techniques. The resulting information then can be processed and displayed as a TV picture. In the CCD, half the electronic elements form the imaging array and the other half are for storage and read-out. The CCD is being developed for use in all solid-state TV systems and its technology is being applied to such diverse areas as space exploration, closed-circuit television, military programs, surveillange systems, transmission of TV pictures over the telephone system by consumers with home video records, and to the field of broadcast camera applications.

charge coupled devices (CCD) digital memories: These have distinct advantages for memory applications, particularly in the area of high density information storage. Mass-memory applications had advanced to the point where 16 kilobit chips could then be fabricated on wafers about the same size as then-current 4k RAMs—and at between one-quarter and one-half the price. As for operating characteris- tics, such a 16k chip operates at data rates of between 25 and 50 us. With current CCD technology, 32k and 64k memory chips are possible, using electron-beam fabrication as necessary to achieve this density. CCD technology combined with MNOS brings cell areas of 0.5 square mils per bit. This allows the fabrication of 64-bit devices on a chip 245 by 245 square mils.

charge shift: The additional or extra rent required by most holders of various equipment.

charge-storage: Image information is stored on a mosaic of photocells or piezoelectric crystals, especially in camera tubes for television.

chart plugging: A diagrammatic chart displaying where plugs or wires are to be inserted into a plugboard. Other information displayed relates to placement and setting of switches, digit emitters, and other specific uses of the plugboard.

chart printer spacing: A form for developing a layout and spacing or general design of printed output as well as the preparation of the carriage control tape.

chatter: Rapid closing and opening of contacts on a relay, which reduces their life.

check: A process of partial or complete testing of the correctness of machine operations, the existence of certain prescribed conditions within the computer, or the correctness of the results produced by a program. A check of any of these conditions may be made automatically by the equipment or may be programmed.

check bit: A binary check digit; for example, a parity bit.

check character: A parity character added to a group of characters to assist in error-detection/correction.

check digit: Relates to one or several digits generated and carried in computer processes for ascertaining error and accuracy control of data in batch processing, in real-time, or in subsequent operations; often periodically regenerated and compared with the original data.

check, dynamic: A problem chosen to determine whether the computer or a program is operating correctly.

check indicator: A device which displays or announces that an error has been made or that a checking operation has determined that a failure has occurred.

check-indicator instruction: A specific instruction designed to direct a signal device to be turned on to call operator's attention to the fact that there is some discrepancy in the instruction now in use.

checking, marginal: A means of testing circuits for incipient or intermittent failures by varying the voltages applied to the circuits.

checking pre-edit programs: A pre-edit checking of the application or operational program before the test run. A pre-edit run can remove such things as disobedience to established supervisory care, program segmentation rules, and so on.

checking routine: A specific type of diagnostic (error-discovering) program which examines programs or data for the most obvious mistakes as misspelling in keypunching, or miskeypunching, but which does not cause execution of the program itself.

checking routine sequence: 1. That specific set of instructions which results in a review of the order of the instructions to be performed. 2. A set of instructions which reviews the order of data, such as employee table number sequence, etc.

checkless: A concept put forth in the 1960s by the Electronic Funds Transfer System, to develop a checkless, cashless, paperless society.

check, longitudinal parity: A parity check made in a longitudinal direction (as opposed to vertical). See parity check.

check, longitudinal redundancy: An error control check based on the arrangement of data according to a rule.

check number: A number composed of one or more digits and used to detect equipment malfunctions in data transfer operations. If a check number consists of only one digit, it is synonymous with check digit.

checkout: The application of diagnostic or testing procedures to a routine or to equipment. Same as debug.

checkout routine: A routine to aid programmers in the debugging of their routines. Some typical routines are: storage, print-out, tape print-out, and drum print-out.

checkout systems tests: Static and dynamic tests on components and subsystems of aircraft and submarine simulators, aircraft weapons complexes, missles etc, require automatic test facilities.

checkpoint: 1. A place in a routine where a check, or a recording of data for restart purposes, is performed. 2. A point at which information about the status of a job and the system can be recorded so that the job step can be restarted later. 3. To record such information.

checkpoint data set: A sequential or partitioned data set containing a collection of checkpoint entries. If a checkpoint data set is a partitioned data set, each checkpoint entry is a member.

checkpoint records: Records that contain the status of a job and the system at the time the records are written by the checkpoint routine. These records provide the information necessary for restarting a job without having to return to the beginning of the job.

checkpoint/restart facility: 1. A facility for restarting execution of a program at some point other than at the beginning, after the program was terminated due to a program or system failure. A restart can begin at a checkpoint or from the beginning of a job step, and uses checkpoint records to reinitialize the system. 2. Under telecommunications access method (TCAM), a facility that records the status of the teleprocessing network at designated intervals or following certain events. Following system failure, the system can be restarted and continued without loss of messages.

check problem: A problem chosen to determine whether the computer or a program is operating correctly.

check-proof total: One of a number of check totals which can be correlated in some manner for consistency or reconciliation in a range, set or distinct calculation.

check register: A register used to store information temporarily where it may be checked with the result of a succeeding transfer of this information.

check reset key: A pushbutton that acknowledges an error and resets the error detection mechanism indicated by the check light. This is required to restart a program after an error has been discovered in batch mode.

check solution: A solution to a problem obtained by independent means to verify a computer solution.

check sum: The sum used in various summation checks.

check truncation: The conversion of information on checks which flow through the banking system to computer media. The consumer receives a descriptive statement listing his checks, rather than the canceled checks themselves.

check, vertical parity: A check by summation in which the binary digits, in a character or word, are added, and the sum checked against a single, previously computed parity digit; i.e., a check tests whether the number of ones in a word is odd or even (synonymous with odd-even check, and related to redundant check and forbidden-combination check).

Chinese binary code: A code, used with punch cards, in which successive bits are represented by the presence or absence of punches on contiguous positions in successive columns as opposed to rows. Column-binary code is widely used in connection with 35-bit word computers where each group of 3 columns is used to represent a single word.

chip depletion layer: Sensitive zone at the junction on N-type and P-type semiconductors in which there are no current carriers until the device is biased or operated. Also called depletion region.

chip die: A single piece of silicon which has been cut from a slice by scribing and breaking. It can contain one or more circuits but is packaged as a unit.

choke packet: A packet that is triggered only when the system is congested. Each newly arriving packet is checked to see if its output line is in warning state. If so, the interface message processor (IMP) transmists a choke packet back to the source host, giving it the destination revealed in the packet. The packet itself is tagged (a header bit is activated) so that it will not generate any future choke packets, and is forwarded as usual.

chrominance signal: In color television, the signal which gives the combined luminance and color information. The signal is obtained by combining, in a color coding circuit, specified fractions of the separate video signals, which are used to modulate a chrominance subcarrier.

CIOCS: See communications input/-output control system.

cipher: Encrypts a fixed-size unit of plaintext with each operation.

cipher-proof: A method of balancing whereby certain figures are automatically subtracted from a control total. If the balance results in zero, it is proved that all figures were added and listed correctly. Sometimes referred to as zero balance.

ciphertext only problem: Having a quantity of ciphertext and no plaintext.

ciphertext or cryptogram: The output of the encryption process.

circuit: 1. A communications link between two or more points. See channel. 2. The conductor or system of conductors through which an electric current is intended to flow.

circuit breaker: Device for opening an electric circuit under abnormal operating conditions; e.g., excessive current, heat, high ambient radiation level, etc. Also called constant breaker.

circuit capacity: 1. The number of communications channels that can be derived from a given circuit at the same time. 2. The information capacity, measured in bits per second, of a circuit.

circuit chip: In microcircuitry, a single device, either a transistor or a diode that has been cut from a larger wafer of silicon.

circuit clamping: When used in a broadband transmission, clamping reinserts low-frequency signal components which were not transmitted faithfully.

circuit, component: An essential item that becomes an integral part of a circuit.

circuit composition: A fundamental circuit is composed of metallic conductors. Attached to the conductors are combinations of loading coils, equalizers, filters, amplifiers, repeaters, etc.

circuit cycle: The flow of electrons through a circuit.

circuit delay: The time it takes a circuit to change state after receiving an input signal.

circuit diagram: Conventional representation of wiring system of electrical or electronic equipment.

circuit discriminator: 1. Refers to a part of a circuit that extracts the desired signal from an incoming frequency-modulated wave by changing frequency variations into amplitude variations. 2. A device which, when the input voltage surpasses a given level, produces a voltage output. 3. A device which responds only to a pair of frequencies which share some characteristic, such as amplitude.

circuit dropout: The momentary interruption of a transmission because of the complete failure of a circuit.

circuit element: A single active or passive functional item in an electronic circuit such as one diode, one transistor, one resistor, etc., which, when connected to another, forms an electrical current.

circuit grade: The information-carrying capability in speed or type of signal. The grades of circuits are broadband, voice, subvoice, and telegraph. For data use, these grades are identified with certain speed ranges.

circuit layout record card: Card maintained by the telephone company or administration listing the facilities and equipment used to provide each special circuit transiting the facility concerned.

circuit load: Usually a percentage of maximum circuit capability to reflect actual use during a period of time; i.e., peak hour line load.

circuit noise level: The ratio of the circuit noise at any point in a transmission to some arbitrary amount of circuit noise chosen as a reference. This ratio is expressed in decibels above reference noise, abbreviateddbrn, signifying a circuit noise meter reading adjusted to represent an interfering effect under specified conditions.

circuit reliability: The percentage of time a circuit meets operational standards.

circuits, computer: Among the various basic types of circuits used in the construction of digital computers are the following: storage circuits, triggering circuits, gating circuits, inverting circuits and timing circuits. In addition, there may be other circuits used in smaller quantities such as power amplifiers for driving heavier loads, indicators, output devices, and amplifiers for receiving signals from external devices, as well as oscillators for obtaining the clock of frequency.

circuit switch: A communications switching system which completes a circuit from sender to receiver at the time of transmission (as opposed to a messsge switch).

circuit switching applications: Typical circuit switching applications involve a connection being established and held for the duration of a complete data transmission or voice call. When the connection is no longer needed, the corresponding trunk line is freed up and made available for assignment to the next input link desiring a trunk connection.

circuit switching concentration: Involves a switching device which electrically bridges a group of n inputs to a group of m output links on a demand basis (n is typically from 3 to 5 times the value of m in commercial applications). Ordinarily, the input links and the output trunks to which they are switched have similar bandwidth and transmission properties. A communication channel is thus formed by the electrical concatenation of the input and output link segments within the switch. Thus no message queuing delays are introduced at the switch once a connection is established.

circuit types: There are circuits that interconnect the nodes of the network, circuits that connect terminals with the network, and circuits which provide the end-to-end path between communicating processes. Circuits also physically connect nodes in a network. Available circuit capacity ranges from 100 bits per second (bps) for voice grade lines to 250,000 bps for wideband.

circular interpolation: A mode of contouring control that uses the information contained in a single block of the tape to produce an arc of a circle. The velocities of the axes used to generate the arc are varied by the control system.

circular list: An ordered set of items contained within a memory in such a way that only two items are program addressable. These items are the earliest appended (beginning item) and the most recently appended (ending item).

circulating register: A shift register in which data moved out of one end of the register are re-entered into the other end as in a closed loop.

circulating storage: Dynamic storage involving a closed loop. Same as cyclic storage.

circulation time: The time from submission of a job until subsequent re-submission of the same job during the debugging phase.

citation index: An index or reference list of documents mentioned in a specific document or document set. The references are mentioned or quoted in the text. The citation index lists these references.

clamp: Circuit in which a waveform is adjusted and maintained at a definite level when recurring after intervals.

class: 1. A set of individuals, documents, data, etc., with similar characteristics. 2. A subdivision of a category.

Class-D channel: A transmission circuit which can transmit punched paper tape at the rate of 240 words per minute, or punch card data at the rate of approximately 10 cards (80 columns) per minute.

classes of exchange: Class 1: see regional center; class 2: see sectional center; class 3: see primary center; class 4: see toll center; class 5: see end office.

class of channel: Refers to the media through which channels pass: wire, cable, carrier, coaxial cable, radio, and microwave.

CLD: Called line.

clear: 1. In plain language, i.e., not in code or cipher. 2. To repair a fault on a circuit. 3. To give an on-hook signal and release a circuit from occupation. 4. To empty a data storage device. 5. To place one or more storage locations into a prescribed state, usually zero or the space character. Contrast with set.

clear area: In character recognition, a specified area that is to be kept free of printing or any other markings not related to machine reading.

clear collision: In data transmission, the contention that occurs when data terminal equipment (DTE) and data circuit terminating equipment (DCE) simultaneously transfer a clear request packet and a clear indication packet specifying the same logical channel.

clear confirmation signal: In data transmission, a call control signal to acknowledge receipt of the data terminal equipment (DTE) clear request by the data circuit terminating equipment (DCE) or the reception of the DCE clear indication by the DTE.

cleared condition: As related to destructive reading a flux configuration is permanently changed to some predetermined state and is also called the cleared condition. Same as zero condition.

clear-forward signal: A signal sent in the forward direction to terminate the call or call attempt and release the circuit concerned. This signal is normally sent when the calling party clears.

clearinghouse association: An organization of banks established to develop and maintain a clearinghouse. A number of automated clearinghouse (ACH) projects are being undertaken by associations which existed prior to the development of the Electronic Funds Transfer System (EFTS).

Clearing House Interbank Payments System (CHIPS): The Clearing House Interbank Payments Systems is an automated clearinghouse (ACH) of the New York Clearing House Association (NYCHA). CHIPS is used chiefly for funds transfers for international customers of NYCHA banks. This system links a large computer in the ACH to about 100 small terminal computers in the participating banks.

clearings: The incoming cash letters of items which must be proved, sorted, returned if necessary, and for which settlement must be made.

clear instruction: That specific instruction which replaces data or information in storage or in registers, accumulators, etc. with zeros or blanks.

clear signal: The original unscrambled, normal, unprocessed or uncoded signal.

clear-to-send: A code designation (EIA RS-232) applied to a sense circuit used by a terminal or computer to detect that its modem is ready to send data.

clear-to-send circuit: Signals on this circuit are originated in the signal converter. For send-only and full-duplex service, the signal converter shall hold the clear-to-send circuit in the "on" condition at all times. This circuit is not required for receive-only service. For half-duplex service when the send-request signal is switched to the "on" condition, the clear-to-send circuit shall be switched to the "on" condition after a time delay sufficient to effect the reversal of direction of transmission equipment. When the send-request circuit is switched back to the "off" condition, the clear-to-send circuit shall be switched back to the "off" condition.

clear voice override: A specific ability of a scrambler to properly receive a clear message, even when it is set to private or coded operation. Same as autoclear.

click, key: Transient pulses or surges on a transmission line set up by the opening or closing of contacts.

clinical laboratory systems: Development of automated information handling and instrument data aquisition began in the early 1960s. Many hospitals over 400 beds now have computer based systems operational or in development. Activities performed include: specimen collection schedules, laboratory worklists, manual and automatic result recording, quality control reports, exception reports, ward result reports, patient summary reports, and inquiries.

clipper: A specific circuit which removes the portion of a current waveform which would otherwise extend above or below a specified level; i.e., accomplished by tubes, transistors, diodes, etc. and for some an ordinary capacitor can be developed to do some clipping.

CLK: See clock.

clock (CLK): 1. That specific device or unit designed to time events. 2. A data communications clock which controls the timing of bits sent in a data stream, and controls the timing of the sampling of bits received in a data stream.

clock counter: A memory location that records the progress of real time, or its approximation, by accumulating counts produced by a (clock) count pulse interrupt.

clocked signals: Those signals within the control that are synchronized in time by a master oscillator or clock. The timing is accomplished by digital logic gating. The primary purpose of clocking (or gating) the signals is to maintain the correct time and phase relationship among the pulse signals.

clock frequency: A designed type of master frequency of periodic pulses which schedule the operation of the computer.

clock generator pulse: A specifically designed generator which generates pulses for purposes of special timing or gating, i.e., pulses which are used as inputs to gates to aid in pulse-shaping and timing.

clock input: The terminal on a flip-flop whose condition or change of condition controls the admission and the output state of the flip-flop. The clock signal performs two functions: (a) it permits data signals to enter the flip-flop; (b) after entry, it directs the flip-flop to change state accordingly.

clock pulse: A synchronization signal provided by a clock.

clock pulse generator: A specifically designed generator which generates pulses for purposes of special timing or gating in a digital computer, i.e., pulses which are used as inputs to gates to aid in pulse-shaping and timing. Same as time pulse generator.

clock rate: The time rate at which pulses are emitted from the clock. The clock rate determines the rate at which logical or arithmetic gating is performed with a synchronous computer.

clock timing: A pulse positioned next to recorded characters on tapes, drums, disks, etc. to control the timing of read circuits, count characters, or develop and perform related type functions which a clock pulse would perform.

clock track: A track on which a pattern of signals has been recorded to provide a time reference.

closed circuit: 1. In radio and television tranmission, used to indicate that the programs are transmitted directly to specific users and not broadcast for general consumption. 2. A completed electrical circuit.

closed circuit (CC) process code: When the terminal is in the program mode, the user can execute a single statement that he does not want included in the active program. By typing process code CC in columns 1 and 2 and an arithmetic assignment statement or an output statement in columns 7 through 72, the user indicates to the system that the statement is to be executed immediately, but not retained as part of the program (available on some computers).

closed circuit signaling: That type of signaling in which there is current in the idle condition, and a signal is initiated by increasing or decreasing the current.

closed entry: A design entry that specifically limits a mating part to an exact dimension.

closed instruction loop: A group of instructions that can be repeated endlessly, there being no exit point.

closed loop: The complete signal path in a control system represented as a group of units connected in such a manner that a signal started at any point follows a closed path and can be traced back to that point.

closed loop control: An operation where the computer applies control action directly to the process without manual intervention. See closed loop.

closed loop system: A control system involving one or more feedback control loops, which combines functions of controlled signals and commands, in order to keep relationships between the two stable.

close-down: Under the telecommunications access method (TCAM), orderly deactivation of the message control program.

closed routine: A routine which is not inserted as a block of instructions within a main routine but is entered by basic linkage from the main routine.

closed shop: The operation of a computer facility where programming service to the user is the responsibility of a group of specialists, thereby effectively separating the phase of task formulation from that of computer implementation. The programmers are not allowed in the computer room to run or oversee the running of their programs.

closed subroutine: A subroutine not stored in the main path of the routine. Such a subroutine is entered by a jump operation and provision is made to return control to the main routine at the end of the operation. The instructions related to the entry and re-entry function constitute a linkage.

CLPRINT: 1. An automatically programmed tools (APT) language statement which calls for the listing or printout of a cutter location file (CLFILE). 2. A CLFILE listing.

CLT: See communication line terminal.

clutch cycle: That time space or interval between basic operations on a clutch-driven device, i.e., the time between input/output operations on fixed-size sections when at maximum speed.

clutch point: Affects the usage time for the reading or writing parts of input/output equipment. Synchronous clutches can be engaged at limited points in the operation cycle.

CMOS: See complementary metal-oxide semiconductor.

coarse index: First of a pair of indexes consulted to locate particular records, etc.; the secondary index is the fine index.

coast time: The time which multiplied by the nominal tape speed gives the nominal distance travelled by the tape after receipt of a stop command.

coaxial cable: A cable consisting of one conductor, usually a small copper tube or wire, within and insulated from another conductor of larger diameter, usually copper tubing or copper braid.

coaxial eccentricity: Measure of the concentricity of conductors in a cable. This is especially important for coaxial cables that are to be used in wideband transmission systems.

coaxial pair: Consists of a central conductor surrounded by an insulator which in turn is surrounded by a tabular ouer conductor, which is covered by more insulator.

COBOL: Common Business Oriented Language. A data processing language that makes use of English language statements.

COBOL compiler: A program that translates Common Business Oriented Language (COBOL) statements into assembler input or machine-language programs.

COBOL procedure division: Describes the procedures used in processing the data described in the data division; it contains all the necessary steps to solve a given problem.

COBOL word: One of a group of words having preassigned meanings in the Common Business Oriented Language (COBOL) system.

co-channel: Any two or more television signals are considered co-channel when their video carriers, either off-air or after conversion by community antenna television (CATV) equipment, occupy the same television channel.

co-channel interference: Interference resulting from two or more transmissions in the same channel.

CODASYL: Conference On Data Systems Languages. The conference which developed Common Business Oriented Language (COBOL).

code: Relates to transformations or representations of information in different forms according to a preassigned convention. Digital codes may represent numbers, letters of the alphabet, control signals, etc., as a group of discrete bits rather than as a continuous signal.

code, absolute: A code using absolute addresses and absolute operation codes, i.e., a code which indicates the exact location where the referenced operand is to be found or stored. Same as one level code and specific code and related to absolute address.

code, area: A three-digit number identifying one of 152 geographical areas of the United States and Canada to permit direct distance dialing on the telephone system.

Codec (coder/decoder): A device (chip) which converts analog signals to digital and vice versa.

code-checking time: The time spent checking out a problem on the machine making sure that the problem is set up correctly and that the code is correct.

code conversion: A process for changing the bit grouping for a character in one code into the corresponding bit grouping for a character in a second code.

coded: Relates to the encoded or scrambled signal and results from the coding or scrambling process. It is information in a specifically designed form.

code data: Specific sets of characters designed and structured to represent the items of a data element. An example is to use the digits 01-07 to represent the order of the days of the week.

coded character set: A group of characters to which a code has been assigned.

coded decimal: A form of notation by which each decimal digit separately is converted into a pattern of binary ones and zeros, i.e., in the 8-4-2-1 coded decimal notation, the number 12 is represented as 0001 0010 (for 1, 2).

coded program: A program which has been expressed in the code or language of a specific machine or programming system.

code error: The identification of a particular error by a code in order to draw attention to it during the next stage of operation.

code extension character: A control character used to indicate that one or more of the succeeding code values are to be interpreted according to a different code.

code, five-level: 1. A term frequently used as a synonym for baudot code. 2. Any code using five elements, or bits, to designate one character. Such a code has 32 possible discrete combinations of the five code elements.

code frame: One group of a cyclically recurring number of code characters or signals.

code holes: The information holes in perforated tape, as opposed to the feed or other holes.

code level: This concerns the number of bits used to represent a character. An example is the five-bit baudot code which is a five-level code.

code line: A single instruction written usually on one line, in a code for a specific computer to solve a problem. This instruction is usually stored as a whole in the program register of the computer while it is executed, and it may contain one or more addresses of registers or storage locations in the computer where numbers or machine words are to be obtained or sent, and one or more operations to be executed. Same as program line.

coden: A specialized 5-character identification for periodical titles as developed and maintained by the American Society for Testing and Materials. It will probably be largely supplanted by an 8-digit (7 digits plus an eleven's-complement check digit) code proposed by the American National Standards Institute (ANSI Z39.9-1971).

code position: The positions or sites in various data recording media in which data may be entered or recorded such as hole positions, magnetic spot, etc. Conventions have been adopted to standardize the locations of code positions in almost all media.

coder: A person who prepares instruction sequences from detailed flow charts and other algorithmic procedures prepared by others, as contrasted with a programmer who prepares the procedure and flow charts.

code set: The complete set of representations defined by a code, for example, all of the three-letter international identifications for airports.

code (to): To originate, structure, or devise a program. To code most often concerns the analysis of the problem, preparation of the flow chart, designing and testing a set of developing subroutines, and the specification of the input and output commands and formats.

code-translating terminal: A terminal that can translate one code to another such as translating ASCII to EBCDIC and vice versa.

code value: A value representing any of the elements included in a code set.

codeword: An n-bit unit containing data and checkbits.

coding: The ordered set of computer instructions required to perform a given action or solve a given problem.

coding check: A test performed to determine whether a routine contains errors. This is usually done by following the logic of the routine on paper using test data.

coding line: Generally regarded as a single command or instruction designed for a computer to resolve.

coding optimum: The preparation of a programming routine with a view toward optimizing or idealizing the specific situation.

coding sheet: A preprinted form upon which computer instructions are written.

coefficient constant multiplier: A device, such as a linear amplifier, that develops an output equal to an input multiplied by a constant.

coercive force: A force of magnetic flux density which can be detected and measured.

coherence: Opposite of randomness, especially with reference to radio, light and acoustic waves.

coherent carrier recovery: Modems designed to achieve a high ratio of bits per second per cycle of bandwidth often use coherent detection. This requires the generation of a reference carrier in the receiving modem that is accurately phased with respect to the received signal which may have undergone a frequency offset. In an AM system a straightforward method is to transmit some of the carrier used in modulation at the transmitter and detect it at the receiver by a narrow filter or phase-locked loop.

coherent networks: A network in which input/output, signal levels, bit rates, digital bit stream structures, and signaling information are compatible, throughout the network. If precise matching or coherence is missing, conversion will be needed, which may involve extra harware and/or revised software.

coherent radiation: Light propagation where the phase between any two points in the field is exactly the same or else maintains a constant difference through the duration of the light pulse.

coil blank: Paper tape with only the feed holes punched.

coincidence circuit: A circuit which has two or more inputs and one output. An output signal is produced only when all the input circuits receive inputs of a specified level and within a specified time interval.

coincidence element: A logic element in which the connection between two binary input signals and a single binary output signal is defined by the equivalence operation. The element produces an output signal of 1 when the two input signals are the same and 0 when they are different.

coincidence error: The specific difference as related to time for switching different integrators to the compute mode or the hold mode.

coincidence gate: A specific circuit designed with the capability to produce an output which is dependent upon a specified type of or has the coincident nature of, the input; e.g., an AND gate has an output pulse when there are pulses in time coincidence at all inputs; an OR gate has an output when any one or any combination of input pulses occur in time coincidence. Any gate may contain a number of inhibits in which there is no output under any condition of input, if there is time coincidence of an inhibit or except signal.

coincidence signal: A signal circuit with two or more input wires in which the output wire gives a signal, if and only if, all input wires receive coincident signals.

coincident current selection: The selective switching of one cell or core from an array of magnetic cores by concurrent application of two or more drive pulses to that array.

COL: Computer Oriented Language. Any computer programming language having terms, such as instruction codes and address, that apply to a specific computer or set of similar computers such as machine language programs.

cold cathode gas tube: A gas-filled tube in which the cathode is not heated.

COLINGO: A formalized English-like inquiry system for command and control implementations.

collation: 1. The Boolean operator that gives a truth table value of true only when both of the variables connected by the logical operator are true. 2. The logial operation which makes use of the AND operator or logical product.

collation operation: One of the basic logic elements (gates or operators) which has at least two binary input signals and a single binary output signal. The answer or variable which represents the output signal is the conjunction (set theory) of the variables represented by the input signals. In set theory, the output is 1 only when all input signals represent 1.

collation sequence: An ordered sequence in which the characters are processed to be acceptable to a computer.

collator: A device to collate, merge, or match sets of punched cards or other documents.

collected-data processing: An application in which accumulated data are processed.

color: In optical character recognition, the spectral appearance of the image dependent upon the spectral reflectance of the image, the spectral response of the observer, and the spectral composition of incident light.

color-killer: A tube in a color television receiver which prevents the appearance of color on the picture screen during black and white telecast reception.

Colpitts oscillator: An oscillator in which two resonant circuit capacitors are used, with a tap between the two capacitors.

Columbus Project: The City National Bank and Trust Company of Columbus, Ohio began operating an electronic funds transfer service (EFTS) project in October 1971. It lasted nine months and involved a point-of-sale (POS) system in Upper Arlington, Ohio. This system performed credit authorizations for retail purchase, captured credit card transaction data, debited customers' credit accounts, and credited merchants' accounts. City National concluded that one bank could not support a POS system.

column: 1. A vertical arrangement of characters or other expressions. 2. Loosely, a digit place.

columnar transposition: A cipher where the plaintext is written horizontally, as a series of rows, and the ciphertext is read out by columns, beginning with the column whose key letter is the lowest.

column-binary code: A code used with punched cards, in which successive bits are represented by the presence or absence of punches, in binary notation, in successive columns (as opposed to rows).

column vector: One vertical section of a matrix consisting of a single column. The elements of the column are interpreted as the components of the vector.

combination: A code expression that is defined to be nonpermissible and whose occurrence indicates a mistake or malfunction.

combinational logic element: 1. A device having at least one ouput channel and two or more input channels, all characterized by discrete states, such that the state of each output channel is completely determined by the contemporaneous state of the input channels. 2. A logic element used in combination logic.

combination cable: A cable that has conductors grouped in combinations, such as pairs and quads.

combined head: A relatively small electromagnetic unit used for reading, recording or erasing polarized spots that represent information on a magnetic tape, disk or drum.

combined print and read: A unit, system, or a specific process in which the printing unit operates at the same speed as the reading unit. In this process of recordfor-record simultaneous reading and printing, the computer system does not require storage or buffering due to the uniform synchronization of speeds.

COMIT II: A string-handling and pattern-matching language.

command: 1. An electronic pulse, signal or set of signals to start, stop or continue some operation. It is incorrect to use command as a synonym for instruction. 2. The portion of an instruction word which specifies the operation to be performed.

command control block (CCB):   A 16-byte field required for each channel program executed by physical input/output control systems (IOCS). This field is used for communication between physical IOCS and the problem program.

command control program: A computer program that handles all user console commands sent to the system.

command language: A source language consisting primarily of procedural operators, each capable of invoking a function to be executed.

command language control: Man-machine interaction is provided by the command language control. In this language a hierarchy of command statements is established and validated, with the full set available to the system administrator and a subset available to any terminal in the message switch network. The language is used for changing the status of circuits and terminals, and introducing alterations to the telecommunications network. In addition, it serves to display information on message traffic and on circuit problems. The commands are divided into sets so that control can be maintained over their use and so that only the functions desired are included in a system.

command library: Under time-sharing option (TSO), a partitioned data set consisting of command processor programs. A user command library can be concatenated to the system command library.

command mode: Under time-sharing option (TSO), the entry mode immediately following LOGON, or following completion of command processor. In command mode, the system is ready to accept any command in the command libraries.

command name: The first term in a command, usually followed by operands.

command net: A communications network which connects an echelon of command with some or all of its subordinate echelons for the purpose of command control.

command procedure: Under time-sharing option (TSO), a data set or a member of a partitioned data set containing TSO commands to be performed sequentially by the EXEC command.

command processing: The reading, analyzing, and performing of commands issued via a console or through an input stream.

command processor: A problem program executed to perform an operation specified by a command.

command readout: A display of a commanded dimension.

command repetition rate: Frequency of occurrence at equal time intervals of operational commands such as FWD start, REV start, or stop, expressed in commands per second.

command statement: A job control statement that is used to issue commands to the system through the input stream.

comment: Relates to various types of expressions which serve to identify or explain one or more steps in routines but which have no effect on the execution of such routines or programs.

comment code: Various types of comments can be entered from a terminal when it is in the program mode. Each type of comment is identified by a different comment code.

comment statement: A statement used to include information that may be helpful in running a job or reviewing an output listing.

commonality: A term applied to equipment or systems which have the quality of one entity possessing like and interchangeable parts with other equipment.

common area: A control section used to reserve a main storage area that can be referred to by other modules.

common battery central office: A central office which supplies transmitter and signal current for its associated stations and for signaling by the central office equipment from a power source located in the central office.

common battery signaling: A procedure for bringing a line signal of a supervisory message (usually) to a distant switchboard or end unit by using a direct current to the line.

common block: A block of storage locations in a digital computer which is associated with information or data required both in the main program and in a specific subprogram.

common business oriented language: See COBOL.

common carrier: Organizations licensed and regulated by the U.S. Federal Communications Commission and/or various public utility commissions and required to supply communications services to all users at published prices.

common-carrier exchange: The location of a common carrier's communication equipment for interconnecting subscribers' lines.

common carrier wide band channels: Facilities that the common carrers provide for transferring data at speeds of from 19200 baud up to the 1 million baud region.

common-channel interference: Interference between two broadcast stations using identical or nearly similar carrier frequencies or whose sideband frequencies encroach on one another.

common computer software: Programs or routines which usually have common and multiple applications for many systems; e.g., report generators, sort routines, conversion programs which can be used for several routines in language common to many computers.

common control switching arrangement (CCSA): A dedicated switched network leased by a user to handle his communications requirements between scattered locations (including voice and data). The switching equipment used to interconnect trunks and access lines is located on telephone company premises. Trunks are circuits between switching machines, and access lines provide access to the network from a subscriber location to a switching machine. Long-distance charges between company locations are eliminated, and for a flat monthly charge the user has control over network users.

common control unit: A unit that coordinates the flow of data between the data devices and the communication facility.

common field: A field that can be accessed by two or more independent routines.

common hardware: Expendable items such as plugs, sockets, bolts, etc.; items commonly used to construct or repair machines or components.

common hub: A common connection such as a ground voltage that provides this voltage to other circuits that are connected.

common language: See common machine language.

common language optical character readers (OCR): Universally acceptable language for OCR's adopted by most manufacturers and usually including commonly accepted character shapes.

common machine language: A machine-sensible information representation which is common to a related group of data-processing machines.

common mode interference: A specific type of interference that appears between any measuring circuit terminals and ground.

common mode rejection: The capability of a circuit to discriminate against common mode voltage; usually expressed as a ratio or in decibels.

common programs: See common software.

common segment: In an overlay structure, an overlay segment upon which two exclusive segments are dependent.

common software: Programs or routines which usually have common and multiple applications for many systems, such as report generators, sort routines, and conversion programs which can be used for several routines in a language common to many computers.

common storage area: The system loader automatically allocates common area when it is loading programs. Common storage occupies the same memory space during execution as the system loader does when loading programs. This allows effective utilization of memory storage, since the space taken up by the loader can be used by the program during execution.

common user network: A system of circuits or channels allocated for communication paths between switching centers to provide communication service on a common basis to all connected stations or subscribers. It is sometimes called a general purpose network.

communicated information: Transferred information. It can be a series of letters, a group of tones, or a series of picture scanning elements. This information comprises a message.

communicating terminal: A system for communicating to and from other terminals and computers.

communication ac signaling: Communication with ac signaling is accomplished by a system of frequency-shift keying, in which the dc signals outputed from a teletypewriter are modulated and tones sent down the line. For example, a station may convert a dc marking impulse to a 1070 Hz audio signal and a dc spacing signal to a 1270 Hz audio signal. This frequency-shift keying is a form of frequency modulation (FM) and is often accomplished by data sets and modems.

communication center: 1. Building or room in which communications equipment has been centralized. 2. A facility responsible for the reception, transmission, and delivery of messages. Its normal elements are a message center section, a cryptographic section, and a sending and receiving section, using electronic communications devices.

communication common carrier: A company whose business is to supply communication facilities to the public. Since common carriers serve the public, they must comply with established regulations. A communication common carrier with interstate facilities comes under the jurisdiction of the Federal Communications Commission as well as the state organizations. Common carriers can carry voice, facsimile, telemetry, television, and data messages. There are approximately 2800 common carrier companies operating in the United States.

communication conductor: In electrical communications, a conductor with relatively low electrical resistance, such as copper wire, to link sending and receiving points. These points use a translating device (e.g. telephone) to send and receive the intelligence of the signal.

communication control character: Refers to a specific character which designates the operation to be performed by some peripheral device. As with other characters it is represented by a pattern of printed binary digits or holes in tapes or cards. Its execution usually causes control changes on printers. For example, back space, skip line or rewind on tapes. Other types of characters relate to EOM, such as end-of-message, etc.

communication control procedures: Conventions for controlling the flow of messages between communicating processes. In a network situation, communication control procedures can perform the following: (a) identify the source and destination stations; (b) request permission to send; (c) invite a station to send; (d) arbitrate contention when multiple stations or devices require the same communication channel; (e) provide for error recovery; (f) identify a device or process; and (g) identify a message when multiple messages are outstanding between communicating processes.

communication controls (CCs): To bring distant computers into memory-to-memory communications, a computer provides for single-channel communication controls. Computer installed CCs are connected through one of two types of subsets, to leased or dial network communication lines. Transmission is set in motion by either manual or automatic dialing. In the latter case, the computer working with CC triggers an automatic calling unit to establish line connections more quickly. Data speeds vary with the CC model from 220 bytes per second to 5100 bytes per second.

communication-interface modules: Modules provided to interface communication line terminals (CLTs) with currently available modems in addition to telegraph facilities for which no modem is necessary. The modular concept of the standard communication subsystem permits the addition of new interface modules as new offerings are made available by the common carriers. Jacks are provided on each telegraph interface module which permit a teletypewriter to monitor all data passing through the interface.

communication line adapter for teletype (CLAT): A semiautomatic device used to link buffer units with remote teletype units. The CLAT is incorporated within the buffer cabinet, which is located with the processor at the central site. The purpose of the CLAT is to receive data in serial bit form from the remote inquiry station and convert the data to parallel bit form for use in the inquiry buffer unit. Similarly, data transmitted from buffer to remote inquiry station is converted by the CLAT from parallel to serial bit form.

communication line group: A group of lines with similar characteristics (such as association with the same type of terminal device).

communication line terminal (CLT): Input/output device used when data is to be transmitted to or from the central processor using a commmunications line.

communication line terminal (CLT) display console: Consoles often contain as standard equipment a visual-display (cathode-ray tube) console to enhance operator-system communication. The advantages of a visual display to the operator are obvious and the possible display functions endless. The executive system will include a display of information from the run statement, operator requests associated with input/-output interventions (printer interlocks, etc.) and manually initiated CLT lines. The operator will have the option to request alternate information, such as backlog status. In the event that the available display area becomes filled up, the executive will defer lower-priority displays and compact or summarize displays.

communication link: 1. The means of connecting one location to another for the purpose of transmitting and receiving information. 2. A channel or circuit intended to connect other channels or circuits.

communication modes: Each channel is capable of operating in three different communication modes: input, output, or function. The input and output modes are employed when transferring data to or from the central computer. The function mode is the means by which the central computer establishes the initial communication path with a peripheral subsystem. During this mode of transmission, the central computer sends one or more function words to a peripheral subsystem. These function words direct the units to perform the desired operation (available on some computers).

communication processor applications: Typical examples are: (a) front end processing—interfacing to a host computer. (b) Remote data concentration—multiplying from many low speed to one or more high speed lines. (c) Message-switching—to store, analyze, check, process, then transmit. (d) Terminal control—showing control hardware. (e) Network processing and control-support of local databases, network hardware and protocols.

communication region: Under a disk operating system (DOS), an area of the supervisor that is set aside for interprogram and intraprogram communication. It contains information useful to both the supervisor and the problem program.

communications: A method or means of conveying information of any kind from one person or place to another, except by direct unassisted conversation or correspondence through postal agencies.

communications buffer: In a computer communications network a buffer is a storage device used to compensate for a difference in the rate flow of data received and transmitted along the numerous communication lines converging on the data processing center. The communications buffer orders information from many operators and controls the information so it can be processed by the computer without confusion. The buffer has memory and control circuitry of its own for storing incoming messages that the computer is not ready to process and for storing outgoing messages which have to be delayed because of busy lines.

communications circuits: In a computer network there are circuits that interconnect the nodes of the network, circuits that connect terminals with the network, and circuits, logical or physical, which provide the end-to-end path between communicating processes. As regards the circuits that physically connect the nodes in a network, the transmission media can be voice grade lines or wideband and they can be owned, leased from a common carrier, or dialup. Voice-grade circuits can be modulated to operate in the range of 110 baud to 9600 baud. Wideband lines operate from 19000 to 250000 baud and some economies of scale exist if there is in fact a need for that kind of bandwidth.

communications control devices: The data devices that can be attached directly to the systems channel via a control unit designed to perform character assembly and transmission control.

communications control unit (CCU):   A small computer whose only purpose is to monitor and control the flow of data-communications traffic to and from the CCU's larger, host computer. A CCU is sometimes known as a front end processor.

communications hardware: Devices for transmission, switching, and termination of communications signals, such as data terminals, modems, acoustic couplers, private branch exchange (PBX) equipment, store-andforward message switching computers, etc.

communications input/output control system (CIOCS):   A system that allows the customer's problem program to communicate with remote terminals in the same general manner in which the program utilizes basic IOCS to communicate with magnetic tape or other standard input/-output (I/O) devices.

communications module: In some computer configurations, a high-speed data link connecting the input processor and supervisory computer. Using this link, selected data is passed from the input computer to the supervisory computer for the optimizing and feedforward calculations and the results cascaded to the input computer for adjustments to program limits and set points.

communications multiplexer channel: A data processing and communications coordinator. Systems equipped with a communications multiplexer channel can manage the myriad data-transfer problems inherent in complex configurations. As many as 256 on-line terminals can be connected to the communications multiplexer channel. A combined data rate of 10,000 bytes per second is attainable in systems of practical processing complexity. The communications multiplexer channel wired-in program is stored in a special read-only memory. This design feature eliminates the need for extensive, costly circuitry which would otherwise be required.

communications net: An organization of stations capable of direct communications on a common channel or frequency.

communications preprocessor: The communications preprocessor can handle such diverse problems as point-to-point communications circuits, polled communications circuits, synchronous and asynchronous transmission, contention networks, speed and code differences, and automatic circuit answering and calling. Adding a communications preprocessor is often determined to be the cheapest way to increase the capacity of the larger computer by offloading the communications function. Other possible functions include message accumulation and queuing, message switching and gathering of message statistics. The communications preprocessor can also select the computer to do the processing if the system consists of multiple processors. The communications preprocessor is normally easier to reprogram for new communications functions than are the larger computer systems.

communications processing system: Refers to a system designed for the transmission of data to the central computer for processing from a remote terminal as opposed to a terminal connected directly to the central computer.

communications reliability: Increased reliability can result from the incorporation of more sophisticated error detection and correction techniques, not only at the terminal, but at data concentrators at various points in the computer communications network, and at the front-end communications processor at the central processor location. The front-end communications processor may also increase the cost effectiveness of the system by reducing the load on the more expensive central processor.

communications satellite: An artificial satellite which is projected into a predetermined orbit around the earth to function as a relay station.

Communications Satellite Corporation (COMSAT): A U.S. company created by act of Congress in 1962 to provide communications via satellites. COMSAT leases satellite circuits to many U.S. companies and is active in international communications through partial ownership in the International Telecommounications Satellite Organization (INTELSAT) and the International Maritime Satellite Organization (INMARSAT).

communications signal: Aggregate of electromagnetic waves propagated in a transmission channel that act on a receiving unit.

communications sink: A device which receives information, control, or other signals from communications source(s).

communications software modules: Communications software modules includes those for line handling, terminal control, buffer management, queue control, etc.

communications source: A device which generates information, control, or other signals destined for communications sink(s).

communications status word: A special word location in storage that contains status information.

communications system: A computer system which handles on-line, real-time applications. A typical communications system would consist of the following: a teletype, visual display, or audioanswer-back device connected to an ordinary telephone line through a communication multiplexer, a device which converts the keyedin character to electronic pulses for transmission over the telephone line. An interface device in the computer center translates these pulses into binary code and delivers the character to computer storage. After receipt of the entire message, the central computer searches or stores the requested information and sends back the appropriate response. Important elements of any communications system are the modems (modulator/demodulator) which connect the communications multiplexer from the remote output to the interface device in the computer center. On the transmission end, the modulator converts the signals or pulses to the right codes and readies them for transmissions over a communication line. On the receiving end, a demodulator reconverts the signals for communication to the computer via the computer interface device.

communications system banks: A system that links teller window locations in savings banks, savings and loan associations, and commercial banks with either the main office of the institution or a branch office, where a computer is located. The system consists of the teller terminal which is linked to the processor over communications line through the control unit. Transaction data can be transmitted from a keyboard.

communications traffic: All messages that are transmitted and received.

communications trunk: A telephone line between two central offices that is used to provide communications between subscribers.

communication subsystem control: The standard communication subsystem is controlled by function words which activate external function control lines and instruct a specific communication line terminal (CLT) to perform a particular action. The use of program-generated function words, rather than processor instructions, in controlling the standard communication subsystem, allows the processor logic to be completely independent of the subsystem logic.

communications unit network: A stored program communications processor for real-time systems. It scans communication channels, temporarily stores data, evaluates data priority, and sends it to its destination. Public or private telephone or telegraph lines can be used to carry the data to and from selected units such as terminals or teletypewriters. With little or no operator intervention, it simultaneously supervises a network, receives and disburses messages, and keeps a log.

communication switching unit: A unit which allows any two processors to share a group (one to eight) of communications lines and enables one processor to switch between different groups of communication lines. Additional expansion features can provide a group switching capability of up to 63 lines (on some computers).

communications word arrangement: The standard communication subsystem accommodates four types of computer input/-output words. They are the function word, input-data word, output-data word, and output-data request word.

communication task: A function provided by computers to handle all communication with the operator console.

communication theory: A branch of mathematics concerned with the properties of transmitted messages. The messages are subject to certain probabilities of transmission failure, distortion, and noise.

community antenna relay service (CARS): The 12.7512.95 GHz microwave frequency band which the FCC has assigned to the CATV industry for use in transmitting television signals.

community antenna television (CATV): Refers to television signals from distant broadcasting stations which are picked up by antennae and amplified, then sent by cable or microwave links to sub-scribers. CATV also provides a highly sophisticated cable distribution system in large metropolitan areas in direct and successful competition with direct broadcasting.

community automatic exchange (CAX): A small dial telephone office serving a community.

commutation switch: A device controlling the sequential switching operators required for multichannel pulse communication systems.

commutator pulse: A pulse developed at a particular instant in time relative to a specific reference pulse, which may be a major or minor cycle pulse, and one which is often used to mark, clock, or control a particular binary digit position in a computer work.

Comopt: An international code name for a picture film combined with an optical soundtrack.

compacting: A process of dynamic relocation in which contiguous segments are moved to one end of the memory to combine all unused storage at the other end.

compaction algorithm: An algorithm for data compaction so that data will require fewer bits.

compaction, data: Pertaining to the reduction of space, bandwidth, cost, and time for the generation, transmission, and storage of data by employing techniques designed to eliminate repetition, remove irrelevancy, and employ special coding.

compaction of file records: The reduction of space required for records by compressing or compacting the records by means of specialized coding and formating under a programmed routine. A balance, though, must be maintained in a system between processing time and core storage, and the reduction of file size and channel utilization.

compaction sample-change: A data compaction procedure accomplished when constant levels are specified, or easily defined. Varying levels are stated for value together with deviations in discrete or continuous values, parameters, or variables. Curves can be reconstructed from transmission even if smaller precession numbers than originals are transmitted.

companding (compressing and expanding): 1. Data in bits can often be recorded into a more compact form for transmission, using a compaction algorithm. A related algorithm can recover the original form; the entire sequence represents companding. 2. In voice transmission, to compress the signal amplitude into a narrow range, because the amplifiers are not linear over wide ranges.

compandor communication equipment: Equipment that compresses the outgoing speech volume range and expands the incoming speech volume range on a long distance telephone circuit. Such equipment can make more efficient use of voice communication channels.

comparator check: An accuracy check on reading, writing, sensing, and punching by running newly printed or punched cards and the original ones through a comparator to check for errors.

comparator circuit: A circuit which compares two signals (such as commands from tape and slide displacement from the transducer) and produces an output signal indicating agreement or disagreement of the two signals.

comparing: As a control technique, permits data fields to be machine-checked against each other to prove the accuracy of machine, merging, coding, balancing, reproducing, gang punching, record selection from magnetic drum, disk, and tape storage. In wired control-panel machines this is accomplished by comparing magnets, and in a stored-program machine it is accomplished with compare instruction.

comparing unit: 1. An electromechanical device used to compare two groups of timed pulses and signals, either identity or nonidentity. 2. A machine that automatically checks cards on a match or nonmatch basis. With this machine, feeding, punching, and segregating are controlled by comparing cards from two separate files for a match or nonmatch condition. Comparison of both alphabetical and numerical data may be made on selected columns or fields, or on entire cards.

comparison: The examination of the relationship between two items of data. It is usually followed by a decision.

compatible: Capable of direct interconnection; usually implies no requirement for code, speed, or signal level conversion.

compatible-sideband   transmission: A method of independent sideband transmission wherein the carrier er is reinserted at a lower level after its normal suppression to permit reception by conventional amplitude modulation (AM) receivers.

compendium: An abbreviated summary of the essentials of a subject.

compilation time: The time during which a source language is compiled (translated) as opposed to the time during which the program is actually being run (execution time).

compile: To prepare a machine language program from a computer program written in another programming language by making use of the overall logic structure of the program, or generating more than one machine instruction for each symbolic statement, or both, as well as performing the function of an assembler.

compile-and-go: Concerns specific automatic coding procedures that compile the source language program and immediately execute the generated machine language program. A popular compile-and-go programming system employs FORTRAN as the source language.

compiler: A computer program that will convert a higher level language into machine language.

compiler language: The source language for a procedure oriented programming system, i.e., FORTRAN language.

compiling program: A translating program designed to transform, assemble, or structure programs that are expressed in other languages into equivalent programs which are expressed in terms of a particular computer language for which that machine was designed.

compiling routine: An executive routine which, before the desired computation is started, translates a program expressed in pseudocode into machine code (or into another pseudocode for further translation by an interpreter).

complement: A quantity which is derived from a given quantity, expressed to the base n, by one of the following rules and which is frequently used to represent the negative of the given quantity. 1. Complement on n: subtract each digit of the given quantity from $n - 1$, add unity to the least significant digit, and perform all resultant carries. For example, the twos, complement of binary 11010 is 00110; the tens, complement of decimal 456 is 544, 2. Complement on $n - 1$: subtract each digit of the given quantity from $n - 1$. For example, the ones, complement of binary 11010 is 00101; the nines complement of decimal 456 is 543.

complementary metal-oxide semiconductor (CMOS): A device that combines both N- and P-channel transistors on the same chip by diffusing or implanting isolated, doped substrate regions for the N-channel transistors. Since most CMOS diffused interconnections are similar to conventional P-channel circuits, CMOS has less exposure to leakage current variation than straight Nchannel. However, because extra diffusion is required for the N-channel substrates as well as extra source/drain diffusion, CMOS is more expensive to manufacture than either N- or P-channel. Further, the special substrate region takes up considerable space, giving CMOS lower packing density than either N- or Pchannel. The major CMOS advantage is that since transistors of both polarities are available, one can design circuits with very low quiescent power. Speed and transient power (the major element of power when dynamic circuits are being operated at full repetition rate) are similar for CMOS and N-channel circuits.

complementary metal-oxide semiconductor (CMOS) logic: A logic circuit using CMOS transistors as logic functions. Complementary means that pairs of opposite types of transistors are used together on a push-pull basis, thus eliminating resistors and greatly reducing power consumption.

complementary operator: The logic operator whose result is the NOT of a given logic operator.

complete carry: In parallel addition, a technique in which all of the carries are allowed to propagate.

complete instruction: A specific instruction designed to take in a complete computer operation including the execution of that operation.

completeness (remote-computing system) errors: Errors detected after the user has indicated that his program is complete. All such errors are then extracted and immediately displayed at the terminal in a sequential list. When all the errors have been listed, the user then can correct or disregard them individually before initiating the execution of his completed program. Any disregarded errors, when redetected during execution, are considered as execution errors.

complete operation: An operation which includes: a) obtaining all operands from storage, b) performing the operation, c) returning resulting operands to storage, and d) obtaining the next instruction.

complex relocatable expression: In assembler programming, a relocatable expression that contains two or more unpaired relocatable terms or an unpaired relocatable term preceded by a minus sign, after all unary operators have been resolved. A complex relocatable expression is not fully evaluated until program fetch time.

component error: Error related to the operational amplifier but specifically its components as the input and feedback impedances.

composite cable: In communications use, a cable in which conductors of different gauges or types are combined under one sheath.

composite conductor: One in which strands of different metals are used in parallel.

composited circuit: A circuit which can be used simultaneously for telephony and direct-current telegraphy or signaling, separation between the two being accomplished by frequency discrimination.

composite external symbol dictionary (CESD):   Control information associated with a load module that identifies the external symbols in the module.

composite filter: Combination of a number of filter sections, or half sections, all have the same cutoff frequencies and specified impedance levels.

composite signal: A total television signal comprising video, blanking, synchronizing, and chrominance component signals.

composite video signal: The video signal of a cathode-ray tube, consisting of picture signal, blanking pulses, and sync pulses.

composition error: An error that is detected by the user as soon as he enters it into the computer.

compound logical element: Computer circuitry that provides an output from many inputs.

compound modulation: Use of an already modulated wave as a further modulation envelope. Also called double modulation.

compressing terminal: A system that compresses the data prior to storage or transmission which can include the elimination of spaces between characters and fields, fixed field data, and fields of data that are already in the computer system.

compression, data: 1. A method of increasing the amount of data that can be stored in a given space or contained in a given message length. 2. A method of reducing the amount of storage space required to store a given amount of data or reducing the length of message required to transfer a given amount of information.

comprise network (net):   A network used in conjunction with a hybrid coil to balance subscriber's loop that is adjusted for an average loop length or an average subscriber's set, or both, to secure compromise (not precision) isolation between the two directional paths of the hybrid.

computational stability: The degree to which a computational process remains valid when subjected to effects such as errors, mistakes, or malfunctions.

compute bound: Concerns a restriction in a computer function or program that limits output rate because operations are delayed awaiting completion of a computation operation. Same as compute limited.

compute limited: See compute bound.

compute mode: A mode in which input signals are connected to computing units (analog computers), including integrators for the generation of the solution.

computer: A machine capable of storing information electronically and manipulating that information by means of electronic circuits. A computer possesses a limited set of circuits that can perform certain basic operations—addition, subtraction, and shifting, for example—by opening and closing electronic gates that connect transistors. These basic operations can be combined to create more sophisticated and useful operations.

computer, message switching: A computer designed to perform communication control functions such as reception of message validation, message storage, and login.

computer aided design (CAD): Refers to the capability of a computer to be used for automated industrial, statistical, biological, etc., design through visual devices.

Computer Aided Manufacturing-International (CAM-I): An organization of private companies and government agencies to develop a numerically controlled computer-aided programming language.

computer-aided part programming: Prepares a manuscript in a computer language.

computer applications engineer: An employee who provides primarily hardware-oriented technical sales support to sales personnel. Their work, in varying degrees, involves hardware configuration, special systems, peripheral equipment, modules, and instruments.

computer assisted instruction (CAI): A data processing application in which a computing system is used to assist in the instruction of students. The application usually involves a dialog between a student and a computer program in which the computer informs the student of his mistakes as he makes them.

computer, buffered: A computing system with a storage device which permits input and output data to be stored temporarily in order to match the slow speed of input/-output devices with the higher speeds of the computer. Thus, simultaneous input/output computer operations are possible. A data transmission trap is essential for effective use of buffering.

computer center: A complex of computer equipment, peripheral equipment, program library, personnel and the office space containing it all.

computer check: An accuracy check on reading, writing, sensing, and punching by comparing what has been written on newly printed or punched cards to the information on an original set of cards by running both sets through a comparator.

computer circuits: The various basic types of circuits used in the construction of digital computers. They include storage circuits, triggering circuits, gating circuits, inverting circuits, and timing circuits. In addition, there may be other circuits used in smaller quantities such as power amplifiers for driving heavier loads, indicators, output devices, and amplifiers for receiving signals from external devices, as well as oscillators for obtaining the clock of frequency.

computer code: 1. A system of combinations of binary digits used by a given computer. Also called machine code. 2. A repertoire of instructions.

computer console operator: This job classification covers those employees who set up and operate the console unit and peripheral units of an electronic data processing system such as card-to-tape, tape-to-printer, tape-to-card and other machines used for processing programmed technical data.

computer control state: One of several distinct and selectable conditions of the computer control circuits.

computer decision: 1. Usually by comparison, a verification is completed concerning the existence or nonexistence of a given condition as a result of developing an alternative action. 2. The computer operation of finding out if a certain relationship exists between words in storage or registers, and taking alternative courses of action. This is effected by conditional jumps or equivalent techniques. The process consists of making comparisons, by use of arithmetic, to determine the relationship of two terms (numeric, alphabetic or a combination of both), e.g., equal, greater than, or less than.

computer dependent programs: Programs specifically written using the language and/or features of a specific computer.

computer diagram: A functional drawing showing interconnections between computing elements.

computer efficiency: Determined by the ratio of the number of hours of correct machine operation to the total hours of scheduled operation; e.g., on a 168-hour week scheduled operation, if 12 hours of preventive maintenance are required and 4.8 hours of unscheduled down time occurs, then the operation ratio is 168 to 16.8/168, which is equivalent to a 90% operation ratio).

computer engineering: Automatic control or computer science engineering.

computer equation (machine equation): An equation derived from a mathematical model for more convenient use on a computer.

computer independent language: A programming language which is not a computer language, but which requires translation or compilation to any one of a variety of computer languages. The language which is unique to that machine or one which has compilers for translation to its own machine language.

computer instruction: A machine-language instruction related to a specific computer.

computer instruction set: That particular instruction set which consists of an operator part, one or more address parts, and some special indicators (usually), and which serves to define the operations and operands for the computer. When the total structured group of characters is transferred to the computer, the operation is executed.

computerized microfilm: Microfilm produced from magnetic tapes. Special equipment is used for this conversion.

computer language: A language that is used directly by a computer. Same as machine language.

computer learning: That process by which computers modify programs according to their own memory or experience, e.g., changes of logic paths, parameter values. An example is a chess-playing computer. In process-control, an analog computer can alter its parameters by a continuous process according to temperatures, or other reports it receives.

computer limited operation: Operation of a peripheral device in a mode in which the device can receive or transmit information more rapidly than the computer can supply or accept it (peripheral device operates in start/stop mode).

computer limited switching: A type of storage device wherein access to the next position from which information is to be obtained is not dependent on the position from which information was previously obtained.

computer logic: The logical operations of the computer, consisting entirely of five operations—add, subtract, multiply, divide and compare. This simple processing logic is enough to allow the computer to accomplish its entire potential of tasks when properly programmed.

computer manager: The professional charged with the responsibility of coordinating electronic data processing (EDP) with the other functions of a business. The computer manager must not only be technically qualified, but he must also have a thorough grasp of all the activities of his firm. He must be able to manage the programmers, systems engineers, and systems analysts who translate the ideas of management into a language the computer can understand and follow.

computer matrix: Relating to computers, a logic network in the form of an array of input leads and computer logic.

computer mode: See compute mode.

computer network: A complex network consisting of two or more interconnected computing units.

computer network facilities: Three types of facilities in addition to the host computer are generally required to accomplish computer networking. These consist of: (1) the user communication interface, (2) the communications network, and (3) facilities for the network control function.

computer network services: The services which attract users to networks are: access to computer power, programs, and data bases. They are primarily functions of the host systems on the network. These networks ought to be completely transparent with respect to the delivery of these services.

computer numerical control (CNC):   A numerical control system wherein a dedicated, stored program computer is used to perform some or all of the basic numerical control functions.

computer-oriented language: 1. A programming language that reflects the structure of a given computer or that of a given class of computers. 2. A programming language whose words and syntax are designed for use on a specific class of computers.

computer output microfilm (COM):   Normal printed output of a computer reduced to one of several available microforms by a special output device that takes the place of the line-printer. The COM device allows high-quality output at speeds of 5000 or more lines per minute.

computer peripheral: The auxiliary devices under control of a central computer, such as card punches and readers, high-speed printers, magnetic tape units, and optical character readers.

computer program: A series of instructions or statements, in a form acceptable to a computer, prepared in order to achieve a certain result.

computer run: 1. To process a batch of transactions while under the control of one or more programs, and against all the files that are affected to produce the required output. 2. Performance of one routine, or several routines automatically linked so that they form an operating unit, during which manual manipulations are not required of the computer operator.

computer service organization: Various companies which offer and contract maintenance and operation of computers not owned or leased by them for charges and fees commensurate with the size and complexity of the system.

computer storage: Often called computer or automatic storage, it is a designed part of the automatic data processing system or hardware and may be controlled automatically or without the need for human intervention.

computer system: A group of machines and equipment that provides all the resources necessary to perform useful data processing. A computer system includes a computer, memory devices, input/output devices and other peripherals necessary for specific tasks. A computer system may or may not include facilities for data communications.

computer systems audit: An audit trail concerning the origin and transfer of source document information as traced from its origin. Auditors and accountants usually require approval of techniques for such procedures, together with adequate controls and amendment procedures during data preparation, assembly, and design of master records.

computer utility: Generally refers to the special computational ability of time-shared computer systems. Programs as well as data may be made available to the user. The user also may have his own programs immediately available to the central processor, may have them on call at the computer utility, or he may load them by transmitting them to the computer prior to using them. Certain data and programs are shared by all users of the service; other data and programs because of their proprietary nature, have restricted access. Computer utilities are generally accessed by means of data communication subsystems.

computer word: A sequence of bits or characters treated as a unit and capable of being stored in one computer location. Same as machine word.

computing: A generic term for all mathematical and logical operations carried out according to precise rules of procedure.

computing, multi-access: This implies that more than one identical input/output terminal may be directly used with the system. Usually they are remote, such as teletype or other typewriter-like units, or cathode-ray tube types in the most modern systems.

computing element: A computer component that performs the mathematical operations required for problem solution. It is shown explicitly in computer diagrams.

computing machinery: Data processing equipment and systems.

computing system request for price quotation (RPQ): A customer request for a price quotation, of alterations or additions to the functional capabilities of the computing system. The RPQ may be used in conjunction with programming RPQs to solve unique data processing problems.

concatenated data set: A temporary data set formed by uniting the content of several independent data sets in a specified sequence.

concatenation: The process of linking a collection of facts together.

concatenation character: In assembler programming, the period (.) that is used to separate character strings that are to be joined together in conditional assembly processing.

concentration: The process of allowing a large group of users to share a smaller group of facilities. This is generally achieved by sequentially switching each user onto a facility one at a time as they become available.

concentration processor: The polling of local lines of resolution of contending terminals, the checking and formatting of messages, the correction of errors, guidance to operators, and similar tasks are typical of those conveniently performed by a concentrator with a reasonable degree of processing power.

concentration   vs.   multiplexing: Multiplexing generally refers to static channel derivation schemes in which given frequency bands or time slots on a shared channel are assigned on a fixed predetermined (a priori) basis. Thus a multiplexer has the same instantaneous total input and output rate capacities. Concentration, by contrast, refers to sharing schemes in which some number of input channels dynamically share a smaller number of output channels on a demand basis. Concentration thus involves a traffic smoothing effect not characteristic of multiplexing. Since the aggregate input bit rate and output bit rate need not be matched in a concentrator, statistics and queuing play an important role.

concentrator: A functional unit that permits a common path to handle more data sources than there are channels currently available within the path. A concentrator usually provides communication capability between many low-speed, usually asynchronous channels and one or more high-speed, usually synchronous channels. Usually, different speeds, codes, and protocols can be accommodated on the low-speed side. The low-speed channels usually operate in contention and require buffering.

concentrator error control: Error control procedures and message reassembly may be implemented in the concentrator as well as terminal speed recognition and code conversion. The concentrator may reformat the data in order to interface the different speeds and protocols of the network and terminal circuits.

concept-coordination: A term used to describe the basic principles of various punched card and mechanized information retrieval systems which involve the multidimensional analysis of information and ordinate retrieval. In concept coordination, independently assigned concepts are used to characterize the subject contents of documents, and the latter are identified during searching by means of either such assigned concepts or a combination of the same.

conceptual modeling: A method of making a model to fit the results of a specific experiment, then conducting another experiment to find out whether the model is right or wrong. The models are created continuously, and are tested and changed in a cyclic manner. The physical sciences have developed through the years in this way, but there has been little use of the approach in biology, mainly because the kind of mathematics that developed is not well suited to biology. But now computers can get around this problem, and the important technique of conceptual modeling is beginning to be used in biology.

concordance: An alphabetic list of words and phrases appearing in a document, with an indication of the place those words and phrases appear.

concurrency control: Uses algorithms that maximize the amount of parallel activity in a distributed database system, while maintaining the semantic integrity (i.e., accuracy) of the database.

concurrent: Pertaining to the occurrence of two or more events or activities within the same specified interval of time. Contrast with consecutive, sequential, simultaneous.

concurrent control system: Relates to an environment which allows the system to react immediately to the inquiries, requests and demands of many different users at local and remote stations; it allows for the stringent demands of real-time applications; it is able to store, file, retrieve, and protect large blocks of data; and it makes optimum use of available hardware facilities, while minimizing turnaround. Only through central control of all activities can this environment of the combined hardware and software be fully established and maintained to satisfy the requirements of all applications; this responsibility for efficient, centralized control is borne by the executive. This system controls and coordinates the functions of the complex internal environment, and by presenting a relatively simple interface to the programmer, relieves him of concern for the internal interaction between his program and other coexistent programs.

concurrent input/output: The acceptance, listing, and processing of all requests for input/output (I/O) functions from the operating programs. This function of the executive system makes possible the concurrent operation of several programs using the same I/O channels without the danger of one program interferring with another program's I/O functions. Requests for I/O operations are submitted to the executive in the form of a parameter specifying the location of an execution packet which defines the function to be performed. An attempt is made to recover from I/O errors whenever feasible.

concurrent operations: This term is used to refer to various methods in electronic data processing in which multiple instructions or operations of different instructions are executed simultaneously. Concurrent operations refers to computers working as contrasted to computers being programmed. This concept is one of the basic tenets of time-sharing, priority processing, etc.

concurrent peripheral operations: Same as spooling.

concurrent processing: See concurrent operations

concurrent real-time processing: Allows data to be processed while a business transaction is taking place.

condensed instruction deck: An output card deck from an assembly program that contains several instructions per card.

condition: In the COBOL system: (a) one of a set of specified values that a data item can assume, (b) the status of a switch as specified in the special-names paragraph of the environment division, (c) a simple conditional expression. See conditional expressions.

conditional: Subject to the result of a comparison made during computation, or to human intervention.

conditional assembly: An assembler facility for altering, at pre-assembly time, the content and sequence of source statements that are to be assembled.

conditional assembly expression: An expression that an assembler evaluates at pre-assembly time.

conditional branch instruction: Transfers control to another program instruction if, and only if, some specific condition is satisfied. Also known as conditional transfer or conditional jump.

conditional breakpoint instruction: A conditional jump instruction which, if some specified switch is set, will cause the computer to stop, after which either the routine may be continued as coded or a jump may be forced.

conditional expressions: In list processing languages (LISP) conditional expressions are the means used to test conditions and act according to the result of the test.

conditional implication gate: A binary (two-input) logic coincidence circuit for completing the logic operation of A OR NOT B; i.e., the result is false only if A is false and B is true.

conditional implication operation: Relates to a Boolean operation where the result for the values of the operands p and q is given by the table:

Operands		Result
p	q	r
0	0	1
1	0	0
0	1	1
1	1	1

conditional information content: 1. The negative of the logarithm of the conditional probability of the first symbol, given the second symbol. 2. The choice of logarithmic base determines the unit of information content. 3. The conditional information content of an input symbol given an output symbol, averaged over all input/output pairs, is the equivocation. 4. The conditional information content of output symbols relative to input symbols, averaged over all input/output pairs, has been called spread, prevarication, irrelevance, etc.

conditional jump: See conditional branch instruction.

conditional stop instruction: This can cause a program to be halted if some given condition is discovered; i.e., the program may be required to stop if it finds that a console switch has been set by the operator.

conditional transfer: 1. A transfer which occurs only when a certain condition exists at the time the transfer instruction is executed. 2. An instruction which interrupts the normal process of obtaining the instructions in a normal ordered sequence and specifies a different address if certain programed conditions occur.

conditional transfer of control: An instruction which results in a transfer of control when specific sets of circumstances arise or exist, i.e., a computer decision on the next instruction could be one of several courses of action available and the selection would relate to alternative conditions of predetermined calculations.

condition code: A code that reflects the result of a previous input/output, arithmetic, or logical operation.

conditioned circuit: A circuit that has conditioning equipment to obtain the desired characteristics for voice or data transmission.

conditioning: The addition of equipment to a leased voice-grade channel to provide minimum values of line characteristics required for data transmission.

conditioning schedules (U.S. Dept. of Defense): Type D is used for data transmission circuits, Type N for teletypewriter speed circuits, Type S for secure voice circuits, Type V for facsimile, slow data or nonsecure voice circuits, and Type Z for wideband (up to 50 kHz) secure voice circuits.

conductance: 1. A measure of the ability of a substance to conduct electricity. It is the reciprocal of resistance, and is expressed in siemens. 2. The real part of admittance.

conduction: Transfer through a medium, such as the conduction of electricity by a wire, or of heat by a metallic frame, or of sound by air.

conductivity: Specific conductance, i.e., conductance per unit length. The reciprocal of resistivity.

conductor: Anything, such as a wire, which is suitable for carrying an electric current; that part of an electrical circuit which carries the current, as opposed to the dielectric.

conduit: Pipes installed underground to carry telephone distribution network cables; ducts.

configuration: A group of machines which are interconnected and are programmed to operate as a system.

configuration services: In Systems Network Architecture (SNA), these deal with managing the network configuration (e.g., bringing nodes on-line and off-line).

confined area cables: Lightweight cables for inside wiring permit compact installation in confined areas. Specially formulated vinyl jackets have low moisture absorption, making them ideal in damp areas. These cables are used for interconnecting keysets to the PBX and for low-speed data transmissions.

conflation algorithm: A procedure for retrieving information. It reduces all words with the same root to a single form by removing the derivational parts. This algorithm is of particular value when using natural language terms for indexing.

conformity accuracy: This includes the combined conformity, hysteresis and repeatability errors. The units being used are to be stated explicitly. It is preferred that a + and/or − sign precede the number or quantity. The absence of a sign infers a + sign. It can be expressed in a number of forms.

congestion: A specific condition that develops when the number of calls arriving at the various communications input stations of a network exceeds the network handling capacity or capability in a particular time allotment, or that condition which arises when arriving "traffic" exceeds the number of "servers."

congestion theory: A particular theory of mathematics which relates to the study of delays and losses which affect the traffic of items which move through a communications system.

conjunction: The logical operation which makes use of the "and" operator or logical product. The conjunction of two variables, or expressions, may be written as a and b, a or b, or just plain ab. These may also be described as an intersection when using Venn diagrams.

conjunctive search: A search defined in terms of a logical product.

connecting cable: The cable used to transfer an electrical impulse between two pieces of equipment.

connection: The current-carrying junction which results when two conductors are clamped, wrapped, or wrapped and soldered into electrical contact. Also, an association of channels and other functional units providing means for the transfer of information between two or more terminal points.

connection box: An electrical distribution panel similar in purpose to that of a plugboard. (A plugboard permits distribution or altering of destinations of signals.) Most often found in punch card machines with mechanical sensing. Wires can be disconnected and changed to different terminals to achieve specific design purposes.

connection delay: The interval from the instant when the information required to set up a through connection in an exchange is available for processing, to the instant that the switching network through connection is established between the inlet and outlet.

connection release: The breaking of a connection in switching networks between calling and called stations.

connector: 1. Generally, a protective device mounted on main distributing frame. In CCITT specification description language, a connector is either an inconnector or an out-connector. Flow is always assumed to be from the out-connector to its associated inconnector. 2. In flow charting, a symbol used to indicate the interconnection of two points in the flow chart.

connect time: The time which elapses while the user of a remote terminal is connected to a time-shared system. Connect time is usually measured by the duration between "sign-on" and "sign-off."

CONS: Carrier Operated Noise Suppression.

conscious error: An error that was instantly recognized as such by an operator, but that his reflex actions were unable to prevent.

consecutive sequence computer: A computer used to execute instructions individually and sequentially without any concurrent activities such as simultaneous reading, writing, and computing.

consistency check: A process designed to verify that a piece of data is consistent with the rules prescribed for its handling.

consistency error (remote-computing system): An erroneous statement detected as soon as the user enters the offending statement. The system rejects the offending statement and the user can substitute a correct statement immediately.

console: 1. The unit of computer, also peripherals and data entry terminals where the control keys and certain special devices are located. This unit may contain the start key, stop key, power key, sense switches, etc., as well as lights which display the information located in certain registers. 2. A portion of the computer which may be used to determine the status of machine circuits, registers, and counters, determine the contents of storage, and manually revise the contents of storage.

console debugging: The programmer may debug at the machine console or at a remote console by slowly stepping the machine through each instruction and observing the contents of appropriate registers and memory locations.

console display: A visual display unit that provides a "window into the computer." It can display a message of thousands of characters of information, or tables, charts, graphs and the lines and curves of drawings as a series of points.

console display keyboard: 1. A keyboard which makes possible interpretive operations. Its function for a particular job is assigned by the computer program and the keys for that job are identified by removable illuminated overlays. 2. An operator control panel for those processors where the display is used in place of the typewriter control console.

console display register: Sets of indicator lights on a computer console that display the bit pattern contents of registers.

console start-up: The standard console interrupt is triggered by a switch on the console, allowing an operator to exert control.

console switch: One which can be set from an operator's console to enable a program to change its actions according to the setting it detects.

consolidate: The final stage of compilation in which subroutines implicitly or explicitly called by a source program are inserted from a library file into the program being compiled.

consolidation: In any proving operation where several packages and totals are to be included in one classification, it is necessary to consolidate the totals for proving purposes. It is also a term used to designate a departmental proof.

constant: 1. The quantity of messages which will be present in the machine and available as data for the program, and which usually are not subject to change with time. 2. A character or group of characters usually representing a value. A key or standard, used by the computer to identify, locate, measure, or test in order to make a decision.

constant area: A location within the computer in which one or more constants may be stored for reference.

constant   FORTRAN: Fixed   point (integer): 1 to 5 decimal digits, optional + or − sign but no decimal point. Floating point: Sequence of decimal digits with decimal point, optional + or − sign; or a sequence of decimal digits, the letter E followed by an integer exponent, + or −sign optional. Constants within a Boolean expression are interpreted as octal numbers (of less than 12 octal digits).

constant instruction: An instruction not intended to be executed as an instruction, written in the form of a constant. Related to dummy instruction.

constant multiplier: A computing element that multiplies a variable by a constant factor.

constant multiplier coefficient unit: Same as scalar.

constant ratio code: A code in which all characters are represented by combinations having a fixed ratio of ones to zeros.

constant section: A specific part of internal storage reserved for invariable data for recurred usage.

constant storage: A part of storage designated to store the invariable quantities required for processing.

construct noise: Noise caused by equipment malfunction.

contact alignment: A term which refers to electrical contacts and the sidewise movement or play in mating contact pins or other devices for plugs or other contact insertions or surfaces.

contact area: The common surfaces between conductors or connectors of electricity flow. They must be large enough to cause a reduction in current density to a value low enough to avoid excessive heat or potential drop across the contact surface.

contact bifurcated: Contacts used in printed circuits with slotted flat springs which increase flexibility of the spring and provide extra points of contact.

contact configuration: A standard or designed arrangement of various contacts in general multiple-contact connectors, i.e., including the spacing, number, orientation, location of the contacts in the connector.

contact, electrical: The path or joint of the two halves of a connector or that point joined in the electrical connection.

contact float: The amount of give movement, or sideplay which a contact has within the insert cavity to thus allow self-alignment of mated contacts, i.e., easy insertion of the plug or other contact surface.

contact sense module: In some systems, a device which is designed to monitor and convert program-specified groups of field switch contacts into digital codes for input to the computer. Inputs are scanned by the computer at programmed intervals.

contact-separating force: The exertion or force necessary to separate or remove pins from sockets.

content addressed storage (CAM): A very important storage device which identifies storage locations by their contents instead of by their names, codes, addresses, or position. It is usually polled or interrogated in parallel throughout its contents to discern if the sought after word is available by comparing it with all other words stored instead of searching for its address. A search key substitutes for the address of the desired data or information. The programmer does not need to specify an address and by requesting a "yes" or "no" answer to whether a particular word is stored, all data associated with such a keyword may be dumped or transferred out. The device can store the keywords and their associated data in any available location, i.e., at random.

content, information (message or symbol from a source): 1. The negative of the logarithm of the probability that this particular message or symbol will be emitted from the source. 2. The choice of logarithmic base determines the unit of information content. 3. The probability of a given message or symbol being emitted may depend on one or more preceding messages or symbols. 4. The quantity has been called self-information.

contention: A condition occurring on a multistation communication channel when two or more stations try to transmit at the same time. This is overcome by station control accomplished through polling and/or calling.

contention PODA (CPODA): A variant of priority oriented demand assignment (PODA), which requires stations to make advance requests before transmitting.

contention ring: A ring which utilizes the contention mechanism required for token recovery to eliminate the channel acquisition delay when the load is light.

contention system: A system in which one or more terminals and the computer compete for use of the line.

contents: The information stored in any storage medium. The symbol ( ) is used to indicate "the contents of", e.g., (M) indicates the contents of the storage location whose address is M. (A) indicates the contents of register A. (T2) indicates the contents of the tape on input/output unit two.

context-dependent compression: Compression of runs of repeated symbols into a count plus the symbol.

context-dependent encoding: Encoding which determines the conditional probability for each symbol for each possible predecessor.

context editing: In systems with time sharing, a method of editing a line data set or file without using line numbers. To refer to a particular line, all or part of the contents of that line are specified.

context-independent encoding: Encoding which assumes that the probability of a symbol occurring is independent of its immediate predecessor.

contiguous alphabet: An alphabet (A through Z) assigned, by code, to a continuous binary sequence.

contiguous segmentation: A design of placement in which each segment is placed in memory locations with contiguous real addresses.

contingency interrupt: The program is interrupted if any of the following events occur at the operator's console: the operator requests use of the keyboard to type in information; a character has been typed in or out; a type-in has been typed in or out; a type-in has been completed; or the operator requests a program stop.

continuation card: A punched card which contains information that was started on a previous punched card.

continuation line: A line of a source statement into which characters are entered when the source statement cannot be contained on the preceding line or lines.

continuity check: A check made to a circuit in a connection to verify that an acceptable path for transmission of data or speech exists. With the increased use of separate or common channel signaling systems, a continuity check on the actual voice path itself is normally carried out before a circuit is put through to the customer.

continuity failure signal: In data common channel signaling, a signal sent in the backward direction indicating that the call cannot be completed due to failure of the forward continuity check.

continuous carrier: A carrier over which transmission of information is accomplished by means that do not interrupt the carrier.

continuous data: 1. Continuous measures are those which may conceivably be found at any point along a continuous scale. The units of measurement may be measured in as fine units as is desired or as related to the problem. 2. Used in a broad sense to indicate all quantitative data, including that of a quantal nature.

continuous forms: A continuous supply of paper made up of several hundred individual sheets separated by perforations and folded to form a pack. It is designed for automatic feeding through the print unit of a line printer and sprocket holes are punched for that purpose, in the margins of each sheet.

continuous function: A function in which the difference between any two consecutive states is less than any assignable quantity. In such a function, if we suppose the independent variable to pass through every possible state from one given value to another, the function will pass, by imperceptible degrees, through every state from the first to the last. A function that follows this law is said to be subject to the law of continuity.

continuous interrogation: Constant electrical activation and observance of an encoder's reported shaft position.

continuous optimization program (COP): A continuous program using linear programming techniques.

continuous path operation: The controlling of the motion of a machine tool in space, as a function of time, such that the machine travels through the designated path at the specified rate. (This generally requires the ability to simultaneously move more than one machine axis at coordinated rates.)

continuous progression code: A particular code in which characters are represented by words of a fixed number of bits, but which are arranged in a sequence so that the signal distance between consecutive words is 1 or unity. Also called cyclic permitted code or CP code.

continuous simulation: The type of simulation which may be represented by continuous variables considered at regular intervals. The system is therefore suitable for representation by a set of differential equations. These may be further classified as linear or nonlinear. Examples: missile flights, respiratory control system, etc. (Contrast with discrete simulation.)

continuous system diagnosis (time-sharing):

A very useful technique which can be included easily in a time-shared system. A collection of diagnostic tasks are placed permanently in the task queue with only a low priority assigned to them. Whenever the queue of user-ready tasks is empty, the system selects and runs one of these test programs sending the results to a special monitor console. Normal preventive maintenance can be interlaced similarly with user tasks eliminating the need for shutting down the entire system at periodic intervals.

continuous system modeling program: A digital computer program that simulates analog systems.

continuous variable: In contrast to discrete variables, a variable is continuous if it can assume all values of a continuous scale. Such quantities as length, time, and temperature are measured on continuous scales and their measurements may be referred to as continuous variables.

continuous wave (CW): The method of dot-and-dash transmissions.

contour analysis: In optical character recognition (OCR), a reading technique that employs a moving spot of light which searches out the character outline by bouncing around its outer edges.

contouring: Continuous tool-path control. A system in which the cutting path results from the coordinated simultaneous motion of two or more axes. It can produce contours, three-dimensional complex curves, and socalled warped surfaces, depending on the number of axes under control.

contracts preventive maintenance: The arrangement between the customer and manufacturer for periodic maintenance of equipment.

contrast: The range of light and dark values in a picture, or the ratio between the maximum and minimum brightness values. A high-contrast picture would contain intense blacks and whites; a lower-contrast picture would contain only shades of gray.

control: 1. The part of a digital computer or processor which determines the execution and interpretation of instructions in proper sequence, including the decoding of each instruction and the application of the proper signals to the arithmetic unit and other registers in accordance with the decoded information. Frequently, it is one or more of the components in any mechanism responsible for interpreting and carrying out manually-initiated directions. Sometimes it is called manual control. 2. In some business applications, a mathematical check. 3. In programming, instructions which determine conditional jumps are often referred to as control instructions, and the time sequence of execution of instructions is called the flow of control.

control, error: The improvement of digital communications through use of certain techniques such as error detection, forward-acting error correction, and use of block codes.

control action: The correction a controller makes for a deviation or error.

control action, proportional plus integral plus derivative: Specific control action in which the output is proportional to a linear combination of the input, the time integral of the input and the time rate-of-change of input.

control-action system: Concerns the nature of the change of the output effected by the input. The output may be a signal or the value of a manipulated variable. The input may be the control loop feedback signal when the set point is a constant of an actuating error signal, or the output of another controller.

control algorithm: A mathematical representation or procedure design of the control action to be performed.

control and data acquisition system: A system designed to handle a wide variety of real-time applications, process control, and high-speed data acquisition. Each system is individually tailored with modular building blocks that are easily integrated to meet specific system requirements. A large family of realtime process input/output (I/O) devices is included, such as analog input, contact sense, and contact operate, as well as data processing I/O units—magnetic tape, disk storage, line printer, graph plotter, card and paper tape input and output. Data are received and transmitted on either a high-speed sysle-steal basis or under program control, depending on the intrinsic data rate of the I/O device.

control and orthotronic error: Accuracy of information on magnetic tape is orthotronic control which provides unique ortho-correction—the automatic detection and correction of erroneous data. Basically, orthotronic control can be compared to the accounting technique of "crossfooting," in which a zero balance in rows and columns of figures confirms accuracy and a nonzero balance indicates an error. When information is written on tape, a special checking digit, called a parity bit, is automatically computed and placed at the end of frames (rows) of data in an information word.

control block: A storage area through which a particular type of information required for control of the operating system is communicated among its parts.

control block queue: A special control block which is designed to be used in the regulation of the sequential use of some programmer-defined facility by a set of competing tasks.

control block task: The accumulation of control data relating to a particular task.

control block unit: A nine-word area of core storage describing an input/output (I/O) device connected to the computer. These blocks are generated during system assembly for use by the I/O executor (on some systems).

control break: Commonly used in connection with a computer report program whereas comparing control change is used in punched card terminology.

control carriage.: The device that controls the feeding of continuous forms through a printer.

control character: 1. A character whose occurrence in a particular context initiates, modifies, or stops a control function. A control character may be recorded for use in a subsequent action. A control character is not a graphic character, but may have a graphic representation in some circumstances. 2. A character whose occurrence starts, changes, or stops a process.

control character, switching: A specific character that controls switching of devices to on or off, usually in telecommunications systems, but also used in other data processing equipment.

control circuits: The circuits which cause the computer to carry out the instructions in proper sequence, and which can control by permitting only the coded conditions to continue or function.

control codes: There are special codes used for purposes other than scrambling. They may be used for control functions, such as auto-clear or for synchronization.

control computer: A computer which, by means of inputs from and outputs to a process, directly controls the operation of elements in that process.

control console or panel: Two methods of operator control are provided in conjunction with the control unit: a control panel and an operator's console. Either method provides a visual indication of the status of the entire system and permits manual intervention in the system's operation. The control panel contains various control switches by which the operator can start and stop the machine and can load and interrogate both main and control-memory locations. Sense switches may be used in conjunction with programmed instructions to stop processing or to select predetermined program paths, thereby increasing the flexibility of a program.

control counter: A special counter contained in the control unit.

control C station: A switching network station directing operations such as polling, alerting, recovering, selecting control, and tape sequence. Same as tape program.

control cycle: A particular cycle of the operation of a punch card machine's main shaft during which the feeding is stopped due to a control change, i.e., a choice often given the user as to how many intercycles arise for a control change, which may or may not be determined within the machine.

control data: One or more items of data used as control to identify, select, execute or modify another routine, record, file, operation, data value, etc.

control desk: Desk-like console or group of panels from which operators or service personnel actually control the computing system or communicate with it.

control device character: A control character which is used to control various devices associated with computing or telecommunications systems, i.e., particularly the switching to on or off of the devices.

control dictionary: The portion of a program deck that contains symbolic information necessary to relocate and/or load the deck, including the names and locations of control sections.

control director: 1. A centralized control device in an automatic telephone office which combines the functions of registers, translators and senders. Used in some major metropolitan areas to control the routing of junction and tandem calls, particularly between stepby-step central offices. 2. A parasitic element in an antenna on the major lobe side of the active dipole, i.e., facing the transmitter whose signal is to be received.

control edit character: A special character designed for accuracy control.

control element: The final controlling means actuating the load. Also referred to as actuator.

control field (sorting): A continuous group of characters within a record which form all or part of the control word.

control forms: A specific function of a supervisor or manager whose task is to take care to avoid excess or unneeded forms to be used in the computing system.

control function: An action that affects the recording, processing transmission or interpretation of data, e.g., starting or stopping a process; carriage return; font change; rewind; end of transmission. Same as control operation.

control group: The number of people, one or more, required to spend their full time in decision-making when a system is being programmed.

control guidance system: A specific system in which deliberate guidance or manipulation is used to achieve a prescribed value of a variable. It is usually subdivided into a controlling system and a controlled system.

control input/output (I/O) module: Provides control signals, parity checks, time interface, and data transformations for I/O devices. It consists of an instruction register and associated decoding circuitry, a data register, and a manipulation register with associated timing circuits. Each control module is capable of controlling any standard device of the I/O complement. There can be as many simultaneous I/O operations as there are I/O control modules. The I/O exchange automatically connects control modules with any of the I/O devices on command from processor modules. The I/O control modules also provide interface with associated data-processing systems.

control instruction: A computer instruction causing a jump in the sequence of instructions to occur.

control instruction register: A distinct register in which the content is the address of the next instruction.

control job statement: Individual statements used to direct an operating system in its functions, as contrasted to information needed to process a job but not intended directly for the operating system itself.

control keys: Control keys move and control the cursor, switch the terminal from one application to another, and switch the communication disciplines.

control language: The language used to prescribe the course of a linear programming problem run on a computer. The language consists mainly of verbs (agendum names), which call in a body of code (program or subroutine) embodying the desired algorithm for execution.

control language, job (JCL): Specifications (usually on punched cards) that declare the environment in which a job (series of computer programs) is to be run.

controlled carrier: Transmission in which the magnitude of the carrier is controlled by the signal, so that the depth of modulation is nearly independent of the magnitude of the signal.

controlled variable: A quantity, condition, or part of a system which is subject to manipulation, regulation, or control by a computer.

controller: A module or specific device which operates automatically to regulate a controlled variable or system.

controller, proportional plus integral plus derivative: A specific controller which produces proportional plus integral (reset) plus derivative (rate) control action.

controlling system: Usually refers to a feedback control system; i.e., that portion which compares functions of a directly controlled variable and a set point, and adjusts a manipulated variable as a function of the difference. It includes the reference input elements; summing point; forward and final controlling elements, as well as feedback elements (including the sensing element).

control logic: The sequence of steps or events necessary to perform a particular function. Each step or event is defined to be either a single arithmetic or a single Boolean expression.

control loop: The path along which control-affecting signals travel from the error detecting point, through the controller, and back to the error detecting point.

control marks (CM): The central mark (any one-slab block) supplies special control features which can be utilized by the programmer. However, several specified CM configurations have been reserved for particular features on data tapes, as EF for end of file, etc.

control message illegal error: A control message that has been read and not defined. If the message is typed in it may be retyped. Otherwise, only the compile or assemble phase of the job is processed and a job error is given.

control mode: The state that all terminals on a line must be in to allow line discipline, line control, or terminal selection to occur. When all terminals on a line are in the control mode, characters on the line are viewed as control characters performing line discipline, that is, polling or addressing.

control number: This is the quantity or number (value) which must be the result of a process or problem in order to prove the accuracy of the process or problem.

control office: A central office, switching center or telephone exchange in which switching equipment at each selection level is actuated directly by signals dialed in by the calling subscriber.

control output module: A device in some systems that stores computer commands and translates them into signals which can be used for control purposes. Some can generate digital outputs to control on/off devices or to pulse set-points stations. Others can generate analog outputs – voltage or current – to operate valves and other process control devices.

control panel: 1. An interconnection device, usually removable, that employs removable wires to control the operation of computing equipment. The panel is used on punch-card machines to carry out functions which are under the control of the user. On computers it is used to control input and output functions. 2. A device or component of some data-processing machines, which permits the expression of instructions in a semifixed computer program by the insertion of pins, plugs, or wires into sockets, or hubs in the device, in a pattern representing instructions, and thus making electrical interconnections which may be sensed by the dataprocessing machine. Same as plugboard.

control panel, central: The group of displays, manual buttons, and switches which are used by the operators, engineers and maintenance personnel of the computer center.

control pen (light): A pen-like device with a light on the tip used to communicate with a computer by "writing" on a CRT display.

control procedure: A basic key to achievement of high operating efficiency in a computing or data-processing installation. This procedure must include many functions: (a) administrative control of job schedules, workflow, and computer usage records; (b) control over data and program libraries; (c) control over computer operations; and (d) control over the flow of programs and data within the computer system during job runs.

control program: A sequence of instructions which prescribes the series of steps to be taken by a system, a computer, or other device. Control programs contain many routines that would otherwise have to be put into each individual program. Such routines include those for handling error conditions, interruptions from the console, or interruptions from a communications terminal. There are also routines for handling input and output equipment. Because these routines are prewritten, the programmer is saved a good deal of effort and the likelihood of programming errors is reduced.

control programming system: Programming that is fundamental to the operation and maintenance of a system. It serves as an interface with program products and user programs and is available without additional charge.

control punching: Punches which determine how the data on a punched card is to be treated within a machine, or which functions the machine is about to or is capable of performing.

control ratio: Concerns that specific limitation in the relationship between two quantities as expressed in direct or percentage comparison.

control record: 1. A record that contains data used to intiate, modify, or stop a control operation or to determine the manner in which data is processed. 2. Under telecommunications access method (TCAM), a record included in a checkpoint data set that keeps track of the correct environment records, incident records, and checkpoint request records to use for restructuring the message control program environment during restart.

control register: A register which stores the instruction currently governing the operation of the computer. Same as program register.

control relationship: A particular relationship between any two units of equipment to indicate the nature of the control of either unit by the other, i.e. if one unit can be controlled by the other without human intervention, the first is said to be on-line to the second, and is under the direct control of the second during its exercise.

control routine: 1. A routine which controls loading and relocation of routines and in some cases makes use of instructions which are unknown to the general programmer. Effectively, control routine is part of the machine itself (synonymous with monitor routine, supervisory routine, and supervisory program). 2. A set of coded instructions designed to process and control other sets of coded instructions. 3. A set of coded instructions used in realizing automatic coding.

control section: A sequence of instructions or data within a program that can be referred to from outside the program segment in which it is contained. A control section can be deleted or replaced with a control section from other program segments.

control sequence: The normal order of selection of instructions for execution. In some computers one of the addresses in each instruction specifies the control sequence. In most other computers, the sequence is consecutive except where a transfer occurs.

control signal: The actuating signal in automatic control systems.

control statements: 1. Statements that direct the flow of the program, either causing specific transfers or making transfers dependent upon meeting certain specified conditions. 2. Instructions which convey control information to the processor, but do not develop machine-language instructions, i.e., symbolic statements.

control station: That point within the general maintenance organization that fulfills the control responsibilities for the circuit, group, supergroup or line section assigned to it. In a data network, the station that selects the master station and supervises operational procedures such as polling, selecting, and recovery. The control station has the overall responsibility for the orderly operation of the entire network.

control storage: Monolithic storage, used primarily for microprograms.

control switching point (CSP): The class 1, 2 and 3 offices (regional, sectional and primary centers) used for nationwide dialing.

control system inventory: A systems approach to inventory control.

control tape: See carriage tape.

control terminal: In timesharing systems, any active terminal at which the user is authorized to enter commands affecting system operation.

control total: A sum of numbers in a specified record field of a batch of records, determined repetitiously, during the processing operation so that any discrepancy from the control indicates an error.

control transfer instruction: A computer instruction causing a jump in the sequence of instructions to occur.

control unit: The portion of a computer which directs the sequence of operations, interprets the coded instructions, and initiates the proper commands to the computer circuits preparatory to execution.

control utility console: A computer console that is primarily used to control utility and maintenance programs.

control volume: Volume containing one or more indices of a specific catalog.

control word (sorting): Refers to a continuous group of characters within a record which are designed to form all or part of the control word.

convenience files: Unofficial desk files, or other unofficial files, physically located near the point of usage (copies) for convenient reference.

conventional equipment: That equipment which is generally considered to be part of the computer system but which is not specifically part of the computer itself. Various card handling devices, tape handlers, and disk units, if not built into the mainframe or wired in, would be conventional equipment.

conventions: Standard and accepted procedures in program and systems analysis. The abbreviations, symbols, and their meanings developed for particular systems and programs.

convergence: Intersection of beams in a multi-beam electron tube, such as a color TV tube.

convergence connector: A flowchart connector that is used to indicate the convergence of multiple flowlines into one line, or form on-line into multiple flowlines.

conversational: Pertaining to a program or a system that carries on a dialog with a terminal user, alternately accepting input and then responding to the input in a real-time mode. See also interactive.

conversational language: A language utilizing a near English character set which facilitates communication between the computer and the user. For example, BASIC is one of the more commonly used conversational languages.

conversational processing: The user is said to be communicating with the system in a "conversational" manner when each statement he enters through the terminal is processed (translated, verified, and, if desired, executed) immediately. The system then sends a reply to the terminal. The information contained in the reply varies. For example, it might be a message indicating that the previous statement contained an error. Operations in the conversational manner must be in either of two possible modes: the program mode or the command mode.

conversational programming: A technique used in instructing the computer to perform its operations, whereby common vocabulary can be utilized by the user to describe his procedures most accurately. If a statement cannot be understood by the computer, it asks the user for a clarified instruction. The conversational procedure continues until the user has selected the series of statements in the proper sequence which will solve his problem. Conversational programming saves the user the inconvenience of having to study other programming languages extensively before he can solve his problem.

conversational remote job entry (CRJE): An operating system facility for entering job control language statements from a remote terminal, and causing the scheduling and execution of the jobs described in the statements. The terminal user is prompted for missing operands or corrections.

conversational time-sharing: Use of a computer system by many users in a conversational mode.

conversation mode: A condition of real-time communication between one or more remote terminals and a timesharing computer, in which each entry from a terminal elicits an immediate response from the computer. The remote terminal thus can control, interrogate, or modify a task within the computer.

conversion: 1. A procedure to change information from one form of representation to another; for example, from punch cards to magnetic tape or from one language to another. 2. The procedure of changing a number written in one number base to the base of another number system. 3. The procedure of changing from one data processing method to another, or from one type of equipment to another.

conversion, code: 1. The conversion of character signals or groups of character signals in one code into corresponding signals or groups of signals in another code. 2. A process for converting a code of some predetermined bit structure (for example, 5, 7, or 14 bits per character interval) to a second code with approximately the same number of bits per character interval. No alphabetical significance is assumed in this process.

conversion costs: One-time expenses which are incurred when an organization installs a computer for the first time or when it applies an existing computer to a new application area. Conversion costs often constitute a significant part of the total investment of the organization in its computer. They consist mainly of costs in preparing files for the computer, preparation of air conditioned rooms and storage.

conversion device: A particular device or piece of peripheral equipment which converts data from one form into another form or medium, but without changing the data, content, or information.

conversion mode: Communication between a terminal and the computer in which each entry from the terminal elicits a response from the computer and vice versa.

conversion time: The time taken for a converter to complete its measurement.

convert: 1. To change numerical information from one number base to another. 2. To transfer information from one recorded medium to another.

converter, dc-dc: Unit which converts one dc voltage value to a different one. Much used in transmission equipment, where power is fed to each rack and converted to the different dc voltages needed.

cooperative installation: A computer installation serving many users who share the costs of a bigger system than they could afford individually.

coordinate dimensioning: A system of dimensioning where a point is defined as being a certain dimension and direction from a reference point as measured with respect to a defined axis.

coordinate dimension word: A word defining an absolute dimension.

coordinate geometry (COGO): A language useful for solving coordinate geometry problems in civil engineering. It can be used as a geometrically oriented urban data-management system under ICES.

coordinate indexing: An indexing scheme by which descriptors may be correlated or combined to show any interrelationships desired for purposes of more precise information retrieval.

coordinate paper: Marginally punched, continuous form graph paper normally used for printout on an XY plotter.

coordinates: Coordinates are elements of reference by means of which the relative positions of points in a plane may be determined with respect to the ordinate and abscissa axes. These elements, the objects to which reference is made, and the method of making the reference constitute a system of coordinates.

coordinate storage: A storage unit whose elements are arranged in a matrix so that access to any location requires the use of two or more coordinates; i.e., a cathode-ray tube store and a core store using coincident-current selection.

core: A tiny doughnut or magnetizable metal that can be either in an on or off state and can represent either a binary 1 (on) or a binary 0 (off). Commonly called magnetic core.

core array: A rectangular grid of cores containing a given number of words each of a given number of bits making up the rectangular array.

core plane: An electronic device or grid which has wires and magnetic cores arranged in parallel. It is used in internal storage with particular bit positions for several addresses.

core resident: Pivotal programs permanently stored in core memory for frequent execution.

core switch: A magnetic core in a switching device used to route signals to a selected destination.

corner frequency: A defined value of abscissa of the confluence in the asymptotic approximation of a log amplitude vs. log frequency relation. Used to characterize instrument response capabilities.

corpus: A body or mass of data, most often in unreduced form and as selected for study or analysis.

correct and copy: Refers to the procedure in which a designated record is copied from one tape to another with specified corrections. In manipulating magnetic tapes, either a record-counting method or a file-identification method may be employed. The file option provides added convenience in that it permits operation over an entire tape or file, rather than over a specified number of records.

correction from signals: A system or correction in which the maintenance of synchronous equipment is controlled, not by a special correcting signal, but by the position of the characteristic instants of restitution of telegraph signals comprising the text.

correction program: See correction routine.

correction routine: A routine used in or after a computer failure, malfunction, or program or operator error. It reconstitutes the routine executed before the error occurred and from the closest rerun point.

corrective maintenance: The activity of detecting, isolating and correcting failures after occurrence.

corrective maintenance time: Scheduled or unscheduled time, used to perform corrective maintenance.

correlation measurements: The three important measures of correlation are: 1. The line of regression that is fitted to the points on the scatter diagram in such a way that the sum of the squared deviations from the line is at a minimum. The line of regression gives the average change in y resulting from any given change in x. 2. The standard error of estimate (S_y) equals $\sqrt{\Sigma d^2/N}$, where d represents the deviation from the line of regression. S_y indicates, in absolute terms, the error that may be expected from any group of estimates made from the line of regression. 3. The coefficient of correlation (r) is a relative measure of the degree of relationship between two variables. It indicates the degree of improvement in the ability to estimate y from x over estimates of y made from the mean of the y variable alone.

cost analysis: Used to determine the cost of production of any job, process, or service in an industrial or commercial organization.

cost data center accounting: A type of financial accounting designed so that charges of all kinds are recorded, edited, sorted and posted. The charges are first posted to the job or cost center account that applied so management has records of where expenditures are made and which jobs may be too expensive. The same information is then used as input to the computer to post the required formal ledger.

cost-effectiveness: A designed measure of performance for distinct evaluations of systems, products, or endeavors. It is most often expressed as a ratio of some reference measure of cost and/or performance.

cost problem dynamic programming: A method for optimizing a set of decisions which must be made sequentially. Characteristically, each decision must be made in the light of the information embodied in a small number of observables called state variables. The incurred cost for each period is a mathematical function of the current state and decision variables, while future states are functions of these variables. The aim of the decision policy is to minimize the total incurred cost, or equivalently, the average cost per period. Mathematical treatment of such problems involves the theory of functional equations and usually requires a digital computer for implementation.

counter: A device or location which can be set to an initial number and increased or decreased by an arbitrary number by stimuli applied one at a time.

counter, read/write: Data is transferred between the main memory and peripheral devices via read/write channels. Associated with each channel are two read/write counters. These counters store the starting and current addresses of the data being transferred by the read/write channel.

count-pulse interrupt: An interrupt level that is triggered by pulses from a clock source. Each pulse of the clock source causes an instruction in a (clock) count pulse interrupt location to be executed, thus modifying the contents of a particular location (byte, halfword, or word) in memory. Each count pulse interrupt level is associated with a count zero interrupt level.

country-or-network identity: Information sent in the backward direction consisting of a number of address signals indicating the identity of a country or network in which the call has been transit-switched internationally.

coupled circuits: Two or more circuits electrically connected so that they react on each other, leading to energy transfer.

coupled computers: An installation in which computers are joined to carry out special applications, such as two computers operating in parallel and used as a check on one another, or when they are coupled or joined so that the off-line computer is programmed to watch the on-line computer and, if needed, switch operation to itself.

Coursewriter III: A simple language for preparing computer-assisted instruction courses.

CPB: See channel program block.

CPU: See central processing unit.

CPU busy time: See CPU time.

CPU cache: A distributed computation model where each user has a minicomputer inserted between his terminal and the mainframe, or large central computer. Part of the computation is performed on the central computer and part on the minicomputer.

CPU time: The amount of time devoted by the central processing unit to the execution of instructions. Same as CPU busy time.

cramping: The contraction of either side or of the central section of a TV picture; it may arise, for example, from poor emission of certain thermionic valves.

crash: A complete failure of a hardware device or a software operation.

CRC: See cyclic redundancy check.

creation: In file processing, a term referring to initial data collection, and the organization of this raw data into a file.

credit message: When a user calls RECEIVE, this message is sent to the transport station on the receiving machine and is entered in the conn array.

credit verification terminal: Credit verification terminals are specific types of terminals closely related to point-of-sale recorders and electronic cash registers. Credit verification is one of the functions performed by a complete electronic cash register, but there are requirements for simpler, and much less expensive, terminals which service the on-line real-time credit card, permit manual entry of the amount of purchase (and in some cases the credit card number), provide some fixed data entry (e.g., store identification), communicate with a central computer containing credit files, provide a go/no-go/maybe response for the transaction, and in some applications imprint a sales slip.

crippled leapfrog test: A variation of the leapfrog test, so that it repeats the tests from a single, rather than a changing, set of storage locations. See leapfrog test.

criteria sorting: 1. A character group usually forming a field, utilized in the identification or location of an item. 2. That part of a word, record, file, etc., by which it is identified or controlled. 3. The field by which a file of records is sorted into order; i.e., the key or a file of employee records by a number, department, or letter.

criterion: A value used for testing, comparing, or judging, e.g., in determining whether a condition is plus or minus, true or false; also a rule or test for making a decision by computer or by human thought.

critical path: The longest time path in a project which has to be done as quickly as possible. Because the overall time required to complete the project can not be less than that required along the critical path, it requires the most careful monitoring. Any delay along this path causes the project to be delayed, while minor delays along non-critical paths do not.

critical path scheduling: A monitoring system that continuously checks progress in programming needs of an operating system to report and prevent slippage. Reports generated by this monitoring of computer programming needs, in which jobs to be done are sorted, will indicate the most critical items on the critical path of the computer.

critical regions: Sets of operations on a common data structure which exclude one another in time.

cross assembler: A program run on one computer for the purpose of translating instructions for a different computer.

crossbar: An automatic telephone switching system using switches mounted on movable bars. Information dialed into the system is stored in common equipment that tests and selects the switching paths and controls the operation of the switching mechanism.

crossbar switch: A switch having a plurality of vertical and horizontal paths, and electromagneticallyoperated mechanical means for interconnecting any one of the vertical paths with any of the horizontal paths.

crossbar-switching system: A line-switching system using mechanisms called crossbar switches. These consist of contact spring units operated in coordination by horizontal and vertical members.

cross channel switching: A feature that permits program access to input/output devices through two channels.

crosscheck: To check the computing by two different methods.

cross coupling: Undesired transfer of interfering power from one circuit to another by induction, leakage, etc.

crossed-fields multiplier: Analog device which incorporates a cathode-ray tube and is specifically designed for the single input signal to produce a proportional electrostatic field perpendicular to the axis of the tube. The other input signal, which represents the other variable, produces an axial magnetic field to thus deflect the beam perpendicular to the two fields to make it proportional to the product of the two input signals.

cross-fade: To fade in one channel while fading out another in order to substitute gradually the output of one for that of the other; e.g., to create the impression of a change of scene. Same as dissolve or mix.

crossfire: Interfering current in one telegraph or signaling channel resulting from telegraph or signaling currents in another channel.

crossfooting: Crossfooting is the addition and/or subtraction of factors in a horizontal spread to prove processing accuracy. It can be used on a payroll register to prove that the final totals of net pay and deductions equal the final total earnings; this provides control on report preparation as well as calculating and card-punching operations. In posting transactions to records that are stored in a computer (i.e., accounts receivable), crossfooting is used to prove the accuracy of posting, either as each transaction is posted, or collectively at the end of the run, or both.

cross-hatch pattern: A test pattern of vertical and horizontal lines used on a television picture tube.

cross isle: The place where operators tear off tape and transfer it to an outgoing circuit in a torn tape system.

cross modulation: A form of signal distortion due to modulation of the carrier of the desired signal by an undesired wave.

crossover frequency: The point of division between separated frequency bands of the crossover network.

crossover network: The device between audio amplifier output and speakers which divides the high from the low audio frequencies.

cross-parity checking codes: Method of using a character parity check as well as a block check to detect errors.

crosspoint switch: A shared memory system with a rectangular grid-organized system of busses and interconnections. In this system, a separate bus goes into each memory module, with each processor attached to each memory bus.

cross reference: A notation in a file or on a list showing that a record has been stored elsewhere.

cross reference dictionary: A special printing or listing that identifies all references of an assembled program to a specific label.

This listing is provided immediately after a source program has been assembled.

cross-sectional testing: Tests used to get a representative sampling of system performance.

crosstalk: Crosstalk happens when signals on one circuit emerge on another circuit as interference. The circuit which is the source of the signals is known as the disturbing circuit, and the one which the signals are heard is the disturbed circuit.

crosstalk, far-end: Crosstalk which is propagated in a disturbed channel in the same direction as the propagation of a signal in the disturbing channel. The terminals of the disturbed channel where the far-end crosstalk is present and the energized terminals of the disturbing channel are usually remote from each other.

cross-tracking: A crosslike array of bright dots on the display, used for locating points and lines or for drawing curves.

CRT: See cathode-ray tube.

CRT consoles: Cathode-ray tube (CRT) display consoles used as CRT terminals overcome most of the disadvantages of a typewriter console. The CRT display rate is very fast—thousands of characters per second. It is quiet and its output is flexible, easily modified and rearranged. The more sophisticated forms of CRT consoles have pictorial capabilities allowing line segments to be displayed. Pointing facilities, such as light pens, allow users to easily designate symbols or vectors of interest.

CRT deflection beam: See cathode-ray deflection beam.

CRT display: Indicates the memory word parity. Other display bits may indicate: (a) the next instruction, (b) the contents of any memory location, (c) the contents of the accumulator, (d) the contents of index registers, (e) the status of the traps. When the computer halts, the display register will indicate the next instruction word, while a register will contain the address of the halt instruction that stopped the computer. To display anything else, the appropriate push-button display switch must be pressed. When the display-M button is pressed, the contents of the memory location specified by a register will be displayed. When either the display or other buttons are pressed, the contents of other registers or the condition of the tapes are displayed. The display register is also used as an entry register. Push-buttons which may clear all or various parts of the display register are provided. The contents of the display register may be entered in any memory location.

CRT display point-mode: In this mode, individual points may be established and/or plotted at random locations on the tube face. A point is established by two independent 18-bit words. The first word determines the vertical position, the second word sets up the horizontal position. Once an initial point has been established, subsequent plots may be made by single word changes (on some computers).

CRT electron gun: A hot cathode that produces a finely focused stream of fast electrons, which are necessary for a cathode-ray or television tube. The gun is made up of a hot cathode electron source, a control grid, accelerating anodes, and usually focusing electrodes. This device makes up an essential part of instruments such as cathode ray tubes, TV receivers, and video display units.

CRT field: Sometimes considered to be a "standard" 256 scan lines spaced evenly down the screen.

CRT graphic terminals: Graphic terminals are primarily of two types: CRT displays and electromechanical plotters. CRT terminals for graphic applications require the ability to draw lines and move spots on the face of the CRT, as well as printing alphanumeric characters. Since most graphic applications require a two-way interaction between the user and the computer, some form of graphic input, such

as a light pen, a RAND tablet, or a cursor, is required. Most graphic applications also require an alphanumeric keyboard for manual input.

CRT point mode: A mode of operation in which points may be established and plotted on the display.

CRT stand-alone terminals: A completely self-contained stand-alone CRT terminal is usually used in applications in which a single terminal (or a very limited number of terminals) is used at a site that is remotely located from the central computer. In this case the stand-alone terminal must contain all of the control logic and buffering functions necessary to its operation and must contain a communication modem to interface with the communications line to the central computer.

CRT storage: 1. The electrostatic storage characteristics of cathode-ray tubes in which the electron beam senses the data. 2. The storage of data on a dielectric surface, such as the screen of a cathode-ray tube, in the form of the presence or absence of spots bearing electrostatic charges; these spots can persist for a short time after the removal of the electrostatic charging force.

CRT terminal: A terminal device that uses a cathoderay tube as a screen on which information may be displayed. The unit may or may not include a keyboard. Also known as a keyboard display or video-data terminal.

CRT terminal controller: If several terminals are used at a site which is remotely located from the central computer, hardware and operating economies are achieved by using a multistation configuration in which several terminals are connected to and controlled by a local controller which in turn interfaces with the communications line to the central computer. These economies are achieved through sharing control, logic, buffering, and communications functions in the controller rather than providing these capabilities independently in each terminal.

CRT terminal types: CRT terminals are used for both alphanumeric and graphic applications; i.e., the display of text alone and the display of mixtures of text and diagrams. Much higher performance is required in most graphic terminals with consequent higher costs. They have in common the ability to display alphanumeric information in lines on the face of a CRT, to accept information from a remote source such as a computer, to enter information from a manual keyboard to edit and rearrange data, and to transmit data to remote destinations. A small buffer memory is usually provided to permit refreshing of the information on the face of the CRT at a sufficiently fast rate to avoid noticeable flicker.

crush strength: The physical limit of an optical fiber or cable to withstand an applied force or weight perpendicular to the axis of the fibers.

cryogenic element: Various high speed circuits which use the superconductivity characteristics of materials operating at or near absolute zero temperatures.

cryogenic memory: Superconductive memory that operates at very low (or at near absolute zero) temperatures.

cryogenics: The science of physical phenomena at very low temperatures, approaching absolute zero, $0°K$ or $-273°C$.

cryogenic storage: Depends for its operation on the properties of specific materials, which can become superconductive when their temperatures and the magnetic fields in which they are situated fall below certain very low temperatures. Since superconductors have zero resistance, they can maintain or store a current permanently.

cryostat: A device that uses evaporative and condensing cycles to achieve extremely low temperatures, and is often used to liquefy gases.

cryotron: A device utilizing properties or metals at near absolute zero temperatures

so that large current changes can be obtained by relatively small magnetic field changes.

cryptanalysis: The steps and operations performed in converting encrypted messages into plaintext without initial knowledge of the key employed in the encryption.

cryptographic, crypto: Pertaining to equipment which transforms data to conceal its actual meaning, usually by secret code conversion.

cryptography: The art of devising ciphers.

cryptology: Refers to disguised, or encrypted communications. It embraces communications intelligence.

crystal diode: Specific diodes which are manufactured with a junction of a base metal and some types of crystalline elements, for example, silicon or germanium. Such diodes contrast with vacuum diodes and are used in computing equipment to perform logic, buffering current conversions necessary for switching and storage transfers. Same as crystal rectifier.

crystal rectifier: See crystal diode.

csc: Abbreviation for cosecant.

csect: See control section.

CSW: Channel status word.

CTT: Central trunk terminals.

cue: Same as call.

current: The flow of electrons through a circuit.

current amplification: Ratio of output current to input current of valve amplifier, magnetic amplifier, transistor amplifier, or photomultiplier, often expressed in decibels.

current attenuation: Ratio of output to input currents of a transducer, expressed in decibels.

current balance: A form of balance in which the force required to prevent the movement of one currentcarrying coil in the magnetic field of a second coil carrying the same current is measured by means of balancing mass.

current beam position: On a CRT display device, the coordinates on the display surface at which the electron beam is presently aimed. Same as starting point.

current-carrying capacity: A measure of the maximum current which can be carried continuously without damage to components or devices in a circuit.

current density: Current flowing per unit crosssectional area of conductor or plasma; expressed in amperes (or milliamperes) per unit area.

current, disturbance: The unwanted current of any irregular phenomenon associated with transmission which tends to limit or interfere with the interchange of information.

current feed: Delivery of radio power to a current maximum (loop or antinode) in a resonating part of an antenna.

current gain: In a transistor, the ratio of ultimate change in collector current at a constant voltage, resulting from a change in emitter current.

current instruction register: The control section register which contains the instruction currently being executed after it is brought to the control section from memory. Same as instruction register.

current law, Kirchoff's: This law states that the sum of the currents leaving a junction must be exactly equal to the current entering the junction.

current line pointer: In systems with timesharing, a pointer that indicates the line of a line data set with which the user is currently working.

current mode logic (CML): Logic in which transistors operate in the unsaturated mode as distinguished from most other logic types which operate in the saturation region. This logic has very fast switching speeds and low logic swings. Same as emitter-coupled logic (ECL).

current record: The record pointed to by the current line pointer.

current transformer: One designed to be connected in series with the circuit, drawing predetermined current. Applied to an instrument when the line current is transformed down to changed range.

cursor: 1. A position indicator frequently employed in a display on a video terminal to indicate a character to be corrected or a position in which data is to be entered. 2. A solid underscore which may appear under any character location on the screen. In the basic system the cursor always appears under the location where the next character will appear.

curtain antenna: A large number of vertical radiators or reflectors in a plane, as in an original beam system.

curtate: A portion of a punched card consisting of adjacent punched rows.

curve conformity: Relating to curves, the closeness to which it approximates a specified functional curve (i.e. logarithmic, parabolic, cubit, etc.) and usually expressed in terms of nonconformity; i.e., the maximum deviation between an average curve and a specified functional curve. The average curve is determined after making two or more full range traverses in opposite directions. The value of nonconformity is referred to the output unless otherwise stated.

curve fitting: The process of obtaining a specific representation of a curve by a mathematical expression or equation.

curve fitting, compaction: A specific method of data compaction developed by substituting analytical expressions for data to be stored or transmitted. An example is the breaking of curves into straight line segments, and then transmitting only the slope, intercept and acceptable range for each line segment.

customer device circuits: Many circuits connect customer devices—time-sharing terminal, remote job entry station, mini-computer-based system, etc.—with the network interface, possibly a multiplexer or concentrator. These circuits, part of the low-speed channel side of the multiplexer or connector, can operate at a maximum speed equal to that of the circuit connecting nodes, but is usually sharing that high-speed circuit with a number of low-speed circuits and thus operates at a considerably lower rate.

customer engineer (CE): The technical specialist that installs, maintains and fixes equipment at customer sites for its supplier.

customer engineering monitor (CEMON): A monitor developed by IBM for customer engineering.

customer station equipment: Refers to various units of communications common carrier transmitting and receiving equipment used in connection with private line services and located on the customer's premises.

customer testing time: Computer time utilized in certifying the validity of a computer program prior to doing actual production work with it.

cut form: In optical character recognition (OCR), a document, receipt, etc, of standard dimensions which must be issued a separate read command in order to be recognized.

cutter location data (CLDATA): The input to the postprocessor that consists of such items as x, y coordinates, postprocessor commands, etc. The actual data is contained in the CLFILE or CLTAPE.

cutter location file (CLFILE): The storage medium name of the cutter location data (CLDATA). It is common to random access storage systems.

C voltage: A former term for bias voltage.

cybernetics: Concerns relationships between animal and machine behavior and the study of control system theory. This is a diverse field encompassing (a) integration of communication, control, and systems theories; (b) development of systems engineering technology; and (c) practical applications at both the hardware and software levels. Recent and projected developments in cybernetics are taking place in at least five important areas: technological forecasting and assessment, complex systems modeling, policy analysis, pattern recognition, and artificial intelligence. Applications have moved far beyond the feedback control systems described in Norbert Wiener's "Cybernetics", first published 25 years ago.

cycle: 1. A complete sequence of a wave pattern that recurs at regular intervals. The number of cycles occurring in 1 second is the frequency of the wave, now expressed in hertz. 2. An interval of space or time in which one set of events or phenomena is completed. In alternating current, the time for a change of state from a value through a positive and negative maximum and back to the same value. 3. A non-arithmetic shift in which the digits dropped off at one end of a word are returned at the other end in circular fashion, cycle right and cycle left. 4. To repeat a set of operations a prescribed number of times including, when required, supplying necessary address changes by arithmetic processes or by means of a hardware device such as a b-box or cycle-counter. 5. See also major cycle.

cycle, action: Refers to the complete

operation performed on data. Includes the basic steps of: origination, input, manipulation, output, and storage.

cycle billing: Use of a time basis for repeated billing (e.g. four weeks).

cycle count: To increase or decrease the cycle index by unity or by an arbitrary integer.

cycle criterion: 1. The total number of times the cycle is to be repeated. 2. The register in which that number is stored.

cycled interrupt: The change (by sequence or specific operation cycle) of control to the next or a specific function in a predetermined manner or order.

cycle index: The number of times a cycle has been executed, or the difference, or negative of the difference, between the number that have been executed and the number of repetitions desired.

cycle index counter: Utilized to count the number of times a given cycle of a program instructions has been done. It can be examined at any selected time to determine the number of repetitions still required in a loop.

cycle reset: The return to an initial value in a cycle index.

cycle shift: Removal of the digits of a number (or characters of a word) from one end of a number or word and their insertion, in the same sequence, at the other end.

cycles per second: Same as hertz.

cycle time: A specific interval of time that recurs regularly and in the same sequence. For example, the interval required for completion of one operation in a repetitive sequence of operations or the time interval required to execute a specific group of operations which can be repeated in their entirety.

cyclically-magnetized condition: The condition of a magnetic core after it has been influenced by a magnetizing force varying between two limits.

cyclic availability: That specific time period during which stored information can be read.

cyclic binary code: 1. Positional binary notation for numbers in which any two sequential numbers, whose difference is 1, are represented by expressions that are the same except in one place or column, and in that place or column differ only by one unit. 2. A type of cycle unit-distance binary code.

cyclic check: A method of error detection which checks every nth bit, n + 1 bit, n + 2 bit, etc. It is more powerful and efficient than horizontal checks, vertical checks, or combinations of both.

cyclic decimal code: A four-bit binary code word in which only one digit changes state between any two sequential code words, and which translates to decimal numbers. Categorized as one of a group of unit-distance codes.

cyclic feeding: A system employed by character readers in character recognition which senses the trailing edge of the preceding document and automatically triggers the feeding of the following document. This system allows character recognition of varying sized documents.

Cyclic Permuted (CP) Code: A specific code in which characters are represented by words of a fixed number of bits but which are arranged in a sequence so that the signal distance between consecutive words is 1 or unity.

cyclic redundancy check character: An operations character designed as a redundant character introduced for error detection purposes, in various modified cyclic codes.

cyclic redundancy check (CRC): A method of error detection using specific characters. A CRC character is generated at the transmitting terminal based on the contents of the message transmitted. A similar CRC generation is performed at the receiving terminal. If the two characters match, the message was probably received correctly.

cyclic shift: 1. A shift in which the data moved out of one end of the storing register are re-entered into the other end, as in a closed loop. 2. A shift in which the digits dropped off at one end of a word are returned at the other in a circular fashion.

cyclic storage: Same as circulating storage.

cyclic storage access: A storage unit designed so that access to any location is only possible at specific, equally-spaced times; e.g., magnetic drums, delay lines, etc.

cyclic transfer: This optional channel provides continuous cyclic word communication with from one to four equal-length blocks of memory. The blocks are continuous and contain from 1 to 4096 words. Both input and output modes are accomodated. The cyclic feature of this channel is beneficial in such applications as telemetry or other high-speed repetitive operations because once initiated, this channel continues to function without the need of a program instruction to start each cycle (on some computers).

cycling: Periodic change imposed on a controlled variable or a function by a controller. See also hunting.

cylinder: The tracks of a disk storage device that can be accessed without repositioning the access mechanism.

D

D format: A data set format in which ASCII records are variable in length.

DA: See differential analyzer; data acquisition.

DAC-1 monitor: A system which provides: a) a table which contains the location and size of each subroutine in memory; b) a table which contains the location and size of all global variables in memory; c) the basic codes required to retrieve programs and data stored in the auxiliary disk and drum; and d) a relocation program which, when given data in the form of a subroutine in memory, will relocate the subroutine and assign memory addresses to its above-mentioned variable tables.

daisy chaining: A time-shared bus system consisting of a single bus request line onto which all processors are tapped in parallel. A bus grant line runs serially through all the processors. When the arbiter sees a bus request come in, it sends its reply on the bus grant line. Non-requesting processors ignore the bus and let the grant signal pass while the requesting processor assumes that the grant is for it and retains the signal.

daisy-wheel printer: A wheel used in fast printers.

damped natural frequency: The frequency of an oscillator following a transient input, usually a step function or pulse.

damper: A diode in the flyback power supply which prevents ringing.

damping: A characteristic built into electrical circuits and mechanical systems to prevent rapid or excessive corrections which may lead to instability or oscillatory conditions. For example, a register is connected to the terminals of a pulse trans-

former to remove natural oscillations; a moving element is placed in oil or sluggish grease to prevent mechanical overshoot of the moving parts.

damping, signal: The final manner in which the output settles to its steady-state value after a change in the value of the measured signal; i.e., when the time response to an abrupt stimulus is as fast as possible without overshoot, the response is said to be "critically damped." It is "underdamped" when overshoot occurs and "overdamped" when response is slower than critical.

damping factor: A measure of damping for the free oscillation of a second-order linear system. It is expressed (without sign) as the quotient of the greater by the lesser of a pair of consecutive swings of the output (in opposite directions) about an ultimate steadystate value.

DARAF: The unit of elastance equal to the reciprocal of capacitance.

DARPA: Defence Advanced Research Projects Agency of the Department of Defense, sponsor of the ARPA network. See Advanced Research Project Agency Network.

DASD: See direct access storage.

DASPAN: RCA's Data Communications network facilities.

DAT: See dynamic address translation.

data: 1. A general term loosely used to denote any or all facts, numbers, letters, symbols, etc. which can be processed or produced by a computer. 2. In a more restricted sense, data refers to numerical information as contrasted with non-numerical information. 3. Implying source data or raw data as contrasted with information which is then defined to mean the knowledge obtained by the processing of data.

data access protocol (DAP): In Digital Equipment Corporation Network (DEC-NET), used to achieve remote access. It allows the user to request specific records in a file rather than the entire file.

data acquisition and control system (DAC): A system designed to handle a wide variety of real-time applications, process control and high-speed data acquisition. Each system is individually tailored with modular building blocks that are easily integrated to meet specific system requirements. A large family of realtime process input/output (I/O) devices is included, such as analog input, analog output, contact sense, and contact operate, as well as data processing I/O units, such as magnetic tape, disk storage, line printer, graph plotter, card and paper tape input and output. Data are received and transmitted on either a highspeed cycle-steal basis or under program control, depending on the intrinsic data rate of the I/O device.

data-adapter unit (communications): A unit that greatly expands the input/output capabilities of the system. It provides direct connection of a variety of remote and local external devices to a system. These devices include (a) the data-collection system, (b) the datacommunication system, (c) the process-communication system, (d) telegraph terminals, (e) telemetry terminals, and (f) control and data acquisition equipment.

data analysis display unit: The facility offered by cathode-ray tube (CRT) visual display unit for on-line analysis of data.

data bank: 1. A collection of libraries of data. 2. A comprehensive collection of libraries of data. For example, one line of an invoice may form an item. A complete invoice may form a record. A complete set of such records may form a file. The collection of inventory files may form a library,

and the libraries used by an organization are known as a data bank. 3. Computer files created to store and furnish on-line or off-line information for man on man or for some aspect of accumulated knowledge. The information may be retrieved selectively or in mass.

database inquiries and library browsing (time-sharing): Retrieval from data or document libraries generally using remote terminals.

database management: A systematic approach to storing, updating, and retrieval of information stored as data items, usually in the form of records in a file, where many users, or even many remote installations, will use common data banks.

database server: In distributed computation, this accepts queries about the database, analyzes them itself, and returns the answers. Same as backend machine.

data bits: Represent the actual binary data being transferred. In many applications the characters are often 8-bits long with the least significant bit being sent out or received first.

data break: An automatic input/output channel which provides external communications or peripheral equipment with direct access to core memory.

data bus: See bus.

data capture: Bringing in data from one or more points to a central point. May be in-plant or off-site. See point-of-sale.

data capture speech synthesis: A method of using speech as a direct form of input.

data carrier: The selected medium used to transport or carry (communicate) data or information. Punched cards, magnetic tapes, and punched paper tapes are examples.

data carrier storage: This type of storage usually requires some action by an operator such as selection and loading before automatic control becomes operable.

data cell: A direct access storage module containing strips of tape on which data is stored.

data chaining: The gathering (or scattering) of information within one physical record, from (or to) more than one region of memory, by means of successive I/O commands.

data channel: The bidirectional data path between the input/output (I/O) devices and the main memory in a digital computer that permits one or more I/O operations to happen concurrently with computation.

data channel multiplexer: Expands the data-break facilities of the computer to allow large numbers of input/output devices to transfer data directly with the main memory, via the memory buffer register. Simultaneous data-break requests are serviced by the multiplexer according to prewired priority.

data channels cycle stealing: A technique used to "steal" a memory cycle; a data channel steals the cycle for an input unit to use. Data channels give the processor-controller (P-C) the ability to delay the execution of a program for communication of an input/output (I/O) device with core storage. For example, if an input unit requires a memory cycle to store data that it has collected, the data channel with its cycle stealing capability makes it possible to delay the program during execution of an instruction and store the data word without changing the logical condition of the P-C. After the data is stored the program continues as though nothing had occurred. This capability should not be confused with interrupt which changes the contents of the instruction register. Cycle stealing by the data channels can occur at the end of any memory cycle. The maximum delay before cycle stealing can occur is one memory cycle time.

data circuit: The electrical means for two-way transmission of binary signals.

data circuit terminating equipment (DCE) waiting: A call control signal at the DCE/data terminal equipment interface which indicates the DCE is waiting for another event in the call establishment procedure.

data code: 1. Sets of symbols which are used to represent various data items for data elements on a one for one basis. A single number or symbol might represent a particular week or month. 2. Specific sets of characters designed and structured to represent the data items of a data element. A typical example might be to use the digits 01-07 to represent the order of the days of the week.

data-code conversion: The translation of alphanumeric data into a form acceptable to the computer. Usually, this is done by the computer itself during the input of the data.

data-coding system: A system of coordinate indexing.

data collision: 1. In a data transmission system, the situation that occurs when two or more demands are made simultaneously on equipment that can handle only one at any given instant. 2. In a computer, the situation that occurs when the same address is obtained for two different data items that are to be stored at that address.

data-collection stations: Devices on production floors used to collect employee payroll data and other information, for entry into computer systems.

data communication multiplexer (DCM):   Hardware, usually supported by software for synchronous or asynchronous or direct-connection terminal control.

data communications (DATACOM):   A global communications network used by the U.S. Air Force.

data communications control unit (DCCU):   The unit that scans the central terminal unit buffers for messages and transfers them to the central processor.

data communications exchange: A particular hardware unit which connects a control unit of a central processor to a communications network. It is used in realtime applications where data is to be sent and received simultaneously over several communications channels, perhaps operating in many different modes.

data communications system (banks):   A system that links teller window locations in savings banks, savings and loan associations, and commercial banks with either the main office of the institution or a branch office, where a computer is located. The system consists of the teller terminal which is linked to the processor over communications lines through the control unit. Transaction data can be transmitted from a keyboard.

data compaction: See data compression.

data compression: A technique that saves storage space by eliminating gaps, empty fields, redundancies, or unnecessary data to shorten the length of records or blocks.

data concentrator network: A typical cost data concentrator multiplexes four or eight asynchronous terminals over a single communications link. This type of concentrator is well suited for minicomputer users, with composite data rates to 19.2k bps. Fifteen channel data rates, downline loading, diagnostics and performance monitoring, and local echoplex are typical performance features. The series of network concentrators support both asynchronous and bisynchronous channels, at any mix.

data connection: The interconnection of a number of data circuits on a tandem basis by means of switching equipment to enable data transmission to take place between data terminal equipment. Where one or more of the data circuits which are interconnected is a virtual data circuit, the overall connection is known as a virtual data connection. The overall connection includes the data circuit terminating equipment at the respective data terminal installation locations.

data control block (DCB):   A control block combined with access routines for the purpose of receiving information required to store and receive data.

data definition name (DDNAME):   A name appearing in the data control block of a program which corresponds to the name field of a data definition statement.

data definition (DD) statement: A job control statement that describes a data set associated with a particular job step.

data delimiter: Usually a flag character that marks the ends or bounds of a series or string or bits or characters; it is thus not a part or member of such a string unless it is the first or last member. Most frequently, certain special patterns of data are proposed and used by each computer center as a convention or rule of that center and are used as markers, endof-message signals, etc.

data description: The input of entries in the data division used to describe the characteristics of a data item.

data descriptor: Describes data (i.e., a data area). By pointing sequentially, a particular data descriptor may be concerned with many memory locations. More than this, however, a data descriptor is also concerned with the presence, in core, of the data it describes. This is due to the data overlay capabilities of the computer. A descriptor is concerned with many aspects of storage. These aspects are indicated by various bits in the descriptor.

data destination address: Information sent in the forward direction consisting of a number of address signals indicating the complete address of the called customer.

data display unit: A visual display unit where data stored in memory can be selected and displayed as characters or graphs upon a screen. It may sometimes incorporate a light pen to enable graphs to be modified by a user under program control.

data element: A specific item of information appearing in a set of data.

data element dictionary (DED):   An organized listing of a file containing specifications, descriptions, and sometimes source and usage information for data elements belonging to a given system. Specifications commonly include: data type (numeric/-character, coded/uncoded, check digit, etc.), valid range, valid codes, interfield validity conditions and data level in a hierarchy. Descriptions include labels for the variable name and for the coded values. Source/usage information includes locations, forms, devices, people involved in data collection and reporting. A DED may exist as a table in a disk file for use in editing input data, search and sort procedures, and table-driven automatically formatted output listings.

Data Encryption Standard (DES):   The encryption algorithm of a product cipher developed by IBM. The cipher was adopted by the U.S. government in 1977 as an official standard for unclassified information. The algorithm has since been implemented by many manufacturers and other users of hardware.

data escape character: A transmission control character that changes the meaning of a limited number of contiguously following characters or coded representations, and is used exclusively to provide supplementary transmission control characters.

data exchange system: A system in which data is accepted from input channels, processed, and retransmitted as output channels become available.

data extent block (DEB):   An extension of the data control block that contains information about the physical status of the data set being processed.

data file: Aggregations of data sets for definite usage. The file may contain one or more different data sets. A permanent data file is one in which the data is subject to being updated perpetually; e.g., a name and address file. A working data file is a temporary accumulation of data sets which is destroyed after the data has been transferred to another form.

data flowchart: A flowchart representing the path of data through a problem solution. It defines the major phases of the processing as well as the various data media used. Same as data flow diagram.

data flow diagram: See data flowchart.

data flow model: A distributed computation model where the problem is described by a graph, with each graph node corresponding to a processor. Results are moved among the processors as messages. The collection of processors cooperate on running a single program.

data format: Describes the way data is held in a file or record, whether in character form, a binary number, etc.

data-formatting statements: These statements instruct the assembly program to set up constants and reserved memory areas and to punctuate memory to indicate field boundaries.

dataframe: A unit of information normally represented as a page of data, including the margin.

data generation (planning):   Its purpose is to show integration of specific procedures for developing optimal solutions of problems or ranges of feasibilities using general and broad range scientific method framework. The principle steps are define, design, and delimit the problem (or model) with a clear, succinct statement of hypothesis, scope, and objective. Affirm positively the aspiration level desired (algoristic, stochastic, or heuristic) and confidence base required. Determine exploration methodology; environment and special circumstances; types of variables and degree of uncertainty; values of constants and parameters; reliability and validity criteria, sources, measurements and control of errors.

datagram: A model in which the network layer accepts messages from the transport layer and attempts to deliver each as an isolated unit.

datagram identification: In X.25, the first two bytes of the user data field.

datagram or internet layer: A layer associated with transmission control protocol (TCP) which routes datagrams around the network(s), fragments datagrams and then reassembles them transparently for delivery to the destination transport station.

datagram service signal: In X.25, a notification packet which tells whether the datagram was delivered or not, and if not delivered, why not (congestion, incorrect addressing, etc.).

data handling system: A system in which data is sorted, decoded or stored in a particular form; related to data reduction.

data hierarchy: A data structure consisting of sets and subsets such that every subset of a set is of lower rank than the data of the set.

data-initiated control: Jobs can be initiated and run automatically, according to present rules, upon receipt of a signal or message from an external source. For example, in a teleprocessing application, jobs are performed upon receipt of messages from remote terminals. Data from a remote terminal can initiate loading of a program from the library; the program then processes the data and makes appropriate responses to the originating terminal. Messages can be logged and queued on a secondary device, routed, and transmitted to other terminals. Inquiry by name, account number, or other key data can initiate a search of files stored in the system, find the requested information, and respond to the requester.

data interchange code: A variant of ASCII code, including various nonprinting control characters.

data layout: 1. A predetermined arrangement of characters, fields, lines, punctuation, page numbers, etc. 2. A defined arrangement of words, totals, characters, stubs, heading, etc. for a desired clear presentation of data or print output, such as a financial record.

data line: A line of 32 alphanumeric characters or spaces displayed on a cathode-ray tube (CRT) screen.

data line occupied: A designation applied to a sense circuit in an automatic calling unit. When on, the circuit indicates to the computer that the telephone circuit is in use and unavailable.

data line terminal: Transmits and receives data on a block-by-block basis, using synchronous tramsmission. A data block consists of data characters preceded by a start-of-block (SOB) character and followed by end-ofblock (EOB) and block parity (B/P) character. Transmission characters are 8 bits in length; 6 data bits, one control bit, and an odd-parity bit. Each block transmission is completely protected by both character and block parity. The block parity character uses an even-parity check for each longitudinal bit level in the data block (in some systems).

data link: 1. Terminal installations and the interconnecting network operating in a particular mode that permits information to be exchanged between terminal installations. 2. A bidirectional transmission path for data comprising two data channels in opposite directions which operate together at the same data rate.

data link encryption: Refers to when a hardware encryption device is spliced into the host interface message processor (IMP) line just after it exits the host, and a decryption device is spliced into the line just before it enters the IMP. In this way the entire encryption/decryption process can be retrofitted without affecting existing software.

date link escape (DLE): Used in the text of a message to change the meaning of a limited number of following characters. Typical applications of this character are supplement control information, and transparent text mode of operation.

data link escape character: A data communications term representing a control character which when combined with one or more succeeding characters forms an escape sequence and the development of additional data communications control operations.

data logging: Refers to the recording (logging) of data events relative to time.

data loop transceiver (DTR): Station arrangement (data set) for Western Union's Class D leased data channels.

data management: Functions of the control program that provide access to data sets, enforce data storage conventions, and regulate the use of input/output devices.

data manipulation: The performance of data-processing chores common to most users, such as sorting, input/output operations, and report generation.

data medium: A specific material, in, on, or by which data can be stored, represented, or communicated by static use or by variation of one or more of its physical characteristics or parameters.

data migration: The moving of data from an on-line device to an off-line or low-priority device, as determined by the system or as requested by the user.

data mode: A move mode in which the data portions of all segments of a spanned record are accessed.

data modem: A modulation/demodulation device that enables computers and terminals to communicate over telephone circuits.

data modem clocking: The derivation of synchronous clocking signals from the modem, rather than from the terminal or computer.

data monitor: A typical data monitor is made easy to operate by automatically determining the speed, protocol, bits-per-character value and parity of lineunder-test. Powerful start/stop trapping capability can be user programmed to allow for selective monitoring and troubleshooting. Often printer/poll options give the unit powerful emulation capability for: 1. Asynchronous, synchronous byte-controlled, and synchronous bit-oriented monitoring and emulation; 2. Simultaneous accomodation of X.25 (levels II and III) analysis display.

data-name: A name assigned by the programmer to a data item for use in a COBOL program.

DATANET: A General Electric model that can be used for production control. A message exchange which receives and transmits automatically. Other uses include a data-collection system for the purpose of transmitting data from a remote station to a central unit and permitting an operator to dial and send perforated-tape data over a phone line.

data network: A network linking terminals through which data is telecommunicated.

data network service companies: Communicate data and provide data processing, with remote data communication as an incidental service. As long as processing is involved, the data network services are not subject to regulation by governmental agencies. A data network that does no processing but provides data communication is operated by Western Union. Their own TWX/TELEX network was formed by the merger of their own TELEX network with the TWX network purchased from the Bell System in April 1971.

data origination: 1. The translation of information from its original form into a machine-sensible form. 2. The act of creating a record in a machine-sensible form, directly or as a by-product of a human-readable document.

Data-Phone: A trademark of the A.T. & T. Company to identify the data sets manufactured and supplied by the Bell System for transmitting data over the telephone network. It is also a Bell System service mark to identify the transmission of data over the telephone network. (Data-Phone Service).

data processing: A generic term for all the operations carried out on data according to precise rules of procedures; a generic term for computing in general as applied to business situations.

data processing conversational mode: A mode of operation of a data processing system in which a sequence of alternating entries and responses between a user and the system takes place in a manner similar to a dialogue between two persons.

data processing management: Includes many of the same management functions of any operating organization (a) supervision and administration, (b) reporting, (c) long-range planning, (d) project control maintenance of standards, (e) liaison, etc. In data processing, however, these functions have some unusual aspects. Supervision of a data processing function is not an easy task without a thorough knowledge of the technical details and skills. A combination of rigid, detailed operations and creative development must often be supervised simultaneously.

Data Processing Management Association (DPMA) certificate: A certificate that indicates a person has a certain level of competence in the field of data processing. The certificate is obtained by passing an examination offered yearly throughout the United States and Canada.

data processing standards: Cover activities such as systems analysis, programming, operating, and clerical procedures that relate to basic functions. (a) Communications, which specifically are between systems analyst, programmer and operating staff, and refer to a standard form or presentation, terminology, and documentation. (b) Control, which generally refers to a prescribed quality, timetables, responsible definitions. (c) Continuity, refers to standard methods and documentation followed and dependent upon by all individuals of the computer, management, and scientific teams.

data processing system: A network of machine components capable of accepting information, processing it according to a plan, and producing the desired results.

data processor: A system designed to operate with large quantities of actual information upon which extensive calculation is usually not required but which must be sorted or otherwise manipulated.

data protection: Safeguards against loss or destruction of data.

data purification: The reduction of data errors prior to using the data in an automatic data processing system.

data record: A collection of facts, numbers, letters, symbols, etc., that a program can process or produce.

data record format: The predetermined arrangement of the contents of a data record.

data reduction: 1. The art or process of transforming masses of raw test or experimentally obtained data, usually gathered by instrumentation, into useful, ordered, or simplified intelligence. 2. The process of transforming raw data into useful form by smoothing, adjusting, scaling and ordering experimental readings.

data reliability: A ratio that relates the extent to which data meets a specific or given standard, usually concerning the accuracy of data, or the degree to which data is error free. Other examples relate to the probabilities of the correctness of data, i.e., the degree to which data is unchanged after transmission or recording operations.

data representation: The utilization of numerals, letters, and special symbols to represent values and descriptive data. In a digital computer all program instructions and data are recorded as electrical impulses in coded form.

Dataroute: Canada's nationwide commercial network designed for digital data transmission.

data rules: The unique group of conditions surrounding data elements, sets, and files, and the action to be taken when the conditions are satisfied. The rules are expressed in tabular form, rather than narrative, to insure complete, consistent, and accurate documentation of the processing methodology, and at the same time to provide flexibility for change.

data scaling: See scaling.

data security: The protection of data against unauthorized disclosure, transfer, modifications, or destruction, whether accidental or intentional.

data selecting: The process of extracting various pertinent or specific information from a large body of data, or the removal of certain records from the file.

data set: 1. An electronic device that provides an interface for the transmission of data to remote stations. 2. The terms modem and data set are often used interchangeably. 3. A collection of similar and related data records that is recorded for use by a computer. A recordable medium such as a data file.

data set clocking: A time base oscillator supplied by the data set for regulating the bit rate of transmission.

data set control block (DSCB): A standard-format control block specifying the parameter, for one data set, needed to describe and manipulate the data set in a direct-access device.

data set extension (DSE): Under time-sharing option (TSO), a control block containing control information for each of a terminal user's data sets.

data set label (DSL): A generic term covering data set control block's (DSCB's) for direct-access devices and the data set labels used on sequential access devices.

data set name: The term or phrase used to identify a data set. See also qualified name.

data set organization: The arrangement of information in a data set. For example, sequential organization or partitioned organization.

data-set-ready circuit: A circuit that indicates that the local modem is connected to the channel and is ready to receive data or to accept a request to transmit. This circuit is off at all other times and is an indication that the data terminal equipment is to disregard signals on any other interface lead.

data-set-ready lead: One of the basic data set interchange leads defined in Electronic Industries Association Standard RS-232-B.

data set system: A data set that has a particular system use and/or content and a predefined relationship to a system unit.

data set utility programs: Programs that can be used to update, maintain, edit, and transcribe data sets.

data signaling rate transparency: A network parameter which enables the transfer of data between users without placing any restrictions, within certain limits, on the data signaling rate used.

data sink: In communications, a device capable of accepting data signals from a transmission device. It may also check these signals and originate error control signals. Contrast with data source.

data skew: Distortion of a signal due to lack of synchronization between the source of the signal and the receiver.

data source: In communications, a device capable of originating data signals for a transmission device. It may also accept error control signals. Contrast with data sink.

data statements: Written as part of a source program to show and specify the format of data items used in the program.

data station: A multipurpose remote-terminal device which can be used for a broad range of communications applications, as well as for off-line jobs. This device gives branch offices, warehouses and remote reporting locations throughout a plant, or any other company outposts, the power to prepare source data locally and communicate directly with a centrally located computer. The data station features a wide choice of input/output devices, including paper tape and punched-card equipment, a keyboard, page printers, and often an optical bar-code reader that introduces many applications possibilities.

data storage: The utilization of any medium for storing data and suggesting a capability to store large volumes immediately on-line to a central processor, as in a magnetic drum or magnetic disk store.

data stream: A sequence of binary digits used to represent information for transmission.

data switching exchange (DSE): Equipment installed at a single location to switch data traffic. A data switching exchange may provide only circuit switching, only packet switching, or both.

data-system transmission: A series of circuits, modems, or other devices which transfer or translate information from one site or location to another.

data telephone circuit: A specific telephone circuit permitting the transmission of digital data, for example, through use of the Data-phone developed by the American Telephone and Telegraph Company.

data terminal: 1. A device which modulates and/or demodulates the data between one input/output device and a data-transmission link. 2. Various typewriter, audio or visual devices for inputting or receiving output of computers.

data terminal equipment (DTE) clear request: A call control signal sent by the DTE to initiate clearing.

data terminal equipment (DTE) data transfer requested: A call control signal transmitted by the data circuit terminating equipment to the DTE in leased circuit service to indicate that the distant DTE is wishing to exchange data.

data terminal equipment (DTE) waiting: Call control signal condition at the data circuit terminating equipment (DCE)/DTE interface which indicates that the DTE is waiting for a call control signal from the DCE.

data terminal ready: An Electronic Industries Association (EIA) RS-232 designation applied to a control circuit used by a terminal or computer to tell its modem that the terminal or computer is ready for operation. In some applications this circuit is used to enable the modem to answer terminal calls.

data test set: Automatically performs all primary measurements necessary to qualify voice-bandwidth circuits for data transmission. Microprocessor-based, the device offers automatic, unattended operation. It may be controlled from a computer/terminal via an RS-232-C interface or from the front panel. Easy-to-use interface commands facilitate remote operation.

data-text: A language designed for use by social scientists to perform numerical computations and analysis.

data transfer rate: A particular rate at which data is transmitted through a channel, but measured during the time data is actually being transmitted; i.e., tape transfer rates are measured in terms of characters per second, discounting gaps between blocks, words, etc.

data transfer register: The temporary store or device which eases the communication or movement of data within the computer.

data transfer time: The time that elapses between the initial offering of a unit of user data to a network by transmitting data terminal equipment and the complete delivery of that unit to receiving data terminal equipment.

data transmission: The sending of data from one place to another by means of signals over a channel.

data transmission efficiency: The number of data bits correctly received divided by the total number transmitted; the throughput rate.

data transmission ratio: The data transmission ratio of useful or acceptable data output to the total input of data.

data transmission trap: A conditional (unprogrammed) jump to a specific location activated automatically to provide communication or signals between specific input/-output routines and the related programs.

data transmission utilization measure: The ratio of useful data to total data.

data under voice: Bell System service providing wideband digital signals [up to 56 kilobytes per second (kb/s)] to be carried on existing microwave radio systems, in addition to the usual multiplexed voice signals.

data unit: A set of one or more related characters which is treated as a whole. Often used in place of field to specify a particular unit of information.

data validity: A relation or measure of

verifiability of data, i.e., the results of specific tests performed on the data such as the forbidden code check. Such tests and checks verify the reliability of the data and thus its validity or degree of acceptability.

data word length: The selection of one of the word lengths of the equipment as a datum, which can be used to classify different operations as fractions or multiples of this length for working.

data wrap: The transmission of data through a communications system and the return of the data to its source to test the accuracy of the system.

dating routine: A routine in which a computer stores, where needed, a datum such as current day's date, expiration date of a tape, etc.

dating subroutine: A computer program subroutine that processes dates and times related to processing.

datum: A word defining the physical core base location of a program and to which the relative program addresses are added to give the absolute addresses upon which the central processor works.

dB: See decibel.

dBr: The power difference expressed in dB between any point and a reference point selected as the zero relative transmission level point. Any power expressed in dBr does not specify the absolute power. It is a relative measurement only.

dBRN: A unit of measurement of the absolute power of electrical circuit noise.

dBw: Decibels referred to one watt, a unit of power measurement in communication.

dc: Abbreviation for direct current.

dc amplifier: Amplifier capable of amplifying dc and slowly varying alternating signals.

DCB: See data control block.

dc component: The average value of a varying signal such as the luminance of a television picture.

dc couple: A modem or device which transmits a steady state of pulses rather than oscillating or alternating.

dc coupled flip-flop: A flip-flop made up of electronic circuits in which the active elements, whether tubes or transistors, are coupled with resistors.

DCCU: See data communications control unit.

dc-dc converter: Device which converts dc at one voltage to dc at another voltage. These are common in modern telephone switching systems where low voltages (typically 5v) are needed to power transistorized circuitry.

dc dump: The condition resulting when DC power is withdrawn from a computer which uses volatile storage, i.e., loss of stored information.

DCE clear indication: For data: a call control signal transmitted by the data circuit terminating equipment (DCE) to indicate that it is clearing the call.

dc erasure: See erasure.

dc flip-flop: A device which passes the steady state characteristics of a signal and which largely eliminates the transient or oscillating characteristics of the signal.

d-character: A specific character which is used to modify the operations code in some equipment.

D class channel: Used to transmit punched paper tape at approximately 240 words per minute depending upon the code element (5-, 6-, 7-, or 8-level code) employed. It is also used to transmit 80-column punched cards at the rate of 10 to 11 per minute.

dc noise: See noise.

DDNAME: See data definition name.

dead band range: The range through which an input can be varied without initiating response; i.e., a dead band is expressed in percent of span. Resolution sensitivity has been defined as one-half dead band. When the output is at the center of the dead band, they denote the minimum change in measured quantity required to initiate response.

dead front: The joining of a connector that is designed in such a way that the contacts are recessed below the surface of the connector's body in order to prevent accidental short-circuits, and to prevent the contacts from contacting other objects.

dead letter queue: Under telecommunications access method (TCAM), a queue containing messages that could not be placed in the appropriate destination queue for a terminal or application program.

dead line: A telephone line disconnected from a central office.

deadlock: A condition in which two or more processes are waiting indefinitely for events that will quite probably never occur.

dead spot: A region where the reception of radio transmissions over a particular frequency range is extremely weak or practically zero.

dead time: 1. Any definite delay deliberately placed between two related actions in order to avoid overlap that might cause confusion or to permit a particular different event, such as a control decision, switching event, or similar action, to take place. 2. The delay between two related actions, measured in units of time for efficiency study.

dead time measure: The specific interval of time between the initiation of an input change or stimulus and the start of the resulting response.

dead zone unit: A specific unit which offers a constant output over a specified range of the input variable.

DEB: See data extent block.

deblock: To remove records from a block.

debouncing: A delay programmed into software that prevents false input from a keyboard due to the bouncing of the keys. The springs under old or heavily used keyboards can get so tired that they bounce after depression, which sends bogus signals to the computer. Debouncing techniques involve initiating a pause that delays the ability to accept input for a short time (typically a few milliseconds) after already accepting one.

debug: See debugging.

debugged program: A program that will perform actions in the logical sequence expected and produce accurate answers to one or more text problems which have been designed specifically to execute all foreseeable paths through the program.

debugging: The process of determining the correctness of a computer routine, locating any errors in it, and correcting them. Also the detection and correction of malfunctions in the computer itself to assist the programmer in debugging his programs. Among the routines included are the following: (a) changed-word post mortem, a routine to compare the contents of program or data areas with a selected image area; (b) address reference search, a routine to detect all words in the computer memory which reference a particular address; (c) dump selected memory area, a routine to provide the contents of all locations within a specified memory area.

debugging package (DDT): Permits the user to examine, search, change, insert breakpoint instructions, and stop/trace his program at the symbolic level. DDT permits the use of literals in the same manner as the assembler. It can load both absolute and relocatable assembler-produced files. Its command language is geared to rapid interactive operations by the on-line user (in some systems).

debugging statements: Part of operating statements. They provide a variety of methods for manipulating the program in an attempt to identify program errors (bugs"). The user may: (a) Insert or delete statements; (b) Execute selectivity; (c) Print changes of values as the change occurs and transfer control as transfer occurs; (d) Obtain a static printout of all cross-reference relationships among names and labels, and dynamic exposure of partial or imperfect execution.

debug macroinstruction: A macroinstruction that generates a debugging or program testing capability within a particular program.

debug macros: See debug macroinstruction.

decade: A group or assembly of ten units, e.g., a counter which counts to ten in one column or a resistor box which inserts resistance quantities in multiples of powers of 10.

decay: Reduction in amplitude of a signal on an exponential basis.

decay constant: Under time-sharing option (TSO), a weighting factor used in calculating the duration of a job's next time slice based on its use of previous time slices. Recent time slices are more heavily weighted than earlier time slices.

decay time: The time in which a voltage or current pulse will decrease to one-tenth of its maximum value. Decay time is proportional to the time constant of the circuit.

decelerating ring: A metallic ring on the inner wall of an image orthicon tube used to slow down electrons in the scanning beam before they reach the target.

deceleration time: The time which elapses between completion or reading or writing of a tape record and the time when the tape stops moving.

decentralized data processing: The housing of data by individual subdivisions of an organization or at each geographical location of the parts of an organization.

decentralized files: Records located and maintained in or near the office immediately responsible for the function in connection with which they are accumulated.

decibel (dB): A unit for measuring relative strength of a signal parameter, such as power and voltage (technically, one tenth of 1 Bel). The number of decibels is 10 times the logarithm (base 10) of the ratio of the measured quantity to the reference level. The latter must always be indicated, such as 1 mW (milliwatt) for a power ratio.

decibel meter: Meter which has a scale calibrated uniformly in logarithmic steps and labelled with decibel units; used for determining the power levels in communication circuits, relative to a datum power level, now 1 mW in 600 ohms.

decimal: 1. Pertaining to a characteristic or property involving a selection, choice, or condition in which there are ten possibilities. 2. Pertaining to the number representation system with a radix of ten. 3. See binary-coded decimal notation.

decimal arithemtic trap mask: The bit, in the program status doubleword, that indicates whether (if 1) or not (if 0) the decimal arithmetic trap is in effect.

decimal code: A code in which each allowable position has one of ten possible states. The convéntional decimal number system is a decimal code.

decimal coded digit: A digit or character defined by a set of decimal digits, such as a pair of decimal digits specifying a letter or special character in a system of notation.

decimal digit: In decimal notation, one of the characters 0 through 9.

decimal encoder: An encoder having ten output lines for each decade of decimal numbers, one line representing each digit from 0 to 9.

decimal filing: A system for subject-classifying records, developed in units of 10 and coded for arrangement in numerical order.

decimal point: The radix point in decimal representation.

decimal representation: A method of representing ten binary coded distinct characters (primarily the decimal digits) in which each character is represented by some designated binary numeral, i.e., in positional notation utilizing 4 bits standing 8-4-2-1 the decimal 23 is represented by 0010 0011, representing 2 and 3 respectively.

decimal to binary conversion: The process of converting a number written to the base of ten, or decimal, into the equivalent number written to the base of two.

decision, logical: The choice or ability to choose between alternatives. Basically this amounts to an ability to answer yes or not with respect to certain fundamental questions involving equality and relative magnitude, e.g., in an inventory application, it is necessary to determine whether or not there has been an issue of a given stock item.

decision box: The symbol used in flowcharting to indicate a choice or branching in the information processing path.

decision element: A circuit that performs a logical operation on one or more binary digits of input information (represent "yes" or "no") and expresses the result in its output.

decision instruction: An instruction that effects the selection of a branch or program, for example, a conditional jump instruction.

decision integrator: A digital integrator changed in such a way that when used in incrementation computers it has an output increment which is maximum negative, zero, or maximum positive dependent upon the same input values, and which is used when negative feedback is necessary as in various types of adders, i.e., a specific servomechanism used to develop rotational speed of a shaft which is proportional to its input current.

decision rules: The programmed criteria which an online, real-time system uses to make operating decisions. It is important to periodically review the decision rules which are being used by a system, because the nature of the problems to be solved changes over time and new situations may have arisen which were not at first anticipated.

decision table: A table of all contigencies that are to be considered in the description of a problem, together with the actions to be taken. Decision tables are sometimes used in place of flowcharts for problem description and documentation. A table is set up as a set of columns, the upper part of each column contains a list of conditions which may or may not be satisfied. The lower part of the column lists a set of actions to be taken of the set of conditions if satisfied. The rows of the table may indicate the type of conditions or the type of action.

deck: A collection of cards; commonly a complete set of cards which have been punched for a definite service or purpose.

declarative macroinstruction: Utilized as a portion of an assembly language to instruct the compiler or assembly program to perform some action or take note of some condition. When used it does not result in any subsequent action by the object program.

declarative operation: 1. Coding sequence consisting of a symbolic label, a declarative operation code, and an operand. It involves writing symbolic labels and operation codes for data and constants. 2. The process or procedures which provide the object program with various input, output, work ideas, and other constants which may be designed or required.

declare: In assembler programming, to identify the variable symbols to be used by the assembler at preassembly time.

decode: 1. To convert data by reversing the effect of some previous encoding. 2. To interpret a code.

decoder: 1. A device which determines the meaning of a set of signals and initiates a computer operation based thereon. 2. A matrix of switching elements which selects one or more output channels according to the combination of input signals present.

decollate: To separate the plies of a multi-part form or paper stock.

decrement: 1. The quantity by which a variable is decreased. 2. In some computers, a specific part of an instruction word. 3. To decrease the value of a number.

decrement field: A portion of an instruction word set aside specifically for modifying the contents of a register or storage location.

decryption: A method of deciphering encrypted data.

dector: A circuit that extracts the meaningful signal from a carrier (audio or video).

dedicated: 1. Leased or private, usually referring to communications lines or equipment. 2. Reserved or committed to a specific use or application.

dedicated buffering: Assigning a core storage area in a compute memory for the exclusive use of a particular communication line. See dynamic buffering.

dedicated circuit: A communications circuit or channel that has been reserved or committed or allocated for a specific user or use, i.e., for emergency, ultra-high level priorities, or very distinct purposes.

dedicated computer: A computer that is devoted to a singular processing type activity. For example, a minicomputer used in a Direct Numerical Control (DNC) system is dedicated to machine tool activity.

dedicated line: Communication channel devoted to one user; i.e., it is not part of a switched network.

dedicated memory: A section of main memory in a realtime and/or multiprogramming system which is committed to programs and data which must always remain instantly available.

dedicated storage: The allocated, reserved or obligated, set aside, earmarked or assigned ares of storage which are committed to some specific purpose, user, or problem, e.g., exclusively reserved space on a disk storage unit for accounting procedure, problem or data set.

default value: The choice among exclusive alternatives made by the system when no explicit choice is specified by the user.

deferred addressing: Preferred term for indirect addressing in which the address part specifies a location containing an address, and which in turn specifies a location containing an address, etc., until the specified location address is eventually found. A preset or conditioned number of iterations is set by a termination indicator.

deferred entry/deferred exit: An asychronous event causes the deferred entry by passing control of the central processing unit to a subroutine or to an entry point, while this transfer causes a deferred exit from the program having control previously.

deferred maintenance: Maintenance designed to correct an existing fault that does not necessarily prevent continued operation of a system, device, or program.

deferred posting: A term used to describe the posting of items in the bookkeeping department on a delayed basis. All items received during one day's business are intersorted and posted on the next business day, as of the date received.

deferred restart: A restart performed by the system on resubmission of a job by the programmer. The operator submits the restart deck to the system through a system input reader.

define data command: A command language statement used for describing a data set.

define the file (DTF) table: An area of main storage that serves as a logical connector between the user's problem program and a file. The DTF table can also be used to provide control information for any transfer of data.

definite integral: An integral which is the limiting value of a certain summation expression which is frequent in mathematics and responds by a plane curve or curves.

definition: 1. The resolution and sharpness of an image, or the extent to which an image is brought into sharp relief. 2. The degree with which a communication system reproduces sound images or messages.

deflection circuit: Circuit used in various cathode-ray tubes to direct the electronic beam to strike a designated or desired spot on that screen, i.e., to establish the storage location of the data bit which is to be stored.

deflection coils: Coils of wire in which the magnetic field which swings the electron beam in writing tubes is generated.

deflection plates: Relating to cathode-ray tubes, an electrode pair, parallel and set apart by a short distance in which a focused electron beam is sent. Vertical deflection is by an amount proportional to the voltage across the plates. If the plates are vertical, the deflection is horizontal. The beam can be controlled in two dimensions to strike anywhere on the screen the base of oscilloscopes, television displays or an electrostatic storage tube used in a computer terminal. Similar to electrostatic deflection.

deflection sensitivity: Used in connection with cathode-ray tubes, the quotient of the change in displacement of the electron beam at the place of impact, divided by the change in the deflecting field. It is usually expressed in millimeters per volt when applied between the deflection electrode plates for electrostatic field deflection, or in millimeters per gauss for magnetic field deflection.

deflection yoke: The ring around the neck of a writing tube which contains the deflection coils.

deflector plates (or deflecting electrodes):   See deflection plates.

degauss: To demagnetize a magnetic tape. A degausser is a coil that is energized momentarily by an alternating current that disarranges the impulses on a magnetic tape when it is placed close to the coil.

degeneracy: The condition in a resonant system when two or more modes have the same frequency.

degenerative feedback: A technique which returns part of the output of a machine, system or process to input it in a way as to cause a larger quantity to be deducted from the input with an increase of output results.

degit emitter: A character emitter limited to the twelve row pulses in a punched card.

degradation: A condition in which the system operates at reduced levels of service. These circumstances are usually caused by unavailability of various equipment units or subsystems.

degradation factor: A measure of the loss in performance that results from reconfiguration of a data processing system; for example, a slow-down in run time due to a reduction in the number of central processing units.

degradation failure: A gradual and partial failure of a component or device.

degraded-service state: A telecommunication service condition defined to exist during any period over which the established limiting value for at least one of the performance parameters is worse than its specified threshold value.

DEL: See delete character.

delay: The amount of time by which a signal is delayed or an event retarded.

delay circuit: A circuit that is designed to delay a signal passing through it.

delay distortion: 1. The distortion that results when the phase angle of the transfer impedance is not linear with frequency within the desired range, thus making the time of transmission or delay vary with frequency in that range. Also called "phase distortion." 2. A characteristic distortion of a communication channel that causes some of the frequency components within the bandwidths to take longer to be propagated through the channel than others. As a result, the output of the channel is not a replica of its input.

delayed access: Access which is delayed because of procedures relating to batch processing or the inherent slow speed of input/output of storage devices.

delayed duplicates: Duplicated packets. These occur when the routing algorithm gets into a loop or when congestion causes a long delay. The sending host retransmits. If a new route is taken, the next packet may arrive before the original, and the extra packet will be forgotten. If the delayed packet shows up at the receiver after the sequence numbers have wrapped around, it will be accepted, and the correct packet rejected as a duplicate. The user will receive incorrect data from the transport station, and no error will be detected.

delay element: The circuitry or electronic mechanism accepting data temporarily, and then emitting the same data after a specific interval.

delay (D) flip-flop: A flip-flop whose output is a function of the input which appeared one pulse earlier; for example, if a 1 appeared at the input, the output after the next clock pulse will be a 1.

delay flop: Clarified by monostable multivibrator, i.e., a circuit which holds information for a fixed period of time. This period is determined by the nature and design of the circuit elements.

delay line: 1. A line or network designed to introduce a desired delay in the transmission of a signal, usually without appreciable distortion. 2. A sequential logic element with one input channel and in which an output channel state at any one instant, T is the same as the input channel state at the instant T-N, where N is a constant interval of time for a given output channel. e.g., an element in which the input sequence undergoes a delay of N time units.

delay line, acoustic: A delay line basing its operation on the time of propagation of sound waves.

delay line, sonic: A delay line using a medium (such as mercury or quartz) providing acoustic delay. (Related to mercury delay line).

delay line, quartz: A sonic delay line using a length of quartz crystal as an acoustical medium and with sound waves representing digital data being propagated over a fixed distance.

delay line register: A unique register incorporating a delay line, a means for a signal regeneration, and a feed-back channel. Thus, the storage of data in serial representation is achievable through continual circulation.

delay system: A system in which bids that cannot be served immediately are permitted to wait until service can begin.

delay unit: A unit in which the output signal is a delayed version of the input signal, i.e., if the input signal is f(t), the output signal is f(t T) where T is the delay introduced.

delay vs frequency distortion: That distortion in a transmission system caused by the difference between the maximum transit time and the minimum transit time of frequencies within a certain band under specified conditions. Also called time delay distortion and phase distortion.

deleave: See decollate.

delete character: A distinct operational character designed to be used to obliterate erroneous or undesired characters.

delete code: A code used in punched tape to correct errors. Usually a punch in each of the first seven tracks of the tapes. The tape reader bypasses these rows of holes.

deleted representation: Similar to an erase character, i.e., a particular representation to which any other representation can be converted by further operation or recording. In paper tape, which does not lend itself to erasure or deletions, deleted representation consists of a code hole in all of the code positions. Often called null representation. In graphics, the absence of information can be deleted representation.

deletion record: A record which results in some corresponding record(s) being deleted from a master file.

delimiter: A character which limits a string of characters, and therefore cannot be a member of the string.

delimiter macroinstructions: Macroinstructions that group functional macros into various coding subgroups.

delimiter statement: A job control statement used to mark the end of data.

Delphi technique: A unique forecasting method for use when there is no directly relevant historical data available. It is an intuitive forecast made after combining the views of many experts in the particular field.

delta clock: One of the primary uses of this clock is timing subroutine operations. If a momentary fault throws the computer into a closed programming loop, or if a fault occurring during the execution of an instruction halts the computer, the delta clock restarts the computer by means of an interrupt, thus providing automatic fault recovery. The interrupt can be programmed to notify the operator that a closed loop has occurred. If completing an operation takes longer than desired, this clock is also used to interrupt the computer and thereby allow program attention to be diverted to items of more immediate importance.

delta noise: The difference between the 1-state and the 0-state half-selected noise.

delta routing: A hybrid algorithm (centralized and isolated routing) where each interface message processor (IMP) measures the "cost" of each line (i.e., queue length, bandwidth, etc.) and periodically sends a packet to the routing control center (RCC) giving it these values.

delta signal: In coincident-carrier magnetic core storage, a difference is developed between the signal magnitude obtained and the partial-select output signal of a cell when the cell is in a zero condition.

DEM: See demodulator.

demand: An input/output coding technique in which a read or write order is initiated as the need to read a new block or write a new block of data occurs. Operations do not take place in parallel.

demand fetching: A memory multiplexing design in which segments are kept on a backing storage and only placed in an internal storage when computations refer to them.

demand load: 1. In a communication center, the power required by all automatic switching, synchronous and terminal equipment, operated simultaneously on-line or standby, control and keying equipment, plus lighting, ventilation and air conditioning equipment required to maintain full continuity of communications. 2. In an operating receiver facility, the power required for all receivers and auxiliary equipment which may be operated on prime or spare antennas simultaneously, those in standby condition, multi-couplers, control and keying equipment, plus lighting, ventilation and air conditioning equipment required for full continuity of communications. 3. In a transmitter facility, the power required for all transmitters and auxiliary equipment which may be operated on prime or spare antennas or dummy loads simultaneously, those in standby condition, control and keying equipment plus lighting, ventilation and air conditioning equipment required for full continuity of communications.

demand paging: In System/370 virtual storage systems, transfer of a page from external page storage to real storage at the time it is needed for execution.

demand processing time-sharing: The simultaneous accommodations by the executive systems of requests and demands from users at numerous remote inquiry terminals, operating in a demand (or conversational) mode. All facilities available to the batch-processing user are also available in the demand mode; the primary difference is that the executive system utilizes its knowledge of the existence of such demand devices to permit the user additional flexibility in the statement and control of individual runs. The demand user may communicate directly with the executive, a worker program, or he may communicate with a conversational processor.

demand reading (or writing): Method for performing input (or output) operations in which blocks of data are transferred to or from the central processor as needed for processing. No special arrangements are made for storing input or output data in buffer areas to allow operations to take place in parallel.

demarcation strip: A terminal board acting as a physical interface between the business machine and the common carrier. See interface.

DEMOD: See demodulator.

demodulation: The process of retrieving an original signal from a modulated carrier wave. This technique is used in data sets to make communication signals compatible with business machine signals.

demodulator: 1. A device which receives tones from a transmission circuit and converts them to electrical pulses, or bits, which may be accepted by a business machine. 2. A device which detects the modulating signals, then removes the carrier signal and reconstitutes the intelligence.

demount: To remove a volume from a tape unit or a direct access device.

demultiplexing: Dividing of information streams into a larger number of streams (contrasted with multiplexing).

dense binary code: A code in which all possible states of the binary pattern are used.

density: The number of units of useful information contained within a linear dimension, usually expressed in units per inch.

density tracks: The number of bits which can be written in a single position across the width of the tape, including parity bits.

departure frequency: The amount of variation of a carrier frequency or center frequency from its assigned value. This concept was described formerly as frequency deviation, a usage which is now deprecated because of the currency of a different meaning in phase and frequency modulation.

deposit: Protecting the contents of an area of memory by writing to a backing store.

derate: Use of a device or component at a lower current, voltage or power level than it can handle, in order to give longer life or reduce occurrence of stress-related failures.

derelativized coding: Absolute coding with all relative addresses modified by addition of their instruction's base addresses.

derivative action gain ratio: The ratio of maximum gain resulting from proportional plus derivative control action to the gain due to proportional action alone.

derivative action time: Proportional plus derivative control action, and for a unit ramp signal input, the advance in time of the output signal (after transients have subsided) caused by derivative control action as compared to the output signal due to proportional control action only.

derivative control action (rate): A defined control action in which the output is proportional to the rate of change of the input.

descriptive and inductive statistics: Descriptive statistics usually involve methods that, essentially, do not go beyond the data with which we start; inductive statistics involve generalizations, predictions, estimations, and decision.

descriptive statement: Electronic Funds Transfer System (EFTS) projects which eliminate some paper instrument for payment transactions may require that these transactions be printed automatically on descriptive statements. For example, systems which involve check truncation, direct payroll deposit, automated bill payment, or automated tellers will require that the consumer receive a periodic statement describing any of these transactions. Point-of-sale systems might involve periodic statements for both consumers and merchants.

descriptor: A computer word used specifically to define characteristics of a program element. For example, descriptors are used for describing a data record, a segment of a program, or an input/output operation.

designation register: A computer register into which data is being placed.

design augmented by computers (DAC-1): An image processing system in which the combination of computer hardware and software permits "conversational" manmachine graphic communication and provides maximum programming flexibility and ease of use for experimentation.

design system: The creation of a detailed plan for the architecture or structure of a system, usually culminating in a document that specifies how the system is to be built.

desired value: The value of the controlled variable hoped-for, wanted or chosen; i.e., the desired value equals the ideal value in an idealized system.

desk check: Various procedures for analyzing or inspecting a written program or specific instructions for errors in logic or syntax usually without the use of computing or peripheral equipment.

destination code: 1. The name of a terminal or processing program to which a message is directed. 2. In North America, the complete ten-digit number that constitutes a telephone address, comprised of a threedigit area code, a three-digit office code, and a four-digit station number.

destination-code indicator: Data or information sent in the forward direction indicating whether or not the destination code is included in the destination address.

destination field: A field in a message header that contains the destination code.

destination queuer: A group of queues in which the queue control block for each queue resides in main storage, and the message-segment chain for each queue resides on a direct-access storage device. The queues contain message segments that are transmitted to terminals.

destination station: A station to which a message is directed.

destination warning marker (DWM): A reflective spot on magnetic tape that is sensed photoelectrically to indicate the end of the tape is coming.

destruction notification: A general letter or detailed listing sent to departments announcing the scheduled destruction of records.

destructive cursor: On a cathode-ray tube (CRT) display device, a cursor that erases any character through which it passes as it is advanced, backspaced, or otherwise moved.

destructive read operation (DRO) readout: The act of reading information from the store of a computer. If the information is to be retained in the computer's store after it has been read out, it is necessary for the information to be written-in to the store again as a special operation.

detail chart: A flowchart in minute detail of a sequence of operations. The symbols of the detail chart usually denote an individual step or computer operation. A detail chart is more detailed than a logic chart, usually reflects the particular computer characteristics and instructions, and facilitates the actual coding of the program in the manner intended by the programmer preparing the chart.

detail file: A temporary reference file of information, usually containing current data to be processed against a master file at a later time.

detail printing: The printing of one line of data from each punched card passing through the accounting machine.

detecting system (error): A system employing an error detecting code and so arranged that any signal deleted as being in error is (a) either deleted from the data delivered to the data sink, in some cases with an indication that such deletion has taken place, or (b) delivered to the data sink, together with an indication that it has been detected as being in error.

detent: A raised or depressed part of a surface, i.e., a bump, in machinery, perhaps a spring, clamp, etc.

deterministic simulation: A simulation in which a fixed relationship exists between input parameters and output results for each action, value, event, etc., such that given input parameters will always result in the same output.

Deutsche Industrie Normenausschus (DIN): The German standard-setting organization. Plugs, sockets, and photographic film are made to DIN standards worldwide.

development time: A part, portion, or section of operating time during which new routines or hardware are tested and debugged.

deviation alarm: A specific designed alarm caused or developed by a variable departing from its desired value by a specified amount.

deviation from linearity: Concerns the maximum deviation of output from the most favorable straight line that can be drawn through the input/output curve. The method of determining the most favorable line must be stated. This may be expressed in percent of output full scale.

deviation ratio: In a frequency-modulation system, the ratio of the maximum frequency deviation to the maximum modulating frequency of the system under specified conditions.

device, digit delay: A logic device for postponing digit signals; e.g., to accomplish the effect of a carry from one digit position to another in arithmetic circuits.

device control character (DCC): A control character used to switch devices on or off.

device control unit: A hardware device that controls the reading, writing, or display of data at one or more input/output devices or terminals. See also transmission control unit.

device-end before console interrupt: External interrupts are erased by either an external device requiring attention (such as a signal from a communications device), console switching, or by the timer going to zero.

device feedback: 1. The return of a portion of the output of a device to the input; positive feedback adds to the input, negative feedback subtracts from the input. 2. Information returned as a response to an originating source.

device independence: The ability to request input/output (I/O) operations without regard for the characteristics of specific types of I/O devices.

device selection check: 1. A check that verifies the choice of devices, such as registers, in the execution of an instruction. 2. A check (usually automatic) to verify that the correct register, input/output (I/O) device, etc., was selected in the performance of a program instruction.

device selection code: Address code that selects a particular device or interface for an input/output operation.

device status word (DSW): A computer word containing bits whose condition indicates the status of devices.

device type: The general name for a kind of device; for example, 2311, 2400, 2500-1.

DFG: See diode function generator.

D format: A data set format in which ASCII records are variable in length.

DFT: See diagnostic function test.

diad: A group of two items used to express quarternary digits binary form.

diagnosis: The process of locating and explaining detectable errors in a computer routine or hardware component.

diagnostic check: A routine designed to locate a malfunction. Used in debugging a program.

diagnostic function test (DFT): A program used to test overall system reliability.

diagnostic program: A program that facilitates maintenance by detection and isolation of malfunctions or mistakes.

diagnostic routine: 1. Locates a malfunction in a computer. 2. Locates mistakes in programming or data. Routines for diagnosing programming mistakes are most often service routines, whereas routines for diagnosing mistakes in data are usually specific to a particular application.

diagnostics test: The running of a machine program or routine for the purpose of discovering a future or a potential failure of a machine element, and to determine its location or its potential location.

diagnostic trace program: A particular type of diagnostic program for the performance of checks on other programs or for demonstrating such operations. The output of a trace program may include instructions of the program which is being checked and intermediate results of those instructions

arranged in the order in which the instructions are executed.

diagnotor: A combination diagnostic and edit routine which questions unusual situations and notes the implied results.

dialed circuit: A connection established through the switched telephone or message network by dialing or by keying a tone transmitter. Such circuits can be established manually or automatically by a business machine.

dial exchange: An exchange where all subscribers originate their calls by dialing.

dialing: Establishing a connection, through common communication lines, between a central computing system and a remote terminal.

dial line: See switched line.

dial number card: Card inserted in the center of the telephone dial, giving the telephone number.

dialog control: Corresponds to the session layer in the International Standard's Organization (ISO) model. The control of the direction of flow by the data flow control layer.

dial pulse: An interruption in the direct-current loop of a calling telephone. It is produced by the breaking and making of the dial pulse contacts of a calling telephone when a digit is dialed. The loop current is interrupted once for each unit of value of the digit.

dial-up (switched network) characteristics: Several remote terminals may dial into the computer using the same data set and line termination at the computer. The actual number is limited by the size of the messages to and from the terminal, and the required response time, i.e., the allowable delay at an individual terminal due to contention for the computer line termination. If data set is not furnished by the telephone company a data access arrangement is required. (Monthly rental plus a one-time installation charge).

dial-up terminal: A terminal on a switched line.

diamagnetic: A material that tends to move from the stronger to the weaker region of the field when placed in a nonuniform magnetic field. A bar of diamagnetic material placed in a uniform magnetic field tends to swing around so that its longer axis is at right angles to the field. Copper, bismuth, and antimony are diamagnetic.

diametral index of cooperation: In facsimile systems, the product of the drum diameter and the line advance in scanning lines per unit length. The unit of length must be the same as that used for expressing the drum diameter.

diatron: A circuitry design which uses diodes.

dibit: A group of 2 bits. In four-phase modulation, each possible dibit is encoded as one of four unique carrier phase shifts. The four possible states for a dibit are 00, 01,10, 11 (e.g., Bell System 201-type data sets).

di-cap storage: A device capable of holding data in the form of an array of charged capacitors, or condensers, and using diodes for controlling information flow.

dictionary: 1. An alphabetic list of the words of a language, with their accepted meanings. 2. A list of code names or keywords used in a routine or system and an indication of their intended meanings.

dielectric: A non-conducting material through which induction of magnetic lines of force may pass. It is a medium in an electrical field capable of recovering, as electrical energy, all or part of the energy required to establish an electric field (voltage stress). The field is accompanied by displacement or charging currents.

dielectric amplifier: Operates through a capacitor; the capacitance varies with applied voltage.

dielectric constant: A dielectric material's ability to store electrostatic energy, compared to air.

difference engine: As a forerunner to the computer, it was the machine developed by Charles Babbage to solve polynomial expressions or equations by the difference methods.

difference report: A report noting resultant changes from an original computer program after program changes.

differential: Either of a pair of symbols dy, dx associated with the functional relationship y = f(x) in such a way that dy/dx = f'(x) or dy = f'(x)dx. Therefore, it appears that when dy/dx is used as the notation for a derivative it may be treated as a fraction. While this gives consistent results in some circumstances, it is in general not true.

differential amplifier: A circuit which will produce an output signal derived from the difference between two input signals.

differential analyzer: An analog computer using interconnected integrators to solve differential equations.

differential delay: Difference in delay of two specified frequencies of interest in a band or channel.

differential equation: An equation containing derivatives or differentials of an unknown function, i.e., the solution satisfies the equation identically throughout some interval of x. The general solution represents the set of functions that satisfy the equation. Related to physical problems, the arbitrary constants are determined from additional conditions which must be satisfied. Most differential equations result from mathematical relations and descriptions of motion and change.

differential gain: In color television, the change in gain, expressed in dB, for the 3.58 MHz color subcarrier as the level of the luminance signal is varied from blanking to white.

differential gear: In analog computers, a mechanism that relates the angles of rotation of three shafts, usually designed so that the algebraic sum of the rotation of two shafts is equal to twice the rotation of the third. A differential gear can be used for addition or subtraction.

differential modulation: A type of modulation in which the choice of the significant condition for any signal element is dependent on the choice of the previous signal element.

differential phase: Variation in phase of the color subcarrier of a television signal as the level of the luminance signal is varied from blanking to white.

differential resolver: A device used for zero shift or offset in numerical control systems that utilize resolver or flat type feedback. It is connected electrically between the reference and the feedback. When the shaft of the resolver is turned, it shifts the phase of the reference signal to the position feedback unit and creates the signal that tells the slide to move.

differentiate: 1. To find the derivative of a function. 2. To deliver an output that is the derivative with respect to time of the input. 3. To distinguish objects or ideas from others.

differentiating amplifier: A specific amplifier whose output current is proportional to the derivative with respect to time, related to the input current, as used in analog computers.

differentiating circuit: A device whose output function is proportional to a derivative, i.e., the rate of change, of its input function with respect to one or more variables.

differentiator: A resistor-condenser circuit at the input to the horizontal oscillator in a cathode-ray tube (CRT).

diffusion: A process used in the production of semiconductors which introduces minute amounts of impurities into a substrate material such as silicon or germanium and permits the impurity to spread into the substrate. The process is very dependent on temperature and time.

digit: 1. One belonging to the set of the n symbols of integral value, ranging from 0 to n-1 inclusive, in a system of numbering with radix n; for example, the ten digits 0,1,2,3,4,5,6,7,8,9 in the decimal system; 0, 1 in the binary system. 2. One of the ideographic characters 0, 1...9...used to designate a quantity smaller than n for the base n number system. 3. A sign or symbol used to convey a specific quantity of information either by itself or with other numbers of its set; e.g., 2, 3, 4 and 5 are digits. The base or radix must be specified and each digit's value assigned.

digital: Pertaining to the use of discrete integral numbers in a given base to represent all the quantities that occur in a problem or calculation. It is possible to express in digital form all information stored, transferred, processed, or transmitted by a dual-state condition (i.e., on-off, true-false, and open-closed).

digital-analog decoder: A device in an analog computer used to translate digital data into variable electrical flow.

digital backup: A specifically designed alternate method of digital process control initiated through the activation of special purpose digital logic in the event of a failure in the computer system.

digital block: A set of multiplexed equipment that includes one or more data channels and associated circuitry.

digital cable test set: Compares two cable traces on the scope at once. Once device weighs $16\frac{1}{2}$ lbs and measures $11\frac{1}{2}$ inches deep. Range is 1 to 100 feet and then up to 50,000 feet in 10 ranges. Accuracy is better than 1 percent of range. Internal rechargeable battery gives 6 hours of continuous operation.

digital channel: A channel capable of carrying direct current, as opposed to analog channels, which do not.

digital circuit: A circuit which transmits information signals in digital form between two exchanges. It includes termination equipment but not switching stages.

digital clock: Clocks which have output signals in digital representation. They allocate time to each program according to a set of priorities. Used in computing systems with developed time-sharing procedures.

digital communications applications: These will become the common denominator for virtually all forms of remote information transfer. Voice, data, facsimile and video information can all be converted economically to digital form with two major benefits. First, integrated digital communciations networks are feasible economically to replace the separate facilities that have been required traditionally for voice, data, and video. Second, digital information can be processed readily by the low-cost, digital computing elements available from the semiconductor industry. This allows integrated communications switching facilities, and also permits compaction and compression of the many types of digital information in order to reduce transmission bandwidth requirements, thus lowering operating costs.

digital computer: A computer which processes information represented by combinations of discrete or discontinuous data as compared with an analog computer for continuous data. It is a device for performing sequences of arithmetic and logical operations, not only on data but on its own program as well. A storedprogram digital computer is capable of performing sequences of internally stored instructions, as opposed to calculators, such as card

programmed calculators, on which the sequence is impressed manually.

digital control unit: In a digital computer, those parts, devices or modules which affect the retrieval of instructions in proper sequence, the interpretation of each instruction, and the application of the proper signals to the arithmetic unit and other parts in accordance with this interpretation.

digital converter: A modem or device which converts information into digital form.

digital data: Data represented in discrete, discontinuous form, as contrasted with analog data represented in continuous form. Digital data is represented by means of coded characters, i.e., numbers, signs, symbols, etc.

digital data channel: A one-way path for data signals which includes a digital channel and associated interface adaptors at each end.

digital data communications message protocol (DDCMP): The data link protocol in DECNET. The data format consists of the SOH, Count, Sync, Select, Ack, Seq, Addr, Header checksum, Data and Data Checksum fields. DDCMP uses a sliding window, and up to an extreme of 255 packets. Its maximum packet size is 16383 bytes versus 1008 bits. Among its control packets are ACK, NAK, REP, START, and STARTACK.

digital data service (DDS): Bell System's digital data service in the United States.

digital double-ended control: For digital networks, a synchronization control system between two exchanges is double-ended if phase error signals used to control the clock at a particular exchange are derived from comparison of the phase of the incoming digital signal and the phase of the internal clock at both exchanges.

digital encoding: Use of a digital code (binary "M" ary, or pseudorandom) to encode an analog or digital signal.

digital error: A single digit inconsistency between the transmitted and received signals.

digital exchange: An exchange that switches information in digital form.

digital filter: A filtering process performed on a digitized signal by a general or special purpose computer. Although digital filtering is far more flexible than analog filtering, it is slower, more expensive, and largely limited to experimental applications when relatively few frequencies are being filtered. When a power spectrum is desired across a larger frequency range, however, the fast Fourier transform (FFT) method offers advantages.

digital input data: The form of machine-control programming that is established by converting descriptive numerical information into a countable form or code for machine actuation.

digital integrator: An integrating device in which digital signals are used to show increments in input variables x and y and an output variable z.

digital microwave: Transmission of voice or data in digital form on microwave links.

digital microwave radio: Designed and built for industrial/business voice and data communications. This microwave radio offers 96 voice-channel capacity to businesses (e.g., banks, insurance companies, and retailers) that have been excluded previously from digital radio communications due to the narrow bandwidths available in the 2-GHz band. Several companies offer 384-channel radios with voice and data capacity for 2and 6-GHz operational fixed service.

digital multiplex equipment (MUL-DEX): Equipment for combining, by time division multiplexing, a defined integral number of digital input signals into a single digital signal at a defined digit rate (multiplexer); and also for carrying out the reverse function (demultiplexer).

digital multiplier: A specific device which generates a digital product from the representation of two digital numbers, by additions of the multiplicand in accordance with the value of the digits in the multiplier. It is necessary only to shift the multiplicand and add it to the product if the multiplier digit is a one, and just shift the multiplicand without adding, if the multiplier digit is a zero, for each successive digit of the multiplier.

digital overlay: A digital network arranged to overlay an existing analog network with suitable interconnections between the two.

digital radio: A microwave radio system designed for the transmission of digital signals, which are usually pulse code modulated signals.

digital readout: A numerical display of the slide position, usually a lighted display in decimal digit.

digital recording: A method of recording in which the information is coded in digital form, usually in binary code. The most frequently used method of coding is a form in which a change in flux polarity indicates a "one" and the absence of change in flux indicates a "zero."

digital signal: 1. A nominally discontinuous electrical signal that changes from one state to another in discrete steps. 2. A signal that is time-wise discontinuous, i.e., discrete, and can assume a limited set of values.

digital signatures: A method of authentication where the receiver can verify the claimed identity of the sender, and the sender cannot later repudiate the message.

digital subset: A collection of data in a prescribed format described by control information to which an operating system has access and which constitutes the principal unit of data storage and retrieval within the system.

digital switching: A process in which connections are established by operations on digital signals without converting them to analog signals.

digital tape recording: A method of recording in which the information is first coded in a digital form. Most commonly, a binary code is used and recording takes place in two discrete values of residual flux.

digital technology: Using bits instead of analog signals, store and forward abilities have practically eliminated the necessity of interconnection of both (or several) parties to permit widespread use of voice mail. Because bit-error rates have dropped dramatically, direct-dialing technology is now worldwide, transmission speeds, modem, multiplexer and other equipment have improved measurably with digital systems replacing analog in a majority of services. Computerbased PBXs are not at all related to the older analog types and as tariffs change they become volume bound rather than range determined.

digital transmission test set: Serves applications such as digital radio, fibre optic, and T-carrier systems, including multiplexer, switch and line testing. Operating at all three rates, test sets generally include the ability to generate a test pattern at one rate and perform measurements at another rate.

digital volumeter: One which indicates a voltage by its nearest numerical magnitude; e.g., by moving-coil optical deflection, switching of electroluminescent elements, dekatrons, digitrons.

digital-to-analog converter: A device that converts a digital input signal to an analog output signal carrying equivalent information.

digital transmission group: A number of voice or data channels or both that are combined into a digital bit stream for trans-mission over various communications media.

digit-coded voice: A coded voice response that is output from an audio response unit (ARU).

digit compression: Any of a number of techniques used to pack digits.

digit delay device: A logic device that postpones digit signals and achieves the effect of a carry from one digit location to another in arithmetic circuits.

digit delay element: A specific delay element that introduces a delay in a line of signals or pulses of one digit period duration.

digit deletion: A procedure through which a central office deletes unneeded digits dialed into it. A digit deletion stage is able to delete up to six digits if, for example, there are direct tie lines to the wanted central office.

digitization: Conversion of an analog signal to a digital signal, with steps between specified levels. See quantization.

digitized voice/data (on T1 link):   Facilitates management with a system that mixes digitized voice with data on a T1 line. An operating system incorporates voicedigitizing input/output cards. The quality of implementation of continuously variable slope, delta modulation (CVSD) can be compared to a connection by means of normal lines. Data and voice connections can be time division multiplexed by the system on the T1 circuit. Unlike standard frequency division multiplexing, these time-division multiplexing (TDM) methods prevent cross talk between voice channels, while the digitizing technique reduces the bandwidth. Twenty-four voice channels occupy only half the T1 circuit, leaving half for data and other services on this type of system.

digitizer: A low-speed input device that converts graphic and pictorial data into binary, numeric inputs for a digital computer.

digit place: In positional representation, the site where a symbol such as a digit is located in a word representing a number.

digit plane driver: A particular amplifier that drives a digit plane for a magnetic core storage unit.

digit position: In positional notation the specific position of each digit in a number. The digit positions are numbered commonly from the lowest significant digit of the number; e.g., in a system utilizing 12-bit binary representation, the individual positions will be references as follows: 11 10 9 8 7 6 5 4 3 2 1 0.

digit pulse: A particular drive pulse common to magnetic cells corresponding to a one digit position in some or all the words in a storage unit. In some techniques it may always be an inhibit pulse or always an enable pulse which are more acceptable names for the general term.

digit punch: A punch in any of the rows representing 0 through 9 in punched cards; 0 punch also functions as a zone punch in alphabetic representation. Similar punches in paper or plastic tapes relate to other codes.

digit selector: A device which separates a card column into individual pulses corresponding to punched row positions.

digit time: The magnitude of the time interval between the signals that represents consecutive digits at a given point in a channel.

digit-transfer trunk: A set of wires used to transfer electrical pulses (numbers) in a computer.

digrams: Two letter combinations, the most common of which are: th, in, er, re, and an.

dimension: 1. In assembler programming, the maximum number of values that can be assigned to a SET symbol representing an array. 2. A FORTRAN language statement used to define arrays.

diminished radix complement: A complement on N-1 is obtained by subtracting each digit of the given quantity from N-1 (where N = radix); e.g., the ones complement of binary 11010 is 00101; the nines complement of decimal 456 is 543.

diode: 1. A device utilized to permit current flow in one direction in a circuit, and to inhibit current flow in the other direction. In computers, these diodes are primarily germanium or silicon crystals. 2. A vacuum tube with two active electrodes.

diode function generator: A device with the capability of generating an arbitrarily designed or specified (fixed function or family) by using an amplifier whose input or feedback impedance consists of networks of resistors and diodes with connections to bias supplies.

diode rectifier: A device for converting alternating into direct current.

diode-transistor-logic (DTL): A logic circuit employing diodes with transistors used only as inverting samplifiers.

diplexer: A coupling device which permits two radio transmitters to share the same antenna.

dipole: A double antenna often used in vhf and uhf systems.

dipole modulation: The representation of binary digits on a magnetic surface medium such as disks, tapes, drums, cards, etc., but in which a specified part of each cell is saturated magnetically in one of two opposing senses, depending upon the value of the digit represented. The remainder of the cell is magnetized in a predetermined sense and remains fixed.

direct-access: A type of storage medium which allows information to be accessed by positioning the medium or accessing mechanism directly to the information required, thus permitting direct addressing of data locations.

direct access application: A type of computing system application in which master records are processed normally and interrogated in a random (nonsequential) order.

direct access device: Same as a random access device or unit as differentiated from a serial access memory unit.

direct access display channel: Provides automatic collection of data and control information from main memory with a single instruction. This indexible address register contains the memory address of the next display control or data word in memory. Termination of the transfers is controlled by the stop bit which signals the computer upon completion of plotting. The stop bit's location may be determined by examining the contents of the channel register.

direct-access queues: A group of queues, or, more specifically, message-segment chains of queues, residing on a direct-access storage device. The group can include destination and process queues.

direct access storage: Relates to storage device, such as magnetic disks and drums, that are capable of fast and direct access to storage locations.

direct-access storage device (DASD): A queue in which the queue control block resides in main storage, and the message-segment chain resides in a direct-access storage device. These queues contain message segments that are sent to a message processing program.

direct acting: A specific and defined operation of a final control element directly proportional to the control output.

direct acting controller: A unique controller module in which the absolute value of the output signal increases as the absolute value of the input (measured variable) increases.

direct address: An address that designates a storage location of an item of data to be treated as an operand.

direct allocation: A system in which the particular peripheral units and storage locations allotted to a program are defined at the time the program is written.

direct broadcast satellite (DBS): A satellite which gives out signals that can be received by small, inexpensive, dish-shaped antennas. These antennas are usually mounted on rooftops, window ledges, or elsewhere affording an unobstructed view of the satellite. DBS is used to bring television and other related programs to remote or rural areas where television never was obtainable before.

direct call: A procedure which avoids the use of address selection signals. The network interprets the call request signal as an instruction to establish a connection with a single destination address previously designated by the user.

direct circuit: An intertoll or office trunk, in particular a high usage circuit connecting two toll centers.

direct code: A code which specifies the use of actual computer command and address configurations.

direct-connection line: A leased line that carries messages directly to their destination point (that is, without going through a central office exchange.)

direct control: Control of an automatic switching arrangement in which the functional units necessary for the establishment of connections are associated with a given call for its duration and are set directly in response to signals from the calling device.

direct control connection: A device that permits two systems to be coupled together for control purposes by passing the channels control information that can be sent across the connector by a single instruction in each computer.

direct controlled system: A module, process, or machine directly guided or restrained by the final controlling element, i.e., designed to achieve a prescribed value of the directly controlled variable.

direct cost effectiveness: That cost effectiveness related to cost benefits accrued directly by the service provider or manufacturer; e.g., as a result of manhour, space, or raw material savings. The result may be an increase in profit or a decrease in unit cost.

direct coupled flip-flop: A flip-flop made up of electronic circuits in which the active elements, whether tubes or transistors are coupled with resisters.

direct-coupled transistor logic (DCTL): Logic employing only transistors as active circuit elements.

direct coupling: Intervalve and transistor coupling so that zero-frequency currents are amplified to the same extent as higher frequency currents. The correct grid bias for succeeding valves is obtained either by a potentiometer or by a reversed polarity batte.

direct-current balancer: The coupling and connecting of two or more similar direct-current machines so that the conductors connected to the junction points of the machines are maintained at constant potentials.

direct-current bias: In magnetic tape or wire recording, the addition of a polarizing direct current in signal recording to stabilize magnetic saturation.

direct-current component: That part of the picture signal which determines the average or datum brightness of the reproduced picture.

direct-current converter: A converter which changes direct current from one voltage to another.

direct-current coupling: The coupling of the direct-current signals from one to another, usually by resistors and in the low-frequencies, without using series capacitors or transformers.

direct data capture: Automatic recording of transaction data such as at an electronic point-of-sale terminal.

direct data set: A data set whose records are in random order on a direct access volume. Each record is stored or retrieved according to its actual address or its address relative to the beginning of the data set.

direct digital control (DDC): Control action in which control is obtained by a digital device which establishes the signal to the final control element.

direct display: Cathode-ray tubes display various alphanumeric graphic or sketch results from a processor for viewing or photographing for records or animation.

direct distance dialing (DDD): A telephone service which enables a user to dial telephones directly outside the user's local area without the aid of an operator.

direct-distribution satellite: Use of the fixedsatellite service to relay programs from one or more points of origin directly to terrestrial broadcasting stations without any intermediate distribution stages.

direct frequency modulation: The system of FM transmission in which the audio modulates the frequency of the master oscillator through a reactance modulator.

direct information access network for Europe (DIANE): A grouping of otherwise independent computerized information services located throughout Europe.

directing code: Routing digits or a special code dialed before the normal directory number.

direct-insert routine: 1. A separately coded sequence of instructions that is inserted in another instruction sequence directly in low order of the line. 2. A directly inserted subroutine to the main line program specifically where it is required. 3. A subroutine that must be located and inserted into the main routine at each place it is used.

direct instruction: An instruction which contains an operand for the operation specified by the instruction.

directional filter: A combination high-pass and lowpass filter with a common branching point; used to separate the higher and lower transmission bands of a bidirectional system.

directivity gain: The value of the directive gain of an antenna, in the direction of its maximum value.

directivity pattern: A geometrical representation of the output strength in the various directions of a transmitting antenna.

directly controlled system: A module, process, or machine directly guided or restrained by the final controlling element, i.e., designed to achieve a prescribed value of the directly controlled variable.

directly proportional: A condition in which two quantities either increase or decrease together, in a manner such that their ratio is constant.

direct memory access (DMA): High-speed data transfer operation in which an input/-output channel transfers information directly to or from the memory.

direct numerical control (DNC): A system connecting a set of numerically controlled machines to a common memory for part program or machine program storage, with provision for on-demand distribution of data for the machines. Direct numerical control systems typically have additional provisions for collection, display or editing

of part programs, operator instructions, or data related to the numerical control process.

director: Equipment in common-carrier telegraph message switching systems, used for making cross-office selection and connection from input line to output line equipment in accordance with addresses in the message.

directoried data set: A data set in direct access storage that is organized so that the first part contains an index (directory) to the members following.

director-type numerical control (N/C) system: Accepts dimensional data and by interpolation creates the necessary drive pulses to each axis to form the cutter path.

directory: A group of records containing information used in locating and retrieving elements of the diskresident system. There are six directories in the basic operating system, (a) system directory, (b) transient directory, (c) core image directory, (d) macro directory, (e) relocatable directory, and (f) phase directory.

directory file: A disk file that defines the virtual machine configuration of each user.

directory lookup system (DLS): A feature in an integrated voice and data switching system that provides professional operator assistance with update and correction of an organizational directory. A hard copy telephone directory can also be produced. Passwords are used to access the system, protecting the data base's security.

direct outward dialing (DOD): A telephone service in which outgoing calls can be placed directly by dialing an initial digit (access digit) and then the desired number without the aid of an operator.

direct-point repeater: A telegraph function in which the receiving relay controlled by the signals received over a line repeats corresponding signals directly into another line or lines without the interposition of any other repeating or transmitting apparatus.

direct-reading system: Instrument or measuring system set up so that the desired quantity can be obtained direct from a readout or scale without calculation or calibration.

direct recording: A magnetic-tape recording in which some characteristics of the record current, such as amplitude or frequency, are varied continuously in a manner analogous to the time variations of the original signal.

direct recording facsimile: That type of facsimile recording in which a visible record is produced, without subsequent processing, in response to the received signals.

direct reference address: A virtual address that is not modified by indirect addressing, but may be modified by indexing.

direct satellite orbit: A satellite orbit such that the projection of the center of the satellite's mass on the reference plane revolves about the axis of the primary body in the same direction as that in which the primary body rotates. If it revolves in the reverse direction it is called a retrograde orbit.

direct store and forward lockup: A lockup in which neither interface message processor (IMP) can accept any incoming packets from the other.

direct system output writer: A job scheduler function that controls the writing of a job's output data sets directly to an output device during execution of the job.

direct voltage: A voltage which produces a current flowing in one direction only.

disabled: 1. Pertaining to a state of the central processing unit that prevents the occurrence of certain types of interruptions. Same as masked. 2. In communications, pertaining to a state in which a transmission

control unit cannot accept incoming calls on a line.

disabling tone: A selected tone transmitted over a communications path to control equipment.

disarmed state: The state of an interrupt level that cannot accept an interrupt input signal.

disaster dump: A dump or printout which occurs as a result of a nonrecoverable program error.

disciple line: Distinct procedures that adjust the operating parameters of transmission systems to achieve correct or desired values.

disconnect (DISC) command: A protocol command that allows a machine to announce that it is going down.

disconnect signal: A signal sent to a terminal from a central computer that results in the ending of the line connection. Also, a signal transmitted from one end of a subscriber line or trunk to indicate at the other end that the established connection should be disconnected.

discontinuous binary number: A number containing two or more subordinate numbers, each subordinate number treated as a separate binary value.

discontinuous function: A function which does not vary continuously as the variable increases uniformly. The function $b/a \sqrt{x^2 - a^2}$ is a discontinuous function. Note that the step size is not necessarily uniform.

discrete-address beacon system (DABS): Provides ground controllers with aircraft position and identity information.

discrete circuits: Electronic circuits built of separate, individually manufactured, tested and assembled diodes, resistors, transistors, capacitors and other specific electronic components.

discrete component circuit: A circuit designed to be implemented by use of individual transistors, resistors, diodes, capacitors, etc., as contrasted with an integrated circuit.

discrete data: Data that may assume one of two or more states, such as a code for sex, race, number of children, etc.

discrete programming: A class of optimization problems using only integer data. See integer programming.

discrete proportion: One in which the ratio of the first term to the second is equal to that of the third to the fourth; thus, 3:6 :: 8:16. The proportion 3:6 :: 12:24 is not a discrete but a continued proportion, or a geometrical progression. A discrete quantity is discontinuous in its parts.

discrete sampling: A sampling process in which the individual samples are sufficiently long in duration that the accuracy of information transmitted via the channel per unit time is not decreased by the sampling.

discrete series: A discrete action in use in which the differences between successive observations are always finite in character, that is, there are no values falling between the observed values.

discrete simulation: The major components and events of the system are individually identifiable (discrete) and considered at irregular intervals, i.e., only when the system changes state. Contrast with continuous simulation.

discrete unit: Of a digital nature, as opposed to a continuous analog information flow.

discrete variable: A variable that assumes only a whole number value.

discrimination: The skipping of various instructions as developed in a predetermined set of conditions as programmed. If a conditional jump is not used, the next

instructions would follow in the normal proper sequence.

discriminator: A balanced, duo-diode detector cicuit which converts frequency deviations into a variable dc or audio signal.

disjunction: The logical operation which makes use of the -or- operator or the logical sum. The disjunction of two variables, or expressions, may be written as A + B, A or B, A union B. These may also be described as a union when using Venn diagrams.

disk: A magnetic storage medium on the surface of one or more rotating disks, the most modern of which are portable.

disk accessing: The process of or method used in transferring data to and from a disk file. Disk units and access routines vary widely in their sophistication; access can be accomplished either by using physical addresses (actual disk locations) or various levels of symbolic or keyed-record addressing procedures. Some disk drives can locate a desired record using addressing logic contained within the unit itself to find a keyed record, thus leaving more productive time available to the central processing unit while the record is being sought.

disk drive: The mechanism designed to rotate magnetic disks at high speed past read-write heads; sometimes used to drive the entire disk unit.

disk file: 1. A single magnetic disk unit consisting of a drive, channel, and the fixed or removable disks. 2. An associated set of records of the same format, identified by a unique label. 3. Dual-access systems allow simultaneous operations of any two functions-reading, writing, and positioning. Disk capacity may be 200 million bits or more.

disk file addressing: The operation which locates information on a random-access file.

disk file index: A (disk file) table of key fields that identifies the records in another disk file.

disk file subsystem: Provides for large-scale system mass storage. For fast random access to all data files on the disks, there are many reading and writing heads. These are strategically located and can be positioned to provide high-speed access to any storage location. Each record on each side of the disk face has a unique address. Sorting of data before processing is reduced, giving the computer time for other, more important operations.

disk memory: A non-programmable bulk-storage, random access memory consisting of a magnetizable coating on one or both sides of a rotating thin circular plate. Memory latency time is of the order of hundreds of milliseconds.

disk monitor system: An operating system for the various computing systems.

disk-resident system: An operating system that uses disk storage for on-line storage of system routines.

disk servers: In the user/server model, servers whose function is to read and write raw disk blocks, without regard to their contents.

disk storage: The storage of data on the surface of magnetic disks.

disk storage area: The area(s) on magnetic disks used for work in process; not permanent or even semipermanent.

disk storage module: A non-removable assembly of magnetic disks serviced by two access mechanisms.

disk storage unit: A device that provides medium-capacity random access. It is designed for use as an extension of internal main memory, main storage for operating systems and working programs, or where fast direct access is the primary consideration. Typical applications are: handling numerous real-time inputs from an extensive data-gathering system; large data arrays in scientific computation; control of fast-moving inventories, such as a wholesaling or airline passenger reservations.

disorderly closedown: A system stoppage due to an equipment error wherein it is impossible to do an orderly closedown. Special precautions are necessary to prevent the loss of messages and duplication in record updating.

dispatch: A system that enables a user to dispatch vehicles efficiently so as to minimize overall travel time and cost. It obtains from the computer user's existing order-processing system information about the number of shipments to be delivered, where they are to be delivered, and the weight and space requirements for each one. It must also know the delivery and unloading times and will produce an assignment sheet listing the size of trucks to be used, orders to be grouped together, route to be followed, and time of departure from ware house or store.

dispatcher: A resident routine called the dispatcher is at the heart of the communication between the computer and its input/-output devices. The dispatcher maintains a queue of channel requests for each channel and will honor each in turn as the channel becomes available. In addition, the dispatcher controls the operation of the multiprogrammed symbiont routines, interrupting the user's program temporarily to give control to a symboint and returning control to the user when the symbiont has released. The dispatcher maintains a pool of buffer areas for the symbionts and a similar pool of drum symbionts are employed (in some systems).

dispatcher and scheduler: The human being who coordinates the input requirements of production programs, the output requirement of the user department, and the processing capabilities of the data processing equipment. He also sends the output to its ultimate users. Generally, this clerical position requires a knowledge of the technical operation of the system.

dispatcher task: A unique control routine function which selects from the task queue the next task to be processed and gives it control of the central processor.

dispatching priority: A number assigned to tasks, and used to determine precedence for use of the central processing unit in a multitask situation.

dispatching system: One of the basic applications of real-time systems is to respond to demand by assigning resources to meet it, then reporting accordingly. For example, a system that assigns inventory to fill orders. In this case a dispatching system must reduce the recorded balances, prepare the appropriate documents for the warehouses where the items are stocked, and issue recorded documents when inventory levels become too low. The dispatching system also performs such functions as financial accounting, payroll, and management reports on daily operations. The equipment for such a system generally consists of a medium or large computer, magnetic tape transports, magnetic disk files, a card reader-punch, a printer, and perhaps several teletype terminals and a buffer.

dispersal records: The act of placing copies of records in locations other than those housing the originals. May be built-in as part of existing procedures, improvised by rerouting data, or created to provide the needed copy for dispersal.

disperse: A data processing operation in which input items or fields are distributed or duplicated in more than one output item or field.

dispersion: 1. The relationship between refractive index and wavelength. Signal distortion in an optical waveguide is caused by several dispersive mechanisms: waveguide dispersion, material dispersion, and profile dispersion. In addition, the signal suffers degradation from multimode distortion, which is referred to (often erroneously) as multimode dispersion. 2. The scattering of microwave radio radiation by raindrops, or similar obstructions. 3. The allocation of circuits between two points

over more than one geographic or physical route.

dispersion measures: Characteristics of a set of data which describe distribution characteristics, including variance, skewness, kurtosis, moments, etc.

displacement: 1. An amount added to a base address to produce an actual address. 2. The process of shifting or displacing a signal in time or frequency. A bandsplitter uses frequency displacement to encode the signal.

display: The representation of a data item in visible form, for example, lights or indicators on a machine console or other device.

display, vector-moded: Provides a rapid means for displaying straight lines between two points without specifying any in-between points.

display adapter unit: Controls the transmission of data, unit control information, and unit status information, and the sequencing and synchronizing of the various units in the system. In addition, digital data received from computer storage is formatted for deflection commands for the cathode-ray tube (CRT) devices.

display center: That selected position on a display screen for duplicating data or information to an advantage.

display character generator: On a cathode-ray tube (CRT) display device, a hardware unit that converts the digital code for a character into signals that cause the electron beam to create the character on the screen.

display console keyboard: The keyboard, (similar to a typewriter keyboard) on a display console.

display control state: All modes can specify that the display enter the control state in which 12-bit words are decoded as instructions to change display parameters, change mode, or change the address of access to the computer memory.

display control unit: Device for controlling the operation of the display equipment.

display cycle: On a cathode-ray tube (CRT) display device, the sequences of movements of an electron beam needed to create a display image once.

display data module: An optical device which stores computer output and translates this output into literal, numerical, or graphic signals which are distributed to a program-determined group of lights, annunciators, and numerical indicators for use in operator consoles and remote stations.

display editing features: The methods available for the editing function switch (F) or keyboard (K).

display input devices: The techniques available for visual data input: function switch (F), keyboard (K), light pen or pointer (P), or stylus (S).

display line: On a display device, the series of character locations that constitute a horizontal line on the display surface.

display modes: Modes such as vector, increment, character point, etc., that indicate the manner in which points are displayed on a screen.

display plotter: The major element of one plotter unit is a console with a 12-inch-square display screen (a 21-inch cathode-ray tube) on which tables, graphs, charts, alphanumeric characters, or the lines and curves of drawings can be displayed as a series of points. When the full display area is used, 3848 alphanumeric characters—the contents of a page of information—can be viewed. A built-in electronic marker helps the operator edit messages. When the display console is used as a point plotter, it can plot graphs, charts, and drawings with precision.

display points per frame: The measurement of the minimum and maximum number of points which can be drawn flicker-free at the manufacturer's recommended refresher rate.

display position: On a display device, the series of character locations that constitute a vertical line on the display surface.

display processing unit (DPU): The device in a computer graphics system which converts the digital instructions of the computer into the analog voltages which control the CRT. Most DPUs have an enhanced processing capabiltiy which relieves the CRT from most of the computation involved in graphic displays.

display quality: The contract ratio, refresh rate, character size and character clarity combine to produce the quality of the display.

display refresher rate: The manufacturer's recommended number of frames per second for regeneration of a display.

display station: Used to display alphanumeric information in a visual input/output system. It provides rapid man-machine communication by direct cable connection to the computer via a display control, or by remote transmission over telephone lines.

display terminal types: Alternative technologies to cathode-ray tube (CRT) terminals include plasma panel displays, magneto-optic displays, and injection electroluminescense light-emitting diode (LED) displays. In displays having a very small number of characters, plasma panel and LED techniques are being used. From a longer range standpoint the LED technology is perhaps the most promising because of its compatibility with other semiconductor large scale integration (LSI) technologies.

display tube: A cathode-ray tube used to display information.

dissemination: Furnishing or distributing information or data from a storage point; the distribution of output reports.

distance: The number of digit positions by which the corresponding digits of two binary words of the same length are different.

distance code: The minimum binary number that can be added to or subtracted from any character in the code and that will produce another valid character in that code. ASCII, for example, is a distance 1 code, since changing any bit (a difference of 1) in an ASCII character will produce a code for another ASCII character.

distant signal: Television signals originating at a point too far away to be picked up by ordinary home reception equipment; also signals defined by the Federal Communications Commission (FCC) as outside a broadcaster's license area. Cable systems are limited by FCC rules in the number of distant signals they can offer subscribers.

distortion: 1. Caused by transients which, as a result of the modulation, are present in the transmission channel and depend on its transmission qualities. 2. The unwanted change in waveform that occurs between two points in a transmission system.

distortion set: Instrument which measures the extent of a specified type of distortion in a communication system; e.g., distortion in an amplitude (or frequency) modulated signal.

distributed adaptive routing algorithms: Algorithms where each interface message processor (IMP) periodically exchanges specific routing information with each of its neighbors.

distributed architecture: Multiple company facilities, including distant locations, tied together, without investment, in stand-alone systems. A system can employ star architecture which can be extended by fibre optic cable.

distributed capacitance: The electrical capacitance between components and wires (other than that of pure capacitors).

distributed computation: The distribution of computations over multiple machines.

distributed computer system: The arrangement of computers within an organization in which the organization's computer complex has many separate computing facilities all working in a cooperative manner, rather than the conventional single computer at a single location. Versatility of a computer system is often increased if small computers in geographically dispersed branches are used for simple tasks and a powerful central computer is available for larger tasks. Frequently an organization's central files are stored at the central computing facility, with the geographically dispersed smaller computers calling on the central files when they need them. Such an arrangement lessens the load on the central computer and reduces both the volume and cost of data transmission.

Distributed Computer Systems (DCS): Experimental ring network at University of California, Irvine.

distributed database systems: Databases geographically distributed among the network hosts.

distributed intelligence: The concept of distributed intelligence as applied throughout a computer communications system can have the effect of reducing the traffic on communications channels, since the intelligence can be used for such things as providing an echo back to the user, preventing transmission of erroneous data, and compressing of data prior to transmission. The intelligence can also be used to increase the flexibility at the terminal for the user, by providing editing and perhaps even simple processing prior to transmission.

distributed line: A transmission line on which there is a regular distribution along the whole length of the line of its electrical parameters (inductance, capacitance, and resistance) as opposed to lumped loading, or the increase of circuit inductance by insertion of coils at regular intervals.

distributed locking algorithms: Algorithms that attempt to simulate locking in database (i.e., centralized, replicated) systems.

distributed multiprocessing: A computer network which supports computer-to-computer communications (as opposed to just terminal-to-computer communications) may permit programs to be written which operate on more than one computer system simultaneously. This may be called distributed multiprocessing, where different parts of the same program may run simultaneously on the several central processing units (CPUs) of a single computer system.

distributed operating system: A system in which existing operating systems are discarded and a single homogenous distributed operating system is developed.

distributed query processing: Query processing, which follows the assignment of relations to hosts, which involves inquiries concerning information in the database.

distribution list: Under telecommunications access method (TCAM), a list of terminals, each of which is to receive any message directed to the group.

distribution cable: Branch off of a feeder cable.

distribution entry: Under telecommunications access method (TCAM), an entry in the terminals table associated with a distribution list.

distribution frame: A structure for terminating wires and connecting them together in any desired order.

distribution-list entry: A terminal table entry containing information on a group of terminals, each of which is to receive any message directed to the group. The information in the entry includes relative addresses that locate the single terminal in the group.

distribution network: Part of the local exchange cable network, comprising small cables between subscribers' distribution points (DPs) and cabinets, remote line units (RLUs) or other flexibility points.

distribution plant: The hardware of a cable system-amplifiers, trunk cable and feeder lines attached to utility poles or fed through underground conductors like telephone and electric wires.

distribution time pulse: A device (or circuit) used to allocate timing pulses to one or more control lines or paths.

distributor: The electronic circuitry which acts as an intermediate link between the accumulator and drum storage.

disturbance: 1. Considered to be an undesired change in a variable applied to a system and one which tends to affect the value of a controlled variable adversely. 2. A change in condition outside the loop that affects the error signal.

disturbance power: The unwanted power of any irregular phenomenon associated with transmission which tends to limit or interfere with the interchange of information.

disturbed cell: A magnetic cell which has received one or more partial drive pulses in the opposite sense since it was set or reset.

disturbed response signal: The output signal from a core subjected to a partial read pulse after it has been set to a one or zero condition, there having been one or more intervening partial drive pulses.

disturbed response voltage: That output signal from a core which is subjected to a full read pulse after it has been set to a one or a zero condition, after one or more intervening partial drive pulses, to thus cause a disturbed one output signal or a disturbed zero output signal.

disturbed zero output signal: See disturbed response voltage.

divergent series: A divergent series is an infinite series in which the sum of the terms is greater than any definite quantity, if enough terms are taken.

diversity: Involves a method of transmission and/or reception where a single received signal is derived from combining a group of signals in an attempt to gain decibels.

diversity polarization: Transmission methods used to minimize the effects of selective fading of the horizontal and vertical components of a radio signal.

diversity reception: That method of radio reception whereby, in order to minimize the effects of fading, a resultant signal is obtained by combination or selection, or both, of two or more sources of received signal energy which carry the same modulation or intelligence, but which may differ in strength or signal-tonoise ratio at any given instant.

divide check: An indicator that is on when an invalid division is attempted or has occurred.

divided job processing: The task of programming one or more processors to permit the execution of divided jobs.

divided slit-scan: A device that scans characters (photoelectrically) in optical character recognition.

divider block: The task of programming one or more processors to permit the execution of divided jobs.

divide time: The amount of time needed to perform an average division operation.

divisional communication: Communication between the computer department and the other departments of an organization or division.

DLE: See data link escape character

DLT: See data loop transceiver.

DNC: See direct numerical control

document: Any representation of information which is readable by human beings, usually used in connection with information of interest to the originator of a data processing activity, rather than to the operators of the computer, more commonly applied to input information than output.

document alignment: When a transverse or gravitational force is applied to the document to align its reference edge with that of the machine.

documentation: The group of techniques necessary for the orderly presentation, organization and communication of recorded specialized knowledge, in order to maintain a complete record of reasons for changes in variables. Documentation is necessary to give an unquestionable historical reference record.

documentation book: All the material needed to document a computer application, including problem statement, flowcharts, coding and operating instructions.

documentation supervisor: The person in a company's data processing section who has the authority and responsibility to see that programs, flowcharts and other records are complete, accurate, and annotated with the appropriate explanations. This is so that if a programmer becomes ill or leaves the company before his project is completed, his replacement can carry on easily with the work he has begun.

documentation systems: A procedure in which systems analysts develop specification for programmers, explaining how to develop documentation and systems definitions. Such documents usually contain: (a) The name of the responsible individual who ordered or is directing the program. (b) A brief outline of the system, with some notes relating to the benefits to be obtained. (c) A type of "handbook" developed for use by those who will use the system and programs, explaining such things as: paper flow, coding required, and output file instructions. Other items explained are equipment utilization change-over procedure, systems test data, program descriptions, etc.

document imprinter: A device which transfers information to a document.

document misregistration: The improper state of appearance of a document, in character recognition, on site in the character which lengthens the marking impulse by delaying the mark-to-space transition.

documentor: A program designed to use data processing methods in the production and maintenance of program flowcharts, text material, and other types of tabular or graphic information.

document reader: A device for reading marks or characters on sheets of paper.

document reference edge: In character recognition, a specified document edge with which the alignment of characters is defined.

document retrieval: The system of searching, indexing, and identifying of specific documents which contain the desired data being sought.

document transportation: The phase in the reading process in character recognition, which makes the effective delinery of the source document to the read station.

document writer: A typewriter-like machine used to compose, edit and print documents. Such machines normally employ paper or magnetic tape as the storage medium and provide text-editing capabilities so that document copy can be changed and a correct tape generated. Document writers also normally include a right justification capability, but without a full proportional spacing.

docuterm: A word or phrase descriptive of the subject matter or concept of an item of information and considered important for later retrieval of information.

domain: 1. The set associated with the variable. A set could be all real numbers, for example. The set on which the function is defined is the domain of the function. 2. The region in a crystalline structure with parallel electric fields for all molecules.

domain, magnetic: Region in a magnetic material where direction of magnetization is uniform.

domains: In a relational database system, the columns of a relation.

domestic satellite (DOMSAT):   A satellite system used purely for national telecommunications services.

donor: An element which enters or is introduced in small quantities as an impurity into semiconducting materials and which has a negative valence greater than the valence of the pure semiconductor.

donor ion: An atom in a doped semiconductor crystal which gives up an electron.

door-bucket: A storage device that provides complete buffering overlap. Usually a magnetic core storage unit. This device processes data with one section of storage while the other section is being loaded.

dopants: Chemical elements added to the core and cladding of fibers to alter the transmission and reflective properties of the fiber.

dope vector: A specification or dictionary type of record built by a compiler to provide information describing the location, format, length, etc. of a single data element or an element within an array or structure. The specification record is used in generating an object program code to unpack or locate the specific bits or bytes required when a reference is in the source program.

doping: The process of adding alien elements to a semiconductor crystal to supply it with charge carriers–electrons or holes.

doppler effect: Change in apparent frequency (or wavelength) because of relative motion of a source of radiation and an observer.

dot cycle: One cycle of a periodic alternation between two signalling conditions, each condition having unit duration. In teletypewriter applications one dot cycle is a successive mark and a space. Telegraph transmission is sometimes considered in terms of dot cycles per second or dot speed, which is half the speed of transmission as expressed in bauds.

dot-matrix printer: A printer which has five or seven carefully spaced wires instead of a type wheel.

dot speed: Telegraphic transmission speeds as measured in dot cycles per second.

double buffer: The use of two areas of memory as buffer storage during input/-output operations which involve a particular peripheral unit; e.g., if data from an input unit is loaded first into one buffer and then into another, the unit can be driven at its maximum input speed; while the input loads one buffer the central processor can process the data in the other.

double-ended amplifier: The utilization of two areas of memory as buffer storage during input/output operations involving a particular peripheral unit.

double-length numeral: A specific numeral which contains twice as many digits as ordinary numerals in particular computers, and ones which usually require two registers or storage locations. Such numerals are most often used for double-precision computing.

double modulation: Modulation of one wave by another wave which is also modulated.

double-polling: A technique whereby a discrete signal is transmitted twice to a station of a multipoint circuit by a polling device, such as a computer. The station will respond to the first signal with a "ready-to-transmit" signal if it has traffic ready to send, and it will transmit the message after receipt of the second signal.

double-precision: The retention of twice as many digits of a quantity as the computer normally handles.

double-precision arithmetic: Arithmetic used when more accuracy is necessary than a single word of computer storage will provide. Two computer words are used to represent one number.

double-precision hardware: Application problems that require a high degree of precision are solved quickly and easily because of double-precision hardware. By using a word size of 48 bits rather than the ordinary 24, the precision of both fixed- and floating-point operations is considerably greater. The doubleprecision store, load, and add instructions provide swift completion of all double-precision operations.

double-precision operation: An operation in which two registers are treated as a 64-bit double-word register containing a single quantity.

double-precision quantity: A quantity that has twice as many digits as are carried normally in a word of a fixed word-length computer.

double-pulse recording: A specific method for magnetic recording of bits in which each storage cell comprises two regions magnetized in opposite senses with unmagnetized regions on each side.

doubler: A frequency multiplier which multiplies the frequency of an input signal by two.

double rail logic: Self-timing asynchronous circuits in which each logic variable is represented by two electrical lines which together can take on three meaningful states—zero, one, and undecided.

double-sideband transmission: A method of communication in which the frequencies produced by the process of modulation on opposite sides of the carrier are not related to each other, but are related separately to two sets of modulating signals. The carrier frequency may be either transmitted or suppressed.

doubleword: Two computer words, considered as a single, 64-bit quantity, beginning at an even-numbered word location (in some computers).

doubleword length: Many arithmetic instructions produce two word results. With fixed-point multiplication, a double-length product is stored in two A registers of control storage for integer and fractional operations. Integer and fractional division is performed upon a double-length dividend with the remainder and the quotient retained in the A registers (in some systems).

doubleword register: Two computer registers used together to hold a double word.

down-line transmission: A technique used in a computerized message-switching system whereby the stations on one of the multipoint circuits can communicate directly, without each message being received by the computer and transmitted back down the same line.

downstream: Signals traveling from the headend to subscriber's homes.

down time: The period during which a computer is malfunctioning or not operating correctly because of mechanical or electronic failure, as opposed to available time, idle time, or standby time, during which the computer is functional.

downward multiplexing: A system which leaves the transport layer open to multiple network connections, and distributes the traffic among them in a round-robin fashion.

downward reference: In an overlay structure, a reference made from a segment to a segment lower in the path, that is farther from the root segment.

drift: A change in the output of a circuit which takes place slowly. Usually caused by voltage fluctuations or changes in environmental conditions. Circuits can be designed to include correction for drift and are used in analog computers to eliminate the errors which would otherwise occur.

drift corrected amplifier: A high gain amplifier which has been equipped separately with means for reducing drift and thus preventing drift error.

drift equivalent voltage (to account for drift): A voltage measurement which must be applied to the input of a high-gain amplifier to bring the output voltage to zero. This is a hypothetical voltage when applied to the input of the usual equivalent circuit of the amplifier.

drift stabilization: Any automatic method used to minimize the drift of a dc amplifier.

drive pulse: 1. A pulsed magnetomotive force applied to a magnetic core. 2. A particular pulse of current in a winding inductively coupled to one or more magnetic cells which produces a pulse of magnetomotive force.

drive, winding: A coil of wire inductively coupled to a magnetic cell.

driver: A small program which controls external devices or executes other programs.

drop: A connection made available for a terminal unit on a transmission line.

drop dead halt: A halt which may be deliberately programmed or the result of a logical error in programming, but from which there is no recovery.

drop in: The reading of a spurious signal whose amplitude is greater than a predetermined percentage of the nominal signal.

dropout: 1. A momentary loss in signal, usually due to the effect of noise, propagation anomalies, or system malfunction. 2. A failure to read a binary character from magnetic storage, generally caused by defects in the magnetic media, or failure in the read mechanism. 3. In magnetic tape, a recorded signal whose amplitude is less than a predetermined percentage of the reference signal.

dropout count: The number of dropouts detected in a given length of tape. In digital recording, the length specified is normally that of the complete roll.

drum mark: A character used to signify the end of a record on a drum.

dry cell: A small portable battery. The cell operates on Leclanché principles, with a central (positive) carbon electrode and a metal outer case for the negative electrode.

dry contact: That part of a circuit containing only contact points and resistive components.

dry reed contact: An encapsulated switch consisting of two metal wires which act as the contact points for a relay.

dry running: Examination of the logic and coding of a program from a flowchart and written instructions. It also utilizes paper to record the results of each step of the operation before running the program on the computer.

DS: See data set.

DSCB: See data set control block.

DSE: See data set extension.

DSS: See dynamic support system.

dual cable: A method of doubling channel capacity by using two cables installed side by side to carry different signals.

dual channel controller: The controller that permits tape reading and/or writing at the same time.

dual operation: Of any logic operation, another whose result is the negation of the result of the original operation when applied to the negation of its operands. It is represented by writing 0 for 1 and 1 for 0 in the tabulated values of the statements for the original operation. For example, the OR operation is the dual of the AND operation.

dual systems: The use of two computers to receive identical inputs and execute the same routines, with the results of such parallel processing subject to comparison.

dual-tone multi-frequency signaling (DTMF): A signaling method employing set combinations of two specific voice-band frequencies, one of which is selected from a group of four low frequencies, and the other from a group of either three or four relatively high frequencies.

dual track: Use of two tracks on magnetic tape, so that recording and subsequent reproduction can proceed along one track and return along the other, thus obviating rewinding.

dummy: An artificial address, instruction, or record of information inserted solely to fulfil prescribed conditions, such as to achieve a fixed word length or block length, but without itself affecting machine operations except to permit the machine to perform desired operations.

dummy control section: A control section that an assembler can use to format an area of storage without producing any object code.

dummy instruction: An artificial instruction or address inserted in a list to serve a purpose other than the execution as an instruction.

dummy section: See dummy control section.

dump: A small program that outputs the contents of memory onto hard copy which may be listings, tape, or punched cards.

dump, ac: The removal of all alternating current power intentionally, accidentally or conditionally from a system or component. An ac dump usually results in the removal of all power, since direct current is supplied usually through a rectifier or converter.

dump and restart: Software routines for taking program dumps at specified times, and for restarting programs at one of these points in the event of program failure. See dump point and checkpoint.

dump check: A check which usually consists of adding all the digits during dumping, and verifying the sum when retransferring.

dumping: Various techniques designed to provide a periodic write out of a complete program and its data (i.e., the contents of the working storage area) to a backup storage or memory unit. A dumping program usually incorporates restart procedures to enable the program to be resumed at the last dump point in the event of interruption due, for example, to a machine failure, or some other job interruption. A periodic dump avoids having to start from the original beginning if some unforeseen event causes erasure.

dumping storage: A procedure or process for transferring data from one particular storage device to another or from one particular area to another.

dump point: That point in a program at which it is desirable to write the program and its data to a backing storage, as a protection against machine failure. Dump points may be selected to effect dumping at specific time intervals or at predetermined events in the running of the program.

duo: Recording of images on only one-half of the film width during one passage of the film. Film is then turned end-for-end and rerun to utilize the second half of the film. The principle is both useful and economical when filming small documents at high degrees of reduction.

duodecimal: 1. Pertaining to a characteristic or property involving a selection, choice, or condition in which there are twelve possibilities. 2. Pertaining to the numeration system with a radix of twelve.

duo-diode: A vacuum tube containing a double diode.

duoprimed word: A computer word containing a representation of the 6, 7, 8, and 9 rows of information from an 80-column card.

duotricenary notation: Notation using the base 32.

dup: 1. A punched card which is an exact copy of a previous punched card. 2. Improper use of word duplex, but often meant to signify a second set of equipment or computing devices which would substitute for original equipment in case of failure.

duplex: In communications, pertaining to a simultaneous two way and independent transmission in both directions (sometimes referred to as full duplex). Contrast with half-duplex.

duplex channel: A channel providing simultaneous transmission in both directions.

duplex computer: A pair of usually identical computers operating so that if and when one is shut down for maintenance, improvements, checkouts, etc., the other can operate without a reduction in capability of the total system. Use of each computer might alternate, to provide time for preventive maintenance, or one might run relatively low priority problems or act as a slave to the other.

duplex system bridge: A duplex system based on the Wheatstone bridge principle in which a substantial neutrality of the receiving apparatus to the sent current is obtained by an impedance balance.

duplexing: The scheme of combining a master tape with either a tape or a series of punched cards containing pure data, plus the appropriate switching codes to produce a document. This may be done on a Flexowriter, in conjunction with two tape readers or a tape reader and a card reader, working on a "flip-flop" basis. Duplexing permits substantial reductions in the length of data transmissions in that fixed information and most of the function codes can be stored in the master tape and need never be transmitted over the line.

duplicate record: An undesirable record occurring in a file which has the same key as another record in the same file.

duplication check: A check which requires that identical results of two independent performances, either concurrently on duplicate equipment or at different times on the same equipment, of the same operation be identical. Same as redundancy check.

duplication factor: In assembler programming, a value that indicates the number of times that the data specified immediately following the duplication factor is to be generated.

durability index: A measure of the durability of a tape expressed as the number of passes that can be made before a significant degradation of output occurs, divided by the corresponding number that can be made using reference tape. Measurements are made by shuttling a given length back and forth over a transport and monitoring the dropout count and/or decrease in output.

duration pulse: Time interval between the points on the leading and trailing edges at which the instantaneous value bears a specified relation to the pulse amplitude. Frequently, the specified relation is taken as 50 percent.

duration response: That particular time interval between the start of a pulse which influences a storage cell and the end of the resulting response of that storage cell.

DVORAK keyboard: Endorsed by the American National Standards Institute (ANSI) as the Alternate Standard to the QWERTY keyboard. It is designed to provide the typist with more speed, comfort, and less errors than the QWERTY keyboard by placing the most frequently used characters in the center of the board, where the more agile fingers of the hand are. The DVORAK home row of keys can configure 3000 word combinations, compared to the QWERTY's 100. Unlike the QWERTY keyboard, the DVORAK keyboard was named not by its first six keys, but by the man who invented it, August Dvorak.

dwell: A programmed time delay of variable duration, not cyclic or sequential, not an interlock.

dyadic Boolean operation: One of several specific Boolean operations that are applied to pairs of operands, in particular the operators: AND, equivalence, exclusive OR, inclusion. NAND, NOR, OR.

dyadic operation: An operation on two operands.

dyadic processor: A type of computer architecture in which two processors simultaneously execute identical programs and compare results to determine errors. If different results occur, software called "tie-breaking" software attempts to determine which central processing unit (CPU) is in error, or else a third processor will intervene. Dyadic processors are used in real-time fault-tolerant systems to increase their reliability and up-time. One drawback of dyadic processors is their increased cost.

dynamic accuracy: Accuracy determined with a timevarying output.

dynamic address translation (DAT): 1. In System/370 virtual storage systems, the change of a virtual storage address to a real storage address during execution of an instruction. 2. A hardware feature that performs the translation.

dynamic allocation: Method used in multiprogramming computers for assigning main storage, peripheral units, or communications devices to various programs or within a system. These procedures are usually under the control of executive supervisory or operating system programs. They are designed to permit complete flexibility in the loading of programs, especially when depending upon the peripherals and storage available at any one point in time. The essence of this procedure is that the programmer need not specify the particular peripheral he requires, but only the type of peripheral or header label of tape files for example.

dynamic allocation memory: Each time a subroutine is called using this feature, the unique storage area for that subroutine is assigned to the first storage available. Thus, all subroutines called on the same level will share the same storage area. This results in a significant storage saving in many cases. In addition, a recursive subroutine call is possible because a new storage area is assigned each time a subroutine is entered. This feature together with in-line symbolic coding, provides real-time capability (in some systems).

dynamic analysis: The study of control system performance with disturbance inputs affecting the controlled variable or in conditions which affect that variable.

dynamic behavior: How a control system or an individual unit behaves with respect to time.

dynamic buffering: A computer technique using a pool of core storage areas to accumulate message segments prior to transmitting these segments to a secondary storage device.

dynamic check: A check made on the operation of an analog device and on the setup of a problem, by comparing results obtained in the compute mode with some previously computed values.

dynamic circuitry: Uses switch circuits whose outputs are streams of pulses or oscillations occurring at precisely determined instants, rather than dc levels. When the state of the device is changed, the change occurs at one of these instants, and it is necessary to ensure that input signals will occur at the proper instants. The output pulses occur in step with a clock signal which is a continuous stream of pulses at a precise frequency.

dynamic computer check: A problem chosen to determine whether the computer or a program is operating correctly.

dynamic core allocation: A storage allocation procedure used in multiprogramming for more efficient utilization of the core by shifting units of work from location to location within the core.

dynamic database (time-sharing):   The database for the problem area can be very dynamic and changes are frequent. References to the database are equally frequent and require that the database be updated constantly.

dynamic data set definition: The process of defining a data set and allocating auxiliary storage space for it during job step execution rather than before job step execution.

dynamic device reconfiguration (DDR):   A facility that allows a demountable volume to be moved, and repositioned if necessary, without abnormally terminating the job or repeating the initial program load procedure.

dynamic dispatching: A facility that assigns priorities to tasks within an automatic priority group to provide optimum use of central processing unit and input/output resources.

dynamic dump: A dump of a selected area of main storage during the execution of a program at intervals specified by the programmer. A snapshot is a form of dynamic dumping. Such a dump or printout can simulate a page by page or stepped review of register contents.

dynamic error: The error or part of an error related to frequency such as the inadequate dynamic response of some computing device or unit.

dynamic flow diagram: A diagram that shows the operational aspects of a computer program as a function of time.

dynamic gain: That specific magnitude ratio of the steady state amplitude of the output signal from an element or system to the amplitude of the input signal to that element or system, for a sinusoidal signal; i.e., it is expressed as a ratio, or in a decibels as 20 times the log of that ratio for a specified frequency.

dynamic instruction: The sequence of machine steps performed by the computer in a real-time or simulated environment.

dynamic loop: A specific loop stop consisting of a single jump instruction which causes a jump to itself. A loop stop is designed for operating convenience.

dynamic margin: Refers to when step-by-step attenuation is applied to a data test signal; the amount of attenuation added when the receive end gives total errors or "wipe-out" is noted and this becomes the benchmark for future trouble isolation.

dynamic memory: Memory devices in which the stored information decays over a period of time, only milliseconds in some circumstances. The design intention is that information would be read out only nanoseconds after it has been written-in.

dynamic memory relocation: The allocation of memory space in a multiprogrammed computer which most efficiently utilizes the total memory capacity. This allocation is accomplished automatically by the computer when it changes the area of storage occupied by a given program or portion of a program.

dynamic metal-oxide semiconductor (MOS) circuits: Circuits that use the absence or presence of charge on a capacitor to store information, typically with three or four transistors per cell. Fewer transistors give higher packing density and lower cost. Since the capacitor that stores the charge has a leakage current, the stored information degrades slowly and therefore must be refreshed (normally by addressing the memory periodically so that every address is covered eventually).

dynamic page relocation: The segmentation of internal storage into blocks whose addressing is controlled automatically by a memory-protected set of addressable registers.

dynamic printout: A printout of data which occurs duriing the machine run as one of the sequential operations.

dynamic problem check: A problem chosen to determine whether the computer or a program is operating correctly.

dynamic program loading: The process of loading a program module into virtual storage, based on an explicit or implicit reference to that program module by an executing program, rather than loading that program module independent of whether it will be referred to by an executing program.

dynamic program relocation: The action of moving or relocating a program, before it has complete execution and without modification, to another part of storage in a manner that permits subsequent resumption of its execution.

dynamic range: 1. In a transmission system, the difference in decibels between the noise level of the system and its overload level. 2. The difference, in decibels, between the overload level and the minimum acceptable signal level in a system or transducer.

dynamic relocation: See dynamic memory relocation.

dynamic response: The behavior of output as a function of input measure in respect to time.

dynamic scheduling: Job scheduling designed for the computer on a minute-by-minute basis, for analysis by managers.

dynamic storage: The storage of data of a device or in a manner that permits the data to move or vary with time, and thus the data is not always available.

dynamic storage allocation: The allocation of storage space to a procedure based on the instantaneous or actual demand for storage space by the procedure, rather than allocating storage space to a procedure based on its anticipated or predicted demand.

dynamic storage, volatile: A specific unit for storage which depends only on the external supply of power for the maintenance of stored information.

dynamic subroutine: A subroutine which involves parameters, such as decimal point position or item size, from which a relatively coded subroutine is derived. The computer itself is expected to adjust or generate the subroutine according to the parametric values chosen.

dynamic support system (DSS): An interactive debugging facility that allows authorized maintenance personnel to monitor and analyze events and alter data.

dynamic system flowchart: The representation of a dynamic system in a form suitable for manipulating and studying utilization in a computer.

dynamic tape skew: The deviation of a tape from a linear path when transported across the heads, causing a time displacement between signals recorded on different tracks and amplitude differences between the outputs from individual tracks owing to variations in alignment.

dynamic test: 1. A system which determines the correct program and machine function either by running a sample problem with similar programming and a known answer, or by using mathematical or logic checks such as comparing A times B with B times A. 2. A check system built into the program for computers that do not have automatic checking. This check system is concerned with program runs on computers that are not internally self-checking .

dynamic vs. static simulation: In a dynamic system the activity is time dependent; a static system is not time sensitive.

dynamizer: A specific logic element which converts a space distribution of simultaneous states representing digits into a corresponding time sequence. A staticizer is another specific logic element which converts a time sequence of states representing digits into a corresponding space distribution of simultaneous states.

E

Early Bird: The world's first commercial communications satellite. With a capacity equivalent to 240 telephone circuits, Early Bird increased transatlantic telecommunications capacity by 50 percent and made live commercial television possible for the first time across an ocean.

earth: A connection made either accidentally or by design between a conductor and earth. Common ways of obtaining good ground connection are to connect to main water pipes, taking care to insure that these are not plastic. To earth (to ground) is to connect to earth, usually for safety reasons.

earth stations: Ground terminals that use antennas and associated electronic equipment to transmit, receive and process communications via satellite. Future cable systems may be able to interconnect by domestic communications satellites, creating regional and national cable networks.

earth station technology: Significant progress has been made in improving the communications capability and operating efficiency of the standard global satellite system, and in reducing the investment required to build and operate such stations. The first generation stations – used with the Early Bird satellite, for example – required an investment of some $12 million. Today, the highly advanced fourth generation stations can be constructed for about $4 million. The COMSAT Laboratories have made a substantial contribution to this achievement. Earth stations of this capability and cost, however, are neither required nor economical for many specialized applications which require large numbers of earth stations, such as domestic, maritime, aeronautical and other communications. Thus, research and development work has, for the past several years, been aimed at the

development of small and relatively inexpensive earth stations.

EAX: See electronic automatic exchange.

EBR: See electron beam recording.

ECB: See event control block.

echo: A portion of the transmitted signal that has been reflected or otherwise returned with sufficient magnitude and delay to be received as interference.

echo attenuation ratio: A specific ratio of transmitted power at an output terminal to the return or echo power received at or reflected back to the same output terminal; i.e., the output of the transmitter or input to the transmission line, as expressed in decibels. The ratio of the transmitted power to that which is reflected back to the original transmission point.

echo cancellers: Conventional techniques using echo suppressors reduce to a large extent the echoes produced by imperfectly terminated long distance telephone circuits. However, these echo suppressors tend to produce noticeable speech clipping, and also prevent simultaneous talking. COMSAT laboratories developed an adaptive echo canceller which removes the echo without incurring any of the undesirable side effects encountered in the conventional suppressors. Using digital techniques, a replica of whatever echo signal may be encountered is formed, and subtracting the replica from the real echo signal achieves echo-free operation.

echo check: An error control technique whereby the receiving terminal or computer returns the original message to the sender to verify that the message was received correctly.

echo-plex: A communication procedure

wherein characters keyboarded by the operator do not print directly on his printer, but are sent to a computer which echoes the characters back for printing. This procedure, requiring full-duplex communication facilities, provides a form of error control by displaying to the operator an indication of the character received by the computer.

echo power ratio: See echo attenuation ratio.

echo suppressor: A line device used to prevent energy from being reflected back (echoed) to the transmitter. It attenuates the transmission path in one direction while signals are being sent in the other direction.

echo talker: A part of a signal that is returned to the source in time to be received as interference.

ECL: See emitter-coupled logic.

EC mode: See extended control mode.

edge: A document reference edge or a stroke edge.

edge, document loading: The edge which is first encountered during the reading process in character recognition, and whose relative position indicates the direction of travel for the document.

edit: To rearrange, delete, or add information. For example, blanks, spaces, or invariant symbols may be removed from data to be transmitted to allow more efficient use of available circuit time, then replaced after the data has been received.

edit capabilities: Permit checking of many characters at a time doing zero suppress, floating dollar sign, asterisk protect, comma and decimal insertions, sign control, and other routines. Editing time in the central processors is reduced.

edit control character: A special character designed for accuracy control.

editing terminal: A system that provides the following editing capabilities: (a) replacement of characters; (b) insertion, deletion and movement of characters, words, sentences, paragraphs and blocks; (c) field checks which include the numbe of, sequences of and types of digits; (d) zero fill, left or right; (e) batch balance; (f) check digit verification.

edit keys: See editing terminal.

edit mode: In systems with time sharing, an entry mode under the EDIT command that accepts successive subcommands suitable for modifying an existing line data set or file.

editor: A routine which performs editing operations.

EDP: See electronic data processing (EDP) system.

EDS: See exchangeable disk storage.

effective address: The addition of the contents of the base register and displacement plus, in some cases, the index register contents to form the address actually used in addressing main storage. See base displacement addressing system.

effective bandwidth: The bandwidth of an ideal (rectangular) band-pass filter, which would pass the same proportion of the signal energy as the actual filter.

effective ground: Connection to ground through a medium of sufficiently low impedance and adequate currentcarrying capacity to prevent voltage build-up which may be hazardous to equipment or personnel.

effective instruction: To alter a presumptive or unmodified instruction when using a stored program computer. Such alteration produces a complete instruction. When it is executed, it is called an effective instruction or an actual instruction. The modification process uses words called modifiers or index words. These are added to or combined with the presumptive or unmodified instruction by means of arithmetic or logical operations.

effective printing rate: In a printer, the actual printing rate (including the effect of paper advance and information loading cycle times for worst control codes, timing codes and error detection, mode) expressed as lines per minute.

effective speed: Speed (less than rated) which can be sustained over a significant period of time and which reflects slowing effects of control codes, timing codes, error detection, retransmission, tabbing, hand keying, etc.

effective transmission: A system of rating transmission performance based upon subjective tests of repetition rates.

effective transmission speed: An average rate of bits per unit time.

effective word: The accessed word in an operation on a single word.

effector: A device used to produce a desired change in an object in response to its input energy.

EIA: An abbreviation for Electronic Industries Association.

EIA interface: A set of signal characteristics (time duration, voltage and current) specified by the Electronic Industries Association for use in communications terminals. Also includes a standard plug/-socket connector arrangement.

EIA interface standard RS-232 B or C: A standardized method adopted by the Electronic Industries Association to insure uniformity of interface between data communication equipment and data processing terminal equipment. Has been generally accepted by most manufacturers of data transmission and business equipment.

eight-level code: A distinct code designed with eight impulses used to describe a single character, but with additional start and stop elements often used for asynchronous transmission.

elapsed time: The total time taken by a process, as measured between the apparent beginning and the apparent end of the process. See real time clock.

E layer: Layer in ionosphere about 65 miles above the Earth's surface which reflects radio waves. The E layer tends to disappear during darkness.

electrical connector: Any device among thousands which is designed or used to either terminate or connect electrical conductors.

electrical contact: The path, joint, or touching of the two halves of a connector or that point joined in the electrical connection.

electrical impulses: The signals coming from card or magnetic tape readers, and other similar devices, which are converted into the code used by the computer and sent to the computer's memory for processing or storage.

electrical interface: Electrical interconnection between system elements.

electrically alterable read-only memory (EAROM): A memory unit made up in such a way that electrical pulses on appropriate pins can erase some or all of the stored data so that new information can then be written in.

electrically erasable read-only memory (EEROM): A memory circuit in which an applied electric pulse erases all the stored memory, so that it must be rewritten.

electrical schematic diagram: A specific representation in graphics of an electrical circuit in which symbols are used for each circuit element, i.e., resistors, capacitors, inductors transistors, diodes, transformers, switches etc., and wires are represented by lines. The schematic permits tracing of current paths for power and signals; such diagrams most often are furnished by manufacturers of equipment for assistance in repairs or diagnosis.

electrocardiogram (EKG) processing: 1. EKG processing is the single most widely used automated analysis procedure currently in use in medicine. Of primary importance was the practical and well documented work at National Institutes of Health. Rigid certification procedures are available, and programs operating in over six different types of computers have passed the test with several more scheduled for tials. The analog EKG signal is converted to digital form and voltage, duration, and interval measurement tables listed; interpretive messages are selected by reference to decision tables. Special digital and analog magnetic tape recorders and telephone transmission devices are available from several companies. 2. Cardiac catherization on-line acquisition and analysis of blood pressures, dye curves, and other parameters not only simplify report preparation but allow more effective procedural decisions during the tests to maximize diagnostic yield. 3. Cardiac intensive care monitoring—post myocardial infarctions—concentrates mostly on arrythmia detection, offering generally better noise immunity than entirely analog systems.

electrochemical   recording   facsimile: Facsimile recording by means of a chemical reaction brought about by the passage of a signal-controlled current through the sensitized portion of the record sheet.

electrolytic: Describes a type of capacitor with permanent polarity markings.

electromagnetic communications: Light-beam (e.g. laser) communication above the ehf frequency band, and nonlight-beam frequency communications in or below ehf band. The latter devices include radio, television, and radar devices covering the frequency spectrum between vhf and ehf bands. More elaborate translators are required than for electrical communications.

electromagnetic deflection: Moving the beam in writing tubes by means of a magnetic field, i.e., by means of deflection coils.

electromagnetic delay line: A delay line whose operation is based on the time or propagation of electromagnetic waves through distributed or lumped capacitance and inductance.

electromagnetic field: Field associated with electromagnetic waves with magnetic and electric fields at right angles to each other.

electromagnetic relay: An electromagnetic switching device having multiple electrical contacts that are operated by an electrical current through a coil. It is used to complete electrical circuits with an applied control current, and also as a mechanical binary counter.

electromagnetic spectrum: A continuous range of frequencies of electromagnetic radiation (i.e., oscillating electrical and magnetic energy which can travel through space). See frequency.

electron: A stable elementary particle with a negative charge which is responsible for electrical conduction. Electrons move when under the influence of an electric field. This movement constitutes an electric current.

electron beam: A beam of electrons emitted from a source, e.g., a cathode-ray tube (CRT) has a thermionic cathode electron gun which produces the beam.

electron beam recording (EBR): A means of using an electron beam to write computer-generated data direct to microfilm.

electron gun: The device in a writing tube or CRT which generates the electron beam.

electronic: Pertaining to that branch of science dealing with the motion, emission, and behavior of currents of free electrons, especially in vacuum, gas, or phototubes and special conductors or semiconductors. This is contrasted with electric, which pertains to the flow of large currents in metal conductors.

electronic automatic exchange (EAX): The General Telephone Company term for electronic telephone exchange equipment.

electronic calculator punch: A piece of standard peripheral equipment designed to read punched cards, perform mathematical and logic processing and punch the results into cards.

electronic circuit analysis program (ECA-PII): A simple language for analyzing electrical networks. Earlier versions were implemented in varying forms on several computers, in batch and on-line versions.

electronic communications: The specialized field concerned with the use of electronic devices and systems for the acquisition or acceptance, processing, storage, display, analysis, protection, and transfer of information.

electronic computer originated mail (ECOM): The U.S. Postal Service's version of electronic mail.

electronic data processing (EDP) center: A complete complex including one or more computers, the peripheral equipment, personnel related to the operation of the center and its functions, and the office space housing the necessary hardware and personnel.

electronic data processing (EDP) memory thin film: A new thin-film memory computer with wide range of capabilities that is adaptable readily to many typical and specialized applications, such as: (a) tactical data systems; (b)command and control systems; (c) digital communications and switching systems; (d) data reduction and analysis; (e) logistics; (f) scientific computation; (g) traffic control; (h) reservation systems; (i) computation analysis; (j) inventory and scheduling systems; (k) intelligence systtems; (l) systems simulation; (m) missile and satellite dynamics; (n) process control; and many others. Thin-film memory computers have resulted in microminiaturization of computer components, greater reliability, speeds, and accuracy. Whole circuits etched on film 1/20 of an inch thick replace hundreds of separate diodes.

electronic data processing (EDP) system: A machine system capable of receiving, storing, operating on, and recording data, and which also possesses (a) the ability to store internally at least some instructions for data-processing operations, and (b) the means for locating and controlling access to data stored internally. See also computer.

electronic differential analyzer: A form of analog computer using interconnected electronic integrators to solve differential equations.

electronic document distribution: A technique for transmitting correspondence via a data communications system.

electronic funds transfer system (EFTS): Various electronic communications systems which transfer financial information from one point to another. Although EFTS encompasses many diverse electronic automation projects, it is used most frequently to describe three types of systems: (a) automated clearing houses, (b) automated tellers, and (c) point-of-sale systems.

electronic hash: Electrical interfering noise arising from vibrators or commutators.

Electronic Industries Association (EIA) interface: See EIA interface.

Electronic Industries Association (EIA) standard code: A code or coding system conforming to any one of the standards established by the EIA.

electronic jamming: The deliberate radiation, reradiation, or reflection of electromagnetic energy with the object of impairing the use of electronic devices, equipment or systems.

electronic library: A general purpose library system whereby the user sits at a computer terminal and can call for viewing on a cathode-ray tube (CRT) any author, title or subject in the card catalog, or any page of any book in the library. The tremendous potential of the electronic library can be appreciated if one realizes the materials of several libraries may become available to millions of users through the usage of computer utilities.

electronic mail network: Global electronic mail systems have expanded from the United Kingdom, Canada, and the United States to include Australia, Hong Kong, The Netherlands, and Puerto Rico/U.S. Virgin Islands. The ITT Dialcom system operators are the Overseas Telecommunications Commission (OTC) of Australia; Cable & Wireless, Ltd. of Hong Kong; The Netherlands' PTT; ITT World Communications Inc. in Puerto Rico and the Virgin Islands. Each new licensee will offer ITT Dialcom's proprietary electronic mail software, operating on the respective licensee's own computers.

electronic multiplier: An all-electronic device capable of forming the product of two variables. Examples are a time-division multiplier, a square-law multiplier, an AMFM multiplier, and a triangular-wave multiplier.

electronic neuron network simulation: The study and duplication of neuron cells and networks in order to build multiple-purpose systems using analogous electronic components. Computers have been programmed to act as neuron system simulators, and this type of research holds much potential for the future.

electronic private automatic branch exchange (PABX): A type of exchange in which switching is accomplished by the flow of electrons through solid state devices rather than by elecromechanical means.

electronic stylus: A pen-like device which is commonly used in conjunction with a cathode-ray tube (CRT) for inputting or changing information under program control. The electronic stylus is often called a light pen, and works by signalling the computer with an electronic pulse. The computer acts on these signals and can change the configuration plotted across the tube face or perform other operations using the inputted data according to previously programmed instructions.

electronic switch: A circuit element that causes a start and stop action or a switching action electronically, usually at high speeds.

electronic switching system: The Bell Laboratorydesigned switching system for local/national communications is an example.

electronic tutor: A teaching machine which makes use of programmed instructions in the computer to help each student achieve his educational goals. Each student communicates with the computer via his own terminal. The computer will be programmed to adjust its teaching style automatically to the needs of each student, and each student will progress at his own best pace independently of others. Bright students will move from topic to topic rapidly, while slower students will be carefully tutored and given extra practice to raise them to the desired achievement levels.

electron image: The pattern of electrons emitted by the image orthicon photocathode which corresponds to the light and shade in the object before the television camera.

electron multiplier: A tube with several successive plates which multiplies electrons incident on the plates through secondary emission.

electro-optic detector: Any device capable of detecting transmitted light by converting the received radiation into some form of electrical signal.

electrostatic deflection: Swerving the beam in writing tubes, by means of an electrostatic field or CRTs i.e., by means of deflection plates.

electrostatic field interference: A form of interference induced in the circuits of various devices which is due to the presence of an electrostatic field, i.e., it often appears as common mode or normal mode interference in the measuring circuits.

electrostatic printing: A type of printing, now common in photocopying, in which a pattern of electrostatic charges is produced on the surface of paper; a very fine powder is then applied to the paper, which sticks to the charged lines and letters and is made permanent by applying heat.

electrostatic shield: A metal mesh used to screen one device from the electric field of another.

electrostatic storage: The storage of data on a dielectric surface, such as the screen of a cathode-ray tube, in the form of the presence or absence of spots bearing electrostatic charges that can persist for a short time after the electrostatic charging force is removed.

electrostrictive: The relationships and phenomena which are concerned with the changes in dimensions which occur when a dielectric or any other material is polarized, i.e., such materials are used as transducers of electrical energy to mechanical energy.

eleven's complement check digit: A check digit used for numeric data (usually coded numbers such as I.D. numbers) to detect transposition or substitution error. It is calculated by: a) developing a sum composed of each digit in the number multi-plied by an integer which is different for each digit position (e.g., for the code number 1234567, $(1 \times 8) + (2 \times 7) + (3 \times 6) + (4 \times 5) + (5 \times 4) + (6 \times 3) + (7 \times 2) = 112$); b) dividing the sum by 11 (e.g., $112/11 = 10$); c) calculating the remainder and subtracting from 11 (e.g., $11 - 2 = 9$); d) subtracting 1 ($1234567 - 8$). (Note: if the calculated result is 10 an "x" is used.)

ELSE operation: Disjunction, OR Operation, Inclusive OR operation.

else rule: A catch-all rule in decision tables designed to handle the conditions not covered by exact and explicit rules; it is written by leaving all conditions blank. Action then to be taken may be to halt processing, note the condition, or to correct the situation and continue processing.

EM: See end-of-medium character.

embossed plate printer: The data preparation device, in character recognition, which prints through the paper medium by allowing only the raised character to make contact with the printing ribbon.

embossment: As related to optical character recognition, the distance between the nondeformed part of a document surface and a specified point on a printed character.

emergency button: A button on a computer used in case of emergency (such as fire, etc.).

emergency maintenance: A type of corrective maintenance completed on a nonscheduled basis.

emergency off: That particular control switch on most control panels or consoles which, when pushed, will disconnect all power from the computer system. Typically used for fires only since instantaneous removal of power from all system components can result in damage or alteration to electrical and mechanical parts, disk, or tape file. (Normally, a system "power off" results in sequenced removal of power from components effected by timing circuits.)

emergency restart: Procedure that reestablishes signal communication when other signal links fail on a common channel signaling system.

emitter: The transistor terminal which emits charge carriers.

emitter coupled logic (ECL) circuit: A logic circuit in which the circuit generates its own clock pulse independently of the clock pulse for logically preceding or following circuits. This allows different circuits to work at their own speeds and not be dependent on a clock pulse which must run at the speed of the slowest circuit. ECL circuits do not saturate, obviating either Schottky clamps for gold doping. However, to realize ECL's speed potential, one or two extra diffusions are needed in manufacturing. The net result: ECL memories are faster than TTL but more expensive. Certainly, for applications requiring small memories to be mixed with ECL logic, there will always be a requirement for ECL memories. Also, since ECL memories are faster than CMOS and N-channel, they will be used in applications that need extra speed. Since this is not true with TTL, ECL should become a more important memory form than TTL.

emitter follower: A circuit like a cathode-follower but using a transistor rather than a vacuum tube and an emitter rather than a cathode. The base also substitutes for the grid.

empirical: Pertaining to a statement or formula based on experience or experimental evidence.

empiric function generator: A computer program or device capable of generating a mathematical function, curve, or set of values from given values, such as test data or laboratory measurements.

empty medium: Usually printed forms or blank paper tapes, invoices, etc. which are bases or media on which data has been recorded only to develop a frame of reference to determine the feasibility of such instruments to be used later as data carriers.

emulation: A technique using software of microprogramming in which one computer is made to behave exactly like another computer; i.e., the emulating system executes programs in the native machine language code of the emulated system. Emulation is used generally to minimize the impact of conversion from one computer system to another, and is used to continue the use of production programs—as opposed to "simulation" which is used to study the operational characteristics of another (possibly theoretical) system.

emulator: 1. A device or computer program that emulates. 2. The combination of programming techniques and special machine features that permits a given computing system to execute programs written for another system.

emulator generation: The process of assembling and link-editing an emulator program into an operating system during system generation.

emulsion: A light-sensitive chemical coat on materials. Most commonly photographic film.

emulsion-laser storage: A digital data storage medium which uses a controlled laser beam to expose very small areas on a photosensitive surface.

enabled: 1. Pertaining to a state of the central processing unit that allows the occurrence of certain types of interruptions. 2. In communications, pertaining to the state in which a transmission control unit can accept incoming calls on a line.

enabled page fault: A page fault that occurs when input/output and external interruptions are allowed by the central processing unit.

enabled transition: In some protocol models, a transition is enabled if there is at least one input token in each of its input places. If enabled, the transition may "fire" at will, taking one token from each input place and leaving one token in each output place.

encode: Conversion of a character into its equivalent combination of bits.

encoded question: A question set up and encoded in a form appropriate for operating, programming or conditioning a searching device.

encoder: A device capable of translating from one method of expression to another method of expression, e.g., translating a message "add the contents of A to the contents of B," into a series of binary digits.

encrypted voice: Telephone communications which are protected against compromise through use of an approved ciphony system.

encryption: In network security, a method making the data unintelligible to all but its intended recipient. Also called encipherment.

end around carry shift: A carry sent directly from the high order position to the least significant place, i.e., using nine's complement addition to subtract numbers.

end-data symbol: Indicates that no more data will follow.

end distortion: In start-stop teletypewriter signals, the shifting of the end of all marking pulses from their proper positions in relation to the beginning of the start pulse.

ending label file: The gummed paper containing a description of the file content which usually appears at the end of each file and then only once.

end instrument: A device that is connected to one terminal of a loop and is capable of converting usable intelligence into electrical signals, or vice versa. It includes all generating, signal-converting and loopterminating devices employed at the transmitting and/or receiving location.

end mark: An indicator to signal the end of a word or the end of a unit of data.

end-of-address (EOA): A unique character or group of characters at the end of a message header for separating the header from the message text. Under the ASCII conventions, EOA has been superseded by start of text (STX).

end-of-block (EOB) character: A character that represents the end of a line or block of information contained in a machine control tape. On a typewriter equipped with a tape punching unit the carriage return inserts an EOB code in the tape.

end-of-control ticket: A document used during magnetic ink character reader (MICR) document processing that signals the end of a control of items. Identified by an identifying digit in the least significant digit position of the transaction code.

end-of-data (EOD): The signal that is read or generated when the final record of a file has been read or written.

end-of-data (EOD) file: The condition that exists when all of the records in a data file have been read or written.

end-of-data (EOD) marker: A character or code that demonstrates that the end of all data held on a specific storage unit has been reached. Not to be confused with end-of-file marker.

end-of-data (EOD) tag: A value used when entering a list of data items to terminate the reading process. A value is chosen unlike the other data items, such as -1,999, or 'end.' As values are read they are compared to the EOD tag. When the EOD tag is entered, the program exits the reading routine.

end office: Class 5 office of local telephone exchange where subscriber's loop terminates.

end-of-field marker: An additional data element which shows that the end of a field (usually a variable length field) has been reached.

end of file (EOF):　Termination or point of completion of a quantity of data. End-of-file marks are used to indicate this point.

end-of-file (EOF) indicator:　A device associated with each input and output unit that makes an end of file condition known to the routine and operator controlling the computer.

end-of-file (EOF) routine:　A routine which provides the special processing required when the last record of a file of data has been reached, either provided by a housekeeping package or user written routine.

end-of-file (EOF) trailer label:　A record with identification and control data related to previous records of a file. Its first five characters are IEOF.

end of line:　A machine code character which indicates the end or termination of a group of records.

end of magnetic tape (EMIT):　The point on a reel of magnetic tape that indicates the end of usable tape for recording purposes.

end-of-medium character:　A control character specifically designed to indicate either the physical end of the data medium or the end of the portion of the data medium upon which desired data is recorded.

end of message (EOM):　The specific character or sequence of characters which indicates the termination of a message or record.

end of program:　A miscellaneous function that indicates the completion of the program. It stops the spindle, coolant, and feed after completion of all commands in the block. Used to reset the controls and/or the machine. May also rewind the tape or advance a loop tape past the splice area.

end-of-record (EOR):　A code specifying the end of a piece of information.

end-of-record (EOR) word:　The last word of a record on tape. It has a unique bit configuration and may be used to define the end of a record in memory.

end-of-reel trailer label:　A record with identification and control data related to previous records of a file that extends to another reel. This is the last record on all but the last unit of a multi-reel file. Its first five characters are IEOR.

end of run:　The finishing of a program forming a run, usually signaled by a message or indicator from the program.

end-of-run routine:　One provided by the programmer to deal with various housekeeping operations before a run is ended; i.e., rewinding tapes, printing control totals, etc.

end of tape (EOT):　That particular special coating on magnetic tapes which signifies the approaching physical end of magnetic or paper tapes.

end-of-tape (EOT) marker:　A marker on a magnetic tape used to indicate the end of the permissible recording area, for example, a photo-reflective strip, a transparent section of tape, or a particular bit pattern.

end-of-tape (EOT) routine:　One either provided by a housekeeping package or written by the user that supplies the special processing required when the last record on a reel of magnetic tape has been reached.

end-of-text character:　A data communications character designed to indicate the end of the text being transmitted.

end of transmission block (ETB):　Indicates the end of transmitting a block (group of information units) of data.

end-of-transmission-block (ETB) character:　A data communications character designed to indicate where data has been arranged in blocks for transmission, i.e., a control character which indicates the end of a block.

end of transmission (EOT): A unique character or group of characters used to denote the end of a data transmission to or from a remote terminal.

end of transmission text (ETX): An end-of-transmission-block (ETB) message used when the information transmitted represents text.

endorser: A particular feature now almost standard on most magnetic ink character readers (MICRs) which is an endorsement record of each blank after the document has been read.

end point: The final position of the cutter when a span is completed. The end point of any span is also the start point of the next span.

end-to-end circuits: A typical circuit in a computer network can utilize the other circuits in its establishment. This is the end-to-end circuit which connects two processors; for example, a program in a computer with a user at a terminal, or two programs in two different computers. In contrast, other circuits connect two or more physical devices and will be used in part to form this circuit, a physical or logical connection between processes. If the circuit is physical, then switching hardware will establish the circuit, making the proper connection at each switching point. If the circuit is logical, then no direct physical connection necessarily exists at any of the switching points in this type of communication between the input and output lines, but instead, the connection is established in tables of the communications software of the computers establishing the connection, and is executed by other computers at each switching point.

end-to-end encryption: Encryption with the same keys and devices available at both send and receive terminals, so the message is transmitted entirely as an encrypted message.

end-to-end protocols: These prevent overflow and increase efficiency. In a layered structure, flow control breaks into two classes: end-to-end and congestion. Various inexpensive systems are sufficient to keep data flows under control to prevent loss, duplication, and sequential disarray.

end-to-end test: Dynamic test. As used by the Bell System, a test utilizing the 900 series test equipment.

end value: A value designed to serve as a minimum or maximum control value and often compared with the value of some index, count, or signal to determine if the anticipated maximum or minimum has been attained.

energy level diagram: A line drawing that shows increases and decreases of electrical power along a channel of signal communications.

engaging force contact: The exertion or force necessary to insert or engage pins into sockets.

engineering-improvement time: The time set for installing, acceptance testing, or approving equipment which is added.

engineering logic diagram: A specific logic diagram that has been referenced or addended with detailed information relating to circuitry, chassis layout, terminal identification, etc. showing gates, circuits, etc. used in the logic, as well as types and rating of the circuit elements.

engineering measures: Distinct units of measure as applied to a process variable.

engineering time: The time during which the equipment is not productively available because it is undergoing testing, preventive maintenance, repair, or modification.

enquiry character (ENQ): A special control character designed to elicit a response from some remote station, usually for station identification or for the description of the station equipment status.

entering: The process in which a terminal places on the line a message to be transmitted to the computer.

entropy: 1. The measure of unavailable energy in a system. 2. The unavailable information in a set of documents. 3. An inactive or static condition (total entropy).

entropy-energy zero: Energy which is completely predictable in nature and furnishes no information.

entropy per symbol: The minimum number of bits per symbol.

entry: 1. A statement in a programming system. In general each entry is written on one line of a coding form and punched on one card, although some systems permit a single entry to overflow several cards. 2. A member of a list.

entry block: A block of main-memory storage assigned on receipt of each entry into a system and associated with that entry throughout its life in the system.

entry conditions: The initial data and control conditions to be satisfied for successful execution of a given routine.

entry, data: The writing, reading, or posting to a coding form or to a terminal or processing medium, of information or instructions, i.e., a datum or item which is entered on one line, a single entity of processing.

entry instruction: Usually the first instruction to be executed in a subroutine, i.e., it may have several different entry points each of which corresponds to a different function of the subroutine.

entry name: A name within a control section that defines an entry point and can be referred to by any control section.

entry point: 1. A specific location in a program segment which other segments can reference. 2. The point or points at which a program can be activated by an operator or an operating system.

entry symbol: An ordinary symbol that represents an entry name or control section name.

envelope delay: Time delay of the modulation envelope of a signal in passing through a channel or network.

environment: The elements and/or factors influencing or affecting the design and operation of a device or system.

environment control table (ECT):   Under time-sharing option (TSO), a control block that contains information about the user's environment in the foreground region.

environment division: 1. The division of a COBOL program in which the programmer lists the features of the equipment needed to run a program—input/output devices, storage size, and others. 2. The environment division specifies the processor on which the source program is to be compiled, the configuration on which the object program is to be executed, and the relationships between data files and input/output media. The configuration section contains three paragraphs which deal with the overall specifications of the processors involved and equate actual hardware names with mnemonic names supplied by the programmer. The input/output section consists of two paragraphs that identify each file and specify input/output techniques, respectively.

environment record: Under telecommunciations access method (TCAM), a record of the total telecommunciations environment at a single point in time.

EOF: See end of file.

EOM: See end-of-message.

E 13B: The type font chosen by the American Bankers Association as the common machine language (MICR) for the banking industry.

equalization: The process of reducing frequency and/or phase distortion of a circuit by the introduction of networks to compensate for the difference in attenuation and/or time delay at the various frequencies in the transmission band.

equalizer: An elaborate tone control system designed to compensate for frequency distortion in phonograph records.

equate: To establish a variable, segment, or file name which is to be replaced at each appearance by a second named identity; this may be utilized for testing, measuring, etc. or whenever a substitute identity or quantity is desired. Contrasts with equivalence, which establishes identical identities.

equipment failure: A fault in the equipment causing improper behavior or preventing a scheduled task from being accomplished.

equipment-misuse error: Indication that a logical equipment assignment has been made that does not make sense. For example, assigning the binary paper-tape punch as compiler input, or assigning the card reader as the load-and-go unit would be an equipment misuse. The message is given only as a warning. The assignment is made and the job will proceed normally.

equitable sharing: A form of scheduling under which the response ratio is proportional to the number of jobs present in the system.

equivalence: A logic operator having the property that if P is a statement, Q is a statement, R is a statement,..., then the equivalence of P, Q, R,..., is true if and only if all statements are true or all statements are false.

equivalence element: A unique logic element which has two binary input but only one binary output signal; variance or variable of the output symbol signal is the equivalence of the variables represented by the input signals, i.e., a two-input element whose output signal is 1 when its input signals are alike.

equivalent binary digit(s): The number of binary digits required to express a number in another base with the same precision, e.g., approximately 2⅓ binary digits are required to express in binary form each digit of a decimal number. For the case of coded decimal notation, the number of binary digits required is usually 4 times the number of decimal digits.

equivalent equations: Two equations or equation systems (the same unknowns) which have the same set of solutions.

equivalent four-wire system: A transmission system using frequency division to obtain full-duplex operation over only one pair of wires.

equivalent network: One identical to another network either in general or at some specified frequency. The same input applied to each would produce outputs identical in both magnitude and phase, generated across the same internal impedance.

erasable and programmable read-only memory (EPROM): This is an ultraviolet-light-erasable PROM, sometimes called a metal-oxide semiconductor (MOS) PROM. An advantage of using these, though they are likely to be more expensive, is that reprogramming can be done in the field to keep up with software update.

erasable storage: A storage medium which can be erased and reused repeatedly, e.g., magnetic drum storage, magnetic tape storage, magnetic disk storage, etc.

erase: 1. To replace all the binary digits in a magnetic storage device by binary zeros. 2. To replace all the binary digits in a paper tape by punched holes; more correctly called rubout or letter out. 3. To obliterate information from a storage medium, e.g., to clear, to overwrite.

erase character: Same as delete character.

erase field strength: As regards magnetic tape, the minimum initial amplitude of a decreasing alternating field (normally applied in the longitudinal direction) required to reduce the output of a given recorded signal by a specified amount.

erasing head: That unit or part of various reading or writing devices which is designed and used to remove magnetic fields, spots, i.e., bits of data on storage media such as tapes, disks, drums, etc.

erasure: A process by which a signal recorded on a tape is removed and the tape made ready for rerecording. Erasure may be accomplished in two ways: in ac erasure, the tape is demagnetized by an alternating field which is reduced in amplitude from an initially high value; in dc erasure, the tape is saturated by applying a primarily unidirectional field. AC erasure may be carried out by passing the tape over the erase head fed with high freqency ac or by placing the whole roll of tape in a decreasing 60-cycle field (bulk erasure). DC erasure may be carried out by passing the tape over a head fed with dc or over a permanent magnet. Additional stages may be included in dc erasure in order to leave the tape in a more nearly unmagnetized condition.

ERP: See error recovery procedures.

ERR: See error.

error (ERR):   Any discrepancy between a computed, observed, recorded, or measured quantity and the true, specified, or theoretically correct value or condition.

error-actuating signal: A specified reference input signal minus the feedback signal.

error burst: A data transmission technique using a specified number of correct bits interspersed with designed error bits. The last erroneous bit in a burst and the first erronous bit in the successive burst are separated by the specified number of correct bits. The group of bits in which two successive erroneous bits are always separated by less than a specific number of correct bits.

error checking and recovery: Parity is computed or checked on all references to central store. If a parity error occurs, the computer will interrupt to the proper location, an alarm will sound, and the appropriate fault lights will be flashed on the operator's console. For all real-time applications, the system will attempt to recover. Once the computer has recovered satisfactorily, the system will continue normal operation (in some systems).

error code: 1. A specific character that may be punched into a card or tape to indicate that a conscious error was made in the associated block of data. Machines reading the error code may be programmed to throw out the entire block automatically. 2. Illegal control code on a binary card.

error-coded check: Refers to a code used for either detecting or correcting errors in the information as represented and used mainly in transmission or storage of data in computers. Various types of check bits are the main components of such codes.

error condition: The state that results from an attempt to execute instructions in a computer program that are invalid or that operate on invalid data.

error control: 1. An arrangement that will detect the presence of errors. In some systems, refinements are added that will correct the detected errors, either by operations on received data or by retransmission from the source. 2. A periodic or continuous check of such channel characteristics as delay distortion, frequency response, and noise in an effort to reduce or eliminate the causes of errors.

error control character: A specific control character designed to aid in accuracy control.

error control codes: In data transmission, codes used in error detection and correction. Most of these codes depend on extra parity bits or on the use of codes with redundancy.

error control commands: The ideal communication computer will have special commands for generating longitudinal redundancy check characters, cyclic redundancy checks, and vertical redundancy checks. These special commands will perform these functions in a fraction of the time that would be required with a general purpose instruction set.

error control restart procedures: Checkpoints and restart procedures make it possible, in the event of an error or interruption, to continue processing from the last checkpoint rather than from the beginning of the computer run. These techniques are included in applications which require many hours of processing time, since heavy machine scheduling and deadlines generally do not permit a complete rerun. To establish checkpoints, processing intervals are determined, each being based upon a certain number of items, transactions, or records processed. At each interval or checkpoint, the stored program identifies input and output records and then records them along with the contents of important storage areas such as counters and registers; at the same time, accuracy of processing up to that point is established.

error correcting code: 1. A code in which each telegraph or data signal conforms to a specific rule on construction, so that departures from this construction in the received signals can be automatically detected, and which permits the automatic correction, at the receiving terminal, of some or all of the errors. Such codes require more signal elements than are necessary to convey the basic information. 2. An error-detecting code in which the forbidden-pulse combination produced by gain or loss of a bit indicates which bit is wrong.

error correction and detection characters: In addition to the control characters,

which are defined in most formats, one of two error detection characters are specified to be placed at specific points in a transmission. Typically, they immediately follow the end of text (ETX), and their value is derived from characters of text after start of text (STX).

error correction (transmission): Blocks of data containing transmission errors can be retransmitted correctly. Such retransmission is immediate and fully automatic (in some systems).

error detecting and feedback system: A system employing an error detecting code, so arranged that a signal detected as being in error automatically initiates a request for retransmission of that signal. Also known as decision feedback system, requests repeat system, ARQ system.

error detecting code: A code in which each expression conforms to specific rules of construction, so that if certain errors occur in an expression, the resulting expression will not conform to the rules of construction and, thus, the presence of the errors is detected.

error detection data channel: One type of 56 kbits per second (bps) synchronous full-duplex data channel provides error detection, remote and local looping, and polling capability. The unit serves several applications, including facsimile, bulk data-transfer between computers, and local area network gateway applications.

error detection system: A system employing an errordetecting code and so arranged that any signal detected as being in error is deleted from the data delivered to the data link (in some cases with an indication that such a deletion has taken place), or delivered to the data link, along with an indication that it has been detected as being in error.

error detection (treatment): The purpose of error control is to ensure that the information received by an acceptor is as intended by the source. There must be some means for the acceptor to deduce when received information contains errors, and a mechanism for removing them. Two types of error control may be identified: forward error control where sufficient redundant material is included with the information to allow the acceptor to detect an error and to infer the correct message; and feedback error control, where some redundancy is needed to reveal errors, but correction is made by retransmission.

error diagnostics: An erroneous statement is printed with the erroneous part of the statement clearly marked. The entire statement is processed, even when an error has been detected, whenever possible. Some compilers will continue to the end of the program. Thus, complete error diagnostics may be obtained in one compilation. The errors are listed on the same device as the source-language listing.

error dump: The dumping onto tape, etc. by a priority program of information and core storage so that the cause of an equipment or program error interrupt may be assessed by the analysts.

error, generated: The total error determined by combining the effect of using inexact or imprecise argument with the inexact formula. These errors are compounded by rounding off.

error interrupts: Special interrupts are provided in response to certain error conditions within the central computer. These may come as a result of a programming fault (e.g., illegal instruction, arithmetic overflow), a store fault (parity error) or an executive system violation (attempt to leave the locked-in area or violation of guard mode). These faults have special interrupt locations in central store and are used by the executive system to take remedial or terminating action when they are encountered.

error list: A list created by a compiler indicating incorrect or invalid instructions in a source program.

error message: An indication that an error has been detected.

error quantization: A specific gauge or measure of the uncertainty, particularly that of the irretrievable information loss, which occurs as a result of the quantization of a function in an interval where it is continuous.

error range: 1. The range of all possible values of the error of a particular quantity. 2. The difference between the highest and the lowest of these values.

error rate: The ratio of the number of bits, elements, characters or blocks incorrectly received to the total number of bits, elements, characters, or blocks transmitted.

error rate monitor: A common channel signaling system device which receives an indication for each signal unit found in error and that measures the rate of occurrence of errors according to a prescribed rule.

error rate of translation (communications):   Ratio of the number of alphabetic signals incorrectly translated to the number of alphabetic signals in the message, the restitution at the input of the receiving apparatus being without distortion.

error ratio: A transfer function relating the system error to the reference input and equals error/input.

error recovery procedures (ERP):   Procedures designed to help isolate and, where possible, recover from errors in equipment. The procedures are often used in conjunction with programs that record the statistics of machine malfunctions.

error, relative: A ratio of the error to the value of the quantity which contains the error, as contrasted to absolute error.

error report: A list of error conditions generated during the execution of a specific program.

error routine: An error routine provides a means of automatically initiating corrective action when errors occur, such as tape read and write, or disk seek, read, and write. It is executed after the programmed check establishes an error. The error routine should cause the operation to be performed at least one more time (in some cases several). If the error persists, processing is interrupted and the condition is signaled on the console. The operator's instruction manual should include procedures for correction and resumption of processing.

error signal: Relating to closed loops, that specific signal resulting from subtracting a particular return signal from its corresponding input signal.

ERROR status word: The status word indicating that the remote computing system has detected an error.

error tape select: Signifies that a tape transport unit select error has occurred.

error transmission: A change in data resulting from the transmission process.

escape character (ESC): 1. A control character to signal a change in the meaning of one or more of the characters that follow it. 2. A data communications term representing the use of a control character which, when combined with one or more succeeding characters, forms an escape sequence and the development of additional data communications control operations.

ESD: See external symbol dictionary.

ETB: See end of transmission block.

etched circuit: Refers to integrated circuits and the particular construction in a geometric design or pathing arrangement to form active elements by an etching process on a single piece of semiconducting material.

ethernet: A coaxial cable network in which all stations monitor the cable (the ether) during their own transmission, ending transmission immediately if a collision is detected.

ethernet linkage (GTE Telenet): One example is Bridge Communications Inc., Cupertino, CA, which recently received certification from GTE Telecommunications Corp. to operate its ethernet local area network gateway products over GTE Telenet's public and private data networks. Certification allows Bridge's Gateway Server/1 (GS/1) units to connect Xerox Network System (XNS) ethernet networks to host computers or other XNS ethernets by means of GTE Telenet's packet-switching network, using the CCITT X.25 protocol for the LAN-to-Telenet interface. According to GTE Telenet, users wanting to access a remote ethernet previously had to lease costly full period dedicated telephone lines between ethernets. With the GS/1 capability, users have the option of using a high-speed line to connect an ethernet to a nearby Telenet public data network access point and paying a variable charge only for the data packets actually transmitted—lowering the cost of communications many times.

E-time: See execution time.

ETX: See end-of-text.

Euronet: A European packet switching network with master packet switching exchanges (PSES) in London, Paris, Rome, and Frankfurt, and slave remote access points (RAPS) in Dublin, Brussels, Luxembourg, Amsterdam and Copenhagen. The four PSES are linked by a ring of 48 kbit/s digital links and the RAPS feed in to adjacent PSES by 48 kbit/s or 9.6 kbit/s links. Euronet is sponsored by the European Economic Community; its network management center is in London.

European Space Agency (ESA): The European organization responsible for launching rockets carrying spacecraft for various operations.

even-parity check: A parity check in which the number of zeros (or of ones) in a group of binary digits is expected to be even.

event: Use of an input/output device which makes the device busy but does not make the channel busy.

event chain: The series of actions that result from an initial event. An example is order processing, inventory adjustment, shipping document preparation, etc., resulting from a sale.

event control block (ECB): A control block used to represent the status of an event.

exalted carrier: Addition of the synchronized carrier before demodulation, to improve linearity and to mitigate the effects of fading during transmission.

exalted-carrier reception: A method of receiving either amplitude or phase modulated signals in which the carrier is separated from the sidebands, filtered and amplified, and then combined with the sidebands again at a higher level prior to demodulation.

except gate: A gate in which the specified combination of pulses producing an output pulse is the presence of a pulse on one or more input lines and the absence of a pulse on one or more other input lines.

exception principle system: An information system or data processing system which reports on situations only when actual results differ from planned results. When results occur within a normal range they are not reported.

exception reporting: A record of departures from the expected or norm. Often times, maximum or minimum limits are the set parameters and the normal range lies within these end numbers or expectations. Reports that have results which exceed these parameters become the basis for an exception reporting output.

EXCEPT operation: Same as Exclusion, NOT-IF-THEN operation, AND-NOT operation.

EXCEPT operator: A logic process designed for exception, e.g., if P and Q are two statements, then the statement P EXCEPT Q is valid only if P is true and Q is false.

excess-fifty: A representation in which the number (n) is denoted by the equivalent of (n + 50).

excess sixty-four binary notation: In assembler programming, a binary notation in which each component of a floating-point number E is represented by the binary equivalent of E plus sixty-four.

excess-3 binary coded decimal (BCD) (XS-3): A variation of 8421 BCD code in which the natural binary sequence of values from 3 through 12 respectively represents the decimal numbers 0 through 9. Used for convenience in forming nine's complements.

exchange: A unit—consisting of one or more central offices with associated equipment, lines, and stations—established by a telephone company to serve a specified area (not necessarily marked by political boundaries), usually with a single rate of charges that are approved by a regulatory authority and specified in the telephone company's filed tariffs.

exchangeable disk storage: A backing storage device where magnetic disks are loaded into a disk transport as a unit.

exchange buffering: A technique using data chaining for eliminating the need to move data in main storage, in which control of buffer segments and user program work areas is passed between data management and the user program according to the requirements for work areas, input buffers, and output buffers, on the basis of their availability.

exchange facilities: Channels and equipment used by the communications common carriers to provide service to the general public. In a broader sense, any such channels and equipment.

exchange network: The public switched telephone system. Often referred to as the message network, the toll system, or the telephone network.

exchange, private automatic branch (PABX): A private automatic exchange which provides for the transmission of calls to and from the public telephone network.

exchange register: A temporary surge of rights which performs shuffling of internal storage contents.

exchange service: A service permitting interconnection of any two customers' telephones through the use of switching equipment.

exchange station: A communications system designed so that stations of any two customers can be interconnected by an exchange.

excitation: The operating ac voltage fed to synchro motors and generators.

exclusion: Same as NOT, if-then.

exclusion gate: A binary logic coincidence (two-input) circuit for completing the logic operation of A AND NOT B; i.e., result is true only if statement A is true and statement B is false.

exclusive-NOR gate: A two input (binary) logic circuit designed to perform the logic operation of exclusive NOR, i.e., if A and B are input statements, the result is true or 1 when both A and B are true or when both A and B are false. The result is false when A and B are different.

exclusive OR: A logical operator having the property that if P is a statement and Q is a statement, then the OR of P.Q. is true if and only if at least one is true; false if all are false. P or Q is often represented by P + Q, PUQ.

exclusive-OR element: A logic element in which the relationship between the two binary input signals and the single binary output signal is defined by the exclusive-OR operation.

exclusive-OR operation: A reasonable element applied to two operands that will create a result depending on the bit patterns of the operands.

exclusive reference: A reference between exclusive segments; that is, a reference from a segment in storage to an external symbol in a segment that will cause overlay of the calling segment.

exclusive segments: Segments in the same region of an overlay program, neither of which is in the path of the other. They cannot be in main storage simultaneously.

EXEC: See execute statement.

execute: To interpret a machine instruction and perform the indicated operation(s) on the operand(s) specified.

execute cycle: The period of time during which a machine instruction is interpreted and the indicated operation is performed on the specified operand.

execute phase: An alternate part of the cycle of the computer's operation wherein a command in the program register is performed upon the address indicated. The act of performing a command.

execute statement (EXEC): A job control language (JCL) statement that marks the beginning of a job step and identifies the program to be executed or the cataloged or in-stream procedure to be used.

execution: Of an instruction, the set of elementary steps (or primitives) carried out by the computer to produce the result specified by the operation code of the instruction.

execution cycle: That portion of a machine cycle during which the actual execution of the instruction takes place. Some operations (e.g. divide, multiply) may need a large number of these operation cycles to complete the operation, and the normal instruction/operation alternation will be held up during this time. Also called operation cycle.

execution error (remote-computing system): Of a program statement, causes an immediate execution interrupt at the point at which the error is encountered. The error is extracted and displayed at the terminal. The user may then correct the error and resume the execution of his program. If the user chooses to ignore the error and continue the execution, he may do so. For all syntactic errors, the diagnostic message is specific (in that the variable in error is named or the column where the error occurred is specified) and often tutorial in suggesting the procedure for obtaining correct results.

execution instructions: The set of elementary steps carried out by the computer to produce the result specified by the operation code of the instruction.

execution time (E-time): 1. The sum total of the amount of time required to complete a given command. 2. The portion of an instruction cycle during which the actual work is performed or operation executed; i.e., the time required to decode and perform an instruction. (Same as instruction time.)

executive: 1. A routine that controls loading and relocation of routines and in some cases makes use of instructions which are unknown to the general programmer. Effectively, an executive routine is part of the machine itself. Same as monitor routine, supervisory routine, and supervisory program. 2. A set of coded instructions designed to process and control other sets of coded instructions. 3. A set of coded instructions used in realizing automatic coding. 4. A master set of coded instructions.

executive assignment facilities: The assignment of computer memory and facilities in a computer program.

executive communications: Provides for all communication between the operating programs and the computer operator, and between the executive system and the computer operator. These communications take place via the computer keyboard and the on-line typewriter. This function includes the interpretation of all keyboard inputs addressed to the executive system and the transfer of control to the section of the executive to which the input pertains.

executive control program: A main system program designed to establish priorities and to process and control other routines.

executive diagnostic system: A comprehensive diagnostic system available within the executive system to aid the check out of user programs. Both allocation time and compilation or assembly time commands are available to trigger snapshot dumps. Postmortem dumps are also available through the executive control statement.

executive dumping: The facility to obtain printable dumps of the contents of areas of film or core memory in case unexpected errors cause premature termination of supposedly debugged programs. The dumps are recorded on tape for later printing on the high-speed printer.

executive file-control system: Designed to provide a user the highest possible degree of operational flexibility in storing and retrieving data, without requiring concern with the physical characteristics of the recording devices. Thus, most files are made insensitive to input/output media characteristics as the system adjusts the interface between the file and the device. The system invokes security measures to insure that files are not subject to unauthorized use or destruction. Full facilities are provided for rollback of files from mass-storage devices to magnetic tape, as well as the reconstruction of such files on the massstorage devices when they are later referenced by the user; in general, the user need not be aware of the residence of his files.

executive instruction: Similar to supervisory instruction, this instruction is designed and used to control the operation or execution of other routines or programs.

executive language control: 1. A set of control commands capable of performing all of the desirable or mandatory functions required in a modern executive system. The command language is open-ended and easily expanded, so that features and functions may be added as the need arises. 2. The basic format of an executive control statement is quite simple, and is amenable to a large number of input devices. Statements are not restricted to card image format, and may be of variable lengths. Each statement consists of a heading character for recognition purposes, followed by a command (which categorizes the statement), followed by a variable number of expressions. The end of a statement is signified by the end of a card, a carriage return, or an equivalent signal, depending on the type of input device.

executive program: A program that controls the execution of other programs and regulates the flow of work in a data processing system.

executive routine: A routine designed to control the loading, relocation, execution and possibly the scheduling of other routines. An executive routine is part of the basic operating system and effectively may be considered as part of the computer itself. Such a routine maintains ultimate control of the computer at all times and control always returns to the executive routine when any controlled routine finishes its functions or when an unexpected stop or trap occurs.

executive supervisor: 1. The executive-system component that controls the sequencing, set-up, and execution of all runs entering the computer. It is designed to control the execution of an unlimited number of programs in a multiprogramming environment, while allowing each program to be unaffected by the coexistence of other programs. 2. Contains three levels of scheduling—coarse scheduling, dynamic allocation, and central processing unit (CPU) dispatching. Runs entered are sorted into information files, and these files are used by the supervisor for run scheduling and processing. Control statements for each run are retrieved and scanned by the control command interpreter to facilitate the selection of runs for set-up by the coarse scheduler.

executive system control: Primary control of the executive system is by control information fed to the system by one or more input devices that may be either on-line or at various remote sites. This control information is similar in nature to present control-card operations, but allows additional flexibility and standardization.

exit macroinstruction: 1. A supervisory program macroinstruction that is the final instruction in an application program, signifying that processing is complete. The supervisory program takes the needed action such as releasing working storage blocks to return control to other processing. 2. The final macroinstruction in an application program that releases storage—including the message reference block—and resets associative conditions of the transaction if needed.

exjunction: A reasonable element applied to two operands that will create a result depending on the bit patterns of the operands.

expanded order: 1. A symbolic representation in a compiler or interpreter. 2. A group of characters having the same general form as a computer instruction, but never executed by the computer as an actual instruction. (Synonymous with quasi instruction.) 3. An instruction written in an assembly language designating a predetermined and limited group of computer instructions for a particular task. 4. An instruction which must be translated or interpreted before execution in a computer, i.e., one written in a pseudocode. Often a mnemonic operation code or special characters for compilers.

expandor: A unique transducer designed for a given amplitude range of input voltages and which produces a larger range of output voltages. One important type of expandor employs the information from the envelope of speech signals to expand their volume range.

expected values: The summation of the products of all possible outcomes after each is multiplied by the probability that it will occur, and tables constructed to indicate these values.

explicit address: An address reference that is specified as two absolute expressions. One expression supplies the value of a displacement. Both values are assembled into the object code of a machine instruction.

explicit function: A function whose value is expressed directly in terms of the variable; thus, in the equation $Y = AX^2 + BX^{1/2} + C$, Y is an explicit function of $X : (Y = fX)$. The term stands opposed to implicit function, in which the relation between the function and variable is not directly expressed.

explicit route: In systems network architecture (SNA), a sequence of transmission groups onto which the virtual route chosen by the source is mapped.

exponent: A number placed at the right and above a symbol in typography to indicate the number of times that symbol is a factor, e.g., 10 to the 4th power (10^4) equals 10 x 10 x 10 x 10, or 10,000.

exponential equation: A name given to an equation in which the unknown quantity enters as an exponent; thus $A^x = b$ is an exponential equation. Every exponential equation of the simple form $a^x = b$, may be solved.

exponential function: A function in the mathematical form of: $f(x) = kb^x$; k and b are constants.

exponential smoothing: A processor technique of forecasting.

extended-area service: An exchange service, without toll charges, that extends over an area where there is a community of interest in return for a higher exchange service rate.

extended arithmetic element (EAE):   A fundamental central processor logic circuit element which provides hardware-implemented multiply, divide, and normalize functions.

extended control (EC) mode: A mode in which all the features of a System/370 computing system, including dynamic address translation, are operational.

extended-time scale: One computer time ratio is the time interval between two events in a simulation by a computer to the problem time, or the physical system time, i.e., the time interval between corresponding events in the physical system being simulated. When this ratio is greater than 1, the operation is considered to be on an extended-time scale, which is a slow-time scale. When it is less than 1 it is said to be on a fast-time scale, and when it is not constant during the run it is said to be on a variable time scale. Real-time working is involved when it is equal to 1.

extension register: A computer register used as an extension of the accumulator register or the quotient register.

extensiveness: The availability, as either standard or optional features, of: byte manipulate, double precision, translate-edit capability, floating-point instructions, hardware multiply-divide, or logical operations.

extent: A continuous area of direct access storage between defined upper and lower limits.

external arithmetic: Operations performed outside of the computer itself as by peripheral or auxiliary units but which may or may not become part of the total problem or program on interrupt bases, i.e., array processors, fast Fourier transform processors, and other attached support processors.

external clocking: In synchronous communication, when the bit-timing signal is provided by the modem.

external delays: This is lost time which occurs beyond the control of engineers, operators, or maintenance men. Examples are power failure, ambient conditions outside the prescribed range, or transmission difficulties or faults.

external device code: All external devices are connected to the processor by a common cable that carries an external device address code and a code which specifies what operation is to be performed. Only that device whose address is on the lines will respond to an instruction on the common cable. No instruction will be initiated unless it is accompanied by a start signal. When a device recognizes its address and receives a start signal, it will start the essential information from the operation code in flip-flops and initiate the specified operation.

external device (ED) address: Specifies which external device a particular instruction is referring to.

external device (ED) start: Occurs if the specified external device is not busy, the channel the specified external device is connected to is not busy, and Bit 16 of the external device control word (EDCW) is a "0". The ED start signal is transmitted from the central processor to the specified external device and initiates the specified operation.

external device status: External devices respond with both their busy status and interrupt request status whenever they recognize their own address. They do not clear out an interrupt request until the interrupt succeeds. The processor notifies an external device that its interrupt has been recognized by sending out an interrupt reset signal.

external inhibit interrupt: The bit in the program status doubleword that tells whether or not all external interrupts are inhibited.

external interruption: An interruption caused by a signal from the interruption key on the system console panel, from the timer, or from another computing system.

external interrupt lines: Some time-sharing computers can have over 200 priority-ordered interrupts for external lines. If the attached interrupts cover a range of priorities, by selectively arming and disarming the external interrupt lines, the executive program can change the relative priority of a terminal's attention requests, allowing different classes of service or response to be given to the terminal.

external interrupts: Originate with device controllers or interrupt modules on the Byte input/output (1/0) bus. An interrupt module provides control of eight external interrupt signals. Device controllers may also generate interrupts to signify individual data transfers, end of operation, or error conditions. The external interrupt system contains a single interrupt line, a priority line, and a select line. A device may initiate an interrupt request only if priority has been received from higher level interrupts on the priority chain. Devices not requiring interrupt service will propagate priority to the next device in line (in some systems).

external label: A typed or written identification placed on the outside of a reel of magnetic tape.

externally initiated trap: An interruption of central processing unit operations due to an event in a device independent of any activity in the central processing unit.

external memory: A backing store under the control of the central processor, but not connected to it permanently, It holds data in a form directly acceptable to it, to minimize access time delays.

external merge: A sorting technique that reduces sequences of records or keys to one sequence, usually following one or more internal sorts.

external name: A name that can be referred to by any control section or separetely assembled or compiled module; that is, a control section name or an entry name in another module.

external page storage: In System/360 virtual storage systems, the portion of auxiliary storage that is used to contain pages.

external reference (EXTRN):   1. A reference to a symbol that is defined as an external name in another module. 2. An external symbol that is defined in another module; that which is defined in the assembler language by an EXTRN statement or by a V-type address constant, and is resolved during linkage editing.

external registers: Various registers, which can be referenced by the program, are located in control store as specific addresses. These are the locations (registers) which the programmer references when he desires that some sort of computational function be carried out.

external status words interrupt: A status word accompanied by an external interrupt signal. This signal informs the computer that the word on the data lines is a status word; the computer, intepreting this signal, automatically loads this word in a reserved address in core memory. If the programmer or operator desires a visual indication of the status word, it must be programmed.

external storage: 1. The storage of data on a device which is not an integral part of a computer, but in a form prescribed for use by the computer. 2. A facility or device, not an integral part of a computer, on which data usable by a computer is stored, such as off-line magnetic tape units, or punch card devices.

external symbol: A symbol whose value is of interest to a number of program modules, not only the program module in which it is defined by a symbol contained in a program module dictionary.

external symbol dictionary (ESD):   Control information associated with an object or load module which identifies the external symbols in the module.

extracode: A sequence of machine code instructions stored within the operating system, and sometimes in read-only memory, which is used to simulate hardware functions. Extracodes may be used to provide floating-point operations, for example, on a machine which does not have floating-point hardware.

extract: To replace the contents of specific columns of a quantity (as indicated by some other quantity called an extractor) by the contents of the corresponding column of a third quantity. To remove from a set of items of information all those items that meet some arbitrary criterion.

extract instructions: An instruction that requests the formation of a new expression from selected parts of given expression.

extra-large scale integration (ELSI):   More than one million logic gates or bits of memory in one device.

extrapolate: As regards curve characteristics, to extend a curve beyond the limits of known points by continuing the trend established over known points, as, for example, the extension of time-based data into future time-periods following trends, averages, or other measurements.

extremely high frequency (ehf):   Radio signals with frequencies between 30 Ghz and 300 GHz, i.e., wavelengths between 1cm and 1mm.

extremely low frequency: Radio signals with frequencies below 300 Hz, i.e., wavelengths longer than 1000 km. Used for radio communications with submerged submarines.

EXTRN: See external reference.

F

fabricated language: A language specifically designed for ease of communication in a particular area of endeavor, but one that is not yet natural to that area. This is contrasted with a natural language which has evolved through long usage.

facilities: 1. All equipment, sites, lines, circuits, and software available for data processing and data communications. 2. Data processing equipment available for use by the executive system of a computer. 3. Programs and routines used by manufacturer-furnished software, such as compilers, loaders, input/output handlers, etc. 4. Manufacturer-furnished software that programmers may use to perform common operations such as sorts, printing, or punching the contents of a file, copying files, etc.

facilities library: A basic library of general-purpose software manufacturer-furnished to perform common jobs. To this the user can add his own often-used programs and routines. Programs in the library can be assembled conveniently into an object program by the use of macro-instructions.

facility assignment (executive): The assignment of memory and external facilities to meet the requirements which are defined symbolically in a job program selected for initiation. Executive maintains a list of all allocatable facilities which is updated to reflect assignment of facilities to newly initiated programs, and to reflect release of facilities by programs during, or at termination of, a run.

facsimile baseband: The frequency band occupied by the signal before modulation of the carrier frequency to produce the radio or transmission line frequency.

facsimile density: In a facsimile system, a measure of the light transmission or reflection properties of an area. It is expressed by the common logarithm of the ratio of incident to transmitted or reflected light flux.

facsimile (FAX): A system for the transmission of images. The image is scanned at the transmitter, reconstructed at the receiving station, and duplicated on some form of paper.

facsimile modulation: The process by which the amplitude, phase or frequency of the wave in facsimile transmission is varied with time, in accordance with a signal. The device for changing the type of modulation from receiving to transmitting, or vice versa, is known as a converter.

facsimile signal level: An expression of the maximum signal power or voltage created by the scanning of the subject copy as measured at any point in a facsimile system. According to whether the system employs positive or negative modulation, this will correspond to picture white or black, respectively. It may be expressed in decibels with respect to some standard value such as 1 milliwatt or 1 volt.

facsimile transmission: System which transmits a representation of the content and form of documents over a telecommunications link. Digital facsimiles, using data compression methods, can be sent over the link much more quickly than in the analog system.

facsimile transmitter: The means for translating the subject copy into signals suitable for the communication channel. The copy is rotated on a drum and produces differences in the brightness of the light reflected from the copy of the output of a receiving photocell.

fact correlation: A process which is an integral part of linguistic analysis and adaptive learning which uses methods of manipulating and recognizing data elements, items, or codes to examine and determine explicit and implicit relations of data in files, i.e., for fact retrieval rather than document retrieval.

factor blocking: The limit of the data records which can be contained in a given block on tape.

factorial sign: The sign ! placed after a number that indicates it is a factorial number.

factors: Values used in making a computation.

factory data collection system (stations): The data collection system gathers manufacturing information from electronic in-plant reporting stations and transmits it directly to the computer. The information is processed as it is received. Reports can be produced which indicate, for example, job cost or machine utilization. Information can enter the processor in several ways, including punched cards, plastic badge, keyboard, or data cartridge. The latter logs production data on a pocket-sized recording device that the employee maintains at his work station.

factory feedback and reports: Feedback is an all-important aspect of the system. Feedback of factory data is collected and analyzed to control and predict stock requirements. Purchase-order receipts, assembly-labor vouchers, and fabrication-labor vouchers are collected and returned to where they are used to update master open-order records. After the feedback data is checked for validity by the computer, it is compared against master records to adjust inventory balances. The receipt of "first operation vouchers" reduces rawmaterial balances by the amount applied to parts. Last-operation vouchers add to stock on hand for parts and also reduce open-order quantities. A rawmaterial status report is printed weekly to show usage and balance on hand. Reports are prepared based on feedback data to show labor by individual, labor by area, and labor by shop order. This data also becomes input to the accounting system. A report on network, extra work, and scrap losses is prepared by reason code. This data also becomes input to the accounting system.

fact retrieval: The automatic recognition, selection, interpretation, and manipulation of words, phrases, sentences, or any data in any form, but particularly in a textural structure, and the relating of these data for conclusions and useful results.

fade: Phenomenon represented by more or less periodic reductions in the received field strength of a distant station, usually as a result of interference between reflected and direct waves from source. Mitigated by using a specific downcoming wave.

fading: The fluctuation in intensity of any or all components of a received radio signal due to changes in the characteristics of the propagation path.

fail-safe system: A system which continues to process data despite the failure of parts in the system. Usually accompanied by some deterioration in performance.

fail soft: A method of system implementation designed to prevent the irretrievable loss of facilities or data in the event of a temporary outage of some portion of the system.

failure: See fault.

failure logging: An automatic procedure whereby the maintenance section of the monitor, acting on machinecheck interrupts (immediately following error detection), records the system state. This log is an aid to the customer engineer in diagnosing intermittent errors.

failure prediction: A technique which attempts to determine the failure schedule of specific parts or equipment so that they may be discarded and replaced before failure occurs.

Fake Host (ARPANET): A background program in the interface message processor (IMP). These programs include the statistics generation routines, the debug facilities, and the IMP console teletype handler.

fallback: A condition in processing when special computer or manual functions must be employed as either complete or partial substitutes for malfunctioning systems. Such procedures could be used anywhere between complete system availability and total system failure.

fallback procedure: A procedure to circumvent all equipment faults. The fallback may give degraded service and may include switching to an alternate computer or to different output devices.

fallback recovery: The restoration of a system to full operation from a fallback mode of operation after the cause of the fallback has been removed.

false add: To form a partial sum, that is, to add without carries.

false drop: An unwanted reference which does not pertain to the subject.

false retrievals: Library references that are not pertinent to, but are vaguely related to, the subject of the library search, and are sometimes obtained by automatic search methods.

family: In mathematics, a set of functions, curves, etc., which can be generated by varying one or more of the parameters of a general form.

fan-in: The number of devices that can be connected to an input terminal of a circuit without impairing its function.

fan-out: The number of circuits which can be supplied with input signals from an output terminal of a circuit or unit. The changes of digital circuits depend on the number of devices that can drive or be driven by one circuit of a specific type, and the number of elements that one output can drive is related to the power available from the output and the amount of power required for each input.

farad: The derived S1 unit of capacitance: the capacitance of a capacitor between the plates where there is a potential difference of 1 volt when charged by a quantity of electricity of 1 coulomb. This is a very large unit; microfarads (10^{-6}) and picofarads (10^{-12}) are used most commonly.

far-end crosstalk: Crosstalk which travels along the disturbed circuit in the same direction as the signals in that circuit. To determine the far-end crosstalk between pairs 1 and 2, signals are transmitted on pair 1 at station A, and the crosstalk level is measured on pair 2 at station B.

fast-access storage: The section of the entire storage from which data may be obtained most rapidly.

fast connect circuit switching: A system where each line typed at a terminal causes the terminal's microprocessor to "dial" the computer, send the line, and then hang up.

fast modem polling [9600 bits per second (bps)]: Offers 12 ms turnaround time or better. These 9600 bps modems are V.29-compatible and operate synchronously over four-wire unconditioned 3002-type private lines. Designed for point-to-point and multipoint (multidrop) polling networks, they offer advanced technology and provide rapid equalization and retraining to obtain the 12 ms RTS/CTS delay for greater data throughput in polling networks.

fast response: This is dependent on the situation: on a desk calculator, a fast response would be a 30-second answer; in computer-assisted instruction, it would be a response time of up to 10 seconds; in inputting information, it would be an instantaneous response (less than 1 second) to the teletype terminal from the computer.

fast storage: High speed input or access storage usually in a hierarchy of storage units and related to these relatively. An imprecise term.

fast-time scale: The ratio of computer time (time interval between two events in a simulation) to the problem time (physical system time), when greater than one, is said to be an extended-time scale, or slow-time scale; when less than one, it is said to be a fast-time scale.

fault: 1. A physical condition that causes a device, a component, or an element to fail to perform in a required manner, for example, a short circuit, a broken wire, an intermittent connection. 2. See pattern sensitive fault, and program sensitive fault.

fault-location problem: A problem for identification or information regarding faulty equipment. It is designed and used to identify the location or type of fault and is often part of a diagnostic routine.

fault time: The period during which a computer is malfunctioning or not operating correctly due to mechanical or electronic failure, as opposed to available, idle time, or standby time, during which the computer is functional.

fault tolerant: Describes a system or program able to function correctly even with some failed components.

FAX: See facsimile.

FAX scanner: Part of a facsimile terminal with a rotating drum around which the original material is placed. As the drum rotates, the copy is scanned by a moving light beam and the facsimile signal is sent out to line.

FAX signal level: See facsimile signal level.

FAX transmitter: See facsimile transmitter.

FCC: See Federal Communication Commission.

FDM: See frequency division multiplexing.

FD or FDX: See full-duplex.

FE: See format effector.

feasibility study: A study in which a projection of how a proposed computer system might work is made to provide the basis for a decision to develop and implement the system.

feasible basis: A basis such that postmultiplying the inverse of the basis by the constant column yields a solution which satisfies the constraints. This usually requires that structural slack variables are nonnegative and that artificial variables (other than objective row artificials) be zero.

FEB: See functional electronic block.

Federal   Communication   Commission (FCC):   Established in 1934 to regulate interstate and foreign communications by wire and radio. Its authority includes amateur radio, commercial radio, common carriers, television, and citizens' band radio. It regulates operators' licenses, classifies radio stations and delineates their services. By its actions, it insures that the services offered will be in the best interest of the public. The FCC regulates common carriers by requiring that at least 30 days prior to availability, each company submit a schedule outlining those services the company intends to offer.

Federal Reserve Bank System: Consists of 12 Federal Reserve Banks, their 24 branches and the national and state banks which are members of the system. All national banks are stockholding members of the Federal Reserve Bank of their district. Membership for state banks or trust companies is optional.

feed: 1. To supply the material to be operated upon to a machine. 2. A device capable of feeding; i.e., a tape feed or a card feed.

feedback: The transfer of energy from the output of a circuit back to its input.

feedback amplifier: Specific amplifiers often used in analog computers using the feedback principle to perform operations on signals, i.e., feeding some function of the output signal as part of the input signal to produce some performance and execute desired operations on the input signal. Gain, stability and frequency response are often influenced by the nature of the feedback as secondary functions.

feedback circuit: 1. Circuit conveying current or voltage feedback from the output to the input of an amplifier. 2. Circuit for using personnel from a program source elsewhere.

feedback control action: That designated control action through which a measured variable is compared to its desired value in order to produce an actuating error signal that reduces the magnitude of the error.

feedback control loop: A closed transmission path including an active transducer, forward and feedback paths and one or more mixing points. The system is such that a given relation is maintained between the input and output signals of the loop.

feedback control signal: That specific portion of an output signal or pulse which is returned as input or causes an input.

feedback elements: Specific elements (in the controlling system) which change the feedback signal as a response to the directly controlled variable.

feedback impedance: Various operational amplifiers. These consist of input terminals, high gain units, output terminals, and networks for feedback and input impedances. These substantially define the relationships of the input signals to the output signals.

feedback loop: The components and processes involved in correcting or controlling a system by using part of the output as input.

feedback signal: A designed return signal caused by a measurement of the directly controlled variable.

feedback system (error): A system employing an errordetecting code and so arranged that a signal detected as being in error will initiate a request automatically for the transmission of the incorrectly received signal.

feedback transducer: One which generates a signal, generally electrical, depending on quantity to be controlled; e.g., for rotation potentiometer, synchro or tacho, giving proportional, derivative or integral signals respectively.

feeder cable: Principal cable from a central office.

feeder counter: That device which counts punch cards as they are passing into a peripheral equipment unit.

feeder lines: Intermediate cable distribution lines that connect the main trunk line to the smaller house drops that lead into residences.

feedforward control action: Designed so that information concerning one or more conditions that can disturb the controlled variable is converted into corrective action. This minimizes the deviations of the controlled variable, i.e., feedforward control can be combined with other types of control to anticipate and minimize deviations of the controlled variable.

feeding, form: The positioning of paper forms on a computer or business machine printer in a fast, accurate way.

feed pitch: The distance between the centers of feed holes.

feed-through connector: One of many electrical connectors, terminal blocks, etc. most often with dual-ended terminals to permit simple distribution and busing of electrical circuits.

femtosecond: 10^{-15} second, or 0.001 picosecond (1 picosecond is 1 trillionth of a second).

FEP: See front end processor.

ferric oxide: The magnetic constituent of practically all present-day tapes, in the form of a dispersion of fine particles within the coating.

ferrite: A chemical compound which consists of iron oxide and other metallic oxides often combined with ceramic material to form storage devices. Ferrite has characteristics of high magnetic flux properties.

ferrite core: A core composed of various types of magnetic materials (usually toroidal in shape) which are pulsed or polarized by electric currents carried in a wire or wires wound around the core. These devices are capable of assuming and remaining at one of two conditions of magnetization, thus providing storage, gating, or switching functions.

ferroelectric: Pertaining to a phenomenon exhibited by certain materials in which the material is polarized in one direction or the other, or reversed in direction by the application of a positive or negative electric field of magnitude greater than a certain amount. The material retains the electric polarization unless it is disturbed. The polarization can be sensed by the fact that a change in the field induces an electromotive force that can cause a current.

ferromagnetics: The science which deals with the magnetic polarization properties of materials.

fetch: 1. To bring a program phase into main storage from the core image library for immediate execution. 2. The routine that retrieves requested phases and loads them into main storage. 3. The name of a macroinstruction (fetch) used to transfer control to the system loader.

fetch phase: The alternate part of the cycle of the computer's operation wherein the instruction is brought from memory into the program register.

fetch (program): 1. To obtain a requested phase, load it into main storage at the locations assigned by the linkage editor, and transfer control to the phase entry point. 2. A routine that accomplishes 1.

fetch protection: Determines right of access to main storage by matching a protection key, associated with a fetch reference to main storage, with a storage key, associated with each block of main storage.

fetch-time program: The time at which a program in the form of load modules or phases is loaded into main storage for execution.

FF: See flip-flop.

F format: A data set format in which logical records are the same length.

fiber buffer: A material used to protect an individual optical fiber waveguide from physical damage, providing mechanical isolation and/or protection.

fiber bundle: An assembly of unbuffered optical fibers. A bundle is usually used as a single transmission channel, as opposed to multifiber cables, which contain optically and mechanically isolated fibers, each of which provides a separate channel.

fiber harness: In equipment interface applications, an assembly of a number of multiple fiber bundles or cables fabricated to facilitate installation into a system.

fiber optic (FO) cable: Can accommodate between 12 and 144 single mode fiber channels, to handle high density routes and ultra-long distances. Various single mode cables are available for operation at 1300 nm. Cables can be ordered for specific applications with attenuation as low as 0.4 dB/Km and maximum dispersion as low as 3.5 ps/nm-Km.

fiber optics (FO) electrostatic plotting system: Enables on-line electrostatic plotting up to two miles from the host computer without repeaters. Transmission rates in excess of 132 bytes/sec are possible with some systems. Optical signals are immune to electromagnetic and radio frequency interference. They do not generate electromagnetic fields or carry an electrical charge. Thus, the risk of unauthorized access to information is reduced, and the risk of shorts and electrical surges is eliminated. This type of fiber optic system (one transmitting and one receiving fiber optic modem) is compatible with various controllers for printers and plotters.

fiber optic (FO) local area network: Allows up to 24 personal computers with associated disk drives and printers to interact over fiber optic transmission lines. It allows as many as 24 users to crosscommunicate simultaneously. The network supports message transfer or file sharing, thus reducing floppy disk handling. Other fiber optic benefits: (a) increased distance between computers and active star node; (b) small cable size; (c) freedom from electromagnetic interference; and (d) ease of installation.

fiber optic (FO) modem: With an RS-232, RS-422, or CCITT V.35 interface, propagates control functions in both directions to provide terminal to central processing unit link up. Sync speeds are 1.2k to 115k bps. In addition, a typical FO modem has a true T1 interface via a barrier strip that provides 4-wire termination to the T1 link. A Bell 306 modem replacement, CSY-306 is a full-duplex sync fibre optic modem. Electrical interfaces are CCITT V.35 or EIA RS-499/422 or 423. Versions are available for remote loopback or data and external clock only. A high speed fiber optic digital communications link features up to 20M bps NRZ data transmission rate. Equipment electrical isolation, ground loop avoidance, data transmission security, and TTL input/output compatibility are other features.

fiber optic (FO) multiplexer: Can multiplex synchronous data rates from 2.4k to 76.8k bits per second (bps) on each channel. This type of unit can also multiplex asychronous rates up to 100k bps. An 8-channel device may be expanded to 16 channels. It is equipped with either RS-232, V.35, or RS-422 interfaces. Each channel may be provided with a different interface to serve a wide variety of terminal networks. Unlike other standard T1 multiplexers, this type can be powered from office ac lines.

Fibonacci number: An integer in the Fibonacci series.

Fibonacci search: A dichotomizing search; in each step of the search the original set or remaining subset is subdivided in accordance with successive smaller numbers in the Fibonacci series. If the number of items in the set is not equal to a Fibonacci number, the number of items in the set is assumed to equal the next higher Fibonacci number.

Fibonacci series: A number series in which each number is equal to the sum of the two preceding numbers.

fiche: See microfiche.

field: A set of one or more adjacent columns on a punched card or one or more bit positions in a complete word consistently used to record similar information.

field alterable read-only memories (ROMs):   These work with many popular minicomputers. They are packaged on a single printed circuit board. Some field alterable ROMs can be programmed at the single-bit level. With capacitive type units, the alteration is almost as simple as a pencil erasure. Any discrete bit in storage can be reprogrammed repeatedly, even while the system is operating.

Fieldata: A family of automatic data processing equipment designed and built to be used in the field by the U.S. Army. Includes such Fieldata programs as: (a) DYSEAC, (b) FADAC, (c) Basicpac, (d) Compac, and (e) the Mobidic series of systems as applied to control and command plus logistics, intelligence, and fire detection.

Fieldata code: 1. The U.S. Military code used in data processing as a compromise between conflicting manufacturers' codes. 2. A standardized military data transmission code, 7 data bits plus 1 parity bit.

field data: An area located in the computer's main memory which contains a data record.

field developed program: A licensed program that performs a function for the user. It may interact with program products, system control programming, or currently available type 1, type 2, or type 3 programs, or it may be a stand-alone program.

field section: The ability of computers to isolate a particular data field within one computer word (or even in two, three, or four words) without isolating the entire word.

field service technician: An employee who assists field service representatives in the installation and maintenance of computer systems and equipment in the plant or at customer installations.

FIGS: See figures shift.

figurative: Data item which is descriptive of its own magnitude, value, or size, such as, cosin 40° or simply, 100.

figures shift: 1. A control character in the Baudot code after which characters are intrepreted as belonging to the uppercase grouping that contains numerics, punctuation, and special symbols. 2. A physical shift in a teletypewriter (5-level Baudot-coded teletypewriter with a 3-row keyboard) that enables the printing of numbers, symbols, and punctuation marks in the uppercase mode.

file: A collection of records; an organized collection of information directed toward some purpose. The records in a file may or may not be sequenced according to a key contained in each record.

file activity ratio: A ratio pertaining to the number of file elements in which changes or transactions are made during a specific updating run or in a given period, to the total number of records or elements in the file. If out of a total of 100 records, 20 are updated in a specific month, the activity ratio is thus 20 percent for this file.

file addressing: A procedure designed for those data records which have a particular key or code designed to identify the data. When the program is given this key it can locate and use the data at the particular file address.

file analysis: The examination, study, and resolution of file characteristics to determine similarities, number and type of redundancies, and to check labeling and listing of documents which affect data elements contained in files.

file checks: Specific hardware checks for faulty tapes without loss of computer time or manual intervention.

file contention: A conflict which arises in a multiprogramming or multitalking environment when more than one active (i.e., initiated but not completed) program or task requires the use of the same file or files. Special precautions must be taken in sharedfile systems where more than one simultaneously active program can change files so that time is not lost, changes negated, or that file lockout does not occur.

file control system: A system designed to aid in the storage and retrieval of data without restriction as to types of input/-output devices.

file conversion: The transformation of parts of records, customer account records, employee records, and the like from their original documents into magnetic files by the computer.

file event: A single-file access, either reading or writing. The processing of an action usually requires one or more file events.

file feed: An extension device which increases the punch card capacity of the feed hopper peripheral devices.

file forms: A file of all of the forms needed for an activity and usually filed according to function.

file gap: An interval of space or time associated with a file to indicate or signal the end of the file.

file identification: The coding required to identify each physical unit of the output of electronic data processing machine runs.

file label: A set of alphanumeric characters that uniquely identify the contents of a particular roll of magnetic tape or a portion of a roll of magnetic tape. This file label is written on magnetic tape as a block which contains the file name, reel number, date written, and date expired.

file layout: The arrangement and structure of data in a file, including the sequence and size of its components. By extension, a file layout might be the description thereof.

file lockout: An adverse situation which can occur in multiprogramming or multitasking environments. Two simultaneously active programs each request the same two files for updating and each is granted exclusive access to one but cannot proceed without access to the other; hence both programs are "stranded" in an incomplete stage and continue to occupy main storage and epu cycles as well as preventing other tasks from using the files. Several techniques have evolved to prevent this situation.

file maintenance: The activity of keeping a file up to date by adding, changing, or deleting data.

file maintenance (graphic): The process designed to update physical representation such as microfilm, film prints, cathode-ray tube (CRT) output copies, etc.

file management: A designed procedure or set of processes for the creation of files and their maintenance.

file mark: A special indication on an external storage device that informs the program that the end of data has been read on the device. A file mark is written by the input/output label system after the header label, after the check-point recording, if any, and before and after the trailer labels of output files.

file organization: The procedure of organizing various information files; these files are often random-access files to develop maximized use of storage and swift retrieval for processing.

file-oriented system: If reference to file storage is the principle or key basis of a system, it is considered to be file-oriented. Auxiliary storage used as fundamental or essential in many commercial systems might be file-oriented, while generally considered incidental in scientific systems.

file packing density: The number of characters that can be stored per unit of length (e.g., on some makes of magnetic tape drives, the inch).

file preparation: The ordering, sorting, and handling of parts records, customer account records, employee records, and the like from their original or copied documents into a form suitable for transformation via the computer onto magnetic files for storage.

file print: A printout of the contents of a file stored on some storage device, usually for the reason of aiding debugging.

file processing: Modification of a file to incorporate changes that involve arithmetic operations; for example, receipts, issues, returns, and losses of stock items.

file protection: A device or method which prevents accidental erasure of operative data on magnetic tape reels.

file protection ring: A detachable ring which can be fitted to the hub of a magnetic reel to show the status of the reel. In some computer systems write permit rings are used.

file randomizing, key: The location of a record in a random-access file is found by means of a key set of characters that identify the file. The key is converted to a random number, the random number is converted to the address where the item may be stored. If the item is not in this pocket an overflow pocket changed to the first pocket will be searched.

file (secondary) switching center: Telephonic switching in which a group of local centers are all connected by trunk circuits.

file security: The relative privacy or inaccessibility of files from unauthorized users. As computers are used more and more frequently in the future as depositories of many kinds of information, file security will become an important legal issue.

file separator (FS):   The information separator intended to identify a logical boundary between files.

file wire: Tape, wire, or string used to arrange documents for convenient reference and use.

filing system: An organization or set of plans developed to identify records for efficient retrieval. Filing systems may be sequential, alphabetical, numeric, or coded in various ways.

filling: The process of inserting meaningless characters, such as null characters, zeros, or spaces, into the unused portions of a field, record, or fixed-length block of data. For example, if a fixed-length block of data was expected to be 128 bytes long, and only 100 are used, the other 28 bytes would be filled with null characters, spaces, or zeros. Filling is also known as padding.

film circuits: Microelectronic circuits in which the passive components and their metallic interconnections are formed directly on an insulating substrate and the active semiconductor devices (usually in wafer form) are added subsequently.

film frame: A single photograph on a strip of film containing a series of photographs, such as microfilm.

film scanner: A high-speed input device for scanning and digitizing negative microfilm images such as drawings, charts, maps, and graphs. A cathode-ray tube beam, following a programmed scan pattern, provides a digital reading when any one of many levels of program-selected threshold sensitivity is met or exceeded.

filter: A circuit consisting of a choke and one or more capacitors that selects the frequency of desired channels. Used in trunk and feeder lines for special cable services such as two-way operation. It also suppresses noise interference.

final controlling element: A specifically designed forward controlling element which directly changes the value of the manipulated variable.

final electrical test: The final complete static and dynamic electrical testing of 100 percent of the circuits to ensure that all will function within specification over operating voltage and temperature ranges.

final result: The outcome created at the end of a routine or subroutine, essentially a result presented to the user at the end of a major processing operation.

final trunk: 1. In long-distance telephone communications, the line that connects switching centers which are adjacent to each other in the line of communications. 2. A trunk telephone line to a higher-echelon office that does not have an alternate route.

financial utility: A general-purpose computer utility for handling the bulk of a region's financial transactions. In the future there is expected a rapid expansion of on-line real-time banking with computer power for individual banks being supplied by large banking utilities. Retail stores are likely to be tied in, and shopping with "money cards" will become commonplace. As more and more business are included, the money card will replace both checks and currency as the normal medium of exchange.

finding: Identifying and then selecting one object in a group. The operation terminates when the object is found.

fine index: A secondary index in a pair of indexes used to locate a particular file record. The higher or mass index would often be considered the coarse index.

fine sort: A term used to describe the act of sorting and posting media into alphabetic or numeric sequence.

finite: A quantity that has a limit or boundary.

fire control: As used in military services, the control over the aiming, fusing, timing, and firing of weapons, especially those systems which use computers for the firing of guns or flight control of missiles.

firing: The heavy flow of electrons from cathode to plate in a gas tube.

firing potential: The potential applied to the plate of a gas diode or the grid of a thyratron at which firing occurs.

firmware: An extension to a computer's basic command (instruction) repertoire to create microprograms for a user-oriented instruction set. This extension to the basic instruction set is done in read-only memory and not in software. The read-only memory converts the extended instructions to the basic instructions of the computer.

first detector: The heterodyne detector in a superheterodyne.

first generation: The period of technology in computer design utilizing vacuum tubes, off-line storage on drum or disk, and programming in machine language.

first-generation computer: A computer utilizing vacuum tube components.

first-in first-out (FIFO): A queuing technique in which the next item to be retrieved is the item that has been in the queue for the longest time.

first-in first-out (FIFO) buffering: A method of ordering communications messages in the order of their arrival at the receiving end of the communications line. Messages are stacked in a message buffer in order of their arrival. The buffer is serviced periodically, which clears out and processes the messages, by repeatedly processing the oldest messages first.

first-level message: Under time-sharing option (TSO), a diagnostic message which identifies a general condition; more specific information is issued in a secondlevel message if the text is followed by a "+."

first-order time constant: As related to a first-order system, the time required for the output to complete 63.2 percent of the total rise or decay as a result to step change of the input.

first-pass own coding (sorting): Instructions created by the programmer in assembly or absolute form. They are designed to be executed by a sort during the first pass of the file after input program has been loaded, but prior to execution of first-pass sequencing instructions.

five level: Teletypewriter code that uses five impulses (plus the start and stop characters) for describing a character.

five-level code: A telegraph code that is designed to utilize five impulses for describing a character. Start and stop elements may be added for asynchronous transmission. A common five-level code is Baudot.

fix: To convert data from floating-point number representation to fixed-point representation.

fixed area (FX): The specific area on a disk on which data files or core image programs may be stored and protected, and whose physical disk addresses are not changed by disk housekeeping (compaction) programs.

fixed block format: A tape coding format in which the number of words appearing in successive blocks identified by the same block address and the number of rows in every block are constant.

fixed block length: The blocks of data have a constant number of words or characters in a system with a fixed block length requirement. This may be because of hardware limitations of a machine, or determined by the program.

fixed connector: Used in flowcharting to indicate that only the result indicator can exist after process completion.

fixed cycle: A preset series of operations which directs machine axis movement and/or causes spindle operation to complete such actions as boring, drilling, tapping, or combinations thereof.

fixed decimal: Restricts the number of decimals to those preselected.

fixed-format messages: Messages in which line control characters must be inserted upon departure from a terminal and deleted upon arrival at a terminal; fixedformat messages are intended for terminals with dissimilar characteristics.

fixed-form coding: Specific coding instructions with a fixed field assigned to particular labels, operations codes, and operand parts of the instructions.

fixed head: A term which relates to the use of stationary, rigidly-mounted reading and writing heads on a bulk memory device. Each head reads or writes a particular track.

fixed-head disk: A disk memory with a multiplicity of heads, each giving access to one read/write track.

fixed-length record: A record having the same length as all other records with which it is associated logically or physically.

fixed-length record file: A file containing a set of records, each containing the same number of characters or very few predetermined record lengths.

fixed page: In System/370 virtual storage systems, a page in real storage that is not to be paged-out.

fixed-plus-variable structure: A type of computer design which accomodates the needs of all users (a requirement in communications).

fixed point: A notation or system of arithmetic in which all numeric quantities are expressed by a predetermined number of digits with the point implicitly located at some predetermined position; contrasted with floating point.

fixed-point arithmetic: 1. A method of calculation in which operations take place in an invariant manner, and in which the computer does not consider the location of the radix point. This is illustrated by desk calculators or slide rules, with which the operator must keep track of the decimal point. Similarly with many automatic computers, in which the location of the radix point is the programmer's responsibility. Contrast with floating-point arithmetic. 2. A type of arithmetic in which the operands and results of all arithmetic operations must be scaled so as to have a magnitude between certain fixed values.

fixed-point calculation: A calculation made with fixed-point arithmetic.

fixed-point number: A number which is represented in fixed-point form in contrast to floating-point form. Example: FORTRAN variables.

fixed-point operation: A calculation of numbers in which the arithmetic point, binary or decimal, is assumed to be or is held at a specific relative position for each number.

fixed-point part: In a floating-point representation, the numeral or a pair of numerals representing a number, that is the fixed-point factor by which the power is multiplied.

fixed-point representation: A notation or system of arithmetic in which all numerical quantities are expressed by a predetermined number of digits with the point implicity located at some predetermined position.

fixed-position addressing: Permits selective updating of tape information, as in magnetic disk or drum storage devices. Units as small as a single computer word may be stored or recorded on tape without disturbing adjacent information. Data blocks are numbered and completely addressable. Inter-record gaps are eliminated, thereby increasing tape-storage capacity.

fixed program computer: A computer in which the instructions are permanently stored or wired in, performed automatically, and are not subject to change either by the computer or the programmer except by rewiring or changing the storage input. Related to wired program computer.

fixed-radix notation: A positional representation in which the significances of successive digit positions are successive integral powers of a single radix; when the radix is positive, permissible values of each digit range from zero to one less than the radix, and negative integral powers of the radix are used to represent fractions.

fixed-ratio transmission codes: Concerns

various error detection codes using a fixed ratio of bits concept.

fixed sequential format: Means of identifying a word by its location in the block. Words must be presented in a specific order and all possible words preceding the last desired word must be present in each block.

fixed-tolerance-band compaction: A specific type of data compaction for storage or transmission of data, where data becomes significant only when the data deviates beyond preset limits of a range. For example, data transmission will not occur unless numbers are reached between 50 to 100.

fixed type bar: A type bar on a printer which cannot be removed by an operator and thus giving to that printer unit a fixed alphabet.

fixed variable: 1. A variable in the problem (logical, structural, primal, or dual) fixed at zero level for feasibility. 2. A variable to be bounded away from zero is sometimes "fixed" at its bound in a bounded variable algorithm so that the transformed variable associated with it is then feasible at zero level, thus permitting arbitrary upper and lower bounds.

fixed word length: Data are treated in units of a fixed number of characters or bits (as contrasted with variable word length).

fixed word length computer: A computer in which data is treated in units of a fixed number of characters or bits.

flag: A bit (or bits) used to store one bit of information. A flag has two stable states and is the software analog of a flip-flop.

flag-setting peripheral: A peripheral which does not halt central processor activity when a peripheral interrupt occurs. Instead it sets a flag in core and waits until the operating system examines the flag to determine what action to take.

flat cable: A cable containing flat metallic ribbon conductors, all lying side-by-side in the same plane and imbedded in a material which insulates and binds them together.

flat-card resolving potentiometer: A particular type of potentiometer which has an element which is a square slab or card wound with resistance wire.

flat conductor: Wire manufactured in tape form so that multiwire tapes for telephones may be laid easily under carpets or on walls.

flat fading: That type of fading in which all components of the received radio signal simultaneously fluctuate in the same proportion.

flexed-reference modulation: A type of modulation in which the choice of the significant condition for any signal element is based on a fixed reference.

flexi mode: Allows entry of numbers to any decimal setting without the need to enter the decimal point.

flip-flop: A bi-stable device; a device capable of assuming two stable states; a bi-stable device which may assume a given stable state depending upon the pulse history of one or more input points and having one or more output points. The device is capable of storing a bit of information; controlling gates, etc.; a toggle.

flip-flop circuit: An electronic circuit having two stable states, one input line and one output line, such that as each successive pulse is received, the output line changes between two alternative conditions, e.g. high to low or off to on.

flip-flop delay (D): A flip-flop whose output is a function of the input which appeared one pulse earlier; for example, if a "1" appeared at the input, the output after the next clock pulse will be a "1."

flip-flop equipment: An electronic or electromechanical device that causes automatic alternation between two possible circuit paths. The same term is applied to any mechanical operation which is analogous to the principles of the flip-flop.

flip-flop sign: The specific flip-flop used to store the algebraic sign of numbers.

flip-flop sign control: The control of a specific flip-flop which stores the algebraic sign of numbers.

flip-flop storage: A bi-stable storage device which stores binary data as states of flip-flop elements.

flip-flop string: An important computer property is that the state of one flip-flop can be transferred to another by means of special triggering circuits. That is, a number stored in one strip of flip-flops can be transferred to another string. In this way, numbers can be transferred from place to place in a computer. This function is so important that the flip-flop circuits generally include a pair of triggering circuits for this purpose.

float: 1. A general banking term for the amount of funds in the process of collection, represented by checks in the possession of one bank but drawn on other banks. Further current definitions of float include many forms of taking advantage of delays in the payments process. Float is used intentionally or perceived as beneficial by banks, businesses, and individual consumers. Some organizations make systematic short-term use of money made available by float. Faster check processing via Electronic Funds Transfer System (EFTS) will reduce float, as will bill payment and point-of-sale payment mechanisms which involve immediate funds transfer rather than the use of checks. 2. To convert data from fixed-point number representation to floating-point representation.

float factor: The absolute address at the beginning of any area of storage to which reference is made when indirect addressing methods are used to locate items in the storage area. It is also applied to the absolute address of the beginning of the program area in storage.

floating character: A specific character which has as its location one place more significant than the otherwise more significant character position.

floating controller: Concerns a special controller designed so that the rate of change of the output develops a continuous function of the actuating error signal, i.e., the output of the controller can remain at any value in its operating range when the actuating error signal is zero and constant and is then said to "float."

floating decimal: Puts no restrictions on the position of the decimal point.

floating-decimal arithmetic: See floating-point arithmetic.

floating point: A form of number representation in which quantities are represented by a bounded number (mantissa) and a scale factor (characteristic or exponent) consisting of a power of the number base, e.g., $127.6 = 0.1276 \times 10^3$ where the bounds are 0 and 1.

floating-point arithmetic: Arithmetic used in a computer where the computer keeps track of the decimal point (contrasted with fixed-point arithmetic).

floating-point arithmetic hardware: A central processing unit (CPU) circuitry feature usually found on larger computers or on scientific computers which is capable of directly performing operations on floating-point numbers without the use of subroutines.

floating-point base: In floating-point representation, the fixed positive integer that is the base of the power.

floating-point calculation: A calculation made with floating-point arithmetic.

floating-point notation: A form of notation in which quantities are represented by a number multiplied by the number base raised to a power e.g., the decimal number 397 can be written as 3.97×10^2, or 0.397×10^3.

floating-point number: Shifting a number to the right or left of the decimal point. This is done if a problem's solution requires values of numbers that are either too large or too small to be expressed by the computer. For instance, the decimal number 6510 may be expressed as 0.651×10^4, 0.0651×10^5, 0.00651×10^6, etc. The exponent of the number-system base is the scale factor or the number of places the number is shifted. Some systems use fixed-point arithmetic, and have no automatic hardware feature for handling the scaling factor or exponent.

floating-point processor: Executes arithmetic instructions between floating-point accumulators and between memory and any of the floating-point accumulators. When floating-point computation must be interrupted, a single instruction saves the contents of all accumulators and status registers in a hardware stack. Another instruction reverses the process. Distributed parallel logic mounted on the floating-point and the fixed-point processor boards allows a program to execute floatingpoint arithmetic while the central processing unit does other processing.

floating-point radix: See floating-point base.

floating-point representation: A number representation system in which each number, as represented by a pair of numerals, equals one of those numerals times a power of an implicit fixed positive integer base where the power is equal to the implicit base raised to the exponent represented by the other numeral.

floating-significance control: The bit, in the program status doubleword, that indicates whether (if 0) or not (if 1) the result of a floating-point operation is checked for significance.

floating symbol address: A label chosen to identify a particular word, function or other information in a routine, independent of the location of the information within the routine.

floppy: A disk memory based on interchangeable flexible plastic disks, usually with a moveable head able to access many read/write tracks.

flowchart: 1. A graphical representation for the definition, analysis, or solution of a problem, in which symbols are used to represent operations, data, flow, equipment, etc. 2. See data flowchart.

flowchart symbol: Symbols used to represent operations, equipment, data media, etc. in a flowchart.

flowchart text: The descriptive information that is associated with flowchart symbols.

flow direction: In flowcharting, the antecedent-tosuccessor relation, indicated by arrows or other conventions, between operations on a flowchart.

flow-process diagram: A graphic representation of the major steps of work in process. The illustrative symbols may represent documents, machines or actions taken during the process. The area of concentration is on where or who does what, rather than how it is to be done. (Same as process chart.)

flow trace: A debugging device which prints out contents of various registers and memory location in a particular program segment specified by the user.

fluid logic: Used to control the operations of pneumatic computers. Relates to the simulating of logical operations by means of changing the flow and pressure in a fluid – either gas or liquid.

fluorescent screen: The coating on the inner wall of the cathode-ray tube; the means of converting electrical energy into light.

flutter: 1. Distortion due to variation in loss resulting from the simultaneous transmission of a signal at another frequency; 2.

A similar effect due to phase distortion; 3. In recording and reproducing, deviation of frequency which results from irregular motion during recording, duplication, or reproduction. Note: One important usage is to denote the effect of variation in the transmission characteristics of a loaded telephone circuit, caused by the action of telegraph direct currents on the loading coils.

flutter and wow: Changes in signal output frequency caused by tape speed variations occurring at relatively low and relatively high rates.

flux: The lines of force of a magnetic field.

flyback power supply: The high voltage circuit in cathode-ray terminals.

flywheel effect: The effect of a resonant circuit in which an input electrical pulse of less than one cycle produces a complete output cycle.

FM: See frequency modulation.

focusing coil: The coil in a writing tube which guides the electrons in the beam.

following error in servo system (uncompensated): In numerical control (N/C) contouring system, while the machine is moving under servo control, the instantaneous machine position lags the instantaneous command position. This lag can be calculated and is expressend in thousandths per inch per minute (0.001 per in. min.).

follow-up file: A file in which special matters are flagged for attention at the appropriate time (also called a "tickler" file).

follow-up potentiometer: A servo potentiometer that generates the signal for comparison with the input signal.

follow-up servo: A servomechanism which follows changes in the input signal.

font: 1. A family or assortment of characters of a given size and style, for example, 9 point Bodoni Modern. 2. See type font.

font change character (FC): (ISO) A control character that selects and makes effective a change in the specific shape, or size, or shape and size of the graphics for a set of graphemes, the character set remaining unchanged.

font retide: An optical character recognition term referring to a system of lines forming character outlines.

font, type: A type face of a given size.

forbidden combination: A combination of bits or other representations that is not valid according to some criteria.

forbidden-combination check: A check, usually automatic, used to test for the occurrence of a nonpermissible code expression. A self-checking code or errordetecting code uses code expressions such that one or more errors in a code expression produces a forbidden combination. A parity check makes use of a selfchecking code employing binary digits in which the total number of 1s or 0s in each permissible code expression is always even or always odd. A check may be made either for even parity or odd parity. A redundancy check employs a self-checking code that makes use of redundant digits called check digits. Some of the various names that have been applied to this type of check are forbidden-pulse combination, unused commands, improper instruction, unallowable digits, improper command, false code, forbidden digit, nonexistent code, and unused code.

force: To intervene manually in a routine and cause the computer to execute a jump instruction.

forecasting: Various types of plans and determinations concerning potential future situations. Many forecasts are unhappily based on projection and analysis of past results instead of being viewed in the light of very current experience. Statistical procedures and probabilities, as well as new operations research techniques for modern forecasting, make use of such factors and techniques as seasonal variation, trends, random variables, queuing, econometrics, etc.

foreground: 1. In multiprogramming, the environment in which high-priority programs are executed. 2. Under time-sharing option (TSO), the environment in which all programs are swapped in and out of main storage to allow central processing unit (CPU) time to be shared among terminal users. All command processor programs execute in the foreground. Contrast with background.

foreground/background technique: Automatic execution of programs on a priority basis, allowing the lowerpriority programs to execute when higher-priority programs are not utilizing the system.

foregrounding: An important processing procedure in which top-priority processing most often results from real-time entries which usually have precedence, through the use of interrupts into lower priority or background processing.

foreground-initiated background job: Under timesharing option (TSO), a job submitted from a remote terminal for scheduling and execution in the background.

foreground job: 1. A high-priority job, usually a real-time job. 2. A teleprocessing or graphic display job that has an indefinite running time during which communication is established with one or more users at local or remote terminals. 3. Under time-sharing option (TSO), any job executed in a swapped region of main storage, such as a command processor or a terminal user's program.

foreground message processing program: Under timesharing option (TSO), a problem program run in the foreground using the telecommunications access method (TCAM) to handle messages for one or more terminals.

foreground processing: The automatic execution of the programs that have been designed to pre-empt the use of the computing facilities. Usually a real-time program. Contrast with background processing.

foreground program:　1. In multiprogramming, a high priority program. 2. Under time-sharing option (TSO), a program executed in a swapped region of main storage.

foreground region:　A region to which a foreground job is assigned.

foreground routine:　Same as foreground program.

foreign attachments:　Since the 1968 Carterphone decision, "foreign" (i.e., non-Bell) attachments have been permitted on the direct dial network. Formerly, a Data Access Arrangement (DAA) was required between the customer-owned modem and the line. The DAA is said to protect the network from the modem. The low speed asynchronous modem may also be coupled acoustically or inductively through the conventional handset.

foreign exchange (FX):　A service by which a telephone or private branch exchange (PBX) in one city, instead of being connected directly to a central office (CO) in that city, is connected directly to a CO in a distant city via a private line. To callers it appears that the telephone or PBX is located in the distant city.

foreign-exchange service:　That service that connects a customer's telephone to a telephone company central office normally not serving the customer's location.

fore-tape sort:　A specific technique which requires the merging of data from two input tapes and two output tapes, and consequently, merges the data on those tapes to one final output tape, which contains the merged data in proper sequence.

form:　A printed or typed document whch usually has blank spaces for the insertion of information.

formal language:　One specifically designed for ease of communication in a particular area of endeavor, but one that is not yet natural to that area. This is contrasted with a natural language which has evolved through long usage.

formal logic:　The study of the structure and form of valid argument without regard to the meaning of the terms in the argument.

format:　The predetermined arrangement of characters, fields, lines, page numbers, punctuation marks, etc. Refers to input, output and files.

format character nonprint:　A specific control character used to control a printer. This character does not print but may cause backspacing, tabulating, new lines, etc.

format effector (FE):　A control character intended to be used by a printing or display device for controlling the layout or position of information. Same as layout character.

format loop:　The paper tape loop on a line printer used to control the throwing of paper, especially when printing on preprinted stationary.

forms design:　A planned process or procedure for producing specific formats regarding the relationships and arrangements of data and information.

forms designer:　An individual who designs, coordinates, and controls the use and circulation of all company forms.

forms management:　The management function which assures that unneeded forms do not exist, and that needed forms are designed, produced (internal or external) and distributed economically and efficiently.

form stop:　The automatic device on a printer which stops the machine when paper has run out.

FORTRAN:　FORmula TRANslator – the language for a scientific procedural programming system.

Fortran American Standards Association (ASA): A standardized Fortran set as specified by ASA.

fortuituos distortion: A type of telegraph distortion which results in the intermittent shortening or lengthening of the signals. This distortion is random in nature and can be caused by battery fluctuations, hits on the line, power induction, etc.

forty-four repeater: A telephone repeater that employs two amplifiers and operates on a four-wire system, without making use of hybrid arrangments.

forward-acting code: An error-control code that contains redundancy added in such a way that one or more characters received in error can be reconstructed at the receiving end without additional information from the source.

forward controlling elements: Specific design elements in the controlling system which change a variable in response to the actuating error signal.

forward error correction: A method of error correction during data transmission in which the receiving terminal locates and corrects the errors itself, instead of signalling the transmitting terminal to resend the data. For example, data can be transmitted using a Hamming Code. A Hamming Code interleaves a byte in four check bits. Each check bit reflects the states of certain real bits. If an error occurs, the check bits are scanned to determine which real bit is in error. Thus, the error can be self-corrected.

forward path: The transmission path from the loop activating signal to the loop output signal in a feedback control loop.

four-address: An instruction format containing four address parts.

four-address instruction: A machine instruction usually consisting of the addresses of two operands, the address for storing the result, the address of the next instruction, the command to be executed, and miscellaneous indices. Same as three-plus-one-address instruction.

Fourier analysis: The determination of the harmonic components of a complex waveform either mathematically or by a wave analyzer device.

Fourier principle: Shows that all repeating waveforms can be resolved into sine wave components, consisting of a fundamental and a series of harmonics at multiples of this frequency. It can be extended to prove that nonrepeating waveforms occupy a continuous frequency spectrum.

Fourier transform: A mathematical relation between the energy in a transient and that in a continuous energy spectrum of adjacent component frequencies.

four-out-of-eight code: A communication code which facilitates error detection because four of the eight bits representing a character are always marking.

four-phase modulation: A type of modulation designed for the carrier to shift between four distinct phases; the four possible phases serve to encode two bits.

four-plus-one-address: An instruction containing four operand addresses and one control address.

four-quadrant multiplier: A multiplier in which operation is unrestricted as to the sign of the input variables.

four-row keyboard: The keyboard in Model 33 and 35 teletypewriter equipment.

four-tape sort: To sort input data supplied on two tapes, which are sorted into incomplete sequences alternately on two output tapes. The output tapes are used for input on the succeeding pass, resulting in progressively longer sequences after each pass until the data are all in one sequence on one output tape.

four-wire channel: The concept of signals simultaneously following separate and distinct paths in opposite directions in the transmission medium.

four-wire circuit: A two-way circuit using two paths so arranged that communication currents are transmitted in one direction, on one path, and in the opposite direction to the other path. The transmission path may or may not employ four wires.

four-wire repeater: A telephone repeater used in a four-wire circuit. It consists of two amplifiers, one servicing one side of transmission direction of the four-wire circuit and the other servicing the second side of the four-wire circuit.

four-wire system: See four-wire circuit.

four-wire terminating set: Hybrid arrangement by which four-wire circuits are terminated on a two-wire basis for interconnection with two-wire circuits.

fox message: A standard message used for testing telegraph circuits and machines because it includes all the alphanumerics as well as most of the function characters. The message is: THE QUICK BROWN FOX JUMPS OVER THE LAZY DOG'S BACK. 1234567890 STATION NAME SENDING.

fractional part: One of the two elements of the floating-point representation of a number which is not the exponent or power of the base.

fragmenting: The breaking down of a document into a series of terms or descriptors.

frame: 1. An area, one recording position long, extending across the width of a magnetic or paper tape perpendicular to its movement. Several bits or punched positions may be included in a single frame through the use of different recording positions across the width of the tape. 2. A time period encompassing a character, a character group, or a bit-group cycle in a multiplexing process.

frame connector: A portion of metal or plastic which surrounds a multiple-contact connector which has a removable body or insert, i.e., the frame supports the insert and permits a procedure for mounting the connector to a panel.

frame frequency: The frame frequency is the number of times per second that a frame of pulses is transmitted or received.

frame grabber: A device in a visual display unit which allows storage and continuous display of a frame of data.

frame-grounding circuit: A conductor that is bonded electrically to the machine frame and/or to any conducting parts which are exposed to operating personnel. This circuit may further be connected to external grounds as may be required by applicable underwriters codes.

frame header: The four fields which compose a frame, collectively.

frame synchronizing pulse: A frame synchronizing pulse is a recurrent signal establishing each frame.

frame table entry (FTE):   In System/370 virtual storage system, an entry in the page frame table that describes how a frame is being used.

frame (type A):   A distributing frame carrying on one side (horizontal) all outside lines, and on the other side (vertical) the terminations of the central office equipment and protective devices for them.

frame (type B):   A distributing frame carrying on one side (vertical) all outside lines and protective devices for those lines, and on the other side (horizontal) all connections of the outside lines toward the central office equipment.

framing: The process of selecting the bit groupings representing one or more characters from a continuous stream of bits.

framing bits: Noninformation-carrying bits used to make possible the separation of characters in a bit stream.

franchise: Contractual agreement between a community antenna television (CATV) and the governing municipal authority. Under federal regulation, a franchise, certificate, contract, or any other agreement amounts to a license to operate.

free access floor: Raised floor which conceals computer cables and thus improves support for the equipment. Floor panels are removable to permit servicing or inspection.

free field: A property of information processing recording media which permits recording of information without regard to a preassigned or fixed field, e.g., in information retrieval devices, information may be dispersed in the record in any sequence or location.

free oscillations: The oscillating currents and voltages which continue to flow in a circuit after the voltage (impressed) has been removed.

free routing: That method of traffic handling wherein messages are forwarded toward their destination over any available channel without depending on a predetermined routing plan.

freeze point specifications: A point reached in programming any complex system when the functional specifications of the operational program are frozen.

frequency: 1. The number of times an electromagnetic signal repeats an identical cycle in a unit of time, usually one second. One hertz (Hz) is one cycle per second. A KHz (kilohertz) is one thousand cycles per second; a MHz (megahertz) is one million cycles per second; a GHz (gigahertz) is one billion cycles per second. 2. The rate of recurrence of some cyclic or repetitive event, such as the rate of repetition of a sine-wave electrical current, usually expressed in cycles per second, or hertz.

frequency allocation: Frequency on which a transmitter has to operate, within specified tolerance. Bands of frequencies for specified services are allocated by international agreement.

frequency-analysis compaction: A form of data compaction using specific coded expressions to represent a number of different frequencies of different magnitudes that express, compare, or indicate a curve or geometric configuration. Only identifiable coefficients are necessary to compare and thus transmit a whole series of fundamental frequencies.

frequency changer: 1. A machine designed to receive power at one frequency and to deliver it at another frequency. 2. A combination of oscillator and modulator valves used in a superhet receiver to change the incoming signal from its original carrier frequency to a fixed intermediate carrier frequency; also called conversion mixer, conversion transducer, frequency converter.

frequency-change signaling: A telegraph signaling method in which one or more particular frequencies correspond to each desired signaling condition of a telegraph code. The transition from one set of frequencies to the other may be either a continuous or a discontinuous change in frequency or in phase.

frequency departure: The amount of variation of a carrier frequency or center frequency from its assigned value. Note: This concept was formerly described as frequency deviation, a usage which is now obsolete because of the changed meaning in phase and frequency modulation.

frequency discrimination: The operation of selecting a desired frequency (or frequencies) from a spectrum of frequencies.

frequency discriminator: A circuit, the output from which is proportional to frequency or phase change in a carrier from condition of no frequency or phase modulation.

frequency distortion: A type of distortion in which certain frequencies are lost or discriminated against.

frequency distribution: Usually concerns a table showing the number of occurrences of each value displayed in an ordered array or pattern.

frequency diversity: Methods for signal transmission or reception in which some information is transmitted simultaneously on more specific frequency bands to thus minimize the disturbances of selective frequency fading.

frequency divider: 1. A counter with an added gating structure which provides an output pulse after receiving a specified number of input pulses. The outputs of all flip-flops are not accessible. 2. A circuit which reduces the frequency of an oscillator.

frequency division multiplex (FDM): 1. A multiplex system in which the available transmission frequency exchange range is divided into narrower bands, each band used for a separate channel. 2. In this signaling process each signal channel modulates a separate subcarrier which has a frequency spaced to avoid overlapping of the subcarrier sidebands. The selection and demodulation of each signal channel is accomplished on the basis of its frequency.

frequency division multiplexing (FDM) advantages: The primary advantage to end users is its relatively low cost in applications where FDM's aggregate bit-rate limit is not constraining. FDM provides some of this economy by eliminating the need for a separate modem or data set at each remote terminal site, since the multiplexer is designed usually so that it also performs the modulation and demodulation functions. Also, FDMs are cascadable readily or, to put it another way, have features which facilitate dropping and inserting at intermediate points along a multiplexed chan-

nel. Thus FDM is cost effective particularly in multiplexing an unclustered terminal group whose aggregate bit rate does not exceed the above mentioned limit.

frequency division multiplexing (FDM) limitations: One of the limitations of FDM stems from the need for guard bands or safety zones between adjacent subchannels to prevent the electrical overlapping of signals. These guard bands impose a practical limit on the efficiency of an FDM system. For example, with state-of-the-art FDM equipment operating on a private voice grade line, the maximum composite or aggregate low-speed bit rate achievable will typically range from 1800 to 2000 bits per second, although in some cases slightly higher. Generally speaking, other types of sharing must be used if a higher aggregate bit-rate requirement exists.

frequency doubler: Frequency multiplier in which the output current or voltage has twice the frequency of the input. Achieved by simple push/pull tuned circuits.

frequency doubling: Introduction of marked doublefrequency components through lack of polarization in an electromagnetic or electrostatic transducer, in which the operating forces are proportional to the square of the operating currents and voltages respectively.

frequency drift: Change in frequency of oscillation because of internal (aging, change of characteristic or emission) or external (variation in supply voltages, or ambient temperature) causes.

frequency-exchange signaling: A frequency-exchange signaling method in which the change from one signaling condition to another is accomplished by decay in amplitude of one or more frequencies and by the build-up amplitude of one or more other frequencies.

frequency meter: Simple or complex apparatus for relating an unknown frequency to a standard, ultimately the yearly orbiting of the earth around the sun. The basic frequency is that of a quartz-ring oscillator at 10^5 Hz, other frequencies being related to this by dividing, multiplying, or heterodyning. Ultimate standardization is now via an atomic clock.

frequency modulation (FM):   A procedure for varying the frequency of a carrier of fixed amplitude above and below the normal carrier frequency, in accordance with the amplitude variations of an applied signal voltage. Specifically, the rate in hertz or bits per second for a sine wave carrier to be modulated by an intelligence-bearing signal.

frequency modulation (FM) discriminator: Electron tube or transistor device which, after detecting the frequency rate of change of an FM signal, is able to change this to a signal voltage equal to the original modulating signal.

frequency monitor: Nationally or internationally operated equipment to ascertain whether or not a transmitter is operating within its assigned bandwidth.

frequency multiplexing: A method for dividing a circuit into many channels within the bandwidth of the circuit.

frequency multiplier: A circuit which multiplies the frequency of an input signal by a whole number.

frequency response: A measure of the ability of a device to take into account, follow, or act upon a varying condition; e.g., as applied to amplifiers, the frequencies at which the gain has fallen to the one-half power point or to 0.707 of the voltage gain, either at the high or low end of the frequency spectrum.

frequency response characteristic: An established frequency-dependent relation, in both amplitude and phase, between steady-state sinusoidal inputs and the resulting fundamental sinusoidal outputs; frequency response is plotted on a Bode diagram.

frequency response tests: Tests performed on parts of a control system, showing how the output changes when the input is varied in frequency.

frequency shift: System of telegraph-teletypewriter operation in which the mark signal is one frequency and the space signal a different frequency. Also, the difference between mark and space will vary in different systems, e.g., 170 cps U.S.A., 120 cps Europe.

frequency shift keying (FSK):   Most common form of frequency modulation in which two possible states (one and zero) are transmitted as two separate frequencies.

frequency shift modulation (FSM):   A form of frequency modulation in which the carrier frequency is shifted between a mark frequency and a space frequency in response to the impressed intelligence signal (frequency shift keying).

frequency swing: In communications, the frequency above and below the carrier frequency.

frequency, telephone: A frequency lying within a part of the human audio range. Voice frequencies used for commercial transmission of speech usually lie within the range of 200 to 3500 cycles per second.

frequency tolerance: Maximum permissible deviation of the transmitted carrier frequency as related to assigned frequencies, and expressed as a percentage of assigned frequencies or in hertz.

frequency translation: The transfer of signals occupying a definite frequency band (such as a channel or group of channels) from one position in the frequency spectrum to another, in such a way that the arithmetic frequency difference of signals within the band is unaltered.

frictional error: The difference in values measured in percent of full scale before and after tapping, with the measurand constant.

Friction causing this type of error is known as coulomb or dry friction.

front end: The stages between antenna and i-f amplifier in a superheterodyne.

front-end processing: Communications processors are used to interface communication terminals to a "host" data processing system (an information processor).

front-end processor (FEP):   Used as a device driver, controls the peripheral devices of the central computer, and handles all messages between terminals and programs in the central computer. In performance of these tasks, the front-end processor is responsible for the following: (a) Line control of all communication circuits between the central computer and remote terminals; (b) The control of the interface, typically through a memory channel, to the central computer; (c) Message formatting to translate messages to a format compatible with the destination computer or device; (d) Error checking mission; (e) Device multiplexing to insure the efficient use of channels and circuits; (f) Device control allowing for flexibility in the connection of different peripherals to the central facility. The major advantages of front-end processors are in offloading the central computer processor, memory, and storage facilities, and in providing flexibility in the number and variety of devices that can be connected.

front-end processor (FEP) advantages: 1. The cost of hardware to attach lines is often less with a small computer, possibly because different constructional methods are used; 2. The processing load removed from the main computer will increase the power available considerably for computational purposes; 3. It becomes possible to separate the complete system cleanly into two parts: the main processor and the communications network. This gives increased flexibility and may allow one part to be enhanced or replaced without affecting the other.

front-mounted connector: A particular connector usually mounted or attached to the outside of a panel or casing, i.e., a connector which can be installed so that its mating half is inserted and removed only from the outside of the equipment or panel or casing.

FS: See file separator.

fuel cell: An electrochemical cell which produces electrical energy from the chemical energy of a fuel and an oxidant.

full adder (parallel):   An adder which can be developed from as many three-input adders as there are digits in the input words. The carry output of each operation is connected to one input of the three-digit adder corresponding to the next significant digit position.

full carrier: In radio transmission, carrier power emitted at a level of 6 dB or less below the peak envelope power.

full drive pulse: In coincident-current selection, the resultant of the partical drive pulses which, when applied together, cause the selection of, for example, full read pulse, or full write pulse.

full duplex: Simultaneous communication between two points in both directions.

full-duplex channel: A method of operating a communications circuit so that each end can simultaneously transmit and receive.

full-duplex circuit: Communications circuit operating so that each end can simultaneously transmit and receive.

full-duplex facilities: The main reason for implementing these facilities is to increase the data rate. However, in many cases, after the communication facilities and computer equipment have been installed, and the software is running the communication, the link turns out to be nothing more than a full-duplex capability being used in the half-duplex mode. Some of the problems that make complete utilizations of a full-duplex capability difficult are design of available hardware, buffering capability of computer, and message acknowledgement. The hardware and buffering capability problems are a matter of hardware design and core size respectively.

full-duplex service: A service in which the datacommunication channel is capable of simultaneous and independent transmission and reception.

full-duplex telephone lines: Private lines leased from the local telephone company; they are of the same type as those used for voice transmission, with a speed of 1000 bits per second (167 characters per second). The lines are full-duplex, which permits instantaneous responses to control messages.

full-duplex terminal: The separation of input and output to the point where a user at a terminal can be typing input while the computer is sending him output. In this case "echoing" will be delayed until the output has been completed.

full period: Seven days a week, twenty-four hours a day service. Usually used to refer to level of service in communication companies.

full read pulse: In coincident-current selection, the resultant of the partial drive pulses which, when applied together, cause the selection of, for example, full read pulse, or full write pulse.

full scale: In an analog computer, the nominal maximum value of a computer variable or the nominal maximum value at the output of a computing element.

full subtracter: Capable of forming a representation of the difference between two numbers represented by signals applied to its inputs.

full-wave power supply: A power supply using two diodes which draw current during both the positive and negative half-cycles of the input ac voltage.

fullword: See computer word.

fullword boundary: In the IBM 360 computer, an address that ends in 00, a natural boundary for a 4 byte machine word.

full write pulse: In coincident-current selection, the resultant of the partial drive pulses which, when applied together, cause the selection producing full read pulse, or full write pulse.

fully automatic compiling technique (FACT):   A business compiler designed to accept programs written in English-language statements and translate these progams into thousands of corresponding machine instructions. With FACT, all programs make "business sense" and no time is lost in programmer-to-management translation.

function: 1. One quantity (A) is said to be a function of another quantity (B) when no change can be made in B without producing a corresponding change in A and vice versa. Thus, in the equation $Y^2 = R^2 - X^2$, Y is a function of X. 2. A specific purpose of an entity or its characteristic action. 3. In communications, a machine action such as a carriage return or line feed.

functional address instruction format: Contains no operation part of the instruction as it is implied by the address parts.

functional character: A character whose occurrence in a particular context initiates, modifies, or stops a control operation; i.e., a character which controls carriage return.

functional design: The specification of the working relations between the parts of a system in terms of their characteristic actions.

functional diagram: A specific type of block diagram which represents the functional design and special symbols called functional symbols. Functional design relates to the specification between all parts of a system, including the logic design and equipment used. A graphic representation shows the operational aspects of a system.

functional electronic block (FEB): Another name for a monolithic integrated circuit or thick film circuit.

functional interleaving: The procedure or process designed to have input/output and computing operations proceed independently of one another but interleaved in their sharing of the memory.

functional macroinstructions: Macroinstructions that operate on message segments and perform functions such as (a) message editing, (b) checking validity of codes used in the header, (c) routing messages to specified destinations, (d) maintaining logs of messages, and (e) checking for errors in transmission or specifications.

functional multiplier: A device which takes in the changing values of two functions and puts out the changing value of their product.

function generator: A computing element designed with an output of a specified nonlinear function of its input or inputs. Normal usage excludes multipliers and resolvers.

function generator curve-follower: A function generator that operates by following a curve drawn or constructed on a surface.

function generator map-reader: A bivariant function generator using a probe to detect the voltage at a point on a conducting surface and having coordinates proportional to the inputs.

function keys: Keys on keyboards of input/output or specialized terminals which are used to query the system or have it perform certain operations. For example, on a remote-inquiry terminal used in a stock quotation system, a three letter combination identifies any stock, and earnings, sales, dividends, volume, etc. can be displayed, by punching the right function key.

function relay: In an analog computer, a relay used as a computing element.

functions mode: The modem performs a transformation between the digital signal acceptable to the terminal, and network ports and the host computer and the analog signal employed for transmission. In the modem, the square-edged pulse train from the computer or terminal is transformed to fit in the telephone channel frequencies between 300 and 3000 Hz.

function switch: Has a fixed number of inputs and outputs designed so that the output information is a function of the input information, each expressed in a certain code, signal configuration, or pattern.

function table: 1. Two or more sets of data so arranged that an entry in one set selects one or more entries in the remaining sets. For example, a tabulation of the values of a function for a set of values of the variable, a dictionary. 2. A device constructed of hardware, or a subroutine, which can either decode multiple inputs into a single output or encode a single input into multiple outputs.

function word: The function word contains the operating instructions for the peripheral units, its format depending upon the particular subsystem.

functor: An improper term to be avoided. This term is sometimes used to designate a logic element which performs a specific function or provides a linkage between variables.

fundamental: The basic frequency of a vibrating object emitting sound.

future labels (one-pass assembly only): Labels referenced by the programmer in the operand field of a statement which have not been defined previously. A future patch is prepared by the assembler as a control record to the loader; future labels are unique with one-pass assemblers.

G

gain: The ratio between the output signal and the input signal of a device.

gain, loop: A calculated ratio of the change in the return signal to the change in its corresponding error signal at a specified frequency.

game theory: A mathematical process of selecting an optimum strategy in the face of an opponent who has a strategy of his own.

Gantt chart: A chart of activity against time; such charts have historically been used to schedule or reserve resources for specific activities. Critical path method (CPM) and project evaluation and review techniques (PERT) are devices which have offered substantial improvement in scheduling and allocations; a Gantt chart can be used to express the resource allocation schedule decided upon using PERT/CPM.

gap: 1. An interval of space or time used as an automatic sentinel to indicate the end of a word, record, or file of data on a tape, e.g., a word gap at the end of a word, a record or item gap at the end of a group of words, and a file gap at the end of a group of records or items. 2. The absence of information for a specified length of time or space on a recording medium, as contrasted with marks and sentinels which are the presence of specific information to achieve a similar purpose. Marks are used primarily internally in variable word length machines. Sentinels achieve similar purposes either internally or externally. However, sentinels are programed rather than inherent in the hardware. 3. The space between the reading or recording head and the recording medium, such as tape, drum, or disk.

gap azimuth: In multi-channel digital magnetic record/playback heads, the angle between the parallel lines measuring gap scatter and the nominal direction of tape motion over the head assembly.

gap depth: The dimension of the gap measured in the direction perpendicular to the surface of a reading or recording head.

gap digit: Included in a machine word for various technical reasons; but not used to represent data or instructions.

gap-filler input: Data generated by a specific gapfiller type radar and transmitted by ground data lines to the input lines of a computer system.

gap length: The dimension of the gap of a reading and recording head measured from one pole face to the other. In longitudinal recording, the gap length can be defined as the dimension of the gap in the direction of tape travel.

gap loss: The loss in output attributable to the finite gap length of the recording head. The loss increases as the wavelength decreases, amounting to approximately 4 dB when the wavelength is equal to twice the gap length, and subsequently increases rapidly towards a complete extinction of output when the wavelength is equal to approximately 1.15 times the gap length.

gap scatter: In multi-channel digital magnetic tape record/playback heads, the distance expressed in micro-inches between the closest pair of parallel lines which bound all gap trailing edges of a stack.

garbage: Unwanted and meaningless information in input, storage, or output.

garbage in/garbage out (GIGO): Refers to the data into and out of a computer system—that is, if the input data is bad (garbage in) then the output data will also be bad (garbage out).

gas tube: An electron tube into which a chemically inactive gas has been injected.

gate: 1. A device having one output channel and one or more input channels, such that the output channel state is determined by the input channel states, except during switching transients. 2. A combinational logic element having at least one input channel.

gateable clock: One which has a start-up time equal to ½ a bit time, and whose frequency equals the baud rate of the line being sampled.

gate circuit: An electronic circuit with one or more inputs and one output, with the property that a pulse goes out on the output line if some specified combination of pulses occurs on the input lines. Gate circuits provide much of the hardware by means of which logical operations are built into a computer.

gate electrodes: Many metal-oxide semiconductor variations can be produced with either metal gates (aluminum) or silicon gates. In the metal-gate process, the gate elctrode is positioned after the source and drain regions have been formed. To accommodate effective gate-electrode positions, the gate electrode must overlap the source and drain regions. This overlap produces parasitic capacitance that slows the circuits. In the silicon-gate process, source and drain regions are formed after the gate electrode has been positioned; the gate electrode defines the edge of the source and drain regions, reducing overlap. Silicon is used because aluminum could not withstand the processing temperatures needed to produce the source and the drain. Silicon gate has an advantage in P-channel memories, since its lower threshold makes it easier to interface the memory circuit with bipolar logic. Silicon gates must have aluminum for low-resistance interconnection. In more complicated memory cells, silicon and aluminum layers are used together to produce inter-

connection, with higher packing density. With simple memory cells (i.e., three transistors per bit) interconnection is so simple that the silicon gate does not deliver significant increase in packing density over aluminum.

gate pulse: A pulse which enables a gate circuit to pass a signal. Usually the gate pulse is of longer duration than the signal to make sure that coincidence in time occurs.

gate time: A transducer that gives output only during chosen time intervals.

gather-write/scatter-read: Gather-write is the ability to place the information from several nonadjacent locations in core storage (for example, several logical records) into a single physical record such as a tape block. Scatter-read is the ability to place information from a physical record into several nonadjacent locations in core storage.

gating: Selection of part of a wave on account of time or magnitude. Operation of a circuit when one wave allows another to pass during specific intervals.

gating pulse: A pulse which permits the operation of a circuit.

gauss: As related to magnetic tape, the cgs unit of magnetic flux density, equal to 1 maxwell per square centimeter.

Gaussian curve (random-error concept):   A random error of sampling is a variation due to chance alone. If the sample is truly random, small errors will be more numerous than large errors and positive errors will be likely negative errors, thus giving rise to the symmetrical, bell-shaped "normal curve of error." This concept was first investigated by the German mathematician Karl F. Gauss, and the curve is often called the Gaussian curve.

Gaussian noise: Noise where the particular voltage distribution is specified in terms of probabilities related to a "normal" curve.

G code: A command in manufacturing process control changing the mode of operation of the control such as from positioning to contouring or calling for a fixed cycle of the machine.

GDG: See generation data group.

GE: Greater than or equal to.

generalized routine: A routine designed to process a large range of specific jobs within a given type of application.

Generalized Simulation Language (GSL): A FORTRAN-like language which provides facilities for both continuous and discrete simulation. Compiler is written in ALGOL and produces FORTRAN programs.

generalized sort: A sort program which will accept the introduction of parameters at run time and which does not generate a program.

generalized sort/merge program: A program that is designed to sort or merge a wide variety of records in a variety of formats.

general numerical control (NC) language processor: A computer program developed to serve as a translating system for a parts programmer to develop a mathematical representation of a geometric form with the use of symbolic notation.

general program: A program designed to solve a class of problems.

general purpose computer: A computer designed to solve a large variety of problems, e.g., a stored program computer which may be adapted to any of a very large class of applications.

general purpose function generator: A function generator not constrained by design or commitment to a specific function only.

general purpose language: Combined programming languages which often use English words and statements where they are convenient as mathematical notation for procedures conveniently expressed mathematically. COBOL, FORTRAN, and ALGOL are widely used general purpose programming languages in both science and business. They are designed to be used in a wide variety of application areas as opposed to a special purpose language designed for a specific application.

general purpose operating programs: Plans or instructions for controlling input/output operations, remote data transmission, and multiple users.

general purpose operating system: An operating system designed to handle a wide variety of computing system applications.

general purpose program: A program designed to perform some standard operations. The particular requirements of any run of the programs are provided by means of parameters which describe the needs of the run. It is similar to a generator, but differs in that it requires parameters each time it is run, whereas a generator produces a specific program which can later be used without parameters.

general purpose systems simulation (GPSS): A simulation program (language) developed by IBM.

general register: A register used for operations such as binary addition, subtraction, multiplication, and division. General registers are used to compute and modify addresses in a program. They have also found increasing utilization as replacements for special registers, such as accumulators, particularly in microprogrammable processors.

general register address: A value in the range 0 through 15 that designates a register in the current register block, whether by means of the R field of the instruction word or by means of an effective virtual address (in some systems).

general routine: A routine expressed in computer coding designed to solve a class of problems, concentrating on a specific problem when appropriate parametric values are supplied.

general switched telephone network: Facilities provided by the telephone companies in the United States that permit each telephone subscriber to communicate with any other telephone subscriber.

General Telephone and Electronics Corporation: The General System has the second largest portion of the telephone business in the United States. It has two subsidiaries that manufacture telephone equipment both for General and for the rest of the telephone industry: Automatic Electric and GTE Lenkurt Incorporated (formerly Lenkurt Electric). Other subsidiaries of General are Sylvania Electric, and the British Colombia Telephone Company in Canada.

general use open subroutine: A subroutine for general use which must be relocated and inserted into a routine at each place it is used.

general utility functions: Auxiliary operations such as tape searching, tape-file copying, media conversion, dynamic memory, and tape dumps.

generate: 1. To produce a program by selection of subsets from a set of skeletal coding under the control of parameters. 2. To produce assembler language statements from the model statements of a macro definition when the definition is called by a macroinstruction.

generating routine: A form of compiling routine; capable of handling less fully defined situations.

generation: A technique for producing a complete routine from one which is in skeletal form, under control of parameters supplied to a generator routine.

generation data group (GDG): A collection of data sets kept in chronological order; each data set is called a generation data set.

generation data set: One generation of a generation data group.

generation number: One which forms a portion of the file label on a reel of magnetic tape which serves to identify the age of the file.

generation system (SYSGEN): A process that creates a particular and uniquely-specified operating system i.e., set of control and utility programs.

generator: A controlling routine that performs a generate function, for example, report generator, input/output generator.

generator, clock-pulse: A specifically designed generator which generates pulses for purposes of special timing or gating in a digital computer, i.e., pulses which are used as inputs to gates to aid in pulseshaping and timing.

generator, data: A computer program that standardizes test data for program testing.

generator program: A large detailed program which permits a computer to write other programs automatically. Generators are usually of two types. (a) The character controlled generator, which operates like a compiler in that it takes entries from a library tape, but unlike a simple compiler in that it examines control characters associated with each entry, and alters instructions found in the library according to the directions contained in the control characters. (b) The pure generator is a program that writes another program. When associated with an assembler a pure generator is usually a section of program which is called into storage by the assembler from a library and then writes one or more entries in another program. Most assemblers are also compilers and generators. In this case the entire system is referred to as an assembly system.

generator pulse, timing: See generator, clock-pulse.

generic: 1. Of, applied to, or referring to a kind, class or group. 2. Inclusive or generally-opposed to specific and special.

geometric mean: This is the nth root of a product of n numbers. G.M. = $\sqrt[n]{(X_1, X_2....n,)}$ Where a large number of values are involved, it is more convenient to find the logarithms of the numbers. Divide the sum of the logarithms by the number of items, and look up the antilogarithms of the quotient.

geometric organizational syndrome: Related to the interaction of people, e.g., there is one communication path with 2 people, 3 with 3, 6 with 4, 10 with 5, etc.

germanium detector: A type of photoinductive detector where germanium doped with other elements acts as a semiconductor in the range of 600 to 1100 nm.

germanium diode: A crystal diode that uses crystalline germanium.

get: 1. To develop or make a record from an input file available for use by a routine in control of the machine. 2. To obtain or extract a coded or transformed value from a field (as to GET a numerical value from a series of decimal digit characters). 3. To locate and transfer a record or item from storage.

ghost: 1. Duplicated image on a television screen arising from additional reception of a delayed, similar signal which has covered a longer path; e.g., through reflection from a tall building or mast. Also double image. 2. A specimen for use in radioactivity measurement which behaves similarly to biological tissue. Also Phantom.

gibberish total: A total accumulated for control purposes when handling records by the addition of specific fields of each record, although the total itself has no particular sense or meaning; i.e., an accumulation of indicative data such as customer's account number, etc.

giga: A prefix for one billion, i.e., 10^9, times a specific unit.

gigacycle: Same as kilomegacycle (1 billion cycles per second).

gigahertz circuit: A computer logic circuit, or other electronic circuits, which have gradient pulse rise or fall times measured in billionths of seconds or less. A nanosecond is 1 billionth of a second.

giro: A bill payment system widely used in Europe. In giro systems, a single payment order can implement money transfers from a customer's account to many other accounts on the books of the same institution. The giro system is characterized as a credit transfer system, while the U.S. check system is characterized as a debit transfer system. Some Electronic Funds Transfer System's bill payment systems in this country are similar to European giro systems.

G-line: Coated wire used to transmit microwave energy.

glitch: If one applies a counter output to the input of a digital-to-analog converter (DAC) to develop a staircase voltage, the number of bits involved in a code change establishes major and minor transitions. The most major transition occurs at ½-scale when the DAC switches all bits, from 011...11 to 1000...00. If they switch faster off than on, for a short time the DAC will provide zero output, and then return to the required 1 LSB above the previous reading. This large transient spike is known as a glitch. The better the switching times are matched and the faster the switches, the smaller the glitch energy will be.

global: Pertaining to that part of an assembler program that includes the body of any macro definition called from a source module and the open code portion of the source module. Contrast with local.

global variable: A variable whose name is accessible by a main program and all its subroutines.

global variable symbol: In assembler programming, a variable symbol that can be used to communicate values between macro definitions and between a macro definition and open code.

goal-setting: Use of the computer in economic and financial planning and control. Modern computer communication networks provide corporate and governmental planners with the database, mathematical tools, and simulation capabilities necessary for effective planning. Using modern simulation techniques, decision makers are able to try out, on-line, the effects of different changes before any final decisions are made.

go back n: A method for dealing with pipelining errors in which the receiver simply discards all subsequent frames, sending no acknowledgments. If the sender's window is filled before the timer expires, the pipeline begins to empty. The sender eventually will time out and retransmit all unacknowledged frames, beginning with the lost or damaged one. Corresponds to a receive window of size 1.

gold-doped transistor-to-transistor (TTL) process: Two major TTL process variations are "Schottky" and "gold doped" techniques. Consider that the transistor in standard TTL circuits saturate. To prevent severe speed degradation, one must either provide a special clamping device to prevent the transistors from saturating (the Schottky diode), or dope the silicon to reduce transistor recovery time in saturation (gold dope). The manufacturing processes required to produce Schottky diodes or to gold dope the silicon are simple, and thus have insignificant effects on manufacturing cost. Schottky-clamped TTL is slightly faster than gold-doped TTL, but has poorer characteristics over wide temperature ranges.

government channel: FCC rules require cable systems in the top 100 markets to set aside one channel for local government use,
to be available without cost for the "developmental period." That period runs for five years from the time that subscriber service began, or until five years after the completion of the basic trunk line.

graded-index optic fiber: An optic fibre that possesses a core which has varying refraction indices. The refraction index of the core continuously decreases radially outward from the core's axis. Since light travels faster in the low-index regions close to the core/cladding interface, the outer ray paths have a higher average propagation velocity and are equalized to those travelling axially in the higher-index region. Also, the ray paths gradually change direction as they enter lower-index regions, thus insuring shallow-degree reflections from the core/cladding interface. This greatly reduces the modal dispersion of the rays and therefore increases the possible data transmission rates and bandwidth, as compared to a step-index optic fiber. Although graded-index fibers reduce modal dispersion, they actually increase material dispersion, and thus require a narrow bandwidth interval, even though the magnitude of bandwidth is less limited than step-index fibers.

grade of channel: The relative bandwidth of a channel: narrowband, voiceband, wideband.

grade service, voice channel: Originally, a service provided by the common carriers that included a circuit capable of carrying a voice transmission. Now, when used in reference to the transmission of data, it also refers to a circuit of sufficient bandwidth to permit a data transfer rate of up to 2400 bits per second. Primarily the term distinguishes this service from teleprinter grade service in reference to regulatory agencies' tariffs.

gradient: The instantaneous direction of a curve at any point is the direction in which the curve tends to rise or fall. This is indicated by the tangent to the curve at the point. A usual measure of this direction of the curve is the gradient of the tangent. This gradient varies as the tangent varies from point to point on the curve. The mathematical description or graphic representation shows that it always is given as the limiting value of the gradient of any chord PQ as Q approaches P.

grammar: The word order in a communication or a portion of a communication.

grandfather cycle: The period during which magnetic tape records are retained before re-using so that records can be reconstructed in the event of loss of information stored on a magnetic tape.

grandfather file: A magnetic tape or disk containing basic information used on a second file, and this second file is updated according to the latest transactions or changes. When this second file is copied, it becomes the new grandfather file, and a series of grandfather files is the historical record or statistical base for further manipulation, analysis, or an audit trail. They are also backup files in case of accidental erasure or loss of current files.

grandfathering: Exempting cable systems from the federal rules because: (a) they were in existence or operation before the rules, or (b) substantial investments were made in system construction before the rules. Grandfathering applies to signal carriage, access channels, and the certification process.

grant chart: A chart of activity against time; such charts have historically been used to schedule or reserve resources for specific activities. Critical path method (CPM) and project evaluation and review techniques (PERT) are devices which have offered substantial improvement in scheduling and allocations.

graph: A sheet of paper onto which have been placed curves, lines, points, and explanatory alphabetic and numerical information representing numerical data.

graphetic level: An example is a character, either handwritten or printed, usually then capable of being copied, reproduced, transmitted, or manipulated by an ordered set.

graph follower: A device that reads data in the form of a graph, i.e., usually an optical sensing device.

graphic: Pertaining to a pictorial representation of displayed information or material, usually legible to humans, such as, the printed or written form of data, mathematical curves, or a cathode-ray tube display.

graphic arts quality: Automated composition techniques that provide the capabilities of traditional composition methods for printing, such as changes of type face and font, variable spacing and right-hand justification, proportional spacing for characters, and variable leading between lines.

graphic character: A character that can be represented by a graphic. Whether it is one or not usually depends upon one or more of the various types of optical character equipment in use or available, i.e., whether it is readable or copyable by various equipment. Contrast with control character.

graphic data reduction: A process of converting physical representations such as plotter output, graphs, or engineering drawings into digital data.

graphic display program: A program designed to display information, in graphic or alphanumeric form, on the face of a television-like display tube.

graphic-display unit: A communications terminal (linked to a computer) which displays data on a television-like screen.

graphic job processing: An optional feature of multiple fixed number of tasks (MFT) that enables users at display units to define and start jobs quickly and conveniently that are processed under the operating system. The feature also allows interactive use of graphic display programs.

graphic job processor (GJP): A program that elicits job control information from a user as he selects and performs job control operations at a particular display unit or at a specific display station; it interprets the information entered by the user and converts it into job control language.

graphic method: One in which the quantity is photographed in the process of change. The entire range of variation of a quantity, presented in this vivid pictorial way, is comprehended easily at a glance.

graphic panel: A master control panel which, pictorially and usually colorfully, traces the relationship of control equipment and the process operation. It permits an operator at a glance to check on the operation of a far-flung control system by noting dials, valves, scales, and lights.

graphics: The use of diagrams or other graphical means to obtain operating data and answers. The use of written symbols and visual displays.

graphic solution: A solution which is developed and obtained with graphs or other pictorial devices, as contrasted with solutions obtained by the manipulation of numbers.

graphic transmission: A letter or other character symbol reproduced or transmitted in some way through an electronic data system, usually by an ordered set of pulses.

graph plotter: 1. A visual display or board on which a dependent variable is graphed by an automatically controlled pen or pencil as a function of one or more variables. 2. A device that inscribes a visual display of a dependent variable.

grass: The visible evidence of electrical noise in an A-scope display.

gray code: A binary code in which sequential numbers are represented by expressions which are the same except in one place and in that place differ by one unit.

gray code (reflected binary): A unit distance code obtained by a reflection of each bit in the natural binary code.

gray cyclic code: A specific positional code for numbers which has the property that when some or all of those of a given length are arranged in sequence, the signal distance between consecutive numbers is one. The gray code is thus a cyclic binary unit-distance code.

grid: 1. A thin wire mesh between cathode and plate in a triode. 2. In optical character recognition, two mutually orthogonal sets of parallel lines used for specifying or measuring character images.

grid bypass: A small fixed capacitor which bypasses the signal away from the grid leak.

grid leak: A grid resistor through which dc grid current flows.

grid leak detector: A detector which depends on the flow of grid current for its operation.

grid modulation: A system of modulation in an amplitude modulation (AM) transmitter in which the modulating signal is applied to the grid circuit of an r-f amplifier.

grid-spaced contacts: Specific types of electrical contacts, usually surfaces, spring types, or pins arranged in parallel or equally-spaced rows and columns on any type connector, or edges of printed circuit boards.

GROPE-1 system: Human factor problem, using control system engineering and computer program analysis.

Grosch's law: A theory that the power of a computer is equivalent roughly to its cost squared.

gross index: The first of a pair of indexes consulted to locate particular records, etc.; the secondary or supplemental index is the fine index.

ground: A point considered to be at nominal zero potential and to which all other potentials in the circuit are referred, often, but not always, connected to the actual surface of the earth; as a verb to connect to a ground. Also called earth.

grounded potentiometer: A potentiometer with one end terminal attached directly to ground.

ground, signal: Establishes the electrical ground reference potential for all interchange circuits except the frame-grounding circuit.

ground loop: A potentially detrimental loop formed when two or more points in an electrical system, nominally at ground potential, are connected by a conducting path. Note: The term usually is employed when, by improper design or by accident, unwanted noisy signals are generated in the common return of relatively low-level signal circuits by the return currents or by magnetic fields from relatively high-powered circuits or components.

ground wave: The earth-bound wave from a low frequency transmitter antenna.

group address: 1. An address assigned to a group of terminals sharing a single communication channel. 2. A coded representation of several stations; used to activate a group of stations simultaneously.

group-address message: A message with one address to be delivered to a fixed predetermined set of destinations.

group-code entry: A terminal table entry containing information on a pre-specified group of terminals with the group code feature; this feature facilitates simultaneous transmission of a message to all members of the group through the specification of a single set of unique address characters.

group displays: The display system consists of two elements: the basic display unit (BDU) containing the display generation and control equipment; and the projection unit, containing the camera, processor, and projector to produce the large screen images. The BDU changes the stored information received from the display data controller to any of 128 different type symbols and to map-forming lines that appear on the face of a 5-inch cathode-ray tube. The film is developed automatically by the film processor, and the display is projected onto one of the two 12' x 16' wall screens provided as part of the group display. Only ten seconds are required between film exposure by the cathode-ray tube (CRT) and the presentation of the seven-color projection upon the screen.

grouped records: Records combined into a unit to conserve storage space or reduce access time.

group frequency: The frequency which corresponds to the group velocity of a progressive wave in a waveguide or transmission line.

group indicate: The printing of indicative information from only the first record of a group.

group indication: A device on some tabulators which permits the first item of a series of same or similar data or information to be printed and also inhibits some of the printing of the rest of the set of series.

grouping: A mass of data having common characteristics are arranged into related groups.

group mark: A mark that identifies the beginning or end of a set of data, which could include words, blocks, or other items.

group modulation: Use of one carrier for transmitting a group of telephone or telegraph channels, with demodulation on reception and ultimate separation. Side frequencies of the said carrier may represent different groups.

group name: A generic name for a collection of input/output devices.

group printing: The function of a machine which does not print data from every card. Instead it summarizes the data contained in a group of cards and prints only the summarized total.

group separator (GS): A device that identifies logic boundaries between groups of information.

group theory: A study in the mathematical sense of the rules for combining groups, sets, and elements, i.e., the theory of combining groups.

GT: Greater than.

guard: Signal which prevents accidental operation by spurious signals or avoids possible ambiguity.

guard bands: Unused frequency bands between two used frequencies, which provides protection against mutual interference or disruption.

guard bit: 1. A special bit contained in each word or specific groups of words of memory designed to indicate to computer hardware units or software programs whether or not the content of that memory location may or may not be altered by a program. 2. A bit designed to indicate whether a core or disk memory word or group of words is to be filed—protected.

guard digit: A low-order hexadecimal zero appended to each operand fraction in a single-word floating-point arithmetic addition or subtraction operation.

guard mode multiprogramming: The system operates in a multiprogram or multiprocessing environment and to initiate and preserve this, the executive routine must be in complete control of the total system. Special hardware features are provided to permit this control. The multiprogramming and multiprocessing capabilities of the system are based upon guard mode operation, the setting aside of certain instructions, registers, and storage locations for the exclusive use of the executive routine, assuring protection against the interaction of unrelated programs.

guard signal: 1. A signal which allows values to be read or converted only when the values are not in a changing state. 2. An extra output, which is generated when all values are complete, to be used as a guard signal. Used in digital-to-analog or analog-to-digital converters or other converters or digitizers.

guidance control system: A specific system in which deliberate guidance or manipulation is used to achieve a prescribed value or a variable. It is subdivided into a controlling system and a controlled system.

guided wave: Electromagnetic or acoustic wave which is constrained within certain boundaries as in a waveguide.

guide edge: The edge on which paper or magnetic tape is guided while being fed, if such a method is used.

gulp: A small group of bytes, similar to a word or instruction.

H

half-add: A computer instruction that performs bit-by-bit half additions (i.e., logical EXCLUSIVE OR without carry) up on its operands.

half-duplex (HD or HDX): In communications, pertaining to an alternate, one way at a time, independent transmission.

half-duplex channel: A channel capable of transmitting and receiving signals, but in only one direction at a time.

half-duplex circuit: A duplex intercity facility with single loops to the terminals capable of two-way nonsimultaneous operation.

half-duplex facilities: Quite often there is a tendency by many people to implement full-duplex facilities when a half-duplex arrangement will do the job. The primary reason for such a decision is because of the great degree of difficulty that half-duplex operation causes. However, a half-duplex facility is less than the price of a full-duplex facility. The main problem that arises when using a half-duplex facility is the question of priorities (contention) and the acknowledgment of messages. The problem is solved in one of two ways, dependent upon application, Master Station and Idle communications mode.

half-duplex transmission: Alternate, one-way-at-a-time, independent transmission.

half-pulse read: A pulse of a magnitude which by itself cannot switch a magnetic core, and thus cannot interrogate the content, but when combined with a second pulse in the same direction can then switch the core to some prescribed state, i.e., one half-pulse (read) can drive a row or cores in an array, another the column.

half-shift register: Another name for certain types of flip-flops when used in a shift register. It takes two of these to make one stage in a shift register.

half-sinusoid: The entire positive or negative portion of a single cycle of a sine wave.

halftime emitter: A device which emits synchronous pulses midway between the row pulses of a punched card.

half-wave power supply: A power supply using a single diode which draws current during one phase of the input alternating voltage.

halfword: A contiguous sequence of bits or characters which comprises half a computer word and is capable of being addressed as a unit.

halt: A condition which occurs when the sequence of operations in a program stops. This can be due to a halt instruction being met or to some unexpected halt or interrupt. The program can continue normally after a halt unless it is a drop dead halt.

halt instruction: A machine instruction that stops the execution of the program.

hammer code: See Hamming code.

Hamming code: 1. An error-correcting code system that was named after the inventor, R. W. Hamming of Bell Telephone Laboratories. A Hamming code contains four information bits and three check bits. 2. A data code capable of being corrected automatically.

handshaking: The exchange of identifying or alerting signals between two data communication devices prior to any transfer of information.

hands-on background: The prior work experience developed by actually operating the hardware and often used as a criterion of programmer capability and knowledge.

hang: See hang-up.

hang-up: 1. An unplanned computer stop or delay in problem solution, e.g., caused by the inability to escape from a loop. 2. A nonprogrammed stop in a routine. It is usually an unforeseen or unwanted halt in a machine pass; it is most often caused by improper coding of a machine instruction or by the attempted use of a nonexistent or improper operation code.

hang-up prevention: The computer logic must be designed or modified so that no sequence of valid or invalid instructions can cause the computer to come to a halt or to go into a nonterminating uninterruptible state. Examples of this latter case are infinitely nested executions or nonterminating indirect addressing.

hard copy: A printed copy of machine output in a visually readable form; for example, printed reports, listings, documents, and summaries.

hard copy/live copy: Paper copy of a vital record which is dispersed for protection as opposed to microfilm or magnetic tape. Documents which are available immediately for active use without processing.

hard-copy log: In systems with multiple console support or a graphic console, a permanent record of system activity.

hard-copy plotting board: A hard-copy output device which presents the results of a plotter system, which is designed to develop curves, graphs, chart, and other graphic output.

hard facility: A vital records center con-

structed above or below ground of special explosive-proof materials.

hard-limited integrator: A design or set-up relating to an integrator in which the inputs cease to be integrated when output tends to exceed specified limits, i.e., in a hard-limited integrator the output does not exceed the limits, which is not so for soft-limited integrators.

hard limiting: A circuit of nonlinear elements that restrict the electrical excursion of a variable in accordance with some specified criteria. Hard limiting is a limiting action with negligible variation in output in the range where the output is limited. Soft limiting is a limiting action with appreciable variation in output in the range where the output is limited. A bridge limiter is a bridge circuit used as a limiter circuit. In an analog computer, a feedback limiter is a limiter circuit usually employing biased diodes shunting the feedback component of an operational amplifier; an input limiter is a limiter circuit usually employing biased diodes in the amplifier input channel that operates by limiting the current entering the summing junction.

hardware: Physical equipment, as opposed to the computer program or method of use, e.g., mechanical, magnetic, electrical, or electronic devices.

hardware assembler (microprocessor):   Often consists of programmable read-only memory (PROMs) that plug into simulation boards, enabling the prototype to assemble its own programs.

hardware check: A hardware provision used for verifying the accuracy of information transmitted, manipulated, or stored by any unit or device in a computer. Same as built-in check, built-in automatic check.

hardware priority interrupt: A programmed or designed hardware implementation of priority interrupt functions. See priority interrupt.

hard-wired numerical control: A numerical control system wherein the response to data input, data handling sequence, and control functions is determined by the fixed and committed circuit interconnections of discrete decision elements and storage devices. Changes in the response, sequence, or functions can be made by changing the interconnections.

harmonic: 1. The resultant of harmonic frequencies (due to nonlinear characteristics of a transmission line) present in the response when a sinusoidal stimulus is applied. 2. A frequency equal to a wholenumber multiple of a fundamental.

harmonic distortion: 1. Distortion, due to the nonlinear characteristics of a transmission, which results in the presence of harmonic frequencies in the response when a sinusoidal stimulus is applied. 2. Form of interference involving the generation of harmonics according to the frequency relationship $f = nf_1$ for each frequency present, where n is a whole number equal to 2 or more.

harmonic excitation: 1. Excitation of an antenna at one of its harmonic modes. 2. Excitation of a transmitter from a harmonic of the master oscillator; also called harmonic drive.

harmonic filter: One which separates harmonics from fundamental in the feed to an antenna; also called harmonic suppressor.

hartley: A unit of information content, equal to one decadal decision, or the designation of one of ten possible and equally likely values or states.

hartley oscillator: An oscillator circuit in which the coil of the resonant circuit is tapped.

hash addressing (hashing):   A calculation of the approximate address of a record in a file by some semiempirical function (related to address calculation access).

hash total: A summation for checking purposes of one or more corresponding fields of a file that would ordinarily not be summed.

HD or HDX: See half-duplex.

head: A device that reads, writes, or erases data on a storage medium, e.g., a small electromagnet used to read, write, or erase data on a magnetic drum or tape, or the set of perforating, reading, or marking devices used for punching, reading, or printing on paper tape.

headend: Electronic control center—generally located at the antenna site of a community antenna television (CATV) system—usually including antennas, pre-amplifiers, frequency converters, demodulators, modulators, and other related equipment which amplify, filter and convert incoming broadcast television signals to cable system channels.

header: 1. Data (usually for identification) placed at the top of a page. 2. The part of a message which contains the data necessary to guide the message to its destination(s).

header card: A card that contains information related to the data in cards that follow.

header label: A block of data at the start of a magnetic tape file which contains descriptive information to identify the file; e.g., file name, reel number, file generation number, retention period, and the date when the data was written to tape.

header record: A record containing common, constant, or identifying information for a group of records that follows. Same as header table.

header segment: A part of a message that contains any portion of the message header.

header table: See header record.

head gap: 1. The space between the reading or recording head and the recording medium, such as tape, drum or disk. 2. The space or gap intentionally inserted into the magnetic circuit of the head in order to force or direct the recording flux into the recording medium.

heading: In ASCII and communications, a sequence of characters preceded by the start of heading character used as machine sensible address or routing information.

heading control: A title or short definition of a control group of records which appear in front of each such group.

heading information: Contains the following: (a) identification of the originating station; (b) indentification of the sending and receiving device or process; (c) the priority of the message; (d) the security class of the message; (e) routing information concerning the distribution of the message once it has reached its destination; (f) message processing information concerning its status as data or control.

head pressure solenoid: An electromechanical device which upon being energized, maintains a pressure via a roller forcing magnetic tape toward the read-write heads.

head-to-foot: Printing the reverse side of a sheet upside down so that it can be read by turning the sheet over from top to bottom instead of turning it as you would the pages of a book.

head-to-head: Printing on the reverse side of a sheet so that it can be read by turning the sheet over as you would the pages of a book.

head-to-tape contact: The degree to which the surface of the magnetic coating approaches the surface of the record or relay heads during normal operation of a recorder. Good head-to-tape contact minimizes separation loss and is essential in obtaining high resolution.

heavy duty tape: A classification of tape implying a high durability index and high reliability under conditions of prolonged use.

height control: The cathode-ray tube (CRT) receiver hand control which varies the height of the picture.

hermaphroditic connectors: Those connectors whose mating parts are identical at their mating face, i.e., those which have no female or male members but still can maintain correct polarity, sealing, mechanical and electrical couplings.

hertz: 1. A wave used in radio communication; produced by an alternating current at the sending station and received by the aerial of the receiving set. Named after Heinrich Hertz (1867-94), a German physicist. 2. A generalized expression referring to all radio waves or oscillations of electricity in a conductor producing electromagnetic radiation. 3. A unit of frequency; one hertz (1Hz) equals one cycle per second.

Hertzian waves: Electromagnetic waves which have been found useful for communicating information through space – the frequency range 10^4 to 10^{10} Hz, for example.

hesitation: A temporary halt or temporary suspension of operations in a sequence of operations of a computer in order to perform all or part of the operations from another sequence.

heterodyne: Combination of two sinusoidal radio frequency (RF) waves in a nonlinear device with the consequent production of sum and difference frequencies. The latter is the heterodyne frequency, and will produce an AF beat note when the two original sine waves are close in frequency.

heterodyne conversion: Change in the frequency of a modulated carrier wave produced by heterodyning it with a second unmodulated signal. The sum and difference frequencies will carry the original modulation signal and either of these can be isolated for subsequent amplification. The frequency-changing stage of a supersonic heterodyne (superhet) radio receiver uses this principle, an oscillator being tuned to a fixed amount above the signal frequency so that the difference frequency (intermediate frequency signal) remains constant for all incoming signals.

heterodyne interference: Arising from simultaneous reception of two stations, the difference between whose carrier frequencies is an audible frequency.

heterodyning: Mixing two signals in a detector to obtain the beat frequency.

heuristic: A solution which could contribute to the reduction of time and funds necessary for an algoristic solution (i.e., as closed linear-programming models) which require highly structured models. Heuristic models provide resolutions of problems which are more flexible to model, permit faster testing and evaluation, and fit any type of problem which contains elements which can be measured and associated.

heuristic binary file index (HBFI): An index used on a sequential (i.e. records in ascending order by key or identifier) file in batch processing which is developed "de novo" at execution time by "remembering" the keys and record addresses during each binary search for a record so that successive records can be located using any portion of the in-core key/location index previously developed without requiring record addresses.

heuristic routine: A routine by which the computer attacks a problem by a trial and error approach frequently involving the act of learning.

hexadecimal: A number system with a base of 16; valid "digits" range from 0 through 9 and from A through F, where F represents the highest units position (15). Same as sexadecimal.

hexadecimal base: Pertaining to the numeration system with a radix or base of sixteen. That is, the hexadecimal system has 16 "digits": 0, 1, 2, 3, 4, 5, 6, 7, 8, 9, A, B,

C, D, E, F. For example, the decimal number 11,983 would be represented in hexadecimal as 2ECF and would be interpreted in the following way:

$$
\begin{array}{cccc}
16^3 & 16^2 & 16^1 & 16^0 \\
\times 2 & \times E & \times C & \times F \\
+ & + & + & = \\
16^3 & 16^2 & 16^1 & 16^0 \\
\times 2 & \times 14 & \times 12 & \times 15 \\
8{,}192 + & 3{,}584 + & 192 + & 15
\end{array}
$$

$$= 11{,}983$$

hexadecimal notation: A notation of numbers in the base 16.

HF: An abbreviation for high frequency, i.e., frequencies between 3 and 30 megahertz.

HF bias: An ultrasonic signal which reduces distortion in tape recorders.

hierarchical file: 1. A file system or mass storage system in which elapsed processing time is balanced against the unit cost of memories of varying access speeds. Frequently used items may be kept in main memory itself or on drums (expensive), less frequently used items on disks (slower but less expensive), and infrequently used items on data cell or high-speed, high-density tape drives (slowest and least expensive).

hierarchy: A specified rank of order of items. A series of items classified by rank or order.

high: One of two distinct states in digital logic elements. The two states are called true and false, high and low, on and off, or "1" and "0." In computers they are represented by two different voltage levels. The more positive level (or less negative) than the other is called the high level, the other the low level. If the true ("1") level is the most positive voltage, this logic is referred to as positive true or positive logic.

higher-order language: A computer programming language that is less dependent on the limitations of a specific computer:

for instance pseudo-languages; problemo-riented languages; languages common to most computer systems, such as ALGOL, FORTRAN, and COBOL, as opposed to the assembly languages.

high fidelity: A system which reproduces sound with a minimum of distortion.

high frequency: Any frequency above the audible range; i.e., above 15kHz, but especially those used for radio commu-nication.

high-frequency amplification: That at fre-quencies used for radio transmission. In a receiver, any amplification which takes place before detection, frequency conver-sion or demodulation.

high-frequency   carrier   telegraphy: Carrier telegraphy in which the frequency of the carrier currents exceeds the range which is transmitted over a voice-frequency telephone channel.

high-frequency transformer: One de-signed to operate at high frequencies, taking   into   account   self-capacitance, usually with bandpass response.

high-gain amplifier: A special voltage amplifier in analog computers having the characteristic of arbitrary feedback. Same as dc amplifier.

high-level data link control (HDLC):   A version of synchronous data link control (SDLC) modified by the International Standards Organization (ISO).

high-level language: A language in which each instruction or statement corresponds to several machine code instructions. High-level languages allow users to write in a notation with which they are familiar rather than a language oriented to the machine code of a computer.

high-level modulation: Modulation pro-duced at a point in a system where the power level approximates that at the output of the system.

highlighting display: Reversing the field, blinking,   underlining,   changing   color, changing light intensity or some combina-tions of the above. A keyboard terminal should have at least three different methods of emphasizing or highlighting information on the display.

high-limiting control action: A designed control action in which the output never exceeds a predetermined high limit value.

high-low   bias   check: A   preventive-maintenance procedure in which certain operating conditions, such as supply voltage or frequency, are varied about their nom-inal values in order to detect and locate incipient defective parts. Same as marginal test.

high-on-the line: A   momentary   open circuit on a teletypewriter loop.

high order: Pertaining to the weight or significance   assigned   to   the   digits   of   a number; i.e, in the number 123456, the highest order digit is one; the lowest order digit is six. One may refer to the three high-order bits of a binary word as another example.

high-order digit: A digit that occupies a more significant or highly weighted position in   a   numerical   or   positional   notation system.

high or low selector: A specific device designed to select automatically either the highest or the lowest input signal from among two or more input signals.

highpass: The operation of a circuit or a device which permits the passage of high-frequency signals and highly attenuates the low frequency signals, e.g., a filter or other types of devices.

highpass (lowpass) filter: Freely passes signals of all frequencies above (or below) a reference   value,   known   as   the   cutoff frequency.

high performance equipment: Equipment producing signals transmittable via teleprinter and telephone circuits.

high-speed bus: A set of wires that transfers electrical pulses which represent data and instructions to various registers and counters. However, onoff and similar transfer lines or control signals are not considered as digit transfer buses.

high-speed carry: Any technique in parallel addition for speeding up carry propagation, for example, standing-on nines carry. Contrast with cascaded carry.

high-speed data acquisition (HSDA): A monitoring and controlling facility used to acquire, evaluate and record data in a testing situation.

high-speed line printer: Provides printed output at the rate of 1000 alphanumeric lines per minute or more. Since the production of some records or reports require the skipping of many lines, the printer has the timesaving ability to skip vertically between print lines regardless of the number of lines. The control of skipping is accomplished by either program control or by means of a punched-tape control loop on the printer. The automatic-interrupt feature for optimum timesharing is part of the printer, allowing processing time to be shared between cycles (in some systems).

high-speed memory: A unit capable of producing information at relatively higher speeds than other peripheral or memory units connected or related to a computer system; also an indication of the lower average access time.

high-speed reader (HSR): A reading device capable of being connected to a computer without seriously holding up the computer. A card reader reading more than 250 cards per minute would be called a high-speed reader. A reader which reads punched paper tape at a rate greater than 50 characters per second could also be called a high-speed reader.

high-usage trunk: A group of trunks for which an engineered alternate route is provided, and for which the number of trunks is determined on the basis of relative trunk efficiencies and economic considerations.

high very-high-frequency (vhf) band: Part of the frequency band which the Federal Communication Commission (FCC) allocates to VHF broadcasting, including channels 7 through 13, or 174 through 216 MHz.

hill-and-dale: A method of disk recording in which the stylus moves up and down.

hi-mode bias testing: The destructive read-off or use caused by overloading or underloading the computer components causing failure of substandard units to thereby minimize nonschedule down time.

hi-speed memory: See high-speed memory.

histogram: Represents the measurements or observations constituting a set of data on a horizontal scale and the class frequencies on a vertical scale. The graph of the distribution is then constructed by drawing rectangles, the bases of which are determined by the corresponding class frequencies.

hit: 1. Momentary electrical disturbance on a circuit. 2. A successful comparison of two items of data.

hit-on-the-fly printer: A printer where either the paper, the print head, or both are in continuous motion.

hit rate: The percentage of records in a file which are accessed compared to the total number of records in that file.

hit ratio: The ratio of the number of successful references to main storage to the total number of references.

hits: Momentary line disturbances which could result in mutilation of characters being transmitted.

hold: The function of retaining information in one storage device after also transferring it to another device.

hold button (analog):   Causes the solution to be temporarily suspended, permitting the user to study the various quantities. The integrating capacitors are disconnected during hold so that they will neither charge nor discharge.

hold controls: A pair of cathode-ray tube (CRT) receiver hand controls which help synchronize the picture horizontally and vertically.

holding beam: A diffuse beam of electrons used to restore negative charges on the inside storage surface of a cathode-ray tube (CRT). The holding beam is the source of charges for regeneration and replenishment of those which leak off.

holding gun: A device which generates an electronic holding beam.

holding time: The period of time a trunk or circuit is in use for each transmission, including the operator or switching-equipment time in making the connection, plus the user's transmission time; that is, it includes both operating time and message time.

hold instruction: A computer instruction which causes data called from storage to be retained in storage after it is called out and transferred to its new location.

hole count check: A checking feature in punched card equipment.

Hollerith system: A widely used system of encoding alphanumeric information onto cards. The mainstay Hollerith card is synonymous with punch card. Such cards were first used in 1890 for the U.S. census, and are named after the inventor, Herman Hollerith.

hologram: Means of optical imaging without the use of lenses, now a practical reality with the advent of the laser. The laser beam is split into two portions, one part directly illuminating a photographic film (or plate) while the other first illuminates the scene. The two portions produce an optical interference pattern on the film which, when illuminated by a laser beam, will produce two images of the original scene. One of these is virtual but the other is real and may be viewed without a lens.

holographic lens: A hologram of a lens. More precisely, it is a recording of the optical characteristics of a lens and prism. When a laser beam passes through the hologram, it acts in the same way as if it had passed through an actual lens and prism. Holographic lenses take far less space and are much less expensive than conventional lenses. As a result, they are used widely in supermarket bar code scanners and office copying machines.

home address: An address written on a direct access volume denoting a track's address relative to the beginning of the volume.

home loop: 1. A short, local transmission path. 2. An operation involving only those input and output units associated with the local terminal.

home record: The first record in a chain of records.

homostasis: The dynamic condition of a system wherein the input and output are balanced precisely, thus presenting an appearance of no change, hence a steady state.

hop: Distance along Earth's surface between successive reflections of a radio wave from an ionized region.

horizontal automatic frequency control (afc):   The automatic frequency control in the horizontal sync circuit of a cathode-ray tube (CRT).

horizontal check parity: Compares the number of bits tallied and totalled along channels to a previously determined quantity.

horizontal control tube: The comparator stage of the horizontal automatic frequency control (afc) system.

horizontal display: The width, in inches, of the display area of the cathode-ray tube.

horizontal format: The horizontal arrangement of data, as viewed by an observer of a document.

horizontally-deflecting coils: The deflecting coils of a writing tube which exert a sidewise force on the writing beam.

horizontally-deflecting plates: The deflecting plates in a writing tube which exert a sidewise force on the writing beam.

horizontal oscillator: The relaxation oscillator in the cathode-ray tube (CRT) horizontal sync circuit.

horizontal output stage: The power amplifier stage in the cathode-ray tube (CRT) receiver's horizontal sync circuits.

horizontal parity check: A checking procedure counting bits along a horizontal direction to compare them with a previous count. See parity.

horizontal raster count: The number of coordinate positions addressable across the width of the cathode-ray tube.

horizontal sorter: A sorter rack which slides backward and forward.

horizontal sync signal: The signal which instructs the television set to return its beam tto the left hand side of the screen and begin a new scan line.

horizontal tabulation character: A specific control character designed to cause a printing or display unit to skip forward to the next set of predetermined positions on the same line.

host-based support programs: Provide for the following: (a) The generation of application and installation-oriented system configurations using a suitable system generation macro language and a library of macro definitions. (b) An assembler and link editor to assemble user-written message handling procedures, new device drivers, and application-dependent modules used in generating new system configuration. (c) A loader to allow the transfer (down-line loading) of diagnostic test routines and previously generated operating software on request from the host system or the communications processor. (d) Dump programs to help isolate and correct error conditions.

host computer: 1. The primary or controlling computer in a multiple computer operation. 2. A computer used to prepare programs for use on another computer or on another data processing system; for example, a computer used to compile, link edit, or test programs to be used on another system.

host-to-host protocol: A specific level of protocol that allows hosts to initiate and maintain communication between processes running on distributed computers. A process (e.g., a user program) running on one computer requiring communication with a process running on a remote computer requests its local supervisor to initiate and maintain the communication link under the host-to-host protocol. This protocol utilizes the lower level protocols and maintians responsibility for initiating the communication link between processes on remote computers and controlling the flow of messages between those processes.

house drop: The coaxial cable that connects each building or home to the nearest feeder line of the cable network.

housekeeping: Operations in a routine which do not contribute directly to the solution of the problem at hand, but which are made necessary by the method of operation of the computer.

housekeeping operation: A general term for the operation which must be performed for a machine run before actual processing begins, i.e., establishing controlling marks, setting up auxiliary storage units, reading in the first record for processing, initializing, setup verification operations, and file identification.

housekeeping routine: The initial instructions in a program which are executecd only one time, i.e., clear storage.

HP: See highpass filter.

hub: A socket on a control panel or plugboard into which an electrical lead or plug wire may be connected in order to carry signals, particularly to distribute the signals over many other wires.

hub-polling: The computer invites the first terminal to send a message, if none is ready the first terminal passes the request to the second terminal and so on. This is efficient particularly when terminals are inactive and lines are very long. Whenever a terminal replies with an information message the computer deals with it, and then resumes the polling sequence by inviting the next terminal to proceed. In this way an active terminal near the beginning of the ciruit is prevented from monopolizing the attention of the computer.

human factors: The application of psychology and related social sciences to systems involving humans and human behavior.

human frequency range: The human ear can detect sounds over a range of frequencies; it can hear sounds of different pitch. Although the nominal range is 20 to 20,000 Hz most people can hear a range smaller than this (especially at the high frequency end), depending on age, state of health, and so on.

human-oriented language: A programming language that is more like a human language than a machine language.

hunting: A continuous attempt on the part of an automatically controlled system to seek a desired equilibrium condition, the system usually contains a standard, a method of determining deviation from this standard and a method of influencing the system so that the difference between the standard and the state of the system is brought to zero.

hybrid coil: An arrangement using one or more transformers wired as a balanced bridge to provide two-to-four wire conversion for long distance telecommunication circuits.

hybrid computer: A computer designed with both digital and analog characteristics, combining the advantages of analog and digital computer when working as a system. Hybrid computers are being used extensively in simulation process control systems where it is necessary to have a close representation of the physical world. The hybrid system provides better precision that can be attained with analog computers and greater control than is possible with digital computers, plus the ability to accept input data in either form.

hybrid computer system checkout: Programs that provide checkout of hardware, the analog wiring and the digital program.

hybrid hardware control: A program group that provides the control and communication between various elements of the hybrid system. The programmer can control analog computer modes and operation of automatic features of the analog device.

hybrid integrated circuit: A class of integrated circuits wherein the substrate is a passive material such as ceramic and the active chips are attached to its surface.

hybrid interface: A channel for connecting a digital computer to an analog computer.

hybrids: Circuits fabricated by interconnecting smaller circuits of different technologies mounted on a single substrate.

hybrid-system checkout: Implements checkout of system hardware, analog wiring, and digital programs. Normal maintenance checks are performed in conjunction with a standard, wired analog patch board. Digital utility programs and analog status check programs are also provided.

hybrid systems: 1. The result of a number of efforts to utilize the best properties of both digital and analog computers by building hybrid systems. In the hybrid system, a digital computer is used for control purposes and provides the program, while analog components are used to obtain the continuous solutions. 2. A combination of an on-site minicomputer for immediate response processing and an off-site large scale computer for processing of large blocks of data.

hybrid telecommunications: Has some characteristics (as seen by the user) of both switched and leased line offerings. (This is not to be confused with a composite or hybrid data processing/data communications service in which both data processing and communications services are packaged into a single offering.) Also known as a value added network service, it provides an important new category of domestic common carrier service in which common carriers (in the form of the value added network vendors) depart from numerous time-honored concepts.

hysteresis error: The maximum difference in readings of the value of the output at a specified value of the measurand. The readings are taken as the measurand approaches the specified value from the maximum limits of the measurand value from each direction. Hysteresis error is expressed in percent of full scale of the measuring system.

hysteresis loop: A graphical repesentatin centered around the origin of rectangular coordinates, depicting the two values of magnetic induction for each value of·magnetizing force — one when the magnetizing force is increasing, and one when the magnetizing force is decreasing.

hysteresis or backlash: Difference in output value achieved when approaching the same value of input from both directions.

Hz: See hertz.

I

iconographic model: A pictorial representation of a system and the function relations within the system.

ICTD: See interchannel time displacement (skew).

idealized system: A conceptual system whose ultimate controlled variable has a stipulated relationship to specified set points. For measurements, it is a basis for performance standards.

ideal value: The expected or desired value of the indication, output, or ultimately controlled variable of an idealized device or system; most often it is assumed that an ideal value continually exists even though it may be impossible to determine.

identifier: A symbol whose purpose is to identify, indicate or name a body of data.

identifier word: A full length computer word associated with a search or a search-read function. In a search or search-read function, the identifier word is stored in a special register in the channel synchronizer and compared with each word read by the peripheral unit (in some systems).

identity: An equation; a statement that two expressions are equal. When an equality is true at all times and for all values of the symbol for which the numbers are defined, it is an identity. The symbol $\equiv$ means, "is identically equal to" and is generally used to emphasize this trait of relationship.

identity element: A logical element operating with binary signals that supply one output signal from two input signals. The output signal will be 1 when, and only when, the two input signals are the same; i.e., both inputs are 1 or both 0.

identity gate: A specific n-input gate which yields an output signal of a particular kind when all of the ninput signals are alike. Same as identity unit.

identity sign: A mathematical symbol, $\equiv$ designed to indicate that two expressions are identical.

identity unit: A n-input unit that yields a specified output signal only when all n-input signals are alike.

IDF: See intermediate distributing frame.

idle character: A character transmitted on a communications line that does not print or punch at the output component of the accepting terminal.

idle communications mode: Primary advantages over the master system mode of operation are as follows: (a) Provides equal priority for both stations. (b) Provides a continuous check of both stations' performance and communication link reliability. In the idle communication mode of operation, idle information is transferred between stations (usually two computers) when text is not being transferred. During this idle mode of operation, data flows from station A to station B for a fixed period of time, and then the flow changes from station B to station A. The only time a station can initiate a transfer is when it is idling the line. The information that is transferred during the idle mode is usually one of three patterns: (a) All ones. (b) SYN or some other predefined character. (c) Test patterns.

idle time: 1. The period between the end of one programmed computer run and the commencement of a subsequent programmed run. 2. The time normally used to assemble cards, paper, tape reels, and control panels required for the next computer operation. 3. The time between operations when no work is scheduled.

IDP: See integrated data processing.

i-f alignment: The process of tuning the resonant circuits in the i-f strip to their proper frequencies.

IF-AND-ONLY-IF operation: Same as equivalence.

IF-B-THEN-A gate: Same as A OR NOT B gate.

IF (E) N_1, N_2, N_3, FORTRAN: E is a meaningful sequence of variables, operators, and functions. The program will branch to statement number N_1, N_2, or N_3 depending on whether E is less than, equal to, or greater than zero, respectively.

i-f strip: The intermediate frequency amplifier stages in a superheterodyne.

IF-THEN: Same as inclusion.

IF-THEN gate: Same as A OR NOT B gate or B OR NOT A gate.

IF-THEN operation: Same as: inclusion, conditional implication operation.

i-f trimmer: A small variable capacitor in the i-f amplifier resonant circuits of an amplitude modulation (AM) broadcast band receiver.

ignore: 1. A typewriter character indicating that no action whatsoever be taken, i.e., in teletype or flexowriter code, a character code consisting of holes punched in every hole position is an ignore character, this convention makes possible erasing any previously punched character. 2. An instruction requiring nonperformance of what normally might be executed, i.e., not to be executed. This instruction should not be confused with a no-op or do nothing instruction, since these generally refer to an instruction outside themselves.

ignore block character: One of the main control characters which indicates that an error in data preparation or transmission has occurred and certain predetermined amounts of coming or recently transmitted data should be ignored. In this particular case, the amount to be ignored is a partial block of characters back to the most recently occurring block mark.

ignore gate: Same as A IGNORE B gate and B IGNORE A gate.

illegal: The status of a program which has attempted to perform a nonexistent instruction, or to violate the program area reservation check.

illegal character: A character or combination of bits not accepted as a valid representation by the machine or by a specific routine.

illegal code: A code character or symbol which appears to be the proper element but really is not a true member of the defined alphabet or specific language. If forbidden patterns, characters, or symbols present themselves, they are judged to be mistakes or the results of malfunctions.

illegal-command check: A specific check, usually programmed or automatic, to test for the use of or occurrence of codes which have no real assigned meaning or validity, i.e., illegal characters. Checks can be designed to have a flip-flop signal occur when the presence of illegal digits occur, i.e., to record or indicate the event.

illegal operation: The process which results when a computer either cannot perform the instruction part or will perform with invalid and undesired results. The limitation is often due to built-in computer constraints.

image: An exact duplicate array of information or data stored in, or in transit to, a different medium.

image dissector: In optical character recognition, a mechanical or electronic transducer that sequentially detects the level of light intensity in different areas of a completely illuminated sample space.

image interference: A failing peculiar to superheterodynes in which two stations separated by a frequency equal to twice the intermediate frequency (i-f) of the receiver may be received simultaneously.

image processing system: Consists of: (a) a graphic console which includes a display tube, control buttons and lights, an alphanumeric keyboard and a position indicating pencil; (b) a fling-spot or other type of scanning device which permits computer controlled scanning of film images; (c) a display adaptor unit; (d) a set of programs which allow contrast adjustments, subtractions, smoothing, and other image manipulation activities. Image processing is in use in a few locations to assist in morphologic studies of tissue cells (cytology, differential white-cell counts), chromosome typing, and x-ray diagnosis.

image sensors: Sensors known as charge-coupled devices (CCD), and nickel-size silicon chips containing over 120,000 electronic elements. When an image is focused on the CCD, the sensor's electronic elements transform the picture into individual electrical charge packets. These packets are then read out very rapidly by charge transfer techniques. The resulting information then can be processed and displayed as a television picture. In the CCD, half the electronic elements form the imaging array and the other half are for storage and readout. The CCD is being developed as part of broadly-based efforts aimed at developing all solidstate television systems and applying CCD technology to a wide range of other applications such as space exploration, closed-circuit television, military programs, surveillance systems, telephone systems transmitting television pictures, by consumers with home video records, and in broadcase camera applications.

imaginary number: 1. A number whose square is negative. 2. A number multiplied by itself yielding a negative number, e.g., the square root of—4 does not exist in the number system, it is neither +2 or—2. The symbol is used in mathematics to denote the imaginary unit.

IMIS: Integrated management information system.

immediate access: Pertaining to the ability to obtain data from or place data in a storage device or register directly, without serial delay due to other units of data, and usually in a relatively short time period.

immediate access store: A store whose access time is negligible in comparison with other operating times.

immediate   addressing: A   particular system of specifying the locations of operands and instructions in the same storage location, i.e., at the same address. This is contrasted with normal addressing in which the instruction word is stored at one address or location and contains the addresses of other locations where the operands are stored.

immediate symbol: A symbol that is assigned a specific value during the first pass of the assembly program.

impact strength: As related to magnetic tape, a measure of the work done in breaking a test sample of tape or base film by subjecting it to a sudden stress. Commonly used methods of applying the stress are by means of a free-falling or pneumatically driven projectile.

impedance: The total opposition offered by a component or circuit to the flow of an alternating or varying current: a combination of resistance and reactance.

impedance matching: When connection of a load impedance to the output terminals of a system does not result in maximum possible power being transferred to the load, or leads to excessive energy being reflected back towards the source, an impedance matching device (transformer, sub-line, etc.) may be connected between the output and the load to minimize or overcome these effects.

imperative statement: Action statement of a symbolic program that is converted into actual machine language.

implementation: The several steps concerned in installing and starting successful operation of computer systems or related machines. The steps begin with feasibility studies, applications studies, equipment selection, systems analysis (present) and design of proposed new system, physical location of equipment, operations analysis, and critical review.

implication: 1. A foreign particle imbedded in an otherwise uniform or homogeneous material; e.g., a foreign particle that changes the optical reflectance of paper being used for optical character recognition. 2. A logic operation with the property of "if-then." For instance, "A" is a statement and "B" is another statement, then, "A" inclusion "B" is false if "A" is true and "B" is false.

implicit address: In assembler programming, an address reference that is specified as one absolute or relocatable expression. An implicit address must be converted into its explicit base-displacement form before it can be assembled into the object code of a machine instruction.

implicit computation: An analog or digital computation which uses a self-nulling principle. For example, the variable sought first is assumed to exist, after which a synthetic variable is produced according to an equation and compared with a corresponding known variable. The difference between the synthetic and the known variable is driven to zero by correcting the assumed variable. Although the term applies to most analog circuits, even a single operational amplifier, it is restricted usually to computation performed by (a) circuits in which a function is generated at the output of a single high-gain dc amplifier in the feedback path, (b) circuits in which combinations of computing elements are interconnected in closed loops to satisfy implicit equations, or (c) circuits in which linear or nonlinear differential equations yield the solutions to a system of algebraic or transcendental equations in the steady state.

implicit function: An expression in which the form of the function is not expressed directly but which requires some operation to be performed, to render it evident. Thus, in the equation $ay^2 + bxy + cx^2 + dy + ex + f = 0$, y is an implicit function of x.

implicit instruction format: Contains no address part because it is used either when no address is required or when it is shown in some way.

impulse: A change in the intensity or level of some medium, usually over a relatively short period of time; e.g., a shift in electrical potential of a point for a short period of time compared to the time period, i.e., if the voltage level of a point shifts from -10 to +20 volts with respect to ground for a period of two microseconds, one says that the point received a 30-volt, 2-microsecond pulse.

impulse noise: A form of noise characterized by high amplitude and short duration, sometimes occurring as a group of impulses, or burst. Heard on the line as sharp clicks, impulse noise is a common source of error, originating from switching equipment, electrical storms, etc.

inactive station: A station that is ineligible currently for entering or accepting messages.

inband signaling: The transmission of signaling tones at some frequency or frequencies within the frequency band normally used for voiceband transmission.

incident record: See control record.

inclusion: 1. A foreign particle imbedded in an otherwise uniform or homogeneous material; for instance, a foreign particle that changes the optical reflectance of paper being used for optical character recognition. 2. A logic operation with the property of "if-then," for instance, "A" is a statement and "B" is another statement, then, "A" inclusion "B" is false if "A" is true and "B" is false.

inclusion gate: See B OR NOT A gate.

inclusive OR operator: A logical operator which has the property that P or Q is true, if P or Q, or both, are true.

inclusive reference: A reference between inclusive segments; that is, a reference from a segment in main storage to an external symbol in a segment that will not cause overlay of the calling segment.

inclusive segments: Overlay segments in the same region that can be in main storage simultaneously.

incoming group: Under telecommunications access method (TCAM), the portion of a message handler designed to handle messages arriving for the message control program.

incoming trunk: A trunk coming into a central office.

inconnector: A flow chart symbol which illustrates continuation of a broken flowline.

increment: An added part or portion as differentiated from decrement representing a decreasing portion. Mathematically, an increment is the average rate of change of a variable, y, with respect to a variable, x, within a given interval or $\Delta y/\Delta x$ where delta (Δ) represents a small change.

incremental: An arrangement of 2-bits phased 90 degrees (electrical) apart, from which direction of rotation can be sensed. Repeated sequentially and summed algebraically in an external counter.

incremental compaction: A procedure for data compaction using only the initial value, and all subsequent changes in storage for transmission. A saving in time and space is achieved only when the changes at specific intervals are transmitted or processed.

incremental computer: A computer in which changes in the variables rather than the variables themselves are represented. Those changes correspond to a change in an independent variable as defined by the equations being solved.

incremental coordinates: Coordinates measured from the preceding value in a sequence of values.

incremental data: Data which represents only the change from that data which just preceded it; hence, in incremental positioning each move is referenced to the prior one.

incremental dimension: A dimension expressed with respect to the preceding point in a sequence of points.

incremental feed: A manual or automatic input of present motion command for a machine axis.

incremental integrator: A digital integrator modified so that the output signal is maximum negative, zero, or maximum positive when the value of the input is negative, zero, or positive.

incremental representation: 1. A method of representing a variable in which changes in the values of the variable are represented, rather than the values themselves. 2. See binary incremental representation.

incremental tape: A type of magnetic tape written one character at a time as opposed to the usual record blocking approach used in computer systems; used for digital data logging.

incremental tape units: Magnetic tape modules that require a tape flow for reading and writing.

incremental transducer: Rotary or linear feedback device with discrete on-off pulses.

All pulses are the same, and there is always the same number of signals per unit length or per revolution. Direction is determined by special logic circuits.

independent events: Two events are said to be independent if the occurrence of either in no way effects the occurrence of the other.

independent modularity: The property of a system which allows it to accept changes and adjust processing accordingly to yield maximum utilization on all modules without reprogramming. This system is used in multiprocessing. To achieve this objective, the computer system incorporates master control programs to exercise at an unprecedented degree of automatic control.

independent operations: Operations which do not inhibit the operation of any unit which is not connected or concerned in the operation concerned.

independent routine: A routine executed independently of manual operations, but only if certain conditions occur within a program or record, or during some other process.

independent sector designating device: A device utilized for group indication.

independent sideband transmission: A type of transmission in which frequencies produced by modulation of a carrier wave are symmetrically spaced both above and below the carrier frequency and all are transmitted.

independent utility programs: A group of utility programs that support, but are not part of, the main computer operating system. They are used chiefly by the system programmer to initialize and prepare direct access storage devices for use under operating system control.

independent variable: A variable whose value is not a direct function of some other variable and does not depend on another variable. The independent variable is usually plotted as the abscissa (horizontal line) on an axis.

index: An integer used to specify the location of information within a table or program.

index (data management):   1. Table in the catalog structure used to locate data sets. 2. A table used to locate the records of an indexed sequential data set.

indexed sequential access method (ISAM):   See basic indexed sequential access method.

indexed sequential data set: A data set in which each record contains a key that determines its location. The location of each record is computed through the use of an index.

indexed sequential file: A file composed of records with keys (or identifiers) in which the records are arranged in ascending sequence by key value and for which a file index is continuously maintained.

indexed sequential organization: A file organization in which records are arranged in logical sequence by key. Indexes to these keys permit direct access to individual records.

index entry: An individual line or item of data contained in an index, such as, an entry in a dictionary.

index field value: The contents of the three bit index (X) field of an instruction word (bit 12-14) designating one of the current general registers 1-7 as an index register.

indexing: A technique of address modification often implemented by means of index registers.

index number: Used to measure the changes in the large number of constantly varying items in the data. The index number measures fluctuations during intervals of time, group differences of geographical position or degree, etc.

index positions: Specified areas, e.g., the row-column intersects, on a punch card where holes may be punched.

index register: A special register designed to modify the operand address in an instruction or base address by addition or subtraction, yielding a new effective address.

index word: 1. A storage position or register the contents of which may be used to modify automatically the effective address of any given instruction. 2. An index based on the selection of words as used in a document, without giving thought to synonyms and more generic concepts related to the term selected.

index word register: A register which contains a quantity which may be used to modify addresses (and for other purposes) under direction of the control section of the computer. (Sometimes known as b-box.)

indicating instrument: A specific measuring instrument in which the value of the measured quantity is developed to be indicated visually.

indicator chart: One used by a programmer during the logical design and coding of a program to record items about the use of indicators in the program. A portion of program documentation.

indicators: The devices – usually lights on the operator's console – which register conditions, such as high or equal conditions resulting from a comparison of plus or minus conditions resulting from a computation. A sequence of operations within a procedure may be varied according to the position of an indicator.

indicator, volume: See plugboard.

indirect control: When one peripheral unit controls another through various types of electronic ties that require human intervention.

indirect cost effectiveness: That cost effectiveness related to the benefit accrued primarily by the consumer rather than the provider; i.e., a shorter hospital stay, a tool which may accomplish a task more quickly. Note that the unit cost may increase.

indirectly controlled system: A specific portion of the controlled system in which the indirectly controlled variable is changed in response to changes in the controlled variable.

indirectly controlled variable: A distinct variable which does not originate a feedback signal, but which is related to, and influenced by, the directly controlled variable.

indirect reference address: A reference address in an instruction that contains a 1 in bit position 0; the virtual address of the location that contains the direct address. If indirect addressing is called for by an instruction, the reference address field is used to access a word location that contains the direct reference address; this then replaces the indirect reference address and is used as an operand address value. Indirect addressing is limited to one level and is performed prior to indexing (in some computers).

individual line: A subscriber line arranged to serve only one main station, although additional stations may be connected to the line as extensions. An individual line is not arranged for discriminatory ringing with respect to the stations on that line.

induced failure: An equipment failure caused by the environment around the failed item.

induction coil: An apparatus for transforming a direct current by induction into an alternating current.

inductive potentiometer: A type of toroidally-wound autotransformer with one or more adjustable sliders.

industrial data processing: Data processing for industrial purposes, most often relating to numerical control of machines, or management reporting and planning.

industrial process control: Some application areas are: (a) precious metals production, (b) cement production, (c) environmental control, (d) pilot plants, (e) chemical processes, (f) petroleum refining and many others. The data acquisition and control system provides maximum flexibility in the types of process data that it can accept, and the variety of output signals and data format that a computer may exercise.

inequivalence: 1. The Boolean operator which gives a truth table value of true if only one of the two variables it connects is true. 2. A logical operator which has the property that if P is a statement and Q is a statement, then P exclusive or Q is true if and only if either but not both statements are true, false if and only if both are true or both are false. P exclusive or Q is often represented by PQ.

infinite pad method: In optical character recognition, a method of measuring reflectance of a paper stock such that doubling the number of backing sheets of the same stock will not change the measured reflectance.

infix notation: A method of forming one-dimensional expressions (i.e., arithmetic, logical, etc.) by alternating single operands and operators. Any operator performs its indicated function upon its adjacent terms which are defined subject to the rules of operator precedence and grouping brackets which eliminate ambiguity.

info field: A field of a data frame containing a single transport message. The info field of a control frame is not used.

information: 1. The meaningful contents of a databearing signal. 2. An aggregation of data that may or may not be edited and formatted.

information bit: One of those bits which is used to specify the characters of a given code group (opposed to framing bits).

information bits: In telecommunications, bits that are generated by the data source and which are not used for error-control by the data-transmission system.

information channel: The transmission and intervening equipment involved in the transfer of information in a given direction between two terminals. An information channel includes the modulator and demodulator, and any error-control equipment irrespective of its location, as well as the backward channel when provided.

information content: The negative of the logarithm of the probability that this particular message or symbol will be emitted from the source. 1. The choice of logarithmic base determines the unit of information content. 2. The probability of a given message or symbol being emitted may depend on one or more preceding messages or symbols. 3. The quantity has been called self-information.

information efficiency: A measure composed of the actual negative entropy divided by the maximum possible entropy using the same set of signs.

information feedback system: In telecommunications, an information transmission system that uses an echo check to verify the accuracy of the transmission.

information flow analysis: The development of organizing and analyzing techniques to obtain facts and information about the organization, initialization, and flow to the final users of reports throughout the enterprise or organization.

information function: A special mathematical function which describes a source of information.

information link: The physical means for connecting two locations for telecommunications purposes.

information loss: 1. That progressive irreversible process in a magnetic cell which is caused by successive partial drive pulses or digit pulses in an incorrectly operating storage unit or medium. 2. A reduction of information content which results from restrictive input or processing procedures by reason of limited size, for an information element, or inexact or oversimplified coding.

information processing: 1. The processing of data representing information and the determination of the meaning of the processed data. 2. Usually a less restrictive term than data processing, encompassing the totality of scientific and business operations performed by a computer.

information processing system: A system that receives, processes, and delivers information.

information rate (from a source, per second): The product of the average information content per symbol and the average number of symbols per second.

information rate (from a source, per symbol): See average information content.

information rate (through a channel, per second): The product of the average transinformation per symbol and the average number of symbols per second.

information rate (through a channel, per symbol): See average transinformation.

information retrieval: The methods and procedures for recovering specific information from stored data. See also retrieval, message.

information retrieval system: A computing system application designed to recover specific information from a mass of data.

information retrieval techniques: Recovering, collecting, and segmenting particular items of information which are required at a specific time and for a specific purpose. The basis of most techniques relates to communication, clarification, and indexing. Information enters the system, is analyzed, clarified, and stored. The user then trans-

lates his requirement and a search of storage is developed. This index technique can be assisted by a technique such as key word in context (KWIC), indexes, and other systems.

information separator: Any of several control characters used to mark logical boundaries between sets of information.

information source: An information generator. This output is assumed to be free from error.

information, supervisory, and unnumbered frames: The three kinds of frames in bit-oriented protocols.

information system: The network of all communication methods within an organization. Information may be derived from many sources other than a data processing unit such as by telephone, by contact with other people, or by studying an operation.

information theory: 1. The branch of learning concerned with the study of measures of information and their properties. 2. The branch of learning concerned with the likelihood of accurate transmission or communication of messages subject to transmission failure, distortion, and noise.

information transfer: When the total information outside a channel or component equals the total information within. If the information outside is less than the information inside it is said to be "nonconservative."

information transmission system: A system which receives and delivers information without changing it.

information word: An ordered set of characters that have at least one meaning and are handled by the computer as a unit.

infrared: That portion of the radiation spectrum having a wavelength in the range which adjoins the visible ray spectrum and extends to the microwave radio frequencies.

inherited error: The error in the initial values, especially the error inherited from the previous steps in the step-by-step integration.

inhibit: 1. To prevent an event from taking place. 2. To prevent a device or logic element from producing a specified output.

inhibiting input: A gate input that, if in its prescribed state, prevents any output which might otherwise occur.

inhibition rules: Used in resolving conflicts when two interrupts occur at the same time or when one occurs before another is processed.

inhibit wire: 1. The conductive core which carries the pulse that is capable of restoring a part magnetic state to a magnetic core. Such ability prevents the loss of a stored bit. 2. Wire used in memory cores when the core is required to remain in a zero state.

in-house: System development or operation performed by an organization's own staff, as opposed to contracting the work to an outside organization.

in-house line: A privately owned or leased line separate from a public right of way.

initial condition mode: In analog computing, the integrators are inoperative, and the required initial conditions are applied or reapplied, as contrasted to the operate mode when the input signals are connected to the computing units, including integrators for the generation of the solution.

initial error: The error caused when there is a difference between the true and actual value of an argument and the value used for the computation.

initial flow data: A flowchart that represents the path of data in the solving of a problem, and that defines the major phases of the processing as well as the various data media used.

initial instruction: A procedure stored within a computer to ease the loading of programs.

initialize: 1. A program or hardware circuit which will return a program, a system or a hardware device to an original state. 2. To set an instruction, counter, switch, or address to a specified starting condition at a specified time in a program.

initial program load (IPL): The initialization procedure that causes an operating system to commence operation.

initial start: Beginning of data processing upon loading a system into a computer.

initiating task: The job management task that controls the selection of a job and the preparation of the steps of that job for execution.

initiation area discriminator: A unique cathode-ray tube (CRT) combined with a photoelectric cell to discern unmapped or uncorrelated long-range radar data for processing by various specific programs in defenseoriented procedures.

injection laser diode: A semiconductor device where lasing occurs within at least one positive/negative junction, where light is emitted from the edge of the diode.

ink ribbon: Continuous ribbon of ink used in a computer line printer or a punched card tabulator. In a computer line printer a typical ribbon is 16 inches wide and several feet long and is fed vertically through the print unit while the printer is operating. A tabulator ribbon is typically only half as wide and is fed laterally across the print unit.

in-line: A system whereby transactions are processed in the line, or in the sequence, in which they arrive without the need for sorting.

in-line processing: The processing of data in random order, not subject to preliminary editing or sorting.

in-line subroutine: A subroutine inserted directly into the linear operational sequence. Such a subroutine must be recopied at each point that it is needed in a routine.

inner macroinstruction: A macroinstruction that is nested inside a macro definition.

in-plant: A communication system operating within a central office or factory.

in-processing: Same as on-line.

input: 1. (ISO) Pertaining to a device, process, or channel involved in an input process or to the data or states involved in an input process. In the English language, the adjective "input" may be used in place of "input data, " "input signal," "input terminal," etc., when such usage is clear in a given context. 2. Pertaining to a device, process, or channel involved in the insertion of data or states, or to the data or states involved. 3. One, or a sequence of, input states. 4. Same as input channel. 5. Same as input data. 6. Same as input device. 7. Same as input process. 8. The process of transferring data from an external storage to an internal storage. 10. The data to be processed. 11. An adjective referring to a device or collective set of devices used for bringing data into another device. 12. A channel for impressing a state on a device or logic element.

input area: The area of internal storage into which data are transferred from external storage.

input block: 1. A section of internal storage of a computer reserved for the receiving and processing of input information. Synonymous with input area. 2. An input buffer. 3. A block of computer words considered as a unit and intended or destined to be transferred from an external source or storage medium to the internal storage of the computer.

input blocking factor (B): In a tape sort, the number of data records in each record of the input file.

input-buffer register: A device that receives data from input devices (tape, disk) and then transfers it to internal computer storage.

input channel: A channel for impressing a state on a device or logic element. Same as input.

input (communications): 1. The current, voltage, power, or driving force applied to a circuit or device. 2. The terminals or other places where current, voltage, power, or driving force may be applied to a circuit or device.

input data: Data to be processed. Same as input.

input device: The mechanical unit designed to bring data to be processed into a computer, e.g., a card reader, a tape reader, or a keyboard.

input editing: Inputs may be edited to convert them to a more convenient format for processing and storage than that used for entry into the system; and to check the data for proper format, completeness, or accuracy. Often, inputs must be formatted as most convenient for preparation by humans, and then must be reformatted for computer use.

input equipment: 1. The equipment used for transferring data and instructions into an automatic data processing system. 2. The equipment by which an operator transcribes original data and instructions to a medium that may be used in an automatic data processing system.

input impedance: Impedance measured at the input terminals, such as a typewriter terminal, cathode-ray tube (CRT), transmission line or gate, or an amplifier, all under no-load conditions.

input job stream: A sequence of job control statements entering the system which may include input data.

input limiter: A circuit of nonlinear elements that restrict the electrical excursion of a variable in accordance with some specified criteria. Hard limiting is a limiting action with negligible variation in output in the range where the output is limited. Soft limiting is a limiting action with appreciable variation in output in the range where the output is limited. A bridge limiter is a bridge circuit used as a limiter circuit. In an analog computer, a feedback limiter is a limiter circuit usually employing biased diodes shunting the feedback component of an operational amplifier; an input limiter is a limiter circuit usually employing biased diodes in the amplifier input channel that operates by limiting the current entering the summing junction.

input loading: Amount of load imposed upon the sources supplying signals to the input.

input medium: The mode of information presentation, i.e., punched card, punched tape, etc.

input mode: Under time-sharing option (TSO), an entry mode that accepts successive lines of input under the EDIT command for a line data set. The lines are not checked for the presence of subcommands.

input module: The device or collective set of devices used to bring data into another device, or a channel, or process device for transferring data from an external storage to an internal storage.

input/output cable: Refers to a wire, bus or trunk used to connect the various input or output devices to the computer.

input/output channel control: The transfer of data between external devices and their associated assembly registers proceeds under the control of the external device. Input/output channels may transfer data simultaneously in multichannel operation. The access to main memory from the in/out channel is made available as needed, subject to channel priority. This is provided by channel priority logic which selects the channel of highest priority requesting transfer; that is, the lowest numbered channel requesting transfer of data. The data rate and active channels are not restricted except that the program must not require data transfer which exceeds a peak word rate of 55 kc considered over all input/output channels (in some computers).

input/output channel selection: Permits the computer to designate a particular channel in the terminal.

input/output control extensiveness: Includes (a) physical and logical control over I/O records, files, and units; (b) buffer control; (c) teleprocessing terminal and message handling; (d) random access I/O control; (e) labeling of files; and (f) error-recovery procedures.

input/output control program: The control of input/output operations by the supervisory (computer) program.

input/output equipment: Pertains to those specific units of the total computing system which are designed to accept data and output the results of computing and processing in a form readable either by humans or other processing units.

input/output information messages: Listed on the operator message device and the system output device. The operator message device is defined by the available equipment in the system. Normally it is the console typewriter but may be the line printer if no typewriter is available. The system output device may be different from the operator message device. For example, the operator message device may be the console typewriter and the system output device may be the line printer. This gives the operator an indication of the operations being performed and also gives a complete list of the job operations on the system output device for the programmer. Messages are not duplicated when the system output device and operator message device are the same.

input/output interrupt inhibit: The bit, in the program status doubleword, that indicates whether (if 1) or not (if 0) all internal interrupts of the I/O group are inhibited.

input/output (I/O): 1. A device that gets data in and out of the computer. 2. The data that goes into a computer and comes out of a computer. 3. The media carrying the data such as card, tape, disk, etc. 4. The process of transmitting data to and from the computer.

input/output processor (IOP): Transfers operations to and from main memory.

input/output real-time control: All I/O data transfers are controlled automatically by signals emanating from the central processor or from the peripheral subsystems themselves. Any general purpose I/O channel can accommodate a real-time system peripheral device. All I/O channels are buffered. Each I/O device has associated with it a control unit which, once activated by the central processor, carries out the entire operation of the instruction given it, while the central processor proceeds with other tasks.

input/output register: Registers that temporarily hold I/O data.

input/output routines: Computer program routines used to simplify the programming task.

input/output unit control: Directs the interaction between the processing unit and input/output devices.

input process: The transmission of data and its reception from peripheral hardware or as an exchange of external storage to internal storage.

input program: 1. A specific routine, sometimes stored permanently in a computer, designed to allow the reading of programs and data into the machine. 2. A routine which directs or controls the reading of programs and data into a computer system. Such a routine may be stored internally, wired, or part of a "bootstrap" operation and may perform housekeeping or system control operations according to rules.

input queue: See input work queue.

input record: 1. One read into memory from an input device during a run. 2. The current record stored in an input area ready for processing.

input reference: The specific reference designed and used to compare the measured variable resulting in a deviation or error signal. Also referred to as set point, or desired value.

input rotem: That particular set of instructions which cause data to be accepted by a computer system and generally designed as a built-in feature.

input routine: A routine, sometimes stored permanently in a computer, to allow reading of programs and data into the machine.

input signal: The control-loop signal when it enters a data block.

input state: The state occurring on a specified input channel.

input storage: 1. Holds each bundle of facts while it awaits its turn to be processed. This allows successive bundles to be compared to make sure they are in the right order or for other control purposes. 2. Any information that enters a computer for the purpose of being processed or to aid in processing. It is then held until signaled for use by the control program.

input stream: The sequence of job control statements and data submitted to an operating system on an input unit especially activated for this purpose by the operator. Same as input job stream.

input stream control: Same as job entry substream (JES) reader.

input tape (sorting): The process used for data introduction to particular devices using tapes, either plastic, metallic, or paper tape —chadded or chadless—or fabric tape loops, e.g., the data links or channels used to read data from tape, such as, tape readers, stations, handlers, transports, etc.

input tape test: A method of testing and simulation, wherein a test input tape is prepared from an input message tape, which is then read by the test supervisory program in a manner as if it had actually arrived from regular input devices.

input translator: A section of a computer program that converts the incoming programmer's instruction into operators and operands understood by the computer. This scan or search also checks the input items for desired properties and, in many cases, outputs appropriate error messages if the desired properties of the input do not conform to the proper syntax.

input unit: Any peripheral unit which provides input to the central processor computer, such as a card reader, paper tape reader.

input work queue: A queue of summary information of job control statements maintained by the job scheduler, from which it selects the jobs and job steps to be processed.

inquiry: A technique whereby the interrogation of the contents of a computer's storage may be initiated at a local or remote point by use of a keyboard, touchtone pad, or other device.

inquiry and communications systems: Computer systems are now provided with facilities for diversified onsite and long distance inquiry and data communications networks. Centralized records and data processing operations can be tied in with information sources at remote locations and will provide instant on-line response to interrogations and input data from a large number of inquiry stations. Communication networks may include standard tele-type stations, and electric typewriter stations.

inquiry and transaction processing: A type of teleprocessing application in which inquiries and records of transactions received from a number of terminals are used to interrogate or update one or more master files maintained by the central system.

inquiry answer (remote): In an operating teleprocessing network, several inquiries simultaneously might come into the system from distant cities concerning information that is contained in a disk file. The appropriate records world then be taken from the disk file and the appropriate responses would be prepared and returned to the original cities. Although this appears to be a simple function, it requires design balance to achieve the required variety of terminal speeds and functions, simultaneous operation of many devices operating through a single economical channel, the time-sharing and space-sharing programs that control these devices, and the range of disk file capacity and speed. Furthermore, it has to do all these things concurrently with batch job processing.

inquiry character: Designed to elicit a response from some remote station, usually for station identification or for the description of the station equipment and status.

inquiry-response: Requests for information are transmitted from a remote terminal to a central processor, where a response is generated and transmitted back to the terminal. The inquiry-processing function may be combined with on-line updating.

inquiry station: 1. (ISO) A user terminal primarily for the interrogation of an automatic data processing system. 2. Data terminal equipment used for inquiry into a data processing system.

inquiry-terminal display: Information is placed into the computer through the alphanumeric keyboard and is simultaneously displayed on the screen. The unit then displays a reply to the inquiry on the screen. Information is displayed many times faster than that produced by an operator by means of a type-out. To re-use the display after the inquiry has been answered requires only a press of the erase button.

inscribe: The action of reading the data recorded on documents and writing the same data on the same document. The document thus becomes available and suitable for the application of automatic reading by optical character readers or other reading devices.

inserted subroutine: 1. A separately coded sequence of instructions that is inserted in another instruction sequence directly in low order of the line. 2. A directly inserted subroutine to the main line program specifically where it is required. 3. A subroutine that must be relocated and inserted into the main routine at each place it is used.

insertion method (sorting):   The technique of internal sorting in which records are moved to permit insertion of other records.

instability: Tendency for a circuit to break into unwanted oscillations.

installation: A particular computing system, in the context of the overall function it serves and the individuals who manage it, operate it, apply it to problems, service it, and use the results it produces.

installation time: Time spent in installing and testing either hardware, or software, or both, until they are accepted.

instantaneous access: Obtaining data directly from, or placing data into a storage device or register without serial delay due to other units of data, and usually in a relatively short period of time.

instantaneous frequency: The instantaneous rate of change of phase with respect to time (expressed in radians per seconds) divided by two.

instantaneous-transmission rate: A rate at which data is transmitted through its channel, but measured during the time data is actually being transmitted.

in-stream procedure: A set of job control statements placed in the input stream that can be used any number of times during a job by naming the procedure in an execute (EXEC) statement.

instruction: A set of bits which will cause a computer to perform certain prescribed operations. A computer instruction consists of: 1. an operation code which specifies the operation(s) to be performed; 2. one or more operands (or addresses of operands in memory); 3. one or more modifiers (or addresses of modifiers) used to modify the operand or its address.

instruction address: The address that must be used to fetch an instruction.

instruction address register (IAR):   A computer register that contains the address of the next instruction to be executed.

instructional constant: A constant to be used in a computer program that is written in the form of an instruction, but is really a piece of data (one form of a dummy instruction).

instructional cycle: The steps involved in the processing of an instruction.

instruction area: 1. A part of storage allocated to receive and store the group of instructions to be executed. 2. The storage locations used to store the program.

instruction characters: Characters, when used as code elements, can initiate, modify, or stop a control operation. Characters may be used, for example, to control the carriage return, etc.

instruction code: The symbols, names, and definitions of all the instructions which are directly intelligible to a given computer or a given executive routine.

instruction control circuits: The circuits which cause the computer to carry out the instructions in proper sequence, and which can control by permitting only the coded conditions to continue or function.

instruction control unit: A specific device or unit which causes the retrieval of instructions to appear in proper sequence and to be individually interpreted with the proper signals to the arithmetic unit or other computer segments in accordance with the interpretation it makes.

instruction counter: The computer register that keeps track of the next instruction to be executed.

instruction external devices: The computer sends instructions to external devices which tell those devices to initiate special operations. After an external device operation has been initiated, all control of events passes to the logic associated with that external device until the operation is completed. During the operation the external device will respond busy to attempts by the processor to initiate further operations. The sequencing of events during this operation derives its timing from the external devices and its logic.

instruction format: The allocation of bits or characters of a machine instruction to specific functions.

instruction modification: A change in the operationcode portion of an instruction or command such that if the routine containing the instruction or command is repeated, the computer will perform a different operation.

instruction register: See program counter.

instruction repertoire: 1. The set of instructions a particular computer can perform. 2. The set of operations that can be represented in a given operation code.

instruction set: Same as instruction repertoire (1).

instruction short: The use of an index specification in a FORTRAN READ or WRITE statement.

instruction statement: See instruction.

instruction time: The portion of an instruction cycle during which the control unit is analyzing the instruction and setting up to perform the indicated operation.

instruction word: 1. A grouping of letters or digits handled by the computer as a distinct unit to signify the provision of definitions of operations to be performed or the description of further data. 2. A part of a word or all of a word which is executed by the computer as an instruction.

instrumentation: 1. Various types of equipment capabilities related to automatic data acquisition. 2. The application of devices for the measuring, recording and/or controlling of physical properties and movements.

instrumentation calibrate: A procedure to ascertain, usually by comparison with a standard, the locations at which scale/chart graduations should be placed to correspond to a series of values of the quantity which the instrument is to measure, receive, or transmit.

instrumentation correction: The calculated difference between the true value and the indication of the measured quantity; i.e., a positive correction denotes that the indication of the instrument is less than the true value.

insulator: A nonconducting material.

INTCP: See intercept.

integer: A whole number as distinguished from a fraction; that is, a number that contains the unit (one) an exact number of times.

integer constants (FORTRAN): An integer constant is a number without a decimal point, using the decimal digits 0,

1,...,9. A preceding + or − sign is optional, and an unsigned integer constant is assumed to be positive.

integer numbering system: Whole numbers; i.e., numbers without fractional parts. Digital computers can handle fractions, mixed numbers, or single integers (which includes zero). Most computer users distinguish digit, integer, number, and numeral systems.

integer programming: 1. In operations research, a class of procedures for locating the maximum or minimum of a function subject to constraints, where some or all variables must have integer values. 2. Loosely, discrete programming.

integral: 1. The result of integration either of a function or of an equation; an expression whose derivative is the integrand. 2. An expression which after being differentiated will produce a given differential.

integral action limiter: A program or unit which limits the value of the output signal due to integral action to a predetermined value.

integral action rate: Relates to proportional plus integral or proportional plus integral plus derivative control devices; a step input, the ratio of the initial rate of change of output due to integral control action to the change in steady-state output due to proportional control action; i.e., integral action rate usually is expressed as the number of repeats per minute due to the fact it is equal to the number of times per minute that the proportional response to a step input is repeated by the initial integral response. Concerning integral control devices, for a step input, the ratio of the initial rate of change of output to the input change.

integral boundary: A location in main storage at which a fixed-length field, such as a halfword or doubleword, must be positioned. The address of an integral boundary is a multiple of the length of the field, in bytes.

integral control action (reset): A specifically designed control action in which the output is proportional to the time integral of the input, i.e., the rate of change of output is proportional to the input. Same as high-limiting control action.

integral reset controller: A unique single action controller which produces integral control action only.

integrated adapter: An integral part of a central processing unit that provides for the direct connection of a particular type of device and uses neither a control unit nor the standard I/O interface. See also integrated communications adapter, integrated file adapter.

integrated circuit, hunting: A special type of integrated circuit which has a substrate of a passive material with active chips attached to its surface, i.e., a combination circuit.

integrated circuit (IC): Complete module of components manufactured as single, solid units made by either a film deposition or a diffusion process. Integrated circuits may be used as logic circuitry or as storage modules capable of recording many individual bits of information. Integrated circuits offer the advantage of higher speeds because pulses have shorter distances to travel and require less power, and because manufacturing techniques have made integrated circuits relatively inexpensive, a user can obtain a given level of computing power for less cost or more computing power for a given cost. Integrated circuits are contrasted to the discrete components—transistors, diodes, capacitors, and resistors—which were assembled into circuits that were plugged into receptacles in the computer.

integrated communications adapter: An integrated adapter that allows connection of multiple communication lines to a processing unit.

integrated data processing (IDP): 1. A system that treats as a whole all data processing requirements to accomplish a sequence of data processing steps, or a number of related data processing sequences, and which strives to reduce or eliminate duplicating data entry or processing steps. 2. The processing of data by such a system.

integrated emulator: An emulator program whose execution is controlled by an operating system in a multiprogramming environment.

integrated file adapter: An integrated adapter that allows connection of multiple disk storage devices to a processing unit.

integrated injection logic (I^2L): Characterized by some observers as the bipolar large-scale integration (LSI) of the future. Its primary advantages are increased density, good speed-power product, versatility, and low cost. The technology is capable of squeezing 1000 to 3000 gates, or more than 10000 bits of memory, on a single chip. It has speed-power product as low as 1 picojoule (pj) compared to 100 pj with transistor-to-transistor logic (TTL). It can handle digital and analog functions on a single chip and is made with a five mask process without the need for currentsource and load resistors.

integrated monolithic circuit: Several logic circuits, gates, and flip-flops are etched on single crystals, ceramics, or other semiconductor materials and designed to use geometric etching and conductive ink deposition techniques all within a hermetically sealed chip. Some chips with many resistors and transistors are extremely tiny, others are in effect "sandwiches" of individual chips.

integrated system: The combination of processes which results in the introduction of data which need not be repeated as further allied or related data is also entered. For example, shipment data may also be the basis for inventory inquiries, invoicing marketing reports, etc.

integrated terminal equipment (ITE): Provides voice features simultaneously with data transmission, using common two-pair telephone wire. Data terminals attach directly to built-in RS-232-C or RS-449 connectors. Instruments range from 12-button to 30-button models. In a distributed system, ITEs may be placed up to 54000 feet apart.

integrating amplifier: An analog computer amplifier whose output voltage is proportional to the time integral of the input voltage. Thus, the output voltage is proportional to the area under a time-curve plot of a variable between a given reference time and an arbitrary point in time.

integrating circuit: A device whose output function is proportional to the integral of the input function with respect to a specified variable; e.g., a watt-hour meter.

integrating mechanism: A specific integrator that has input/output variables presented by the angles of rotation of shafts, i.e., basically a gear of infinitely variable ratios.

integrator: 1. A resistor-condenser circuit at the input to the vertical oscillator. 2. A device whose output is proportional to the integral of the input variable with respect to time.

integrator capacitors: May be shunted by a resistor to permit the zero balance of an integrator.

integrator (computing unit): 1. A device which has two input variables (x and y) and one output variable (z), the value of z being proportional to the integral of y with respect to x. 2. One with one input and one output variable, the value of the output variable being proportional to the integral of the input with respect to elapsed time.

integrity: Preservation of data or programs for their intended purpose.

intellectronics: The use of electronics to extend man's intellect. For example, the use of a computer to recall facts and formulas, and by applying logic to a situation, to arrive at the logical conclusion.

intelligence amplifier: The computer becomes an intelligence amplifier when its enormous manipulative and computational powers are combined with the imagination, intuition, and evaluation capabilities of man. The computer becomes an intelligence amplifier by multiplying the orders of magnitude of the capabilities of man's mind and providing him the freedom to explore in depth all the ramifications of his ideas.

intelligence sample: A part of a signal that indicates the quality of the population.

intelligent keyboard systems: An intelligent keyboard system must provide the following functions: keying, displaying, editing, calculating, storing, compressing, communicating, and printing.

intelligent minicomputer terminals: General purpose computers have been used frequently in remote job entry terminals to allow local processing and to handle the functions of communicating with a larger computer. Now however, built-in minicomputers are being used in lower speed, manual, interactive-type terminals. It has become economical to let a general-purpose computer handle the communications control functions formerly performed by special-purpose logic. In addition, minicomputers are now built-in and can do other things such as local editing of the data to be transmitted, and compression of the data to minimize the amount of communications required. They can also handle a certain amount of error correction for the user.

intelligent terminal: A terminal with some level of programmable "intelligence" for performing preprocessing or post-processing operations.

INTELSAT I: See Early Bird.

INTELSAT II: Early Bird was followed by the successful launching of three

INTELSAT II series satellites during 1967. One of these was positioned over the Atlantic Ocean and two were placed in operation over the Pacific, thereby extending satellite coverage to more than two-thirds of the world.

INTELSAT III: The more powerful satellites of the INTELSAT III series were positioned over the Atlantic, Pacific and Indian Oceans during 1968-70. The Indian Ocean satellite completed global coverage by the satellites, a goal toward which COMSAT and INTELSAT had worked since inception.

INTELSAT IV: The capacity and flexibility of the global system was greatly expanded with the introduction of the INTELSAT IV series of satellites, the first of which was launched in January 1971 and began service the following March. These advanced high-capacity satellites each provide an average capacity of about 4000 telephone circuits.

INTELSAT IV-A: New INTELSAT IV-A satellites, planned for launch beginning late in 1975, have almost twice INTELSAT IV capacity, and introduce frequency re-use through spot beam separation. After evaluating the alternatives of employing proven technology (an improved INTELSAT IV satellite), and a completely new INTELSAT V satellite, the INTELSAT governing body chose to rely upon proven techniques and, accordingly, approved the construction of three INTELSAT IV-A satellites at a cost of $72 million for delivery beginning the late part of 1975.

INTELSAT IV-A spot beam separation: Frequency re-use by beam separation permits a given frequency band to be used in different directions by different transponders and antenna beams, thereby increasing the total bandwidth available for use by a single satellite. The increased bandwidth results in higher satellite communications capacity and was the first commercial application of this concept in satellite communications.

INTELSAT V studies: Systems engineering studies were conducted with the intent to arrive at the definition of the characteristics of the satellites of the INTELSAT V series. This actively constitutes an extension of the follow-on studies on the INTELSAT IV satellites which led in 1971 to the design, eventually adopted, for INTELSAT IV-A series. Fundamental concepts and subsystems requirements were reviewed in terms of assumed various models for the entire INTELSAT system. Thus, a variety of spacecraft configurations, communications subsystems, including earth station technology, were examined, leading to the definition of two generic spacecraft designs.

intenet packet controllers (IPCs): A family of format and protocol conversion packages; they support dissimilar devices, allowing them to communicate without altering the devices themselves. IPCs are available for certain word processing systems, entry to X.25 networks such as Telenet and Tymnet, and for ASCII CRT emulation of 3270 IBM devices. Usage is transparent to the user.

interacting control algorithm: Specific control action which is produced by an algorithm whose various terms are interdependent.

interaction: The acceptance by a system of a line of input from a terminal, processing of the line, and a return of data, if any, to the terminal. See also interaction time.

interaction time: In systems with time-sharing, the time between acceptance by the system of a line of input from a terminal and the point at which it can accept the next line from the terminal. Contrast with response time.

interactive: A system which performs processing or problem-solving tasks by carrying on a dialog with the user.

interactive console uses: A particular interactive terminal user may control one or more batch processes at remote systems from the same terminal. Here, and in the previous modes, it is implicit that the user is responsible for specifying host systems to be used and for overtly scheduling the subtasks of a complete network job in a meaningful and sensible manner. This usage mode is the predominant activity on the Advanced Research Project Agency (ARPA).

interactive graphics: Graphics where the viewer can manipulate or change the display in some way.

interactive processing: A development made possible by the advent of time-sharing; involves the constant interplay of creative and routine activities with the routine jobs being relegated to the computer.

interactive system: Specific computer capability relating to direct communication between man and machine with real-time rapidity; i.e., the thought process of humans remains uninterrupted by machine delays.

interactive terminals: Equipped with a display, a keyboard, and an incremental printer. Optionally they also include a tape subsystem. Such terminals support interactive, conversational, demand, inquiry, and transaction oriented applications.

interairline network: All major U.S. carriers interconnect their reservation computers.

inter-arrival time: The interval between messages or processing requests. Important in queuing theory.

interblock gap: The space on magnetic tape separating two blocks of data or information.

intercalcate: The following or insertion of data as an interfiling or punched card into a file of cards.

intercarrier signal: The 4.5 megacycle signal in a television receiver.

intercept: The action taken by a control station whereby messages addressed to an inoperative station are accepted and stored at the control station unit until they can be sent to the destination station. The control station may be a computer in a messages-witching system.

intercepting: Routing of a call or message placed for a disconnected or nonexistent telephone number or terminal address to an operator position or to an especially designated terminal.

intercepting trunk: A trunk to which a call for a vacant number or changed number or a line out of order is connected for action by an operator.

interception: The route of a call directed to an invalid telephone number or terminal address to an operator or to a specially designated terminal when a normal call is not completed.

interchangeable card feed: A device which usually converts an 80 column card feed to a 52 column card feed.

interchangeable connector: Connectors from one manufacturer which can mate with connectors designed by other manufacturers or a multivariable connector, i.e., ones which have inserts for various contact configurations which can be interchanged in the standard holder.

interchangeable variable length block format: Data that is not constrained to a fixed length or position format.

interchannel time displacement (skew): Maximum time difference between earliest and latest bits of a single parallel bit character. ICTD for a tape transport, head, and guide assembly is based on the full width of the tape, includes the effects of interchanging tapes between machines, and is measured after the start time has elapsed. Tape width and tape speed must be stated with each ICTD specification. Note: ICTD is simply the total time delay between a pair of bits and tolerance values are of no significance.

intercommunicating system: A privately owned system without a switchboard capable of two-way communication, normally limited to a single unit, building or plant. Stations may or may not be equipped for originating a call, but they can answer any call.

intercomputer communication: Increased bit transmission speeds permit very favorable economies to be made in computer/-communication systems. Of particular interest is matching of the asymmetrical characteristics of the information flow found in many situations, such as systems using keyboard entry with visual display output.

interconnect: To link community antenna television (CATV) headends, usually with microwave, so that subscribers to different cable systems can see the same programming simultaneously.

interconnected business system: Specific systems composed of combinations of smaller business systems or units but integrated for extra efficiency and speed.

interconnector: A flowchart symbol which illustrates continuation of a broken flow-line.

intercoupler: The connection of two or more hardware units, usually electronically or electrically.

interelectrode capacitance: The effective capacitance between electrodes in a vacuum tube.

interexchange channel: A channel connecting two different exchange areas.

interface: 1. A common boundary—for example, physical connection between two systems or two devices. 2. Specifications of the interconnection between two systems or units.

interface CCITT: The world recommendation for interface requirements between data processing terminal equipment and data communication equipment. The CCITT recommendation resembles very closely the American EIA Standard RS-232-B or C. This standard is considered mandatory in Europe and on the other continents.

interface channels (communication): Buffered input/output (I/O) channels permit the central processor to continue with computation while input and output communications are proceeding. Access to the memory is time-shared between the operating program and I/O data transfer. Access also is controlled automatically by the I/O rate of the external device; it is not a programming consideration. Any cycle of the memory time is available for I/O data transfer in preference to its use by the program. The buffers built into the I/O units permit the synchronization or interface of the varying speeds of the faster central processing units with the slower I/O units.

interface design: For unique user applications such as on-line installations which require specialized input/output equipment, engineering staff will design the necessary interface units as part of services to their customers. Then, they will fabricate these units for particular systems under close supervision by the same engineers that designed them. These engineers, who are naturally quite familiar with the logic and requirements, are best qualified to do this important work.

interface message processor (IMP) computer: Small computers which handle the store-and-forward communications of a packet network, and also have the capability of collecting message handling statistics.

interface message processor (IMP) throughput: The throughput of an IMP is defined as the number of host data bits that traverse it each second; it is the ratio of the number of data bits to the computational load per message. The principal parameters involved are the number of packets per message, the program processing time per packet, the I/O time for packets and message acknowledgments, and the overhead for various periodic IMP processes such as its routing computations.

interface message processor (IMP)-to-host interface: Advanced Research Project Agency Network (ARPANET) communications between IMP and host are conducted through a full-duplex, bit-serial unit at a rate of 10000 bits per second. Bit transfer is asynchronous and is controlled by a "ready-for-the-next-bit, here's-your-bit" handshaking procedure. The IMPs are interconnected through wideband, 50-kilobit per second leased lines.

interface message processor (IMP)-to-host protocol: Provides for the transmission of messages between hosts and IMPs and, combined with the IMP-to-IMP protocol, creates a virtual communication path between host computers. The IMP-to-host protocol is a set of procedures that permits a host to transmit messages to other hosts on the network and to receive information on the status of those transmitted messages. These conventions constrain the host computer in its network transmissions so that it makes efficient use of the available communications capacity without locking out other host computers from a portion of that capacity.

interface message processor (IMP)-to-IMP protocol: The lowest level protocol on the Advanced Research Project Agency Network (ARPANET); provides for reliable communication among IMPs. This protocol handles flow control and error detection and correction in a manner similar to the basic control procedures developed. Another function of the IMP-to-IMP protocol is routing. The routing routine in each IMP attempts to transmit a message along the path for which the total estimated transit time is smallest. These estimates appear in routiing tables in the IMPs and are updated dynamically according to internally estimated delays and delays estimated by neighboring IMPs. The estimates are based upon both queue lengths and the recent performance of the connecting communication circuit.

interface (microprocessor) system: Devices that interconnect all other support hardware and often a teletype unit (TTY) for program assembly, simulation, programmable read-only memory (PROM) programming, prototype operations, and debugging.

interface—MIL STD 188B: The standard method of interface established by the Department of Defense. Presently, it is mandatory for the installation of all new equipment. This standard provides the interface requirements for connection between data communication security devices, data processing equipment, or other special military terminal devices.

interface module: Makes the necessary conversion between the electrical operating levels of the communication terminals and the particular, external circuit. The terminations offered and electrical potentials supplied, and signals presented and responses anticipated by each module conform to the Electronic Industries Association (EIA) standard for that type of data communication. Different interface modules are required for any one of the following applications: printing telegraph equipment employing dc circuits, any transmission rate employing data sets, and a specialized application such as dialing. Some data-set interface modules are equipped for unattended answering and have the ability to resend to remotely originated dial connections.

interface processor: The transfer of data between the processor and the standard communication subsystem takes place through input data leads, connected to the processor output channel. In addition to the data leads, there are several control leads that are used to control the flow of data (in some systems).

interface routines: Routines for linking one system to another system.

interface-system communications: An interface device in the computer center translates pulses into binary code and delivers the character to computer storage. After receipt of the entire message, the central computer searches or stores the requested information and sends back the appropriate response.

interfacing terminal: The communication adapter can provide the EIA RS-232 interface or other interface between the terminal and the communication system.

interference: A term used to describe an operating characteristic of many systems. Since both the processor and the channels require storage cycles for references from main storage, and since only one access from storage can be made in any given storage cycle, the processor and the channels must time-share main storage. This contention for storage cycles is termed interference. The interference characteristics of a channel or channels are a measure of the input/output (I/O) computer overlapping capability of a computer system.

interfield validity check: A data validity check procedure (usually table-driven) which determines the validity of an otherwise valid value in a given field by reference to the value contained in another field. An important capability of a medical record system, e.g., if diagnosis = ovarian carcinoma, sex must = female.

interfix: A technique which allows the relationships of keywords in an item or document to be described so that very specific inquiries can be answered without false retrievals due to crosstalk.

interim (post burn-in) electrical test: A final electrical test for most procurements. For other procurements with the highest screening requirements, the test will be used to determine the number of devices that failed the burn-in test. The result will give an indication of the quality of the entire lot and may serve as a basis for rejection of the lot if more than the prescribed number of devices fail by more than some pre-scribed limit.

interim (pre burn-in) electrical tests: The electrical tests performed at this point uncover electrical failures that have been caused by mechanical and thermal stresses applied in previous tests. Data recorded at this point serves as a starting point for parameters to be monitored through burn-in.

interim reports: Single-record inquiries, or interim reports, may be produced in seconds or minutes on a demand basis. Exception reports may be prepared auto-matically to signal activity requiring man-agement attention.

interlace: To assign successive storage location numbers to physically separated storage locations in order to reduce access time.

interlaced memory: A memory with sequentially addressed locations occupying physically separated positions in the storage media.

inter language: A modification of comm-on language suitable for automatic transla-tion by the equipment into machine or computer usable language.

interleave: 1. To insert segments of one program into another program so that the two programs can be executed simultane-ously, i.e, a technique used in multipro-gramming 2. The facility of accessing in core store more than one of the normal units of access in any one core cycle. The number of units accessed depends on the number of address logic units in the central processor and also the number of core highways. 3. To send blocks of data alternately to two or more stations on a multipoint circuit.

interleaved code: A method of data communications protocol. The process interleaves control information with its data in order to facilitate the detection of data errors due to the communications lines. The receiving terminal must know the type of interleaved code used so that it may inter-pret the incoming information and signal the transmitting terminal if an error occurs.

interleaving, functional: The process of having input/output (I/O) and computing operations proceed independently of one another but interleaved in their sharing of the memory.

interlock: To prevent a machine or device from intiating further operations until the operation in process is completed.

interlock circuit: The signal on this circuit usually originates in the signal converter and is in the "on" condition only when all the following conditions are met: 1. Its internal switching circuits are arranged for signaling on a communication facility; 2. It is not in any abnormal or test condition which disables or impairs any normal func-tion associated with the class of service being used.

interlock switch: An automatic safety circuit breaker which cuts off the power.

interlock time print: The time necessary for the printer to accept data from storage and complete the printing of it.

interlude: A minor subprogram designed for preliminary computations or data organizations, such as, calculating the value of some parameter or clearing parts of the storage. It is usually overwittten after it has served its purpose, as it is usually no longer needed in the program.

intermediate carrier: A communications carrier which may be modulated by one or more subcarriers.

intermediate control: The grouping of various minor controls into a category other than beginning or ending.

intermediate control change: A specific control change of expected or average moderate magnitude.

intermediate cycle: An unconditional branch instruction may address itself, i.e., a branch command is called, executed, and a cycle is set up, which may be used for stopping a machine.

intermediate distributing frame (IDF): In a local central office, the primary purpose of the distributing frame is to cross-connect the subscriber line multiple to the subscriber line circuit. (In a private exchange its purpose is similar.)

intermediate frequency (i-f): The signal in a superheterodyne which appears at the output of the first sector.

intermediate memory storage: An electronic scratchpad for holding working figures temporarily until they are needed, and for releasing final figures to the output.

intermediate pass (sorting): That part of a merging operation which because of the number of strings or otherwise, does not reduce the file to a single sequenced string.

intermediate subcarrier: A carrier which may be modulated by one or more subcarriers and used as a modulating wave to modulate a carrier.

intermediate total: The result when a summation is terminated by a change of group which is neither the most nor the least significant.

intermediate zones: Those zones which are not bounded by a range limit.

intermittent fault: A fault that occurs in no predictable or regular pattern .

intermodulation distortion: 1. Form of interference involving the generation of interfering beats between two or more carriers according to the frequency relationship $f = nf_2 \pm mf_2$, where n and m are whole numbers (but not zero), with appropriate expansion for additional carriers. 2. As related to magnetic tape, non-linearity characterized by the appearance of frequencies in the output equal to the sums and differences of integral multiples of the component frequencies present in the input signal. Harmonics are not included as part of the intermodulation distortion.

internal analog transmission: Network transmission is performed in the analog domain with the modems being supplied by the carrier. These modems may be located remotely from the customer's equipment. "Dataroute" in Canada is an example of this approach.

internal and external interrupt: A special control signal which diverts the attention of the computer to consider an extraordinary event or set of circumstances; i.e., it causes program control to be transferred to a special subordinate which corresponds to the stimulus. Many levels of control can be exercised by the numerous forms of interrupts provided. The interrupts from external sources serve to synchronize the computer program with the readiness of peripheral devices, including other computers, to transmit or receive data. Internal interrupts serve to synchronize the computer program with termination of input/output transfers and to signal the occurrence of an error.

internal arithmetic: The computations performed by the arithmetic unit of a computer.

internal bias: The bias, either marking or spacing, occurring within a start-stop receiving mechanism, and having the same effect on the markings of operation as a bias which is external to the receiver.

internal bias (teletypewriter): The marking or spacing bias that may occur in a start-stop teletypewriter receiving device.

internal checking: The equipment characteristics designed for the improvement of accuracy such as hole counts, parity checks, validity checks and others.

internal clocking: In synchronous communication, occurs when the bit-timing signal is provided from within the terminal or computer, rather than from a modem.

internal code: A system of character-word structure that is used by the IBM 360 computer series to replace the bit/block relationship of older systems. Data representation is character- or word-oriented.

internal control system: A system in some computers in which an interrupt source meets automatic and immediate response.

internal data: Data from within the company itself, such as payroll, inventory, etc.

internal digital transmission: Although the bandpass characteristics of even a simple short length of transmission line, not to mention a large physical plant including switching centers, echo suppressors, and amplifiers, do not permit the transmission and reception of a rectangular pulse (with an infinite number of harmonics), a specially engineered physical plan can be constructed for all digital transmission. In this approach the analog amplifiers are replaced by digital repeaters; this being an electronic adaptation of telegraphic repeaters of days gone by. The Bell system T1 carrier is an example of this approach.

internal hemorrhage: An internal hemorrhage is when a program produces gibberish output, but continues to run. Internal hemorrhaging can occur when a program reads bad data, either from a bad disk or by receiving it over a noisy communications line. Sometimes a small hardware failure can result in internal hemorrhaging, which can affect other programs or the entire system on which it is working.

internal interrupt: A feature of peripheral equipment using an external device which causes equipment to stop in the normal course of the program and perform some designated subroutine.

internally initiated trap: An interruption of central processing unit operations because of a currently scheduled activity on a data channel.

internally stored program: The set or sequence of instructions (i.e., program or routine) that is stored within the computer (internal memory) as contrasted to those programs which might be stored externally on cards, paper, or magnetic tapes, etc.

internal magnetic recording: Representation of information within magnetic material such as in magnetic cores (of core storage).

internal manipulation instruction: A computer instruction that causes a change in format or location of data.

internal memory: 1. The storage of data on a device that is an integral part of a computer. 2. The storage facilities forming an integral physical part of the computer and directly controlled by the computer. In such facilities all data are accessible automatically to the computer; e.g., magnetic core and magnetic tape on-line. (Contrasted with external storage.) 3. All memory or storage which is accessible automatically to the computer without human intervention.

internal-memory terminal: The internal memory should be designed so that it can be shared for programming and/or internal storage. Most terminal systems provide for 2 or 4K of memory with options to add an additional memory in 2 or 4K segments up to 32 or 64K.

internal sort: A sorting technique that creates sequences of records or keys. Usually it is a prelude to a merge phase in which the sequences created are reduced to one by an external merge.

internal storage: 1. The storage of data on a device which is an integral part of a computer. 2. The storage facilities forming an integral physical part of the computer and directly controlled by the computer. In such facilities all data are accessible to the computer, e.g., magnetic core, and magnetic tape on-line.

internal timer: An electronic timer which

facilitates monitoring or logging events at predetermined intervals.

internal visual inspection: A thorough preseal visual inspection, performed under a microscope, designed to eliminate circuits with potential reliability problems. Die mounting, wire bonding, metallization, oxide and diffusion defects, general mechanical integrity, and workmanship are among the things inspected. Precap visual inspection weeds out many potentially unreliable circuits that will pass other screening tests.

international algebraic language (IAL): The language which preceded ALGOL.

international code: The system used in radio telegraph in which a group of dots and dashes stands for a letter of the alphabet.

International Computer Center: Located in Rome and sponsored by UNESCO.

International Organization for Standardization (ISO): An organization established to promote the development of standards to facilitate the international exchange of goods and services, and to develop mutual cooperation in areas of intellectual, scientific, technological, and economic activity.

International Radio Consultative Committee: One of four permanent organs in the International Telecommunication Union.

International Telecommunication Union (ITU): The specialized telecommunications agency of the United Nations, established to provide standardized communications procedures and practices including frequency allocation and radio regulations on a worldwide basis.

interoffice trunk: A direct trunk between local central offices in the same exchange.

interpolation: The operation of finding terms between any two consecutive terms of a series which conforms to the given or assumed law of the series taken at fixed and regular intervals.

interpreter: 1. A computer program that translates and executes each source language statement before translating and executing the next one. 2. A device that prints on a punched card the data already punched in the card.

interpreter (interpretive routine): An executive routine which, as the computation progresses, translates a stored program expressed in some machine-like pseudo-code into machine code and performs the indicated operations, by means of subroutines as they are translated. An interpretive routine is essentially a closed subroutine which operates successively on an indefinitely-long sequence of program parameters (the pseudo-instructions and operands). It may be entered as a closed subroutine and exited by a pseudo-code exit instruction.

interpreter/reader: A specialized service routine designed to read an input stream, store programs and data on random access storage for later processing, identify the control information contained in the input stream, and store this control information separately in the appropriate control list.

interpreter transfer: Machines that print data on punched cards; this information is interpreted and punched into another card through a transfer interpreter.

interpreting: Printing on a paper tape or cards the meaning of the holes punched on the same tape or cards.

interpretive programming: The writing of programs in a pseudo-machine language, which is converted by the computer into actual machine language instructions.

interpretive routine: A routine which carries out problem solution by the processes of: (a) Decoding instructions written in a pseudo-code, and selecting and executing an appropriate subroutine to carry out the functions called for by the pseudo-code. (b) Proceeding to the next pseudo-instruction. It should be noted that an interpretive routine carries out its functions as it decodes the pseudo-code, as contrasted to a compiler, which only prepares a machine-language routine which will be executed later.

interpretive trace program: A trace or diagnostic program used to perform a desired check on another program and may include instructions as its output. Intermediate results of those instructions can be arranged in the order in which the instructions are executed.

interpretive translation program: A specialized program which relates and handles the execution of a program by translating each instruction of the source language into a sequence of computer instructions and allows these to be executed before translating the next instruction.

interprocessor communication: Communication between two independent processors can occur at three levels. At the software level, information stored in core memory by one processor can be accessed by the other processor. At the firmware level, microcommands in one processor can be used to generate internal interrupts in the other. And, finally, byte input/output (I/O) interfaces on the I/O buses can be externally interconnected to provide a third level of communication.

interrecord gap (IRG): An interval of space or time deliberately left between recording portions of data or records. Such spacing is used to prevent errors through loss of data or overwriting, and permits tape stop-start operations.

interrogating typewriter: One connected to a central processor for communicating with a program in main memory; i.e., able to insert data into the program to receive output from the program.

interrogation pulse: Periodic synchronous or asynchronous electrical activation and observance of an encoder's shaft position.

interrogator-control terminal: Provides facilities for simultaneous operation of video-data interrogators on a single line and performs the required communications with the rest of the system. It provides standard callable formats for automatic allocation of information to prescribed positions on the video screen. In both the video-data terminal and interrogator units, the display and keyboard elements can be separated physically. They feature completely solid-line characters for high visibility, and instantaneous erase to either correct errors or clear the display for the next message.

interrupt: A break in the normal flow of a system or program occurring in such a way that the flow can be resumed from that point at a later time. Interrupts are initiated by signals of two types: (a) Signals originating within the computer system to synchronize the operation of various components. (b) Signals originating exterior to the computer system to synchronize the operation of the computer system with the outside world; i.e., an operator or a physical process.

interrupt control routine: A routine entered when an interrupt occurs that provides for such details as the storage of the working details of the interrupted program, an analysis of the interrupt to decide on the necessary action, and the return of control to the interrupted program.

interrupt device: External interrupts are caused by either an external device requiring attention (such as a signal from a communications device), console switching, or by the timer going to zero.

interrupted continuous waves: Continuous waves that are interrupted at a constant audio-frequency rate.

interrupter code: The programmed or arbitrarily selected code which requires translation to computer code in order to result in machine language.

interrupt feedback signal: A steady signal, indicating that an interrupt signal has advanced its associated interrupt level to the waiting or active state; the signal is dropped when the interrupt level is reset to the disarmed or the armed state.

interruptible: Same as enabled.

interrupt independent processor: An input/output (I/O) finished condition caused by the I/O hardware when an I/O operation has been completed.

interruption: A break in the normal sequence of instruction execution. It causes an automatic transfer to a preset storage location where appropriate action is taken.

interruption network: A network of circuits in a computing system that continuously monitors its operation. The network detects events that normally require intervention and direction by the supervisor, and initiates interruptions.

interrupt logging: The logging or listing of interrupts during program testing, or when a system is being monitored, so that possible program errors caused by interrupts may be classified and corrected.

interrupt log word: Contains bits set to indicate the number and type of interrupts that occur in a segment of a program.

interrupt mode: See analog hold mode.

interrupt priority table: A table that lists the priority sequence of handling and testing interrupts used when a computer does not have fully automatic interrupt handling capability.

interrupt servicing: The process by which an interrupt handler, whenever an interrupt occurs, performs operations to halt the central processing unit's (CPU's) processing, satisfy the interrupting device, and return the interrupted process to the CPU.

interrupt signal feedback: See interrupt feedback signal.

interrupt-signal switch: One of the more powerful control signals governing the

input/output (I/O) operations of the central computer and the peripheral subsystems. This signal demands the immediate attention of the central computer. It switches program control to a special address connected with the event or circumstances that initiated the interrupt. Interrupts from external sources synchronize the computer program with the status of the subsystem units, and indicate error conditions occurring within the peripheral subsystems. Internal interrupts synchronize the computer program with the termination of I/O transfers.

interrupt-signal trigger: A signal that is generated, either internal or external to the central processing unit, to interrupt the normal sequence of events in the central processor.

interrupt system: Provides for internal processor interrupts, input/output peripheral device interrupts, and groups of individual external interrupts, each with its own unique interrupt memory address and priority assignment.

interstage punch: A system for punching in which only odd numbered rows or cards are used.

interstate: Operating terminations located in at least two states; crossing a state boundary.

interstation interference: That from another transmitter on the same or an adjacent wavelength, as distinct from atmospheric interference.

intersystem communications: Many users will want to install systems of different sizes to meet a diverse number of data-processing problems. And in many cases it is desirable for the two configurations to be linked so that the flow between the two environments need not be slowed by mechanical transfer. The user of certain configurations will be able to join two configurations together. Any two configurations can share input/output devices or be linked channel to channel. Some configurations can be linked through main or large core storage.

intersystem unit: An input/output unit that is to be reserved so that information may be passed between job segments.

intertoll office trunk: A trunk between toll offices in different telephone exchanges.

interval: If a variable, x, can take as its values all real numbers lying between two given numbers, a and b, then its range is called the interval (a, b). This is written $a < x < b$ or $a \leq x \leq b$ according to whether the values a and b are excluded or included. The expressions "near to" or "neighborhood of" can be stated more precisely by using the concept of an interval.

interval polling timer: Enables the control program to keep track of time of day and to interrupt periodically as required. More than one interval can be controlled at once. For example a five-second interval between successive polling of a teleprocessing line can be specified, and at the same time a two-minute limit on the duration of a new program undergoing test can be in effect.

interval resolution: The smallest interval between two adjacent discrete details which are distinguishable from the other. The terms fine or coarse are used to designate the interval as small or large.

interval timer: A clock device that cycles a value stored in core. It can be used for job accounting by measuring the duration of time for each job, for interrupt to prevent a runaway job from gaining control of the system, for time recording, and for polling a communication network on a regular basis, for example, every minute, every half-hour, etc.

interword gap: The time period and space permitted between words on a tape, disk, drum, etc. Usually, such space allows for controlling specific or individual words, for switching.

intrastate: That which is enclosed completely within the boundaries of a state.

intrinsic coercivity: As related to magnetic tape, the maximum value of the intrinsic coercive force corresponding to the saturation flux density of the material.

intrinsic flux: As related to magnetic tape in a uniformly magnetized sample of magnetic material, the product of the intrinsic flux density and the crosssectional area.

intrinsic hysteresis loop: As related to magnetic tape, a curve showing the relation between intrinsic flux density and magnetizing field strength when the magnetizing field is cycled between equal negative and positive values. Hysteresis is indicated by the fact that the ascending and descending branches of the loop do not coincide.

intrinsic induction (magnetic tape): As related to magnetic tape, in a sample of magnetic material, for a given value of the magnetizing field strength, the excess of normal flux density over the flux density in vacuum. Using the cgs system of units, the intrinsic flux density is equal numerically to the ordinary flux density minus the magnetizing field strength ($B_i = B - H$).

intrinsic semiconductor: A crystal, germanium, or silicon substance which conducts electric currents of an electric field due to the presence of mobile holes and electrons.

introspective program: A self-monitoring computer program.

invalid exclusive reference: An exclusive reference in which a common segment does not contain a reference to the symbol used in the exclusive reference.

inventory control: The practice to hold stocks to meet demands. Even though stocks are held, temporary shortages are sometimes experienced, probably due to a sudden rise in demand or delay in production.

inventory data control: A multipart invoice form used to determine inventory requirements.

inventory master file: Permanently stored, regularly updated inventory information retained for future use.

inventory records: A complete listing of file contents by records series together with sufficient supporting information to enable a proper evaluation of file functions and activities.

inventory stock report: A specific report showing the current amount of inventory on hand for each item carried in inventory.

inversion: To invert or reverse such as in frequency inversion where the high frequencies are shifted to low and the low to high frequencies.

invert: To place in a contrary order. To invert the terms of a fraction is to put the numerator in place of the denominator, and vice versa.

inverted file: A method of file organization in which a keyword identifies a record, and all item numbers or documents described by that keyword are indicated.

inverter: A circuit which takes in a positive pulse and puts out a negative one, or takes in a negative pulse and puts out a positive one. The physical meaning of positive and negative depends on the specific circuit and the conventions established for it.

inverting amplifier: An amplifier whose output voltage is equal in magnitude to the input voltage but opposite in sign.

inverting circuits: Signals are inverted as they pass through gate circuits. Some types of circuits provide complementary outputs; that is, there are two output terminals instead of one, with the normal output appearing at one terminal and the inverted output at the other. In some dynamic circuits, transformer coupling is used, in which case the secondary windings may be connected to furnish either normal or inverted outputs.

invertor: 1. An electronic or electromechanical device which changes dc to ac (or vice versa). 2. A circuit used for this purpose.

invitation list: Under telecommunications access method (TCAM), a sequence of polling characters or identification sequences associated with the stations on line; the order in which the characters are specified determines the order in which the stations are invited to enter a message.

invitation to send (ITS): A Western Union term that indicates a character transmitted to a remote teletypewriter terminal which polls its tape transmitter.

involuntary interrupt (program): An interrupt which is not caused by an object program in core but which affects the running of such a program. For example, the termination of a peripheral transfer will cause the operating system to stop the object program momentarily while the interrupt is serviced.

inward dialing: A feature of private branch exchanges and Centrex systems that allows callers to dial from the public network straight to a wanted extension on a private automatic branch exchange without intervention by an operator. It is called direct dialing in Britain.

inward WATS: A telephone service similar to WATS but applicable to incoming calls.

I/O: Input-output.

I/O appendage: A user-written routine that provides additional control over I/O operations during channel program operations.

I/O buffer: The temporary storage area for input and output of a computer.

I/O channel: A device which allows independent communication between the memory exchange and the input/output exchange. It controls any peripheral device and performs all validity checking on information transfers.

I/O (communications) device: Any subscriber (user) equipment designed to introduce data into or extract data from a data-communications system.

I/O control: Includes physical and logical control over I/O records, files, and units; buffer control; teleprocessing terminal and message handling; random access I/O control; labeling of files; and errorrecovery procedures.

I/O controller (I/OC): An independent, wired logic processor that provides: (a) indpendent data paths between peripheral subsystems and main storage; (b) high-speed communications capability; (c) enhanced systems performance through chained buffer operations; (d) the ability to expand the number of I/O channels available to the system. The data paths of the I/OC provide transfers between peripheral subsystems and main storage independent of the cyclic operation of the central processors. Operations are initiated from a central processing unit (CPU) by sending functional commands to the I/OC via the normal CPU channel interface. The I/OC accepts these commands and then sequences the independent data transfer.

I/O control manager: Involves keeping records of all the documents received and transmitted, working closely with operating departments to insure that processed information is timely, and routing the work according to procedures developed for the installation. In addition, this function usually controls the data processing supplies and inventories such as magnetic tapes, printer paper, punch cards, etc.

I/O control section: The input/output functions as a small processor. Programmed input/output instructions load the access-control word locations and establish desired peripheral activity. From this point, I/O control automatically scans the input/-output channels, accepting data from the peripheral subsystem at the natural rate of the equipment. When a peripheral subsystem presents or asks for a word of data, its associated access-control register is referenced and I/O control transfers the data word to or from central store, updates the access-control word, and tests for a terminal condition. All of the access-control word indexing and testing is performed in the index section in effectively zero-time, in parallel with normal construction execution and indexing.

I/O control system (IOCS): A group of macroinstruction routines for handling the transfer of data between main storage and external storage devices. IOCS consists of two parts: physical IOCS and logical IOCS.

IOCS: See I/O control system.

I/O device: The hardware of the computer by which data is entered into a computer, or by which the finished computations are recorded for immediate or future use.

I/O equipment: Specific units of the total computing system designed to accept data and output the results of computing and processing in a form readable either by humans or other processing units.

I/O exchange: An electronic switch designed to route I/O messages.

I/O exchange buffering: A specific technique for I/O buffering that prevents or avoids the internal movement of data. Buffers are either filled, empty, or actively in use, by an I/O device. Exchange buffering relates to distinct areas set aside for work and for buffering. This technique requires some additional programming but allows both I/O units and central processing unit (CPU) to be active a greater percentage of the time than in single-buffered I/O schemes. Same as double buffering.

I/O instructions: Computer instructions

which operate input-output devices like card readers, printers, and terminals.

I/O interface control module: The micro-circuit modules that use all computer inputs and outputs, with the number and type determined by system applications and the peripheral equipment used. There is also a provision to connect an I/O interface directly with a memory module under program control to allow an efficient method of resolving conflicts in memory access.

I/O interrupt indicators: Used to determine the I/O unit originating an interrupt and the cause of the interrupt by testing the indicators associated with each I/O channel. When the cause of the interrupt has been determined and corrective action has been taken, the indicators may be reset and the interrupted program resumed. These instructions also provide the facility for setting, resetting, and testing the inhibit I/O interrupt indicator.

I/O interruption: An interruption caused by the termination of an I/O operation or by operator intervention at the I/O device.

I/O limited: A system or condition where the time for input and output operation exceeds other operations.

I/O limited tape: A sort program in which the effective transfer rate of tape units determines the elapsed time required to sort.

I/O magnetic tape: The most common size of tape is ½ inch wide, available in lengths up to 2400 feet on a 10½ inch diameter reel and it is conventional to record each tape character as a 7-bit code across the tape, containing only 6 information bits, the seventh bit being the parity check or in a 9-bit code with 8 information bits and a parity bit.

I/O models: Such classes of models as these are derived from assumptions about economic variables and behavior which take account of the general equilibrium phenomena and are concerned with the empirical analysis of production, i.e., especially intermediate uses and final output. The problem is to investigate what can be produced and the quantity of each intermediate product which itself must be used up in the production process. Various data are obtained initially which attest to available resources and current state of the technology.

ion: An atom with an electric charge.

ion implantation (I^2):   Allows accurate control of dopants or impurities introduced into the silicon; a more expensive and controllable alternative to thermal diffusion. The process can change the threshold voltage of metal-oxide silicon transistors selectively and produce devices with no overlap capacitance. Although it has not yet demonstrated significant advantage in memories, I^2 is a potentially valuable processing tool, and may be used to varying degrees in all complex integrated circuits eventually.

ionization: Since the atom is electrically neutral to begin with, the loss of an electron will endow it with a positive charge. Such a charged atom is called an "ion," and the process which creates it is known as ionization.

ionospheric disturbance: An abnormal variation of the ion density in part of the ionosphere. It is produced by solar flares and affects radio communication.

ion trap: A permanent magnet clamped to the neck of a kinescope which prevents ions from striking the kinescope screen (in some systems).

I/O operation: 1. Each channel is capable of operating in three different transfer modes: input, output, or function. The input and output modes are employed when transferring data to or from the central computer. The function mode is the means by which the central computer establishes initial communication paths with a peripheral subsystem. During this mode of transmission, the central computer sends one or more function words to a peripheral subsystem directing the specified units to perform the desired operation. 2. The I/O section acts as an autonomous processor which runs independently of the instruction-execution cycle, scanning the input channels for the presence of I/O word transfer requests and transferring data between the channels and central storage, control led by the I/O access-control location associated with the channels.

I/O parity interrupt: Each time control is given to the monitor, the I/O parity trap is armed and the interrupt location is patched with an instruction. When an I/O parity occurs, the computer halts at the instruction at which the parity occurred with the console I/O parity indicator light on.

I/O printer: Alphanumeric characters and such functions as shifting, tabulating, carriage return, etc. are coded into tape or edge cards for subsequent processing by the equipment. Output is in the form of typewriter printing. Printout is automatic or manual in accordance with the program. Information may be entered manually at continuous speeds. A "diskinterlock" prevents inadvertent depression of two keys at once, yet maintains the touch essential for speed typing.

I/O priority and interrupt: Features used to divert program attention to new input data, the completion of output buffer transfers, or emergency conditions (inquiries, errors) existing on peripherals. The interrupt feature relieves need for much program checking of status of units.

I/O processing unit (IOP) multiplexer: Performs bidirectional data transfer between core memory and standard-speed peripheral devices, with up to 32 such devices operating concurrently.

I/O processing unit (IOP) selector: Performs bidirectional data transfer between core memory and high-speed peripheral devices. Up to 32 devices can be attached to a selector IOP, but the high data transfer rates associated with devices allow only one

device to operate at a given time (in some systems).

I/O referencing: Reference to input and output data on tape or disk are made symbolically.

I/O-request word: A control word that is stored in the message reference block until the I/O is completed.

I/O subroutines: Generalized computer program subroutines used to process input, output, formatting, etc.

I/O switching: Connecting input/output devices to more than one channel and using channel switching to optimize processing.

I/O table: A plotting device used to generate or to record one variable as a function of another variable.

I/O tape limited: Computer instructions created by the programmer, in assembly or absolute form, which are executed by a sort during the first pass of the file after input program has been loaded but prior to execution of first-pass sequencing instructions.

I/O test program (microprocessor): A special programmable read-only memory (PROM) which plugs into prototyping boards for complete check-out.

I/O traffic control: Directs the time-sharing of the main memory by the various peripheral devices and the central processor. This control element makes possible the concurrent performance of central processing computing and up to eight simultaneous I/O operations. For example, the computer can read or write tape, read cards, punch cards, store information in a randomaccess drum device, print two separate reports, and compute simultaneously.

I/O trunks: Can be connected to a peripheral control which handles both reading and writing (e.g., a magnetic tape control connects to a pair of trunks). Data are transferred between main memory and a trunk (and a peripheral device) via the read/write channel specified in the instruction which initiates the transfer. Additional peripheral devices can be connected to the system simply by adding more I/O trunks to the basic configuration. The number of peripheral devices in a system depends only on the number of I/O trunks available.

I/O unit: Those devices, modems, terminals or various pieces of equipment whose designated purposes relate to manual, mechanical, electronic, visual or audio entry to and from the computer mainframe unit.

IPCs: See intenet packet controllers.

IPL: See initial program load.

ipot: Abbreviation or slang for inductive potentiometer, a precision type of toroidally-wound automatic transformer provided with one or more adjustable sliders.

irrational number: A number such as $\sqrt{2}$ which can be shown to exist and upon which the operations defined upon the rational numbers can be shown to be defined, but which cannot be expressed as a quotient of a pair of integers.

irreversible magnetic process: A mechanism with a flux change within a magnetic material in which the flux does not return to its initial state when the disturbing magnetic field is removed.

IS: See information separator.

ISAM: See basic indexed sequential access method.

isochronous modulation: Modulation (or restitution) in which the time interval separating any two significant instants is theoretically equal to the unit interval or to a multiple of this.

isolated locations: Locations of storage by a hardware device that prevents them from being addressed by the user's program and protects their contents from accidental mutilation.

isolater/regulator: A device that combines the characteristics of isolation devices and voltage regulators, providing protection against voltage spikes, noise and fluctuations. The cost is not much higher than that of an individual isolator or voltage regulator. Some do not protect against transverse voltage spikes or low frequency (less than 1 Hz) spikes; others cannot protect against voltage swings greater than $\pm$ 15 percent.

ITE: See integrated terminal equipment.

item: 1. A set of one or more fields containing related information. 2. A unit of correlated information relating to a single person or object. 3. The contents of a single message.

item advance: In grouping of records, a technique for operating successively on different records in memory.

item advance technique: A programming technique which groups records in specific arrangements disregarding location aspects of the data.

item counter: Counts the number of calculations preceding the final result.

item design: Specifies which fields make up an item, the order in which the fields are to be recorded, and the number of characters to be allocated to each field.

item sorting: Concerns the basic elements of a file in which the sorting of the file constitutes the reordering of file records.

iterate: To execute a loop or series of steps repeatedly, e.g., a loop in a routine.

iterative process: A process for calculating a desired result by means of a repeating cycle of operations, which comes closer and closer to the desired result, e.g., the arithmetical square root of n may be approximated by an iterative process using additions, subtractions, and divisions only.

ITF: basic: A simple, algebra-like language designed for ease of use at a terminal.

ITF: PL/1:   A conversational subset of PL/1 designed for ease of use at the terminal.

ITS: See invitation to send.

J

jack: A connecting device to which a wire or wires of a circuit may be attached and which is arranged for the insertion of a plug.

jack part: An electrical connector at the end of a wire designed to fit into a hub.

jackplug: An electronic connector at the ends of wires designed to fit into particular type hubs.

jamming: Deliberate interference of a transmission on one carrier by transmission on another approximately equal carrier, with wobble or noise modulation.

jargon: The technical vocabulary of a special trade group or scientific group.

JCL: See job control language.

jitter: A shift in the time or phase position of individual pulses, causing difficulty in synchronization and/or detection. Also called peak distortion.

J-K flip-flop: A flip-flop having two inputs designated J and K. At the application of a clock pulse, a "1" on the "J" input and a "0" on the "K" input will set the flip-flop to the "1" state; a "1" on the "K" input and a "0" on the "J" input will reset it to the "0" state; and "1's" simultaneously on both inputs will cause it to change state regardless of the previous state. $J = 0$ and $K = 0$ will prevent change.

job: 1. One or more applications specified by the programmer to be executed as a logical unit. A job is delimited by the job card. 2. An externally specified unit of work for the computing system from the standpoint of installation accounting and operating system control. A job consists of one or more job steps.

job batch: A succession of job definitions that are placed one behind another to form a batch. Each job batch is placed on an input device and processed with a minimum of delay between one job or job step and another.

job control: A program is called into storage to prepare each job or job step to be run. Some of its functions are to assign input/output (I/O) devices to certain symbolic names, set switches for program use, log (or print) job control statements, and fetch the first program phase of each job step.

job control language (JCL): A programming language used to code job control statements.

job control processor: The processing program that reads and interprets job control statements and sets up the system to execute a specific program using specific resources.

job control statement: Any one of the control statements in the input stream that identifies a job or job step or defines its requirments and options.

job definition: A series of job control statements that define a job.

job description: A personal report of background, training, education, skills, etc. of various personnel used to determine which capabilities of individuals are required for particular tasks or assignments; a description and listing of experience of such individuals in several particular former job classifications.

job dividing: The task of dividing a job into a number of parts, some of which can or have to be performed simultaneously, but some of which require the completion of other parts before they can be executed.

job input device: A device assigned by the operator to read job definitions and any accompanying input data.

job input file: A data file (or data set) consisting of a series of job definitions and accompanying data.

job input stream: The input consisting of punched cards (usually) which is the first part of an operating system. The stream contains the beginning of job indicator, directions, programs, etc.

job library: A concatenation of user-identified partitioned data sets used as the primary source of load modules for a given job.

job management: Functions performed by special programs such as job schedulers or master schedulers.

job name: The name assigned to a job statement; it identifies the job to the system.

job-oriented terminal: 1. A terminal designed for a particular application. 2. A terminal specifically designed to receive source data in an environment associated with the job to be performed, and capable of transmission to and from the system of which it is a part.

job output device: A device assigned by the operator for common use in recording output data for a series of jobs.

job output file: A data file (or data set) consisting of output data produced by a series of jobs.

job processing: The reading of job control statements and data from an input stream, the initiating of job steps defined in the statements, and the writing of system output messages.

job processing control: The portion of the control program which starts job operations, assigns input/output units, and performs needed functions to proceed from one job to another.

job processing system: Composed of a series of individual programs that work together to form a complete operating system. The system also contains a complete description of the primary operating system routines-the monitor program, executive program, system loader, system-preparation routine, and input/output routines.

job queue: Same as input work queue.

job scheduler: The control program function that controls input job streams and system output, obtains input/output resources for jobs and job steps, attaches tasks corresponding to job steps, and regulates the use of the computing system by jobs.

job statement: A special control statement related to input job stream which marks the beginning of a series of job control statements for a specific job. The previous history (e.g., termination circumstances of the last job) has no impact on subsequent steps if separated from them by a job statement, whereas steps not separated by job statements may abort succeeding ones if errors occur.

job step: A unit of work for the computing system from the standpoint of the user, presented to the control program by job control statements as a request for execution of an explicitly identified program and a description of resources required by it. A job step consists of the external specifications for work that are to be done as a task or set of tasks. Also, it is used to denote the set of all tasks which have their origin in a job step specification.

job step initiation: The process of selecting a job step for execution and allocating input/output devices for them.

job step restart: Same as step restart.

job step task: A task that is initiated by an initiator/terminator in the job scheduler in accordance with specifications in an execute (EXEC) statement.

job stream: The set of computer jobs in an input queue awaiting initiation and processing.

job support task: A task that reads and interprets job definitions or converts job input and output data from one input/-output medium to another.

join: Same as logical sum, union, EITHER-OR operation, OR-ELSE operation, disjunction.

joint denial gate: The specific gate whose output is true when, and only when, all inputs are false.

joint probability: The probability that both A and B will occur. If A and B are independent, neither influencing the other, joint probability is the product of their separate probabilities.

joint use: The simultaneous use of a pole, line, or plant facility by two or more kinds of utilities.

JOSS: A time-sharing language developed by the Sperry-Rand Corporation originally to make quick calculations of a nature too involved for a calculator.

journal: A record of all the system events which have taken place in the installation. It is usually maintained by an operating system and stored on disk or tape.

JOVIAL (Jules Own Version of IAL): A language containing facilities for numerical computations and some data processing. Most widely used for command and control applications. A new version of JOVIAL called JOVIAL/J73 has been developed; it will probably become the new standard language for command and control applications.

julian date: The day of the year, e.g., February 1st would be day 32 (contrasted to calendar date). Widely used in computer notation.

jump: An instruction or signal which, conditionally or unconditionally, specifies the location of the next instruction and directs the computer to that instruction. A jump is used to alter the normal sequence control of the computer. Under certain special conditions, a jump may be forced by manual intervention.

jumper: An electrical conductor of relative short length used to permanently or temporarily complete a circuit or bypass an existing circuit.

jump operation: The computer departs from the regular sequence of instruction executions and jumps to another routine or program, or even some preceding or forward instructions to alter control, repeat a process or loop, etc.

junction: The contact interface surface or immediate area between N-type and P-type semiconducting material. Transistor action takes place at the junction of these differently doped materials. Junction transistors may be P-N-P type or N-P-N type for the emitter, base, and collector electrode materials, respectively.

junction diode: The basic element of an injection laser where the semiconductor diode has the dproperty of essentially conducting current in one direction.

junction P-N type: A transition region between P and N (positive and negative) as doped and of the acceptor and donor type semiconductor materials in developing electric charge distributions and potential (voltage) gradients to permit diode and transistor action.

junction, summing: In computing amplifiers or operational amplifiers, various input impedances are connected each from a separate input terminal of a unit to a common point which is called a summing junction and is connected to the feedback impedance.

junk: A garbled or otherwise unintelligible sequence of signals or other data, especially as received from a communications channel, i.e., hash or garbage.

justification: The act of adjusting, arranging or shifting digits to the left or right, to fit a prescribed pattern. 1. In printing or listing, the alignment of a margin. 2. In the COBOL system, the alignment of characters with respect to the left or right boundaries of data items.

justified: Aligned, as by shifting to the right or left, to fit a prescribed pattern relative to a word or boundary field.

justify: 1. To control the printing positions of characters on a page so that both the left-hand and right-hand margins of the printing are regular. 2. To shift the contents of a register, if necessary, so that the character at a specified end of the data that has been read or loaded into the register is at a specified position in the register. 3. To align characters horizontally or vertically to fit the positioning constraints of a required format.

justify, margin: To adjust exactly by spacing to align a set of characters horizontally or vertically to the right or left margins. To develop exact format or spacing in words, fields, items, or data as designed by context of exact specifications.

juxtaposition: The positioning or placing of items adjacent to each other or side by side.

K

k: A symbol standing for the number 1024, or 2^{10}. Frequently used as a synonym for thousand.

karnaugh map: An arrangement in tabular form which facilitates combination and elimination of duplicate logical functions by listing similar logical expressions.

kayser: Unit for wave number, the reciprocal of a wavelength (in cm).

kc: See kilocycle.

KeV: 1,000 electron volts.

key: 1. One of a set of levers or parts pressed to operate a teletypewriter, console, etc. 2. To depress a lever (as in 1), thus causing an associated function to occur.

keyboard: 1. A device for the encoding of data by key depression which causes the generation of the selected code element. 2. The portion of the supervisory printer via which the operator can communicate with the system.

keyboard display station: A valuable tool for on-line program debugging. Programs are displayed on the keyboard/display station with mnemonic and location in a format identical to the programmer's coding sheet, a page of coding at a time. The editing features of the keyboard/display station are used to make corrections to the program. The programmer may thumb through the pages of his program stored in memory just as he can thumb through his coding sheets. In a data-acquisition system, the keyboard/display station may also be used for quick-look display of test data or results, as the test progresses. The ability to address locations on the keyboard/display station screen by the computer permits the output of only the changing information by the computer at very rapid per character rate, rather than requiring a complete page of information for each change. This light demand on computer time permits a continuous presentation of important test parameters as they change.

keyboard entry and inquiry: The use by an operator of a keyboard to provide a computer with information and to establish what is stored in any specific location.

keyboard features: Designed to make the operator as efficient as possible. The most important design features are: (a) layout, (b) N-key rollover, (c) edit keys, (d) function keys, (e) numeric pad, and (f) control keys.

keyboard function keys: These make it possible to strike one or two keys to call out strings of characters and formats, send a distinct code to the computer which may represent any amount of data, and easily activate the terminal peripherals (in some systems).

keyboarding: A procedure for operating at typewriter-like keyboards to produce copy and machine readable data.

keyboard inquiry: A technique whereby the interrogation of the contents of a computer's storage may be initiated at a keyboard.

keyboard layout: A typewriter keyboard layout should be used for all applications. The current practice is to have separate layouts for typewriter, keypunch and teletype. Standardizing on the typewriter layout will make it easy to switch operators from one terminal to another without loss in efficiency.

keyboard lockout: An interlock feature

which prevents sending from the keyboard while the tape transmitter or another station is sending on the same circuit; this avoids breaking up the transmission by simultaneous sending.

keyboard N-key rollover (at least 3-key rollover): Strikes a series of keys simultaneously and displays the characters in the order that the keys are released. N-key rollover is necessary for a typist to type at full speed without locking the keyboard or dropping characters.

keyboard printer: Permits keyboard insertion of transaction data and printed page output of computer responses at speeds related to the common-carrier service available. Either telegraphic or voice grade lines can be utilized. The keyboard and printer can be used separately or in combination. The keyboard contains a full four-bank set of keys, 10 numeric, 26 alphabetic, 10 special character keys, and a space bar. The printing unit prepares a copy of all transaction data as it is typed on the keyboard. Computer responses are also printed by the printing unit (in some systems).

keyboard send/receive (KSR): A combination teletype-writer transmitter and receiver with transmission capability from keyboard o nly.

keyboard types: Two basic types: (a) alphanumeric and (b) numeric. Alphanumeric keyboards are used for word processing, text processing, data processing and teleprocessing. Numeric keyboards are only used on touchtone telephones, accounting machines and calculators. The touchtone telephones have come into significant use as a calculator and data input and voice output device.

key change: Occurs when an input record has a different key from its immediate predecessor.

key click: Transient pulses or surges on a transmission line set up by the opening or closing of contacts.

key-click filter: A filter that attenuates the surges produced each time the keying circuit contacts of a transmitter are opened or closed.

keying: The forming of signals, such as those employed in telegraph transmission, by the interruption of a direct current or modulation of a carrier between discrete values of some characteristics.

keying chirps: Sounds accompanying code signals when the transmitter is unstable and shifts slightly in frequency each time the sending key is closed.

keying terminal: A combination alphanumeric/numeric keyboard for entering, editing, calling out character strings, operating peripherals, and changing the function of the terminal.

keypunch: A keyboard-actuated device that punches holes in a card to represent data.

key search: Information that is to be compared with specific parts of data items, labels, or identifiers for identification when conducting a search.

key-verify: To use the punch card machine known as a verifier, which has a keyboard, to make sure that the information supposed to be punched in a punch card has been properly punched. The machine signals when the punched hole and the depressed key disagree.

keyword: A significant or informative word in a title, abstract, body, or part of the text that is utilized to describe a document. A keyword or set of keywords may describe the contents of a document, label the document, and/or assist in identifying and retrieving the document.

keyword-in-context index (KWIC): Lists available programs arranged alphabetically by the keywords in the program titles. There is an index entry for each significant keyword in the title. Certain words are not accepted as indexing words but will be printed as part of the title. A KWIC index is prepared by highlighting each keyword of the title in the context of words on either side of it and aligning the keywords of all titles alphabetically in a vertical column.

keyword-out-of-context (KWOC): Similar to a KWIC index, except that keywords are listed separately from the title in which they appear, with the title itself printed in its normal order of words. A KWOC index is easier to read than a KWIC index, but increases the overall amount of printing and pages for the index.

keyword parameter: A parameter that consists of a keyword, followed by one or more values.

kick off: To remove a job or task from access to a computing system, either under direct control of the system operator, or under control of the system monitor.

kilobauds: New and higher capacity data channels. For special applications, some data channels capable of 20 kilobauds have been placed in service. See also baud.

kilocycle: A thousand cycles per second, or 10^3 cycles per second. See also megacycle, gigacycle, and teracycle.

kilomega: A prefix meaning one billion; i.e. a kilomegacycle means one billion cycles (same as billicycle and gigacycle), and a kilomegabit means one billion bits (same as billibit).

kilomegacycle: One billion cycles. Same as billicycle.

kilovolt-ampere: A unit of apparent electrical power equal to 1000 volt-amperes.

kilowatt: A unit of electrical power equal to 1000 watts.

kilowatt-hour: Unit of work equal to 1000 watts acting for one hour.

kind field: Tells whether or not any data is in the frame.

kinescope: The writing tube in a television receiver which converts the picture signal into light.

Kipp relay: A monostable multivibrator, i.e., a circuit which has one stable or quasi-stable state and one unstable state and which undergoes a complete cycle of change in response to a single triggering excitition.

Kirchhoff's current law: This law states that the sum of the currents leaving a junction must be equal to the current entering the junction.

klystron: A uhf oscillator tube containing its own cavity resonator, which depends on the bunching of electrons for its operation.

KSR: See keyboard send/receive.

KWIC: See keyword-in-context index.

KWOC: See keyword-out-of-context.

L

label: 1. A set of symbols used to identify or describe an item, record, message, or file. Occasionally it may be the same as the address in storage. 2. A code name that classifies or identifies a name, term, phrase or document. See header label, end-of-file trailer label, and end-of-reel trailer label. 3. See tape label.

label (program): An ordered set of characters used to symbolically identify an instruction, a program, a quantity, or a data area. The label also symbolically designates the memory location which is to contain the instruction, etc. The label is, therefore, the symbolic analog of an address. A label may be absolute, relative, direct, or indirect.

label record: A record used to identify the contents of a file or reel of magnetic tape.

laboratory instrument computer (LINC): Performs several of the functions that normally external devices or people are required to perform. Data recording, analog-digital conversion, experiment monitoring, control, and analysis are built-in capabilities of the computer. LINC gives direct assistance to the research worker in many ways.

lag: A relative measure of the time delay between two events, states, or mechanisms.

lag (communications): Lag in a communications system is the time lapse between the operation of the transmitting device and the response of the receiving device.

lag or lead: See lead or lag.

lambertian emitter: An optical light source where the transmitted radiation is distributed uniformly in all directions.

landline facilities: Domestic communications common carriers' facilities that are within the continental United States.

language: 1. A defined set of characters and rules which are used to form symbols, words, etc., and the rules for combining these into meaningful FORTRAN, COBOL, etc. 2. A combination of a vocabulary and rules of syntax.

language converter translator: 1. A program which converts language to equivalent statements in another computer language, usually for a different computer. 2. Any assembler or compiling program which brings forth equivalent output from human-readable statements.

language digit: On international telephone calls, an additional digit inserted, usually automatically, as an indication of the language desired to be spoken by an operator at the distant end.

language for conversational computing (LCC): A powerful language for on-line computing in the style of ALGOL 60 with many features from JOSS.

language, problem oriented: 1. A language designed for convenience of program specification in a general problem area rather than for easy conversion to machine instruction code. The components of such a language may bear little resemblance to machine instructions. 2. A machine-independent language where one needs only to state the problem, not the method of solution.

language processor: A general term for any assembler, compiler, or other routine that accepts statements in one language and produces equivalent statements in another language.

language statement: A statement that is coded by a programmer, operator, or other user of a computing system, to convey information to a processing program such as a language translator or service program, or to the control program. A language statement may request that an operation be performed or may contain data that is to be passed to the processing program.

language subset: A part of a language that can be used independently of the rest of the language.

language theory parsing: Various procedures designed to break down the components of a sentence into structural forms.

language theory, production: In formal language theory (BNF), the input string translation into an output string.

language translation: The translation of information from one language to another.

language translator: 1. A program which converts a language to equivalent statements in another computer language, usually for a different computer. 2. A routine which aids in the performance of natural language translations such as French to English. 3. Any assembler or compiling program which brings forth the same or equivalent output from human-readable statements.

large capacity storage (LCS): An optional extension to processor storage.

large-scale integration (LSI): The accumulation of a large number of circuits (say 500 or more) on a single chip of a semiconductor. Characteristic of many central processing units (CPU's) circuits and memories introduced since 1970.

laser: A device which emits an extremely narrow and coherent beam of electromagnetic energy in the visible light spectrum.

laser-emulsion storage: A digital data storage medium which uses a controlled laser beam to expose very small areas on a photosensitive surface, producing desired information patterns.

laser memory: Experiments over the past four or five years have indicated the feasibility of using extremely fine laser beams to produce and to read optical patterns (films or holes) so small that an entire telephone directory would be contained on an area the size of a postage stamp. While not yet commercially available, such devices could solve problems which currently are not approachable due to unavailable cheap and large memory capacity.

laser mode: A well-defined distribution of the radiation amplitude in a cavity which results in the corresponding distribution pattern in the laser output beam. In a multimodal system the beam will tend to diverge.

laser scanner: A hardcopy output device that uses photographic film and a laser to create images. The film is mounted inside a lightproof drum that rotates rapidly. At the same time, a laser, mounted on a track that runs the length of the drum, moves back and forth, exposing the film with a highly precise, modulated beam of light. Laser scanners are used in applications where high resolution and high precision is essential, such as satellite shots.

laser threshold: The minimum pumping power (or energy) required to operate a laser.

last-in, first-out (LIFO): A queue discipline wherein the newest entry in a queue or file is the first to be removed.

latency time: 1. The time lag between completion of instruction staticizing and the initiation of the movement of data from its storage location. 2. The rotational delay time from a disk file or a drum file.

layer-to-layer adhesion: As related to magnetic tape, the tendency for adjacent layers of tape in a roll to adhere, particularly after prolonged storage under conditions of high temperature and humidity.

layer-to-layer signal transfer: The magnetization of a layer of tape in a roll by the field from a nearby recorded layer. The magnitude of the induced signal tends to increase with storage time and temperature, and to decrease after the tape is unwound, these changes being a function of the magnetic instability of the oxide.

layout: The overall plan or design such as flowcharts of diagrams, format for card columns or fields, outline of the procedure, makeup of a book or document, etc.

layout character: Same as format effector.

LC: A prefix or suffix which indicates a Library of Congress subject or document number.

LCB: See line control block.

LCL: See local.

LCS: See large-capacity storage.

LE: Less than or equal to.

lead-acid storage cell: An individual cell used in central office batteries. The plates are made of lead, lead/antimony or lead/-calcium and the electrolyte is dilute sulfuric acid. The charge/discharge action is reversible; cells may be charged and discharged many times or kept "floating" in a fully charged condition. Nominal voltage is 2 volts per cell, rising to 2.15 if fully charged and falling to 1.85 volts when discharged.

lead computer operator: Assists in scheduling the operations and in assigning personnel. Coordinates activities of the section with other sections in the data processing department. Many act as shift supervisor.

leader: 1. A record which precedes a group of detail records, giving information about the group not present in the detail records, e.g., beginning of batch 17. 2. An unused or blank length of tape at the beginning of a reel of a tape preceding the start of the recorded data.

leader record: A record that contains the description of or information held in a group of records.

leading control: A title of a control group of records that appears in the front of the group.

leading edge, document: The edge first encountered during the reading process in character recognition and whose relative position indicates the direction of travel for the document.

leading end: That particular end of a wire, tape, ribbon, line, or document that is processed first.

leading zeros: Zeros preceeding the first non-zero integer of a number. Leading zeros may be employed in the numeric fields of numerical control input blocks to indicate the assumed position of the decimal point within the field.

lead or lag: An advance or delay of the output signal with respect to the input.

lead systems analyst: Usually considered as the assistant manager of systems analysis, or has full technical knowledge of the activity. Comparable to a senior but also has supervisory duties of instructing, directing and checking the work of other system analysts, including the senior systems analysts.

lead time: The period of time between the actual ordering of parts or equipment and the delivery of same.

leakage: 1. Undesirable conductive paths in certain components; specifically, in capacitors, a path through which a slow discharge may take effect; in problem boards, interaction effects between electrical signals through insufficient insulation between patch bay terminals. 2. Current flowing through such paths.

leapfrogging: Community antenna television (CATV) operators' practice of skipping over one or more of the nearest television stations to bring in a farther signal for more program diversity on the cable. Federal Communication Commission (FCC) rules establish priority for carrying stations that lie outside the cable system's service area.

leapfrog test: A routine to test the internal operation of a computer which consists of a series of arithmetic or logical operations on one section of storage, a transfer to another section, including a check on the transfer, and then a repetition of the operations.

learning, computer: That feature of various unique programs designed to improve the efficiency of computers by altering programs using the computer's own experience as the basis. Instructions for program modification are written which analyze programming and processing results and then take corrective action based on predesigned branches or alterations due to a specific computer's characteristics and happenings.

leaseback: The practice by telephone companies of installing and maintaining community antenna television (CATV) distribution systems, and leasing the facilities back to separate contractors for operation of the system.

leased channel: 1. A point-to-point channel reserved for use by a single leasing customer. 2. In addition to the designated channels (education, government and public access) and over-the-air broadcast channels, cable systems must make the remainder of their channels available for lease. At least one channel is to be available for lease by part-time users. Channels can be leased by groups for individuals for the sole use of the lessee at posted rates. The operator must not censor or control program content in any way, under Federal Communications Commission rules.

leased circuit: A service offering which provides a customer with permanent (rather than dialed) connections to all points on the circuit for the duration of a contract.

leased facility: A facility reserved for sole use of a single leasing customer.

leased line: A communication channel leased for exclusive use from a common carrier, and frequently referred to as a private line.

leased line availabilities: Available from the same common carriers who provide switched-network service. The telephone companies and Western Union offer line rates as Type 1002, type 1005, 3000 Series, etc., which are tariff designation numbers used by most of the common carriers. Following is a tabulation of the leasedline facilities available for data communication.

Type 1002	55 baud
Type 1005	75 baud
Type 1006	150 baud
Type 3002	1200 bps to 9600 bps, depending upon conditioning applied to line and capabilities of associated modems. The fundamental, unconditioned bandwidth is that of a voice-grade line: 300 Hz to 3,000 Hz.
Type 8800	Approximate bandwidth: 48,000 Hz, handles data at 40,800 bps. (Known as a "Wideband" channel.)
Type 5700	Approximate bandwidth: 240,000 Hz, equivalent to 60 voice-grade channels.
Type 5800	Approximate bandwidth: 1,000,000 Hz, equivalent to 240 voice-grade channels.

Most of the services described are related in one way or another to the voice network. Typically the 1000 series services are fractions of a voice channel, and the wider bandwidth services are multiples of a voice channel.

leased-line network: A network reserved for the exclusive use of one customer.

least count: Thousandths or ten-thousandths of an inch per pulse or impulse.

least significant digit or character: That occupying the extreme right-hand position in a number of words.

left-justify: 1. To adjust the printing positions of characters on a page so that the left margin of the page is regular. 2. By extension, to shift the contents of a register so that the most significant digit is at some specified position of the register. Contrast with normalize.

left shift: A shift operation where the digits of a word are displaced to the left. This has the effect of multiplication in an arithmetical shift.

length-pulse modulation: Pulse-time modulation in which the value of each instantaneous sample of the modulating wave is caused to modulate the duration of a pulse. Note: In pulse modulation the modulatin a wave may vary the time of occurrence of the leading edge, the mailing edge, or both edges of the pulse.

length (record or word): The number of characters, digits or words which comprise a data record in some specific file or data set of fixed or variable size.

letter: One of a set of symbols combined to represent written words; an alphabetic character.

level: 1. The power relationship between different circuits, or different parts of the same circuit. The level at some particular point is the gain or loss of power, expressed in decibels (dB) between that point and some arbitrary reference point. The level at the reference point is zero. 2. In describing codes or characters it is synonymous with bit, element, or channel (for example, the levels or rows of recorded information on paper tape).

level compensator: An automatic gain control device used in the receiving equipment of a telegraph circuit.

level-enable flip-flop: The flip-flop, set by the level-enable signal, that partially controls the ability of an interrupt level to advance from the waiting state to the active state.

level-enable signal: A signal generated by the central processing unit (CPU) for the purpose of changing the state of the level-enable flip-flop from 0 to 1.

level of addressing: 1. Zero level addressing, the address part of an instruction is the operand, for instance, the addresses of shift instrucitons, or where the address is the date (in interpretive or generating systems). 2. First level addressing, the address of an instruction is the location in memory where the operand may be found or is to be stored. 3. Second level of addressing (indirect addressing), the address part of an instruction is the location in memory where the address of the operand may be found or is to be stored.

level system: A given embodiment of operational characteristics differing significantly from predecessor and successor levels by virtue of improvement modifications either for efficiency or for expanded capability.

lexiographic scan: An analysis that only concerns itself with one character at a time, possibly taking into account the immediate neighbor of the character.

LF: See line feed character.

librarian: A program that creates, maintains and makes available the collection of programs, routines and data that make up an operating system.

librarian program: Provides maintenance of library programs used as part of the operating system. The library may be stored on a single secondary storage unit, or it may be distributed over several different storage units. In either case, the librarian program keeps the library up to date by adding, deleting, and modifying as required. User-written application programs can be incorporated into the library along with subroutines, the control program itself, compilers, sort/merge, and utility program.

library: An ordered set of standard and proven routines and subroutines by which problems may be solved; usually stored in relative or symbolic coding. (A library may be subdivided into various volumes, such as floating decimal, double-precision, or complex, according to the type of arithemetic employed by the subroutines.)

library automation: The application of machines to improve library services by increasing the quantity and quality of the work performed by the library staff. Some automation, as in circulation control systems, increases the amount of work accomplished per man hour; other kinds of automation, as in the on-line retrieval services, greatly increase the capabilities of a library in meeting user demands.

library facilities: A basic library of general-purpose software furnished by manufacturers to perform oftenused programs and routines. Programs in the library can be conveniently assembled into an object program by the use of macroinstructions.

library link: A special set of data used by execute statements such as attach, link, load, etc.

library macro definition: A macro definition stored in a program library; for example, the IBM-supplied supervisor and data management macro definitions.

library programs: A software collection of standard and proved routines and subroutines by which problems may be solved on a given computer.

library routine: A checked-out routine which may be incorporated into a larger routine; maintained in a library as an aid to programmers.

library (SYSLIB) system: A partitioned data set in which the members constitute the programs of TSS/360.

library system: The organized collection of absolute programs, relocating specialized systems, creating and maintaining the library sections, and loading and editing programs onto the resident device. These programs are linkage editor and librarian.

library tape: Usually a magnetic tape taken from storage that contains an indexed collection of tapes held for immediate use; also library tapes contain various subroutines of a general nature or related exclusively to the particular system to which it belongs.

library terminal: A special terminal for use in the bibliographic system of a large library. It has a keyboard, alphanumeric cathode-ray tube (CRT), a slowspeed printer, an extended alphabet keyboard, a badge reader, a unit document reader, a magnetic-tape cassette, and a communications interface. Most importantly, special terminals must be oriented toward the specific user—layout, operation procedure, output format, input technique, etc.

librious: Provides library operations for file maintenance of installation-oriented programs and subroutines. Includes standard input/output (I/O) routines, utility routines, and mathematical subroutines.

lighthouse tube: An ultra-high frequency (uhf) triode resembling a miniature lighthouse.

lightning surge: The current surge in a communication system resulting from a lightning discharge.

light pen: When used in conjuction with the incremental display, greatly extends its usefulness. It is a high speed, photosensitive device that can cause the computer to change or modify the display on the cathode-ray tube. As the pertinent display information is selected by the operator, the pen signals the computer by generating a pulse. Acting upon this signal, the computer can then instruct other points to be plotted across the tube face in accordance with the pen movements, or exercise specific options previously programmed without the need for separate input devices.

light pen attention: An interruption generated by a light pen when it senses light on the screen of a cathode-ray tube (CRT) display device. Same as selector pen attention.

light pen tracking: The process of tracing the movement of a light pen across the screen of a cathode-ray tube (CRT) display device.

light-sensitive: Describes thin surfaces of

which the electrical resistance, emission of electrons, or generation of a current depends on incidence of light.

light stability: In optical character recognition, the resistance to change of color of the image when exposed to radiant energy.

light stylus: See light pen.

limit: A value toward which a varying quantity may approach less than any assignable quantity, but which it cannot pass. Thus, the quantity $a^2 + 2ax^2$ varies with x, or it is a function of x, and approximates towards a^2 in value as x is diminished, and may, by giving a suitable value to x, be made to differ from a^2 by less than any assignable quantity. Thus a^2 is a limit of the expresion, which in this case may be found by making x = 0.

limit checks: A check made on input data to insure that it does not exceed a maximum figure.

limited: A word often attached to another word or term to indicate the particular machine activity which needs the most time, i.e., tape-limited, input-limited, etc.

limited distance adapter: A short-range modem (thirty miles or less).

limited integrator: An arrangement or set-up which involves an integrator where the inputs cease to be integrated when the output tends to exceed specified limits. In a hard limited integrator the output does not exceed the limits, while in a soft limited integrator, with limited precision, the output may exceed the limit.

limiter circuit: A circuit of nonlinear elements that restrict the electrical excursion of a variable in accordance with some specified criteria. Hard limiting is a limiting action with negligible variation in output in the range where the output is limited. Soft limiting is a limiting action with appreciable variation in output in the range where the output is limited. A bridge limiter is a bridge circuit used as a limiter circuit. In an analog computer, a feedback limiter is a limiter circuit usually employing biased diodes in the amplifier input channel that operates by limiting the current entering the summing junction.

limiting: A limiting action with negligible variation in output in the range where the output is limited. Soft limiting is a limiting action with appreciable variation in output in the range where the output is limited. A bridge limiter is a bridge circuit used as a limiter circuit.

limit priority: A priority specification associated with every task in a multitask operation, representing the highest dispatching priority that the task may assign to itself or to any of its subtasks.

limit priority or range limit: The upper bound to the priority list for dispatching or designing a priority rating to various tasks or subtasks, i.e., active, inactive, top priority, lowest priority or batch processing.

line: 1. A horizontal row of characters printed across a page or card, such as in line-at-a-time printers. 2. A channel or conductor capable of transmitting signals.

line adapter unit: Provides for installation of line adapters to permit attached transmission control units to communicate with similarly equipped terminals. Adapters modulate and demodulate signals over communication facilities in a manner similar to common-carrier provided data sets that would otherwise be required for these functions. Three types of line adapters can be installed to provide for: (a) limited distance (8 miles) communication, (b) communication over privately owned or leased common-carrier facilities, and/or (c) simultaneous sharing of voice-grade line by up to four low-speed terminal lines. Each low-speed line maybe operated either point-to-point or multipoint.

line address: A character or set of characters designating a specific communication channel.

line amplifier: In broadcasting, that which supplies power to the line, either to a control center or to a transmitter.

linear: The order in an algebraic equation in which all of the variables are present in the first degree only, i.e., an equation in which none of the variables are raised to powers other than unity or multiplied together.

linear amplifier: One for which the output signal level is a constant multiple of the input level.

linear circuit: A circuit whose output is an amplified version of its input or whose output is a predetermined variation of its input.

linear coding: A linear operation that is predictable and uses an additive process such as $2 + 2 = 4$ or modulo 2 addition. The operation is performed on a signal to encode it. Linear operations are less secure than nonlinear.

linear displacement transducer (LVDT): An electromechanical device which produces an electrical output proportional to the displacement of a separate movable core.

linear distortion: Distortion independent of the signal amplitude.

linear equations: Graphed as a straight line. Since a straight line is determined by two points, to plot the graph of a linear equation, plot two points and draw a straight line through them.

linear integrated circuit (IC):   Uses implanted junction bipolar technology to provide 200V drive capability in order to directly drive a cathode-ray tube's (CRT's) cathode. The use of this technology eliminates the need for separate driver transistors and associated components, thus eliminating the need for approximately twenty to thirty printed circuit board components. The chip uses standard diffusion technology instead of the more costly dielectric-isolation process formerly required for high-voltage capability. This IC accomplishes a purportedly exceptional slew rate and low power dissipation.

linear interpolation: A mode of machine tool contouring control which uses the information contained in a block to produce constant velocities proportional to the distance moved in two or more axes simultaneously.

linearity: A constant ratio of cause and effect (as in a straight line representation).

linearity controls: The cathode-ray tube (CRT) receiver hand controls which help correct distortion in the picture.

linearity error: An error due to or caused by the departure from linearity of a nominally linear unit.

linearization: A mathematical procedure incorporated in a post-processor to subdivide simultaneous linear and rotary machine slide motions into smaller segments so the tool motion resulting from the consecutive subdivisions will result in a straight line on the surface of the part within a part programmer's specified tolerance.

linear language control programming: The language used to prescribe the course of a linear programming run on a computer. The language consists mainly of verbs (agendum names) which call in a body of code (program or subroutine) embodying the desired algorithm for execution.

linear modulation: Modulation in which the change in the modulated characteristic of the carrier signal is proportional to the value of the modulating signal over the range of the audio-frequency band.

linear optimization: Procedures for locating maximum or minimum values of a linear function of variables which are subject to specific linear constraints which may or may not be inequalities.

linear potentiometer: A potentiometer in which the voltage at a movable contact is a linear function of the displacement of the contact.

linear programming (LP): In operations research, a procedure for locating the maximum or minimum of a linear function of variables that are subject to linear constraints.

linear selection switch: A specific fixed or permanent storage device which stores coded data in the form of an array of cores and wires, but the wiring holds the information rather than the cores, and these are wound through or to bypass the core.

linear threshold: The basic elements of machine intelligence, including ultra-reliability, multichannel capacity, associative memory and adaptivity.

line average edge: In optical character recognition, an imaginary line that traces and smooths the form of the printed or handwritten character to better convey the intended form.

line bias: The effect of the electrical characteristics of a transmission line on the length of the teletypewriter signals.

line circuit: Line switching establishes a physical circuit path, physically connecting the input path to the appropriate output path at each switching point, and exists for the duration of interaction between processes.

line coding: A single command or instruction for a computer to solve.

line conditioning: Designated as Type C1, Type C2, and Type C4, improves the frequency response of a line and improves its envelope-delay characteristics. There is a charge for conditioning the line, and if the line is used in a multipoint configuration, the charges are higher.

line control: 1. A system or method of presenting incoming information to the central processor and outgoing information to the terminal lines in a manner that optimizes the utilization of the hardware and software involved (for computer systems). 2. Sets of procedures that designate how line usage will be controlled.

line control block (LCB): An area of main storage containing control data for operations on a line. The LCB can be divided into several groups of fields, most of these groups can be identified as generalized control blocks.

line control unit: A special-purpose computer used to control input and output from communications lines that are not connected directly to the main computer.

line coordination: The procedure of insuring that equipment at both ends of a circuit are set up for a specific transmission.

line coupling: Transfer of energy between resonant (tank) circuits in a transmitter, using a short length of line with small inductive coupling at each end.

line data set: A telephone line disconnected from a central office.

line deletion character: A terminal character specifying that all characters are to be deleted from a line of terminal input.

line discipline: Distinct rules and procedures which adjust the operating parameters of transmission systems to achieve correct or desired line control; includes considerations of contention, polling, queuing priority, etc.

line distortion: Arises in the frequency content or phase distribution in a transmitted signal, as a result of the propagation constant for the line.

line driver: A power amplifier used to drive many points such as logical elements, input/output units using a conductor of a low-impedance bus, e.g., a transfer, checking or clock-pulse bus. Alternately, it is an amplifier used to allow signals to be sent over long distances.

line drop: The potential drop between any two points on a transmission line due to resistance, leakage, or reactance.

line dropout: A large, momentary change in the transmission characteristics of a telephone circuit.

line editing: In some systems, especially those using typewriter terminals, the message editor may be required to scan each input line for editing-control codes, which indicate the logical functions of deleteprevious-character (backspace) and delete-previousline (cancel). These codes are inserted by the terminal operator when a correction in the message is required. Additional operations may involve the generation of format-effector codes used to control the position of the printing element.

line equalizer: Device which compensates for attenuation and/or phase delay for transmission of signals along a line over a band of frequencies.

line equipment: Circuit in a central office directly associated with a particular line.

line error: A deviation from correctness in data caused by conditions in a transmission medium.

line feed character (LF):   A format effector that causes the printing or display position to be moved to the next printing or display line.

line finder (telegraphic):   A piece of switching apparatus which electromechanically seeks an idle current to a given destination from among all of the circuits to that destination.

line generator (display):   Typical is the model LG-9 line generator which receives digital on- or off-line inputs and generates straight lines between any two points on a straight line between any two points on a 512×512 matrix on a cathode-ray tube at a constant writing rate. Dotted, dashed, or blank lines can be generated.

line group: A set of one or more communication lines of the same type, over which terminals with similar characteristics can communicate with the computer.

line hit: An electrical interference causing the introduction of spurious signals on a communications circuit.

line impedance: The impedance of a transmission line. It is a function of the resistance, inductance, conductance, and capacitance of the line, and the frequency of the signal. Same as characteristic impedance.

line level: The signal level in decibels at a particular position on a transmission line.

line load: Percentage of maximum circuit capability in actual use during a given period of time.

line load control: Selective denial of call origination capability to specified subscribers' lines when excessive demands for service are offered to a switching center. It does not affect the capability to receive calls. Normally, in North America, a central office is divided into three groups of lines and control is rotated, with one or two groups being denied outward service at a time.

line loading: The use of resistors, capacitors, and inductors to compensate for the frequency distortion and delay distortion characteristics of telephone lines.

line loop: A communication line from an input at one terminal to output units at a remote terminal.

line loop resistance: The metallic resistance of the local loop (often called loop resistance).

line network, leased: A communications network reserved for the sole use of one customer.

line noise: Noise originating in a transmission line.

line number: 1. A number associated with a line in a printout or display. 2. In systems with time sharing, a number associated with a line in a line data set.

line number editing: In systems with time sharing, a mode of operation under the EDIT command in which lines to be modified are referred to by line number.

line-off unit: Input/output device or auxiliary equipment not under direct control of the central processing unit.

line-of-sight: As far as the eye can see; the range of very high frequency signals.

line parameters: Those necessary (series impedance and shunt admittance) to specify the electrical characteristics of a transmission line.

line print: A set of printed characters and spaces, arranged in a horizontal row and considered as a unit.

line printer: A printer in which all characters across an entire line of type are printed in one print cycle.

line procedure specifications: A sequence of userselected macroinstructions that (a) specify the manner in which control information in the message header is to be examined and processed, and (b) specify other functions (such as translating) to be performed.

line program: A single instruction usually written on a standard coding form and stored as a single entity.

line reflection: The reflection of some signal energy at a discontinuity in a transmission line.

line relay: A relay activated by the signals on a line.

line scanning: Uses the small computer to establish and maintain line synchronization, character assembly, and completed character detection. This technique requires the use of a small computer that is communication oriented and has an instruction execution speed capable of handling many lines. The trade-off factors for this approach are that a greater percentage of processor time is required in order to service the line, and the system is limited in the speed of the lines it can service.

line speed: 1. The maximum rate at which signals may be transmitted over a given channel. 2. The normal operating speed of a communications system.; the automatic machine speed, as opposed to the slower speed of any associated manual operations.

lines per second (LPS) control routine: A QTAM routine that performs initialization functions and obtains the address of the LPS line group routine to be used for processing a particular message segment.

lines per second (LPS) line group routine: A userdefined routine comprised of subroutines necessary to prepare a message segment for processing, and examine and process the control information in the message segment. The functions performed are based on the userselected macroinstructions that determine the configuration of each line group routine. One line group routine must be provided for each line group included in the system.

line status: The status of a communication line such as receive, transmit, or control.

line stretcher: An impedance matching device for coaxial transmission lines.

line switching: A switching technique where the connection is made between the calling party and the called party prior to the start of a communication, e.g., telephone switching.

line termination controller: The controller terminates the line with a buffer or a terminal adapter, which is addressable by the central processing unit (CPU). This is a specific piece of hardware (it maybe as simple as a few circuit boards) that is mounted in the controller rack. The receive and transmit operations of the communications medium are analogous to the read and write operations of computer peripheral devices. Controller designs vary and in some systems more than one controller may be required. The number of lines that can be attached depends on factors such as the throughput capacity of the processor, the scanning rate, and the total data rate of the lines. Controllers may or may not handle both start-stop and synchronous transmissions, interface both half- and full-duplex lines, and be designed to handle a mix of low, medium, and highspeed data rates. Thus, a controller that has this type of flexibility may be desirable in many systems.

line turn-around: In half-duplex communication, the switching of modems and communication channels from transmission in one direction to transmission in the opposite direction.

link: In automatic switching, a path between two units of switching apparatus within a central office.

link access procedure (LAP):   A version of high-level data link control (HDLC) modified by the CCITT, later modified again to LAPB.

linkage: A means of communicating information from one routine to another.

linkage editor: 1. A system service program that edits the output of language translators and produces executable program phases. It relocates programs or program sections and links together separately assembled (or compiled) sections. 2. A program that produces a load module by transforming object modules into a format that is acceptable to fetch, combining separately produced object modules and previously processed load modules into a single load module, resolving symbolic cross references among them, replacing, deleting, and adding control sections automati-

cally on request, and providing overlay facililties for modules requesting them.

linkage, slide: A system of mechanical elements interconnected by arms or bars, i.e., in a slide linkage, the elements are constrained to move only in the direction of their lengths in contrast to pin-jointed linkages.

link bit: A specific one-bit register which contains an indicator for overflow from the accumulator, and usually, other registers. It can be tested under program control.

link group: Consists of those links which employ the same multiplex-terminal equipment.

linking loader program: A special computer program used to combine links as they are loaded into computer storage for execution.

LISP: See list processing.

listing: A printout, usually prepared by a language translator, that lists the source language statements and contents of a program.

list posting: A bookkeeping procedure of grouping checks of a specific account into a single total for posting to the customer account record.

list processing (LISP):   (ISO) A method of processing data in the form of lists. Usually, chained lists are used so that the logical order of items can be changed without altering their physical locations.

list processing languages: Specific languages developed by symbol manipulation and used primarily as research tools. Most have proved valuable in contruction of compilers and in simulation of problem solving. Other uses have included verification of mathematical proofs, pattern recognition, information retrieval, algebraic manipulation, heuristic programming, and exploration of new programming languages.

list structure: A specific set of data items combined because each element contains the address of the successor item or element, i.e., a predecessor item or element. Such lists grow in size according to the limits of fixed storage capacity, and it is simple to insert or delete data items anywhere in a list structure.

list (to): In punched card equipment, to print every relevant item of input data on the general basis of one line of print per card, as contrasted to tabulate.

literal: 1. A symbol that names itself and is not the name of something else. 2. A symbol or quantity in a source program that is itself data rather than a reference to data. 3. A character or group of characters, used in a COBOL program to represent the value literally expressed. Thus, the literal 7 represents the value 7, whereas seven is a name that could be used to represent the value 7.

literal operands: Operands, most often in source language instruction, that specify precisely the value of a constant rather than an address in which the constant is stored. This method enables the coding to be written more concisely than if the constant had been allocated a data name.

literal pool: An area within an assembled program segment where the literals used in a program section are stored. Within an area, duplicate literals may be eliminated.

literature search: A systematic and exhaustive search for published material on a specific subject, and usually the preparation of abstracts on that material.

live copy/hard copy: Paper copy of a vital record which is dispersed for protection, as opposed to microfilm or magnetic tape. Documents which are available immediately for active use without processing.

liveware: The personnel associated with all aspects of a computer.

live zone: The zone in which a value of the output exists.

load: 1. The process of reading the beginning of a program into virtual storage and making necessary adjustments and/or modifications to the program so that it may have control transferred to it for the purpose of execution. 2. To take information from auxiliary or external storage and place it into core storage.

load address: The absolute storage location into which a word or the first of a series of contiguous words is loaded.

load and go: An automatic coding procedure which not only compiles the program creating machine language, but also proceeds to execute the created program. Load and go procedures are usually part of an operating system.

load balancing mode: In this mode the user submits a complete job to the network via his local complex; however, he does not know or care where the job gets run. In effect he tells the network control program to find all the necessary data sets, construct the job control sequence properly, and assign it to be processed by the aggregate resources of the network in the best way.

load control: A procedure designed to prevent thrashing by measuring the utilization of processors and backing storage, and (if necessary) pre-empting processes to reduce the computational load.

load, dummy: 1. A device (i.e., a resistor) in which the output power can be absorbed. A dummy load is used for simulating conditions of operation for test purposes. 2. To effect the finding, and transfer to storage of a program or set of programs without execution to determine that all relevant specifications and components exist in the proper forms in the library.

loader: A program that operates on input devices to transfer information from off-line memory to on-line memory.

loader application: Relates to that set of instructions which brings other data and instructions into storage and which is often built into various computer models.

loader system: One of the supervisor routines. It is used to retrieve program phases from the core image library and load them into main storage.

load factor: Ratio of average load to peak load over a period.

load impedance: A specific impedance presented to the output of a device by the load.

loading: Adding inductance (load coils) to a transmission line to minimize amplitude distortion.

loading error: The error found in the output of the computer which came about as a result of a change in value of the load supplied.

loading-location misuse errors: 1. A loading location specification was made but no load or execute was specified. 2. The loading location specified was not within the available range of memory. 3. The loading location is assigned as the first available location.

loading procedure: A procedure to place data and instructions into storage. System, object, and library routines are loaded in a similar manner. A program may have a fixed origin or may be relocatable. Fixed origin programs are loaded into the specified memory address. Programs are relocated by a base address initially set by the executive routine. After the main program has been loaded, any library subroutines or equipment drivers called will then be loaded. When all the necessary routines are in memory, the loader returns to the job processor.

loading routine: A set of instructions used to bring data and instructions into storage.

loading routine (bootstrap): 1. A developed routine placed in a storage for the purpose of reading into storage another program, routine, or various data. 2. A single subprogram that loads a complete object program.

load map: A memory address map listing the location of program segments for a given core load.

load matching: Adjusting circuit conditions to meet requirements for maximum energy transfer to load.

load mode: In some variable-word-length computers, delimiters that are moved in data transmission.

load module library: A partitioned data set that is used to store and retrieve load modules.

load point: A preset point at which magnetic tape is initially positioned under the read/write head to start reading or writing.

load program: A set of instructions used in conjunction with the console to enter a program on punched cards into computer storage.

load regulation: A deviation from steady-state of the controlled variable when the set point is fixed. Such an offset resulting from a no-load to a full-load change (or other specified limits) is often called an offset deviation or "droop."

load sharing: Computers placed in tandem to share the peak period processing load of a system.

load stabilization: Method of stabilization by variation of apparent load.

load system program: One of the system service progams. It is used to build a resident system from punched cards.

load voltage regulation: A change in output voltage of a power source for a specified change in the load. This is often expressed as the percentage ratio of the voltage change from no-load to rated load divided by the no-load voltage.

local: In assembler progamming, pertaining to that part of a program that is either the body of any macro definition called from a source module or the open code portion of the source module.

local area networks: Designed for on-line, real-time data communication environments. Among other allied products are statistical and switching multiplexers and microwave radio systems, providing reliable, short range communications links. Some also include duplex digital data encryption/decode unit, operating at data rates up to 2M bits per second. Typically the local communciations network combines data switching capabilities, distributed architecture, and high capacity to allow large numbers of dispersed users access to multiple computers in a flexible, cost-effective way.

local central office: Central office arranged for terminating subscriber lines and provided with trunks for establishing connections to and from other central offices.

local channel: In private line services, that portion of a through channel within an exchange provided to connect the main station with an interexchange channel.

local control: That carried out directly and not from a remote control console.

local distribution system (LDS):   A wide band microwave system or cable system capable of transporting a number of television signals simultaneously. Used to interconnect cable system headends.

local exchange center: A telephone switching center not included in the switching centers that handle traffic in the long distance trunk network.

local (load-on-call):   A program overlay procedure for loading one of several subprograms into main memory for execu-tion only when required by the currently executing program.

local loop: A channel connecting the subscriber's equipment to the line terminating equipment in the central office exchange. Usually a metallic circuit (either two-wire or four-wire).

local origination channel: A channel on a cable system (exclusive of broadcast signals) programmed by the cable operator and subject to his exclusive control.

local oscillator: The front-end oscillator in a superheterodyne.

local-service area: The area containing the telephone stations that a flat rate customer may call without incurring toll charges.

local signals: Television signals received at locations within the station's predicted grade B contour. Cable systems must carry all commercial local signals in their areas.

local station: A station whose control unit is connected directly to a computer data channel. Contrast with remote station.

local switching center: A telephonic switching center designated to handle traffic in the long distance trunk network.

local variable symbol: In assembler programming, a variable symbol used to communicate values inside a macro definition or in the open code portion of a source module.

locate mode: A way of providing data by pointing to its location instead of moving it.

location: A place in memory in which one or many words or characters may be stored, identified by an address. Same as cell position.

location counter: 1. The control section register which contains the address of the instruction currently being executed. Also, it is called the instruction counter, program address counter, etc. 2. A counter that is incremented by one for each word the assembly program generates in the object program.

location delimiter: A specific delimiter designed for use within a storage area or part of a specific storage area, i.e., as a subdivision for very efficient area utilization.

location, effective: The actual storage location of interest.

location-free procedure: Procedure which, for the purpose of execution, is independent of its location in storage; the procedure does not contain any constants which must be changed as a result of relocating the procedure in storage.

locations, buffer storage: A set of locations used to compensate for a difference in a rate of data flow, or time or occurrence of events, when transmitting data from one device to another, and importantly also to retain temporarily a copy of the data as safeguard against faults and unintentional erasures.

locator run: A routine that locates the correct run on a program tape, whether initiated by another routine or manually.

lock: To terminate the processing of a magnetic tape in a way that its contents are no longer accessible.

locking: Code extension characters that change the interpretation of an unspecified number of following characters.

locking relay: Contacts made or broken when the relay is energized are unaffected by de-energization.

lock mode: Under telecommunications access method (TCAM), a mode in which the connection between a terminal and an application program is maintained for the duration of a message and its response.

lockout: 1. In a telephone circuit controlled by an echo-suppressor, the inability of one or both subscribers to get through because of either excessive local circuit noise or continuous speech from one subscriber. 2. In data communications, to place unaddressed terminals on a multipoint line in control state so that they will not receive transmitted data.

lockout switch: A manual switch provided with drum memory, and associated with individual drum memory segments. It provides the contents of such segments with selectable protection from alteration.

lock-up: A method of controlling the location to which a jump or transfer is made. It is used especially when there are a large number of alternatives, as in function evaluation in scientific computations.

log: 1. A record of everything pertinent to a machine run including, (a) identifications of the machine run, (b) record of alternation switch settings, (c) identification of input and output tapes, (d) copy of manual key-ins, (e) identification of all stops, and (f) a record of action taken on all stops. 2. A collection of messages that provides a history of message traffic.

logarithm: The exponent of a number indicating the power to which it is necessary to raise a given number, called the base, to produce the original number.

logarithm characteristic: The non-negative decimal part of a logarithm is called the mantissa, and the integral part is called the characteristic of a logarithm. For example, in the log 1830 = 0.2635 + 3, 0.2625 is the mantissa and 3 is the characteristic, or 1 less than the number of integers.

logger: A device that automatically records physical processes and events, usually with respect to time.

logging routine: A procedure that creates a record of all transactions on a secondary storage device such as magnetic tape or magnetic disk.

logic: 1. The science dealing with the criteria or formal principles of reasoning and thought. 2. The systematic scheme which defines the interactions of signals in the design of an automatic data processing system. 3. The basic principles and application of truth tables and interconnection between logical elements required for arithmetic computation in an automatic data processing system. See also symbolic logic.

logic add: An operation performed in Boolean algebra on two binary digits simultaneously in a way that the result is one if either one or both digits are a one, or zero if both digits are zero. The logic operator is the OR operator.

logical choice: To make the correct decision where alternates or even a variety of possibilities are open. The variety of logical choices a computer can make and the speed with which it makes them is a pretty accurate measure of its intelligence quotient (I.Q.).

logical circuit: A group or set of logic elements interconnected or integrated to carry out the design of the processing task as part of the total computer logic design.

logical comparison: The consideration of two things, with regard to some characteristic, to obtain a yes if they are the same, or a no if they are different.

logical connectives: The operators or words, such as AND, OR, OR ELSE, IF THEN, NEITHER, NOR, and EXCEPT, which make new statements from given statements and which have the property that the truth or fallacy of the new statements can be calculated from the truth or fallacy of the given statements and the logical meaning of the operator.

logical design: 1. The planning of a data processing system prior to its detailed engineering design. 2. The synthesizing of a network of logical elements to perform a specified function. 3. The result of 1 and 2, frequently called the logic of a computer or of a data processing system.

logical difference: In set theory, all members of one set which are not members of another, given the elements of each specific set; i.e., if set A includes 1,3,5,7,9 and 11 and set B includes 2,3,4,5,6,7 the difference is 3, 5, and 7.

logical element: The smallest building block in a computer or data processing system which can be represented by logical operators in an appropriate system of symbolic logic. Typical logical elements are the AND gate and the OR gate which can be represented as operators in a suitable symbolic logic.

logical element symbol: That circuitry which provides an output resulting from input of two variables.

logical expression: In assembler programming, a conditional assembly expression that is a combinatin of logical terms, logical operators, and paired parentheses.

logical file: 1. A data set that is composed of one or more logical open records. 2. A data file that has been described to the disk or tape operating systems through the use of a file-definition (DTF) macroinstruction. Note that a data file is described to the operating system through a different defining method. Operating system publications refer to a data file described in this different manner as a data set.

logical flowchart: See logic flowchart.

logical inclusive OR: A logical operator that produces a "true" result when either or both of two logical variables are true.

logical input/output control system (IOCS): A set of macro routines provided to handle the creation, retrieval, and maintenance of data files. Contrasted with physical IOCS.

logical leading end: The first end of the tape for the decoding process.

logical multiply: Same as AND operator.

logical one or zero: Represents two possible states of binary systems (equivalent to mark or space).

logical operation: Computer operations of comparing, selecting, or taking alternative action.

logical record: A record identified from the standpoint of its content, function, and use rather than its physical attributes. It is meaningful with respect to the information it contains. Contrasted with physical record.

logical relation: In assembler programming, a logical term in which two expresions are separated by a relational operator.

logical shift: A shift in which the sign is treated as another data position.

logical sum: A result, similar to an arithmetic sum, obtained in the process of ordinary addition, except that the rules are such that a result of one is obtained when either one or both input variables is a one, and an output of zero is obtained when the input variables are both zero. The logical sum is the name given the result produced by the inclusive OR operator.

logical symbol: A sign used as an operator to denote the particular operation to be performed on the associated variables.

logical term: In assembler programming, a term that can be used only in a logical expression.

logical unit: A self-contained unit.

logical unit number: A number assigned to peripheral units during autoload or system generation time. Such numbers can be altered whenever convenient, in contrast to a physical unit number. For example, a card reader may be assigned logical unit number 5 and a read operation from unit 5 will result in reading a card.

logical variable: A variable which may only have a "true" or "false" value.

logic analysis: The delineation or determination of the specific steps required to produce the desired output or intelligence information from the given or ascertained input data. The logic studies are completed for many computer processes, programs, or runs.

logic card: A grouping of electrical components and wiring circuitry mounted on a board allowing easy withdrawal and replacement from a socket in the equipment. Each card is related to a basic machine function and on discovery of a bug in that function, the card can be replaced.

logic circuit: One of many types of switching circuits such as AND, OR, NAND, etc.; gates that perform various logic operations or represent logic functions.

logic-controlled sequential computer: Executes instructions in a sequence designed by built-in logic; i.e., a fixed sequence, but one which can be overridden or changed by an instruction; a highly unique and almost single purpose computer with little or no concurrent action.

logic design: The specification of the working relations between the parts of a system in terms of symbolic logic and without primary regard for hardware implementation.

logic diagram: A diagram that represents a logic design and sometimes the hardware implementation.

logic difference: See logical difference.

logic element: 1. A device that performs a logic function 2. See combinational logic element, sequential logic element.

logic flowchart: The particular detailed solution of the work order or arrangement in terms of the logic, or built-in operations and characteristics, of a specific machine. Concise symbolic notation is used to represent the information and describe the input, output arithmetic, and logical operations involved. The chart indicates types of operations by use of a standard set of block symbols. A coding process normally follows the logical flowchart.

logic instruction: An instruction that executes an operation that is defined in symbolic logic, such as AND, OR, NOR.

logic levels: Nominal voltages which represent binary conditions in a logic circuit.

logic module: The logical input/output control system (IOCS) routine that provides an interface between a processing program and physical IOCS.

logic operator: Any of the switching operators or gates such as AND, OR, NAND, etc.

logic shift: A type of shift in which all bits or characters are treated identically, i.e., no special consideration is made for the sign position as in an arithmetic shift.

logic swing: The voltage difference between the two logic levels "1" and "0."

logic symbol: 1. A symbol used to represent a logic element graphically. 2. A symbol used to represent a logic operator.

logo: A recursive procedure-based language designed for educational applications. Used in teaching mathematics, heuristics and formal methods in courses ranging from elementary to university levels.

long distance (LD) trunk: A type of trunk that permits trunk-to-trunk connection and which interconnects local, secondary, primary, and zone centers.

long grain: In character recognition, a favorable machine paper arrangement which is achieved: 1. when the grain obtained during the formation of the paper runs in the direction of its longest dimension, and 2. when such paper, as a cutform document, travels through a character reader in the direction of its longest dimension.

long instruction format: An instruction which occupies more than one standard instruction position or length (e.g., a two-word instruction); the second word may be used for address modification or as an operand.

longitudinal circuit: A circuit formed by one telephone wire (or two or more telephone wires in parallel) with a return through the earth or through any other conductors except those which are taken with the original wire or wires to form a metallic telephone circuit.

longitudinal mode delay line: Delay lines are often named according to a propagating medium, such as mercury delay line, quartz delay line, or according to vibrational modes as longitudinal.

longitudinal parity check: Generated by the data line terminal at the transmitting end to count for even parity of all of the bits in each one of the bit levels for all data characters in the message including the start-of-message code but not the end-of-message code. This same count is also being generated for the bits of the data characters entering the data-line terminal of the receiving end.

longitudinal redundancy check: An error control device or system based on the arrangement of data in blocks according to some preset rule, the correctness of each character within the block being determined on the basis of the specific rule or set.

longitudinal testing: Interactive tests to compare earlier performance with later performances.

longitudinal transmission check: A parity check at fixed intervals of data transmission. See parity check.

long-line effect: Frequency-jumping by an oscillator supplying a load through a long transmission line; due to admittance of the line being suitable for oscillation at more than one frequency.

Long Lines: A department of AT&T headquarters which provides most intercompany transmission facilities in the Bell System.

long-space disconnect: A feature of some modems which causes the modem to terminate a telephone call in response to the receipt of a spacing signal for an extended period of time.

long-term storage: Data storage in reference to the length of time data is stored in core memory.

look-up: See table look-up.

loop: 1. A self-contained series of instructions in which the last instruction can modify and repeat itself until a terminal condition is reached. The productive instructions in the loop generally manipulate the operands, while bookkeeping instructions modify the productive instructions, and keep count of the number of repetitions. A loop may contain any number of conditions for termination. The equivalent of a loop can be achieved by the technique of straight line coding, whereby the repetition of productive and bookkeping operations is accomplished by writing the instructions for each repetition. 2. A communications circuit between two private subscribers or between a subscriber and the local switching center.

loop actuating signal: The combined input and feedback signals in a closed-loop system.

loopback test: A test in which signals are looped from a test center through a data set or loopback switch and back to the test center for measurement. See also bussback.

loop box: A specific register used as an index register but only to modify instructions immediately prior to their execution. For example, a number or symbol is addended to an instruction as the last step before the instruction is executed and the instruction is thus modified, but without changing the instruction as it is stored in memory.

loop checking: A method of checking the accuracy of data transmission in which the received data are turned to the sending end for comparison with the original data, which are stored there for this purpose.

loop code: The repetition of a sequence of instructions by using a program loop. Loop coding requires more execution time than straight line coding but results in a savings of storage.

loop computing: Those instructions of a loop that perform the primary function of the loop, as distinguished from loop initialization, modification and testing, which are housekeeping operations.

loop counter: In assembler programming a counter used to prevent excessive looping during conditional assembly processing.

loop difference signal: Output signal at a point in a feedback loop produced by an input signal applied at the same point.

loop error: The departure of the loop output signal from the desired value. If used as the loop actuating signal it is known as the loop error signal.

loop execution: The execution of the same set of instructions where, for each execution, some parameter or sets of parameters have undergone a change, e.g., a new value for a variable; or the addresses of various data may be modified, often through the use of an index register, to modify the address part of the instruction automatically.

loop feedback signal: The part of the loop output signal fed back to the input to produce the loop actuating signal.

loop gain: A calculated ratio of the change in the return signal to the change in its corresponding error signal at a specified frequency.

loop gain characteristic: Relating to closed loop, the characteristic curve of the ratio of the change in the return signal to the change in its corresponding error signal for all real frequencies.

looping execution: See loop execution.

loop initialization: The instructions immediately prior to a loop proper which set addresses and/or data to their desired initial values.

loop input signal: An external signal applied to a feedback control loop in control systems.

loop jack switchboard: A patch panel with rows on jacks for physical access to local loops (maximum capacity of 90 channels). Each column of four jacks accesses one local loop and consists of looping jacks, a set jack, and a miscellaneous jack.

loop modification: Those instructions of a loop which alter instruction addresses or data.

loop operation: A loop which has an associated set of instructions which restore modified instructions or data to their original or initial values at each entry to the loop, or a sequence of instructions which may be obeyed repetitively.

loop output signal: The extraction of the controlling signal from a feedback control.

loop termination: This may be accomplished in different ways. When reading data from cards, the cards can run out causing a hang-up or stop. More commonly, in reading data, the last card contains some particular code number which may be

tested and used to terminate the loop. Most often, the first card contains the number of data sets to be read, and this number is put into a counter location and tested for zero to end the loop.

loop test: Insulation test on a transmission line or cable made by connecting the conductors to form a closed loop.

loop transmission: A mode of multipoint operation in which a network is configured as a closed loop of individual point-to-point data links interconnected by stations that serve as regenerative repeaters. Data transmitted around the loop is regenerated and retransmitted at each station until it arrives at its destination station. Any station can introduce data into the loop.

loop update: The process of supplying current parameters associated with a particular loop for use by that loop's control algorithm in calculating a new control output.

loss: A decrease in signal power as measured between two points.

loss factor: The ratio of the average power loss to the power loss under peak loading. Of a dielectric, the product of dielectric constant and the tangent of its dielectric loss angle; a measure of the heating effect which occurs in dielectrics.

loss, hysteresis: See hysteresis.

loss insertion: An attenuation or loss instead of a gain.

lot: A collection of product units bearing identification and treated as a unique entity from which a sample is to be drawn and inspected to determine conformance with the quality criteria. Microcircuits sealed within a six week period are considered one lot.

low: Digital logic elements which operate with two distinct states. The two states are called variously true and false, high and low, on and off, or "1" and "0." In computers they are represented by two different voltage levels. The level that is more positive (or less negative) than the other is called the high level, the other the low level. If the true ("1") level is the most positive voltage, such logic is referred to as positive true or positive logic.

lower curtate: The bottom 18 rows on a punched card containing the bottom 9 rows of holes.

lower sideband: Band of frequencies of modulated signals below the carrier frequency.

low frequency: 1. Vague term used to indicate audio frequencies as distinct from radio frequencies. 2. Indicates radio frequencies between 30 and 300 KHz.

low-frequency amplifier: One for amplifying audio-frequency signals.

low-level language: One in which each instruction has a single corresponding machine code equivalent.

low-level modulation: Modulation produced at a point in a system where the power level is low compared with the power level at the output of the system.

low limiting control action: A specifically designed control action in which the output is never less than a predetermined low limit value.

low order: That which pertains to the weight or significance assigned to the digits farthest to the right within a number; e.g., in the number 123456, the low order digit is six.

low-order digit: A digit that holds the low weighted position in a numeral in a positional notation system.

low or high selector: A specific device designed to select automatically either the highest or the lowest input signal from among two or more input signals. Also referred to as low or high signal selector.

lowpass: A type of pass relating to the operation of a circuit or a device, as a filter which permits the passage of low frequency signals and attenuates high frequency signals.

lowpass filter: A filter that greatly attenuates signals of higher than a specific frequency, but passes with minimal attenuation all signals lower in frequency.

low-performance equipment: Equipment having insufficient characteristics to permit its use in trunk or link circuits. Such equipment may be employed in subscriber line circuits whenever it meets the line circuit requirments.

low speed: Usually, data transmission speed of 600 bits per second (bps) or less.

low-speed storage: A storage module or device with access time more lengthy in relation to the speeds of arithmetic operations of the central processing unit (CPU) of the computer and more lengthy when compared to other faster access peripheral units.

low tape: An indication that the supply of paper tape in a perforator is nearly depleted.

LP: See linear programming.

LPS: See lines per second control routine.

LRC: See longitudinal redundancy check.

LSD: See least significant digit.

LSI: See large-scale integration.

LT: Less than.

lumen: Unit of luminous flux, being the amount of light emitted per second in unit solid angle by small source of one candela output. In other words the lumen is the amount of light which falls on unit area per second, when the surface area is at unit distance from a source of one candela.

lumerg: A unit of luminous energy; e.g., one erg of radiant energy which has a luminous efficiency of 1 lumen per watt is equal to 1 lumerg of luminous energy.

luminance: Measure of brightness of a surface; e.g., candela/cm^2 of the surface radiating normally.

luminance signal: The signal controlling light values in the color cathode-ray tube receiver.

luminesence: That particular property of emitting light while exposed to excitation, i.e., the phosphors, such as aquadag, used as a coating on the interior surface of cathode-ray tube screens, emit light when excited by the electron beam, having persistence characteristics.

lumped: Relates to elements of electrical impedance concentrated in discrete units rather than being distributed over transmission lines or through space.

lumped loading: Inserting uniformly spaced inductance coils along the line, since continuous loading is impractical. See also loading.

M

machinable: The capability of being sensed or read by a specific device, i.e., one that has been designed to perform the reading and sensing function, e.g., tapes, cards, drums, discs, etc. are capable of being machine readable.

machine check handler (MCH): A feature that analyzes error and attempts recovery by retrying the failing instruction, if possible. If retry is unsuccessful, it attempts to correct the malfunction or to isolate the affected task.

machine check indicator: A protective device which will be turned on when certain conditions arise within the machine. The machine can be programmed to stop or to run a separate correction routine or to ignore the condition.

machine code: 1. A set of binary digits used by a business machine. 2. An operation code.

machine code instruction: 1. Composed of the absolute numbers, names, or symbols assigned by the machine designer to any part of the machine. 2. Those symbols that state a basic computer operation to be performed. 3. A combination of bits specifying an absolute machine-language operator, or the symbolic representation of the machine-language operator. 4. That part of an instruction that designates the operation of arithmetic, logic, or transfer to be performed.

machine code language: Same as machine code, and contrasted with symbolic code. op

machine cognition: Optical machine reading and pattern recognition. Certain machines have the capability to sense optically a displayed character and to select from a given repertoire of characters the specific character nearest in shape to the displayed character. The various shapes of characters are based on statistical norms, and if different shapes arise, new characters join the repertoire. This suggests a type of artificial learning, i.e., perception and interpretation are based on experience. Optical character recognition must be part of the scheme. Machine learning is based on artificial perception or machine cognition.

machine cycle: The specific time interval in which a computer can perform a given number of operations. 2. The shortest complete process of action that is repeated in order. 3. The minimum length of time in which the foregoing can be performed.

machine error: A deviation from correctness in data resulting from an equipment failure.

machine-independent: An adjective used to indicate that a procedure or a program is conceived, organized, or oriented without specific reference to the operating characteristics of any one data processing system. Use of this adjective usually implies that the procedure or program is oriented or organized in terms of the logical nature of the problem, rather than in terms of the characteristics of the machine used in solving it.

machine instruction: An instruction that a machine can recognize and execute.

machine instruction code: A particular group of circuits which cause other circuits to be completed with the occurrence of a particular pattern of electric pulses. These pulse patterns are the operation code of a machine instruction; the instructions are thus executed.

machine instruction part: Part of machine instructions; consists of codes indicating the operation to be performed. The balance may be addresses of the operands or may also contain the address of the next instruction, or information essential to the proper execution of the operation, e.g., a command to shift a datum within a machine register.

machine interruption: An interruption caused by an error being detected in the machine checking circuits.

machine language: 1. The binary data that can be executed or used by the processing unit. 2. The system of codes by which instructions and data are represented internally within a particular data processing system.

machine learning: The ability of a device to improve its performance based on its past performance.   Related   to   artificial intelligence.

machine logic: 1. Built-in methods of problem approach and function execution: (a) the way a system is designed to do its operations: (b) what those operations are; and (c) the type and form of data it can use internally. 2. The capability of an automatic dataprocessing machine to make decisions based upon the results of tests performed.

machine   operation: A   predetermined operation set which a computer is designed, built and operated to perform directly, e.g., a jump, etc.

machine operators: Personnel who load and unload, set up, and control the equipment in the data processing installation.

machine-oriented   language: 1. A language designed for interpretation and use by a machine without translation. 2. A system for expressing information which is intelligible to a specific machine, e.g., a

computer or class of computers. Such a language may include instructions which define and direct machine operations, and information to be recorded by or acted upon by these machine operations. 3. The set of instructions expressed in the number system basic to a computer, together with symbolic operation codes with absolute addresses, relative addresses, or symbolic addresses. Same as machine language, object language, and contrasted with problem-oriented language.

machine-oriented   programming   system: Uses a language oriented to the internal language of a specific computer. Systems considered to be machine-oriented are assembly systems and macro systems.

machine-processible media: The physical character of the mode of input or output such as punch cards, magnetic tape, disk packs, etc., in an optical scanning unit; such media are hard copy.

machine readable: Data in a form or medium that can be sensed (read) by a machine.

machine-readable   characters: Symbols (printed, typed or written) that can be interpreted by both people and optical character recognition equipment.

machine-readable   medium: A medium that can convey data to a given sensing device. Same as automated data medium.

machine reel: The reel which accepts tape in the rewrite heads; often called the take-up reel or file reel.

machine run: The execution of one or several machine routines which are linked to form one operating unit.

machine sensible: In machine language, or capable of being interpreted by a machine.

machine spoiled work-time: Time wasted during runs due to faults, i.e., faults which may not stop a run, but measurably hamper it, causing an overrun on its schedule.

machine translation: The automatic translation from one representation to another. The translation may involve codes, languages, or other systems of representation.

machine word: A unit of information of a standard number of characters which a machine regularly handles in each transfer, e.g., a machine may regularly handle numbers or instructions in units of 36 binary digits.

macro assembler: A two-pass assembler is available with subprogram, literal, and powerful macro facilities. It resembles the standard Meta-Symbol assembler. The output, which can be directly processed by the debugging program (DDT) provides symbol tables for effective program checkout in terms of the source language symbols (in some systems).

macro-assembly language program: A language processor that has characteristics of both an assembler and a compiler.

macro-assembly processor: A language processor that accepts words, statements, and phrases to produce machine instructions. It is more than an assembly program because it has compiler powers. The macro assembler permits segmentation of a large program so that portions may be tested separately. It also provides extensive program analysis to aid in debugging.

macro call: See macroinstruction.

macro code: A system of coding which assigns a name to a block of coding, after which every appearance of that name as an operator causes the assembler to insert a copy of that coding into the object program.

macro definition: The specification of a macro operation. This includes specifying the name of the macro operation and the prototype cards, which indicate which fields are to be fixed, and which are to be variable (substitutable arguments).

macroelement: A particular group or ordered set of data elements handled as a unit and provided with a single data use identifier.

macro expansion: 1. The sequence of statements that result from a macro generation operation. 2. Same as macro generation.

macro flowchart: A chart utilized in designing the logic of a specific routine in which the various segments and subroutines of a program are represented by blocks.

macro-generating program: Designed and developed to construct a group of instructions in the object language appropriate to a particular macroinstruction in the basic source language.

macro generation: An operation in which an assembler produces a sequence of assembler language statements by processing a macro definition called by a macroinstruction. Macro generation takes place at preassembly time.

macro generator: Particular types of generating programs designed and developed to construct the group of instructions in the object language appropriate to a particular macroinstruction in the basic source language.

macroinstruction: 1. Either a conventional computer instruction (e.g., ADD MEMORY TO REGISTER, INCREMENT, and SKIP, etc.) or device controller command (e.g., SEEK, READ, etc.). 2. A symbolic language statement for a macro-assembly programming system. A statement can correspond to several computer instructions.

macroinstruction exit: A supervising program macroinstruction that is the final instruction in an application program signifying that processing is complete. The supervising program takes the needed action such as releasing working storage blocks to return control to other processing.

macroinstruction link: An operating system instruction which causes the named program module to be located in an external library and loaded into an available position of storage. Control passes to the named module exactly as though a call macroinstruction had been used. If a copy of the named program module is present in storage, the process is bypassed, and an ordinary call is completed.

macroinstruction operand: In assembler programming, an operand that supplies a value to be assigned to the corresponding symbolic parameter of the macro definition called by the macroinstruction.

macroinstruction sorts: Separate programs furnished by manufacturers to sort data stored on random-access disks and drums. These programs strip off the item keys of data stored on a random-access device, sort the keys, and then store on the disk or drum a table containing the keys and the addresses of the corresponding file items. Items may be brought in from the disk or drum in the order of the sorted keys by using macroinstructions.

macroinstruction system: A predefined macroinstruction whose expansion provides some system service or linkage to a system service routine, e.g., get, put, call and save.

macro language: The representations and rules for writing macroinstructions and macro definitions.

macro library: A collection of macro definitions cataloged onto the resident disk pack by the librarian.

macro parameter: The symbolic or literal that is in the operand part of a macro statement and will be substituted into specific instructions in the incomplete routine to develop a complete open subroutine.

macro processing instruction: An assembler instruction that is used in macro definitions and processed at pre-assembly time.

macroprogramming: The process of writing machine procedure statements in terms of macroinstructions.

macro prototype: Same as macro prototype statement.

macro prototype statement: An assembler language statement that is used to give a name to a macro definition and to provide a model (prototype) for the macroinstruction that is to call the macro definition.

macro skeleton table: A macro assembly program internal table that contains the prototypes of all the macro definitions in a program.

macro-statement number: A number associated with a single macro statement so that reference may be made to that statement in terms of its number.

magamp: See magnetic amplifier.

"magic eye" tube: A vacuum tube used as a tuning indicator.

magic paper: An on-line system for manipulation of symbolic mathematics.

magnetic amplifier: A heavy duty current amplifier for driving large motors. The input to the magnetic amplifier is low level direct current to a control winding. The output is high level alternating current. Sometimes called a saturable reactor or saturable transformer.

magnetic card memory: A card, usually designed with a rectangular flat surface, of special materials coated with various types of magnetic substances on which data is recorded so that it can be read by an automatic device.

magnetic character reader: Reads magnetically inscribed data from card and paper documents into the computer. Pocket selection may be controlled by the program. Fixed field length and readability checks provide techniques for controlling accuracy. May be used for both on-line and off-line sorting. An adapter is required for attachment to the multiplexer channel or to a select channel.

magnetic character sorter: A machine that reads magnetic ink and sorts the documents with this ink on them.

magnetic coating: Refers to a magnetic layer of oxide particles that is applied to a base.

magnetic delay line: 1. A delay line using magnetic material; i.e., a drum channel used as a delay line, or combinations of cores and other components used as a delay line. 2. A delay line consisting of a magnetic medium and basing its operation on the time of propagation of magnetic waves.

magnetic disk: A random access storage device consisting of magnetically coated disks accessible to a reading and writing arm similar to an automatic record player. Data are stored on the surface of each disk as small, magnetized spots arranged in circular tracks around the disk. The arm is moved mechanically to the desired disk and then to the desired track on that disk.

magnetic disk file: A file of data held on a magnetic disk.

magnetic ferrite core memory: The physical construction of memory in which cores are placed in the same number of columns and rows on a flat surface.

magnetic field: State in a medium, produced either by current flowing in a conductor or by a permanent magnet, that can induce voltage in a second conductor in the medium when the state changes or when the second conductor moves in prescribed ways.

magnetic field interference: A special type or form of interference induced in the circuits of a device due to the presence of a magnetic field. It often appears as common mode or normal mode interference in the measuring circuits.

magnetic film storage: Magnetic material is coated on standard or special types of motion picture-type film as a base and the presence or absence of magnetic spots determines codes.

magnetic hysteresis loop: A closed curve designed to indicate the hysteresis in the relation between magnetizing force and the magnetic induction in a magnetic material.

magnetic induction: A specific vector associated with the mechanical force exerted on a current-carrying conductor which is located in a magnetic field.

magnetic ink: Ink containing particles of magnetic substance which can be detected or read by automatic devices, i.e., the ink used for printing on some bank checks for magnetic ink character recognition (MICR).

magnetic ink character recognition (MICR) code: A code that consists of a set of 10 numeric symbols and four special symbols standardized as Font E 13B developed for the American Banker's Association. The characters are readable visually through the use of magnetic sensing heads in verious types of magnetic ink recognition equipment. The special symbols mentioned above are: (a) amount, (b) dash, (c) transit number and (d) "on us."

magnetic ink character recognition (MICR) scan: The sensing of characters printed in magnetic ink as by codes developed and used by the American Banker's Association for bank checks with standardized characters, inks, etc. developed by the USA Standards Institute.

magnetic ink document reader: Reads specified fields of magnetized ink characters from documents and translates information read into a coded format, most often for direct insertion into an input area of a computer's core storage.

magnetic ink document sorter/reader: A machine capable of reading information from documents containing magnetized ink characters and sorting the documents into order according to the digits recorded in a particular field.

magnetic ink scanners: Machines which read numbers or characters printed in a magnetic (iron oxide) ink.

magnetic instability: The property of a magnetic material that causes variations in the residual flux density of a tape to occur with temperature, time, and/or mechanical flexing. Magnetic instability is a function of particle size, magnetization, and anisotropy and tends to increase layer-to-layer signal transfer and causes decreases in short-wavelength output with time and/or use.

magnetic path: The route followed by magnetic flux lines, i.e., a closed line which involves all media through which the lines of flux pass.

magnetic read-write head: A small electromagnet used for reading, recording, or erasing polarized spots on a magnetic surface.

magnetic shift register: A register which makes use of magnetic cores as binary storage elements, and in which the pattern of binary digital information can be shifted from one position to the next left or right position.

magnetic storage, static: A storage device in which binary data are represented by the direction of magnetization in each unit of an array of magnetic material, usually in the shape of toroidal rings, but also in other forms such as wraps on bobbins.

magnetic stripe recording: Magnetic material deposited in stripe form on a document or card.

magnetic strip file: A file storage device which uses strips of material with surfaces that can be magnetized for the purpose of storing data.

magnetic tape: A storage device consisting of metal or plastic tape coated with magnetic material. Binary data are stored as small, magnetized spots arranged in column form across the width of the tape. A read-write head is associated with each row of magnetized spots so that one column can be read or written at a time as the tape is moved relative to the head.

magnetic tape check: Hardware checks for faulty tapes without loss of computer time or manual intervention.

magnetic tape deck: A complete tape transport and its associated read-write heads; capable of either reading from or writing to a magnetic tape file.

magnetic tape drive: The mechanism that moves magnetic or paper tape past sensing and recording heads. This mechanism is associated with data processing equipment.

magnetic tape file: A reel of magnetic tape that contains records of information arranged in an ordered sequence.

magnetic tape file checks: Specific hardware checks for faulty tapes without loss of computer time or manual intervention.

magnetic tape file operation: Magnetic tape is provided for the storage of information to accomplish sequential file updating. It is also used as an interim means of storage in off-line conversion of input to magnetic tape, and when "working tapes" are utilized in operations such as sorting.

magnetic tape gap width: The dimension of the gap measured in the direction parallel to the head surface and pole faces. The gap width of the record head governs the track width. The gap widths of reproduced heads are sometimes made appreciably less than those of the record heads to minimize tracking errors.

magnetic tape group: A set of magnetic tape decks built into a single cabinet. Each deck is capable of independent operation and occasionally arranged to share one or more interface channels for communication with a central processor.

magnetic tape head: The portion of a magnetic tape deck that reads or writes information to the tape.

magnetic tape (input-output): The most common size of tape is ½ inch wide, available in lengths up to 2400 feet. on a 10½ inch-diameter reel and it is conventional to record each tape character as a 7-bit code across the tape, containing only 6 information bits, the seventh bit being the parity check.

magnetic tape label: One or more records at the beginning of a magnetic tape that identifies and describes the data recorded on the tape and contains other information, such as the serial number of the tape reel.

magnetic tape strip: Lists hundreds of individual records. As a specific record is needed, a computer signal similar to the combination of a safe causes the proper strip to drop from the deck. The strip then whips around the fast-moving drum that searches for the current record, reads, or writes on it, and transmits its data to the computer for further processing.

magnetic tape systems: These are semi-automatic systems that consist of a magnetic tape control and one magnetic tape transport. Data transfer is completely under program control and timing is controlled almost exclusively within the compatible system in some operations.

magnetic tape unit: The mechanism normally used with a computer which handles magnetic tape and consists of a tape transport, reading or sensing and writing or recording heads, and associated electrical and electronic equipment. Most units may provide for tape to be wound and stored on reels. However, some units provide for the tape to be stored loosely in closed bins.

magnetic tape wind: The way in which tape is wound on a reel (uniform or uneven, etc.).

magnetic thin film: A layer of magnetic material, usually less than one micron thick, often used for logic or storage elements.

magnetic thin-film storage: See thin-film memory.

magnetic wire: A wire made of or coated with a magnetic material and used for magnetic recording.

magnetizing field strength: As related to magnetic tape, the instantaneous strength of the magnetic field applied to a sample of magnetic material.

magnetizing force: See magnetizing field strength.

magnetoelectric: The property of certain materials (e.g., chromium oxide) of becoming magnetized when placed in an electric field. Conversely, they are electrically polarized when placed in a magnetic field. Such materials may be used for measuring pulse electric or magnetic fields.

magnetostriction: A phenomenon wherein certain materials increase in length in the direction of the magnetic field when subjected to such a field, and return to their original length when demagnetized.

magnetostrictive delay-line: One which utilizes the magnetostrictive property of materials. Magnetostriction is a property of materials causing them to change in length when they are magnetized.

magnetron: An ultra high frequency (uhf) diode oscillator containing its own cavity resonator in which electrons are whirled in a circular path by a magnetic field.

main distributing frame (MDF): A distributing frame, on one part of which terminates the permanent outside lines entering the central office building and on another part terminate the subscriber line multiple cable line, trunk multiple cabling, etc. It is used for associating any outside line with any desired terminal in a multiple or with any other outside line. It usually carries the central office protective devices and functions as a test point between line and office. In a private exchange the main distributing frame is for similar purposes.

main frame: The main part of the computer, i.e., the arithmetic or logic unit. The central processing unit.

mainline program: That module of code which constitutes a root module for a job or a separable job set; the mainline program usually exists as a load module or as a core-image program for production execution and in this form includes all required subprograms necessary for execution. Contrast with subprogram or subroutine.

main memory: The fastest storage device of a computer and the one from which instrucitons are executed. Contrasted with auxiliary storage.

main station: A telephone station with a distinct call number designation that directly connects to a central office. Also, in leased lines for customer equipment, the main point where such equipment interfaces the local loop. See also extension station.

main storage: Program addressable storage from which instructions and data can be loaded directly into registers from which the instructions can be executed or the data can be operated upon. Usually an internal storage.

main storage dump: 1. To copy the contents of all or part of main storage onto an output device, so that it can be examined. 2. The data resulting from 1. 3. A routine that will accomplish 1.

maintainability: The ease and effectiveness with which a system can be kept in good operating condition.

maintenance: 1. The periodic checking, testing, and repairing of hardware circuitry. Maintenance that is performed before an actual problem occurs is called preventive maintenance. 2. The continuing process of correcting program bugs, making minor code modifications, and generally updating a program to accomodate changing needs and applications.

maintenance control: A panel of indicator lights and switches that display a particular sequence of routines, from which repairmen can determine changes to execute.

maintenance, emergency: When a known fault or malfunction is repaired or corrected using adjustments or replacements after measurements and tests to locate, diagnose, and remove the fault. The service is called corrective maintenance. Same as unscheduled maintenance or remedial maintenance.

maintenance programmer: An individual who codes and tests revisions to the production programs needed to maintain operations. He must also be able to debug these programs.

maintenance program procedures: Diagnostic checking and test routines designed by manufacturers or software companies for purposes of removing machine malfunctions, human errors, or programmer mistakes. Other procedures help to maintain programs and routines in proper working order and in a steady status with current information.

maintenance time: Time used for hardware maintenance including preventive maintenance time and corrective maintenance time. Contrast with available machine time.

major control change: A control change characterized as being of greater importance or a control change which is relatively of greater magnitude.

major control cycles: A series of control cycles on a punched card tabulator initiated automatically during the processing of a file of punched cards as a result of detection of a change of major control data.

major control data: The items of data, one or more of which are used to select, execute, identify, or modify another routine, record, file, operation or data value.

major control field: The most significant control field in a record; the control field upon which sorting according to the collating sequence is first attempted.

major cycle: The maximum access time of a recirculating serial storage element, the time for one rotation, e.g., of a magnetic drum or of pulses in an acoustic delay line. A series of minor cycles.

majority carrier: In a semiconductor, the type of carrier which predominates, either electrons (in N-type material) or holes (in P-type material).

majority decision gate: A binary input unit which has the capability of implementing the majority logic operator.

majority element: A threshold element or a decision element, e.g., if the weights are equal to 1 and the threshold is equal to $(n + 1)/2$, the element is called a majority element.

majority gate: A hardware item designed to implement the majority logic operator.

majority logic operator: A logic operator having the property that if P is a statement, Q is a statement, R is a statement,..., then the majority of P, Q, R,..., is true if more than half of the statements are true, false if half or less are true.

major state: The control state of a computer. Major control states in some systems include fetch, defer, execute, etc.

major state generator: One or more major control states are entered to determine and execute an instruction. During any one instruction, a state lasts for one computer cycle. The major state generator determines the machine state during each cycle as a function of the current instruction, the current state, and the condition of

the break request signal supplied to an input bus by peripheral equipment.

major state logic generator: The logic circuits in the central processor that establish the major state for each computer cycle.

major time slice: In time-sharing option (TSO), the period of time during which a terminal job is in main storage. See also minor time slice.

major total: The result when a summation is terminated by the most significant change of group.

make connection: Manual connection in switching equipment or networks.

makeup time: That measured fraction of available time consumed in reruns developed by malfunctions or mistakes as they occur during the previous operating time.

malfunction: Equipment failure.

management information system (MIS): 1. (ISO) Management performed with the aid of automatic data processing. 2. An information system designed to aid in the performance of management functions.

management reports: 1. Reports prepared on a recurring basis and distributed at specific intervals, passing from one level of company management to another and/or one organization to another. They contain statistical and/or operating information reflecting utilization of resources, status of operations or provide other administrative information useful in judging progress, forming decisions, or directing operations. 2. The management function which assures that administrative reports are kept to a minimum and that those required are well presented, accurate, and timely.

management services: Pertains to that specific category of consulting or other assistance made available from accounting or management consulting firms related to data processing service, systems, or specific problems.

man-auto: A type of locking switch that indicates and controls methods of operation, e.g., automatic or manual.

manipulated direct controlled variable: That specific quantity or condition which is varied as a function of the actuating signal so as to change the value of the directly controlled variable. Most practical control systems have several manipulated variables. In process control activity, the one immediately preceding the directly controlled system is intended.

manipulated variable: In a process that is desired to regulate some condition, a quantity or a condition that is altered by the computer in order to initiate a change in the value of the regulated condition.

manipulative indexing: An indexing technique where the interrelations of terms are shown by coupling individual words. An indexing scheme by which descriptors may be correlated or combined to show any interrelationships desired for purposes of more precise information retrieval.

man/machine dialog: A specialized form of interactive processing between man and machine in which the human operator carries on a dialog with the computer through a console or some other input/-output device.

man/machine digital system: An organization of people, digital computers and equipment to regulate and control events and achieve system objectives.

man/machine simulation: Includes models of systems in which human beings participate (operational or behavioral models). However, the possibility also exists of incorporating people within the model. In other words, the model is no longer completely computer based but requires the active participation of a human.

man/machine package (MMP): A sophisticated human/computer interface providing data base management for moves, additions and changes to an integrated voice and data switching system. Designed for easy training and use, MMP is accessed through an ASCII cathode-ray tube (CRT) terminal and uses simple English language commands.

manual backup: An often used alternate method of information handling or process control by which manual activities or adjustments of final control elements take place in the event of a failure in the computer system.

manual control: The direction of a computer by means of manually operated switches.

manual data access arrangement: The name associated with the A.T. & T. switched network protective device, which provides for the connection of modems other than those supplied by A.T. & T.

manual data entry module: In some systems, a module or device designed to monitor a number of manual inputs from one or more operator consoles and/or remote data entry devices and transmit information from them to the computer.

manual exchange: An exchange where calls are completed by an operator.

manual input generator: A device that accepts manually input data and holds the contents which can be sensed by a computer, controller, and other devices, i.e., used to insert a word manually into commputer storage for hold until it is read during the execution of a program.

manual operation: Processing of data in a system by direct manual techniques.

manual part programming: The preparation of a manuscript in the machine control language and format required to accomplish a given task. The necessary calculations are performed manually.

manual product reference record: One page of the master product file.

manual storage switch: Sets of switches used for manual entry of data into the computer.

manual switch: The hand operated device designed to cause alternate actions contrasted with electronic switch.

manual word unit: A device that an operator can use to set up a word of information for direct entry into memory.

manufacturers' customer engineer: An individual who installs the equipment and, once it is installed, keeps it running. Other duties involve performance of periodic routine preventive maintenance and tracking down problems.

map: 1. To transform information from one form to another. 2. A listing provided by a compiler to enable a programmer to relate his data names to the core addresses within the program.

MAP: See model and program.

mapped buffer: A display buffer in which each character position has a corresponding character position on the display surface.

mapping: 1. A transformation from one set to another set. 2. A correspondence.

margin: That fraction of a perfect signal element through which the time of selection may be varied in one direction from the normal time of selection, without causing errors while signals are being received. There are two distinct margins, determined by varying the time of selection in either direction from normal.

marginal: The derivatives or rate of change of a function with respect to quantity. Incremental and variable are often used in a synonymous sense. Thus the composite terms (a) marginal cost (of production), (b) marginal revenue (from sales), (c) marginal value (of a capacity, of sales, of supplies, etc.). The coefficients of a linear programming model are themselves all marginal figures, for example, the cost coefficient of an activity is the marginal cost of performing the activity; the coefficient in a material-balance row is the marginal consumption or production of the material.

marginal check: See high-low bias check.

marginal check components: A special preventive maintenance design or procedure in which various certain operation conditions are varied about their normal value in order to aggravate borderline components into detectable faults.

marginal errors: Occur irregularly in tapes, and most often disappear simply because the writing is done over a slightly different section of tape.

marginal tests (voltage and registers): Built into some computers is a network for marginal test of computer subsections. Two features of the marginal test system make routine checks fast and accurate: the marginal check voltage is variable continuously, and all working registers are displayed simultaneously on the console lights.

marginal voltage check: A means of testing the control unit by reducing the power supply voltage on the logic modules. The theory is that if there is a marginal module, it will fail at the reduced voltage.

margin control: See range finder.

mark: 1. A sign or symbol used to signify or indicate an event in time or space, e.g., end of word or message mark, a file mark, a drum mark, an end of tape mark. 2. One of the two possible conditions of an information element (bit); a closed line in a circuit.

mark detection: A type of character recognition system that detects from marks placed in areas on paper or cards—called site areas, boxes, or windows—certain intelligence or information. Mark reading results from optical character recognition or mark-sensing systems which seek out the presence or absence of pencil marks or graphite particles, such as on college or school exams, census returns, etc.

marker: A symbol used to indicate the beginning or the end of some set of data, e.g., the end of a record, block, field, file, etc.

mark field: A symbol used to indicate the beginning or the end of some set of data, e.g., group, file, record, block...in this case a particular field.

mark-hold: The normal no-traffic line condition whereby a steady mark is transmitted. This may be a customer-selectable option.

mark impulse: Presence of signal. In telegraph communications a mark represents the closed condition or current flowing. A mark impulse is equivalent to a binary 1. See also neutral circuit.

marking: The "idle" condition on a telegraph circuit where the circuit is closed but no transmission is taking place. This condition also exists when transmission is taking place and a bit of intelligence corresponding to a "yes" is being sent. Marking is the normal information condition.

marking typewriter pulse: The signal pulse which, in dc neutral operation, corresponds to a "circuit closed" or "current on" condition.

marking wave: Same as keying wave.

Markov chain: A model often used for determining the sequence of events in which the probability of a given event is dependent only on the preceding event.

mark reader: A device capable of reading pencil marks on documents up to a size of 13 inches X 8 inches. The marks can be positioned anywhere on the document. The reader's sensing cells are switched on by special block dial clock track marks.

mark scanning: Optical sensing of data in the form of marks.

mark-sense: To mark a position on a punched card with an electrically conductive pencil, for later conversion to machine punching.

mark sense cards: Punched cards divided into card columns to facilitate mark sensing. The columns are usually the width of two or three normal punching columns.

mark sensing: 1. The electrical sensing of manually recorded conductive marks on a nonconductive surface. 2. The automatic sensing of manually recorded marks on a data medium.

mark-space multiplier unit: An electronic analog multiplier unit in which one input voltage is used to control the amplitude of a square wave and the other input voltage controls the mark-to-space ratio of this square wave.

mark-to-space ratio: The ratio of the duration of the positive and negative cycles of a square wave. A space is negative cycle, a mark a positive cycle.

mark-to-space transition: The transition, or switching, from a marking impulse to a spacing impulse.

"M" ARY: More than two states or conditions as com- pared with binary, meaning two states.

mask: A machine word that specifies which parts of another machine word are to be operated on.

mask bit: A special pattern of bits used to extract selected bits from a string.

masking: A technique for sensing specific binary conditions and ignoring others. Typically accomplished by placing zeros in bit positions of no interest, and ones in bit positions to be sensed.

mask matching: A method employed in optical character recognition to correlate or match a specimen character and each of a set of masks representing the characters to be recognized, i.e., the characters are deliberately registered on the reference masks and no allowance is made for character misregistration. Such types are: (a) Holistic masks (exact), (b) Peep-hole masks (more lenient but still exacting), and (c) Weighted area masks, (probability assignments).

mass data: A relative amount of data, usually larger than can be stored in the central processing unit of a computer at any one time.

mass memory: Disk, drum, or tape memory. See also bulk memory.

mass storage: An auxiliary storage of very large storage capacity used for storage of data to which infrequent reference need be made.

mass storage device: Storage units with large capacity such as magnetic disk, drum, data cells, etc.

mass storage file: A type of secondary, and usually slower, storage designed to supply the computer with the required information and data for immediate up-todate reports on a given program segment.

mass storage (on-line): The storage of a large amount of data readily accessible to the central processing unit of a computer.

master: A file of data considered permanent or semipermanent; i.e., an arrangement or ordering of a series of records; also, a single record from such a file.

master-active file: A master file containing items which are relatively active.

master clock: The primary source of timing signals used to control the timing of pulses.

master console: In a system with multiple consoles, the basic console used for communication between the operator and the system.

master control interrupt: A signal generated by an input/output device, or by an operator's error, or by request of the processor for more data or program segments, which permits the master control program to control the computer system.

master control program (MCP): 1. Controls all phases of a job set-up—directs program compiling and debugging, allocates memory, assigns input/output activity, schedules and interweaves multiple programs for simultaneous processing. 2. Directs all equipment functions and the flow of all data; provides for comprehensive automatic error detection and correction. 3. Directs the operator with printed instructions. 4. Adjusts system operation to changes in system environment. Thus, the program-independent modularity of the computer, combined with the automatic schedule and control features of the master control system, provides true multiprocessing ability of the system. A good example of this is shown by the ability of a system to perform four read/write operations simultaneously with the program executions on two processors.

master control routine: Part of a program consisting of a series of subroutines. It controls the linking of the other subroutines and may call the various segments of the program into memory as required. It is also used to describe a program which controls the operation of a hardware system.

master data: 1. A set of data which is altered infrequently and supplies basic data for processing operations. 2. The data content of a master file. Examples include names, badge numbers, or pay rates in personnel data, or stock numbers, stock descriptions, or units of measure in stock control data.

master file: (ISO) A file used as an authority in a given job and relatively permanent, even though its contents may change.

master file utility routines: Contained as an integral part of the system. These are programs that are useful for data conversion, editing, etc. A description of the individual utility routines provided with the system is given in the individual write-ups of the utility routines. Utility routines are loaded and executed from the master file by an executive control statement. Frequently used object programs may be added to the system as utility routines. These programs may then be called through from the executive master file.

master instruction tape: A tape on which all the programs for a system of runs are recorded.

master library tape: A tape on which all the programs for a system of runs are recorded.

master oscillator: The carrier-generating stage of the transmitter.

master payroll file: A file that contains payroll information about each employee.

master program: Controls all phases of the job set-up: (a) directs program compiling and debugging, (b) allocates memory, (c) assigns input/output activity schedules, (d) interleaves multiple programs for simultaneous processing, (e) directs all equipment functions and the flow of all data, (f) provides for error detection and correction, and (g) communicates with the operators.

master program tape: A tape, most often magnetic, which contains the main program or master data file with most or all of the routines and programs for various main runs. A fundamental part of the operating system.

master program update file: Programs from the old master file are deleted, corrected or left unchanged and new programs are added from the transaction tape. Updating can include changing program job assignments. A new program master file is produced.

master record: A record in a master file; contains semipermanent data.

master routine: 1. A routine that controls loading and relocation of routines and in some cases makes use of instructions which are unknown to the general programmer. Effectively, a master routine is part of the machine itself. 2. A set of coded instructions designed to process and control other sets of coded instructions. 3. A set of coded instructions used in realizing automatic coding. 4. A master set of coded instructions.

master scheduler: Permits the function of a control program that allows an operator to initiate special actions or to cause requested information to be delivered which can override the normal control functions of the system.

master/slave multiprogramming mode: A specific feature designed to guarantee that one program cannot damage or access another program sharing memory. The unique operating technique in changing from slave to master mode makes multiprogramming practical and foolproof.

master/slave system: A special system or computer configuration for business or scientific use (as production automation) in which one computer, usually of substantial size or capability, rules with complete control over all input/output and schedules and transmits tasks to a slave computer. The latter computer often has a great capacity, and it performs the computations as directed and controlled by the master unit.

master station: 1. A unit having control of all other terminals on a multipoint circuit for purposes of polling and/or selection. 2. Pertains to a switching network and to a station which sends data to a slave station, but under its control.

master synchronizer: A primary source of

timing signals. Often a ring counter synchronized by a crystalcontrolled oscillator.

master time: 1. The primary source of timing signals used to control the timing of pulses. 2. The electronic or electric source of standard timing signals, often called "clock pulses," required for sequencing computer operation. This source usually consists of a timingpulse generator, a cycling unit, and sets of special pulses that occur at given intervals of time. In synchronous computers the basic time frequency employed is usually the frequency of the clock pulses.

master unit: That specific unit that executes jobs simultaneously and has the capability of regrouping several units together to control independently a complete automatic data processing system or job.

match: A data processing operation similar to a merge, except that instead of producing a sequence of items made up from the input, sequences are matched against each other on the basis of some key.

matched filter: A method employed in character property detection in which a vertical projection of the input character produces an analog waveform which is then compared to a set of stored waveforms for the purpose of determining the character's identity.

matching: Used to verify coding. Individual codes are machine-compared against a group of master codes to select any that are invalid.

matching transformer: Inserted into a communication circuit to avoid reflection losses because the load impedance differs from the source impedance. In designing for optimum matching, the ratio of the impedances equals the square of the ratio of the turns on the windings.

match-merge: The comparison of two files, usually based on key words designed to place them in the prearranged sequential order of those records which match the arbitrarily selected key words.

material dispersion: The spreading of a light pulse inside an optic fiber due to the different wavelengths of light emitted by a source. Because different wavelengths travel at different speeds within a fiber, material dispersion occurs. Because of this property, when determining the maximum bandwidth performance of a fiber, a narrow bandwidth source, such as a laser diode, must be used. Most laser diodes emit over 2 to 4 nm wavelength intervals. Light-emitting diodes (LEDs), however, have an emission bandwidth of 10 to 20 times this. Both modal and material dispersion pose limitations on optic fiber bandwidth, their effects varying with the type of fiber. Step-index fibers are limited primarily by modal dispersion and perform almost equally for laser diodes and LEDs. Graded-index fibers are constructed to reduce the amount of modal dispersion, but are sensitive to material dispersion, and thus require a laser diode source to fully use their bandwidth potential.

mathematical analysis: Includes arithmetic and algebra; deals with numbers, the relationships between numbers, and the operations performed on these relationships.

mathematical check: A check which uses mathematical identities or other properties, occasionally with some degree of discrepancy being acceptable, e.g., checking multiplication by verifying that $A \cdot B = B \cdot A$. Same as arithmetic check.

mathematical control mode: A specific type of control action such as proportional, integral, or derivative.

mathematical expectation: The product of the amount we stand to receive and the probability of obtaining it. e.g., if the probability of winning an amount A is $P(A)$, our mathematical expectation is $A \cdot P(A)$.

mathematical model: The general characterization of a process, object or concept which enables the relatively simple manipulation of variables to be accomplished in order to determine how the process, object, or concept would behave in different situations.

mathematical programming: A mathematical theory for optimizing a set of variables controlling a process for a given set of parameters.

mathematical span: The algebraic difference between upper and lower range values.

matrix controller: A device that will generate a list of recommended connections for each line and line group so that front-end ports, modems, multiplexers, and complete front ends can be "spared-out" even during emergency conditions. These devices maintain a file of open trouble reports so that service and maintenance tickets are not lost. Signal calling becomes relatively simple. Various datacom matrices and control processors help to keep networks up and maintenance costs down.

matrix table: A specific set of quantities in a rectangular array according to exacting mathematical rules and designs.

maximal: Highest or greatest.

maximum flux: Referring to magnetic tape, in a uniformly magnetized sample of magnetic material, the product of the maximum intrinsic flux density and the cross-sectional area.

maximum induction: The greatest value, positive or negative, of the intrinsic flux density in a sample of magnetic material which is in a symmetrically, cyclically magnetized condition. Usually the maximum intrinsic flux density of a tape is measured in the orientation direction, using an alternating magnetizing field of amplitude oe.

maximum operating frequency: The maximum repetition or clock rate at which the modules will perform reliably in continuous operation, under worst-case conditions, without special trigger pulse (clock) requirements.

maximum printer lines: The maximum number of lines which can be printed by the computer in the time stated. Unless otherwise noted each line is considered to be 120 columns wide.

maximum transfer rate: The maximum number of binary digits per second which can be accommodated on the channel. For a duplex channel (input/output) the transfer rate is shown for one direction only.

maxterm: A Boolean sum of n variables, each variable being present in either its true or complemented form.

Mayday: Verbal international radio-telephone distress call or signal, corresponding to SOS in telegraphy.

Mbit: See megabit.

Mc: See megacycle.

MCH: See machine check handler.

MCP: See master control program.

MDF: See main distributing frame.

mean: The mean of two quantities is the quantity lying between them and with them by some mathematical law. There are several types of means, the main ones being the arithmetical mean and the geometrical mean. The arithmetic mean, or average, of several quantities of the same type, is their sum divided by their numbers. For example, the arithmetical mean of 10, 12, 17, and 25 is 64/4 or 16. The arithmetical mean is understood when the word mean is used alone. The geometrical mean of two quantities is the square root of their product; the geometrical mean of 2 and 8 is $\sqrt{16} = 4$. The greater of the given quantities is as many times greater than the mean, as the mean is greater than the least quantity. Such is the idea of the geometrical mean. In a geometrical progression, each term is a geometrical mean between the preceding and succeeding terms; in an arithmetical progression each term is an arithmetical mean between the preceding and succeeding terms.

mean repair time: The average repair time over a given period. Used as a measure of assessing equipment reliability.

mean time between failure: The special limit of the ratio of the operating time of equipment to the number of observed failures as the number of failures approaches infinity.

mean time to failure: The average time the system or a component of the system works without faulting.

measurand: A specific physical quantity, condition, or property to be measured, often referred to as a measured variable. Common measured variables are: (a) pressure, (b) rate of flow, (c) thickness, (d) temperature, and (e) speed.

measure: In set theory, that particular property of a set which denotes how many objects are contained in that set.

measured signal: A designed electrical, pneumatic, mechanical, or other variable applied to the input of a device. It is the analog of the measured variable produced by a transducer, if such is used.

measured variable: A physical quantity, condition, or property which is to be measured, often referred to as the measurand.

measurement error: The total anticipated error due to (a) sampling inadequacy or variability; (b) sample preparation variability; (c) instability or lack of precision in read-out or transducer systems.

measurement reproducibility: The degree of closeness among repeated measurements of output for an input value employing the same operating conditions.

mechanical dictionary: The language-translating machine component which will provide a word-for-word substitution from one language to another. In automatic-searching systems, the automatic dictionary is the component which substitutes codes for words or phrases during the encoding operation. Related to machine translation.

mechanical differential: A mechanical device in analog computers which provides an output mechanical rotation equal to the sum or difference of two input rotations.

mechanical interface: Mechanical mounting and interconnections between system elements.

mechanical shock: A test that determines the capability of parts to withstand rough handling encountered in shipment or in field operation. The test consists of suddenly applied forces or abrupt changes in motion. It is considered to be one of the least important tests because of the low mass of individual microcircuits.

mechanical translation: Language translation by computer or similar equipment.

media: 1. Printed matter. 2. Plural form of medium.

media codes: Code sets assigned to media.

media conversion: Some program libraries have a complete set of routines to perform media conversions of all kinds. Media conversion is efficiently done in the multiprogramming mode rather than with off-line equipment or smaller computers.

median: The value of the middle item when the items are arranged according to size. If there is an even number of items, the midpoint is taken as the arithmetic mean of the two central items. The median is an average of position while the arithmetic mean is a calculated average. The median is computed as follows (a) Arrange the items according to magnitude (this is called an array), (b) Record the size of the middle value. If there is an even number of items in the array there will be two central values; thus, the arithmetic mean of these two values is taken as the median.

medical index: A comprehensive index of articles published in medical journals used to produce several publications in conjunction with automated search programs (MEDLARS, AIM-TWX, MEDLINE).

medium: The physical substance upon which data are recorded, e.g., magnetic tape, punch cards and paper.

medium distance modem: Provides low cost, 9600 bits per second (bps) point-to-point synchronous data transmission at distances ranging from 25 to 200 miles depending on the carrier facility used. This autoequalized, microprocessor-controlled modem is based on innovative digital signal-processing technology. Diagnostic loopbacks, test pattern generator, and error detector are provided for testing.

medium frequency (mf): Frequencies between 300 and 3000 kilohertz. See frequency spectrum.

medium-scale integration (MSI): The accumulation of several circuits (usually less than 100) on a single chip of semiconductor.

medium speed: Data transmission speed between 600 bits per second (bps) and the limit of a voice-grade facility.

medium-term scheduling: A specific portion of a scheduling algorithm that initiates and terminates processes in accordance with the policy of computer management towards users. This level of programming (a) establishes the identity and authority of users, (b) inputs and analyzes their requests, (c) initiates and terminates jobs, (d) performs accounting of resource usage, and (e) maintains system integrity in spite of harware malfunction.

medium, virgin: A storage medium in which no data is recorded, e.g., paper completely unmarked, or paper tape which has no hole punched in it.

MEDLARS: A computer-based system of the National Library of Medicine (NLM) designed for sophisticated searching of medical literature references. The service is available from most medical school libraries.

meet: The Boolean operator that gives a truth table value of true only when both of the variables connected by the logical operator are true.

meet operation: A logical operation applied to two operands that will produce an outcome depending on the bit patterns of the operands and according to rules for each bit position. For example, p = 110110, q = 011110, then r = 010010.

mega: 1,000,000 or 1024K for memory devices.

megabit (Mbit): One million binary bits.

megacycle (Mc): A million cycles per second, 10^6 cycles per second.

member: 1. An entity within a directoried data set, indexed in the data set's directory and having data content. 2. An element of a program activated indpendently of the rest of the program in a multiprogramming environment. See subprogram.

memory: The capacity of a machine to store information subject to recall, or the component of the computer system in which such information is stored. See storage.

memory address register: 1. Contains the address of the selected word in memory. 2. The location in main memory selected for data storage or retrieval. Some registers can directly address all 4096 words of the standard main memory or of any preselected field extended main memory.

memory, backing: Units whose capacity is larger than working (scratchpad or internal) storage but of longer access time, and in which transfer capability is usually in blocks between storage units. See auxiliary storage.

memory cell: Basic storage unit in a semiconductor or magnetic data store.

memory core: A programmable random access memory consisting of many ferromagnetic toroids strung on wires in matrix arrays. Each toroid acts as an electromagnet to store a binary digit.

memory cycle: 1. The process of reading and restoring information in magnetic core memory. 2. The time required to complete this process.

memory cycle time: The minimum time between two successive data accesses from a memory.

memory dump: To write all or part of the contents of a storage, usually from an internal storage, onto an external medium, e.g., to be displayed on an output device.

memory dump (monitor control):   A memory dump may be specified in the control information for a job. Upon termination of the job, the dump routine is loaded from the system unit and executed. The dump routine overlays the monitor and produces a complete dump of the object program. Upon completion of the dump, the monitor is reloaded to process the next job.

memory, erasable: A store used repeatedly; when new information is written in, the earlier information is erased before the new is stored.

memory exchange: An electronic switching device that allows connection between any memory module and input/output channel or processor.

memory fill: Storage in areas of memory not used by a particular routine of some pattern of characters which will stop the machine if the routine tries to execute instructions from areas not intended to contain coding. An aid to debugging.

memory guard: Electronic or program guard inhibiting or preventing access to specific sections of storage devices or areas concerning the main or internal memory of the central processor.

memory hierarchies: Created because there is a speed mismatch between core memory and semiconductor logic and between core and other random access storage media (drums or disks). Program and data parts can be scattered in both main memories and in disks or drums for swapping between main and auxiliary storage automatically on demand. Normally copies of all pages in main memory are retained on an auxiliary drum or disk and when changes are made in page contents while in main memory, copies are written back onto the drum or disk when no longer needed. Access to semiconductor memories is in nanoseconds.

memory latency time: The time required for the memory's control hardware to move physically the memory media containing the desired data to a position where it can be read electrically. Alternately the reading device may be moved to the desired data. Latency is associated with serial memories and certain random access memories.

memory light: A light which indicates there is a number in the memory.

memory lock write: A write protection field in the memory of some computers.

memory map list: A listing of all variable names, array names, and constants used by the program, with their relative address assignments. The memory map is provided at compile time on an optional basis. The listing will include all subroutines called and last location when called.

memory parity interrupt: Each time control is given to the monitor the memory parity trap is armed and the interrupt location is patched with an instruciton. When a memory parity occurs, the computer halts at the location at which the parity occurred, with the console memory parity indicaor light turning on.

memory + and – keys: These keys provide direct access to the memory for storing numbers.

memory protect: A hardware function which provides positive protection to the system executive routine and all other programs against being destroyed by storing data into the program area. It protects not only against processor execution, but also against input/output data area destruction. Because it is a hardware function rather than software, it reduces multiprogramming complexities.

memory protect violation program: A special program which is generated when a detection is made that a memory alteration or modification is being attempted on the contents of sections of memory which are protected by the presence of a guard bit.

memory register: 1. A register involved in all transfers of data and instructions in either direction between memory and the arithmetic and control registers. It may be addressed in some machines. Also called distributor, exchange register, high speed bus, arithmetic register, auxiliary register. 2. A register in which the contents can be added to or subtracted from. The contents are available until the register is cleared.

memory-switched traffic: A routing function necessary to extract the destination logic identifier, determine the destination link and station tables, complete the control block for output with the appropriate routing data and queue the control block for output. Similar functions are necessary for disk-switched traffic.

memory unit: 1. Storage from which the data to be operated on are normally obtained. It may be under the control of the computer, but the data must be transferred to secondary or internal storage before operations commence, and are returned to external storage only after operations are completed. External storage devices usually have larger capacities and lower access speeds than internal and secondary storage. 2. A storage device outside the computer that can store information in a form acceptable to the computer.

menu: A technique to display a list of alternatives to an operator and request a choice of one of them.

mercury delay line: A sonic or acoustic delay line in which mercury is used as the medium of sound transmission, with transducers on each end to permit conversion to and from electrical energy. Related to acoustic delay line.

mercury memory: Delay lines which use mercury as the medium for storage of a circulating train of waves or pulses. Also called mercury storage.

mercury storage: A storage device that utilizes the acoustic properties of mercury to store data (related to mercury delay line.)

mercury tank: A component of a mercury acoustic delay line, i.e., pairs of transducers, such as quartz crystals, are placed at each end of a container of mercury, and are used to launch the acoustic waves representing the data.

mercury-wetted relay: Device using mercury as the relay contact closure substance.

merge: To produce a single sequence of items in a specifc order from two or more sequences without changing the items in size, structure, or total number. Merging is a special case of collation.

merge-match: The comparison and possible merging of two files. This comparison is usually based on key words designed to place records in a prearranged sequential order which matches arbitrarily selected key words. Further, the resulting segregation of those records which do not match are mated to combine or join two different units of equipment.

merge order: The number of files or sequences to be combined during a merge operation. Abbreviated m.

merge pass: In sorting, the processing of records to reduce the number of sequences by a factor equal to the specified merge order.

merge/sort: A three-phase program which utilizes the cascade method of merge sorting. Unsorted data are read from magnetic tape, sorted according to programmer-specified parameters, and ultimately written on magnetic tape.

merging (sorting): See merge.

message: A communication of information or advice from a source to one or more destinations in suitable language or code. In telegraphic and data communications, a message is composed of three parts: (a) a heading containing a suitable indicator of the beginning of the specific message together with information on the source and destination, date and time of filing, and routing or other transmission information; (b) a body containing the information to be communicated; (c) an ending containing a suitable indicator of the conclusion of the specific message, either explicit or implicit.

message blocking: The concatenation of several messages into a single transmission or physical record, in order to reduce transmission overhead. Messages exchanged between such devices as line printers and card readers are blocked together and transmitted as a single unit in order to cut down on the frequent delays due to changing the transmission direction of the communications. Messages and application programs may be blocked and unblocked at various points in the system.

message buffer: A common data structure designed to be used to exchange data between concurrent processes.

message circuit: A long-distance telephone circuit used to furnish regular long-distance or toll service to the general public.

The term is used to differentiate these circuits from circuits used for private line services.

message (communications): A transmitted series of words or symbols intended to convey information.

message control program: A program used to control the sending or receiving of messages to or from remote terminals.

message data: Transmitted characters that are recorded as part of a message. A message data area is the area in a buffer that receives message data.

message display console: Contains a symbol generator and a cathode-ray tube (CRT). Displayed symbols are presented in a typewriter format on a 21-inch CRT in the order received. A flicker-free message is displayed under full daylight ambient light conditions. The 64symbol repertoire is placed in a format of 18 lines of 80 symbols each. Control logic and memory are contained within a modular data processing system, which provides the overall automatic supervision of the message processing system.

message drain: A means for accepting an overflow of accumulated messages in a store and forward message switching system.

message exchange: A device placed between a communication line and a computer in order to take care of certain communication functions and thereby free the computer for other work.

message format: The specific rules for writing a message. The mesage heading, address test, and end of message must be written and placed in a specific order or format.

message handler: Under telecommunications access method (TCAM), a sequence of user-specified macroinstructions that examine and process control information in message headers, and perform functions necessary to prepare message segments for forwarding to their destinations. One message handler is required for each line group having unique message handling requirements.

message intercept processing: Done for messages that have been queued for transmission but cannot be delivered properly to either the primary or alternate destination. This is required whenever a connection cannot be made, when a line becomes inactive, and if either the terminal does not respond to its selection codes or the message is not acknowledged positively. As a general rule the intercepted messages are returned to an input queue of the appropriate user task, to the message switch which selects alternate terminals, or for re-submission at a late time.

message network: Used to refer to the dialed teletypewriter netwrk as opposed to the dialed telephone system. Same as exchange network.

message numbering: The identification of each message within a communications system by the assignment of a sequential number.

message processing program: A program that processes or otherwise responds to messages received from terminals, priority, and the type of message. See also message text.

message protection: Assures message delivery by maintaining the message log, checking for missing serial numbers, and analyzing the message addresses for accuracy and validity.

message queue: A line of messages that are awaiting processing or waiting to be sent to a terminal.

message reference block: The storage areas and working storage set aside by the system when more than one message is being processed in parallel by the system. This mesage reference block is associated with that message so long as it registers in the computer for processing.

message retrieval: The capability to retrieve a message after it has entered an information system.

message routing: The function of selecting the route, or alternate route if required, by which a message will proceed to its destination.

messages, input/output information: Messages listed on the operator message device (probably on console typewriter).

message source: The location in a communication system from which the message originates.

message switching applications: The use of a computer to accept messages from terminals, route the messges over trunk lines to remote message switching computers, and to provide certain reliability functions such as an audit trail and error control. Message switching is a somewhat different application of computer communications in that there is no user processing involved. The sole purpose of the system is to communicate messages from one point to another point.

message switching center: A location where an incoming message is automatically or manually directed to one or more outgoing circuits, according to the intelligence contained in the message.

message switching concentration (MSC) techniques: Involve multiplexing of entire messages or fixed-length portions of long messages, respectively. They are categorized as concentration techniques since a buffer queue stores entire blocks in its buffer until one is assembled and the high-speed line is available to transmit it. The high-speed line transmits variable-length frames of data with appropriate addressing and control information; all data characters in each frame are generally associated with the same source-sink terminal pair.

message switching (MS): A telecommunications application in which a message is received at a central location, stored on a direct-access device until the proper outgoing line is available, and then transmitted to the appropriate destination.

message switching procedures: A message switching system accepts, transmits, and delivers discrete entities called messages. In such a system, no physical path is set up between the source and the destination, and no resources (e.g., capacity, buffer storage, etc.) are allocated to its transmission in advance. Rather, the source includes a destination address at the beginning of each message. The message switching system then uses this address to guide the message through the network to its destination, provides error control, and notifies the sender of its receipt.

message switching system components: Point-to-point communication circuits and switching nodes which are connected so that a message arriving on one circuit may be transmitted to another. Communication over a message-switched system occurs via a sequence of transmitted messages, each consisting of its address followed by text. The address is inspected by each node in routing the message to the next node on the way to its destination.

message text: The part of a message consisting of the actual information that is routed to a user at a terminal or to a program.

metallic circuit: A telephone circuit providing a direct-current connection between terminating points, without intervening transformers, amplifiers, etc.

metal oxide semiconductor (MOS):   A type of transistor for large-scale integrated (LSI) components for computer memory units. In MOS technology, amplification or switching is accomplished by applying a signal voltage to a gate electrode. The resulting electrostatic field creates a conduction channel between the two diffused regions in the silicon crystal structure, called the source and the drain.

metal   oxide   semiconductor   (MOS) memory: A memory using a semiconductor circuit; generally used in high speed buffer memory and read-only memory.

method study: The utilization of certain methods for recording and examining existing and proposed techniques of working in order to improve them.

metron: A unit which expresses a quantity of metrical information.

MFT with subtasking: An option of MFT in which each task can attach a number of subtasks that can execute in the same partition.

MICR: See magnetic ink character recognition.

microampere (μA):   Equal to 10^{-6} ampere.

microcircuits: 1. Miniaturized circuitry components common to the third generation of computer equipment. Microcircuits reduce cost, increase reliability, and operate faster than tubes and transistors. 2. A specialized circuit composed of fabricated and interconnected elements that make them inseparable and miniaturized.

micro code: 1. An instruction written by a programmer or systems analyst in a source program to specify and execute a routine to be extracted from the computer library to give the processor program information and instructions required to regularize the routine to fit into the specific object program. 2. A system of coding making use of suboperations not ordinarily accessible in programming; e.g., coding that makes use of parts of multiplication or division operations. 3. A list of small program steps. Combinations of these steps, performed automatically in a prescribed sequence to form macro operations like multiply, divide, and square root.

microcommand: A command specifying an elementary machine operation to be performed within a basic machine cycle.

microcomputer: A complete small computing system that usually sells for less than $500 and whose main processing blocks are made of semiconductor integrated circuits. In function and structure, it is similar to a minicomputer.

microelectronics: The entire body of electronic art together with, or applied to, the realization of electronic systems by using extremely small electronic parts.

microfarad (μF): One millionth of a farad; the unit of electrical capacity.

microfiche: A microfilm mounted on a card.

microfilm: Microphotographs on film.

microfilm counter: An automatic device used on microfilm cameras to record the number of exposures made.

microfilm duplex: The method of microfilm operation which allows the simultaneous recording of both the front and back of a document, side-by-side on the film.

microfilm frame: A length of microfilm representing one exposure.

microfilm image: The reproduction on microfilm of the words, numbers, and other document information.

microfilm leader: A strip of film or paper at the beginning of a roll of film and used for threading.

microfilm reader: 1. A device for viewing a microimage; consists of a projector and a screen. 2. A unit of peripheral equipment which projects film to permit reading by clients or customers of the stored data on the film, such as microfilm or microfiche, or a device which converts patterns of opaque and transparent spots on a photofilm to electrical pulses which correspond to the patterns.

microfilm reader-printer: A machine which both displays micro-images and produces hard-copy reproductions.

microinstruction: A bit pattern stored in a microprogram memory word; specifies the operation of individual large-scale integration computing elements and related subunits, such as main memory and input/-output interfaces.

microinstruction sequence: The series of microinstructions that the microprogram control unit (MCU) selects from the microprogram to execute a single macroinstruction or control command. Microinstruction sequences can be shared by several macroinstructions.

microminiaturization: The process of reducing the size of parts, photographs, or printed materials for more economical, convenient storage or packing. Microminiaturized circuits are usually etched, evaporated, or electronically deposited metals, inks or other materials to form extremely tiny monolithic chips, blocks, or other integrations.

micromodule: A tiny electronic device with standardized dimensions (usually fabricated using semiconductor techniques) capable of performing one or more functions in a circuit.

micron: A unit of length equal to one-thousandth of a millimeter, i.e., one-millionth of a meter or 39millionths of an inch.

microprocessing unit (MPU): The main piece of hardware of the microcomputer. It consists of the microprocessor, the main memory (composed of read-write and readonly memory), the input/output interface devices, the clock circuit, the buffer, the driver circuits, and the passive circuit elements.

microprocessor: The semiconductor central processing unit (CPU) and one of the principal components of the microcomputer. The elements of the microprocessor are contained either on a single chip or within the same package. In a microcomputer with a fixed instruction set, it consists of the arithmetic logic unit and the control logic unit. In a microcomputer with a microprogrammed instruction set, it contains an additional control memory unit.

microprogram: 1. A program of analytic instructions which the programmer intends to construct from the basic subcommands of a digital computer. 2. A sequence of pseudo-commands which will be translated by hardware into machine subcommands. 3. A means of building various analytic instructions as needed from the subcommand structure of a computer. 4. A plan for obtaining maximum utilization of the abilities of a digital computer by efficient use of the subcommands of the machine.

microprogramming: The technique of using a certain special set of instructions for an automatic computer, that consists only of basic elemental operations which the programmer may combine into higher level instructions.

microroutine: See microprogram.

microsecond: One-millionth of a second.

microwave: 1. All electromagnetic waves in the radio frequency spectrum above 890 megahertz. 2. Line-ofsight, point-to-point transmission of signals at high frequency. 3. Ultra high frequency waveforms used to transmit voice or data messages.

microwave dish: A parabolic antenna.

microwave interference: Interference to a satellite terminal created by radiation from other communications systems. Microwave networks crisscross the nation to serve a variety of communications applications. The antennas in these systems radiate in the same frequency band. Consequently, even at a considerable distance, one of these installations can cause severe interference to the reception of a small standard satellite terminal.

microwave transmission: Transmission of voice, television, or data signals by means of highly directional, high-frequency radio waves. The microwave signals are electromagnetic waves in the super-high frequency portion of the ratio frequency spectrum [above 890 megahertz (MHz)]. Their wavelengths are sufficiently short to exhibit some of the properties of light. Microwaves are used in point-to-point communication because they are concentrated into a beam easily. In addition to the microwave transmission used by the communcication common carrier, many privately owned microwave systems are in service.

mid band: The part of the frequency band that lies between television channels 6 and 7, reserved by the Federal Communication Commission for air, maritime and land mobile units, frequency modulation (FM) radio, and aeronautical and maritime navigation. Mid band frequencies, 108 to 174 megahertz (MHz), can also be used to provide additional channels on cable television systems.

middleware: Software tailored to the specific needs of an installation.

midpoint (coordinate): A coordinate point necessary in the formation of a parabolic span.

millimicro second: Same as nanosecond; one billionth of a second.

millisecond: One-thousandth of a second.

millivolt: One thousandth of a volt.

mill timer: A clock device which adds up the time during which each program, in a multiprogramming machine, is utilizing the central processing unit.

miniaturization: Size reduction to increase packing density of magnetic, electromechanical parts, or components of circuits.

minicomputer communication processor: Connects a central computing facility with a communications network, performing communications control functions for the central computer.

minicomputer device controller: Controls the high speed readers and printers of the central computing facility, relieving the central computer of that task; also controls high speed readers and printers at remote locations.

minimal latency routine: In serial storage systems, a routine coded so that the actual latency is less than the expected random access latency.

minimum access coding: Techniques of coding that minimize the time used to transfer words from auxiliary storage to main storage.

minimum access programming: Programming in such a way that minimal waiting time is required to obtain information out of storage.

minimum delay code: A system of coding that minimizes delays for data transfer between storage and other machine components.

minimum distance code: A binary code in which the signal distance does not fall below a specified minimum value.

minimum latency coding: A procedure or method for programming computers in which the waiting time of a word depends on its location, i.e., locations for instructions and data are chosen so that access time is reduced or minimized. Same as minimum delay coding or optimum coding.

minimum latency program: Programming that requires minimum waiting time to obtain information out of storage.

minor control change: A specific control change of relatively less importance or at least of smaller magnitude in the hierarchy of major, intermediate, and minor ranges of significance.

minor control data: Data used to select, execute, identify, or modify another routine, record, file, operation, or data value.

minor control field: Any control field of less significance than the major control field in a sorting operation.

minority carrier: In a semiconductor, the type of carrier which constitutes less than 50 percent of the total.

minor time slice: Under time-sharing option (TSO), the time within a major time slice when a terminal job has the highest priority for execution. See also major time slice.

minus zone: The bit position in a computer code which represents the algebraic minus sign.

miscellaneous function: An on-off function of a machine such as spindle stop, coolant on, and clamp.

miscellaneous intercept: In Bell System leased telegraph message switching systems, the act of intercepting single-address messages containing a nonvalid call direction code and/or the action of intercepting multiple-address messages without a proper multipleaddress code.

misfeed: Cards, tapes, or other data fail to pass into or through a device properly. Causes may be damaged, misprogrammed, or mis-sensed input.

misregistration: A character recognition term: the improper state of appearance of a character, line, or document, on site in a character reader, with respect to a real or imaginary horizontal baseline.

missing page interruption: Same as page fault.

mission factor: A ratio developed by dividing the number of nonretrieved documents by the total number of relevant documents in the file, e.g., zero would be perfection.

mis-sort: A check drawn by a depositor wrongly sorted to a book or bank other than that in which the account is kept.

misuse failure: Failure because an item has been exposed to conditions outside its proper working range.

mixed processing on-line access: The procedure and provision in the same computers for both on-line realtime services and batch processing.

mixed radix notation: A radix notation that uses more than one radix in a numeration system.

mixed storage: A type of storage whose elements are arranged in a matrix so that access to any location requires the use of two or more coordinates, e.g., cathode-ray tube storage, core storage, etc., which use coincident-current selection.

mixer: See OR circuit.

mix instruction: Specific computer instructions selected to complete particular problems. The optimum mix of instructions determines the speed and accuracy.

mnemonic address: A simple address code, e.g., CA for California, LAX for Los Angeles Airport.

mnemonic instruction codes: 1. Computer instructions written in a meaningful notation, e.g., add, mpy, sto. 2. Codes devised and written in symbolic notation for easier human recognition and retention. 3. The writing of operation codes in a symbolic notation which is easier to remember than the actual operation codes of the machine.

mnemonic operation code: An operation code in which the names of operations are abbreviated and expressed mnemonically to facilitate in remembering the operations they represent. A mnemonic code normally needs to be converted to an actual opera-

tion code by an assembler before execution by the computer. Examples of mnemonic codes are ADD for addition, CLR for clear storage, and SQR for square root.

mnemonics: The art of improving the efficiency of the memory (in computer storage). See also label.

modal dispersion: The pulse spreading that occurs when a light pulse travels through an optic fiber. Because a light ray at an angle close to the angle of incidence undergoes more reflections than a ray traveling parallel or near-parallel to the axis, it travels a longer path than the latter, and arrives at the fiber output after the axial rays. This spreading increases with the diameter and overall length of the fiber. Both modal and material dispersion pose limitations on the fiber bandwidth, but the magnitude of their effects varies with the type of fiber.

mode: 1. A method of operation, e.g., the binary mode, the interpretive mode, the alphanumeric mode, etc. 2. The most frequent value in the statistical sense.

model: 1. Representation in mathematical terms of a process, device, or concept. 2. A general, often pictorial, representation of a system being studied.

model and program (MAP):   The pre-installation techniques and procedures recommended to users of some types of electronic data-processing systems.

model file: The model is an analog of the processing files. It can be originated, added to (posting), compared with others, held aside, filed for later use, sent somewhere, and so on. Sets of symbols are the simple analogs for these happenings.

model, iconographic: A pictorial representation of a system and the functional relationships within.

model statement: A statement in the body of a macro definition or in open code from which an assembler language statement can be generated at pre-assembly time. Values can be substituted at one or more points in a model statement; one or more identical or different statements can be generated from the same model statement under the control of a conditional assembly loop.

modem pooling: Allows several modems to support hundreds of stations. Data calls queue for modem access and usage is transparent to users.

modem, synchronous short-haul: This type of short-haul modem provides high speed, short range synchronous data transmission at switch selectable speeds up to 19200 bps. It operates on 4-wire full-duplex or 2-wire half-duplex circuits in point-to-point applications. The operating range extends to 17Km at 4800 bps on 0.4mm cable. Both internal and external clocks are provided. The interface meets the requirements of EIA RS232C and CCITT V.24/V.28. Rack mount equivalent available.

mode, real-time: Real-time is a mode of operation in which data that are necessary to the control and/or execution of a transaction can be processed in time for the transaction to be affected by the results of the processing. Real-time processing is most usually identified with great speed, but speed is relative. The essence of real time is concurrency—simultaneity. Real-time is refinement in the integration of data processing with communications. Real-time eliminates slow information-gathering procedures, dated reporting techniques and lax communications; insures that facts within the system are as timely as a prevailing situation, as current as the decisions which they must support. Real-time provides answers when answers are needed, delivers data instantly whenever the need for that data arises. Incoming information is edited, updated and made available on demand at every level of responsibilty. Imminent departures from established standards are automatically detected, and management is notified in time for action.

modifier: A quantity used to alter the address of an operand, e.g., the cycle index.

modify: 1. To alter in an instruction the address of the operand. 2. To alter a subroutine according to a defined parameter.

modular: A degree of standardization of computersystem components to allow for combinations and large variety of compatible units.

modular connector: An electrical connector with sections that are used like "building blocks" or modules.

modular electronics: The electronics of miniaturization, i.e. electronic circuits that are so tiny that single or small quantities of molecules are used.

modularity: 1. A condition in the determination of the design of the equipment and programming systems such that the hardware and software components can be identified, altered, or augmented readily without replacements of particular units or sections. 2. Operating system programs conform to specific standards, so that control programs will have an identical interface with all processing programs. These standards are well documented so that user-written programs can follow the same conventions. The user is free to supplement supplied programs to meet special situations. By following the rules indicated in the standards, portions of control or processing programs can be changed or replaced in modular fashion.

modulate: The adjusting to a required standard such as conversion of signals emitted by output to a signal standard required for transmission.

modulated carrier: A frequency which can be transmitted or received through space or a transmission circuit, with a superposed information signal that, by itself, could not be transmitted and received effectively.

modulated radio frequency (RF):   Composite video "carried" by a high frequency signal which simulates the broadcast television signal and which can successfully enter the antenna terminal of the television set.

modulation: The process of varying some characteristic of the carrier wave in accordance with the instantaneous value or samples of the intelligence to be transmitted.

modulation capability: The maximum percentage modulation which can be used without exceeding a specified distortion level.

modulation code: A code used to cause variations in signal in accordance with a predetermined scheme; normally used to alter or modulate a carrier wave to transmit data.

modulation index: In a frequency-modulated wave, the ratio of the frequency deviation to the maximum modulation frequency.

modulation meter: That placed in shunt with a communication channel, giving an indication that interprets, in a stated way, instant-to-instant power levels in varying modulation currents.

modulation noise: 1. Those extra bits or words that must be ignored or removed from the data at the time the data is used. 2. Errors introduced into data in a system, especially in communication channels. 3. Random variation of one or more characteristics of any entity such as voltage, current, and data. 4. Any disturbance tending to interfere with the normal operation of a device or system.

modulation pulse width: The duration of a pulse in the time interval between the points of the leading and trailing edges at which the instantaneous value bears a specified relation to the pulse amplitude.

modulation rate: Reciprocal of the units interval measured in seconds. (This rate is expressed in bauds.)

modulation recording phase: A procedure or method for magnetic recording of bits in which each storage cell is split into two parts, and each is magnetized in opposite senses, with the sequence of these senses indicating whether the bit represented is zero or a one.

modulation suppression: Reduction of modulation in wanted signal in presence of an unwanted signal.

modulation transformer: One which applies the modulating signal to the carrier wave amplifier in a transmitter.

modulator: 1. A device that varies a repetitive phenomenon in accordance with some predetermined scheme usually introduced as a signal. 2. The stage in a transmitter which varies the wave shape of the master oscillator output.

module: 1. A program unit that is discrete and identifiable with respect to compiling, combining with other units, and loading, e.g., the input to, or output from, an assembler, compiler, linkage editor, or executive routine. 2. A packaged functional hardware unit designed for use with other components.

module dissipation: The dissipation of the module calculated from the voltage-current product, plus an allowance for transistor dissipation for load currents being supplied to other modules.

module library: A directoried data set containing selected modules and serving as an automatic source of input to the linkage editor.

module (programming):   The input to, or output from, a single execution of an assembler, compiler, or linkage editor; a program unit that is discrete and identifiable with respect to compiling, combining with other units, and loading.

module testing: The destructive read-off or use caused by overloading or underloading the computer components, causing failure of substandard units and minimizing nonscheduled downtime.

modulo: A mathematical operator which yields the remainder function of division.

modulo-n check: 1. A check that makes use of a check number that is equal to the remainder of the desired number when divided by n, e.g., in a modulo-4 check, the check number will be 0, 1, 2, or 3 and the remainder of A when divided by 4 must equal the reported check number B, otherwise an equipment malfunction has occurred. 2. A method of verification by congruences, e.g., casting out nines.

modulus (modulo): The number of distinct integers in a finite system of numbers. For example, in a modulo 5 system, the numbers are 0, 1, 2, 3, and 4. In this system larger numbers are expressed by dividing them by the modulus until a remainder less than the modulus is obtained. For example, 19 is 4 in the modulo 5 system. If a counter is modulo 5, when it is set at 4, an increment of 1 will result in a setting of 0.

molecule: A group of atoms.

monadic boolean operator: A boolean operator having only one operand, for example, NOT.

monadic operation: An operation on one operand, for example, negation. Same as unary operation.

monitor: 1. (ISO) A device that observes and verifies the operations of a data processing system and indicates any significant departure form the norm. 2. Software or hardware that observes, supervises, controls, or verifies the operations of a system.

monitored instructions: As shown in the input/output instruction repertoire, instructions calling for input, output, or function transfers may be executed either with or without a monitor. When executed with a monitor, an internal interrupt will be generated upon completion of the transfer.

When an instruction is executed without a monitor the interrupt is inhibited.

monitoring and design simulation: The building of a model of a system in the form of a computer program by the use of special languages. The models of a system can be adjusted easily, and the system that is being designed can be tested to show the effect of any change.

monitor operating system: The monitor exercises primary control of the routines that compose the operating system. It is this operating system which turns the computer into a flexible tool allowing the user to achieve maximum use of the hardware's advanced design features.

monitor operator: An individual who initiates and monitors either the operation of a computer or of a process.

monitor printer: A device that prints all messages transmitted over the circuit to which it is connected.

monitor system: A programming system in control of all systems functions (a subprogram of a control program). The monitor simulates the operator at processor speed. It maintains continuity between jobs and maintains status of input/output devices, while providing automatic accounting of jobs. A logical outgrowth of advanced programming systems, it is the only practical way to operate real-time systems and the only efficient method for priority applications.

monolithic: The single silicon substrate in which an integrated circuit is constructed.

monolithic integrated circuit: One of several logic circuits etched on chips of material.

monolithic storage: Storage made up of monolithic integrated circuits.

monomial: An algebraic expression consisting of one term. For example, xy, 3ab, and 2y are monomials.

monostable circuit: A circuit with one stable or quasi-stable state and one unstable state; undergoes a complete cycle of change in response to a single triggering excitation.

monostable device: One which has only one stable state.

monostable multivibrator: A circuit which holds information for a fixed time as it is determined by the nature of the circuit elements.

Monte Carlo method: A trial and error method of repeated calculations to discover the best solution of a problem. It is used when a great number of variables are present, with interrelationships so extremely complex as to forestall straight-forward analytical handling.

morse code: A system used in signaling or telegraphy, which consists of various combinations of dots and dashes.

MOS: See metal oxide semiconductor.

most significant digit (MSD):   The significant digit contributing the largest quantity to the value of a numeral, i.e. the leftmost digit.

motion register: A register whose contents control the motion of a tape-drive.

m out of n code: A form of fixed weight binary code in which m of the n digits are always in the same state.

movable heads: Movable reading and writing heads on bulk memory devices.

move: 1. In communications applications, to transmit. 2. As a variety of program activity, to duplicate the contents of a given section of core or disk memory in another location.

move mode: A transmittal mode in which data are moved between the buffer and the user's work area.

moving average: An average performed on data in which the values closest to a given time are more heavily valued than others. Used as a filtering method to eliminate high frequency noise.

moving head disk: A multitrack disk with a single head which moves to access any read/write track.

MRDOS: Mapped real-time disk operating system.

MS: See message switching.

msec: Millisecond, one thousandth of a second.

MSI: See medium-scale integration.

mu: Greek letter used as symbol for amplification factor; micro-; micron; permeability.

multi-access systems: Permit several people or groups to transact with the computer through the operator's console or many on-line terminals. Access points are connected to the central processor by data transmission lines from remote terminals which can be typewriters, visual display units, cathode-ray tubes, or satellite processors. Multi-access multiprogramming systems have been installed by many universities, laboratories, businesses, and research groups. Most operate in a conventional mode with fast response time and are controlled by operating systems.

multi-address: See multiple address message.

multi-address instruction: An instruction consisting of an operation and more than one address.

multi-aspect: Systems which permit more than one aspect of information to be used in combination to effect identifying and selecting operations.

multi-aspect search: 1. A method of cataloguing vast amounts of data, all related to one field of interest, so that one can call out any or all of this data at any time it is needed. 2. A branch of computer science relating to the techniques for storing and searching large or specific quantities of information that may or may not be a real-time system.

multicomputer system: The use of more than one computer in a system.

multicomputing unit: A computer with multiple arithmetic and logic units.

multicycle feeding: A specific method of processing punched cards during which several fields of an individual card are read in succession on successive machine cycles, e.g., multiread feeding achieves the result by feeding the same card past the reading station several times.

multidrop: A line or circuit interconnecting several stations.

multidrop circuit: A communication system configuration using a single channel or line to serve multiple terminals.

multi-element control system: A specific control system designed to utilize input signals derived from two or more process variables for the purpose of jointly affecting the action of the control system. Some examples are input signals from pressure or temperature or from speeds, flows, etc.

multifont optical arena: Basic character reading equipment having the ability to discern many fonts of formats of characters, usually from hard copy.

multifunctional data transmission: The integration of asynchronous and synchronous circuit switched data transmission. In some systems this occurs at speeds up to 57.6 kilobytes per second (Kbps). Data calls are established by keying in a port name or number.

multijob operation: The simultaneous, concurrent or interleaved execution of job parts or segments from more than one job.

multilength arithemtic: Arithmetic accomplished using two or more machine words to store each operand to attain greater precision in the result.

multilength working: The use of two or more machine words to represent a number and enhance precision.

multilevel addressing: A reference address in an instruction that contains a 1 in bit position 0; the virtual address of the location that contains the direct address. If indirect addressing is called for by an instruction, the reference address field is used to access a word location that contains the direct reference address; this then replaces the indirect reference address and is used as an operand address value. Indirect addressing is limited to one level.

multilevel interrupt structure: Communication interfaces and modem controllers capable of generating interrupts requesting service from the program, and notifying the program of changes in the condition of some of the communication control lines such as data carrier, data set ready, clear-to-send, etc. For a dynamic communication system, the program should have the capability of supressing interrupts and/or selectively modifying the conditions which can cause interrupts.

multilevel priority interrupts: In many large systems interrupt provisions have been made to facilitate the priority requirements of various subroutines. Specifically, the interrupt requests of these subroutines are handled by the central processor in the sequence of the highest priority. If a priority subroutine requests an interrupt, it will have priority over all subroutines of lower priority, even though they have requested previously an interrupt.

multipass sort: A particular sort program designed to sort more data than can be contained within the internal memory of a central computer. Intermediate storage, such as disk, tape, or drum, is required.

multiphase program: A program in absolute form that requires more than one fetch or load operation to complete execution.

multiple access: A system from which input/output can be received or dispatched from more than one location.

multiple address code: An instruction code in which an instruction word can specify more than one address to be used during the operation. In a typical instruction of a four address code the addresses specify the location of two operands, the location at which the results are to be stored, and the margin location of the next instruction in the sequence. In a typical three address code, the fourth address specifying the location of the next instructions is dispensed with, the instructions are taken from storage in a preassigned order. In a typical two address code, the addresses may specify the locations of the operands. The results may be placed at one of the addresses or the destination of the results may be specified by another instruction.

multiple address instruction: 1. A type of instruction that specifies the addresses of two or more items which may be addresses of locations of inputs or outputs of the calculating unit, or the addresses of locations of instructions for the control unit. 2. An instruction that has more than one address part.

multiple address message: A message to be delivered to more than one destination.

multiple aperture core: A specific magnetic core with multiple holes through which wires pass to create more than one magnetic closed path, e.g., used in nondestructive reading.

multiple computer operation: As related to the work to be done, the multiplexer channel can provide linkage for a few or a great many communications lines. Up to 248 communications lines can, for instance, be connected to the processing unit through some eight transmission control units, each line holding a great many separate terminals. Many computers are equipped with a

multiplexer channel. Multiplexer operation is a collateral function for the logic circuits. That is, circuits are borrowed from normal duties as each character is taken into the processing then they are returned to the program being run at the time. This interleaving of functions provides both logic and channel functions with the same circuits. The multiplexer channel consists of circuits reserved for this function.

multiple connector: A connector to indicate the merging of several lines of flow into one line, or the dispersal of one line of flow into several lines.

multiple document indexing: 1. A system of indexing individual documents by descriptors of equal rank, so that a library can be searched for a combination of one or more descriptors. 2. An indexing technique where the interrelations of terms are shown by coupling individual words.

multiple graphs: More than one graph plotted, utilizing a set or sets of data. Thus, a set of data may furnish data required for plotting more than one graph.

multiple index address (time-sharing): The problem of relocating a program, that is, the modification of instruction address to allow the program to operate from the positions in core memory to which it has been assigned is a critical one in time-sharing. Main memory is shared among many users and no user can preplan the execution location of his programs. Moreover, user programs must be swapped in and out of main memory constantly. It is desirable that programs be easily movable from one main memory area to another with minimum address modification.

multiple job processing: Controlling the performance of more than one data processing job at a time.

multiple modulation (compound modulation): A succession of processes of modulation, where the wave from one process becomes the modulating wave for the next.

multiple names: In a directoried data set, more than one name entry in the directory referring to the same member.

multiple precision: The use of two or more computer words to represent a single numeric quantity or numeral, i.e., with twice as many or more digits as are normally carried in a fixed-length word.

multiple regression: A special type of mathematical analysis.

multiple-speed floating controller: A unique type of floating controller; the output may change at two or more rates, each corresponding to a definite range of values of the actuating error signal.

multiple-task management: Managing the performance of more than one data processing task at a time.

multiple user control: This subtask provides scheduling for the user tasks so that their requests are in the proper priority. The processing of requests from user tasks in lower priorities is such that they are overlapped with I/O activity of higher priority requests.

multiplex: The concurrent transmission of more than one information stream on a single channel.

multiplex channel: A data channel which can operate either in burst or multiplexer mode. In the latter mode, several slow input/output (I/O) devices can be served simultaneously by time-slicing.

multiplex data terminal: A device that modulates and/or demodulates data between two or more input/output devices and a data transmission link.

multiplexed operation: A simultaneous operation which shares the use of a common unit of a system in such a way that it can be considered an independent operation.

multiplexer: A technique or device which uses or controls several communication channels concurrently, sending and receiving messages.

multiplexer channel: Depending on the work to be done, the multiplexer channel can provide linkage for a few or a great many communications lines. Up to 248 communications lines can, for instance, be connected to the processing unit through some eight transmission control units. Each line can hold a great many separate terminals. Many computers are equipped with a multiplexer channel. Multiplexer operation is a collateral function for the logic circuits. That is, circuits are borrowed from the normal duties as each character is taken into the processing unit, then returned to the program being run at the time.

multiplexer operations channel: The multiplexer expands the data break facilities of the computer to allow large numbers of input/output devices to transfer data directly with the core memory, via the memory buffer register. Simultaneous data break requests are serviced by the multiplexer according to prewired priority.

multiplexer terminal unit: A unit used to connect multiple terminal stations to and from the central processor of a computer.

multiplexing: 1. The transmission of a number of different messages simultaneously over a single circuit. 2. Utilizing a single device for several similar purposes or using several devices for the same purpose, i.e., a duplexed communications channel carrying two messages simultaneously. 3. The division of various transmission channels or facilities into two or more channels.

multiplexing frequency: A specific method for sectioning a circuit into many channels.

multiplex mode: A means of transferring records to or from low-speed input/output (I/O) devices on the multiplexer channel by interleaving bytes of data. The multiplexer channel sustains simultaneous I/O operations on several subchannels. Bytes of data are interleaved and then routed to or from the selected I/O devices or to and from the desired locations in main storage. Multiplex mode is sometimes referred to as byte mode.

multiplexor: Same as multiplexer.

multiplex, time-division: A system in which a channel is established by intermittently connecting its terminal equipment to a common channel, generally at regular intervals and by means of an automatic distribution. Outside the times during which these connections are established, the section of the common channel between the distributors can be utilized in order to establish other similar channels in turn.

multiplicand: The quantity multiplied by each digit of the multiplier to form the product in the operation of multiplication.

multiplication: Actions or processes which result in multiplying, i.e., determination of the product by repeatedly adding the same quantity (multiplicand) a discrete number of times (multiplier) which involves the shifting of the radix point (or decimal point in decimal computer or values) to the right.

multiplier: The operand which controls the repetitive addition of the multiplicand in the operation of a multiplication.

multiplier, constant: A computing element that multiplies a variable by a constant factor.

multiplier quarter-squares: In some analog computers, a multiplication unit which operates by means of a special identity.

multiplier-quotient register: The register used to contain a multiplier in multiplication and the quotient in division.

multiplier register: One used to hold the multiplier while multiplication is being performed.

multiplier unit: A unit capable of generating a product from the representations of two numbers, often formed by repeated additions of the multiplicand or multiples of it.

multipoint circuit: A system consisting of a circuit connecting three or more terminals, any or all of which may simultaneously receive information flowing in the common circuit.

multipoint line: See multidrop.

multiposition controller: A specially designed controller which has two or more discrete values of output.

multiprecision arithmetic: A form of arithmetic similar to double precision arithmetic except that two or more words may be used to represent each number.

multiprocessing: 1. A computer configuration consisting of more than one independently initiable processor, each having access to a common, jointly-addressable memory. 2. Processing several programs or program segments concurrently on a time-share basis. Each processor is only active on one program at any one time while operations such as input/output may be performed in parallel on several programs. The processor is directed to switch back and forth among programs under the control of the master control program.

multiprocessing environment: A typical system operates in a multiprogram or multiprocessing environment and to initiate and preserve this, the executive routine must be in complete control of the total system. Special hardware features are provided to permit this control. The multiprogramming and multiprocessing capabilities of the system are based upon guard mode operation, the setting aside of certain instructions, registers, and storage locations for the exclusive use of the executive routine, assuring protection against the interaction of unrelated programs.

multiprocessing executive control: The

executive routine that keeps the processor constantly computing on various programs.

multiprocessing interleaving: A process of addressing adjacent storage modules in an even/odd fashion. It significantly reduces storage-access conflicts in a multiprocessor system and increases overall system performance. With interleaving, the modules are divided into even and odd lcoations (although the addressing structure within the modules themselves remains unchanged). For example, in a fully expanded eight module system, modules 0, 2, 4, 6 are referenced for even address while modules 1, 3, 5, 7, are referenced for odd.

multiprocessing system: A computing system employing two or more interconnected processing units to execute programs simultaneously.

multiprogramming: A technique for handling numerous routines or programs by overlapping or interleaving their execution, that is, by permitting more than one program to time-share machine components.

multiprogramming dispatching: The priority assigned to an active task in a multiprogramming or multitask environment. An active task is nonreal-time and nonforeground. The dispatch priority establishes precedence for the use of the central processing unit (CPU) when the operating system prepares to return control to the problem program.

multiprogramming executive: The master contol program in a multiprogrammed system.

multiprogramming (executive control logic): Capabilities of the system are guard mode operation, setting aside certain instructions, registers, and storage locations for the exclusive use of the executive system assuring maximum protection against the interaction of unrelated programs.

multiprogramming input/output control system (IOCS): Two or more independent programs sharing one computer facility in the same time period. Multiprogramming in the simplest case is program segmentation into two parts, such as the use of IOCS with a problem program. At a higher level, multiprogramming involves foreground and background jobs and the related job scheduling.

multiprogramming internal function register (IFR): In some large systems the internal function register (IFR) is a one-word representation of various states and conditions germane to the currently running program. The information in this register is continuously updated by hardware during the execution of a program. Whenever an interrupt occurs, the contents of the IFR are stored in the temporary register where they are available to the executive system and are used to reestablish program conditions at the time of interrupt. In a multiprogram situation, each program will have an associated IFR word. When the program in control is interrupted, its IFR word is stored automatically, thereby capturing the current status of the carry and overflow designators and the store address assignments.

multiprogramming priority: The concurrent operation of several types of applications. Assignment of priority levels is at the discretion of the user, for example, one priority level can be reserved for a program that must provide rapid responses to realtime devices, such as communications control. Another can be reserved for the peripheral control package to accomplish several media conversions — card to tap, tape to printer, etc. The third priority level could then be used to run either a production or monitor job.

multiprogramming system (MPS): A system that can process two or more programs concurrently by interleaving their execution.

multireel file: A file of data stored on magnetic tape that exceeds the capacity of one reel of magnetic tape and is stored on two or more reels.

multisequential system: A particular computing system which works much like a multiprocessor, e.g., one computer controlling several satelite computers, capable of interleaving the execution of instructions which can also execute more than one instruction at a time.

multitasking: The activation of several separate but interrelated tasks under a single program identity; differs from multiprogramming in that common routines and data space as well as disk files may be used.

multitask operation: Parallel processing of programs and of a single re-enterable program used by many tasks.

multithread: Used on a program which can have more than one logical path execed simultaneously.

multitone circuit: A telegraph transmission system in which it is necessary to use two or more channels simultaneously in the same direction for transmitting a signal btween the same two points.

multivibrator: A type of relaxation oscillator used for the generation of nonsinusoidal waves in which the output of each of its two tubes is coupled to the input of the other to sustain oscillations. Used in a cathode-ray tube's sync circuits.

MUMPS language: Massachusetts General Hospital Utility Multiprogramming System. An interpretive language designed for use in the medical environment particularly for interactive data acquisition programs. Basically procedure-oriented, it contains relatively sophisticated editing, list processing and file manipulation capabilities in addition to FORTRAN and BASIC type statements.

muting: Suppression of an output of electronic equipment unless there is adequate signal/noise ratio.

muting circuit or switch: Attenuates amplifier output unless paralyzed by a useful incoming carrier; used with automatic tuning devices.

mv: Abbreviation of millivolt.

mylar: A Dupont trademark for polyester film often used as a base for magnetically coated or perforated information media.

N

NAK: See negative acknowledgment.

name entry: In assembler programming, the entry in the name field of an assembler language statement.

name field: The first field of a map symbolic instruction, punched in card columns 1-6. It may contain a symbol by which other instructions can refer to the instruction named. The name field is also referred to as the location field.

name recognizer: A left-to-right lexicographic scan until a non-alphanumeric character is recognized.

NAND: A logical operator having the property that if p is a statement, q is a statement,..., then the NAND of p, q, r,... is true if at least one statement is false, false if all statements are true.

nano: Prefix for 10^{-9} (a billionth) times a specified unit.

nanosecond circuit: A computer logic circuit, or another electronic circuit, which has gradient pulse rise or fall times measured in billionths of seconds or less. A nanosecond is 1 billionth of a second.

nanosecond (nsec): One billionth of a second. One nanosecond is to 1 second as 1 second is to 32 years.

narrative: Statements included in the coding of a program serving as explanatory documentation of the coded procedures. They are not translated into program instructions but serve as useful aids during the amending or debugging of a program.

narrow bandline: A communication line similar to the common voice-grade line but which operates on a lower frequency.

Communications lines are an essential element of computer communications systems. The selection of a communication service to provide a specific bandwidth depends on the volume and speed requirements of the system.

n-ary code: A code in which each code element may be any one of n distinct values or kinds. For example, the code elements of a binary code have two different values; quaternary code elements have four possible values, etc.

natural binary: A number system to the base (radix) 2, in which the ones and zeroes have weighted value in accordance with their relative position in the binary word.

natural frequency: The frequency of free oscillation of a system.

natural function generator: An analog device or a specific program based on some physical law, such as one used with a digital computer to solve a particular differential equation.

natural language: A language whose rules reflect and describe current usage rather than prescribed usage.

natural noise: Noise caused by natural phenomena such as thermal emission, static, etc.

natural wavelength: That corresponding to the natural frequency of a tuned circuit; e.g., that of an open aerial by virtue of its distributed capacitance and inductance.

NB: Narrow band.

N/C system: A system which uses prerecorded intelligence prepared from numerical data to control a machine or process. The N/C system consists of all elements of the control system and of the machine being controlled that are, in fact, a part of the servomechanism.

n-cube: A term used in switching theory to indicate two n-1 cubes with corresponding points connected.

NE: Not equal to. See relational operator.

near-end crosstalk: Crosstalk which is propagated in a disturbed channel in the direction opposite to the direction of propagation of the current in the disturbing channel. Ordinarily, the terminal of the disturbed channel at which the near-end crosstalk is present is near to or coincides with the energized terminal of the disturbing channel.

negate: To perform the logic operation NOT.

negation element: A device or modem with capability of reversing a signal, condition, state, or an event into its alternate or opposite.

negation gate: A device with capability of reversing a signal, condition, state, or an event into its alternate or opposite.

negative: Relating to gating, the same as NOT, e.g., negative AND is the same as NOT AND or NAND, negative OR is the same as NOT OR or NOR, etc.

negative   acknowledgment   (NAK):   In binary synchronous communications, a line control character sent by a receiving terminal to indicate that an error was encountered in the previous block and that the receiving terminal is ready to accept another transmission of the erroneous block.

negative feedback: The return of some of the output of a device, such as an amplifier, to its input, but 180 degrees out of phase with the normal input voltage. When adjusted correctly, negative feedback will

reduce any distortion in the device, but also reduce the gain.

negative frequency deviation: A drop of the frequency modulation (FM) carrier frequency below the resting frequency.

negative ignore gate: Same as negative gate (A ignore B) and negative gate (B ignore A).

negentropy: 1. In information theory, the average information content—a measure of nonrandomness in a signal. 2. In communications and information systems, a measure of the definition, nonambiguous coding, relational definition of an information or data structure and hence of its manageability and general usefulness.

neper: A unit similar to the decibel but differing from it in magnitude. One neper is equivalent to 8.686 decibels.

nest: 1. To imbed a subroutine or block of data into a larger routine or block of data. 2. To evaluate an nth degree polynomial by a particular algorithm which uses $(n-1)$ multiply operations and $(n-1)$ add operations in succession.

nesting level: In assembler programming, the level at which a term or subexpression appears in an expression, or the level at which a macro definition containing an inner macroinstruction is processed by an assembler.

nesting loop: Contains a loop of instructions which contains inner loops, nesting subroutines, outer loops, and rules and procedures relating to in and out procedures for each type.

nesting storage types: As data is transferred into storage, each word in turn enters the top register and is then "pushed down" the column from register to register to make room for the subsequent words as they are assigned. When a word is transferred out of the storage, again only from the top register, other data in the storage moves back up the column from register to register to fill the space left empty. This is accomplished either through programs or the equipment itself.

net control station: The station that coordinates the use of a communications network by all of the stations.

network: 1. A series of points connected by communications channels. 2. The switched telephone network is the network of telephone lines normally used for dialed telephone calls. 3. A private network is a network of communications channels confined to the use of one customer.

network analysis: An analytical method based upon defining completion times (least, probable, most) and interdependency relationships between stages and components of a complex task. The longest time path in a project; i.e., the specific succession of events upon which overall completion is identified for possible addition of resources so that it may be done as quickly as possible. Because the overall time required to complete the project cannot be less than that required along the critical path, it requires the most careful monitoring. Any delay along this path causes the project to be delayed, while minor delays along noncritical paths do not. This technique has been applied to such complicated and time-critical procedures as organ transplant operations involving simultaneous and interdependent operations on donor and recipient.

network analyzer: A device that simulates a network such as an electrical supply network.

network calculator: An analog device designed primarily for simulating electrical networks.

network capacity: Network capacity can be measured in the maximum number of bits transmitted on the network in a second.

network circuit: 1. A pair of complementary channels that provide bidirectional communication, with associated equipment

terminating in two exchanges. 2. A network of circuit elements (resistances, reactances and semiconductors) which perform specific functions. 3. A schematic diagram of a circuit.

network compromise: An electronic network used with hybrid coils to develop reasonable isolation between the two directions of transmission.

network control language standards: Sets of standard commands to perform common, simple, and intermediate system control functions regardless of the system being used on the network. For example, there is a set of simple functions such as logging in, listing files and directories, etc., which should be standardized in addition to some of the intermediate functions such as running common compilers and executing jobs.

network control needs: Governed by a multitude of factors including the size of the network, protocol, topology, and code set used in transmission. The type of user community served, along with the cost of short- and long-term outages, must also be considered. These control needs will change over time.

network data phase: That phase of a data call when data signals may be transferred between data terminal equipment which is interconnected via the network.

network design criteria: The criteria for network design are (a) function; (b) distribution; (c) volume; (d) language; (e) urgency; (f) accuracy; and (g) cost.

network disconnect command: A unnumbered command used to terminate the operational mode previously set.

network equalize: To insert in a line a network with complementary transmission characteristics to those of the line, so that when the loss or delay in the line and that in the equalizer are combined, the overall loss or delay is approximately equal at all frequencies.

network filter: Attenuates unwanted frequencies; a device for use on power or signal lines, specifically designed to pass only selected frequencies. The two basic types of filters are: active filters, those which require the application of power for the utilization of their filtering properties; and passive filters, those which use inductance-capacitance components and do not require the application of power for the utilization of their filtering properties.

network/guard system: A stand-alone system that enables users to connect, control, monitor, and communicate with networked personal computers. It integrates any direct-connect or dial-up device to a host, regardless of protocol or speed. Access to system and applications is secured through multilevel passwords. A network/-guard monitors, measures, and analyzes real-time data and historical network status. The system typically communicates with users by broadcast message or by direct, two-way conversation.

networking device modem: A range of networking devices entering the market include the metro modem. One type is a 9600 bits per second (bps) synchronous modem optimized for metropolitan applications. Based on digital signal processing, the device is auto-equalized and fully microprocessor controlled. Along with this device is a pocket-sized synchronous short-haul modem. This unit is ac-coupled to provide better protection against line surge voltages. It also has encoded signaling for better noise immunity.

networking microplexer: Combines the flexibility of switching with the economy of statistical multiplexing. Often, a large host-end channel capacity provides numerous local ports at central site. Integral port contention and switching permits more users to access a fewer number of ports. Some systems feature faulttolerance to eliminate catastrophic failures, and comprehensive diagnostics.

network modes: Five modes of computer network usage with important functional

differences can be identified: (a) remote job entry (jobs transferred only); (b) remote batch processing (jobs and data sets transferrd); (c) interactive consol (user controlled); (d) dynamic file access/transfer; and (e) load sharing (system automatically allocates jobs to resources).

network node: Performs a number of network internal functions. A node controls outgoing traffic on some or all of the channels connected to it through a channel allocation mechanism. If the node is a multiplexer, this function is performed by hardware that multiplexes the outgoing channels in either the frequency or time domain.

network noise: Noise caused by interaction of another signal with the signal under consideration.

network, private switching: A series of points interconnected by leased voice-grade telephone lines, with switching facilities or exchange operated by the customer.

network processor: Improves the efficiency of the network by permitting more sophisticated line control procedures, which may also facilitate recover from failure situation. Some of the functions previously performed by the main computer, or the front-end processor, may be delegated to the concentrator giving a more immediate response to the terminal.

network size: The number of nodes and distribution or actual location of those nodes. A network can support on the order of thirty to fifty nodes with a national, and possibly, international distribution.

network synthesis: Process of formulating a network with specific electrical requirements.

network system: A collection of individual communications networks, transmission systems, relay stations, tributary stations, and terminal equipment capable of interconnection and interoperation to form an integral whole. These individual components often serve common purposes, are compatible technically, employ common procedures, respond to some form of control, and operate in unison.

network-teletype: A system of points, interconnected by private telegraph channels, which provide hard copy and/or telegraphic coded (5-channel) punched paper tape at both sending and receiving points. Typically, up to 20 way-stations share send-receive time on a single circuit, and can exchange information without requiring action at a switching center. If two or more circuits are provided, a switching center is required to permit cross-circuit transmission. Such networks are available on a monthly rental plus one-time installation charge basis.

network topology: This can be centralized or distributed. Centralized networks, also called star networks, are those in which all nodes connect to a single node. This is a description of topology only and implies nothing about location of computing power, network control, or user distribution. The alternative topology is distributed where, in the limit, each node is connected to every other node, although the terminology is applied commonly to topologies approaching this full connectivity. There exists a third alternative which describes a certain condition of a distributed network. This is the ring configuration commonly used in describing a distributed computer system. Observing the topology a ring can be seen connecting the nodes of the network.

network virtual terminal (NVT): Permits the user to choose the type of terminal to be used at each location independently. The network translates the code, speed, and protocol of many terminal types into the NVT format. A user computer supporting this network virtual terminal will have the capability to handle a wide range of terminal types without the need for additional software. Consequently terminal users can access several systems from the same terminal, thereby increasing the utility of the terminal, and host computers will be able to handle more terminal types.

neural net: A unique function of memory and information processing necessary for a biological type of computer memory. It includes (a) random organization; (b) the distribution of memory traces through the entire system; (c) the simultaneous participation of any element in many memory traces; (d) no catastrophic failure; (e) implicit or response reinforcement memory; and (f) automatic response (no search and comparison would be needed).

neutral circuit: A teletypewriter circuit in which there is current in only one direction. The circuit is closed during the marking condition and open during the spacing condition.

neutral keying: Form of telegraph signal which has current either on or off in the circuit with "on" as mark, "off" as space.

neutral transmission: The technique which transmits teletypewriter signals, whereby a mark is represented by current on the line and a space is represented by the absence of current. By extension to tone signaling, neutral transmission is a method of signaling employing two signaling states, one of the states representing both a space condition and also the absence of any signaling.

neutral zone: An area in space or an interval of time in which a state of being other than the implementing state exists; e.g., a range of values in which no control action occurs, or a brief period between words when certain switching action takes place. (Similar to dead band.)

new input message queue: A group or a queue of new messages that are in the system and are waiting for processing. The main scheduling routine will scan them along with other queues and order them into processing.

new-line character (NL): A format effector that causes the printing or display position to be moved to the first position of the next printing or display line. Contrast with carriage return character.

new program language (NPL): The predecessor to programming language 1 (PL/1).

new sync: A feature of some data sets that allows for a rapid resynchronization during transition from one transmitter to another on a multipoint private-line data network.

New York Clearing House Association (NYCHA): The first banks to make use of an automated clearing-house at the New York Fed. In June 1971 these banks were linked to the New York Fed's clearing system via teletype terminals. The Fed Wire was tied in via high-speed computer communication lines through the Culpepper Switch; this linked the New York Fed to the other reserve banks, the Board of Governors and the Treasury Department. The system accomplishes same-day transfers of federal funds for banks to meet reserve requirements, electronically transfers government securities and provides end-of-day summary information relating to cash accounting and securities settlement. NYCHA operates the Clearing House Interbank Payments Systems (CHIPS), an automated clearing-house that has handled international accounts. See Clearing House Interbank Payments System, and automated clearing-house.

next-available register block: Address register of available blocks of core storage that are chained together for use by the line control computer, i.e., for the allocation of incoming information.

nexus: A connection or interconnection. A tie or link.

nickel delay line: A delay line utilizing the magnetic and/or magnetostrictive properties of nickel to delay a pulse for retardation or for data storage by circulation.

NIP: See nucleus initialization program.

nixie tube: A glow tube which converts a combination of electrical pulses including binary numbers, as a pattern of pulses, into visual numbers, i.e., the light is used to give a visual display of decimal numbers on computer terminals, panels of consoles, etc. variously showing the contents of registers, data in storage locations, or reading of various instruments or controls, and especially those important items which are subject to changes in rates to which many mechanical devices are not able to respond.

NL: See new-line character.

N-level address: An indirect address that specifies N level of addressing.

n-level logic: Pertaining to a collection of gates so connected that not more than n gates appear in series.

no address instruction: An instruction specifying an operation which the computer can perform without having to refer to its storage unit.

no-bit: The absence of a bit, pulse, or data.

no-charge time: That period of time for which there is no rental charge or cost for the equipment, generally as a result of a machine malfunction and the manufacturer's warranty.

node concentration: Combines inputs from a number of slower speed channels for transmission on a higher capacity outgoing channel in addition to performing the opposite data distribution function to the slower speed channels.

node switching: In some networks a node performs circuit or direct channel switching, directly connecting channels or derived subchannels to other channels terminating at the node. Control of this switching may be by a minicomputer at that node.

noise: 1. Random variations of one or more characteristics of any entity such as voltage, current, or data. 2. A random signal of known statistical properties of amplitude, distribution, and spectral density. 3. Loosely, any disturbance tending to interfere with the normal operation of a device or system.

noise digit: A digit, usually zero, produced during the normalizing of a floating-point number, and inserted during a left shift operation into the fixed point part.

noise factor: The ratio developed by dividing the difference between the number of documents retrieved and the number of relevant documents retrieved, i.e., a measure of the efficiency of the informational retrieval system. A zero would be optimum.

noise generator: A special device designed to generate a random signal of known value, considered normalized if its first digit is not zero.

noise immunity: A measure of the insensitivity of a logic circuit to triggering or reaction to spurious or undesirable electrical signals or noise, largely determined by the signal swing of the logic. Noise can be either of two directions, positive or negat1ve.

noise mode: A floating-point arithmetic procedure associated with normalization in which digits other than zero are introduced in the low-order positions during the left shift.

noise peak: A spurious signal of short duration that occurs during reproduction of magnetic tape, of a magnitude considerably in excess of the average peak value of the ordinary system noise.

noise ratio (NR): Noise power in a terminated filter or circuit divided by the signal power; expressed in decibels.

noise resistance: One for which the thermal noise would equal the actual noise signal present, usually in a specific frequency band.

noise-signal ratio: The ratio of the amount of signals conveying information to the amount of signals not conveying information.

noise source: The origin of any unwanted signal.

noise spike: See noise peak.

noise suppressor: Circuit which suppresses noise between usable channels when these are passed through during tuning. An automatic gain control which cuts out weak signals and levels out loud signals.

noise types: The two main forms of electrical noise are known as steady-state and impulse noise. Steadystate noise is known also as Gaussian noise, thermal noise, white noise, electron hiss grass (a radar term), and random noise. This is the background noise that is present on all electronic circuits. The data signal must be kept at a higher level than this noise after attenuation. Impulse noise is characterized by peaks of large amplitude and pulses of short duration, that is, pulse widths measured in milliseconds. Pulses of this duration have little or no effect on the human ear and will be heard merely as a click or crack without destroying voice intelligence. Impulse noise can block out data signals and is a significant source of errors in data. This is true especially with high-speed data transmission, where more bits are affected in a given time period.

noise weighting: Accomplished by using a filter with a specific amplitude frequency characteristic. It is designed to give numerical readings which approximate the amount of transmission impairment due to the noise, to an average listener, using a particular class of telephone subset. The noise weightings generally used were established by the agencies concerned with public telephone service and are based on characteristics of specific commercial telephone subsets, representing successive stages of technological development. The coding of commercial apparatus appears in the nomenclature of certain weightings. The same weighting nomenclature and units are used in the military versions as well as the commercial noise measuring sets.

noisy digit: A specific digit chosen to be inserted into the units position of a mantissa during leftshifting manipulation associated with the normalizing of various floating-point numbers.

noisy mode: See noise mode.

no job definition error: An error that occurs when the job definition control card cnnot be processed in a run.

nominal bandwidth: The maximum band of frequencies, inclusive of guard bands, assigned to a channel.

nominal (rated) speed: The maximum speed or data rate of a unit or facility which makes no allowance for necessary delaying functions such as checking, tabbing, etc.

nominative testing: Standards of performance established for the testing of both quantitative and qualitative system performance.

non-add key: Enters numbers that do not affect calculations; used for entering data and notations.

non-arithmetic shift: A shift in which the digits dropped off at one end of a word are returned at the other in a circular fashion.

non-blocking voice/data switching: A communications system providing simultaneous, two-way voice and data transmission. Configured with as many as 8192 ports, it allows all stations to be simultaneously engaged in voice conversations and data transmission without blocking calls or degrading performance.

non-charge non-machine fault time: Unproductive time due to errors other than those caused by the computer itself.

nonconductor: An electrical insulator in which there are few free electrons.

non-data input/output (I/O) operations control: Process which relates to I/O operation as differentiated or exclusive of data manipulation such as tape rewinding.

non-data operation: Any use of an input/-output device that does not involve the transfer of data.

non-data set clocking: A time base oscillator supplied by the business machine for regulating the bit rate of transmission. This is referred to by IBM as internal clocking and by the common carriers as external clocking.

nondestructive cursor: On a cathode-ray tube display device, a cursor that can be moved within a display surface without changing or destroying the data displayed on the screen. Contrast with destructive cursor.

nondestructive readout: 1. A storage area that cannot be erased and re-used, e.g., punched cards or perforated paper tape. 2. A reading process that does not destroy the data in the source.

non direction sensing incremental code: A series of pulses representing equal intervals of angle or equal increments of linear motion.

nonequivalence element: A specific logic element which has two binary input signals and only one output signal. The variance or variable represented by the output signal is the nonequivalence of the variable represented by the input signals, i.e. a two-input element whose output signal represents 1 when its input signals are different from each other.

non-erasable storage: A storage device whose information cannot be erased during the course of computation, e.g., punched-paper tape, and punched cards, and silvered or aluminized paper.

non-graphic character: A character that, when sent to a screen or printer, does not produce a printable character image.

Examples of non-graphic characters include the carriage return, tabs, line feed, etc. Same as control character.

non-interacting control system: A multi-element control system. Designed to avoid disturbances to other controlled variables due to the process input adjustments which are made for the purpose of controlling a particular process variable.

non-interactive system: An operating system designed not to permit computations to interact with the environment of a computer.

nonlinear code: A nonlinear operation such as multiplication by numbers or codes. For example, multiplying each number of a group by 3 is more complex than adding 3 to each number. The solution to a nonlinear operation must be found by solving nonlinear equations, a more formidable task than solving linear equations.

nonlinear distortion: Distortion dependent upon signal amplitude, e.g., compression, expansion.

nonlinearity: A relationship between the output and input which is not representable by a straight line. The output signal does not vary directly as the input signal but is also related to other operating parameters such as hysteresis or friction.

nonlinearity distortion: Distortion which occurs due to the transmission properties of a system being dependent upon the instantaneous magnitude transmitted signal.

nonlinear system: A system whose operation cannot be represented by a first order mathematical equation.

nonloaded lines: Cable pairs or transmission lines with no added inductive loading.

nonlocking: A process indicating any of various code extension characters which apply to and change the interpretation of just a specified number of characters.

nonlocking character shift: A control character that causes one (sometimes more) character following to shift to that of another total set of characters; i.e., to caps, or italics.

nonlocking key: Key or relay which returns to its unoperated condition when the hand is removed, or the current ceases, usually by the action of a spring which is extended on operation. The key is said to operate and restore, and the relay to make and release, or operate and deoperate or fall-off.

nonmapping mode: One in which virtual addresses are not transformed through a memory map (i.e. the virtual address is used as an actual address).

non-numeric: Any character or symbol other than a digit.

non-numerical data processing: Specific languages developed by symbol manipulation and used primarily as research tools rather than for production programming. Most have proved valuable in construction of compilers and in simulation of human problem solving. Other uses have been generalized: (a) verification of mathematical proofs, (b) pattern recognition, (c) information retrieval, (d) algebraic manipulation, (e) heuristic programming, and (f) exploration of new programming languages.

non-operable instruction: One whose only effect is to advance the instruction index counter. Often written as "continue." **nonperformance instruction:** An instruction requiring nonperformance of what normally might be executed, i.e., not to be executed. This instruction should not be confused with a NO OP or Do Nothing instruction.

nonpolarized return-to-zero recording: A technique of magnetization coding for a return-to-reference recording indicated by magnetization of specified levels and polarity.

non-preemptive scheduling: Refers to a type of scheduling in which jobs can use resources exclusively until they release them again.

nonprinting character: A byte value for which there is no corresponding character on a printing device. Most high speed printers have a maximum of 96 characters in their printable character set; however, an 8 bit byte may have any one of 256 possible values, 160 of which would not be printable.

nonprint instruction: An instruction that transmitted in a form which prevents the printing of a line or character.

nonprogrammed halt: An inadvertant machine stoppage, not due to the results of a programmed instruction, such as an automatic interrupt, manual intervention, machine malfunction, power failure, etc.

nonreproducing codes: Codes punched into master tapes that cause functions to be performed, but are not reproduced in the product tape.

nonresident portion (of a control program): Control program routines that are loaded into main storage as they are needed and can be overlaid after their completion.

nonresident routine: A routine that does not reside permanently in main memory.

nonresonant line: One which is matched perfectly and shows no standing-wave pattern.

non-return-to-change recording: A method of recording in which ones are represented by a specified condition of magnetization and zeros are represented by a different condition.

non-return-to-reference recording: Specific techniques designed to effect a non-return-to-zero recording.

non-return-to-zero change recording: A special method of recording developed to use 0s and 1s as represented by two specified but different conditions of magnetization.

non-return-to-zero mark recording (NR-ZC): A recording device or process in which a change on the condition of magnetization represents a 1, the absence of such a change indicates a 0.

non-return-to-zero (NRZ): A mode of recording in which each state of the medium corresponds to one binary state. In the mode, the state of the recording medium changes when the information changes from 1 to 0 or from 0 to 1. Note: NRZ modified is also often called NRZ.

non-return-to-zero recording: A recording process to develop a reference condition as provided by a change between the states of magnetization representing 0 and 1.

nonreusable: The attribute that indicates that the same copy of a routine cannot be used by another task.

nonscheduled downtime: The idle machine time during which the hardware is being repaired because of failures or unforeseen circumstances other than normal servicing or maintenance time. Usually, it is expressed as a percent of total available time.

nonscheduled-maintenance time: The time (during regular working hours) between failure discovery and equipment operation.

nonsequential computer: The address of the next instruction is contained in the prior instruction. Contrasted with sequential computer.

nonsimultaneous transmission: Transmission in only one direction at a time.

nonspecific volume request: In job control language (JCL), a request that allows the system to select suitable volumes.

nonstandard labels: Labels that do not conform to American National Standard label conventions.

nonstop operation protection: Ensures against program hold-ups due to infinite indirect address loops or execute instruction loops.

nonswitched line: A connection between a remote terminal and a computer that does not have to be established by dialing.

non-temporary data set: A data set that exists after the job that created it terminates.

nonvolatile storage: A storage medium which retains information in the absence of power and which may be made available upon restoration of power, e.g., magnetic tapes, cores, drums and disks.

NO OP: An instruction commanding the computer to do nothing, except to proceed to the next instruction in sequence.

no-operation memory protect: A special procedure developed to protect the contents of specific sections of storage from alteration by inhibiting the execution of any type of memory modification instruction upon detection of the presence of a guard bit associated with the accessed memory location. Such instructions which access protected memory are most often executed as a no operation or a special violation program interrupt is generated.

NOR circuit: A circuit that has an output only when all inputs are down.

normal binary: 1. Numbering system based on 2s rather than 10s which uses only the digits 0 and 1 when written. 2. A characteristic, property, or condition in which there are but two possible alternatives; e.g., the binary number system using 2 as its base and using only the digits zero (0) and one (1).

normal direction flow: A flow in a direction from left to right or top to bottom on a flowchart.

normalization routine: A floating-point arithmetic operation related to normalization of numerals in which digits other than zero are developed in the low order; i.e., less significant positions during the left shift.

normalization signal: A generation, or a restoration, of signals which comply with specified requirements for amplitude, shape, and timing, i.e., such signals are often generated from another signal, and such requirements are most often conventions or rules of specific computers, with little consistency among a great many systems.

normalized floating control: The bit, in the program status doubleword, that indicates whether (if 0) or not (if 1) the result of a floating-point operation is to be normalized.

normalized form: A special form taken by a floatingpoint number which has been adjusted so that its mantissa lies in a specified range.

normalizing pulse: A generation of signals which comply with specified requirements for amplitude, shape, and timing.

normally closed circuit: A pair of electrical contacts which usually complete the circuit unless positioned to do otherwise. Contrasts with normally open circuit.

normally closed contacts: Specific pairs of contacts on relays which are open only when the relay coil is energized.

normally open circuit: A pair of electrical contacts which usually do not complete the circuit unless positioned so as to complete the circuit.

normally open contacts: Specific pairs of contacts on relays that are closed only when the relay coil is energized.

normal memory: A set of main memory locations which are contiguous and specifically located for storage of programs, data, data sets, and most often organized in a logical or subject order or sequence. If some programs are larger than main memory, overlays to auxiliary memory may be used.

normal mode interference: A distinct form or type of interference which appears between measuring circuit terminals.

normal mode rejection: The capability of a circuit to discriminate against normal mode voltage, most often expressed as a ratio or in decibels.

normal mode voltage: Considered to be an extraneous voltage as induced across the circuit path (traverse mode voltage).

normal operating conditions: Relating to the design of various devices, that range of operating conditions within which the unit is to operate and under which operating influences are stated.

normal state: The condition of operation wherein the instructions are concerned with the conventional aspects of computation (adding, subtracting, information transfer, etc.) The detection of an exceptional condition (interrupt) that occurs while in this state suspends operation in this state and processing continues in control state.

NOT: A logic operator having the property that if P is a logic quantity then the quantity NOT P assumes values as defined in the following table:

P	NOT P
0	1
1	0

The NOT operator is represented in electrical notation by an overline, e.g., P, and in FORTRAN by a minus sign in a Boolean expression.

NOT AND: Same as NAND.

notation: The act, process, or method of representing facts or quantities by a system or set of marks, signs, figures, or characters.

not-busy interrupt: A response sent from a device to the computer if the device is not busy.

NOT IF-THEN: A logic operator possessing the property that if A is a statement and B is a statement, then NOT (if A then B) is true if A is true and B is false, false if A is false and B is true, and false if both statements are true.

NOT IF-THEN gate: Same as A AND NOT B gate and B AND NOT A gate.

nought output: That particular output from a magnetic cell in the zero condition, e.g. when a read pulse is supplied.

N + 1: A formula which refers to the Federal Communications Commission (FCC) requirements that provide for expansion of channel capacity for non-broadcast use. If the governmental, educational, public access and leased channels are in use 80 percent of the weekdays for 80 percent of the time during any three-hour period for six consecutive weeks, the system operator must expand the system's channel capacity within six months.

n-plus-one address instruction: A multiple-address instruction of which one address specifies the location of the next instruction of the normal sequence to be executed.

N-P-N: A transistor composed of two N-type crystals separated by a P-type.

NRZC: See non-return-to-zero mark recording.

nsec: See nanosecond.

n symbol: An arbitrary or unspecified real number which may be restricted to integral or rational values either by definition or context.

n-tuple: A collection of n elements, usually ordered, e.g., X1, X2,..., XN.

N-type: 1. Various semiconductor crystals doped to provide excess electrons. 2. A symbol in flowcharting depicting several options.

N-type conductivity: In a semiconductor, conductivity due to electron movement.

N-type semiconductor: A semiconducting crystal material that has been doped with minute amounts of an impurity which will produce donor-type centers of electrons in the crystal lattice structure. Because electrons are negative particles, the material is called N-type, and conduction is primarily by electrons as the majority carrier of electric current.

nucleus initialization program (NIP): The program that initializes the resident control program; it allows the operator to request last minute changes to certain options specified during system generation.

NUL: See null character.

null character (NUL): A control character that serves to accomplish media fill or time fill. Null characters may be inserted into or removed from, a sequence of characters without affecting the meaning of the sequence, but control of equipment or the format may be affected.

null character string: Same as null string.

null cycle: The time necessary to cycle through a program without introducing data. This establishes the lower bound for program processing time.

null instruction: One which performs no action during the operation of a program. Occasionally used to provide for future changes to the program, but more often used to complete a set of instructions where the machine code system requires instructions to be written in complete groups.

null representation: An empty or blank representation, for example, on a paper tape which controls a printer, a null representation does not cause movement of the printing position, as does a space character.

null set: A logic or set theory term, i.e., a set which contains no members; an empty set.

null statement: A job control statement used to mark the end of a job's control statements and data.

null string: An empty string.

null suppression: The bypassing of all null characters in order to reduce the amount of data to be transmitted. Same as data compaction.

number cruncher: Machines that have great computational power, where the stress is on the ability to handle large figures rather than to process large amounts of data in the form of invoices, etc.

number sequence: A number assigned to an item to indicate the relative position in a series of related items.

number system: A defined set of numbers.

numeral: A digit, or digits, normally used to represent a number.

numeral, decimal: A number written in the notation system with a radix of 10, which is positional and has the digits 0 through 9.

numeration system: A system for the representation of numbers, e.g., the decimal system, the roman numeral system, the binary system.

numerator: In a fraction, the number which is understood to be divided by the other.

numeric: In the COBOL system, having a numeric value.

numerical: Composed of or having to do with numbers.

numerical analysis: The study of methods of obtaining useful quantitative solutions to mathematical problems, whether or not an analytic solution exists, and the study of the errors and bounds on errors in obtaining such solutions.

numerical aperture: The measure of the degree of light acceptance of a fibre defined by $NA = (N\ core^2 - N\ cladding^2)^{1/2}$, where N is the refractive index.

numerical code: A restrictive type of code which has a character set consisting of digits only.

numerical data: Data in which information is expressed by a set of numbers or symbols that can only assume discrete values or configurations.

numerical forms file: A file containing copies of all forms used in any activity, filed in straight numerical sequence. A separate folder is maintained for each form and may also contain specifications, order history, correspondence, and design history.

numerically controlled machine tools: Computer controlled machinery in manufacturing.

numerical system: A system of encoding numbers into numerals and numerals into numbers as 7.26×10^{50} or Roman numeral XXIV or even $9\frac{3}{4}$.

numeric arrangement: To arrange in ascending order or sequence 1, 2, 3, 4, and so on.

numeric atomic symbol: In list processing languages, decimal integers, octal integers, or floating-point numbers.

numeric character: A single graphic selected from the coded character set consisting of the decimal digits and other selected symbols up to a total of 16, which can be represented by a 4-bit binary code.

numeric code: The code used to represent letters and numbers inside a computer. Examples of numeric codes are ASCII, binary coded decimal (BCD), extended binary coded decimal interchange code (EBCDIC), and EXCESS-3. Each of these codes uses a different binary code to encode numbers and letters.

numeric coding: Coding which uses digits only to represent data and instructions.

numeric data: Data represented exclusively by numerals and special characters.

numeric punching: Data represented by the punching of single holes in each column of a field on a punched card. For example, alphabetic characters and other symbols may be punched as two holes per column.

numeric shift: A control for selecting the numeric character set in an alphanumeric keyboard-printer.

numeric word: A word composed exclusively of characters from a numeric code.

Nyquist interval: A special interval of time occupied by each code element when a communications channel is being used at the Nyquist rate.

Nyquist limit (or rate): Maximum rate of transmitting pulse signals through a system. If B is the effective bandwidth in hertz (Hz), then 2B is the maximum number of code elements (bands) per sec which can be received with certainty, 1/2B is known as the Nyquist interval.

O

O and M analysts: Analysts concerned in the broad field of an organization's financial dealings.

object: An energy or information sink within a system.

object code: Output from a compiler or assembler which is itself executable machine code or is suitable for processing to produce executable machine code.

objective function: An objective function of the independent variable function whose maximum or minimum value is sought as an optimization problem.

object language: A language which is the output of an automatic coding routine. Usually object language and machine language are the same, however, a series of steps in an automatic coding system may involve the object language of one step serving as a source language for the next step and so forth.

object machine: The computer on which the object program is to be executed.

object module: The output of a single execution of an assembler or compiler, which constitutes input to a linkage editor. An object module consists of one or more control sections in relocatable, though not executable, form and an associated control dictionary.

object module library: A partitioned data set used to store and retrieve object modules. See also load module library.

object program: 1. A set of machine language instructions for the solution of a problem, obtained as the end result of a compilation process. It is generated from the source program. 2. The absolute coding output by a processor program.

OCR: See optical character recognition (OCR).

octal: 1. Eight; usually describing a number system of base or radix eight, e.g., in octal notation, octal 214 is 2 times 64, plus 1 times 8, plus 4 times 1, and equals decimal 140. Octal 214 in binary-coded octal is represented as 010, 001, 100, octal 214, as a straight binary number is written 10001100. Note that binarycoded octal and straight binary differ only in the use of commas. In the example shown, the initial zero in the straight binary is dropped. 2. The number base eight. 3. Any set of exactly eight characteristics.

octal digit: A digit which is a member of the 8 digits of the octal system which consists of numerals 0 through 7, in a positional notation system with a radix of 8.

octal tube: A tube with a standard eight-pin base.

octaves: A specific area or array of data segregated from the other area.

octonary signaling: A communications mode in which information is passed by the presence and absence or plus and minus variation of eight discrete levels of one parameter of the signaling medium.

odd/even interleaving: In the splitting of memory into several sections and independent paths, addresses are in alternate sections. This allows even further segmenting than normal memory interleaving of the readwrite memory cycle.

odd/parity check: A check by summation in which the binary digits, in a character or word, are added, and the sum checked against a single, previously computed parity digit; i.e., a check tests whether the number of ones in a word is odd or even.

off emergency: The particular control switch on most control panels or consoles which disconnects all power from the computer system.

Office of Telecommunications Policy (OTP): Division of the Executive Office of the President staff that advises the Executive Branch on communications policy, studies policy questions, and develops legislative proposals.

off-line: Equipment or devices not under direct control of the central processing unit; also terminal equipment not connected to a transmission line.

off-line (adjective): Operation of input/-output and other devices not under direct computer control, most commonly used to designate the transfer of information between magnetic tapes and other input/-output media.

off-line computer: 1. Equipment or programs which are not under the direct control of a central processor. 2. A computer which is not actively monitoring or controlling a process or operation. 3. A computer operation completed while the computer is not monitoring or controlling a process or operation.

off-line memory: Any memory medium capable of being stored remotely from the computer, which can be read by the computer when placed into a suitable reading device.

off-line mode: Indicates that the devices are not hooked up together.

off-line remote batch: The preparation of punched cards or magnetic tapes from source documents; the transmission of data to produce duplicate punched cards or magnetic tapes at the computer site. In an on-line system, data is fed directly into the

host computer though some form of communications adapter.

off-line storage: Storage not under control of the central processing unit.

off-line system: In teleprocessing, a system in which human operations are required between the original recording functions and the ultimate data processing function. This inlcudes conversion operations as well as the necessary loading and unloading operations incident to the use of point-to-point or data-gathering systems.

off-premise standby equipment: A duplicate set of equipment available at another location ready to substitute.

off-punch: A punch not correctly positioned in a column of a card.

offset deviation: A deviation from steady-state of the controlled variable when the set point is fixed. Such an offset resulting from a no-load to a full-load change (or other specified limits) is often called "droop" or "load regulation."

offset duplicating machine: A duplicating machine in which an ink image on the master is transferred to a rotating roller, and from there is "offset" onto the copy paper.

offset stacker: A card stacker which can stack cards selectively under machine control so that they protrude from the balance of the deck to give physical identification.

off-the-shelf: 1. Production items available from current stock that do not need to be either newly purchased or immediately manufactured. 2. Computer software equipment used by customers with little or no adaptation, thereby saving them from the time and expense of developing their own software or equipment.

Ohm's law: A law, applicable only to electric components carrying direct current, which states that in metallic conductors the resistance is independent of the current at a constant temperature and zero magnetic field.

Olsen memory: A specific fixed or permanent storage device designed to store coded data in the form of an array of cores and wires. The wiring holds the information rather than the cores.

OLTEP: See on-line test executive program.

omission factor: In information retrieval (IR), the ratio obtained in dividing the number of nonretrieved relevant documents by the total number of relevant documents in the file. Ideally, the omission factor should be close to zero, as it is a measure of the efficiency of the system.

omnidirectional antenna: One receiving or transmitting equally in all directions in the horizontal plane, with little effect outside.

on-call circuit: A circuit activated when asked for by the user.

on-demand system: A system from which information or service is available at the time of requiest.

one-address: Single address; a system of machine instruction such that each complete instruction explicitly describes one operation and one storage location.

one-address instruction: An instruction consisting of an operation and exactly one address. The instruction code of a single-address computer may include both zero and multi-address instructions as special cases.

one condition: In magnetic cells, the state which represents one.

one-core-per-bit storage: A storage unit in which each magnetic cell uses N cores when N stands for the appropriate figure, as one-core-per-bit or two-core-perbit, etc.

one digit adder: A logic element which has two input channels to which signals may be applied, which represent two input digits, the addend and the augend. The two output channels from which the signals may emerge are those which represent the sum and carry digit.

one element: An electrical gate or mechanical device which implements the logical OR operator. An input signal occurs whenever there are one or more inputs on a multichannel input. An OR gate performs the function of the logical "inclusive OR" operator.

one-for-one: An assembly routine in which one source language instruction is converted to one machine language instruction.

one-for-one translation: Conversion of one source language instruction to one machine language instruction.

one-level address: Same as direct address.

one-level storage: A concept which treats all on-line storage as having one level of appearance to a user; a technique which makes all on-line storage appear as main storage.

one output signal: The output of a magnetic cell in the one condition when a read pulse is supplied.

one output to partial output ratio: A special ratio either of the magnitude or the instantaneous amplitude at some specified time, of a one output signal to a partial one output signal.

one-plus-one instruction: A computer instruction containing two addresses.

one-quadrant multiplier: A multiplier in which operation is restricted to a single sign of both input variables.

one's complement: That binary bit which, when added to 1 or 0, equals 1. Same as the inverse binary state of any given bit.

one state: The electronic condition of a major storage position in which the direction of magnetic force has been determined arbitrarily as being the specific direction for that state.

one-to-zero ratio: 1. The ratio of either the maximum amplitude, or the instantaneous amplitude at some specified time, of a one output signal to a zero output signal. 2. The ratio of a 1 output to the 0 output.

one-way channel: A specific channel that permits transmission in one direction.

one-way trunk: A trunk between central exchanges where traffic can originate at only one end.

on-line: Equipment or devices in direct interactive communication with the central processing unit. May also be used to describe terminal equipment connected to a transmission line.

on-line access scheduling: The procedure in a timeshared system for scheduling algorithms.

on-line computer: A computer which is actively monitoring or controlling a process or operation.

on-line data processing: Data processing in which all changes to relevant records and accounts are made at the time that each transaction or event occurs. The process usually requires random access storage.

on-line data reduction: The processing of information as rapidly as the information is received by the computing system or as rapidly as it is generated by the source.

on-line debugging: The act of debugging a program while time-sharing its execution with an on-line process program. On-line debugging is accomplished in such a way that any attempt by the "slave" program undergoing debugging to interfere with the operation of the process program will be detected and inhibited.

on-line diagnostics: The running of diagnostics on a system while it is on-line but off-peak to save time and to take corrective action without closing down the system.

on-line disk file: Complements the powerful advanced systems concept of the computer. With its head-per track design, the disk file provides all-electronic access to any record throughout the file in an average of 20 milliseconds. File organization, programming, and use are simplified because access is entirely by electronic switching, with no moving arms, card drops, or the like. Each record segment is available regardless of physical location on the disks. Multiple segments can be transferred with a single instruction. Module size is four disks totalling 9.6 million alphanumeric characters of information capacity. Up to 100 of these modules may be used with the computer, effectively extending the memory of the computer system by almost a billion characters. Transfer rate is 100,000 characters per second (in some systems).

on-line equipment: Equipment which is in direct communication with a switching center or distant terminal.

on-line file (central): A large data file available to computer terminal users (in a central computer).

on-line implicit calculations: Process variables which cannot be measured directly but can be calculated continuously from implicit relationships by relatively simple analog circuits. Calculated quantities, such as composition or the variance of a key variable, are helpful as operator guides or may even be used as inputs to conventional control systems.

on-line memory: A memory medium used as a nonremovable part of a computer system.

on-line processing: Direct and immediate access to the computer system via terminal devices. Information and instructions may be inputted via a terminal, processing by the computer is then begun immediately, and a response is received as soon as possible, often within seconds. Users of on-line devices usually process individual transactions which require quick responses. Contrasts with batch processing.

on-line storage: Storage devices under the direct control of a computing system.

on-line system: 1. A system which eliminates the need for human intervention between source recording and the ultimate processing by a computer. 2. A system in which the input enters a computer from the point of origin and the output goes directly to where it is used.

on-line test executive program (OLTEP):   A facility that controls activities and provides communication with the operator. This program is part of a set of programs that can be used to test input/-output devices, control units and channels concurrently with the execution of programs.

on-line test system (OLTS):   A system that allows a user to test input/output (I/O) devices concurrently with execution of programs. Tests may run to diagnose I/O errors, verify repairs and engineering changes, or to periodically check devices.

on/off controller: A specific controller (multiposition) which has two discrete values of output, i.e., fully on, or fully off.

on/off keying: Keying in which the output from a source is transmitted and suppressed alternately to form signals.

onomasticon: A vocabulary of proper or special names, e.g., a list of titles, chemical compounds, companies, executives, etc.

on-the-line hit: A momentary open circuit on a teletypewriter loop.

OP code: Same as operation code, i.e., a command to a computer.

open: A condition in which conductors are separated so that current cannot pass.

open circuit: Nondelivery of current from a source then said to be not loaded. Constant-current sources, e.g., pentode output valves, must be loaded, or destructive high voltages can result even with normal drive.

open-circuit impedance: Input or driving impedance of a line or network when the far end is free, opencircuited, not grounded or loaded.

open-circuit signaling: When there is no current while the circuit is in the idle condition.

open code: In assembler programming, that portion of a source module that lies outside of and after any source macro definitions that may be specified.

open-ended: The quality by which the addition of new terms, subject headings, or classifications does not disturb the preexisting system.

opening a file: Identifying a file and checking the header label against details furnished in the user's program to insure that the file can be utilized for the purpose defined by the program.

open loop: 1. Pertaining to a control system in which there is no self correcting action for misses of the desired operational condition, as there is in a closed loop system. 2. A family of automatic control units, one of which may be a computer, linked together manually by operator action.

open-loop control: An operation when computerevaluated control action is applied by an operator. See open loop.

open-loop control system: A special control system in which the output variable is controlled directly by the system input, i.e., without feedback.

open-loop gain: A calculated ratio of the change in the return signal to the change in its corresponding error signal at a specified frequency.

open-loop system: A control system that has no means of comparing the output with the input for control purposes.

open orders: The items or procedures on order, but not yet delivered to inventory or accomplished.

open routine: A routine which can be inserted directly into a larger routine without a linkage or calling sequence.

open running: A teletypewriter connected to an openline or a line without battery. The teletypewriter receiver appears to be running, as the type hammer continually strikes the type box, but does not move across the page.

open shop: The operation of a computer facility where computer programming, coding and operation can be performed by any qualified employee of the organization, not necessarily by the personnel of the computing center itself and where the programmer may assist in or oversee the running of his program on the computer.

open subroutine: A subroutine inserted directly into the linear operational sequence, not entered by a jump. This subroutine must be recopied at each point that it is needed in a routine.

open-wire line: A pole line whose conductors are principally in the form of open wire.

operand: A quantity entering or arising in an instruction. An operand may be an argument, a result, a parameter, or an indication of the location of the next instruction, as opposed to the operation code or symbol itself. It may even be the address portion of an instruction.

operand call syllable: A syllable which specifies that an operand be brought to the stack, either directly from the program reference table or indirectly by means of a descriptor.

operand sum: Automatically sums first factors of sequence multiplication or division problems. Used when obtaining average unit price and standard deviation.

operate: In an analog computer, the computer control state in which input signals are connected to all appropriate computing elements to generate the solution.

operating conditions: Conditions to which devices are subjected, e.g., ambient temperature, ambient pressure, and vibration.

operating conditions, reference: A particular range of operating conditions of a device, within which operating influences are negligible, i.e., the range is usually narrow and the conditions under which reference performance is stated and the base from which the values of operating influences are determined.

operating instructions: A step-by-step description of the activities to be performed by an operator. This is most often provided by a programmer or systems analyst as part of the program documentation.

operating ratio: The ratio of the number of hours of correct machine operation to the total hours of scheduled operation, e.g., on a 168-hour week scheduled operation, if 12 hours of preventive maintenance are required and 4.8 hours of unscheduled downtime occurs, then the operating ratio is (168-16.8)/168, which is equivalent to a 90 percent operating ratio.

operating system (OS):   An integrated collection of service routines for supervising the sequencing of programs by a computer. Operating systems may perform debugging, input-output, accounting, compilation, and storage assignment tasks. Synonymous with monitor system and executive system.

operating time: The calculated part of any available time during which the hardware is operating and yielding results for which there is a high confidence level of correctness.

operation: 1. The action specified by a single computer instruction or pseudo-instruction. 2. An arithmetical, logical, or transferal unit of a problem, usually executed under the direction of a subroutine.

operational: The status of a computer or program when it has been running correctly, using line data, for some time.

operational amplifier: Combines functions of amplification and performance of operations. Operational amplifiers are often summing amplifiers, analog adders, or sign reversing amplifiers.

operational character: Characters used as code elements to initiate, modify, or stop a control operation. Characters may be used, for example, to control the carriage return, etc.

operational instruction halt: An instruction that can stop the computer either before or after the halt instruction is obeyed, depending on the governing criterion.

operational programs: The application program, the processor, and the programs that do the work as against the supervisory program (the staff) and the service program (maintenance).

operational relay: A relay that may be driven from one position or state to another by an operational amplifier or a relay amplifier.

operational-stop instruction: An instruction that can stop the computer either before or after the halt instruction is obeyed, depending on the governing criterion.

operational-use time: The time in which equipment is in actual use, such as production time, incidental time, development time (program), etc.

operation code field: The portion of an instruction word that contains the operation code.

operation control: An action that affects the recording, processing, transmission or interpretation of data, e.g., starting or stopping a process, carriage return, font change, rewind and end of transmission. Same as control function.

operation cycle: Relates specifically to that portion of a machine cycle during which the actual execution of the instruction takes place. Some operations (divide, multiply) may need a large number of these operation cycles to complete the operation, and the normal instruction/operation alternation will be held up during this time. Same as execution cycle.

operation decoder: A device that selects one or more control channels according to the operation part of a machine instruction.

operation field: The second field of a map symbolic instruction, punched-in card columns 8-14. It contains the instruction mnemonic, pseudo-operation, or macro operation code of the instruction. An asterisk may follow a machine code to indicate indirect addressing.

operation (OP) code: That part of an instruction designating the operation to be performed.

operation overhead: See housekeeping.

operations manual: Contains instructions and specifications for a given application. Typically includes components of operators' manual, programmer reference manual, and a log section.

operations research: The use of the scientific method to provide criteria for decisions concerning the actions of people, machines, and other resources in a system involving repeatable operations.

operations research (OR) dynamic programming: A procedure for optimization of a multistage problem solution wherein a number of decisions are available at each stage of the process.

operation, storage: Data movement within storage from one location to another.

operative limits: A calculated range of operating conditions to which a device may be subjected without permanent impairment of operating characteristics. Most often such performance characteristics will not be stated in the region between the limits of normal operating conditions and operative limits.

operator: A symbol which represents an operation to be performed on one or more operands.

operator command: An instruction issued to the control program through a console unit which causes requested information to be developed, new operations to be initiated, regular operations to be altered, or existing operations to be terminated.

operator console: A particular device or part of the mainframe which enables the operator to communicate with the computer, i.e., it is used to enter data or information, to request and display stored data, to actuate various preprogrammed command routines, etc. (in some systems).

operator control: A central control console provides supervision of the computer system. Through the console, the operator can control the processor and peripheral units, observe, and monitor processing functions. A console typewriter provides direct communication with the processor memory.

operator control panel: Contains all the switches and indicators for the operation of the central processor. Bit-by-bit register display and manual entry into the registers are provided by convenient indicator pushbuttons. The control panel is used primarily for initial set-up prior to a program run or for debugging purposes, rather than to exercise control over a running operation.

operator control station: Under telecommunications access method (TCAM), any station that is eligible to enter operator commands.

operator indicators: The displayed lights (on the console of the computer) showing indicator conditions .

operator intervention section: That portion of the control equipment in which operators can intervene in normal programming operations on control.

operator message: A message from the operating system or a problem program directing the operator to perform a specific function, such as mounting a tape reel, or informing him of specific conditions within the system, such as an error condition.

operator monitor: An individual who initiates and monitors either the operation of a computer or of a process.

operators: The characters that designate mathematical or logical operations, such as +, -, etc.

operator unit console: In some systems, that particular device or part of the mainframe which enables the operator to communicate with the computer, i.e, it is used to enter data or information, to request and display stored data, to actuate various preprogrammed command routines, etc.

optical cement: A permanent and transparent adhesive, usually epoxy or methacrylate, capable of handling extreme temperatures.

optical character (OCR) background reflectance: An optical character recognition term related to the reflectance of the background of a document surface within the area reserved for printing (clear band) as compared to a reference standard.

optical character (OCR) mark matching: A method employed in optical character recognition to correlate or match a specimen character and each of a set of masks representing the characters to be recognized, i.e., the characters are registered deliberately on the reference masks and no allowance is made for character misregistration. Such types are: (a) holistic masks (exact); (b) peephole masks (more lenient but still exacting); and (c) weighted masks (probability assignments).

optical character (OCR) photocell matrix: A device capable of projecting an input onto a fixed two-dimensional array of photocells to develop a simultaneous display of the character's horizontal and vertical components. The time necessary to scan the character is related to the response time of the photocells themselves.

optical character recognition (OCR): The machine recognition by machines of printed or written characters based on inputs from photoelectric transducers. Contrast with magnetic ink character recognition.

optical character recognition technology (OCRT): Converts printed characters to machine-compatible language for storage on the system's magnetic medium.

optical document reader: See optical scanner.

optical fiber: A small transparent filament that guides energy in the form of visible light or infrared energy. The fiber consists of an inner transparent silica core and an outer transparent material called cladding. Light is guided through the core by repeated reflections at the interface between the core and the cladding. These reflections occur because of the difference between the core's high refractive index and the cladding's low refractive index. Because of this relationship between the refractive indices of both media, total internal reflection occurs. Optic fibers are used in the communications industry for data transmission in areas where electromagnetic interference (EMI) is not allowed, or where higher security is needed, as well as in many other applications.

optical incremental display: A powerful new general purpose incremental cathode-ray tube diaplay which permits rapid conversion of digital computer data into graphic and tabular form. Its combined capabilities offer the user an unusual degree of versatility and accuracy.

optical journal reader: A specific optical-reader that can provide input to a computer from journal tapes that can be output from adding machines, cash registers, etc.

optical mark page reader: Can be attached to a system for direct reading of marks made by an ordinary lead pencil in specified positions on 8½ by 11 inch sheets of paper. The sheets can be read at a maximum rate of 2000 per hour, or one each 1.8 seconds. The reader is attached to the multiplexer channel and operation is in the multiplex mode. Applications for the reader are in payroll, order entry, accounts payable, inventory control, sales analysis, general ledger work, and many other phases of business, government, and institutions.

optical reader: A device that reads hand-written or machine printed symbols into a computing system.

optical scanner: A special optical device which scans patterns of incident light and generates analog/digital signals which are functions of the incident light synchronized with the scan, the primary purpose being to generate or "read" digital representations of printed or written data.

optical scanning: A technique for machine recognition of characters by their images.

optical type font: Developed as a medium that could be read by both people and machines—a major advance in simplifying the creation of input for data processing systems. As the salesperson or machine operator records the original entry on an adding machine, accounting machine, or cash register, the information is printed on the journal tape in the stylized font that can be read by the optical reader. The optical reader can operate on-line with the computer for immediate processing of reports. The reader can also operate off-line—converting the journal-tape information into punched paper tape.

optical waveguide: Any material structure capable of guiding radiation along a path parallel to its axis containing the light within its boundaries or adjacent to its surface.

optimization: See linear optimization.

optimize: To arrange the instructions or data in storage so that a minimum amount of machine time is spent for access when instructions or data are called out.

optimizing control action: Various control actions which automatically seek and maintain the most advantageous value of a specified variable, instead of maintaining it at one set value.

optimum code: A computer code which is particularly efficient with regard to a particular aspect, i.e., minimum time of execution, minimum or efficient use of storage space, and minimum coding time.

optimum merging patterns: The method of determining a sequence in which specific sorted tapes in a file should be processed so as to minimize the total number of merge passes required to create a single file of sequenced records.

optimum programming: Constructing a program so that the time required to obtain both data and instructions out of memory is at a minimum. This is significant particularly in computers with magnetic drum memories.

optional stop: A miscellaneous function command similar to a program stop except that the control ignores the command unless the operator has actuated a manual selection previously to validate the command.

OR: A logical operator having the property that if P and Q are logic quantities then the quantity "P OR Q" assumes values as defined by the following table:

P	Q	P OR Q
0	0	0
0	1	1
1	0	1
1	1	1

The OR operator is represented in both electrical and FORTRAN terminology by a "+," i.e., P + Q.

OR circuit: An electrical gate or mechanical device which implements the logical OR operator. An output signal occurs whenever there are one or more inputs on a multichannel input. An OR gate performs the function of the logical "inclusive OR operation." order: 1. A defined successive arrangement of elements or events. 2. To sequence or arrange in a series. 3. The weight or significance assigned to a digit position in a number.

order: 1. A defined successive arrangement of elements or events. 2. To sequence or arrange in a series. 3. The weight or significance assigned to a digit position in a numgber.

order block: A group of computer words or a record being transferred out of the equipment; a section of storage reserved to handle each such outlet.

order fulfillment: The delivery of items and billing of customers.

ordering bias: The degree to which a set of data departs from random distribution. An ordering bias will increase or decrease the effort necessary to order a set of data from the effort anticipated for random distribution.

orderly close-down: The stopping of the system in such a way that ensures an orderly restart and no destruction of messages. When a system is forced to stop, an orderly close-down provides that all records are updated that should be updated and that no records are erroneously updated again when the restart is made. Furthermore, all incoming and outgoing transmissions are completed, with a message sent to the terminals which notifies the operators of the close-down.

order of merge: The number of files that can be combined into a consolidated file during a merging operation.

ordinary binary: Expression of binary numerals in a system of positional notation in which each successive digit position is weighted by a factor of two times the weight of the prior position. An example: 1011 binary represents: $1 \times 2^3 + 0 \times 2^2 + 1 \times 2^1 + 1 \times 2^0 = 11$, i.e., eleven.

ordinary symbol: In assembler programming, a symbol that represents an assembly-time value when used in the name or operand field of an instruction in the assembler language. Ordinary symbols are also used to represent operation codes for assembler language instructions.

ordinate: Vertical or Y distance on a graph.

OR ELSE logic: A logical operator which has the property that if P and Q are two statements, then the statement (P or else Q) is true or false. The OR-ELSE operator is represented by an inverted vee. This operator is the same as EITHER/OR.

OR gate: Same as OR circuit.

orientation ratio: The ratio of the residual flux density in the orientation direction to the residual flux density perpendicular to the orientation direction. The orientation ratio of conventional tapes is typically about 1.7.

origin: In coding, the absolute memory address of the first location of a program or program segment.

original document: The document, initially used by a data processing system, that supplies the basic data to be input to the data processing system. Many resulting errors are attributed to errors in the source document.

OR NOT gate: Same as A OR NOT B gate and B OR NOT A gate.

OS: See operating system.

oscilloscope: An instrument for showing visually the changes in a varying current or voltage.

oscilloscope tube: A cathode-ray tube (CRT) used to display waveshapes and forms, most often as part of research or laboratory instrument measuring and checking.

outconnector: In flowcharting, a connector that indicates a point at which a flowline is broken for continuation at another point.

outer macroinstruction: In assembler programming, a macroinstruction that is specified in open code. Contrast with inner macroinstruction.

outgoing group: Under telecommunications access method (TCAM), the portion of the message handler designed to handle messages sent from the message control program to any of the lines, line groups, or application programs.

outline input: When the input device transmits data directly to, and under the control of, the control processing unit.

out-of-band signaling: Signaling which utilizes frequencies outside the intelligence band.

out-of-line coding: A portion of coding stored away from the main path of a routine.

out-of-service time: The time a machine is not used due to a system failure.

output: Information transferred from the internal storage of a computer to output devices or external storage.

output block: 1. A block of computer words considered as a unit and intended or destined to be transferred from an internal storage medium to an external destination. 2. A section of internal storage reserved for storing data which are to be transferred out of the computer. Synonymous with output area. 3. A block used as an output buffer.

output blocking factor (Bo):   In a tape sort, the number of data records in each record in the output file.

output bus driver: All major output signals from the standard computer used in programmed and data-break information transfers.

output capability: The number of unit loads that can be driven by the output of a circuit.

output capacitance: The anode-cathode impedance of a thermionic valve or the capacitive component of the output impedance of a transducer.

output channel: That   particular   or dedicated channel reserved for removal or carrying of data from a peripheral device.

output data: Data to be delivered from a device or program, usually after some processing.

output device: The part of a machine which translates the electrical impulses representing data processed by the machine into permanent results such as printed forms, punched cards, or magnetic writing on tape.

output device, calibrate: A procedure to adjust the output of a device and bring it to a desired value within a specified tolerance for a particular value of the input.

output equipment: The equipment used for transferring information out of a computer.

output gap: An interaction gap through which an output signal can be withdrawn from an electron beam.

output impedance: Impedance measured at the output terminals as a transmission line or gate, or amplifier, under no-load conditions.

output process: A procedure designed to deliver data through various devices, systems, subsystems, or programming commands.

output processor test: The automated processing of output to check for errors (in a complex system).

output record: 1. A record written to an output device. 2. The current record stored in the output area prior to being output.

output register: A specific register which holds data until it can be outputted to an external device.

output routine generator: A generator that produces an output routine to given specifications.

output section: Storage block from which output takes place.

output signal: Specific signal delivered by a device, system, or element.

output state: The state occurring on a specified output channel.

output stream: Output data issued by an operating system or a processing program on output devices activated by the operator. Same as job output stream.

output table: 1. An output device that plots the curves of variables as functions of other variables. 2. A hard copy output device which presents the results of a plotter system, which is designed to develop curves, graphs, chart, and other graphic output.

output tape (sorting):   A tape which contains a file in sequence as a result of a sort/merge process.

output transformer: A step-down iron core transformer between output tube and the speaker voice coil.

output unit: A computer system unit which delivers information from within the computer to the outside.

output unit (SYSOUT), system: 1. An on-line device that is the destination of all system messages that concern the user during the processing of a task. 2. The data set containing the system output.

outside loops: Considered for nested loops when loops within it are contained entirely. The outside loop executes the control parameters that are being held constant while the current loop is being carried through possible values.

outside request foreground program: A special designation of a time-dependent program initiated via an outside request whose urgency pre-empts operation of a background program.

oven: An enclosure and associated sensors and heaters for maintaining components at a controlled and usually constant temperature.

overall loss: A conventional term adopted to represent the composite attenuation, the transducer loss and the insertion loss, of a circuit in a particular case where the impedances between which the circuit is inserted are both equal to a resistance of 600 ohms (in this particular case these 3 losses are the same). Note: The equivalent of a circuit must not be confused with the reference equivalent of a circuit which implies direct or indirect comparison with the fundamental reference systems effected by the voice and by the ear.

overcapacity: The information contained in an item of information which is in excess of a given amount.

overcoupling: Two electrical circuits or mechanical systems tuned to the same frequency when there is sufficient interaction between them for the frequency response curve of the system to show two maxima, displaced to opposite sides of the maximum for either circuit alone.

overflow: 1. Occurs when the result of an arithmetic operation exceeds the capacity of the storage space allotted in a digital computer. 2. The digit arising from (1) if a mechanical or programmed indicator is included. 3. In arithmetic operation, the generation of a quantity beyond the capacity of the register or location which is to receive the result; overcapacity; the information contained in an item of information which is in excess of a given amount.

overflow bucket: One used to accomodate overflow records in a direct access file.

overflow check indicator: Indicates incorrect or unplanned operations in the execution of an arithmetic instruction, particularly when an arithemetic operation produces a number too large for the system to handle.

overflow error: A floating-point arithmetic operation resulting in an overflow condition.

overflow indicator: A bi-stable trigger which changes state when overflow occurs in the register with which it is associated. It may be interrogated and/or restored to the original state.

overflow position: An extra position in the register in which the overflow digit is developed.

overflow record: On an indirectly addressed file, a record whose key is randomized to the address of a full track or to the address of a home record.

overhead (operating systems): The distribution of operating time of the checking, monitoring, scheduling, etc. portions of the executive system over all jobs or tasks related to the total cost of the complete system. It is usually developed by percentages and ratios.

overlap: To perform central processor functions simultaneously on several instructions, for example by obeying an instruction in, say, three states. These may be decode, access operands, and perform functions. The central processor can then have three separate instructions passing through these stages together.

overlapped-operations buffer: Magnetic core buffers outside the main processor memory compensated for speed differences between slower electromechanical input/-output devices and processor speeds. Operations are overlapped, with all units operating simultaneously at rated speeds. Buffering eliminates the need for more expensive, multiple I/O channels, and eliminates complex I/O timing considerations from the programming job.

overlapping data channel: A data channel that allows asynchronous operation of its input/output devices and program processing by the central processing unit.

overlay: 1. A technique for bringing routines into high-speed memory from some other form of storage during processing, so that several routines will occupy the same storage locations at different times. It is used when the total memory requirements for instructions exceed the available high-speed memory. 2. Several sets of information which time-share a block of storage to conserve space. New information which is required is laid over information no longer needed. Generally the sets of information are not related, except that they are needed in the same program at different times. The same data for successive cases is not an overlay. The overlay concept thus permits the breaking of a large program into segments which can be used as required to implement problem solution.

overlay (load) module: A load module that has been divided into overlay segments, and has been provided by linkage editor with information that enables overlay supervisor to implement the desired loading of segments when requested.

overlay path: All of the segments in an overlay tree between a particular segment and the root segment, inclusive.

overlay program: A program in which certain control sections can use the same storage locations at different times during execution.

overlay region: A continuous area of main storage in which segments can be loaded independently of paths in other regions. Only one path within a region can be in main storage at any one time.

overlay segments: An overlay program structure that is not resident in main memory simultaneously with other parts. Very large programs are often segmented into overlays, and such segments are called into memory from auxiliary storage and thus main memory capacity is not overstrained. Overlay segments are ordered as "first level," "second level," etc.

overlay supervisor: A control routine that initiates and controls fetching of overlay segments on the basis of information recorded in the overlay module by linkage editor.

overlay tree: A graphic representation showing the relationships of segments of an overlay program and how the segments are arranged to use the same main storage area at different times.

overload: A condition existing within or at the output of a computing element that causes a substantial computing error because of the saturation of one or more of the parts of the computing element in an analog computer.

overload module testing: The destructive read-off caused by overloading or underloading the computer components. This causes failure of substandard units. The test is designed to minimize nonschedule downtime.

overmodulation: The overloading of an amplitudemodulated transmitter in which the modulating current is greater than that which gives 100 percent modulation.

overrun: Occurs when data are transferred to or from a non-buffered control unit operating with a synchronous medium, and the total activity initiated by the program exceeds the capability of the channel.

overshoot rise-time: The time necessary for the output of a system (other than first order) to change from a small percentage to a large percentage either before overshoot or in the absence of overshoot.

overwrite: To place information in a location and destroy the information previously contained there.

oxide: A chemical coating usually applied to the electron-producing element in an electronic tube.

oxide build-up: The accumulation of oxide or wear products in the form of deposits on the surface of the heads. Oxide build-up causes a loss in output, particularly at short wavelengths, and accelerates tape wear.

oxide-isolation-isoplanar: A novel variation applicable to bipolar processes. This technique primarily results in higher packing densities and slightly higher speeds and is accomplished by using silicon oxide to isolate the various components. A common form of oxide isolation is called isoplanar. The other bipolar processes achieve electrical isolation of the circuit elements with reverse biased P-N junctions, but these junctions occupy more space and have higher capacitance than oxide isolation circuits. The technique will probably be applied to the complex bipolar products to achieve cost reduction.

P

PABX: See private automatic branch exchange.

pack: To combine two or more units of information into a single physical unit to conserve storage or transmission time.

package: A common program written for a major application so that a user's specific problems of data or organization will not make the package less useful.

packed decimal: A means of data representation. Two digits per character can be used to increase speed and capacity in fields where alphabetics and special characters are not being used.

packed format message: Reduces message length and speeds transmission.

packets data flow: Flow control is the primary consideration in these systems. Useful throughput and transmission delay measurements can be conducted taking into account a number of variables such as: packet length, routes to be followed inside the network, and the link control used on various transmission lines.

packet-switched network characteristics: Maintains high average utilization of transmission facilities by (a) combining the traffic of many users, whose peaks do not occur simultaneously; (b) using all network lines in both directions simultaneously; and (c) balancing the asymmetric traffic of many users. Thus, the cost per bit transmitted is reduced.

packet-switching center: Routes traffic according to the current status of the network. Instead of following a predetermined path, data sent through the network are routed automatically by each switching center along the path most likely to mini-

mize the total delay encountered by the data in passing through the network. If certain internodal links become congested with traffic, data are routed automatcially over other links with spare capacity. If a link fails entirely, data will be sent automatically over alternative pathes.

pack field strength: A limit of magnetizing forces associated with a field.

packing factor: The number of units (words, bits, characters, etc.) that can fit into a defined size (per inch, per record, etc.).

packing fraction: The ratio of the active fiber core area to the total cross-sectional area of the fiber bundle.

pack relocation: 1. An act designed to include several discrete items of information in one unit of information. 2. The relocation of programs and data in a procedure to make efficient use of available storage capacity.

pad: Device which introduces transmission loss into a circuit. It may be inserted to introduce loss or match impedances.

pad character: A character inserted to fill a blank time slot in synchronous transmission, or inserted to fulfill a character-count requirement in transmissions of fixed block lengths.

padding: A technique used to fill out a block of information with dummy records, words or characters.

page: 1. Often a set of 4096 consecutive bytes. Applied to main storage, a set of 4096 consecutive bytes, the first byte of which is located at a storage address that is a multiple of 4096 (an address whose 12 loworder bits are 0). 2. The subdivision of a program which can be moved into main memory by an operating system or hardware whenever the instructions of that subdivision need to be performed. A program will be divided into pages in order to minimize the total amount of main memory storage allocated to the program at any one time. The pages will be stored on a fast direct access store.

page addressing: A procedure of memory addressing utilized with some specific computers. The addressing capability is limited to less than the total memory capacity available. But, using page addressing, memory is ivided into segments (pages) each of which can be addressed by the available addressing capability.

page copy: Same as hard copy.

paged segmentation: A designed type of placement in which the memory is divided into units of equal length, called page frames, while segments are divided into units of the same length, called pages. During execution, a page can be placed in any available page frame.

page memory system: The address of the first word or byte within a page of memory; i.e., a memory address expressed as a number having 9 to 12 low-order zeros; the exact number of trailing zeros is related to the size of the page used by a specific computer. All programs in a paged-memory system should begin on a page-boundary address.

page migration: The transfer of pages from a primary paging device to a secondary paging device to make more space available on the primary paging device.

page printer: A printer in which an entire page of characters is composed and determined within the device prior to printing.

page reclamation: The process of making addressable the contents of a page in real storage that has been marked invalid. Page reclamation can occur after a page fault or after a request to fix or load a page.

paging: The process of transmitting pages of information between main storage and auxiliary storage, especially when done for the purpose of assisting the allocation of a limited amount of main storage among a number of concurrently executing programs.

pair: Two like conductors employed to form an electric circuit.

paired cable: Cables which have individually insulated conductors.

panel, maintenance control: A panel of indicator lights and switches on which are displayed a particular sequence of routines, and from which repairmen can determine changes to execute.

paper document conveyor: A device which carries paper documents.

paper low condition: A warning showing that the supply of continuous paper on a printer is about to run out.

paper-tape reader: A device capable of sensing information punched on a paper tape in the form of a series of holes.

paper-tape speed: A rate in characters per second that a paper unit reads or punches.

parallel: The simultaneous transmission of processing the individual parts of a whole, such as the bits of a character or the characters of a word. When characters are dealt with simultaneously (not one after another), the transmission is serial by character and parallel by bit.

parallel action: Binary addition in which all digits are added simultaneously.

parallel addition: Simultaneously processes the addition of corresponding pairs of two-numbered digits within one cycle of execution. One or more cycles are used to propagate and adjust for any carries which may have been generated. Contrasts with serial addition.

parallel data medium: A medium for recording or entering data and as an input/output media for computers such as cards, tapes, paper, and disks. Usually the data carrier is transported easily.

parallel data transmission: Simultaneous transmission of each element of a code. For example, a five-level code would have five channels in a parallel transmission set-up.

parallel digit computer: Specific equipment which processes digits in concurrent procedures or fashion as contrasted to serial computing.

parallel full adder: Developed or formed from as many three-input adders as there are digits in the input words, with the carry output of each connected to one input of the three-digit adder corresponding to the digit position of the next significance.

parallel operation: Simultaneous performance of several actions by providing identical devices for each action. Parallel operation is performed to save time over serial operation, but it requires more equipment.

parallel output: Simultaneous availability of two or more bits, channels, or digits.

parallel-plate package: A technique for packaging circuits that increases high packing density and provides for easier automatic production, assembly, and maintenance.

parallel processing: Computer operation in which programs for more than one run are stored simultaneously, and executed concurrently.

parallel running: 1. The running of a newly developed system in a data processing area in conjunction with the continued operation of the current system. 2. The final step in the debugging of a system; this step follows a system test.

parallel-search memory: A memory where the storage locations are identified by their contents rather than the addresses. Enables faster interrogation to retrieve a particular data element.

parallel search storage: A storage device in which one or more parts of all storage locations are queried simultaneously.

parallel storage: Storage in which all bits, characters, or words are equally available in space. When words are in parallel, the storage is said to be parallel by words. When caracters within words (or binary digits within words or characters) are dealt with simultaneously, the storage is parallel by characters (or parallel by bits, respectively).

parallel transfer: A method of data transfer in which the characters of an element of information are transferred simultaneously over a set of paths.

parallel transmission: The simultaneous sending of data either over different channels, or by different carrier waves over the same channel.

parameter: In a subroutine, a quantity which may be given different values when the subroutine is used in different main routines. In a generator, a quantity used to specify input/output devices, to designate subroutines to be included, or to describe the desired routine to be generated.

parameter potentiometer: A potentiometer used in an analog computer to represent a problem parameter.

parameters sorting: The response to the requirement for specification for a sort/merge generator. Parameters are used to fix input and output formats, computing configuration, location of keys, etc.

parametric oscillator: An oscillator which relies for its operation on the fact that certain nonlinear reactors when driven by a pump or other source of frequency, f, may exhibit negative resistance at frequencies of f/2, f/3,..., f/n where n is determined by the form the nonlinearity takes; if the reactor is an inductor, the device is referred to as a parametron.

parametric subroutine: A subroutine which involves parameters, such as a decimal-point coded subroutine. The computer is expected to adjust or generate the subroutine according to the parametric values chosen.

parametron: A unique device composed of two stable states of oscillation, one is twice the frequency of the other and has the capability of storing one binary digit.

parasitic element antenna: Element of an antenna which is not fed directly by the transmitters (or connected electrically with a receiver) but reflects or directs radio waves to provide directivity to the antenna.

parasitic emission: Spurious emission that is generated accidentally at frequencies which are independent both of the carrier of characteristic frequency of an emission and also of frequencies of oscillations resulting from the generation of the carrier or characteristic frequency.

parasitic oscillation: Unwanted oscillation of an amplifier, or oscillation of an oscillator at some frequency other than that of the main resonant circuit. Generally of high frequency, it may occur during a portion of each cycle of the main oscillation.

parent page: In videotex, routing pages lead the user to the desired page. The routing page immediately preceding the desired page is the parent page.

parity: Equivalence of value in the check digit of the transmitted and received data.

parity bit: A binary digit appended to an array of bits to make the sum of all the bits always odd or always even.

parity character: A column of parity bits representing the modulus-2 sum (binary) of each horizontal row of bits in a medium.

parity check: Addition of noninformation bits to data, making the number of ones in a grouping of bits either always even or always odd. This permits detection of bit groupings which contain single errors. It may be applied to characters, blocks, or any convenient bit grouping.

parity error: Indicates that during a course of the previous block transfer of data a parity error was detected, or one or more bits have never been picked up or dropped out from either the timing track or the mark track.

parity error module: A storage-access module that checks parity. If a parity error is detected, the module will issue a parity-interrupt signal to the processor and rewrite the word in its correct form.

parity interrupt: An interrupt signal that indicates a parity error.

partial differential equation: A differential equation which contains more than one independent variable and/or derivatives (differentials) of more than one independent variable.

partial failure: A fault condition which degrades service but does not interrupt it completely.

partial full-duplex: A method of operation of a communication circuit in combination with a datacommunications terminal in which information may be transmitted full-duplex.

partially selected cell: In an array of magnetic cells, the selective switching of one cell in the array, termed the selected cell, by the simultaneous application of two or more drive pulses such that the resulting magnetomotive-force exceeds the threshold value only in the selected cell; the other cells, although changed magnetically, are not switched and are termed partially selected cells.

partially switched cell: A particular magnetic cell which after being set or reset has received one or more partial drive pulses in the opposite sense.

partial program: A program that is incomplete by itself and specifies a process to be performed on data. It may be used at more than one point in any particular program, or it might be made available for inclusion in other programs.

particle impact noise detection (PIND) test: An audio screening test to locate and eliminate those parts that have internal loose particles. This test cannot discriminate between conductive particles and nonconductive particles.

particle orientation: The process by which acicular particles are rotated so that their longest dimensions tend to lie parallel to one another. Orientation takes place in magnetic tape by a combination of the sheer force applied during the coating process and the application of a magnetic field to the coating while it is still fluid. Particle orientation increases the residual flux density.

partition: A segment of a computer's main memory allocated for running one or more computer jobs so that several jobs, residing in separate partitions, can be processed at the same time.

partitioned data set (PDS): A data set that is divided internally into parts.

part-operation: The part in an instruction that specifies the kind of arithmetical or logical operation to be performed, but not the address of the operands.

part program: Defines the machining functions to be performed on a part with a set of instructions in accordance with some part programming language.

part programmer: A person who prepares the part program. He may also plan the sequence of operations to be performed by a numerically controlled machine tool.

part programming language: A set of symbols, codes, format, and syntax (grammar) definitions used to describe machining operations which are understandable to computers or controls.

part programming manual: The manual preparation of a manuscript in Electronic Industries Code and format to define a sequence of commands for machining a part on a numerical control (NC) machine.

party-line circuit: A multistation net in which all stations are on a single circuit. The stations must share the circuit since only one station may transmit at a time. (Synonymous with multidrop line or circuit.) Terminals can also use a single line simultaneously by any of various multiplexing devices.

PASCAL: A language designed to enable teaching of programming as a systematic discipline. PASCAL is based on ALGOL, emphasizing aspects of structured programming, and extending ALGOL primarily with convenient data structuring facilities.

pass: One phase of a computer run which may comprise several phases. A pass is a logical distinct group of operations in a run with several such groups. For example, during compilation the first pass might be the reading of source instructions and production of object instructions on backing store.

passive element: An electrical device which receives energy from one source and performs some operation on that energy.

passive transducer: A transducer whose input waves are independent of the actuating waves.

password: 1. A unique string of characters that a program, computer operator, or user must supply to meet security requirements before gaining access to data. 2. In systems with time-sharing, a symbol that the user may be required to supply at the time he logs on the system. The password is confidential, as opposed to the user identification.

patch: A section of coding inserted into a routine to correct a mistake or alter the routine.

patch cord: A handy flexible connector conductor with connectors at each end and used to interconnect sockets or plugboards.

patching: Correcting or changing the coding by overlaying it with another instruction or group of instructions.

patch panel: 1. An interconnection device, usually removable, that employs removable wires to control the operation of computing equipment. It is used on punch-card machines to carry out functions that are under control of the user. On computers it is used primarily to control input/output functions. 2. A device or component of some data-processing machines that permits the expression of instructions in a semifixed computer program by the insertion of pins, plugs, or wires into sockets or hubs in the device, in a pattern to represent instructions. 3. The group of displays, manual buttons, and switches which are used by the operators, engineers, and maintenance personnel of the computer center.

path: A series of segments that form the shortest distance in a region between a given segment and the root segment.

path, magnetic: The track or route followed by magnetic flux lines, e.g., a closed line that involves all media through which the lines of flux pass such as the interior of a ferrite toroidal core.

pattern recognition: The recognition of shapes or other patterns by a machine system.

pattern sensitive fault: A fault that appears in response to some particular pattern of data.

PAX: See private automatic exchange.

payments mechanism: A device, instrument or system which transfers money. Existing payments mechanisms are: (a) cash; (b) checks; (c) credit cards; and (d) traveler's checks. Electronic Funds Transfer System devices or systems are also payments mechanisms, e.g., automated check clearing, point-of-sale systems, automated tellers, bill payment systems, etc.

payroll journal: A document or book for listing of payments made to all employees in a given pay period.

payroll register: The document that contains employee payroll information.

PBX: See private branch exhange.

PCS: See print contrast signal.

PDAID: See problem determination aid.

PDS: See partitioned data set.

peak cathode current: The highest instantaneous current drawn from the cathode of a thermionic tube.

peak data transfer rate: The maximum rate that data is transmitted through a channel.

peak distortion: Worst time displacement of the transmission wave components.

peak envelope power: The average power output of a transmitter as measured over one radio frequency cycle at the peak of the modulation envelope.

peak flux density: A maximum magnetic condition of various magnetic materials.

peak forward voltage: The maximum instantaneous voltage in the forward flow direction of anode current as measured between the anode and cathode of a thermionic rectifier or gas-filled tube.

peaking circuit: One which produces a sharply peaked output from any input wave.

peaking network: An interstage coupling circuit which gives a peak response at the upper end of the frequency range that is handled. This is achieved with a resonant circuit and minimizes the fall-off in the frequency response produced by stray capacitance. Not to be confused with peaking circuit.

peak load: The maximum instantaneous rate of power consumption in the load circuit. In a power-supply system the peak load corresponds to the maximum power production of the generator(s).

peak magnetizing field strength (H_m):   The positive or negative limiting value of the magnetizing field strength associated with a symmetrically, cyclically magnetized condition. The peak magnetizing field strength most commonly used in measuring tape properties is 1000 oe.

peak power: Average radio frequency power at maximum modulation.

peak printing rate: The printing rate excluding the effects of paper advance and information loading cycle times, expressed as lines per minute.

peak transfer rate: A rate at which data is transmitted through its channel, but measured during the time data is actually being transmitted, i.e., tape transfer rates are measured in terms of characters per second, discounting gaps between blocks, words, etc.

pentagrid converter: A converter tube with five grids.

pen travel: The length of the path described by the pen in moving from one end of the chart scale to the other. Such a path may be an arc or, in some cases, a straight line.

penumbral: The specific headings that are relevant to the data being sought.

PER: See program event recording.

perforated: Punched.

perforator: A keyboard device for punching paper tape.

performance evaluation: The analysis in terms of initial objectives and estimates, and usually made onsite, of a data processing system's productivity and capabilities, to provide information on operating experience and to identify corrective actions required, if any.

performance reference: The performance attained under reference operating conditions, e.g., a band, hysteresis, linearity, repeatability, etc.

performance standards: The minimum technical criteria that must be met by community antenna television (CATV) systems, consistent with standards set by the Federal Communications Commission (FCC) or the local ordinance.

peripheral: Input/output equipment used to make hard copies or to read in data from hard copies (typer, punch, tape reader, line printer, etc.).

peripheral controls: Regulate the transfer of data between the central processor and peripheral devices. Specifically, they reconcile the mechanical speeds of the peripheral devices with the electronic speed of the central processor, and minimize the interruption of central processor activity due to peripheral data transfers.

peripheral control switching unit: A unit which permits any two processors to share the same peripheral devices.

peripheral conversion program: Handles all those jobs normally done by a separate peripheral processor. The priority interrupt system and multiple memory accumulators in the computer eliminate virtually all loss in running time. Such processing is done through the arithmetic processor.

peripheral equipment: (ISO) In a data processing system, any equipment, distinct from the central processing unit, that may provide the system with outside communication or additional facilities.

peripheral interface channel: That interface form (matching) previously designed or agreed upon so that two or more units, systems, programs, etc., may be joined or associated easily.

peripheral limited: A system in which the overall processing time is dictated by the speed of the peripheral units.

peripheral transfer: The process of transmitting data between two peripheral units.

peripheral units: Machines and equipment operating under computer control.

permanent connection: Connection made without the use of switching equipment.

permanent dynamic storage: A type of storage in which the maintenance of the data stored does not depend on the energy flow.

permanent error: An error not eliminated by reprocessing the information a limited number of times.

permanent fault: Faults are failures in performance in the manner required or specified. Sporadic faults are intermittent while permanent faults are repetitious, but these may either escape attention when they do not result in failure to perform some particular tasks, or are known and easily correctable.

permanent file: A data file that is permanent.

permanent memory: Storage of information which remains intact when the power is turned off.

permanent read/write error: An error that cannot be eliminated by retrying a read/write operation.

permanent storage: Storage in which the maintenance of data does not depend on a flow of energy such as magnetic disk, drum, etc.

permuted index: A form of document indexing developed by producing an entry in the index for each word of specific interest and by including the context in which it occurs, most often restricted to title words.

persistence: The length of time in which the fluorescent screen of a writing tube holds the written image.

pertinency factor: The ratio obtained by dividing the total number of relevant documents retrieved by the total number of all documents retrieved.

PH: Abbreviation for page heading.

phantom channel: A communications channel which has no independent conductive path. The signal information for this type of channel is added to that of other channels in such a manner that no additional paths are required. All signals are recoverable with negligible interaction.

phantom circuit: A superposed circuit derived from two suitably arranged pairs of parallel wires.

phase: 1. Variation of frequency modulation. 2. A varying of the carrier frequency by a signal, with the maximum deviation being at the point of maximum phase angle. 3. A constant amplitude.

phase angle: A measure of the time by which an output lags or leads an input.

phase-by-phase build-up: The modular growth of a system.

phase class name: Non-terminal nodes in formal language theory.

phase dictionary: An abbreviated table of contents that contains the phase name and load addresses of the phases to be loaded for a given application.

phase difference:　The phase angle of the output minus the phase angle of the input, between sinusoidal input and output of the same frequency.

phase discriminator:　A circuit preceding the demodulator in a phase-modulation receiver. It inverts the carrier to an amplitude-modulated form.

phase distortion:　In a transmission system, the difference between the maximum transit time and the minimum transit time for frequencies within a specified band.

phase-frequency distortion:　Distortion due to the difference between phase delay at one frequency and at a reference frequency.

phasing:　In facsimile transmission and reception, adjustment of a reproduced picture to correspond exactly with the original.

phase inverter:　A type of amplifier which supplies a positive and negative half-cycle of output for every half-cycle of input voltage.

phase jitter:　A type of unwanted random distortion which results in the intermittent shortening or lengthening of the signals.

phase library:　The directoried data set that contains program phases, processed and entered by the linkage editor, the source from which program phases are loaded for execution.

phase-locked oscillator:　A parametric oscillator which can be made to oscillate in one of two phases relative to the pump frequency, and thus can act as a storage cell.

phase modulation (PM):　1. A method of angle modulation in which the amplitude of the carrier wave remains constant while varying in phase with the amplitude of the modulating signals. 2. One of three ways of modifying a sine wave signal to make it "carry" information. The sine wave or carrier has its phase changed in accordance with the information to be transmitted.

phase modulation recording:　A procedure or method for magnetic recording of bits in which each storage cell is split into two parts and magnetized in opposite senses, with the sequence of these senses indicating whether the bit represented is a zero or a one.

phase response characteristic:　The phase displacement versus frequency properties of a telemetering system or device.

phase shift:　A change in time relationship of one part of a signal waveform with another, with no change in the basic form of the signal. The degree of change varies with frequency as a signal passes through a channel.

phase splitter:　A means of producing two or more waves which differ in phase from a single input wave.

phoneme:　A primitive unit of auditory speech in a given language.

phosphor:　The fluorescent material which coats the screen of a CRT. When the electron beam strikes the phosphor its electrons become exicted and move to a higher energy level. When the electrons return to their original level they give off the light that forms the display on the screen.

phosphor dots:　Elements in a cathode-ray tube screen which glow in the three primary colors.

phosphorescence:　A property of emitting light for a period of time after the source of excitation is taken away, e.g., in electrostatic storage tubes and cathode-ray tubes (CRTs).

photocathode:　The electrode in the image orthicon which emits the electron image when struck by light from the televised object.

photocell:　A vacuum tube which converts light into electrical energy.

photocell matrix: In optical character recognition (OCR), a device that projects an input onto a fixed two-dimensional array of photocells to simultaneously achieve the character's horizontal and vertical components. Since the reflectance at every point in the input character is measured in parallel rather than sequentially, the amount of time required to scan the character is limited only by the response time of the photocells, which is a fraction of a microsecond. The biggest shortcoming of the photocell matrix has been its relative inability to allow for and correct character misregistration. Consequently, various mechanisms are employed that sense the position of individual characters before projection onto the matrix.

photocomposition: A procedure for typesetting which uses a computer and a film recording system and develops a photograph on the face of a cathode-ray tube display. The characters, words, etc., to be used for a printed plate are produced by the computer on the face of the tube for copying and usually in full page format.

photoconductive cell: A semiconductor device whose resistance is affected by the amount of light falling on it.

photoelectric detection: A form of mark detection using a photoelectric device to locate and verify information as coded or marked in special boxes or windows on prepared forms for such reading purposes. The scanner unit reads a row by reflected light from the document. The cells which "read" or sense the marks are assigned to one column of windows or boxes and detect the presence or absence of reflected light.

photoelectric mark reading: A form of mark detection that uses a photoelectric device to locate and verify information as coded or marked in special boxes or windows on pre-prepared forms. The unit reads a row by reflected light from the document. The cells which sense the marks are assigned to one column of windows or boxes and detect the presence or absence where reflectance falls.

photoemissive: Electrons are emitted from the surfaces of certain specific materials at particular threshold levels of frequency of incident electromagnetic radiation, e.g., visible light, infrared or ultraviolet.

photoformer: A function generator that operates by using a cathode-ray beam to optically track the edge of a mask placed on a screen.

photographic storage: 1. High-density storage of data in binary form on photographic disks for quick reference purposes. 2. Photographic copies of data shown on direct-display cathode-ray tubes. 3. Facsimile copies of readable documents or of direct output of the processor. 4. Any storage schemes utilizing photographic processes. This includes various micro-image systems, computer-output microfilm and binary data storage on photographic media.

photo-optic memory: A specific memory or storage unit that uses an optical medium. For example, a laser might be used to record on photographic film.

phototypesetting: In optical character recognition (OCR), a process of reproducing type matter onto photographic film or paper in order to improve its quality.

photovoltaic cell: A semiconductor device which generates a voltage when light falls on it. It is used as solar cell.

physical circuit: A metallic two-wire channel.

physical end: Either the end of the source program or the end of a data file.

physical record: A meaningful record with respect to access.

physical systems simulation: A development representation of physical systems, e.g., a chemical process in which information provided to the computer is represented by the process variables. The processing completed by the computer is a representation of the process itself and the output of the computer represents the results of the process simulated.

physical-system time: The ratio of computer time to the problem time (in simulation).

pick-up plate: A conducting plate which is situated close to or cemented on the face of the screen of the tube, e.g., copper foil or copper wire. When the plate is coupled to each element of the screen inside the cathode-ray tube, any alternation of the charge stored by the element causes an output signal to be developed by the pick-up plate and thus forms the basis for electrostatic storage and interrogation.

pick-up tube: Converts an image of an external scene into a video signal. Essential component in a television camera channel.

picofarad: One millionth of one millionth of a farad which is a unit of electrical capacity. Also equal to one-thousandth of a millimicrofarad.

picosecond (psec): One thousandth of a nanosecond.

pictorial data representation: Made graphic by bar charts, pie charts, statistical maps, etc. Usually the tabulations will contain: (a) main titles, (b) statistical units, (c) captions (labels of rows), (d) body of data, (e) footnotes, and (f) publisher's source of data.

picture carrier: The television carrier modulated by the video signal.

picture inversion: Conversion of negative to positive image (or vice versa) when carried out electrically. In facsimile transmission it will correspond to the reversal of the black and white shades of the recorded copy.

picture-phone®: A special two-way telephone service that permits the user to see as well as talk with the person at the distant end.

picture signal: The portion of a television signal which carries information relative to the picture itself.

piezoelectric crystal: A crystal which converts mechanical pressure into an electrical signal, or converts a signal into pressure.

piggybacking: The method of temporarily delaying outgoing acknowledgments so that they can be attached to the next transmitted data frame.

pilot: A signal wave in a transmission system, usually a single frequency transmitted over the system to indicate or control its characteristics.

pilot channel: A channel over which a pilot signal is transmitted.

pilot system: A specific collection of file records and supplementary data obtained from the actual operations of a business over an extended period. It is used to effect a realistic system for testing by closely simulating the real world environment.

pinboard: A type of control panel which uses pins rather than wires to control the operation of a computer.

pin contact: A male-type contact used to mate with a socket, i.e., a female contact.

PIND test: See particle impact noise detection test.

pinfeed forms: Continuous strip forms that are aligned by fitting marginally punched holes on pins or sprockets mounted on the rollers of writing machines.

pinfeed platen: A cylindrical platen which drives the paper by using integral rings of pins engaging perforated holes, rather than pressure.

pin-jointed linkages: A system of mechanical elements interconnected by bars, i.e., in a pin-jointed linkage, they are constrained only by fixed or moving rotating joints as contrasted with slide linkages where elements are constrained to move only in the direction of their lengths.

pin-pong: The programming technique that uses two magnetic tape units for multiple reel files and switches between the two until the complete file is processed.

pip: Significant deflection or intensification of the spot on a cathode-ray tube giving a display for identification or calibration. Particularly applied to the peaked pattern of a radar signal.

pipelining: A technique whereby the receiver fetches the next instruction before completing execution of the previous instruction, in order to increase processing speed.

pixels: Short for picture elements. The smallest distinguishable area of a display device which can be individually illuminated. A larger number of pixels will mean a better picture. Some monitors have over one million pixels.

placement algorithm: An algorithm designed to determine where, in an internal storage, segments should be placed prior to their use.

plane: A screen of magnetic cores that are combined to form stacks.

plane driver: A particular amplifier that drives a digit plane for a magnetic core storage unit.

planned stop: Optional stop.

planning data gathering: To display integration of specific procedures for developing optimal solutions of problems or ranges of feasibilities using general and broad range scientific method framework. Define, design, and delimit the problem with a clear succint statement of hypothesis, scope, and objective. Affirm positively the aspiration level desired (algoristic, stochastic, or heuristic) and confidence base required.

plan position indicator (PPI): A radar scope on which a map of the area surrounding the radar antenna is plotted.

plant: Facilities used by common carriers such as: (a) switching equipment, (b) service department, (c) central officer personnel, (d) cable, etc.

plastic conduit: One of the most popular materials for telephone cable ducts today is polyvinyl chloride (PVC) because it is easy to pull long lengths of plasticsheathed cables through PVC ducts.

plastic-disk optical memory: A disk drive that uses a solid-state laser diode, a rotating-mirror assembly, and an inexpensive plastic medium to store up to 1 Gbyte (10^9 bytes) of user data on one surface. Typically, the disk itself is 12 inches in diameter and contains 38,500 tracks per surface, with 25 1k-byte sectors per track. The system records data by using a stationary laser beam which travels through a movable mirror assembly for precise positioning. The beam deforms the disk's surface into bubbles which are confined to preslotted areas. Like most optical memory devices, data cannot be erased for re-recording, however, backup or distribution copies are made easily. Plastic-disk optical memory drives are much less expensive and easier to handle than glass-based optical memory devices.

plate: The electrode in a vacuum tube which collects electrons.

plate modulation: Same as Heising modulation.

platen: A backing, commonly cylindrical, against which printing mechanisms strike to produce an impression.

playback record: A machine tool control system for which the program tape is recorded from the actual motions of the machine. The tape can then be used in the playback mode as a program to make similar parts. For this system the part programmer is not necessary.

plot: 1. To map or diagram. 2. To connect the point-by-point coordinate values.

plotter: A visual display or board in which a dependent variable is graphed by an automatically controlled pen or pencil as a function of one or more variables.

plotting board: An output unit which plots the curves of one or more variables as a function of one or more other variables.

plugboard: 1. A removable panel in punched card-machines consisting of an array of terminals that may be interconnected by short electrical leads according to a prescribed pattern. An entire prewired panel may be inserted for different programs. 2. A control panel or wiring panel.

plugboard computer: A computer which uses plugboard input and output, and where program instructions are delivered by means of interconnecting patch cords on a removable plugboard.

plug compatible: A peripheral device that can function or work with another manufacturer's computer system by direct link-up.

plug-in unit: 1. A self-contained circuit assembly. 2. An assembly of electronic components that are wired together and can be plugged in or pulled out easily.

plug wire: A device that consists of a flexible cord with a metal pin at each end for connecting the sockets of a plugboard.

plumbing: Waveguides and cavities in ultra high frequency equipment.

plus-90 orientation: A specific position which indicates line elements on a document appear perpendicular with the leading edge of the optical character recognition (OCR).

pneumatic computer: One in which signals are sent and information is stored by means of the flow and varying of pressure in fluid.

P-N-P: A transistor composed of two P-type crystals separated by an N-type.

P-N-P type junction: The contact interface surface or immediate area between N-type and P-type semiconducting material. Transistor action takes place at the junction of these differently doped materials. Junction transistors may be P-N-P type or N-P-N type for the emitter, base and collect or electrode materials, respectively.

pocket-size reels: Three and one-half inch tape reels.

point (base): The dot that marks the separation between the integral and fractional parts of a quantity, i.e., between the coefficients of the zero and the minus one powers of the number base. It is usually called, for a number system using base two, a binary point. For base ten, a decimal point, etc.

point, clutch: Input and output equipment requires a clutch for their continuously operating motors to affect the time for the use of the reading or writing parts of this machinery. Synchronous clutches can be engaged at specific limited times or points in the operating cycle, i.e., in the usual card punches, while asynchronous clutches, i.e., on various tape units, can be engaged at any time.

pointer: A word giving the address of another core storage location.

point-of-sale terminal: Provides an easy interface for an unskilled operator, has built-in means of controlling or improving the users' accuracy, and provides a means of automatically reading some form of coded label or tag on the merchandise. Point-of-sale terminals are used in department stores and other large retail outlets.

points-per-frame display: The measurement of the minimum and maximum number of points which can be drawn flicker-free on a cathode-ray tube at the manufacturer's recommended refresher rate.

point-to-point circuits: Private communication lines for the exclusive use of the purchaser that join together one or more points.

point-to-point control system: A control system which is concerned only in going from one point to another without regulating the path it takes to arrive at the second point.

point-to-point line: A line that connects a single remote station to the computer; it may be either switched or nonswitched.

point-to-point transmission: Transmission of data between two points without the use of any intermediate terminal or computer.

polar: A situation in which a binary 1 is represented by current flow in one direction and binary 0 is represented by current flow in the opposite direction.

polar   coordinates: A   mathematical system of coordinates for locating a point in a plane by the length of its radius vector and the angle this vector makes with a fixed line.

polarity: 1. A distinction between positive and negative electric charges 2. A distinction between positive (north) and negative (south) magnetic poles of an electromagnet or permanent magnet; these poles do not exist, but describe locations where magnetic flux leaves or enters magnetic material. 3. The difference between two points in a system which differ in one respect.

polarization: 1. In optics, makes light vibrate in a definite form. 2. In electronics, specifies the direction of an electric vector.

polarization   diversity: Transmission methods used to minimize the effects of selective fading of the horizontal and vertical components of a radio signal.

polar keying: A telegraph signal in which circuit current flows one direction for marking, and another for spacing.

polar mode: 1. A device that separates or breaks up a quantity, particularly a vector, into constituent parts or elements; i.e., the mutually perpendicular components of a plant vector. 2. A device for resolving a vector into its mutually perpendicular components.

polar relay: A relay containing a permanent magnet that centers the armature. The direction of movement of the armature is governed by the direction of current flow.

polar transmission: A method for transmitting teletypewriter signals, whereby the marking signal is represented by direct current flowing in one direction and the spacing signal is represented by an equal current flowing in the opposite direction. By extension to tone signaling, polar transmission is a method of transmission employing three distinct states, two to represent a mark and a space and one to represent the absence of a signal

Polish notation: A specific form of prefix Notation.

poll: A flexible, systematic method, centrally controlled, that permits stations on a multipoint circuit to transmit without contending for the line.

polled circuit: A multidrop or party-line circuit utilizing polling ("Anything to Send?" signals) as a method of line discipline.

polling: 1. A flexible, systematic, centrallycontrolled method of permitting terminals on a multi-terminal line to transmit without contending for the line. The computer contacts terminals according to the order specified by the user, and each terminal contacted is invited to send messages. 2. A centrally controlled method of calling a number of points to permit them to transmit information.

polling characters: A set of characters peculiar to a terminal and the polling operation. Response to these characters indicates to the computer whether or not the terminal has a message to send.

polling interval: A time interval set between polling operations if no data is being transmitted from the polled station.

polling list: A list containing control information and names of entries in the terminal table. The order in which the names are specified determines the order in which the terminals are polled.

poll reject message: A message sent when the polled terminal has no data to send.

poll train (poll list): A list of the stations in a polled network showing the sequence in which they are to be polled. The station identification is usually a 1- or 2-character transmitter start code, and in a computer system this poll train is retained in a program. For a multi-line system, of course, there will be a poll train for each line.

polymorphic system: A system which can take on various forms ideally suited to the problems at hand, usually by altering, under its own control, its interconnections and the functions of its component parts, i.e., it may occur with respect to logic construction or organization.

polynomial cyclic code: A code which detects single, double, and odd numbers of errors.

polyphase: A set of ac power-supply circuits (usually three) carrying currents of equal frequency with uniformly-spaced phase differences.

polyphase merging: A technique designed used in a sort program that merges strings of sequenced data.

polyvalence: The property of being inter-related in several ways.

polyvalent notation: A method for describing salient characteristics, in condensed form, using two or more characters, where each character or group of characters represents one of the characteristics.

port: 1. An entrance to or exit from a network. 2. The part of a data processor which is dedicated to a single data channel to receive data from or transmit data to one or more external remote devices.

portable computer: A self-contained microcomputer. It can be taken anywhere because it is small, lightweight, and powered by a rechargeable battery pack and/or an ac adapter cord.

portable data medium: The selected medium used to transport or carry (communicate) data or information. Punched cards, magnetic tapes, and punched paper tapes, and lately portable disks, are examples most often easily transported independently of the devices used in reading or interpreting such data or information.

positional operand: In assembler programming, an operand in a macroinstruction that assigns a value to the corresponding positional parameter declared in the prototype statement of the called macro definition.

positional parameter: A parameter that must appear in a specified location, relative to other parameters.

positional representation: Same as positional notation.

position control system: A positioning system in which the controlled motion is required only to reach a given end point, with no path control during the transition from one end point to the next.

positive acknowledgment with retransmission (PAR): Protocols in which the transmitter waits for a positive acknowledgment before continuing to the next data item.

positive feedback: Returning of a portion of the output of a device, such as an amplifier, to its input, in phase with the original. This is the basis of operation of most oscillators.

positive frequency deviation: A change in the frequency-modulation carrier to a frequency higher than its resting frequency.

post: 1. To enter a unit of information on a record. 2. To record in a system control block the occurrence of an event for later interrogation by a procedure whose action is dependent upon the status of the event.

post billing system: A system by which the customer invoices are prepared after items have been shipped to the customers.

post editing: An editing procedure or process on the output of a prior operation, especially those related to accounting, or programs which might have syntax or construction errors.

posterior probability: The revised estimate or probability incorporating additional information, usually developed using the Bayes equation.

posting: A procedure for adding data or information to an existing record.

post-installation review: The special on-site examination of procedures, operations, and results of a system in order to recommend or complete correction of deficiencies or determine rates or completion of goal achievement.

post mortem: A routine which, either automatically or on demand, prints information concerning the contents of the registers and storage locations at the time the routine stopped, in order to assist in the location of a mistake in coding.

post mortem dump: A listing of the contents of a storage device taken after a routine has been run in order that the final condition of sections of storage may be recorded for debugging purposes.

postprocessor: A set of computer instructions which transform tool centerline data

into machine motion commands using the proper tape code and format required by a specific machine control system. Instructions such as feed rate calculations, spindle speed calculations, and auxiliary function commands may be included.

postulate: To assume without specific proof; to accept a proposition without immediate empirical evidence; to accept as evident from general life experience or general acceptance.

pot: A reserved area of storage for accumulating certain data.

potential: Scalar magnitude, negative integration of the electric (or magnetic) field intensity over a distance. Hence all potentials are relative, there being no absolute zero potential other than a convention; i.e., earth, or distance from a charge at infinity.

potential difference: Algebraic difference between voltages at two points.

potentiometer: A voltage divider which has a variable contact arm that permits the selection of any portion of the potential applied across its total resistance.

potentiometer multiplier: A multiplying unit which has a position control and the capability of multiplying each of several different variables by a single variable, represented by analog voltages.

power amplification: 1. That provided by valves when delivering power, as contrasted with voltage amplification. 2. Difference between output and input power levels of an amplifier, expressed in decibels.

power amplifier: A tube or circuit designed to amplify both voltage and current.

power diversity factor: The ratio of the total of all individual power loads of different elements to the demand power load for the complete system composed of all these elements.

power dump: The removal of all power accidentally or intentionally.

power factor: The ratio of total watts to total rootmean-square volt amperes, i.e., the active power to the apparent power.

power fail and automatic restart: The power-fail interrupt provides an interrupt when a loss of primary power is detected. Typically a minimum of one millisecond of computer operation is assured after the interrupt. Power restart interrupt occurs when the power is applied and is up to normal operating levels and the processor is placed in the run mode.

power fail logic: Logic circuits that protect a system in the event of primary power failure. Circuits automatically store current operating parameters. When power is restored, the circuits make use of this information to continue proper operation.

power failure interrupt: A signal that occurs on many machines for the purpose of informing the machine that the external power is failing. Usually a power failure interrupt will not destroy the operating status of the machine because most machines store enough power internally to go through a predetermined number of instructions.

power interference filter: A filter in series with the public power input to a rectifier which passes the fundamental frequency of the power supply but greatly attenuates higher interfering frequencies.

power level: The ratio of the power at a point to some arbitrary amount of power chosen as a reference.

power loss: 1. The ratio of the power absorbed by a transducer to that delivered to the load. 2. The energy dissipated in a passive network or system.

power pack: Power-supply unit for an amplifier; i.e., in a radio or television receiver, wherein the requisite steady voltages are obtained by rectifiers from mains. Also the last or power stage of an amplifier when this is integral with the power supply proper.

Powers code: A punched-card code designed by James Powers for the 1910 census.

power supply: An electronic circuit which converts an input ac voltage into an output dc voltage.

power-supply, reference: A stable power supply of constant voltage used to assist in improving the accuracy of the computer with voltage analog representation, i.e., initial or limit conditions are derived directly from the reference supply, and voltages of other values or variables are measured as fractions of the reference supply, most often by potentiometers.

power transformer: In electronics, a transformer introduces the energizing supply into an instrument or system (distinct from a signal transformer).

power transistor: A transistor capable of being used at high power ratings.

PPM (pulse-position modulation): A pulse modulation method whereby the position of the pulse follows the modulating function.

pragmatics: A study of the range or extent to which practical use may be used in constructions of a language.

preamplifier: A one- or two-stage amplifier required to strengthen the output of a weak electrical device to the point where it can drive a main amplifier.

pre-analysis: An initial review of the task to be accomplished by the computer in order to increase the efficiency of that task.

pre-assembly time: The time at which an assembler processes macro definitions and performs conditional assembly operations.

precedence prosign: A character group which indicates how a message is to be sent to communcations personnel.

precision: The degree of discrimination with which a quantity is stated.

precision ratio: The ratio of relevant documents retrieved through use of a query or search formulation to the total number of documents retrieved through that query.

precision/recall measure: The combination of recall and precision ratios for a query or search formulation. A restricted search should have a lower recall ratio and a higher precision ratio than a broad search. That is, the searcher having a very specific query should not have to look through a large number of retrieved documents, while the searcher with a more general query is likely to want many documents to be sure of getting all of the information he wants.

predicate: To affirm or deny, in mathematical logic, one or more subjects.

predicted grade A contour: The line representing the service area in which a good picture is computed to be available 90 percent of the time at 70 percent of the receiver locations. Signal contours determine what educational channels are carried on a cable system and, in smaller markets, what stations must be carried from other small markets.

predicted grade B contour: The concentric area marking a television station's service area in which a good picture is computed to be available 90 percent of the time at 50 percent of the receiver locations.

pre-edit checking program: The application or operational progress before the test run. A pre-edit run can remove disobedience to established supervisory or programmer segmentation rules.

pre-emphasis: Marked alteration of response at the beginning of a part of a transmission system (as in magnetic recording and reproduction, frequency modulation and demodulation, disk recording and reproduction) for a technical reason, such as noise level or restriction of amplitude.

pre-emptive scheduling: A form of scheduling designed so that jobs can be interrupted and their resources transferred to more urgent jobs. An interrupted job can be either terminated completely or resumed later.

prefix: In a system with a complex priority structure the stopping of the scheduling routine from transferring control among programs by the use of suppression bits by which the application program registers its status in a priority table by means of prefixes and suffixes for the use of the scheduling routine.

prefix notation: A method of forming one-dimensional expressions without need for brackets by preceding, with a string or vector of operators, an operand string or vector which may itself contain operators upon operands.

preliminary proposal review: An on-site review to provide guidance to proponent agencies in the preparation of automatic data-processing system proposals.

preliminary review: Evaluation that matches an organization's needs with a computer system.

preparatory function: A command changing the mode of operation of the control.

preprocessor: In emulation, a program that converts data from the format of an emulated system to the format accepted by an emulator.

preselection: A technique for saving time available in buffered computers. A block data is read into computer storage from the next input tape to be called upon before the data are required in the computer. The selection of the next input tape is determined by instructions to the computer.

preserve: The function or procedure designed to retain information in one storage device after transferring it to another device.

preset: 1. To set the contents of a storage location to an initial value. 2. To establish the initial control value for a loop.

preset mode: The monitor is not resident in memory. Each absolute program is loaded into memory with the preset button on the computer console. The processing of individual jobs is the same as in the batch processing mode, except that the EOJ (end of job) card places the computer in a halt state. To begin processing a new job, the absolute compiler, assembler, loader, or utility program for the job must be preset into memory.

preset parameter: A parameter incorporated into a subroutine during input.

prestore: To store a quantity before it is needed.

preventive maintenance: Maintenance specifically intended to prevent faults from occurring. Corrective maintenance and preventive maintenance are both performed during maintenance time.

primary center: A control center connecting toll centers together; a Class 3 office. It can also serve as a toll center for its local end offices.

primary colors: The colors red, yellow, and blue which serve as the basic tints of color television.

primary constants: Those of capacitance, inductance, resistance, and leakance of a conductor to earth (coaxial or concentric) or to return (balanced) conductor, per unit length of line.

primary current: That formed by primary electrons, as contrasted with secondary electrons, which reduce or even reverse it.

primary data: Data published by the same source as that which collected it.

primary element (detector): The first system element that performs the initial measurement operation and responds quantitatively to the measured variable, i.e., the primary element performs the initial conversion of measurement energy.

primary key: The major file record key; all records with the same primary key are members of the same "case" (e.g., the same patient, account, etc.).

primary operator control station: Under telecommunications access method (TCAM), the operator control station that can receive an error recovery procedure message, send operator commands, and receive related responses.

primary service area: The area in which ground wave reception of a broadcast transmission is sufficient, in relation to interference and ionospheric reflections, to give consistently good reproduction of programs without fading.

primary sort chart: Displays the sort pattern for item distribution on the first pass of deposited items through the proof operation. This is distinguished from the inclearing sort chart, which is the distributional chart for inclearing and Federal Reserve cash letters.

primary storage: The main internal storage. Most often the fastest storage device of a computer and the one from which instructions are executed (contrasted with auxiliary storage).

primary switching center: A location which performs telephonic switching which is a selected switching center and also a local switching center, and all secondary centers of the particular group to which controls are connected by trunk circuits.

primary track: On a direct access device, the original track on which data is stored.

primary unit: The symbolic unit on which a file begins.

prime shift: The conventional or normal business hours during which equipment usage is most important.

primitive: A basic or fundamental unit, often referring to the lowest level of a machine instruction or lowest unit of language translation.

principal maintenance period: Each installation may select any period of time which may be scheduled, usually on a daily basis, for the performance of preventive maintenance of the mainframe and the majority of principal peripheral equipment units.

print bar: The print bar, type bar or type wheel is the part of the printer which is responsible for the form of the printed character.

print contrast ratio: The ratio of the difference between the maximum reflectance within a specified distance from the given area to the maximum reflectance at the specified distance.

print contrast signal (PCS): An indication or measurement of the contrast between printed characters and the paper on which the characters are printed.

print control character: A control character for print operations such as line spacing, page ejection, or carriage return.

printed-circuit card: A card, usually of laminate or resinous material of the insulating type, which is used for the mounting of an electrical circuit. Together the base and circuit make up the card.

printer: A device which expresses coded characters as hard copy.

printer skipping: The rate at which the unit advances a form through the carriage without printing.

print format: Describes the manner information is to be printed on a printer, most often provided as part of a program specification.

print hammer: On some types of printers, a device which is activated in order to force paper into contact with the character to be printed.

printing technique: The method by which the unit produces hard copy; impact-type (I) or nonimpact-type (N), the latter implying an electrostatic process.

printing terminal: An impact or nonimpact device for providing the data desired in a hard-copy form.

print line: The normal set of printed characters and spaces arranged in a horizontal row and considered as a unit.

print-out: See hard copy.

print restore (PR) code: A code that causes a printer to resume printing.

print-such editor: A subroutine controlling the printing and the punching of cards and editing operations.

print timing dial: A control knob on a printer.

print wheel: A single element providing the character set at one printing position of a wheel printer.

priority circuit: The priority circuits of the control unit grant memory access to the various units of the system in a sequence that enables each input/output device and system running-time to be used most efficiently. The priority circuits receive, store, and grant requests for access to memory made by the input/output synchronizers and the central processor. When simultaneous requests are made, the priority circuits select the synchronizer that is to be granted memory access according to the relative data-transfer rate of the input/output device controlled by each synchronizer. A synchronizer that controls a unit with a relatively slow transfer rate, such as the cardpunch unit, requires access to memory less often than a synchronizer that controls a unit with a relatively fast transfer rate, such as a tape unit; thus, the cardpunch unit synchronizer has a lower priority than the tape-unit synchronizer. The central processor has the lowest priority, since delaying a central-processor request for memory access will not disrupt the execution cycle or cause loss of information (in some systems).

priority indicator: Group of characters which indicate the relative urgency of a message and its order of transmission.

priority interrupt function: (a) distinguishes the highest priority interrupt active; (b) remembers lower priority interrupts which are active; (c) selectively enables or disables priority interrupts; (d) executes a jump instruction to a specific memory location; (f) stores the program counter register in a specific location.

priority interrupt module: A device which acts as the monitor for a number of priority-designated field contacts and immediately notifies the computer when any of these external priority requests have been generated. This assures servicing of urgent interrupt requests on the basis of programmer-assigned priorities when requests occur simultaneously on the same system.

priority interrupt system: A system in which each class of interrupts is assigned a priority.

priority level: The degree of precedence or urgency assigned to a message or operation.

priority modes: The organization of the flow of work through a computer. The mode depends upon the sophistication of the system and the machine, and will vary from a normal noninterrupt mode to a system in which there are several depths of interrupt.

priority multiplexing: Permits high-speed facilities to be serviced more frequently than low-speed facilities on a completely random basis.

priority or precedence: Controlled transmission of messages in a specific value order of their designated importance; i.e., urgent or routine.

priority, program: Positions which are assigned to computer programs in sequencing of operations on computers.

priority routine: In an interrupt, the leaving of the program by the processor to work on the program connected with the interruptor, the priority routine.

priority scheduling system: A unique type of job scheduler, in larger systems, designed so that a resultant improved system performance is achieved by means of input/-output queues.

priority switch table: A specific table which is included in the priority interrupt handling routine and contains the current status of all devices operating in the interrupt mode.

private: The secure or coded mode of operation. "Private" also can indicate military use.

private automatic branch exchange (PABX): Provides for the transmission of calls to and from the public telephone network.

private automatic exchange (PAX): The specific feature of various programs which restrict the use of input/output devices to special sets of instructions.

private branch exchange (PBX): A manual or dial exchange which is connected to the telephone network, located on a customer's premises and operated by his employees.

private circuit: Private communication line for the exclusive use of the purchaser, or lessee.

private code: An unnamed control section.

private facilities: Channels and equipment used by the communications common carriers to provide service dedicated to the use of one subscriber exclusively. Contrasts with exchange facilities.

private leased line: See private line.

private library (of a job step): A partitioned data set which is neither the link library nor any part of the job library.

private line: A service offered by the common carriers in which a customer may lease a circuit between two or more geographic points.

private line teleprinter service: Provides circuits for the exclusive use of particular subscribers. Keyboard printers, paper-tape punches, and paper-tape readers are used with these services. One circuit can connect two or more teleprinter machines.

private line voiceband: Circuits in which data set will operate at 4800 bits per second.

private line voice service: Provides a private voicegrade line for the exclusive use of a particular subscriber. This service can be used for either voice communication or data in transmission using a modem. The charges for private line service are based on a per mile, per month basis.

private line wire service: A channel furnished to a subscriber for his exclusive use.

private memory: The high-speed integrated-circuit memory of a central processing unit or input/output processor.

private switching network: A series of points interconnected by leased voice-grade telephone lines, with switching facilities or exchanges operated by the customer.

privileged: 1. A user entitled to execute certain system control commands from a terminal. 2. The level of access in a shared

data set (e.g., read-only access, read/write access, unlimited access, no access).

probability theory: A measure of likelihood of occurrence of a chance event, used to predict a behavior of a group.

problem board: 1. A removable panel containing an array of terminals that may be connected by short electrical leads according to a prescribed pattern. The entire prewired panel may be inserted for different programs. 2. A control panel or wiring panel.

problem definition: Compiling logic in the form of general flowcharts and logic diagrams which clearly explain and present the problem to the programmer in such a way that all requirements involved in the run are presented.

problem description: (ISO) In information processing, a statement of a problem. The statement may also include a description of the method of solution, the solution itself, the transformations of data and the relationship of procedures, data, constraints, and environment.

problem determination: The process of identifying a hardware, software, or system failure and determining whether the vendor or the user is responsible for diagnosis and repair.

problem determination aid (PDAID): A program that traces a specified event when it occurs during the operation of a program.

problem diagnosis: Analysis that results in identifying the precise cause of a hardware, software, or system failure.

problem-oriented language: A programming language that is especially suitable for a given class of problems.

problem program: A special program designed to solve a particular problem.

problem state: A state during which the central processing unit cannot execute input/output and other privileged instructions.

procedural and exception tests: Check machine control and operation before processing.

procedural command language: A source language consisting of procedural instructions, each instruction having the ability to specify a function to be executed.

procedure: The step-by-step process for the solution of a problem, especially the machine instructions embodying the solution.

procedure library: A program library in direct-access storage that contains job definitions. The reader/interpreter can be directed to read and interpret a particular job definition by an execute statement in the input stream.

procedure name: An alphanumeric label used to reference a cataloged procedure. See cataloged procedure.

procedure-oriented language: 1. A problem-oriented language that facilitates the expression of a procedure as an explicit algorithm. For example: FORTRAN, ALGOL, COBOL, PL/I. 2. A programming language designed for the convenient expression of procedures used in the solution of a wide class of problems.

procedure step: A unit of work associated with one processing program and related data within a cataloged procedure.

process: 1. To perform operations on data. 2. A systematic sequence of operations that produce a specified result. 3. A course of events occurring according to an intended purpose.

process chart: See flowchart.

process control: Descriptive of systems in which computers, most frequently analog computers, are used for the automatic regulation of operations or processes. Typical

are operations in the production of chemicals wherein the operation control is applied continuously and adjustments to regulate the operation are directed by the computer to keep the value of a controlled variable constant.

process control computer: A digital computer designed for a process control system.

process control loop: Control devices linked to control a phase or process.

process control system: A system in which a computer (generally analog) continuously controls a process automatically.

process functions: Collective functions performed in and by the equipment in which variables are controlled.

processing: The manipulation, preparation, and handling, of information or data equipment designed with programs to achieve desired results.

processing installation control: Automated scheduling of applications and jobs to reduce job turnaround time and to minimize time wasted in set-up.

processing plan: The interaction of man and machine to process data and control operations of both the organization and the computer system.

processing program: 1. A program that is both loaded and supervised by the control program. 2. A collection of manufacturer-supplied programs, language translators, linkage editor, librarian, autotest, sort/-merge, and utilities. All user written programs are processing programs.

process loop testing: A specific process used to determine the need for loop operations.

processor application: Job segments that are applications of a processor.

processor (CPU): Circuits of a computing system that control the interpretation and execution of instructions (does not include interface, core memory, or peripherals).

processor-independent interrupt: An interrupt that occurs independently of the processor such as upon completion of an input/output operation.

processor interrupts: Automatic procedures designed to alert the system to conditions arising that may affect the sequence of instructions being executed.

processor-limited: A system in which the overall processing time is dictated by the speed of the central processor.

processor storage: General purpose storage that is part of a central processing unit. Same as real storage.

processor verbs: Verbs which specify to the processor the procedures by which a source program is to be translated into an object program. Such verbs do not cause action at object time.

process pressure: The pressure of the process medium at the sensing element.

process-program entry: A terminal table entry containing information on a processing program as the destination for message.

process temperature: Temperature of the process medium at the sensing element.

process time: The time at which a source program is translated into an object program through the action of a processor.

product area: An area in main storage to store results of multiplication operations, specifically (in some systems).

product reference record manual: One page of the master product file.

production time: The part of operating time that is neither development time nor make-up time.

productivity system: A measure of the work performed by a system. Productivity largely depends on a combination of two other factors; the facility (ease of use) of the system and the performance of the system.

profile: A set of subject terms that indicates the subject interests of an information system user.

program: A plan for the solution of a problem; consists of planning and coding, numerical analysis, systems analysis, specification of printing formats, and any other functions necessary to the integration of a computer in a system.

program address counter: See location counter.

program attention (PA) key: On a display device keyboard, a key that produces an interruption to solicit program action that does not require the reading of data from the display buffer.

program check interruption (PCI): An interruption caused by unusual conditions encountered in a program, such as incorrect operands.

program control: Descriptive of a system in which a computer is used to direct an operation or process and automatically to hold or to make changes in the operation or process on the basis of a prescribed sequence of events.

program-controlled sequential computer: Executes instructions in a sequence designed with programs in mind; i.e., each instruction determines the location of the next instruction to be executed, a near-standard four-address computer.

program control transfer: Transfer of operational control among two or more independent programs being operated concurrently.

program control unit: The unit in a central processor that executes computer instructions.

program conversion: The controlled transition from an old system to a new one. It involves careful planning for the various steps that have to be taken, and equally careful supervision of their execution.

program counter: 1. A counter built into the control unit and used for sequencing instructions to be executed. It normally contains the address of the next instruction to be performed. 2. A device that records the storage location of the instruction word which is to be operated upon following the instruction word in current use. The control counter may select storage locations in sequence, thus obtaining the next instruction word from the subsequent storage location, unless a transfer or special instruction is encountered.

program deck: The binary output deck produced by the macro assembly program from the input deck for one compilation or assembly run.

program error: A mistake made in the program code by the programmer, keypuncher, or a machine-language compiler or assembler.

program evaluation and review technique (PERT): Critical path analysis using computer techniques.

program event recording (PER): A hardware feature used to assist in debugging programs by detecting program events.

program execution control: A part of the basic control function is performed by the program execution control. When an interruption occurs, it is the program execution control which determines the nature of the interruption and the appropriate action to be taken. The program execution control determines relative priority of programs ready to run, and loads other programs into storage (in some computers).

program flowchart: A flowchart designed for the representation of the sequence of operations within a program.

program halt: See program stop.

program input/output buffer: A portion of main storage into which data are read, or from which they are written.

program instruction: A set of characters that defines an operation and causes the computer to operate accordingly on the indicated quantities; a machine instruction for specific functions.

program language: A language which is used by programmers to write computer routines.

program library: 1. A collection of available computer programs and routines. 2. Same as partitioned data set.

program loop: A specific series of instructions which are repeated until a terminal condition is reached.

programmable concentrators: Since concentrators are programmable they can perform automatic speed recognition to accommodate automatically different speed devices, whereas multiplexers are limited to a single speed or predetermined set of speeds. Concentration need not be performed on a computer devoted to that application but may be merely a function of a general purpose minicomputer which is also acting as one of the switching computers in a network such as is done in the TYMNET and ARPANET.

programmable controller (PC): Used for industrial controls as direct replacements for electromechanical control relays. PCs provide the user with the benefit of solid-state reliability while avoiding its pitfalls. PCs have shielding or noise immune logic; i.e., designed-in isolation from high voltage input/output.

programmable electronic terminal (ET) phones: A series of microprocessor controlled, hands-free telephones. These instruments, with multi-line and display capabilities, improve office productivity when installed on the various private automatic branch exchange (PABX) communication systems. A speaker and microphone within the ET sets provide hands-free dialing, answer back, and other features which are provided by peripheral units. The various ET sets give single-button access to a variety of PABX features, thus eliminating the need to remember procedures and access codes. The ET display often also serves as a clock/calendar which displays the elapsed time and cost of a call in progress. The units are retrofitted easily to currently installed systems.

programmable frequency synthesizer: A compact transportable signal generator that can send two tones between 20 Hz and 20 Khz simultaneously. On these systems, programs can be entered from the keyboard and functions executed with simple commands. User prompts are shown on an easy-to-read 40-character alphanumeric display. An RS-232 interface for downloading and uploading user programs, as well as remote operations, is included.

programmable logic array (PLA): Uses a standard logic network programmed to perform a specific function. PLAs are implemented in either metal-oxide semiconductors or bipolar circuits and are an alternative to read-only memories.

programmable memory: A memory whose locations are addressable by the computer's program counter, i.e., a program within this memory may directly control the operation of the arithmetic and control unit.

programmable read-only memory (PROM): A semiconductor diode array that is programmed by fusing or burning out diode junctions.

program maintenance procedures: Diagnostics checking and test routines designed by manufacturers or software companies for purposes of removing machine malfunctions, human errors, or programmer mistakes.

programmatics: The study of the techniques of programming and programming languages.

programmed acceleration: A controlled velocity increase to the programmed rate.

programmed check: A check of machine functions performed by the machine in response to an instruction included in a program.

programmed dwell: A programmed code that will cause particular axes to dwell for a given period of time.

programmed input/output (I/O) channel: Program control of information transfer between the central processor and an external device provides the fastest method of operating on data received from peripheral equipment. The programmed input/output channel allows input directly to the accumulator where the data can be acted on immediately, thus eliminating the need for a memory reference by either the channel or the program. Likewise, output data may be sent directly from the accumulator to an external device.

programmed instructions: Special subroutines, called programmed instructions, may be used as if they were single commands by employing one of the programmed instructions of the repertoire. This capability allows the programmer to define his own special command, through the use of subroutines, which may be changed by the operating routine if desired.

programmed learning: As instructional methodology based upon alternating expository material with questions coupled to branching logic for remedial purposes. May be implemented in book form ("programmed text") or in computers [tutorial computer-assisted-instruction (CAI)].

programmed logic: The internal logic design alterable in accordance with a pre-completed program which controls the various electronic interconnections of the gating elements, e.g., the instruction repertoire can be electronically changed, or the machine capability can be matched to the problem requirement.

programmed marginal check: A particular marginal check performed under the supervision of a program.

programmed selective dump: A library subroutine called by object programs at run time. The dump may return control to the calling program or to the monitor upon completion. This allows the programmer to take selective dumps during program execution for debugging purposes.

programmer: A person who designs, writes, and tests computer programs.

programmer analyst: Refines systems plans and diagrams into detailed steps.

programmer-defined macros: Segments of coding used frequently throughout a program that can be defined at the beginning and used and referenced by a mnemonic code with parameters. This increases coding efficiency and readability of the program.

programmer reference manual: Contains instructions for utilizing programs or coding for a given system, language, or application, e.g., a FORTRAN programmer reference manual.

programming: (ISO) The designing, writing, and testing of programs.

programming control panel: A panel made up of indicator lights and switches by which a programmer can enter or change routines in the computer.

programming flowchart: A flowchart representing the sequence of operations in a program.

programming language: A language, other than machine language, used for expressing computer programs.

programming module: A discrete identifiable set of instructions, usually handled as a unit by an assembler, a compiler, a linkage editor, a loading routine, or other type of routine or subroutine.

programming system: A system that consists of a programming language, a computer program, and the processor to convert the language into absolute coding.

program module: A set of programming instructions which is treated as a unit by an assembler, compiler, loader, or translator.

program module dictionary (PMD): A parameter collection of control and descriptive information concerning a program module required by programs that must process that module.

program parameter: A parameter incorporated into a subroutine during computation. A program parameter frequently comprises a word stored relative to either the subroutine or the entry point. It may be altered by the routine and/or may vary from one point of entry to another.

progam patching plug: A small auxiliary plugboard patched with a specific variation of a portion of a program and designed to be plugged into a larger plugboard patched with the main program.

program product: A licensed program that performs a function for the user. It interacts with and relies upon system control programming. A program product contains logic related to the user's data and is usable or adaptable to meet his/her specific requirements.

program reference table (PRT): An area in memory for the storage of operands, references to arrays, references to segments of a program, and references to files. Permits programs to be independent of the actual memory locations occupied by data and parts of the program.

program relocation: The moving of an object program in main memory at run time in order to make the best use of available memory. The object program is not aware of its physical change of position and therefore does not alter its own program addresses.

program restriction: A limitation in the performance of a tape transport falling within the specified normal range of operation of the unit and requiring modification of the command sequences to obtain normal accuracy in recording and reproduction of information.

program segment: The part of a program that is contained in a program deck.

program sensitive fault: A fault that appears in response to some particular sequence of program steps. Contrast with pattern sensitive fault.

program sensitive malfunction: A malfunction that occurs only when some unusual combination of program steps occur.

program sequencing librarian: Tells the librarian the sequence in which the programs are to be put on the library tape. (a) Select: used when the input media is on two or more handlers; when the input media is any combination of punched cards, paper tape, or magnetic tape, or when the input media is on two or more input units. Each time the input media changes it will be necessary to issue a new select instruction. If the input does not change, the original select instruction is sufficient. (b) Copy: performs a straight copy function. It will not make changes to the program(s) copied. The program to be copied is indicated in the operand column. The copy instruction should be used only to copy from one library tape to create another library tape. This instruction cannot be used if the input is a tape punched card, or paper tape.

program signal: The electric waves in an audio system which correspond to the various sounds to be reproduced.

program space allocation: Assigns various spaces in memory for input/output data and temporary (intermediate) results.

programs pre-edit: A checking of the application or operational program before the test run. A pre-edit run can remove disobedience to established supervisory, main memory, or program segmentation rules, etc

program statements: These compose a computer program.

program status word (PSW):   A double-word in main storage used to control the order in which instructions are executed, and to hold and indicate the status of the computing system in relation to a particular program.

program step: A phase of one instruction of command in a sequence of instructions. Thus, a single operation.

program stop: A stop instruction built into the program that will stop the machine under certain conditions, upon reaching the end of the processing, or upon completing the solution of a problem.

program storage: A portion of the internal storage reserved for the storage of programs, routines, and subroutines. In many systems protection devices are used to prevent inadvertent alteration of the contents of the program storage.

program suspending: The task of determining when transfer of control should take place in a multiprogramming system.

program test: A system of checking before running any problem in which a sample problem of the same type with a known answer is run.

program testing time: The machine time expended for program testing, debugging, and volume and compatibility testing.

program test system (PTS):   A system that automatically tests programs and produces diagnostics.

program verbs: Verbs which cause the processor to generate machine instructions which will be executed by the object program.

progression: 1. A discrete series in which the terms increase or decrease according to a uniform law. 2. A discrete series that has a first but no last element and the intermediate elements are related by a uniform law to the other elements.

progressive overflow: On a direct access storage device, the writing of overflow records on the next consecutive track. Contrast with chaining overflow.

prompting: In systems with time sharing, a function that helps a terminal user by requesting him to supply operands necessary to continue processing.

proof: An operation for testing the accuracy of a previous operation, such as relisting the checks and adding their amounts to determine the accuracy of the total shown. Proof is effected when a total agrees with another total of the same items arrived at in a different manner. It is then said to be in balance.

proof department: The department within a bank charged with proving, listing, sorting, and distributing all transactions arising from commercial operations of the bank.

proof listing: A report prepared by a processor which shows the coding as originally written, any comments that may have been written, and the machine language instructions produced.

proof machine: A machine designed to prove all deposits and other credits. The proof machine may also sort and distribute the debits to various sorting compartments for bank processing.

proof tape: Listing of documents used to prove the accuracy of the items listed.

propagated error: An error occurring in one operation which spreads through and influences later operations and results.

propagation: Traveling of a wave along a transmission path.

propagation constant: A number expressed in the Greek letter rho to indicate the effect on a wave in a transmission line propagating through it.

propagation delay: The time necessary for a signal to travel from one point on a circuit to another.

propagation loss: The transmission loss for radiated energy traversing a given path. It is equal to the sum of the spreading loss (due to increase of the wavefront area) and the attenuation loss (due to absorption and scattering).

propagation time: Time needed for an electrical pulse to travel from one point to another.

proper subset: A set, A, can have a subset, A_1 such that A intersection A_1 is not identical with A, and is thus a proper subset.

property sort: A technique for selecting records from a file which satisfy a certain criterion.

proportional band: 1. The specific ranges of values of a condition being regulated. Designed to cause the controller to operate over its full range. 2. A particular change in input required to produce a full range change in output.

proportional control: A method of control in which the intensity of action varies linearly as the condition being regulated deviates from the condition prescribed.

proportional control action: Designed control action in which there is a continuous linear relation between input/output (I/O). Such a condition applies when the I/Os operate within their normal ranges and at a frequency below a limiting value.

proportional control system: A special type of feedback control system designed so that the correction generated is a linear function of the original error.

proportional gain: A specific ratio of the change in output due to proportinal control action to the change in input.

proportionality transducer: A constant ratio of incremental cause and effect. Proportionality is a special case of linearity in which the straight line passes through the origin. Zero-error reference of a linear transducer is a selected straight-line function of the input from which output errors are measured. Zerobased linearity is transducer linearity defined in terms of a zero-error reference where zero input coincides with zero output.

proportional plus derivative control action (rate): Specific control action in which the output is proportional to a linear combination of the input and the time rate-of-change of input.

proportional plus derivative controller: Specific control action in which the output is proportional to a linear combination of the input and the time integral of the output.

proportional plus integral controller: A controller that produces proportional plus integral (reset) control action.

proportional plus integral plus derivative controller: A controller which produces proportional plus integral (reset) plus derivative (rate) control action.

proportional range: The band, range, or set of values of a specific condition which is controlled and will cause the controller to operate over its full linear range. A proportional range is most often expressed in terms of full-scale of the associated instrument.

proportional speed floating controller: A unique single action controller which produces integral control action only.

proposal: A statement by a contracting or consulting firm describing how it would carry out a project described by the sponsoring agency or customer, usually in the form of a Request for Proposal (RFP). They include information describing the qualifications of the people who would work on the project, a project management plan, and a budget or price for the project.

proprietary program: A program release by an owner through the legal right of possession and title. Commonly the title remains with the owner and its use is allowed with the stipulation that no disclosure of the program can be made to any other party without prior agreement between the owner and user.

pro-rated billing: The preparation of bills for each of the multiple responsible parties, properly using applicable allocation and selection formulae to distribute charges.

prosign precedence: A group of characters which indicate to communications personnel how a message is to be handled.

protected check: A check that is prepared in such a manner as to prevent alterations.

protected field: A display field in which the user cannot enter, modify, or erase data from the keyboard.

protected files: Files in a computer system that are accessible only to a specific user. Since most files in a system are protected in this way, one user usually cannot obtain access to the information in another user's files.

protected locations: Block locations reserved for special purposes, such as in main storage or on disk files. Data may be read from, but nothing may be written into, these locations.

protection key: An indicator associated with a task which appears in the program status word whenever the task is in control, and which must match the storage keys of all storage blocks which it is to use.

protection, multiprogramming memory: A method of insuring that each program in a multiprogramming environment is protected against all contemporary programs, and in particular, that each program has inviolate storage areas. This is accomplished by independently establishing reserved areas in each store module, and inhibiting a program from reading, writing, or transferring to a location that is not within its reserved areas. Every instruction which references central store has the final address checked to insure that it falls within a permissible area. Store protection is only effective when the guard mode is operative. When an interrupt occurs, the guard mode is terminated and all existing storage is available for execute use. The previously established limits remain loaded and upon executing the load internal function instruction, these limits are once again effective (in some systems).

protection ratio: The lowest ratio of the signal strength of a required signal to that of the interfering signals, to obtain satisfactory and consistent radio reception.

protocol: A collection of rules and conventions which govern the format and content of isolated data, files, or other messages to be communicated from one terminal to another. Sophisticated systems use a complex hierarchy of protocols in order to ease implementation. These hierarchies consist of high-level protocols which are defined in terms of lower-level protocols. In general, each level of protocols make use of subsequently lower levels of protocol.

prototyping boards (microprocessor): Electronic component boards that form operational microprogrammed computers, often with erasable PROMs in place of maskprogrammed ROMs. Standard types hold up to 16 K bits of PROM and 8 K bits of RAM.

PRR (pulse repetition rate): The number of electric pulses per unit of time experienced by a point in a computer; usually the maximum, normal or standard pulse rate.

pseudo-applications program: An operational program that is written to test the supervisory program.

pseudo-clock: A main storage location used by timer supervision routines to calculate timer intervals and time-of-day.

pseudo-code: 1. A code which expresses programs in source language; i.e., by referring to storage locations and machine operations by symbolic names and addresses which are independent of their hardwaredetermined names and addresses. 2. An arbitrary code, independent of the hardware of a computer and designed for convenience in programming. It must be translated into computer code if it is to direct the computer.

pseudo-instruction: 1. One instruction of a pseudocode which is not part of a computer's built-in instruction repertory as realized by hardware. 2. An instruction to a compiler which does not result directly in object code.

pseudo-instruction form: Data represented in the same form as an instruction.

pseudo-operation: An operation that is not part of the computer's operation repertoire as realized by hardware; an extension of the set of machine operations.

pseudo op (pseudo-instruction): 1. A symbolic representation in a compiler or interpreter. 2. A group of characters having the same general form as a computer instruction, but never executed by the computer as an actual instruction. (Same as quasi instruction.) 3. An instruction written in an assembly language designating a predetermined and limited group of computer instructions for performing a particular task.

pseudo-random: The property of satisfying one or more of the standard criteria for statistical randomness but being produced by a definite calculation process.

pseudo-random codes: Digital codes that appear as a random sequence but are of finite length. Therefore, they repeat and are not truly random. They are useful for synchronization and controlling sequences.

pseudo-random-number sequence: A set of numbers produced by a definite recursive rule and satisfying one or more of the standard statistical tests for randomness. Such numbers may approximate uniform (any number in the set of possible numbers being equally likely), normal or Gaussian (having the property of a normal or Gaussian distribution) or some other type of statistical distribution. See random number sequence.

P-type conductivity: In a semiconductor, conductivity due to the movement of holes.

P-type semiconductor: A semiconducting crystal material which has been doped with very tiny amounts of an impurity that will produce donor-type centers of electrons in the crystal lattice structure. Since electrons are negative particles, the material is called N-type. Electrons are the major carrier of current.

public switched network: Any switching system that provides circuit switching to many customers.

pull operation: An operation in which an operand (or operands) is taken from the top of a pushdown stack in memory and placed in a general register (or registers). The operand remains in the stack unaltered; only a pointer value indicating the current top-of-stack is changed.

pulsating dc: An electric current which flows in a single direction and varies in intensity.

pulse: A change in the intensity or level of some medium over a short period of time.

pulse amplifier: An amplifier with very wide frequency response which can amplify pulses without distortion of the short rise time of the leading edge.

pulse amplitude: The maximum instantaneous value of a pulse.

pulse amplitude modulation (PAM): The coding of a continuous or analog signal onto a uniformly-spaced sequence of constant-width pulses by amplitude-modulating the intensity of each pulse, i.e., similar to AM radio broadcasts except that the carrier is a pulse and not a sine wave.

pulse carrier: A carrier wave composed of a series of equally spaced pulses.

pulse channel: The channel pulse is a pulse representing intelligence on a channel by virtue of its time or modulation characteristic.

pulse code: 1. A code in which sets of pulses have been assigned particular meanings. 2. The binary representation of characters.

pulse code modulation (PCM): The form of modulation in which the modulating signal is sampled and the sample quantized and coded so that each element of the information consists of different kinds and/or numbers of pulses and spaces.

pulse corrector: A circuit incorporated in a pulse repeater which transmits cleaned-up pulses even if distorted pulses have been received.

pulse-counting module: A device which counts and stores a number of high or low-speed pulse channels and transmits their status to the computer upon command (in some systems).

pulse detector: One designed for use with modulated pulse signals.

pulse digit: A drive pulse which corresponds to a one digit position in some or all the words in a storage unit.

pulse discriminator: A device which responds only to a pulse having a particular characteristic, such as duration, or period. The latter is also called a time discriminator.

pulse drive: A particular pulse of current in a winding that is inductively coupled to one or more magnetic cells which produces a pulse of magnetomotive force.

pulse droop: The exponential decay of amplitude which is often experienced with nominally rectangular pulses of appreciable duration.

pulse duration modulation (PDM): Pulse-time modulation in which the value of each instantaneous sample of the modulating wave is caused to modulate the duration of a pulse. Note: In pulse modulation, the modulating wave may vary the time of occurrence of the leading edge, the trailing edge, or both edges of the pulse.

pulse frequency modulation: Modulation in which the pulse-repetition frequency of the carrier is varied in accordance with the amplitude and frequency of the modulating signal.

pulse generator: The circuit in a cathode-ray tube transmitter which generates the basic timing impulses for blanking and sync.

pulse interleaving or interlacing: Adding independent pulse trains on the basis of time division multiplex along a common path.

pulse interrogation: The triggering of a transponder by a pulse or pulse mode.

pulse length: Nominal duration of a standard pulse which is the time-interval between the half amplitude points of the rise and decay points of the curve. For pulses of other shapes, the points on the curve must be stated.

pulse length modulation: Pulse time modulation in which the value of each instantaneous sample of the modulating wave is caused to modulate the duration of a pulse.

pulse mode: Coded group of pulses which select a particular communication channel from a common carrier. A pulse mode multiplex controls these channels by means of pulse demoders.

pulse modulation: The use of a series of pulses designed to convey the information contained in the modulating function. The characteristics of a train of pulses may be modified in one of several ways to convey information, including amplitude (PAM), position (PPM), and duration (PDM).

pulse noise: A spurious signal of short duration that occurs during reproduction of a tape and is of a magnitude that is considerably in excess of the average peak value of the ordinary system noise.

pulse operation: Operation of a circuit or device in which energy is supplied in pulses.

pulse-origin time: A start of a pulse is defined as the time at which it first reaches some given fraction, e.g., 10 percent of its full amplitude.

pulse position modulation: A form of pulse time modulation in which the positions of time pulses are varied, without modifying their duration.

pulse regeneration: The process of restoring a series of pulses to original timing, form, and magnitude.

pulse repetition frequency (PRF): The number of electric pulses per unit of time.

pulse rise-time: The time required for the leading edge of a pulse to rise.

pulse-spacing teletypewriter: A spacing pulse or "space" is the signal pulse which, in dc neutral operation, corresponds to a circuit open or no current condition.

pulse spectrum: The distribution, as a function of frequency, of the magnitudes of the Fourier components of a pulse.

pulse-spreading: The increase in pulse width within a given length of fiber due to effects of model and material dispersion.

pulse stretcher: An electronic unit used to increase the time duration of a pulse.

pulse-swapping standardization: A restoration or generation of specific pulses meeting set requirements for amplitude, shape, timing, etc..

pulse time modulation: Modulation in which the values of an instantaneous sample of modulating wave are called to modulate the time occurrence of some charateristic of a pulse carrier.

pulse train: Groups of pulses which occur in time sequence at a circuit point.

pulse-train generator: A circuitry system or device which, with a signal stimulus, produces a fixed number of equally spaced pulses.

pulse transformer: A transformer which permits impedance matching between circuits or reverses polarity by using square hysteresis loop material for the core and other windings ratios to allow output currents or voltages at proper levels.

pulse-width modulation: The duration of a pulse in the time interval between the points of the leading and trailing edges at which the instantaneous value bears a specified relation to the pulse amplitude.

pulse-width recording: A procedure for magnetic recording of bits in which each storage cell comprises two regions magnetized in opposite senses with unmagnetized regions on each side, i.e., the zero bit is represented by a cell containing a negative region followed by a positive region.

punching positions: The specific areas, e.g., rowcolumn intersects, on a punch card where holes may be punched.

punctuation bits: The use of a variable-length data format requires that there be a method of indicating the actual length of a unit of information. This requirement is fulfilled by two punctuation bits associated with each memory location. These bits can constitute a word mark—used to define the length of a field; an item mark—used to define the length of an item; or a record mark—used to define the length of a record.

pure binary: Expression of binary numerals in a system of positional notation in which each successive digit position is weighted by a factor of two times the weight of the prior position.

pure generator: A unique generator which is a routine capable of writing another routine. When this is tied to an assembler, the pure generator is usually a section of a program found on a library tape and is called into storage by the assembler, which then writes one or more entries in the routine.

purge: To remove unwanted records from a file.

pushbutton dialing pad: A twelve-key device to originate tone keying signals. It usually is attached to rotary dial telephones for use in originating data signnals.

push-down dialing: The use of keys or pushbuttons instead of a rotary dial to generate a sequence of digits to establish a circuit connection.

push-down list: A list of items where the last item entered is the first item of the list, and the relative position of the other items is pushed back one.

push-down queue: A last-in, first-out, (LIFO) method of queuing in which the last item attached to the queue is the first to be withdrawn.

push-down stack: A procedure which develops a reserved area of memory into which operands are pushed and from which operands are pulled on a last-in, first-out basis.

push-down storage: A technique used in which data enters at the top register and information is pushed down from register to register.

push operation: An operation in which an operand (or operands) from a general register (or registers) is stored into the new top location of a push-down stack in memory.

push-pull: 1. General principle of transmission, whereby one leg of a balanced circuit is driven by a periodic waveform, while the other leg is driven by the same waveform with phase reversed. 2. Soundtracks which carry sound recordings in antiphase. Class A soundtracks carry the whole waveform and Class B carries half the waveform, both halves united optically or in a push-pull photocell.

push-to-talk operation: A vocal communication affecting a capability of speaking in one direction at a time by using a switch depressed during transmission.

push-up list: A list of items where each item is entered at the end of the list, and the other items maintain their same relative position in the list.

push-up queue: First-in first-out (FIFO) queue.

put: To place a single data record into an output file.

pyramid reporting: Reporting based upon a constant review of data so that only pertinent information goes up the line of command.

Q

Q address: A source location in internal storage in some types of equipment from which data is transferred.

Q-band: A frequency band used in radar.

QCB: See queue control block.

Q output state: 1. The reference output of a flip-flop. When this output is "1" the flip-flop is said to be in the "1" state; when it is "0" the output is said to be in the "0" state. 2. The second output of a flip-flop. It is always opposite in logic level to the Q output.

Q test: A comparison test of two or more units of quantitative data for their equality or nonequality.

quaded cable: A particular cable in which some or all of the conductors are arranged in groups of four.

quadrant: One of the four quarters of the rectangular coordinate dimensioning system.

quadratic: Indicating or relating to a function of the form $f(x) = ax^2 + bx + c$, where $a \neq 0$.

quadratic programming: In operations research, a particular case of nonlinear programming in which the function to be maximized or minimized is a quadratic function and the constraints are linear functions.

quadrature component: The reactive component of a current or voltage due to inductive or capacitive reactance in a circuit.

quadripuntal: Four random punches on a punch card. This term is used in determinative documentation.

quadruple address: 1. A specific method of specifying the location of operands and instructions in which the storage location of the two operands and the storage location of the results of the operation are cited. The storage location of the next instruction to be executed is cited. 2. Each complete instruction specifies the operation and addresses of four registers.

quadruplex system: A system of Morse telegraphy arranged for simultaneous independent transmission of two messages in each direction over a single circuit.

qualification: The process of uniquely identifying the symbols defined in a given section of a program segment by appending another symbol.

qualification testing: A rigorous and formal test of a computer program or system prior to its delivery from the manufacturer to the user.

qualification time: The time which multiplied by the nominal tape speed gives the start distance.

qualified name: A data set name that is composed of multiple names separated by periods (i.e., tree, fruit, apple).

qualified parts list (QPL): A list of products, qualified under the requirements stated in the applicable specification, including appropriate product identification and test reference with the name and plant address of the manufacturer or distributer.

qualifier: All component names in a qualified name other than the right-most (which is called the simple name).

403

quality: Fidelity of reproduction of an original phenomenon.

quality control: Maintenance of production specification within a specified tolerance, aided by an electronic computer which automatically determines mean or mean-square of deviation of actual measurement from that specified.

quanta: 1. The intervals of a set or group used to quantize a function. Units of time in a queue.

quantal data: A discontinuous form, i.e. larger or smaller amounts occur in jumps or increments (quanta) of equal size.

quantity: A positive or negative real number.

quantization: The subdivision of a continuous range into a finite number of distinct elements; a process similar to analog-to-digital conversion.

quantization error: A measure of uncertainty which occurs as a result of the quantization of a function in a continuous interval.

quantize: To subdivide the range of a variable into a finite number of non-overlapping intervals, each of which is assigned a specific code identity.

quantizer: digitizer.

quantizing uncertainty or error: Since the analog continuum is partitioned into 2^n discrete ranges for n-bit conversion, the same digital code, usually assigned to the nominal mid-range value, represents all analog values within a given quantum. Therefore, an inherent quantization uncertainty of ½ LSB is associated with the resolution, in addition to the actual conversion errors. This uncertainty is a property of system resolution.

quantum: A unit of processing time in a time-sharing system that may be allocated for operating a program during its turn in the computer. More quanta may be allocated to higher priority programs than to lower priority programs.

quantum electronics: Amplification or generation of microwave power in solid crystals, governed by quantum mechanical laws.

quartz crystal: A piezoelectric crystal which regulates an oscillator frequency.

quartz delay line: A sonic delay line using a length of quartz crystal as an acoustical medium and with sound waves representing digital data being propagated over a fixed distance.

quasi-optical waves: Electromagnetic waves of short wavelength so that their laws of propagation are similar to those of visible light.

quaternary signaling: An electrical communications mode in which information is passed by the presence or absence, or plus and minus variations, of four discrete levels of one parameter of the signaling medium.

query station: A specific unit of equipment which introduces requests or queries for data, states of processing, information, etc. while the equipment is computing or processing or communicating.

question/answering system: An interactive system that allows a user to obtain answers generated by the computer from data contained in several different records or files.

queue: Waiting lines resulting from temporary delays in providing service.

queue area system: 1. In OS/360, a main storage are reserved for control blocks and tables maintained by the control program. 2. In OS/VS, an area of virtual storage reserved for system-related control blocks. Abbreviated SQA.

queue, automatic: Refers to a specific series of interconnected registers which are designed to implement either a LIFO (Last-In-First-Out) queue or a FIFO (First-In-First-Out) queue without program manipulation. For a FIFO queue, new entries to the queue are placed in the position and automatically jump forward to the last unoccupied position, while removal of the front entry results in all entries automatically moving forward one position. Also called push-down storage and push-up storage.

queue control block (QCB): A special control block which is designed to be used in the regulation of the sequential use of some programmer-defined facility by a set of competing tasks.

queue control task block: See queue control block (QCB).

queued content addressed memory: An experimental automatic memory structure which contains a series of parallel automatic queues.

queue discipline: A method that determines which of several items awaiting processing should received service.

queued sequential access method (QSAM): A method which forms queues of input data blocks that await processing or queues of output data blocks that have been processed and await transfer to auxiliary storage or to an output device.

queued telecommunications access method (QTAM): A method which transfers data between main storage and remote terminals.

queuing: A study of the patterns involved and the time required for discrete units to move through channels.

queuing list: A list frequently used for scheduling actions in real-time on a time-priority basis. Appends are made following the ending item. The beginning item is always the removed item.

queuing theory: A form of probability theory useful in studying delays or line-ups at servicing points.

quibinary code: A binary-coded decimal code for representing decimal numbers in which each decimal digit is represented by seven binary digits which are coefficients of 8, 6, 4, 2, 0, 1, and 0, respectively.

quick-access memory: A part of memory that has a short access time, as compared to the main memory of the central processing unit.

quick disconnect: A type of connector shell which allows for very quick locking and unlocking of two connector parts.

quick start: See system restart.

quiescent: A system that is waiting to be operated; e.g., a valve ready to amplify.

quiescent carrier transmission: One for which the carrier is suppressed in the absence of modulation.

quiescing: The stopping of a multiprogrammed system by means of the rejection of new jobs.

quietening: A receiving circuit device for the suppression of background noise while tuning between radio stations.

quiet error: Errors that occur in manual-mechanical systems and are corrected before they spread throughout the process or system.

quiting: The level reduction by which background noise is reduced when the tuner of the radio set is fed with a radio-frequency signal of a specified voltage.

quinary: See biquinary code.

quinary notation: Notation using the base 5.

quoted string: In assembler programming, a character string enclosed by apostrophes that is used in a macroinstruction operand to represent a value that can include blanks. The enclosed apostrophes are part of the value represented.

quotient: The quantity resulting from the division of a dividend by a divisor. If the dividend is not an even multiple of the divisor, the quantity left over is the remainder.

QWERTY keyboard: The most common type of typing keyboard.

R

rack: The frame or chassis on which panels of electrical equipment may be mounted.

radar computer simulator: The random-access plan position indicator (RAPPI) mode provides visual monitoring of processed radar data (range and azimuth) including beacon and search radar targets, and map outlines selected by a AN/FYQ-40 message label. The RAPPI displays target and air route surveillance radar. The RAPPI contains a built-in symbol generator for displaying 16 symbols to provide a visual indication of the message label, and test switches which can simulate targets (type, range, and azimuth) on the display.

radiation: Energy propogated through space or through a material medium in the form of high density waves.

radio: A method of signalling through space, without connecting wires, by means of electromagnetic waves generated by high-frequency alternating currents.

radio beam: Concentration of electromagnetic radiation within narrow angular limits, such as is emitted from a highly directional antenna in the form of a curtain or bowl.

radio broadcasting: The transmission of a sound or television program for general reception by means of electromagnetic waves.

radio circuit: A communication system which includes a radio link comprised of a transmitter and antenna, the radio transmission path with possible reflections or scatter from ionized regions, and a receiving antenna and receiver.

radio direction finder: A radio receiver with a special antenna capable of locating the direction of a transmitter; a navigation device.

radio frequency interference (RFI): Unwanted interference of electromagnetic radiation of radio frequency signals into operating circuits.

radio frequency (rf): A frequency residing above the audio range and below the frequency of visible light.

radiographic test: Detects internal defects such as loose or extraneous wires, improperly dressed wire bonds, and voids in the die attach material or in the epoxy when epoxy seals are used.

radio link: A self-contained radio circuit capable of working in both directions for insertion between two land-line circuits.

radio-relay station: An intermediate station receiving a signal from the primary transmitter and re-radiating it to its destination.

radio telephony: Use of a radio channel for transmission of telephonic speed.

radix: The radix of a number system is that system's base, or the total number of symbols used in the system. For example, the binary number system has a radix of two, since it uses only two symbols (0,1). The decimal number system, because it uses the digits (0, 1, 2, 3, 4, 5, 6, 7, 8, and 9) has a radix of 10.

radix complement: See complement.

radix notation, mixed: A radix notation which uses more than one radix in a numeration system. A prime example is biquinary notation.

radix number: See radix.

radix point: The dot that delineates the integer digits from the fractional digits of a number. It delineates the digital position involving the zero exponent of the radix from the digital position involving thq minus-one exponent of the radix. The radix point is identified by the name of the system, e.g., binary point, octal point, or decimal point. In the writing of any number in any system, if no dot is included, the radix point is assumed to follow the rightmost digit.

rain barrel effect: An echo-like effect developed into an audio signal which passes over properly compensated or terminated transmission lines as a result of repeated signal reflections.

RAM: See random-access memory.

ramp response: The total time response (transient plus steady-state) resulting from a sudden increase in the rate of change in the input from zero to some finite value.

ramp-response time: The time interval by which an output follows an input, when both vary at a constant rate.

ramp signal: A signal which changes linearly with time.

random access: The process of obtaining information from or placing information into a storage system where the time required for such access is independent of the location of the information most recently obtained or placed in storage. 2. Describing a device in which random access, as defined in 1, can be achieved without effective penalty in time.

random-access device: A storage device in which the access time is independent of the location of the data, (i.e., disk, drum as opposed to a serial access device such as a magnetic tape drive.)

random-access disk file bank: Stores account records and related information, such as holds and no-book transactions. Since access time to the disk file is so fast (average of 1/50 of a second), its storage provides a virtually unlimited extension of core memory. Consequently, there are virtually no limits to the number of tellers for whom proof totals can be maintained, the variety of transactions which can be handled, the variations in transaction processing that individual institutions require, and the variety of passbook formats that are used. The extreme reliability and fast access of the disk file systems from its head-per-track design. There is no positioning of arms or read-write heads since each track has its own readwrite device.

random-access input/output (I/O) routines: Direct, serial, and random processing of drum and disk files which are provided by specific routines. Macroinstructions are available to direct the performance of the I/O functions.

random (RAM) access memory: A memory whose information media are organized into discrete locations, sectors, etc., each uniquely identified by an address. Data may be obtained from such a memory by specifying the data address(es) to the memory, i.e., core, drum, disk, cards.

random-access sorts: Sorts to be performed on random access devices such as magnetic disk and drum.

random-access storage: A storage technique in which the time required to obtain information is independent of the location of the information most recently obtained.

random error: An error that varies in a random fashion, e.g., an error resulting from radio noise or interference.

random file key: A key set of characters that identify the file. In some cases it is desirable to spread new records evenly throughout a file space. For each new record, a random number is generatied and the random number is converted to the address where the item may be stored. If the item cannot be stored in this pocket an overflow pocket will be used.

randomizing: A technique in which the range of keys for an indirectly addressed file is reduced to successively smaller ranges of addresses by some method of computation until the desired address if found.

random number: 1. A set of digits constructed in a sequence so that each succesive digit is equally likely to be any of n digits to the base n of the number. 2. A grouping or succession of digits or numbers developed entirely as a result of a chance process.

random-number generator: A machine routine or hardware designed to produce a random number or series of random numbers according to specified limitations.

random-number sequence: An unpredictable array of numbers satisfying one or more of the statistical tests for randomness.

random-number table: A table of random numbers, used in statistical calculations.

random processing: 1. The treatment of data without respect to its location in external storage, and in an arbitrary sequence governed by the input against which it is to be processed. 2. The processing of data that are in no predetermined order when they enter the computer system.

random sample: A sample in which every item in the population has an equal chance of being included in the sample. This definition implies that the selection of the sample should be left to chance.

random scan: The type of scan where the electron beam of the CRT can be deflected in any direction and the parts of the display can be drawn in any order. See raster scan.

random-sequential access: A storage device in which the information storage medium is grouped in strips. The computer can gain random access to any one strip as easily as any other, but it is then necessary to scan sequentially along the strip to find the desired word.

random-uniform number: Sets of digits constructed in a sequence so that each successive digit is equally likely to be any of n digits to the base of the number.

random walk method: A statistical term that relates to movement to the next position (related to probability).

range: A characterization of a variable or function; all the values which a function may have.

range disk-operating (DO) statement: All FORTRAN statements included in the repetitive execution of a DO loop operation.

range finder: An adjustable mechanism on a teletypewriter receiver which allows the receiver-distributor face to be moved through an arc corresponding to the length of a unit segment. It is adjusted for best results under operating line conditions.

range value accuracy: This is expressed as a percent of the upper range-value.

rank: To arrange in an ascending or descending order according to importance.

rapid access loop: A small section of storage, particularly in drum, tape or disk storage units, that has much faster access than the remainder of the storage.

rapid storage: Storage with a very short access time.

raster: The bright white glow which covers the cathode-ray tube when no signal is received.

raster burn: Deterioration of the scanned area of the screen of a television picture or camera tube as a result of use.

raster grid: On a display device, the grid of addressable coordinates on the display surface.

raster scan: The type of scan used in television and some computer CRT's where the electron beam always moves left to right, and top to bottom. The drawing is divided into horizontal lines and the appropriate points on each line are illuminated. Computer raster graphics contain anywhere from 256 to 1024 lines; the higher the number of lines, the greater the resolution of the picture. See random scan.

rate center: A geographical location used by telephone companies to determine mileage measurements for the application of interexchange mileage rates.

rated speed: The maximum possible speed at which a data-processing device or a line can operate. In general, a piece of equipment's rated speed is expressed in characters per second (cps), and a communication facility's rated speed is expressed in bits per second (bps). For example, if a printer's rated speed is 150 cps, then it could print up to 150 characters in a second, but could never print more than that in one second.

rate gain: A ratio of maximum gain resulting from proportional plus derivate control action to the gain due to proportional action.

rate of perforation: The determination of the speed of punching holes in paper tape by a punching device, expressed in characters per minute or characters per second.

rate of translation error: The ratio of the number of alphabetic characters incorrectly translated to the number of alphabetic characters in the undistorted and restored message at the input of the receiving apparatus.

ratio controller: A specific controller which maintains a predetermined ratio between two or more variables.

rational number: 1. Belong to one of two groups: integer and repeating decimal fractions. A rational number is one which may be expressed as a quotient of two numbers, such as ½, ⅔, etc. An irrational number cannot be expressed so exactly. The representation of π (pi), most logs and roots are irrational. 2. Any number which can be expressed as a quotient of p and q, where p and q are both integers.

rattle echo: Unmusical multiple echo, generally associated with thunder, which is formed by nearby flashes giving rise to a sharp acoustic impulse which is reflected between mountains for strata of air.

raw data: Unprocessed data which may or may not be in machine sensible form.

rayleigh scattering: A scattering of the incident radiation through a fiber inversely proportional to the fourth power of the wavelength, caused by various heterogeneities in the fiber.

RCT: See region control task.

reactance modulator: A circuit capable of acting as a variable capacitor. A second variety of reactance modulator acts as a variable inductance or coil.

reaction: Positive feedback by coupling between an anode and a previous grid, whereby a small voltage applied to the latter is reinforced by voltage or current of the former.

reactive mode: A condition of communication between one or more remote terminals and a computer, in which each entry causes certain actions to be performed by the computer, but not necessarily including an immediate reply. Contrasts with mode, conversation.

read: To copy, usually from one form of storage to another, particularly from external or secondary storage to internal storage; to sense the meaning of arrangements of hardware; to sense the presence of information on a recording medium.

read-after-write-verify: A function to determine if information currently being written is correct as compared to the information source.

read-around ratio: The number of times a specific spot, digit, or location in electrostatic storage may be consulted before spillover of electrons causes a loss of data stored in surrounding spots. The surrounding data must be restored before the deterioration results in any loss of data.

read-back check: A transmission check in which the information that was transmitted to an output device is returned to the information source and compared with the original information to insure accuracy of output.

reader: A device capable of sensing information stored in an off-line memory media (cards, paper tape, magnetic tape) and generating equivalent information in an on-line memory device (register, memory locations).

reader, optical-journal: A specific optical-reader that can provide input to a computer from journal tapes that can be output from adding machines, cash registers, etc.

reader/interpreter: A service routine that reads an input stream, stores programs and data on random-access storage for later processing, identifies the control information contained in the input stream, and stores this control information separately in the appropriate control list. A reader/interpreter may be considered as the opposite of an output writer.

read in: 1. To place data in storage at a specified address. 2. To sense information contained in some source and transmit this information to an internal storage.

reading: The acquisition or interpretation of data from a storage device, from a data medium, or from another source.

reading-access time: The elapsed time before data may be read or used in the computer during the equipment read cycle.

reading accuracy: Expressed as a percent of actual output reading.

reading head: A magnetic head that reads magnetic media.

reading rates: The designation of the volume unit of reading punched cards, characters, words, and fields or blocks of data which are sensed by a sensing device. This rate is expressed as a unit of time.

reading station: The place where a document or punched card may be read.

reading task: The job management task that controls the reading and interpreting of job control statements, and the reading and analyzing of operator commands in an input stream.

read-only memory (ROM): Used to store the microprogram or a fixed program depending upon the microprogrammability of the central processing unit. The microprogram provides the translation from the higher-level user commands, such as ADD, SUBTR, etc., down to a series of detailed control codes recognizable by the microprocessor for execution. The size of the ROM varies according to user requirements within the maximum allowed capacity dictated by the addressing capability of the microprocessor.

read-only storage (ROS): An inexpensive means of controlling the computer by sending pulses through preselected logic strips, which in turn set up paths for the instruction execution. The patterns of these logic strips are a microprogram which analyzes a particular instruction and determines what control paths are needed for its execution.

read out: 1. The act of removing and recording information from a computer or an auxiliary storage. 2. The information that is removed from computer storage and recorded in a form that the operator can interpret directly. 3. To sense information contained in the internal storage of the computer and transmit this information to an external storage unit.

read output: The voltage induced in the sense winding by a magnetic cell to which a read pulse is then applied.

readout position: A display of slide position as derived from a position feedback attached to a machine element.

read release: A feature of a reader that permits more processing time by releasing the read mechanism.

read screen: The transparent component of character readers through which appears the input document to be recognized.

read-start time: The time between the beginning of a read cycle and the actual card reading (in a cardreading machine).

read time: See access time.

read verify: A function that determines that information read is correct as compared to the information source.

read/wire: 1. Same as read winding and drive wire reading pulse. 2. A particular drive pulse (the drive wire or drive winding) inductively coupled to one or more magnetic cells and thus, the pulse of magnetomotive force which is then produced.

read/write head: A small electromagnet used for reading, recording, or erasing polarized spots, which represent information on magnetic tape, disk, or drum.

read/write indicator check: Usually incorporated in certain computers to indicate upon interrogation whether or not an error occurred in reading or writing. The machine can be made to stop, retry the operation, or follow a special subroutine depending upon the results of the interrogation.

read/write process: To read in one block of data while simultaneously processing the previous block and writing out the results of the preceeding processed block.

ready-record: A signal from a file-access mechanism to the computer that a record whose address was previously provided by a seek command has now been located and may be read into memory.

ready status word: A status word that indicates the remote computing system is waiting for entry from the terminal.

real partition: In disk-operating systems (DOS), a division of the real address area of virtual storage that may be allocated for programs that are not to be paged, or programs that contain pages that are to be fixed.

real storage page table (RSPT): A table that contains an entry for each 2K page frame in real storage. This table is the centralized information interface for real storage management.

real time: 1. The actual time during which a physical process transpires. 2. The performance of a computation during the actual time that the related physical process transpires in order that results of the computation can be used in guiding the physical process.

real-time clock: A register and circuitry which automatically maintains time in conventional time units for use in program execution and event initiation.

real-time clock log: Used to log the receipt times of real-time data.

real-time clock time: This built-in clock is used for a wide variety of program-timing purposes. It can be used to log the receipt times of periodic real-time input data. Each input message and its receipt time may be recorded together. This clock is also used in connection with the preparation of statistical and analytical reports dealing with the frequency of certain transactions.

real-time communication executive: The executive system is designed to interface with programs which have real-time requirements. The standard communication subsystem, together with efficient scheduling and interrupt processing features of the executive system, provides an environment satisfactory for any real-time program.

real-time communication processing: A real-time system is a combined data processing and communications system which involves the direct communication of transaction data between remote locations and a central computer, via communication lines, and allows the data to be processed while the business transaction is actually taking place. A real-time system may be thought of as the communications-oriented data-processing of inquiries or messages where responses are generated in a time interval directly related to the operational requirements of the system.

real-time concurrency: Real-time is a mode of operation in which data, necessary to the control and/or execution of a transaction, can be processed in time for the transaction to be affected by the results of the processing. Real-time processing is most usually identified with great speed, but speed is relative. The essence of real-time is concurrency-simultaneity. Real-time is the ultimate refinement in the integration of data-processing with communications. Real-time eliminates slow information-gathering procedures, dated reporting techniques, and lax communications. It insures that facts within the system are as timely as a prevailing situation, and as current as the decisions which they must support. Real-time provides answers when answers are needed, delivers data instantly whenever the need for that data arises. Incoming information is edited, updated and made available on demand at every level of responsibility. Imminent departures from established standards are automatically detected and management is notified in time for action.

real-time control: System control of events as they occur.

real-time data reduction: The reduction of data as rapidly as it is generated by the source, if the transmission time is not overbearing. The computer must process (reduce) immediately since by storing and then reducing, operations would be on-line but not realtime.

real-time executive: See real-time system executive.

real-time guard mode: Activated by the instruction load internal function which establishes certain operation parameters. When operative, any attempt to perform a restricted operation will result in an interrupt to an address in central store. Guard mode is terminated by the occurance of any interrupt. It is possible for any program to use the prevent-all-interrupts and jump instruction, thereby allowing real-time programs to operate effectively when guard mode is established.

real-time information system: A system that can provide information about the process it is describing fast enough for the process to be continuously controlled by an operator using this information.

real-time   input/output   (I/O): The information involved in an operating condition in which a machine accepts the data as it is generated by a sensor, processes or operates on the data, and furnishes the results so as to affect the operations of the data generator or some other device; i.e., the data received from an industrial process under the control of a computer or the data received from a missile under the guidance control of a computer.

real-time monitor: The executive system is an operating and programming system designed to monitor the construction and execution of programs, to optimize the utilization of available hardware, and to minimize programmer effort and operator intervention. The executive system, as a monitor, provides for concurrent processing and real-time operation in a classical monitor environment. The executive system is of modular construction, tailored to each user's equipment configuration and applications requirements. Extensions to the system for peripheral devices and application programs may be added, altered, or deleted as required.

real-time operation: See real-time program.

real-time output: Output data delivered from a data processing system within time limits that are determined by the requirements of some other system.

real-time processing: Rapid data processing so that the results of the processing are available in time to influence the process being monitored or controlled. Same as real-time system.

real-time processing inventory: A system that provides the information necessary to base decisions on update information.

real-time processing management: Provides the information necessary to base decisions on up-to-date information. The data reflects current condidtions and makes it possible to avoid many difficulties.

real-time program: A program which operates concurrently with an external process which it is monitoring or controlling, while meeting the requirements of that process with respect to time.

real-time ratio: The time interval between two events in a simulation by a computer to the problem time, or the physical system time, i.e., the time interval between corresponding events in the physical system being simulated.

real-time remote inquiry: On-line inquiry stations permit users to interrogate the computer files and receive immediate answers to their inquiries. In industry, the stations can be located at dozens of remote locations such as office, factory, warehouse, and remote branch locations. Such a system permits all levels of industrial management to obtain immediate answers to questions about inventories, work-inprocess, sales, etc.

real-time satellite computer: Used to relieve the larger computer system of time consuming input and output functions as well as performing preprocessing and post-processing functions, such as editing and formatting for print.

real-time system: A system in which information is processed in time to influence a process being monitored or controlled.

real-time system executives: Software designed to coordinate the execution of many concurrent prioritystructured tasks in an essentially multiprogramming environment.

rear end: The receiver circuits following the detector.

reasonableness checks: Program tests made on information reaching a computer system, or being transmitted from it, to ensure that the data falls within a given range. It is one form of error control.

reasonableness tests tape: Tests provide a means of detecting a gross error in calculation or, while posting to an account, a balance that exceeds a predetermined limit. Typical examples include payroll calculations and credit limit checks in accounts receivable. In some cases, both upper and lower limits are established; each result is then machine-compared with both units to make certain that it falls between the two.

recall factor: In information retrieval (IR), the ratio obtained by dividing the number of retrieved relevant documents by the total number of relevant documents in the file.

recapitulation: The assemblage of totals for the final total.

received-data circuit: Includes signals that originate from the receiving-signal converter, in response to signals received over the communication media.

receive interruption: The interruption of a transmission to a terminal by a higher priority transmission from the terminal.

receive not ready frame: Acknowledges all frames up to but not including Next, as does Receive Ready, but it tells the transmitter to stop sending.

receive only: The description of a teletype device which only has printer capabilities. Such a machine can receive information from the computer but cannot send it.

receiver: A device which transforms a varying electrical signal into sound waves or other usable form.

receiver isolation: The attenuation between any two receivers connected to the system.

receiver signal: Equipment controlled by signaling currents transmitted over the line and used generally to send out new signals.

receiving: The process by which a computer obtains a message from a line.

receiving-end crossfire: The crossfire in a telegraph channel introduced from one or more adjacent channels at the terminal end remote from the transmitter.

recirculating   loop: In   some   drum computers, a small section of memory that has much faster access than the rest of the memory.

recognition: The act or process of identifying (or associating) an input with one of a set of known possible alternatives.

record: A   collection   of   fields;   the information relating to one area of activity in a data processing activity, i.e., all information on one inventory item.

record carrier: Organizations that deal with the transmission of printed or written material.

record blocking: Grouping records into data blocks that can be read and/or written to magnetic tape in one operation. This enables the tape to be read more efficiently and reduces time required to read or write the file.

record check time: The elapsed time which is required to verify a record transfer on tape. The volume of time or duration that is based on tape speed or distance between the rewrite heads.

record control program: Simplifies input/-output coding. Programming is file-oriented rather than deviceoriented. Information is requested in deviceindependent fashion.

record-control schedule: A type of master record or schedule designating all activities involved regarding disposition of business records, e.g., transfers, retention, etc.

record count: The total number of records in a file. This is maintained and checked each time the file is updated to provide control information about the performance of a program or a particular computer run.

recorder: A device that makes a permanent record, usually visual, or varying signals, usually voltages.

recorder level or point: That level of stock at which stock will be re-orderd.

record format: The contents and organization of a record, ordinarily a portion of a program specification.

record gap: An interval of space or time associated with a record to indicate or signal the end of the record.

recording channel: One of a number of independent tracks on a recording medium or recorders in a recording system.

recording density: The number of bits in a single linear track measured per unit of length of the recording medium.

recording head: The device, in tape or disc equipment, which contains the electrical recording device.

recording measurement: A type of measurement instrument in which the values of the measured quantity are recorded.

recording mode: In COBOL the, representation of data associated with a data-processing system in external media.

recording spot: The moving element from which a facsimile image is reconstructed.

recording stylus: The cutting tool used in electromechanical recording.

recording surface: Storage of information on the ferric-oxide coating of magnetic tape, magnetic drums, etc.

recording trunk: A trunk from a local telephone central office or private branch exchange to a long distance office, used only for communication between operators.

record layout: The arrangement and structure of data in a record, including the sequence and size of its components.

record length: The number of words or characters that form a record.

record management: The direction of a program designed to provide economy and efficiency in the creation, organization, maintenance, use and retrieval, and disposition of records, assuring that needless records will not be created or kept and valuable records will be preserved and available.

record mark: A special character used in some computers at the end of a record.

record name: A name assigned to a record in a file of data.

records appraisal: The analysis of records for the purpose of establishing retention policy. It includes a review of the opera-

tional and legal value of records by records series.

records center: A low cost, centralized area for housing and servicing inactive or semi-inactive records whose reference rate does not warrant their retention in office space and equipment.

record separator (RS): A character designed to demarcate records within a record group.

record series: Groups of identical or related records which are normally used and filed as a unit, and which permit evaluation as a unit for retention scheduling purposes.

records grouped: A set of records sharing the same label, tag, or key.

record sorting: The basic element of a file such that the sorting of files constitutes the reordering of file records (in some systems).

records retention schedule: A comprehensive schedule showing all actions to be taken in relation to the disposition of all of the records of a business. Schedules include provisions for the periodic transfer of records to record centers, as well as provision for their final disposition or retention.

records search: Extended investigation of requested information resulting from a request for extraction of data or the need to check additional locations for a given record.

record storage mark: A special character that appears only in the record storage unit of the card reader to limit the length of the record read into storage.

record strip: A recording method of information storage on vertical strips.

record transport: The part of the record processor that moves records from the three input locations (primary feeder, auxiliary feeder, single-form-insertion station) to the printing station and, after printing, to either of two output stackers (primary stacker or auxiliary stacker).

recoverable error: An error condition that allows continued execution of a program.

recoverable synchronization: The ability to recover or reestablish synchronization automatically when synchronization is lost. It is an important operational feature because disturbances on a communication channel will often upset synchronization.

recovered signal: A decoded signal or a descrambled signal; recovery after the scrambling process is reversed in the receiving unit.

recovery, fallback: The recovery of a computer system from a fallback mode of operation.

recovery management support (RMS): The facilities that gather information about hardware reliability and allow retry of operations that fail because of CPU, I/O device, or channel errors.

recovery program, automatic: A computer program which enables a computer system to keep functioning when a piece of equipment has failed.

recovery routine: A computer program which enables a computer system to keep functioning when a piece of equipment has failed.

recovery routines, interrupt: The act of providing to the operating program the entrances to subroutines which will handle the error interrupts. Upon occurence of an error interrupt, control is transferred automatically to one of the fixed main-memory addresses. The executive provides jump instructions for these locations. These instructions in turn reference subroutines which will attempt to recover from these errors. Attempts to write into a lockedout area of memory result in program termination when operating under executive control. Recovery routines are permitted for illegal operation code, trace mode, characteristic overflow, characteristic underflow and divide-fault interrupts. All I/O and other interrupts are handled by other parts of the executive system.

rectangular loop: A hysteresis loop that is square or rectangular in shape, i.e., the residual value of the effect after all cause is removed is equal nearly to the maximum possible or saturated level of effect.

rectangular mode: A small section of storage, particularly in drum, tape or disk storage units, that has much faster access than the remainder of the storage.

rectifier: electric component for converting an alternating current into a direct current by the inversion or suppression of alternate half-waves. See diode.

rectifier, crystal: Specific diodes which are manufactured with a junction of a base metal and some types of crystalline elements, for example, silicon or germanium. Such diodes contrast with vacuum diodes and are used in computing equipment to perform logic, buffering current conversions necessary for switching and storage transfers.

rectilinear scan: A raster in which a rectangular area is scanned by a series of parallel lines.

recurrent transmission code: A code in which check symbols are used to detect a burst type of error.

recursion: Repetition of an operation or set of operations.

recycling programs: An organized arrangement for recycling programs through a computer where alterations have been made in one program that may change or have an effect on other programs.

reduction: A process by which data are condensed.

reduction, data: See data compression.

reduction ratio: A measure of the number of times a linear dimension of a document is reduced when photographed onto microfilm, expressed as 16X, 24X. If a drawing measuring 18 inches X 24 inches is microfilmed at 10X, the image will measure 1.8 X 2.4.

redundance, error control: The introduction of redundancy decreases the capacity of the channel for carrying information. The choice of which scheme to employ for a particular application depends upon the ease of introducing the redundancy, the kinds of error possible with a given type of link and the performance criteria to be met. Published error rates of 1 in 50,000 for 50 baud lines to 1 in 500,000 for 600 baud lines give a false impression of a random variable. Switching, impulses, crosstalk, central office problems and maintenance personnel cause transmission lines to exhibit time varying burst error characteristics.

redundance, relative (of source):   The ratio of the redundancy of the source to the logarithm of the number of symbols available at the source.

redundance, vertical: In a parity checking system, refers to an even number of bits in odd parity system or vice versa.

redundancy: In the transmission of information, that fraction of the gross information content of a message which can be eliminated without loss of essential information.

redundancy check: An automatic or programmed check based on the systematic insertion in a message of bits or characters that are used for error-checking purposes; they are redundant, as they can be eliminated without the loss of essential information. Parity checking is a form of redundancy checking.

redundancy check, cyclic: The cyclic parity check character for longitudinal error control is calculated from a devisor polynomial. A typical one is: $X^{16} + X^{15} + X^2 + 1$.

redundancy check, longitudinal: An error control check based on the arrangement of data according to a rule.

redundant: A characteristic of having data, equipment personnel, etc. which are more than the efficient minimum which might be required. Redundant characters often work as checking devices, as in parity and other checks.

redundant character: A character specifically added to a group of characters to insure conformity with certain rules which can be used to detect computer malfunction.

redundant check: See redundancy check.

redundant code: A binary coded decimal value with ans added check bit. Three redundant codes are the biquinary code, the two-out-of-five code and the quibinary code.

reed relay: A special switching device which consists of magnetic contactors which are sealed into a glass tube. The contactors are actuated by the magnetic field of an external solenoid, electromagnet or a permanent magnet.

reed switch: See reed relay.

reel: A spool of tape (magnetic or paper).

re-enterable: The attribute of a program that describes a routine which can be shared by several tasks concurrently, or which can call itself or a program which calls it.

re-enterable load module: A type of load module used repeatedly or concurrently by two or more jobs.

re-entrant: A property of a computer program in which it may be reentered for processing after leaving it to do something else.

re-entrant reusable routine: A routine which can be utilized in two or more tasks simultaneously.

re-entry point: The computer instruction by which a routine is re-entered.

re-entry system: A system designed so that the input data to be read are printed by the computer with which the reader is associated.

reference analysis: A statistical break-down of reference requests to determine the frequency and data usage of individual types of records.

reference block: A block within a numerical control program frequently identified by an "o" or "h" in place of the word address "n." It contains sufficient information to enable resumption of the program following an interruption.

reference debugging aids: A set of routines that help the programmer debug computer programs.

reference excursion: In an analog computer, the range from zero voltage to nominal full scale operating voltage.

reference input elements: The specific part of the controlling system which changes the reference input signal in response to the set point.

reference input signal: One specifically external to a control loop which serves as the standard of comparison for the directly controlled variable.

reference level: Single sideband equipment for voice frequency input powoer, that power of one or two equal tones which together cause the transmitter to develop its full rated power output.

reference listing: A list printed by a compiler to indicate instructions as they appear in the final routine, including details of storage allocation.

reference noise: The magnitude of circuit noise that will produce a circuit noise-meter reading equal to that produced by 10 watts of electric power at 1000 cycles per second.

reference pilot: A different wave from those which transmit the telecommunication signals (telegraphy, telephony). It is used in carrier systems to facilitate maintenance and adjustment of the carriertransmission system.

reference-program table: The section of storage used as an index for operations, subroutines, and variables.

reference record: An output of a compiler that lists the operations and their positions in the final specific routine, and contains information describing the segmentation and storage allocation of the routine.

reference tape: A tape used as a reference against which the performances of other tapes are compared. The use of a reference tape is necessary in specifying most performance characteristics because of the difficulty of expressing these characteristics in absolute terms.

reference time: An instant near the beginning of switching chosen as an origin for time measurements. It is variously taken as the first instant at which the instantaneous value of the drive pulse, the voltage response of the magnetic cell, or the integrated voltage response reaches a specified fraction of its peak pulse amplitude.

reference voltage: In an analog computer, a voltage used as a standard of reference, usually the nominal full scale of the computer; also a constant unit of computation used in normalizing and scaling for machine soluion.

reference volume: The magnitude of a complex electric wave.

refile: To transmit a message from a station on a leased line network to a station not serviced by the leased line network.

This is accomplished by sending the message to a preselected Western Union office for retransmission as a telegram to the addressee.

reflectance: The ability of a surface to reflect light.

reflectance ink: The reflecting characteristic of ink used in optical character recognition.

reflected binary: A code using the binary 0 and 1, and so constructed that each successive code is derived from its predecessor by inverting only one bit. Reflected binary is a particular form of gray code.

reflected binary unit distance code: A binary code in which sequential numbers are represented by expressions which are the same except in one place, and in that place differ by one unit.

reflected code: Any binary code that changes by only one bit when going from one number to the number immediately following. Synonymous with reflected-binary code and cyclic code.

reflected wave: 1. A wave turned back from a discontinuity in a continuous medium. 2. A wave propagated back along a wave-guide or transmission-line system as a result of a mismatching at the termination.

reflection: 1. Occurs when a wave meets a surface of discontinuity between two media, and part of it has its direction changed in accordance with laws of reflection so as not to cross the surface. 2. Reduction of power from the maximum possible; part of the energy transmitted is returned to the source. 3. Reduction in power transmitted by wavefilter because of iterative impedance becoming highly reactive outside the pass bands. In all instances, the loss of power is measured in decibels below maximum possible; i.e., when properly matched.

reflection factor: The ratio of current delivered to load compared to current delivered in a perfectly matched load.

reflection gain: A gain in power received in a load from a source because of the introduction of a matching network, such as a transformer.

reflection loss: Loss of power obtainable from a source into a load because the latter is not matched in impedance to the source.

reflection point: A discontinuity in a transmission line due to a partial reflection of a transmitted electric wave.

reflective spot: A silver strip on magnetic tape at the beginning of the reel of tape.

reflectometer: An instrument that measures the ratio of energy of a reflected wave to that of an incident wave in any physical system.

reflector: The dish or similar device in which radar equipment reflects the main bang outward from the horn.

reformatting: The act of changing the representation of data from one format to another, usually with the data being input from a machine-readable source. Reformatting may include the translation or conversion of data values from one character set to another, such as from ASCII to EBCDIC.

refractive index: The ratio of the velocity of light in a vacuum to its velocity in a given material. The refraction index determines the angle of incidence for that medium. Any angle below the angle of incidence allows the light to reflect off the medium. Any angle equal to or greater than this angle causes the light to refract through the medium. Fiber optics technology relies on the refraction index of materials to determine which materials will permit a fiber to achieve total internal reflection.

refresh: The process by which the electron beam of a CRT repeatedly scans the screen to keep the image constant to the human eye. Pictures should be refreshed 30 times a second if they are to be flicker-free.

refreshable: The attribute of a load module that prevents it from being modified by itself or by any other module during execution. A refreshable load module can be replaced by a new copy during execution by a recovery management routine without changing either the sequence or results of processing.

refresh buffer: A digital memory where graphic displays are stored as a matrix of intensity values. Each bit holds the location and status of a pixel on the screen.

regenerate: To restore information that is stored electrostatically such as on a cathode ray tube (CRT) screen.

regenerative feedback: A technique which returns part of the output of a machine, system, or process to the input in a way that causes a larger quantity to be added to the input with an increase of output results.

regenerative memory: Memory devices that need to be refreshed or the contents will gradually disappear.

regenerative reading: A read operation which involves the automatic writing of data back into the positions from which it is extracted.

regenerative storage: Storage that needs to be regenerated to maintain the image, e.g., the storage in a cathode-ray tube.

region: A group of machine addresses which refer to a base address.

region control task (RCT): Under time-sharing option (TSO), the control program routine that ore and LOGON/LOGOFF.

regional center: A control center (Class 1 office) that connects sectional centers of the telephone system together. Every pair of regional centers in the United States has a direct circuit group running from one center to the other.

regional identity code: A code used in international telephone dialing to route calls to a particular continent.

register: A memory device capable of containing one or more computer bits or words. A register has zero memory latency time and negligible memory access time.

register address field: The part of a computer instruction that contains a register address.

register block: The set of 16 general registers (in some computers).

register capacity: The upper and lower limits of the numbers that can be processed in a computer register.

register length: The number of digits, characters, or bits which a register can store.

registration: Accuracy of positioning for cards, documents, etc. in machines.

registration mark: A preprinted indication of the relative position and direction of various elements of the source document to be recognized.

regression: The rate at which an output changes in relation to the changes in inputs.

reimbursed time: The machine time loaned or rented to another office, agency, or organization either on a reimbursable or reciprocal basis.

reject frame: A negative acknowledgment frame which indicates that a transmission error has been found.

rejection: A logical operation applied to two operands which will provide a result depending on the bit pattern of the operands.

relation: In assembler programming, the comparison of two expressions to see if the value of one is equal to, less than, or greater than the value of the other.

relational operator: In assembler programming, an operator that can be used in an arithmetic or character relation to indicate the comparison to be performed between the terms in the relation.

relative accuracy: Error in relative accuracy is the difference between the nominal and actual ratios to full scale of the analog value corresponding to a given digital input, independent of the full scale calibration. This error is a function of the linearity of the converter and is usually specified at less than $\pm\frac{1}{2}$LSB.

relative address: An address that will be altered to an absolute address at the time the program is being run on the computer.

relative address label: A label used to identify the location of data in a program by reference to its position with respect to some other location in that program.

relative code: A code in which all addresses are specified or written with respect to an arbitrarily selected position, or in which all addresses are represented symbolically in a computable form.

relative data: In a program for a cathode-ray tube display device, values that specify a new position for an electron beam in terms of the number of raster units in the X and Y directions away from the current beam position.

relative delay: The difference between maximum and minimum delays occurring in a band of frequencies.

relative frequency: A calculation of the ratio of numbers of observations in a class (subset) to the total number of observations or elements constituting a population, i.e., universal subset.

relative line number: A number assigned by the user to a communications line at system generation.

relative magnitude: The relationship or comparison of the magnitude of one quantity to another, most often related to base magnitude and expressed as a difference

from or a percentage of the base or reference.

relative order: In a program for a cathode-ray tube display device, a display order that specifies that the data bytes following the order are raster unit displacements in the X and Y directions from the current beam position.

relative origin: A symbolic origin that is assigned to a machine location by the loader.

relative redundancy (of a source): The ratio of the redundancy of the source to the logarithm of the number of symbols available at the source.

relative transmission level: The ratio of the testtone power at one point to the test-tone power at some other point in the system chosen as a reference point.

relative value scale (RVS) code: A specific 5-digit code used to indicate procedures, treatments, etc., for medical insurance billing. It has limited use for activity studies.

relaxation oscillator: An oscillator whose output steadily rises and then quickly drops.

relay: An electomagnetic switching device.

relay amplifier: A device used in an analog system for the comparison of two signals and incorporates an amplifier to drive a switch.

relay center: A system in which data transmissions between stations on different circuits within a network are accomplished by routing the data through a central point. Same as messare switching center. See also switching center.

release: 1. For a computer program or system, an embodiment of operational characteristics. 2. To relinquish either by a program or manually, a storage reservation, protection or location.

release connection: In switching networks, to break a connection between called and calling stations.

release-guard signal: A signal sent in response to a clear-forward signal that indicates the circuit is free at the incoming end.

reliable earth terminal (RET): Improves earth station technology for reliable, unattended operation over extended periods from a remote control.

relocatability: A facility whereby programs or data may be located in a place in memory at different times without requiring modification to the program. In some systems, segments of the program and all data are relocatable independently with no loss in efficiency.

relocatable coding: Absolute coding containing relative addresses, which when derelativized, may be loaded into any portion of a computer's programmable memory to execute the given action. The loader program normally performs the derelativization. In some computers the derelativization is accomplished by hardware. This process is known as dynamic relocatable coding.

relocatable expression: In assembler programming, an assembly-time expression whose value is affected by program relocation. A relocatable expression can represent a relocatable address.

relocatable form: A form of program text wherein the instructions have variable load addresses and symbolic cross-references, plus control information to permit later conversion to absolute form.

relocatable library: Under disk-operating systems (DOS) and tape-operating systems (TOS), a library of relocatable object modules and input/output control system modules required by various compilers. It allows the user to keep frequently-used modules available for combination with other modules without recompilation.

relocatable program: A program written so that it may be located and executed from many areas in memory.

relocatable-program loader: A program that assigns absolute origins to relocatable subroutines, object programs, and data, assigns absolute locations to each of the instructions or data, and modifies the reference to these instructions or data.

relocatable routine: A routine designed and stored so that it may be located anywhere in main memory.

relocatable subroutine: A computer program subroutine designed to be located physically and independently in computer memory as required.

relocatable term: In assembler programming, a term whose value is affected by program relocation.

relocate: To change the location of a computer program or routine.

relocate hardware: Same as dynamic address translation.

relocation: The modification of address constants to compensate for a change in origin of a module, program, or control section.

relocation dictionary (RLD): The part of a program that contains information necessary to change addresses when it is relocated.

relocation pack: 1. Inclusion of several discrete items of information in one unit of information. 2. Program relocation to make efficient use of available storage capacity.

relocation-processor storage: The processor must have the ability to relocate programs in storage during normal processing, since many different types of transactions may necessitate bringing a program from file storage into a location in core storage for which the program was not assembled.

reluctance: The opposition in a magnetic circuit.

remanence: A unit of measure for determining the magnetic flex density after removal of applied magnetic force.

remarks card: A card that is used to inset remarks in a listing.

remedial maintenance: The maintenance performed by the contractor following equipment failure. Therefore, it is performed as required on an unscheduled basis.

remote access: Communication with a data processing facility using one or more stations that are distant from that facility.

remote batch: A method of entering jobs into the computer from a remote terminal.

remote calculator: Allow simultaneous on-line computing service for many engineers, scientists, and mathematicians from their home office. In a timesharing system, the remote calculator provides direct, remote access to the computer. Remote connections can be made anywhere, via standard telephone channels, through the common-user dial network. Through the common-user dial network, users query the computer from a keyboard containing conventional functions and symbols of mathematics...answers are immediately shown on the remote calculator display panel. All features of the powerful digital computers can be made instantly available at low cost.

remote computer: A computer at a location other than where the user is; generally connected by communications lines.

remote computing system consistency errors: Statements that are correctly composed but conflict with other statements (e.g., conflicting declaratives, illegal statement ending a DO range, failure to follow each transfer statement with a numbered statement, etc.). Most errors of consistency are detected as soon as the use

enters the offending statement. The system rejects the offending statement and the user can immediately substitute a correct statement. However, some errors of consistency (e.g., illegal branch into the range of a DO) are not immediately detected. These errors are handled in the same manner as errors of completeness, and should be considered as such.

remote computing system exchange: A device that handles data and messages sent between a central processor and remote consoles. The exchange device allows a number of remote consoles to be run simultaneously without mutual interference. It will receive characters sent from these terminals and form them into statements for transfer to memory, results and messages being returned to the proper terminal as necessary.

remote computing system language: Comprised of two types: program statements and operating statements. Program statements are upwardly compatible with FORTRAN IV and are used to form the user's program. Operating statements allow the user to communicate with the remote computing system. Operating statements include modification, test, display, and output statements.

remote concentrators: Allows terminals at remote locations to share communications circuits. Concentrators allow for the statistical multiplexing of the communication circuits so that bandwidth, unused by some devices, can be given to devices that require it. Remote concentrators are responsible for terminal handling, peripheral device control, buffer management, and error control between terminals or devices and the central computing facility.

remote console: A terminal unit in a remote computing system. Some of the distant consoles may be available, each equipped with facilities to transmit and receive data to and from the central processor. Connection to the processor is made through a remote computing system exchange.

remote control equipment: Control apparatus that works from a distance by electronic means.

remote control language: The remote-computing system language comprised of two types of statements; program statements and operating statements. Program statements which are upwardly compatible with FORTRAN IV are used to form the users program. Operating statements allow the user to communicate with the remote-computing system. Operating statements include modificaiton, test, display and output statements.

remote cutoff pentode: A type of pentode in which an unusually high negative grid voltage is required to drive the tube into cutoff.

remote data stations: Can be installed in any normal office environment without special cooling or electrical requirements. They can be linked as single remote units, or as multiple stations, to one or more computers using conventional voice-grade telephone lines.

remote data terminal: A data terminal not on the site of the central processor, i.e., in a remote location.

remote debugging: The use of a remote terminal to debug computer programs.

remote device: A piece of equipment at a remote location (not near the computer).

remote inquiry: An inquiry made from a remote terminal.

remote intelligent terminal: In more sophisticated remote-batch terminals a small computer is included to store programs, to control the input/output (I/O) equipment, and to do some preprocessing functions (e.g., code conversion and editing) and output processing functions (e.g., formatting).In such terminals the use of a minicomputer reduces the amounts of data transmitted to and from the larger central

computer, provides flexible control and formatting for the I/O equipment.

remote job entry (RJE) processing: Processing of stacked jobs over communication lines via terminals typically equipped with line printers. Small computers also can operate as RJE stations if equipped with communications adapters.

remote message processing: An extension of the full power of the data processing and programming facilities of the computer to remote locations. The operating system can be used to processmessages received from remote locations by way of communication lines and telecommunication equipment.

remote oriented simulation system (ROSS): The system models the airspace of one air-traffic control center in detail. A flight between any two points may be simulated by running programs for each of the intervening air-traffic control centers.

remote processing: The processing of data received from remote locations.

remote station: Input/output devices that are not by the computer, i.e., at a remote location.

remote subsets: Communications subsets at remote locations (not at the same place as the computer).

remote terminal: A device or modem for communicating with computers from sites which are physically separated from the mainframe of the computer, and usually distant enough so that communications facilities rather than direct cables are used.

remote testing: Organizes the flow of work being processed. Programs and associated test data are submitted independently to computer operators to determine the speed of the workflow through a computer system. Other tests evaluate the discipline of the procedure and the debugging of programs, as well as diagnostic aids and the impact on memory units and storage facilities. The operator develops a detailed record of all actions taken during each test run.

remote-batch processing: See remote job entry.

remote-cutoff pentode: A type of pentode in which an unusually high negative grid voltage is required to drive the tube into cutoff.

remote-database access service: A service which provides remote data teminal equipment in one country with access to filed information housed in a foreign database.

remote-data concentrator: A device which accepts messages from many terminals through slow-speed lines and transmits data to the host processor through a single high-speed synchronous line. This process helps reduce line costs and smooths out communications to the host processor.

remote-data terminal: A data terminal not on site of the central processor, i.e., in a remote location.

remote-message processing: A system in which messages are received from remote locations by way of communications lines.

remote-operation display: Indicates that remote connection to an interfacing computer by Dataphone or Dataset is possible.

removable random access: Storage devices like magentic disk packs that can be removed physically.

re-order: A procedure for placing items in a particular organizational or methodical manner or arrangement to facilitate the use of identifying keys which follow a prescribed pattern or set of rules, such as by alphabets, value, time sequence, etc.

re-order quantity: The amount of stock that is reordered when the re-order level is reached.

repair-delay time: Time spent in the repair process (of equipment) waiting for parts or assistance.

repair time: Time used for diagnosis and repair of problems in machines.

repeat counter: The repeat counter is used to control repeated operations, such as block transfer and repeated search commands. To execute a repeated instruction "k" times, the repeat counter must be loaded with "k" prior to the execution of the instruction. A repeated sequence may be suspended to process an interrupt, with circuitry providing for the completion of the repeated sequence after the interrupt has been processed.

repeater: A system component which reconstitutes signals into standard voltages, currents, and timing.

repeater coil: A one-to-one ratio audio-frequency transformer for transferring energy from one electrical circuit to another. In wire communication work, it permits the formulation of simplex and phantom circuits.

repeating-coil side circuit: A repeating coil that functions as a transformer at a side circuit terminal.

repeating group: A set of data or information elements linked to each other as well as to the record in which they are placed. All elements in the set must have the same number of occurrences which have values sequenced in the same order for all.

repertory: The many sets of operations that can be represented in a particular operation code.

repetition instruction: A computer instruction repeated a number of times before going on to the next instruction.

repetitive operation: In an analog computer, a condition in which the computer operates as a repetitive device; the solution time may be a small fraction of a second after which the problem is cycled automatically and repetitively through reset, hold, and operate.

repeat until: A command establishing an infinite loop.

replacement algorithm: An algorithm used in a demand fetching system to determine which segment to remove when another segment must be placed in a full-internal memory.

replica reproduction: Copies of documents produced by copiers or phocopiers.

report delay: The time between the cutoff of an activity to be reported and the delivery of the report.

report generation: A technique for producing complete machine reports from information which describes the input file and the format and content of the output report.

reporting period: The time period covered in a report.

report interval: The length of time between the preparation of a corresponding report. This interval may be fixed or variable.

report program: A program that prints out an an analysis of a data file.

report program generator (RPG) language: A popular, problem-oriented language for commercial programming, especially in smaller installations. Like COBOL, RPG has powerful and relatively simple input/-output file manipulation (including table look-up), and reporting capabilities, but is limited in algorithmic capabilities.

representation: A combination of bits, characters, or other elements to form a unit of data.

representative calculating operation: Serves as the calculating speed of the

machine and is longer than an addition time unit but shorter than several multiplication time units, i.e., a mean time for nine additions and one multiplication time unit, as an example.

representative-calculating time: A method of evaluating the speed performance of a computer. One method is to use one-tenth of the time required to perform nine complete additions and one complete multiplication. A complete addition or a complete multiplication time includes the time required to procure two operands from high-speed storage, perform the operation, and store the result and the time required to select and execute the required number of instructions to do this.

representative-computing time: A method of evaluating the speed performance of a computer.

representative simulation: A system in which the components, processes, and interactions of the model bear a clear relationship to the system under study.

reproducibility: The ability to develop the same output magnitude for a given steady-state magnitude of the measurand after a period of time has elapsed in which the measurand and some environmental conditions have been increased or decreased (by a stated amount) and the measurand has been returned to the original value. The elapsed time between measurements should be stated. Reproducibility is expressed as the maximum variation in output under specified ranges of ambient conditions in units of the measurand or as a percent of the fullscale value of the equipment or a percent of the point. It is not intended to include long-term aging effects which cannot be predicted.

reproducing head: The playback head in a tape recorder.

request for next message (RFNM):   A short transmission which is sent back to the source of the message, the interface message processor (IMP). The RFNM is part of a flow control mechanism which involves logical links between source-destination pairs, with a given link becoming blocked after use until the receipt of an RFNM.

request for proposal (RFP): A formal document prepared by a potential user of data processing services to define the specifications for the system that he wants and to request proposals from qualified bidders to deliver that system.

request operator's control panel: A panel consisting of indicator lights and switches by which an operator can request the computer to perform particular functions.

request-repeat system: A communication system that uses an error detecting code that can initiate a request for retransmission.

request slip: A statement of the requirements of storage and peripheral units of a program.

request to send circuit: 1. Condition the local modem for transmitting data. 2. Controls transmission detection in a half-duplex operation.

rerun: To repeat all or part of a computer program run (on a machine).

rerun point: A point in a computer program at which a rerun may start.

rerun program: A particular routine which is designed to be used after a computer failure, malfunction or program or operator error which reconstitutes the routine being executed from the most recent or closest rerun point.

rerun routine: A routine used after a computer malfunction to reconstitute a routine from the last previous rerun point.

rescue dump: To record the contents of computer memory onto magnetic tape at different points in time.

reservation: The distribution of memory areas or peripheral units to a specific program in a multiprogramming computer.

reserve: To set aside a part of a system to one of several programs, i.e., to inhibit its use by any other program.

reserved unit: A symbolic unit given a unique designation, unavailable for assignment to a file, and may be used only by reference to that designation.

reset: To return a register or storage location to zero or to a specified initial condition.

reset pulse: A pulse used to set a flip-flop or magnetic core to its original state.

reset rate: The number of corrections per unit of time made by the control system.

reshaping signal: A restoration of signals which comply with requirements for amplitude, shape, and timing. These signals generate from another signal.

residence system: The external storage space allocated for storing the basic operating system. It includes on-line tape reel or disk pack that contains the necessary programs required for executing a job on the data processing system.

residence volume system: A defined volume which contains the nucleus of the operating system, has the highest level index of the catalog, and is a portion of a single unit of storage media.

resident: A program located permanently in storage; e.g., the nucleus in main storage or a system library on direct access storage.

resident routine: A routine that exists permanently in memory.

residual error rate: The ratio of the number of bits, unit elements, characters, and blocks incorrectly received but undetected or uncorrected by the error control equipment, to the total number of bits, unit elements, characters, blocks that are sent.

residual-error ratio: The ratio of the number of bits, unit elements, characters and blocks incorrectly received but undetected or uncorrected by the errorcontrol equipment, to the total number of bits, unit elements, characters, blocks that are sent.

resistance box: A box containing carefully constructed and adjusted resistors, which can be introduced into a circuit by switches or keys.

resistance lamp: Used to limit the current in a circuit.

resistive component: Part of the impedance of an electrical system which leads to the absorption and dissipation of energy in the form of heat.

resistor: A component which restricts the flow of current into a circuit and offers direct and easy control of the voltage traveling across it.

resistor-transistor-logic (RTL): Logic performed by resistors; transistors produce an inverted output.

resolution: The number of distinguishable elements per unit of distance in a display or output device. The higher the resolution is, the better the picture will be.

resolution factor: In information retrieval (IR), the ratio obtained by dividing the total number of documents retrieved (whether relevant or not to the use's needs) by the total number of documents available in the file.

resolution sensitivity: Sensitivity which has been as one-half dead band. When the output is at the center of the dead band, it denotes the minimum change in measured quantity required to initiate response.

resolver: 1. A device which separates or breaks up a quantity, particularly a vector,

into constituent parts or elements, e.g., the mutually perpendicular components of a plane vector. 2. A small section of storage, particularly in drum, tape, or disk storage units, that has much faster access than the remainder of the storage.

resonant circuit: A circuit in resonance.

resonant line: Parallel wire or coaxial transmission line short-circuited at the ends. Used for stabilizing the frequency of short-wave oscillators.

resonant mode: Field configuration in a tuned cavity. In general, resonance occurs at several related frequencies corresponding to different configurations.

resonator: Any device exhibiting a sharply defined electric, mechanical, or acoustic resonance effect; e.g., a stub, piezoelectric crystal, or Helmholtz resonator. Originally, a circular wire ring containing a small spark gap, used by Hertz for detection of electromagnetic waves.

resource: Any facility of the computing system or operating system required by a job and including main storage, input/-output devices, the central processing unit, data sets, and control and processing programs.

resource allocation: A program which integrates the allocation of resources (men, machines, materials, money, and space) with scheduling, by time period, of project activities.

resource manager: Control of routines that allocate system resources.

resource protection: The system design of automatic procedures set to ensure that resources are accessed by well-defined operations within computations authorized to use the resources.

resource sharing: The sharing of one central processing unit by several users and/or several peripheral devices. Resource sharing is used in connection with the sharing of time and memory.

respond key typeout: A push button on a console inquiry keyboard used to lock the keyboard to permit automatic processing to continue.

response curve: Exhibits the trend of communication response in a system.

response duration: The time interval between the start of a pulse which affects a storarage cell and the response of that storage cell.

response ratio: A ratio calculated to be a measure of the response time to the service time of a job. Represents the degradation in execution speed experienced by a given job due to the presence of other jobs and the scheduling algorithm.

response time: The amount of elapsed time between generation of an inquiry at a data communications terminal and receipt of a response at that same terminal.

response-time monitor: Provides hard copy reports of all transactions by transaction type, with the first seven characters of each transaction printed.

restart point: One of several points in a computer program at which a restart or rerun may begin.

restart-points sorting: The point at which a restart (or rerun) can be initiated. Memory, registers, and the position of tapes are recorded at this point.

restore: 1. To return a cycle index, a variable address, or other computer word to its initial value. See also reset. 2. Periodic regeneration of charge, especially in volatile, condenser-action storage systems.

restorer pulse generator: Generates pulses for special timing or gating in a digital computer; i.e., pulses which function as inputs to gates for aid in pulseshaping and timing.

resynchronization: On a multipoint circuit, the reestablishment of synchronization with a receiver (or transmitter) with which contact had recently been made.

retentivity: The degree or expression of ability of a material to retain magnetic flux.

retina: In optical character recognition, a major component of a scanning device.

retrieve: To find and select specific information.

retry: In communications, resending the current block of data a prescribed number of times, or until it is entered correctly.

return: A set of instructions at the end of a subroutine which directs control to the proper point in the main routine.

return address: 1. The part of a subprogram that connects it with the main program. 2. A process to unite two or more separately written or assembled programs into single operational entities; e.g., to complete linkage. Some computer systems have programs called linkage editors that correct address components into symbols or relocate symbols to avoid overlapping. 3. A communications line between two or more stations or terminals.

return code: A special code used to affect the execution of subsequently run routines.

return-from-zero-time: The elapsed time between the end of a pulse at full signal strength and the start of the absent electrical flow or some lower level of electrical flow.

return point (sorting): A point at which a computer program can be restarted in case of computer failure, without loss of processing accomplished prior to the interruption.

return signal: In a closed loop, the signal that is sent back to be subtracted from the input.

return-to-bias recording: A specific use of the return-to-reference recording in which the reference condition is zero magnetization.

return-to-reference recording: A procedure for magnetic recording of bits in shich the pattern of magnetization used to represent zeros and ones occupy only part of the storage cell, the remainder of the cell is magnetized to a reference condition.

return-to-zero recording: A specific use of the return-to-reference recording in which the reference condition is zero magnetization.

reusable: A program that performs several tasks without reloading.

reusable routine: A routine which can be utilized in two or more tasks and in some cases, simultaneously.

reverse acting controller: A controller in which the absolute value of the output signal decreases as the absolute value of the input (measured variable) increases.

reverse channel: A means of simultaneous communication from the receiver to the transmitter over half-duplex data transmission systems. Generally, the reverse channel is used only for the transmission of control information.

reverse code dictionary: An alphabetic or numeric alphabetic arrangement of codes, associated with their corresponding English words or terms.

reverse digit sorting method: Sorting on a position at a time from right to left in a field (conventional card sorting method).

reverse direction flow: In flowcharting, a flow in a direction other than left to right or top to bottom.

reverse key (exchange or recall key): Reverses postions of two numbers such as divided and divisor.

reverse scan: A particular editing operation designed to suppress zeros, i.e., to replace them with blanks and eliminate the zero suppression word mark.

reversible magnetic process: A device or mechanism of flux change within a magnetic material whereby the flux returns to its first or initial state when the disturbing magnetic field is removed.

reversible process: A process whereby the flux within a magnetic material returns to its original condition when the magnetic field is removed.

rewind: To return a film or magnetic tape to its beginning or passed location.

rewrite: The process in a storage device of restoring the information in the device to its state prior to reading.

RFNM: See request for next message.

RFP: See request for proposal.

rheostat: An electric component in which resistance introduced into a circuit is readily variable by a knob, handle, or by mechanically-driven means.

ribbon microphone: A high fidelity microphone in which the vibration of a thin metal ribbon in a magnetic field generates the audio signal.

right justified: A field of numbers (decimal, binary, etc.) which exists in a memory cell, location, or register possessing no significant zeros to its right. e.g., 000120000 is considered to be a seven-digit field right justified. 0000001200 is a two-digit field not right justified.

right shift: An operation in which digits of a word are displaced to the right. This effects division in an arithmetical shift.

rigid disk: A disk memory in which the magnetic medium is coated onto a rigid substrate.

ring: The side of the plug used to make circuit connections in a manual switchboard. The ring is the connector attached to the negative side of the common battery which powers the station equipment. By extension, it is the negative battery side of a communications line.

ring counter: A loop of interconnected bistable elements such that one and only one is in a specified state at any given time and such that, as input signals are counted, the position of the element in the specified state moves in an ordered sequence around the loop.

ringdown signaling: A specific procedure for bringing a line signal or a supervisory signal to a distant switchboard or end by using low-frequency alternating current to the line.

ring network: A network structure in which terminals and computers are linked together in a circular pattern. In a ring network each computer or terminal is connected to two others.

RLD: See relocation dictionary.

robot: A device equipped with sensing instruments for detecting input signals or environmental conditions.

role indicator: A code assigned to a keyword to indicate the role of the keyword, e.g., a keyword may be a noun, verb, adjective, or adverb. Therefore, an indicator is used to identify the specific role of the keyword.

roll: As related to magnetic tape, a reel with a standard length of tape.

roll-back snapshot system: A system that will restart the running program after a system failure. Snapshots of data and programs are stored at periodic intervals and the system rolls back to restart at the last recorded snapshot.

roll-back system: A system that can restart the running program after a system failure.

roll-call polling: Polling whereby the controller sends a message to each terminal to find out whether the terminal has anything to communicate.

roll in: To reinstate a task or a set of tasks that had been rolled out.

rolling code: A code that changes with time. Describes a form of bandsplitter that periodically rearranges the frequency displacement of sub-bands.

roll-in/roll-out: A return to a main or internal storage unit of data and programs, which had previously been transferred from main or internal memory units to various external or auxiliary units.

roll-over indexing: Allows depression of a key before releasing the previous key.

ROM: See read-only memory.

root segment: The master controlling segment of an overlay structure which always resides in main memory. Usually this is the first segment within the program, and it is always the first to be loaded at program initiation time; often identical to the mainline segment or program.

rotate: The process of moving in a circular manner each bit in a register either to the right or left.

rotating joint: Short length of cylindrical waveguide, constructed so that one end can rotate relative to the other; used to couple two other waveguide systems, normally of rectangular cross-section.

rotational time: The time required for the unit to make one complete revolution.

round: Deletion of the least significant digit(s) with or without modifications to reduce bias.

round robin: Cyclical multiplexing of a resource among jobs with fixed time slices.

rounding: See round-off.

rounding error: The error resulting from rounding off a quantity by deleting the less significant digits and applying some rule of correction to the part retained; e.g., 0.2751 can be rounded to 0.275 with a rounding error of .0001. Same as round-off error and contrasted with truncation error.

round-off: 1. To delete the least significant digit(s) of a numeral and to adjust the part retained in accordance with some rule. 2. The last digit displayed in an answer is increased by one if the following digit would have been a 5 or greater.

round-off error: See rounding error.

route-control digits: Specify digits to be outpulsed and routes to be used for the establishment of toll calls.

routine: A series of computer instructions which performs a specific, limited task.

routine extremity: Used when initiating a new tape or when reaching the end-of-reel of a multireel file. This routine need not be included in memory if all tapes are set-up or initiated automatically by the system supervisor and the open or close macros are not used. The importance of this routine is that it performs necessary tape housekeeping, checks on the operator, and provides necessary information concerning the program being run.

routine loading: A routine which, once in storage, elicits other information into storage from cards or tape.

routine maintenance: Machine time devoted to repairs. Usually on a regular schedule, during which time preventive maintenance activities are also performed.

routine-maintenance time: The machine time devoted to repairs on some regualr pattern or schedule, during which time preventative maintenance activities are also performed.

routing: The selection of a path or channel for sending data.

routing code: 1. A combination of one or more digits used to route a call to a predetermined area. 2. A code assigned to an operator message and used in systems with multiple console support (MCS), to route the message to the proper console.

routing indicator: An address or group of characters in the header of a message defining the final circuit or terminal to which the message has to be delivered.

RS: See record separator.

RSPT: See real storage page table.

R-S-T flip-flop: A flip-flop having three inputs "R," "S" and "T." RTL: See resistor-transistor-logic.

rub-out-character: See delete character.

ruby laser: An optically-pumped ruby crystal producing a very intense and narrow beam of coherent red light. It is used in light-beam communication and for localized heating.

ruly English: A form of English in which every word has one and only one conceptual meaning and each concept has one and only one word to describe it. This is a hypothetical language based on English which complies uniformly to a definite set of rules, without exceptions.

rumble: Low-frequency noise produced in disk recording when a turntable is not balanced dynamically.

run: 1. One routine or several routines automatically linked so that they form an operating unit, during which manual interruptions are not required. 2. One performance of a routine on a computer involving loading, reading, processing, and writing. 3. The execution of one or more programs that are linked to form one operating program.

runaway: A condition which arises when one of the parameters of a physical system undergoes a large, sudden, undersirable and often destructive increase.

run book: All material needed to code document a computer application, including problem statement, flow charts, coding, and operating instructions.

run duration: On the occasion on which, after compiling, the target program is run during the run phase or target phase. The duration or the run is called the run duration and compiling is called the compiling duration.

run locator: A routine which locates the correct run on a program tape, whether initiated by another routine or manually.

RX: See receiver

S

safety circuit: Gives warning of faults or abnormalities, or operates a trip on a protective device.

safety paper: Specially treated paper to prevent alterations and counterfeiting. Usually, it is used on checks.

sample: Used in process control, weather forecasting, timesharing of equipment, on-line processing for missile guidance, etc. to obtain the status of various events and conditions.

sample-change compaction: A data compaction procedure which is accomplished when constant levels are specified, or at least easily defined varying levels are stated for values together with deviations in discrete or continuous values, parameters or variables. Curves can be reconstructed from transmission even if precision numbers smaller than originals are transmitted.

sample controller: Uses intermittently observed values of a signal such as the set point signal, the actuating error signal, or the signal representiong the controlled variable to affect control action.

sampling: 1. Obtaining the values of a function for discrete values of the independent variable. 2. In statistics, obtaining a sample from a population. 3. In analog-to-digital converters (ADC's), the periodic checking of the voltage of an input waveform. The converter uses these successive samples to represent digitally the analog waveform. Increasing the sampling rate increases the accuracy of the digital representation of the waveform.

sampling distribution: A theoretical frequency distribution of the sample means. It is called a theoretical distribution because, while it can be proved that it exists, only one value in it is known.

sampling error: 1. The error in a statistic due to a finite number of samples. 2. Errors arising from improperly selected samples, or samples improperly collected so that the samples are not representative.

sampling gate: A circuit with an output only when the gate is opened by an activating pulse.

sampling period: A specific measured time interval between observations in a periodic sampling control system.

sampling rate: The rate at which measurements of physical quantities are made, e.g., if it is desired to calculate the velocity of a missile and its position is measured each millisecond, then the sampling rate is 1,000 measurements per second.

satellite: 1. Radio transmitting station depending on, or controlled by, another station. 2. Circulating vehicle at a height above the Earth to reflect or transmit back radio waves as a means of communication, using computer-controlled terrestrial antennae.

satellite communication: Principle of reflection or regeneration of telegraphic or telephonic signals from earth satellites, using highly directive antennae for transmission and reception, oriented by computer calculation of orbit.

satellite community reception: The reception of emissions from space stations in the broadcasting-satellite service by receiving installations, which in some cases may be complex and have antennae larger than those used for individual reception, and intended for use either by a group of the general public at one location, or through a distribution system covering a limited area.

satellite computer: A processor connected locally or remotely to a larger central processor. Performs certain processing tasks; sometimes independent of the central processor, other times subordinate to the central processor.

satellite downlink: The portion of a communication link used for transmission of signals from a satellite or airborne platform to a surface terminal. Converse of uplink.

satellite earth coverage: A condition obtained when a beam is sufficintly wide to cover the surface of the earth exposed to the satellite.

satellite earth stations: Track satellites, both during and after launch. Receive telemetry data from satellites providing information on their performance and status (spin rate, voltage, temperature, etc.). Transmit commands when necessary to change the position of the satellite or activate onboard communications components.

satellite equatorial orbit: The plane of a satellite orbit which coincides with that of the equator of the primary body.

satellite station: 1. Re-braodcasts a directly received transmission on a different wavelength. 2. Transmits to and receives from earth satellites.

satisfy: An equation is said to be satisfied when the right-and left-hand members of the equation are equal after substitution of equivalent quantities for the unknown terms in the equation.

saturating integrator: Relating to incremental computers, a digital integrator modified so that the output increment is maximum negative, zero, or maximum positive, according to whether the value of y is negative, zero or positive. Same as incremental integrator.

saturation noise: 1. Extra bits or words that must be ignored or removed from data when the data is used. 2. Errors introduced into data in a system, especially in communication channels. 3. Random variations of one or more characteristics of any entity such as voltage, current, and data. 4. Any disturbance tending to interfere with the normal operation of a device or system.

saturation testing: Program testing with a large bulk of messages, and either using or simulating the use of all lines and terminals in the system. This may be caused by improbable events, such as two messages arriving at exactly the same time.

sawtooth wave: A particular wave, which when graphed gives the appearance of the teeth of a saw.

scalar: A device that produces an output equal to the input multiplied by a constant.

scalar date: A date inscribed as a single number representing its displacement from a specified uniform base or origin date (e.g., January 2, 1900). Used for internal representation and storage in computers to facilitate calculations.

scale: 1. To alter the units in which all variables are expressed, to bring all magnitudes within bounds dictated by need, register size, or other arbitrary limits. 2. A range of values frequently dictated by the computer word-length or routine at hand.

scale control: A system in which one or more control systems depend on another central system, which determines the index (or desired) point in operation.

scale factor: Coefficients that multiply or divide quantities in a problem in order to convert them so they lie in a given range of magnitude, e.g., plus one to minus one.

scale-of-two: A number system written to the base two notation.

scaling: 1. The process of changing a quantity from one notation to another. 2. To place the actual decimal point of a quantity, by shifting if necessary, in the relationship to the machine decimal point, so that: (1) the quantity remains within the capacity of the machine, (2) various quantities are in the correct relationship to each other for arithmetic operations, (3) the results are computed with the actual decimal point of the quantity in the desired location.

scaling factor: A numerical coefficient used to multiply one or more quantities occurring in a calculation.

scan: To examine every reference or every entry in a file routinely as a part of a retrieval scheme.

scan line: One line of light generated by a television screen as its beam sweeps from left to right.

scanner: An instrument which automatically samples or interrogates the state of various processes, files, conditions, or physical states and initiates action in accordance with the information obtained.

scanner, analog input: A device which will, upon command, connect a specified sensor to measuring equipment and cause the generation of a digit count value which can be read by the computer.

scanner television camera: IN optical recognition, to a device that images an input character onto a sensitive photoconductive target of a camera tube, thereby developing an electric charge pattern on the inner surface of the target.

scanning rate: The speed at which a computer can select, convert, and compare an analog input variable to its high and/or low limits.

scanning-electron microscopic (SEM) inspection: An inspection that is electrically destructive and is performed only on a sample basis. SEM inspection is used to examine the quality of metallization on integrated circuits at very high magnification. It is particularly affective in detecting microcracks which may cause catastrophic device failure.

scanning speed: The speed of a scanning spot across the screen of a cathode-ray tube.

scatter format: A load module attribute that permits dynamic loading of control sections into nonadjoining areas of main storage.

scattering: Irregular reflection or dispersal of waves or particles.

scatter loading: A procedure or process of loading a program into main memory such that each section or segment of the program occupies a single, connected memory area (in some systems a "page") but the several sections of the program need not be adjacent to each other. Usually implemented by a virtual memory structure.

sceptre: A language for use in designing and analyzing circuits. Implemented on several computers.

scheduled-down time: The time the computer or other machine is being serviced for regular maintenance; also known as preventative maintenance time (PM).

scheduled engineering time: The time spent on installing and performing regular maintenance on a computer.

scheduled maintenance: Maintenance carried out in accordance with an established plan.

scheduled maintenance time: Maintenance activities performed in accordance with a planned or established schedule or timetable; published for the information coder, oprators, engineers, maintenance technicians, and users, it does not include supplementary maintenance.

scheduler: See master scheduler, and job scheduler.

scheduling: 1. The task of determining what the succession of programs should be in a multiprogramming system. 2. Designation of time and sequence of projected operations.

scheduling algorithm: An algorithm that determines the order in which competing jobs are allowed to use resources.

scheduling system sequential: A first-come, firstserve method of selecting jobs to be run.

schematic: A drawing using conventional symbols which shows the connection of components in a circuit.

Schneider front-end: A front-end train of amplifiers to interface gas chromatograph instruments to a realtime computer.

scientific language: One designed for writing mathematical or scientific programs.

scientific notation: Quantities are expressed as a fractional part (mantissa) and a power of ten (characteristic).

scientific problems: Mathematical problems solved on a computer.

scientific processing: Data processing in shich mathicatical functions are solved.

scientific sampling: Concerns a designed selection sample that represents the population in a manner that characteristics and conclusions can be theorized concerning the population.

scope: In assembler programming, that part of a source program in which a variable symbol can communicate its value.

scrambled: The encoded or secret form of a signal which is unintelligible except when decoded or descrambled.

scratch tape (sorting):   Any tapes used to hold intermediate-pass data (not permanently saved).

scratch pad: A unique internal storage area, reserved for intermediate results, various notations, or working area. It is quickly erasable main storage.

scratchpad memory: A small immediate access memory area of a central processor, with a significantly faster access time than the larger main store. This is normally used by the hardware and/or operating system for storing extracodes, most frequently used operands, groups of object program instructions, or registers.

screen: 1. The surface in an electrostatic cathode ray storage tube where electrostatic charges are stored and by means of which information is displayed or stored temporarily. 2. To make a preliminary selection from a set of entities, election criteria being based on a given set of rules or conditions. 3. To make a preliminary selection of information or documents in order to reduce the number examined at a later time.

screening: Operations that are done to devices on a 100 percent basis to eliminate present or potential failures. Precap visual inspection, burn-in, hermeticity testing, 100 percent electrical testing, etc., are part of the standard high reliability screening operations.

SDR: See statistical data recorder.

sealed circuits: Circuits that are sealed in place. They are very tiny but are far more rugged than their larger, more cumbersome counterparts. Sealed circuits permit the development of electronic systems that take only a fraction of the space required by ordinary wire circuits.

seal test: A test designed to determine the effectiveness of the seal of cavity devices. Both a fine leak and a gross leak test are required. These tests are made after all mechanical tests have been completed.

They screen out the defective seals that may cause device failures with exposure to moisture or gaseous contaminants.

search: To examine a series of items for any that have a desired property or properties.

search, dichotomizing: A search in which an ordered set of items is partitioned into two parts, one of which is rejected, the process being repeated until the search is completed.

search cycle: The part of a search that is repeated for each item. It consists of locating the item and carrying out a comparison.

search time: The time required to locate a particular field of data in storage. Searching requires a comparison of each field with a predetermined standard until an identity is obtained. This is contrasted with access time which is based upon locating data by means of the address of its storage location.

search-time storage: Time required to locate a particular field of data in storage. Searching requires a comparison of each field with a predetermined standard until an identity is obtained. A contrast with access time, which is based upon locating data by means of the address of its storage location.

secondary: The output winding of a transformer.

secondary console: In a system with multiple consoles, any console except the master console. The secondary console handles one or more assigned functions on the multiple console system.

secondary constants: Those for a transmission line which are derived from the primary constants. They are the characteristic impedance (impedance level) as of an infinite line, and the propagation constant (attenuation and phase delay constant).

secondary data: Data published by an individual or organization other than the one which collected it.

secondary failure: Failure caused by the failure of another item, causing the item concerned to be exposed to stresses or conditions for which it was not designed.

secondary memory: A large-capacity storage area which has a longer access time than a scratchpad memory. Secondary memory permits the transferring of blocks of data between it and the main storage.

secondary operator control station: Under telecommunications access method, any operator control station that can send operator commands and receive related responses.

secondary paging device: An auxiliary storage device that is not used for paging operations until the available space on primary paging devices falls below a specified minimum. Portions of a secondary paging device can be used for purposes other than paging operations.

secondary proof: A program in demand deposit accounting which performs the second sort and breaks the block totals from preliminary proof down into ledger control totals.

secondary storage: Storage facilities forming not an integral part of the computer but directly linked to and controlled by the computer, e.g., magnetic drum, magnetic tapes, etc.

secondary switching center: Telephonic switching in which a group of local centers are all connected by trunk circuits.

second-channel interference: In reception by supersonic heterodyne receivers, the interference from signals which are not desired, but whose frequency differs from local oscillator frequency by the same amount as the wanted signal. Both these signals produce an intermediate frequency output acceptable to the receiver.

second detector: The detector in the superheterodyne which extracts the audio signal from the modulated i-f carrier.

second-generation computer: A computer utilizing solid-state components.

second-level addressing: An addressing computer instruction which indicates a location where the address of an operand can be found.

second-removal subroutine: A subroutine which on a specific occasion is entered from a first remove subroutine, is on particular occasions called a second remove subroutine, whereas, the first remove subroutine is entered directly from a program and returns to it.

sectional center: A designation for a control center connecting primary centers together, i.e., a Class 2 office.

section output: The storage block from which output data is drawn.

sector: A set of bits comprising the smallest addressable unit of information in a drum or disk memory.

security: Prevention of access to or use of data or programs without authorization.

seek: 1. See search. 2. Specifically applied to obtaining records from a random access file. The number of seeks is the number of items inspected before the desired item is found.

seek time: The time that is needed to position the access mechanism of a direct-access storage device at a specified position. See also access time.

segment: A set of data that can be placed anywhere in a memory and can be addressed relative to a common origin. The origin and number of locations of a segment are called its base address and its length.

segmented program: A program written in separate parts. One or more of the segments may fit into memory at any one time, and the main portion of the program, which remains in memory, will call for other segments from backing storage when needed.

segment mark: A special character written on tape to separate one section of a tape file from another.

segments, overlay: Overlaying (replacing) one program segment with another.

seizing signal: A signal which is often translated at the start of a message to initiate a circuit operation at the receiving end of a circuit.

select: 1. To take the alternative A if the report on a condition is of one state, and alternative B if the report on the condition is of another state. 2. To choose a needed subroutine from a file of subroutines.

selected cell: Same as coincident-current selection.

selecting data: The extraction of a desired item or items of data from a larger group of data. Sorters and collators are used in selecting data.

selection: Addressing a terminal and/or a component on a selective calling circuit.

selection check: A check, usually an automatic check, to verify that the correct register or device is selected in the performance of an instruction.

selection-check device: 1. A check that verifies the choice of devices, such as registers, in the execution of an instruction. 2. A check (usually automatic) to verify that the correct register, input/output (I/O) device, etc. was selected in the performance of a program instruction.

selection ratio: The factor of reached magnetic force used to select a magnetic storage location to the maximum available magnetic force, which may not be intended to select a location.

selection-replacement technique: A technique used in the internal part of a sort program.

selective calling: A sending station specifying which station on the same line (channel) is to receive a specific message.

selective-casing routine: Specific sets of instructions which determine various criteria in order to develop a history of enterings during the processing.

selective-clock stretching: A technique capable of resolving digital timing differences among system components and obtaining the maximum performance out of each component.

selective dissemination - of - information (SDI): A system in which literature is searched and a hard copy may be obtained, i.e., a system for selectively distributing information.

selective dump: A dump of one or more specified storage locations.

selective fading: Fluctuation in which the components of a signal fade or wither disproportionately, such as the rise and fall of only the high or low frequency components of an electric or electronic device.

selective interference: Interference concentrated into relatively narrow frequency channel(s).

selective-length field: A fixed number of characters are chosen for each data field. This requires filling out shorter data items with zeros or blanks to reach the fixed number.

selective network: One for which the loss and/or phase shift are functions of frequency.

selective reject frame: Calls for retransmission of only the frame specified.

selective repeat: A method for dealing with pieplining errors in which the receiving interface message processor (IMP) stores all the correct frames following the bad one. Eventually the sender sees that someting is wrong and retransmits the one bad frame. This method corresponds to a receiver wondow greater than 1.

selective sequential: A technique of processing a direct-access sequential file so that selected records in the file are located by means of an index table and are presented in the processing program in key number sequence.

selective trace: A tracing routine wherein only instructions satisfying certain specified criteria are subject to tracing.

selective tracing: Tracing of data most often related to highly specific instructions.

selective-tracing routine: A tracing routine which allows only specific instructions to be selected and analyzed, such as only transfer instructions or inputoutput instructions.

selectivity: The ability of a receiver to choose a particular carrier.

select-minus routine: A routine that examines the results of an input/output activity and determines if any error recovery is required.

selector: A device which interrogates a condition and initiates one of several alternate operations.

selector unit channel: A high-speed data channel dedicated to one input/output (I/O) device at a time, operating in burst mode.

select plus routine: A routine that determines if a device is ready to be used and, if it is, prepares a select instruction, channel command, and device order to accomplish an input/output activity or error recovery procedure.

selectron: An electronic tuning device capable of storing bits with rapid selection and access.

select routine: A routine for a specific input/output device consisting of a select plus routine and a select minus routine.

selenium rectifier: One depending on a barrier layer of crystalline selenium on an iron base. Widely used in cathode circuit taking anode current.

self demagnetization: The process by which a magnetized sample of magnetic material tends to demagnetize itself by virtue of the opposing fields created within it by its own magnetization. Self-demagnetization inhibits the successful recording of short wavelengths or sharp transitions in a recorded signal.

self demarcating code: A code in which the symbols are so arranged and selected that the generation of false combinations by interaction of segments from two successive codes is prevented.

self-adapting: The ability of a computer system to change its performance characteristics in response to its environment.

self-decode: Indicates that all or a part of the scanning is done internal to the encoder. Also self decoding u-scan, v-scan.

self-defining term: In assembler programming, an absolute term whose value is implicit in the specification of the term itself.

self-inductance: Realization in a current-carrying coil, of self-induction.

self-operated controller: A device in which all the energy necessary to operate the signal controlling element is derived from the control system through the sensing element.

self-organizing: Having the capability of classification or internal rearrangement, depending on the environment in accordance with given instructions or a set of rules.

self-relocating program: Can be loaded into any area of main storage. Contains an initialization routine to adjust its address constants so that it can be executed at that location.

self-resetting loop: One which contains instructions restoring all locations affecting the operation of the loop to their initial condition as at entry of the loop.

self-selecting u-scan: See self-decode.

self testing modem: Provided to aid in isolating causes of faulty operation. These include means for connecting the transmitter to the receiver for a local back-to-back test, a digital loop back of the received data to the transmitter so that a complete check of the modem plus line can be made from the distant end, the incorporation of a random bit sequence to simulate typical data, and some indication of signal quality or occurrence of errors.

self-tuning: Automatic modification of control algorithm constants based upon process conditions.

selsyn: An induction machine or device which consists of stator and rotor elements each carrying one or more windings, the mutual inductance depending upon the angular position of the rotor with respect to the stator.

semantics: The relationships between symbols and their intended meanings independent of their interpretation devices.

semi-automatic message-switching center: A center where an operator routes messages according to the information in them.

semicompiled: Use of a program which has been converted from source language into object code by a compiler, but which has not yet had included those subroutines explicitly or implicitly called by the source program.

semiconductive: Often considered an electric device which is composed of high conductive metals and low conductive insulators designed to change the nature or strength of electric flows in various circuits.

semiconductor: A material whose resistivity is between that of conductors and insulators, and whose resistivity can sometimes be changed by light, an electric field or a magnetic field.

semiconductor chip: A small, rectangular slice of material, usually silicon and 4 mm^2 or less, on which a complete semiconductor device has been built. It can be either a simple single function like a transistor used as an amplifier, or a complex integrated circuit replacing thousands of discrete components. Chips are often called integrated circuits.

semiconductor donor: Material added to a semiconductor to increase the number of free electrons; this produces an n-type semiconductor.

semiconductor dopant: An impurity added to a superpure semiconductor in order to produce the required electrical qualities.

semiconductor dual in-line package: A standard method of packaging integrated circuits with input/output pins bent at right angles and in lines along the two long sides of the unit so that they go straight into holes in a printed circuit board.

semiconductor memory: A memory whose storage medium is a semiconductor circuit. Often used for high-speed buffer memories and for read-only memories.

semifixed length record: Can be changed in length under certain circumstances by a programmer.

semifixed length record: A fixed length record that can be changed in length under certain circumstances by a programmer.

sending: The process by which the central computer places a message on a line for transmission to a terminal.

sending point: In a check-collection operation of a transit department, any correspondent or local bank that is sent a cash letter.

send-receive keyboard (KSR): A combination transmitter and receiver with transmission capability from keyboard only.

send-request circuit: Signals on this circuit are originated in the data-terminal equipment to select whether the signal converter is to be conditioned to transmit or to receive. For half-duplex service, when the signal on the send-request circuit is switched to the "on" condition, the signal converter switches to the transmit condition, without regard to any signals that may be received from the communications facility. When this signal is switched to the "off" condition, the signal converter switches to the receive condition, without regard to any signals on the transmitted-data circuit. Data-terminal equipment intended for use with send-only service holds the send-request circuit in the "on" condition at all times. Data-terminal equipment intended for use with receive-only service holds the send-request circuit in the "off" condition at all times. This circuit is not required for full-duplex service.

sense: 1. To examine, particularly relative to a criterion. 2. To determine the present arrangement of some element of hardware, especially a manually-set switch. 3. To read holes punched in paper, tape, or cards.

sense data: Information from an input/-output file control unit indicating error, unusual, or attention conditions.

sense signal: The voltage induced in the sense winding by a magnetic cell to which a read pulse is applied.

sense winding: The change in flux configuration which induces voltage.

sense wire: A distinctly conductive wire that carries a feed-out signal, which is occasioned by a change in polarity of a magnetic core unit.

sensing element: Part of a device which is directly responsive to the value of the measured quantity.

sensing-element elevation: The difference in elevation between the sensing element and the case; the elevation is positive when the sensing element is above the case.

sensitivity: The degree of response of an instrument or control unit to a change in the incoming signal.

sensitivity analysis: A trial of a range of input values to determine the response, interdependence, or friction of the output values. Sensitivity analysis is often called parametric programming because one or more parameters can vary in order to determine whether or not a solution should be modified.

sensitivity ratio: 1. A measurement of the degree of response of an instrument or control unit to change in the incoming signal. 2. A measured ratio of a change in output to the change in input which causes it, after steady-state has been reached, usually expressed as a numerical ratio with the units of measurement of the two quantities stated.

sensor: A transducer or other device whose input is a quantitative measure of some external physical phenomenon and whose output can be read by a computer.

sensor scan: A type of sequential interrogation of lists of information or devices under process control. This develops a collection of data from process sensors by a computer for use in calculations, usually working through a multiplexer.

sensor-based system: An organization of components, including a computer whose primary source of input is data from sensors and whose output can be used to control the related physical process.

sentinel: 1. A symbol marking the beginning or the end of some element of information such as a field, item, block, tape, etc. 2. A tag or flag.

separating control character: One of a set of control characters used to delimit hierarchic units of data. The first separating character in a hierarchy might be used between words, paragraphs, or for nested brackets, etc.

separation loss: The loss in output that occurs when the surface of the coating fails to make perfect contact with the surfaces of either the record of reproduced head. Separation loss may be caused by (a) poor guiding, (b) the use of cupped or otherwise distorted tape, (c) the presence of projections, dust or wear products on the tape surface, (d) the accumulation of wear products on the head surface and ultimately, (e) the imperfect smoothness of the tape surface. The magnitude of the loss introduced depends upon the method of recording. The use of high record currents in digital recording or high ac bias in analog recording, tends to reduce the loss.

septum: Dividing partition in a waveguide.

seq and ack fields: Used for sequence numbers and acknowledgements, respectively.

sequence: 1. To put a set of symbols into an arbitrarily defined order, e.g., to select A if A is greater than or equal to B, or select B if A is less than B. 2. An arbitrarily defined order of a set of symbols, i.e., an orderly progression of items of information or of operations in accordance with some rule.

sequence break (sorting):   Refers to the point in a file between the end of one string and start of another.

sequence check: A data processing operation designed to check the sequence of the items in a file assumed to be already in sequence.

sequence checking routine: A routine which checks every instruction executed and prints out data.

sequence control register: The computer register that keeps track of the location of the next instruction to be processed.

sequence counter: A hardware register which is used by the computer to remember the location of the next instruction to be processed in the normal sequence, but subject to branching, execute instructions and interrupts.

sequence number: An identifying number used to designate a block of data, an operation, or part of an operation.

sequencer: See sorter.

sequence sorting: The fields in a record which determine, or are used as a basis for determining, the sequence of records in a file.

sequence switch: The stage in an active file system which controls transmitted and received signals.

sequence symbol: In assembler programming, a symbol used as a branching label for conditional assembly instructions. It consists of a period, followed by one to seven alphameric characters, the first of which must be alphabetic.

sequencing: Ordering in a series or according to rank or time.

sequencing criteria: The fields in a record which determine, or are used as a basis for determining, the sequence of records in a file.

sequencing key: The field in a record that determines the sequence of records in a file.

sequential access: Obtaining data from an input/output device in a serial manner only.

sequential-alarm module: The device which continuously monitors a group of alarm contacts; i.e., whenever one or more of these contacts close, the module immediately signals a priority interrupt to the computer. The computer then reads the module's contact input states to establish a trip sequence from current and previous readings. (some systems)

sequential collating: A process of sequencing a group of records by comparing the key of one record with another record until it is determined whether the records are equal or whether one is greater than the other.

sequential computer: A computer in which events occur in time sequence, with little or no simultaneity or overlap of events.

sequential control: A mode of computer operation in which instructions are executed in consecutive order by ascending or descending addresses of storage locations, unless otherwise specified by a jump.

sequential-data set: A data set organized so that, given one record, the next record to be processed is determined uniquely.

sequential index: A type of direct access to files of data or information according to an established access criteria.

sequential-logic element: A device having at least one output channel and one or more input channels, all characterized by discrete states, such that the state of each output channel is determined by the previous states of the input channel.

sequentially controlled automatic-transmitter start: A special single-service multipoint teletypewriter arrangement designed to provide for transmission between all stations connected to a network without contention between stations.

sequential operations: The performance of large-scale actions one after the other in time.

sequential processing: The processing of data that have been operated on previous to their entry into the computer system which placed them in a definite and prescribed order.

sequential-scheduling system: A form of the job scheduler which recognizes one job step at a time in the sequence in which each job appears in the input job stream.

sequential-stacked job control: A control system which insures that jobs are performed in the sequence that they are presented to a system.

sequential transmission: A television technique of transmitting pictures so that the picture elements are selected at regular times and are then delivered to the communication channel in the correct sequence.

serial: 1. The handling of one after the other in a single facility, such as transfer or store in a digitby-digit time sequence, or to process a sequence of instructions one at a time, i.e., sequentially. 2. The time sequence transmission of, storage of, or logical operations on the parts of a word, with the same facilities for successive parts.

serial adder: A logical unit which adds two binary words, one binary bit pair at a time. The least significant addition is performed first and progressively more significant additions, including carries, are performed until the sum of the two numbers is formed. Saves hardware at the expense of operating time.

serial-data transmission: See serial transmission.

serial-digital computer: A machine in which the digits are handled in serial manner, especially in the arithmetic unit.

serialize: To change from a parallel-by-bit to serial-by-bit.

serially reusable: 1. A reusable program which is not necessarily reenterable. 2. The attribute of a routine that when in main storage the same copy of the routine can be used by another task after the current use has been concluded.

serially reusable load module: A module that cannot be used by a second task until the first task has finished using it.

serial memory: A memory whose information media is continuous. Data is identified by its content or form. Data may be obtained only by performing a serial search through the contents of the memory.

serial number: Numerals attached to a device, machine, item, or a sequence for spatial position of an item relative to other items, i.e., numbers representing a label or identifier.

serial number control: The control messages by assigning a number at the time of origination and adding additional numbers as the message passes through specific points.

serial operation: The flow of information through a computer in time sequence, usually by bit but sometimes by characters.

serial output: Sequential availability of two or more-bits, channels, or digits.

serial-parallel: 1. A combination of serial and parallel, i.e., serial by character, parallel by bits comprising the character. 2. Descriptive of a device which converts a serial input into a parallel output.

serial printer: A device capable of printing characters, one at a time across a page.

serial processing: The sequential execution of two or more processes in a single device such as a channel or processing unit. Contrast with parallel processing.

serial programming: The programming of a computer by which only one arithmetical or logical operation can be executed at one time, e.g., a sequential operation.

serial storage: Storage in which time is one of the coordinates used to locate any given bit, character, or (especially) word. Storage in which words appear one after the other in time sequence, and in which access time therefore includes a variable latency or waiting time of zero to many word-times.

serial transfer: A method of data transfer in which the characters of an element are transferred in sequence over a signal path in consecutive time positions.

serial transmission: A method of information transfer in which the bits composing a character are sent sequentially. Contrast with parallel transmission.

series: A succession of quantities, each derived from the preceding amount or amounts according to some fixed law. The first and last terms of a series are called the extremes, and the intervening terms the means.

series computer operator: Usually operates the central console. May give some direction to lower level classifications. Studies run sheets. Reruns job steps to recover from machine error or program error, consulting with technical staff where necessary. Maintains machine performance and production records.

series modulation: Anode modulation in which modulator and modulated amplifier valves are connected directly in series, to eliminate the necessity for a modulation transformer or choke coupling.

series-parallel: Same as serial-parallel.

series records: Groups of identical or related records which are used and filed as a unit, and which permit evaluation as a unit for retention scheduling purposes.

service area: Surrounds a broadcasting station where the signal strength is above a stated minimum and not subject to fading.

service band: That allocated in the frequency spectrum and specified for a definite class of radio service, for which there may be a number of channels.

service bureau: Computer service installations where users can rent or lease processing time on a central processor and peripheral equipment. Either can supply the programs and the center will load both program and data to be processed, process the data and transmit or deliver the results to the user in any of several forms: cards, punched tape, magnetic tape, etc. Service bureaus also provide such services as key-punching the data and preparing it for processing.

service message: A transmission between communications personnel pertaining to any phase of traffic handling, communication failures, or circuit conditions.

service program: Any of the class of standard routines that assist in the use of a computing system and in the successful execution of problem programs, without contributing directly to control of the system or production of results.

service routine: 1. A routine designed to assist in the actual operation of the computer. Tape comparison, block location, certain post mortems, and correction routines fall in this class. 2. A routine which assists in the operation, maintenance, or repair of a machine.

service time: The time required to execute a job.

servo link: A mechanical power amplifier which permits low strength signals to operate control mechanisms that require fairly large powers.

servomechanism: Any closed-loop, feedback type of control system. A servomechanism consists of the following elements (which may be distinct or combinedfunction elements of hardware): (a) An input signal or command line, to indicate the desired state. (b) An output sensor, capable of monitoring the actual output state. (c) A comparator which determines the deviation from the desired state, based on the above two signals. (d) An effector, which has the power to modify the output state or condition.

servomechanism repeater: A positional servomechanism in which loop input signals from a transmitting transducer are compared with loop feedback signals from a compatible or identical receiving transducer.

servo multiplier: A multiplying unit with position control; capable of multiplying each of several different variables by a single variable.

session: The period of time during which the user engages in a dialog with the time sharing system.

set: 1. To place a storage device in a prescribed state. 2. To place a binary cell in the one state. 3. A collection of elements having some feature in common or which bear a certain relation to one another.

set normal response mode (SNRM): Allows a machine that has just come back on line (is "up" again) to announce its availability and set all the sequence numbers back to zero. Set normal response mode (SNRM), used by high-level data link control (HDLC) and LAPB, is like SNRM except that an extended frame format is used of 7-bit sequence numbers.

set point command: That specific input variable which sets the desired value of the controlled variable. The setting of the input variable may be completed manually, automatically, or as programmed, most often expressed in the same units as the controlled variable.

set point control: A specific control procedure in which the computer supplies the calculated set point to a conventional analog instrumentation control loop.

set symbol: In assembler programming, a variable symbol used to communicate values during conditional assembly processing.

set theory: A study, in the mathematical sense of the rules, for characterizing groups, sets, and elements; i.e., the theory of delimiting or combining groups.

setting time: The time which the variable will take to line out to within 5 percent of the steady state, for a change in input.

set up: The preparation of pieces of equipment for operation.

set-up diagram: A graphic representation showing how a computing system has been prepared and the arrangements that have been made for operation.

set-up services: The action or services performed on a message before it meets the application program. Services include error checking analyzing the action code, etc.

set-up time: The portion of the elapsed time between machine operations which is devoted to such tasks as changing reels of tape, and moving cards, tapes, and supplies to and from the equipment.

several-for-one: A phrase often associated with a macro instruction, where one source language instruction is converted to several machine language instructions.

severity code: A code assigned to an error detected in a source module.

sexadecimal: See hexadecimal.

sexadecimal (hexadecimal) notation: Notation using the base 16.

shading: 1. Variations in brightness in a televised image becuase of local defects in the signal plate of a camera tube, arising from inadequate discharge. Corrected by injective waveforms in the output signal. 2. The technique of varying the directivity of a transducer by controlling the amplitude and phase distribution over the active area of the transducer.

shadow: Ineffectiveness of reception because of an obstacle; e.g., due to the topography of the terrain, between transmitter and receiver.

shadow mask CRT: The type of cathode ray tube (CRT) which is used in color televisions and some color computer terminals. Three electron beams – one for blue, red, and green color – pass through a perforated metal screen, the "shadow mask", to strike blue, red, or green phosphor dots. To the human eye the colors are seen as a combination instead of separately so a wide variety of hues can be produced.

shannon: A specific unit of measurement of the quantity of information which is equal to that contained in a message represented by one or the other of two equally probable exclusive or exhaustive states.

shannon equation: Equation in information theory which gives theoretical limit to rate of transmission of binary digits with a given bandwidth and signal/noise ratio.

shared data set: A data set for which the originator has granted access to other users.

shared file: A direct access device that may be used by two systems at the same time; a shared file may link two systems.

shared main storage multiprocessing: A mode of operation in which two processing units have access to all of main storage.

shared routine: A routine which can be used simultaneously by several people.

shared-files system: A file system configuration in which two computers have access to the same file storage device, though not necessarily at the same time (some systems).

shared-time control action: A control action wherein one controller divides its computation or control time among several control loops, rather than acting on all loops simultaneously.

sharer: A user who issues a share command to gain access to a data set for which the owner has issued a permit command.

sharing: 1. The interleaved time use on a device-hence, a method of operation in which a computer facility is shared by several users concurrently. 2. The apportionment of intervals of time availability of various items of equipment to complete the performance of several tasks by interlacing (contrasted with multiprogramming). 3. The use of a device for two or more purposes during the same overall time interval, accomplished by interspersing the computer component actions in time. 4. A multiple communications control unit (MCCU) attached to the computer allows many consoles to "time-share" the central processing unit simultaneously during transmission and receiving periods. Timesharing is a computing technique in which numerous terminal devices can utilize a central computer concurrently for input, processing, and output functions.

sharp cutoff tube: An amplifier which provides high amplification but is prone to overloading.

sharpness: The clarity of an image, its similarity of geometry of printed characters to the shape of the original type face used as guides.

shelf life: A length of time, often a maximum, in which inventory of various items can remain in stock or normal storage and still be placed in operations without deterioration to the system of piece of equipment.

shelf lists: A technique for controlling records' center holdings wherein the original transfer document is prepared in several copies and filed by ending organizations and destruction date.

Shell sort: A widely-used exchange sort originated by D.A. Shell. The algorithm has proven considerably more efficient than bubble or tennis-match sorting.

shielded line: 1. Line or circuit shielded from external electric or magnetic induction by shields of highly conducting or magnetic material so that the transmitted energy is enclosed within the shield and not radiated.

shielded pair: A balanced pair of transmission lines within a screen, to mitigate interference from outside.

shielding: A method of preventing interaction between circuits by surrounding the circuits with metal plates.

shift: To move information serially right or left in a register(s) of a computer. Information shifted out of a register may be lost, or it may be re-entered at the other end of the register.

shift character: In telecommunications, a control character that determines the alphabetic/numeric shift of character codes in a message.

shift charge: The additional or extra rent required by the lessor or holders of various equipment. Some manufacturers rent or lease equipment for one shift only and charge extra for shifts which are not in normal business or on monthly hour limit. Extra charges are for over 176 hours per month which, in many cases, is a standard shift.

shift-in (SI): 1. (ISO) A code extension character, used to terminate a sequence that has been introduced by the shift-out character, that makes effective the graphic characters of the standard character set. 2. A code extension character that can be used by itself to cause a return to the character set in effect prior to the departure caused by a shift-out character, usually to return to the standard character set.

shifting register: The register which adapts to perform shifts; e.g., a delay line register whose circulation time may be increased or decreased so as to shift the content.

shift instructions: Instructions that include operations which will shift the number either to the left or to the right within an arithmetic register. A shift opera-

tion is equivalent to multiplying or dividing, depending upon the direction of the shift, by the radix of the number base in use.

shift letters: A function by a teleprinter, when initiated by the letters-shift character, which causes the machine to shift from upper case to lower case.

shift-out (SO): 1. (ISO) A code extension character that substitutes for the graphic characters of the standard character set an alternative set of graphic characters upon which agreement has been reached or that has been designated using code extension procedures. 2. A code extension character that can be used by itself to substitute another character set for the standard character set, usually to access additional graphic characters.

shift register: A register in which the stored data can be moved to the right or left.

short block: A block of F format data which contains fewer logical records than are standard for a block.

short-circuit impedance: Input impedance of a network when the output is short-circuited, shorted or grounded.

short-haul carrier: A carrier system designed for use over distances of 10 to 200 miles.

short instruction format: A "standard" length (e.g., one-word) instruction as opposed to a "long" instruction. Most instructions are of this type.

short-term scheduling: A specific portion of a scheduling algorithm that assigns processors and storage to processes as soon as they become available to maintain efficient utilization of a computer. The level of programming also implements synchronizing operations, which enable processes to interact.

short wave broadcasting: International amplitudemodulation (AM) broadcasting in the frequency vicinity of 20-30 megacycles.

shunt: 1. Addition of a component to divert current in a known way; e.g., from a galvanometer, to reduce temporarily its effective sensitivity. 2. Diversion of some flux from the gap in a magnetic circuit by a magnetic slide or screw in a moving-coil indicating instrument.

shunt circuit: Electric or magnetic circuit in which current or flux divides into two or more paths before joining to complete the circuit; also parallel circuit.

SI: See shift-in.

side circuit: A circuit arrangement for deriving a phantom circuit. In four-wire circuits, the two wires associated with the go channel form one side circuit and those associated with the return channel form another. See also phantom circuit.

side circuit loading coil: A loading coil for introducing a desired amount of inductance in a side circuit and a minimum amount of inductance in the associated phantom circuit.

side-circuit repeating coil: A repeating coil that functions as a transformer at a side circuit terminal. Often used as a means for superimposing one side of a phantom channel on that circuit.

sideband: The frequency band on either the upper of lower side of the carrier frequency.

side frequency: A single frequency in the side band.

side tone: One reaching the receiver of a radiotelephone station from its own transmitter.

sifting: An internal sorting technique where records are moved to permit the insertion of other records.

sign: The symbol or bit which distinguishes positive from negative numbers.

sign changer: As regards scalers, when the constant which is used as a multiplier has the value of -1, the scaler may be called a sign changer, an inverter, or a sign reverser.

sign check: It is possible to detect a change in sign during arithmetic operations and either stop the machine or signal for subsequent review. This sign is also used in accounts receivable, accounts payable, inventory, and general ledger applications. The sign check can be used to recognize any balance that becomes negative.

sign check indicator: An error checking device, indicating no sign or improper signing of a field used for arithmetic processes. The machine can upon interrogation be made to stop or enter into a correction routine.

sign digit: A character, frequently a single bit, used to designate the most significant digit different from zero and ending with the least significant digit whose value is known, i.e., 2300.0 has five significant digits, whereas 2300 probably has two significant digits. However, 2301 has four significant digits and 0.0023 has two significant digits.

sign position: A position, normally located at one end of a numeral, that contains an indication of the algebraic sign of the number.

signal: In communications, a designed or intentional disturbance in a communication system. Contrast with noise.

signal-amplitude sequencing (split ranging): An action in which two or more signals are generated or two or more signal control elements are actuated by an input signal, each one responding consecutively with or without overlap to the magnitude of that input signal.

signal attenuation: The reduction in the strength of electrical signals.

signal compensation: Passing a signal through an element with characteristics which are the reverse of those in the transmission line so that the net effect is a received signal with an acceptable level/-frequency characteristic.

signal conditioning: To process the form or mode of a signal so as to make it intelligible to or compatible with a given device, including such manipulations as pulse shaping, pulse clipping, digitizing, and linearizing.

signal correlation: A check made on received signals of different frequencies; to obtain reliable diversity reception the two received signals must not be likely to fade at the same time.

signal damping: The final manner in which the output settles to its steady-state value after a change in the value of measured signal; i.e., when the time response to an abrupt stimulus is as fast as possible without overshoot, the response is said to be "critically damped." It is "underdamped" when overshoot occurs and "overdamped" when response is slower than critical.

signal-disturbed response: The output signal from a core subjected to a partial read pulse after it has been set to a one or zero condition.

signal element: 1. The part of a signal that occupies the shortest interval of the signaling code. 2. The unit duration in building up signal combinations. 3. A pulse or signal. An absence or presence of voltage or current in a communication medium.

signal-feedback control: The portion of the output signal which is returned to the input in order to achieve a desired effect, such as fast response.

signal frequency noise: Noise that lasts for a significant time period and is localized in frequency.

signal frequency shift: The bandwidth between white and black signal levels in frequency-modulated (FM) facsimile transmission systems.

signal generator: An oscillator that provides known voltages (usually from 1 volt to less than 1 u volt) over a wide range of frequencies; used for testing or ascertaining performance of radio-receiving equipment. It may be amplitude-frequency- or pulse-modulated.

signaling, A-C: Transmission of electronic signals over alternating current power lines.

signaling-in-band: Signaling which utilizes frequencies within the intelligence band of a channel.

signaling rate: The rate at which signals are transmitted.

signal level: In optical character recognition, the amplitude of the electronic response which occurs from the contrast ratio between the area of a printed character and the area of a document library.

signal power: An expression of absolute signal strength at a specific point in a circuit. See level.

signal pulsing: Signals which are transmitted in the forward direction and carry the selective information to route the call in the desired direction.

signal space: 1. The exact number of digit positions in which the corresponding digits of two binary numeric words of the same length are different. 2. The number of digit positions in which the corresponding digits of two words of the same length in any radix notation are different.

signal-starting dialing: In semi-automatic or automatic working, a signal transmitted from the incoming end of a circuit, following the receipt of a seizing signal, to indicate that the necessary circuit conditions have been established for receiving the numerical routine information.

signal start-dialing: A signal transmitted following the receipt of a seizing signal.

signal-to-crosstalk ratio: In line telephony, the ratio of the test level in the disturbed circuit to the level of the crosstalk at the same point, which is caused by the disturbing circuit operating at the test level.

signal-to-noise ratio: The ratio of the amount of signals conveying information to the amount of signals not conveying information.

signal transducer: A transducer designed to convert one standardized transmission signal to another.

signal transformation: A generated signal which meets very specific requirements relating to a specific computer system. If such a signal is transformed or timed to conform to its original detail, as above, the signal is proved to have been regenerated or standardized.

signal wave: One which allows intelligence to be conveyed.

signed-magnitude: A system of representing numbers in a computer system in which the number is composed of the sign position and the magnitude of the number. This is opposed to a complement system where negatives are represented by their complement.

significance: In positional representation, the factor, dependent on the digit place, by which a digit is multiplied to obtain its additive contribution in the representation of a number.

significant: Data that is material and has meaning in its output form for use in analysis or interpretation of problems or solutions.

significant digit: A digit that contributes to the precision of a numeral. The number of significant digits is counted by beginning with the digit contributing the most value, called the most significant digit, and ending with the one contributing the least value, called the least significant digit.

significant figures: Digits of a numeral which have specific meanings for particular purposes. Digits which must be kept to preserve a distinct accuracy and may not be rounded off without losing accuracy or desired precision.

silicon diode: A crystal diode that uses crystalline silicon.

silicon transistor: One formed from a silicon crystal, sometimes specified in preference to germanium because of its higher temperature stability.

silicones: A family of synthetic materials consisting of silicon and oxygen, usually with associated carbon atoms. They generally have a low vapor pressure and withstand extremely high temperatures.

simple buffering: A technique for obtaining simultaneous performance of input/-output operations and computing. This method involves associating a buffer with only one input or output file (or data set) for the entire duration of the activity on that file (or data set).

simple-logic element: A set or circuitry which provides an output resulting from an input of two variables.

simple name: The rightmost component of a qualified name.

simplex (SPX): A communications system or equipment capable of transmission in one direction only.

simplex (SPX) circuit: A circuit derived from an existing two-wire circuit by use of a center-tapped repeating coil. This additional circuit must use another wire conductor or ground return to complete its path.

simplex/duplex modems: Modems may be designed to operate in three modes: (a) Simplex, where data is transmitted (and hopefully received) in only one direction; (b) Half-duplex, where data can be transmitted in only one direction at a time, but that direction can be reversed; and (c) Full duplex, where data may be transmitted in both directions simultaneously.

simplex mode: A communication channel operation in only one direction.

simulate: 1. To represent certain features of the behavior of a physical or abstract system by the behavior of another system, e.g., to represent a physical phenomenon by means of operations performed by a computer or to represent the operations of a computer by those of another computer. 2. To represent the functioning of a device, system, or computer program by another. 3. To imitate one system with another, primarily by software, so that the imitating system accepts the same data, executes the same computer programs, and achieves the same results as the imitated system.

simulated attention: A function that allows terminals without attention keys to interrupt processing. The terminal is queried periodically for a specified character string.

simulation: 1. The representation of physical systems and phenomena by computers, models or other equipment, i.e., an imitative type of data processing in which an automatic computer is used as a model of some entity, e.g., A chemical process. 2. In computer programming, the technique of setting up a routine for one computer to make it operate as nearly as possible like another computer.

simulation manipulation: The activation of a representation achieved by accepting inputs and generating outputs analogous to those of the system. This tends to exclude pure optimization models from the definition, since their computing algorithms do not usually reproduce the behavior of the system.

simulator: A device or computer program that performs simulation.

simulator routing: An interpretive routine designed so that programs written for one computer can be run on a different computer.

simultaneity: The facility of a computer to allow input/output on its peripherals to continue in parallel with operations in the central processor.

simultaneous transmission: Transmission of control characters or data in one direction while information is being received in the other direction.

simultaneous computer: A computer that contains a separate unit to perform each portion of the entire computation concurrently, the units being interconnected in a way determined by the computation; at different times in a run, a given interconnection carries signals representing different values of the same variable, for example, a differential analyzer.

sine wave: 1. A perfectly formed electromagnetic wave with no harmonics. 2. A periodic, mathematical plotted function (quantity) which varies according to y = Rsinwt, which is an amplitude-angular-displacement plot of the projection, on a diameter, of a point moving on the circumference of a circle of radius R.

singing: Sound caused by unstable oscillations on the line.

single-address: An instruction format containing one address part.

single buffering: Having only one area in an object program for the input/output of data associated with any one file. This normally causes the delaying of an object program while the relatively slower file device transmits data.

single-cycle key: A push button on a computer printer that causes an additional line to print in spite of an end-of-form condition.

single-domain particle: All ferromagnetic materials are composed of permanently magnetized regions in which the magnetic moments of the atoms are ordered. These domains have a size determined by energy considerations. When a particle is small enough it cannot support more than one domain and is called a single-domain particle.

single-ended amplifier: A single-stage amplifier using one tube.

single-level address: An address that indicates the location where the referenced operand is to be found or stored with no reference to an index register or B-box.

single length: Relates to the representation of numbers in binary form so that the values of the numbers can be contained in a single word.

single-line repeater: A telegraph repeater utilizing a pair of cross-coupled polar relays which are inserted in series with a circuit to repower the signal.

single-office exchange: An exchange served by a single central office.

single operation: A communications system designed to permit electric contacts in only one direction between stations. Technical arrangements may permit operation in either direction, but not simultaneously.

single-phase: Pertaining to a.c. power supplies, when one outward and one return conductor are required for transmission.

single pole: A switch, relay, etc. in which connections to only one circuit can be made. A single polesingle way switch is a simple on-off switch.

single-precision integer: A fixed-point number that occupies one word of core storage. The value varies dependent on the word length of the computer.

single-program initiator (SPI): Under disk-operating systems, a program that is called into main sob control type functions for foreground programs not executing from batched job input.

single-shot circuit: Circuits or logic elements arranged to perform signal standardization to convert an imprecise input signal into one conforming to the requirements of a particular machine.

single-sideband modulation: The spectrum of the modulating wave is translated in frequency by a specified amount, either with or without inversion.

single-sideband transmission: A method of communication in which the frequencies produced by the process of modulation on one side of the carrier are transmitted, and those on the other side are suppressed. The carrier frequency may be either transmitted or suppressed.

single-speed floating controller: A particular controller designed so that output charges are at a fixed rate but increase or decrease depending on the sign of the actuating error signal.

single-station broadband (communications): Can be connected to a communication terminal station (CTS) by a leased Telepak A line. Leased Telepak A line operation permits continuous data exchange between two fixed locations at a maximum transfer rate of 5,100 characters per second. Data transfer can be initiated by either device, providing the remote hardware can handle such an operation. The data format will be such that character parity, start and end of message limits, message parity, and character synchronization will be established. The CTS will be prepared to receive the data at all times. These modes of operation reflect the influence of presently available communications tariff oferrings. The CTS design and packaging philosophy will allow for future higher-speed operation (up to 100,000 bits/sec) and also for operation with communications hardware using more advanced techniques.

single-step operation: A method of operating an automatic computer manually in which a single instruction or part of an instruction is performed in response to a single operation of a manual control. This method detects mistakes.

single-terminal entry: A terminal table entry containing information on a single terminal.

single-vertical key: A push button on a printer which produces an additional printed line for indication.

single-wire line: A transmission line that utilizes the ground as one side of the circuit.

site address: Addresses contained by polling messages which identify the terminal being addresses. Also called station address.

site code: In medical coding, a code that specifies the location of an organ or organ system.

situation display: A visual display such as on a cathode-ray tube mounted on a console of past, present, and anticipated future events in a time sequence and occuring in space.

skeletal code: The framework of a routine which requires the addition of generalized routines to be entered as input parameters in order to be complete.

skew: 1. In reference to facsimile transmission, skew is the deviation from a rectangular picture (frame) caused by the lack of time coincidence between the scanner and the recorder. 2. In optical character recognition, the condition of a line that is not exactly perpendicular to the reference edge of the document being scanned, or is not exactly parallel with preceding and succeeding lines.

skew failure: In character recognition, the condition that exists during document alignment whereby the document reference edge is not parallel to that of the read station.

skewing: Time delay or offset between any two signals in relation to each other.

skip: An instruction to proceed to the next instruction; a blank instruction.

skip bus: A central processor bus, shared by input/output (I/O) interfaces and utilized in order to test devices associated with each interface and conditional branching of the program as a result of the testing.

skip instruction: An instruction having no effect other than directing the processor to proceed to another instruction designated in the storage portion. Same as skip and NO-OP instruction.

skip-key tape: A particular operator control key which, when depressed, advances the tape until a tape skip restore character is sensed.

skip test: A type of microinstruction designed and utilized for conditional operations based on the state of readiness of various devices or the conditions of a register.

sky wave: A radio wave which travels through space rather than along the ground.

slash sheet: An official government data sheet/procurement specification for parts on the Qualified Parts list.

slave: A unit of electronic gear under the control of signals from the master equipment.

slave mode: The mode of computer operation in which most of the basic controls affecting the state of the computer are protected from the program.

slave station: The station which receives data from a master communications station which it either monitors or with which it complies, or in some cases, repeats to other stations, but whose output is not part of the orignal output.

slave tube: A cathode-ray tube (CRT) connected to a master tube and both tubes are identical, the slave following the master, most often to follow the storage contents of an electrostatic storage tube.

sleeve: A quarter-wavelength coaxial line for coupling a coaxial line in a dipole at its center.

slewing rate: The rate at which the output can be driven from limit to limit over the dynamic range.

slice: The parts of a waveform lying inside two given amplitude limits on the same side of the zero axis.

sliding window protocols: Protocols in which each outbound frame contains a sequence number, ranging from 0 up to a predetermined maximum. At any instant, the sender maintains a list of consecutive sequence numbers identifying with frames it is permitted to transmit. These frames fall within the sending window. The receiver keeps a receiving window corresponding to acceptable frames.

slip scan: A character recognition term relating to a magnetic or photoelectric device that obtains the horizontal structure of an inputted character by vertically projecting its component elements at given intervals.

slope-keypoint compaction: A data compaction procedure accomplished using statements of specific points of departure. Direction or slope of departure are transmitted until the deviation from a prescribed condition exceeds a specified value. At that point, a new slope or keypoint is signalled to reduce the time and space required for transmission.

slow memory: That portion of the memory from which information may be obtained automatically, but not at the fastest rate of various sections.

slow-scan television: Transmits still video images in color by telephone.

slow storage: A storage module or device whose access time is longer in relation to the speeds of arithmetic operations of the central processing unit (CPU) of a computer and more lengthy when compared to other faster access peripheral units.

slow-time scale: A time scale greater than the unit of time in the physical system being studied.

slug: A thick copper band, comparable with a portion of a winding on a telephone-type relay which retards the operation and full-off of the relay.

smart-interactive terminals: An interactive terminal in which part of the processing is accomplished by a small computer or processor contained in the terminal itself.

smooth contact: A socket or pin contact which has a significantly smooth profile, i.e., a flush surface and not one which has a locking spring projecting from its side; one that is locked to the connector body by other methods.

smooth line: Cable pairs or transmission lines with no added inductive loading.

snapshot: A dump usually of a selected area of storage taken at specified times during the execution of a routine, thereby providing a time history of this section of storage for debugging purposes.

snapshot debugging: A type of diagnostics and debugging technique in which the programmer specifies the start and end of program segments where he wishes to examine the contents of various registers and accumulators. The snapshot tracing may indicate the contents not only of the various accumulators and registers but also of specified memory locations.

snapshot dump: A dynamic partial print-out during computing, at breakpoints and checkpoints, or selected items in storage.

sneak current: A leakage current that gets into telephone circuits from other circuits; can cause damage if allowed to continue.

sneak path: An undesired electrical path in a circuit.

socket contact: A female-type contact used to mate with a pin, i.e. male-type contact.

soft copy: A volatile representation of information (i.e., a CRT display).

soft error: Occurs during processing and does not occur when the same process is attempted a second time.

soft facility dispersal: A vital records center which is located at a remote distance from the building housing original records. Such a building is constructed above ground and does not include special explosionproof materials.

soft limited integrator: As regards limited integrators, i.e., which involve integrators in which the inputs cease to be integrated when the output tends to exceed specified limits, in a soft limited integrator, which is used for lower cost or convenience and where precision is of less importance, the output may exceed the limits.

soft limiting: A circuit of nonlinear elements that restrict the electrical excursion of a variable in accordance with some specified criteria. Soft limiting has an appreciable variation in output in the range where the output is limited.

software: 1. The internal programs or routines prepared professionally to simplify programming and computer operations. Uses permit the programmer to use his own language (English) or mathematics (algebra) in communicating with the computer. 2. Programming aids that are frequently supplied by the manufacturers to facilitate

the purchaser's efficient operation of the equipment.

software house: A company which offers softwaresupport service to users. This support can range from supplying manuals and other information to a complete counseling and computer part programming service.

software documents: All the documents and notations associated with the computer; i.e., manuals, circuit diagrams, etc, or programs and routines associated with the computer; i.e., compilers, special languages, library routines.

software modularity: The outstanding modularity and resultant flexibility of hardware have their parallels in the programming and operating aids furnished with the systems. Most types of programs in the software library are offered in several versions to run in systems. Most types of programs in the software library are offered in several versions to run in systems configurations of different sizes and compositions. In particular, it is important to note that software versions written for large systems are designed to take advantage of the increased internal and input/output processing capacities of these systems.

software package: A computer program or set of programs used in a particular application such as a payroll/personal package, scientific subroutines package, etc.

software priority interrupt: The developed programmed implementation of specific priority interrupt functions.

solar cell: A photoelectric cell using silicon, which collects photons from the sun's radiation and converts the radiant energy into electrical power with reasonable efficiency. Used in spacecrafts and for remote locations lacking power supplies; i.e., for telephone amplifiers in the desert.

solenoid: Current-carrying coil of one or more layers. Usually a spiral of closely-wound insulating wire, in the form of a cylinder, not necessarily circular.

solid circuit: 1. Modification of properties of a material; i.e., silicon, so that components can be realized in one mass (i.e., resistors, capacitors, transistors, diodes). 2 Subminiature realization of a circuit in three dimensions; e.g., as built up as parts of a semiconductor crystal or by etching or deposition on a substrate.

solid error: An error that always occurs when a particular piece of equipment is used.

solid-logic technology (SLT): Microelectric circuits used as the basic components of the modern computing system. They carry and control the electrical impulses that represent information within a computer.

solid state: Pertains to various types of electronic components that convey or control electrons within solid materials. Transistors, germanium diodes, and magnetic cores are solid state components; vacuum and gas tubes and electromechanical relays are not.

solid-state component: A component whose operation depends on the control of electric or magnetic phenomena in solids, for example, a transistor, crystal diode, or ferrite core.

solid-state computer: A computer built primarily from solid state electronic circuit elements.

solid-state design: The solid-state components and circuitry of the real-time system offer numerous advantages including standardized production of components and the reduction of maintenance procedures. In addition to ease of maintenance, solid-state circuits also impart a high degree of operating reliability to the computer and reduce the power, polling, and space requirements of the system at the same time.

solid-state device: An electronic component designed to control electrons with-

in solid materials; e.g., transistors, germanium devices and magnetic cores.

solid-state element: An electronic component that functions without requiring current to pass through space or a vacuum. As a direct result, power needed to push current through the element is greatly reduced, and there is no need for special cooling due to reduced heat buildup.

solid-state logic: Microelectronic circuits are a product of solid logic technology (SLT) and make up many systems' basic circuitry. These microminiaturized computer circuits are called logic circuits because they carry and control the electrical impulses that represent information within a computer. These tiny devices operate at speeds ranging from 300 down to 6 billionths-of-a-second. Transistors and diodes mounted on the circuits are only 28 thousandths of an inch thick (some systems).

solid-state magnetic modules: Made by the following process; magnetic alloys are deposited in a vacuum and under the influence of a high magnetic field, on planes of glass so thin that the direction of their magnetic fields can be switched within several billionths of a second. This feature allows information to be stored or retrieved at extremely high speeds. Ths immediate benefits derived from this include savings in processing time, reduced power requirements, and miniaturized storage units.

solid-state physics: A branch of physics which covers all properties of solid materials, including electrical conduction in crystals of semiconductors and metals, superconductivity and photoconductivity.

solver: A FORTRAN subroutine for general mathematical programming. Written in the FORTRAN language, SOLVER will handle linear, quadratic, and nonlinear programming problems in up to 70 variables and constraints. The main reaction is that the objective function and each of the constraint functions be concave and differentiable.

SOM: See start of message.

sonic delay line: A delay line using a medium providing acoustic delay, such as, mercury or quartz delay lines.

sophisticated computer vocabulary: An advanced and elaborate set of instructions. Some computers can perform only the more common mathematical calculations such as addition, multiplication, and subtraction. A computer with a sophisticated vocabulary can go beyond this and perform operations such as to linearize, extract square root, and select highest number.

sort: 1. To segragate items into groups according to specified criteria. Sorting involves ordering, but need not involve sequencing, for the groups may be arranged in an arbitrary order. 2. To arrange a set of items according to keys which are used as a basis for determining the sequence of the items, e.g., to arrange the records of a personnel file into alphabetical sequence by using the employee names as sort keys.

sort application: Job segments that are applications of the generalized sorting system.

sort-blocking factor: In sorting, the number of data records to be placed in each block.

sorter: 1. A person, device, or computer routine that sorts. 2. A punched card device that deposits punched cards, depending on the hole patterns, in selected pockets.

sort generator: A program which generates a sort program for production running.

sorting: The process of arranging data into some desired order according to rules dependent upon a key or field contained in each item.

sorting-collating sequence: Refers to a particular sorting sequence and is usually a description of the sort key for a file of records.

sorting routine: Arranges items of data into sequence according to the values contained within specified fields of the individual records.

sorting-routine generator: A generator in which the object program is sorts a set of items into a given sequence defined by the parameters specified to the generator.

sort/merge generator: Custom programs for sorting files of data.

sort/merge program: A processing program that can be used to sort or merge records in a prescribed sequence.

sort run: See sort application.

sound analyzer: Measures each frequency, or a small band of frequencies in the spectral distribution of energy. Particularly useful for tracing sources of vibration or noise in rotating equipment.

sound carrier: The television carrier modulated by the audio signal.

sound channel: The carrier frequency with its associated sidebands, which are involved in the transmission of the sound in television.

sounder: A telegraph receiving instrument in which an electromagnet attracts an armature each time a pulse arrives. The armature makes an audible sound as it hits against its stops at the beginning and end of each current impulse, and the intervals between these sounds are translated from code into the received message by the operator.

sound field: 1. Region through which sound waves, standing or progressive, propagate from a source. Such fields diverge from point, cylindrical or plane sources. 2. Enclosed space in which the diffused sound waves are random in magnitude, phase and direction, constituting reverberant sound.

soundex: A technique, similar to cutter numbering, for phonetic matching of inquiries in the form of words to compensate for possible spelling errors. The input name is converted to an equivalent phoneme representation and matches to phoneme equivalents of file entries are indicated.

sound strip: The stages in a television receiver concerned with the sound program.

sound-track: Track on magnetic tape or cine film on which sound signals have been or can be recorded. Optical tracks may use variable area or variable density modulation.

source data automation (SDA): The many methods or recording information in coded forms, on paper tapes, punched cards, or tags that can be used over and over again to produce many other records without rewriting; usually refers to a process rendering the data machine readable or actually entering data into a system (via communication lines) at the site where the data is originally collected or generated.

source deck: A stack of program cards ready to insert into compiler of some computers operated by punched cards.

source document: The original paper on which are recorded the details of a trans action.

source impedance: The impedance presented to the input of a device by the source.

source inspection: An observation or performance of screening tests by representatives of the government and/or the procuring activity. Source inspection is most often done at final electrical testing and at preseal visual inspection and other screening tests.

source language: The original symbolic language in which a program is prepared for processing by a computer. It is translated into object language by an assembler or compiler.

source-language debugging: Correcting or debugging information requested by the user and displayed by the system in a form consistent with the source programming language.

source language program translation: The program translation to a target program, for example, to FORTRAN or from FORTRAN, ALGOL, etc. The translating process is completed by the machine under the control of a translator program or compiler.

source-macro definition: In assembler programming, a macro definition included in a source module. A source macro definition can be entered into a program library; it then becomes a library macro definition.

source module: An organized set of statements in any source language recorded in machine-readable form and suitable for input to an assembler or compiler.

source-module library: A partitioned data set that stores and retrieves source modules.

source noise: The origin of any unwanted signal.

source program: 1. A program written in source language. 2. The input program to be processed.

source program library: A collection of computer programs in source language form.

source recording: The recording of data in machinereadable documents, such as punched cards, punched paper tape, magnetic tapes, etc. Once in this form, the data may be transmitted, processed, or reused without manual processing.

source statement: Statements written by a programmer in symbolic terms related to a language translator.

source-statement library: A collection of books (such as macro definitions) cataloged onto the system by the librarian.

SP: See space character.

space: 1. A site intended for the storage of data, e.g., a site on a printed page or a location in a storage medium. 2. A basic unit of area, usually the size of a single character. 3. One or more space characters. 4. To advance the reading or display position according to a prescribed format, e.g., to advance the printing or display position horizontally to the right or vertically down.

space character: An operating and graphic character designed to prevent a print.

space diversity: The transmission or reception methods which employ antennas having common polarization and spatial separations to minimize the effects of flat or selective fading.

space-division matrix (SDM): A process in which a switch matrix establishes a discrete path between two or more telephones. Each telephone call completed by the switch occupies a path (space). Once the connection is established, the path is used continuously to transmit information.

space-hold: The normal no-traffic line condition whereby a steady space is transmitted. May be a customer-selectable option.

space-reception diversity: That form of diversity reception which utilizes receiving antennas placed in different locations.

space suppression: The inhibition of platen and/or paper movement for a line of printing.

spacing condition: One of two conditions that a communication channel can assume. Spacing is usually the indication that intelligence is being transmitted.

spanned record: A logical record that is stored in two or more physical records.

special character: A graphic character that is neither a letter, nor a digit, nor a space character.

special-effects generator: A device permitting combinations of images on a television screen supplied by one or more video inputs.

specialized carriers: The established old line common carriers in the U.S. include the local telephone companies, AT & T long lines, and Western Union. Newer carriers offering, planning to offer, or awaiting approval to offer services include United States Transmission Systems, Inc., a subsidiary of ITT World Communications; CPI Microwave, Inc.; MCI Telecommunications Corp.; United Video, Southern Pacific Communications Corp.; Western Tele-Communications (WTCI); and American Satellite. The newer carriers do not offer uniform geographic coverage.

special-purpose computer: A computer that operates upon a restricted class of problems.

special-purpose intelligent terminals: These terminals contain some logic and are polled by the computer, or conversely, the computer polls some intermediate device, such as magnetic tape or disk. If the computer goes down, the terminal can continue to operate in a limited mode for a certain period of time. Applications include department stores, supermarkets, hotel systems, and banks.

specific address: An address that indicates the exact storage location (related to absolute code).

specific address location: To aid in random access, data may be stored directly and retrieved from a specific addressed location without the need for a sequential search as is necessary with magnetic tape. Examples of such units are magnetic drums, disks.

specification file: 1. A file containing copies of all forms used in an activity, filed by construction characteristic of the form (tab cards, flat forms, tags, continuous pin-feed). This file is developed specifically for procurement packages. 2. A reference data file containing specifications for data characteristics, report production, file layouts, etc., used in a given applications set.

specification sheet: Document used to describe physical appearance, construction, and special characteristics of an approved form. Used in processing internal printing or outside procurement.

specific magnetic moment: The value of the saturation moment per unit weight of a magnetic material, expressed in emu/gm. The specific magnetic moment is the most convenient quantity in which to express the saturation magnetization of fine-particle materials. The specific magnetic moment of pure gamma ferric oxide is approximately 75 emu/gm at room temperature.

specific program: A program for solving a specific problem only.

specific routine: A routine to solve a particular mathematical, logical, or data handling problem in which each address refers to explicitly stated registers and locations.

specific schedules: A records retention schedule issued for each organization independently and containing all the records it processes or maintains.

spectral reflectance: The determined reflectance related or caused by a specific wavelength of incident light from a specified surface.

spectral response: A response type and intensity of a machine, device or receiving unit as regards light, radiant energy, of wavelengths or bands of frequencies i.e., the variation of sensitivities of such devices to light of specific wavelengths.

spectrometer: Instrument used for measurements of wavelength or energy distribution in a heterogeneous beam of radiation.

spectrum: 1. The range of electromagnetic radiations, from the longest known electrical wave to the shortest cosmic ray. Light, the visible portion of the spectrum, lies about midway between the two extremes. 2. A graphical representation of the distribution of the amplitude (and sometimes phase) of the components of a wave as a function of frequency. A spectrum may be continuous or, on the contrary, contain only points corresponding to certain discrete values.

spectrum analyzer: Electronic spectrometer usually working at microwave frequencies and displaying energy distribution in spectrum visually on a cathode-ray tube.

spectrum frequency: The range of frequencies of electromagnetic radiation waves which re divided in low frequency (LF), medium frequency (MF), high frequency (HF), etc.

speech equalizer: Circuit for correcting the excessive low-frequency gain of high-fidelity amplifiers designed for reproduction of records.

speech synthesis data capture: A method of using speech as a direct form of input.

spiral parity checking transmission codes: A method used to detect single bit errors.

split catalog: A library catalog in which the different varieties of entry are filed separately, e.g., subject entry, author entry, title entry.

splitter: A passive device (one with no active electronic components) which distributes a television signal carried on a cable in two or more paths and sends it to a number of receivers simultaneously.

spool: 1. The mounting for a magnetic, paper or plastic tape. 2. A tape reel.

spooling: The process of temporarily storing data on disk or tape files until another aspect of processing is ready for the data (such as printing it).

sporadic fault: See intermittent fault.

spot-beam antenna: A multibeam type capable of reusing frequencies by transmitting and receiving signals from ground areas as small as 150 miles in diameter.

springer-finger action: Operations of electrical contacts to permit a stress-free spring action to develop contact pressure, i.e., used in sockets of printed circuits and in many other types of connectors.

sprocket pulse: 1. A pulse generated by a magnetized spot which accompanies every character recorded on magnetic tape. This pulse is used during read operations to regulate the timing of the read circuit and also to provide a count on the number of characters read from tape. 2. A pulse generated by the sprocket or driving hole in paper tape which serves as the timing pulse for reading or punching the paper tape.

SPX: See simplex.

SPX circuit: See simplex circuit.

square loop: See rectangular loop.

squared error: A mathematical technique for introducing the square of the error in the error term of a linear algorithm so as to produce a non-linear correction.

squareness ratio: The ratio, for magnetic material in a symmetrically cyclically magnetized condition, of the residual magnetic flux density, or the flux density at zero magnetizing force, to the maximum flux or density.

square wave: A wave of rectangular shape.

stabilization bake: Usually a 24 hour bake of unsealed devices at +150°C. This test is not a screen, but a pre-conditioning on stabilizing process. The 24 hour bake may improve some characteristics and degrade others as it redistributes ionic contamination.

stabilization network: As applied to operational amplifiers and servomechanisms, a network used to shape the transfer characteristics to eliminate or minimize oscillations when feedback is provided.

stabilization time: The time from start-of-tape motion until tape speed reaches and remains within a stated limit of fluctuation from the steady state tape speed.

stabilizing capacitor: The large capacitor which steadies the operation of the ratio detector.

stabilizing resistor: An unbypassed resistor in the cathode circuit of an intermediate-frequency amplifier tube which helps keep the tube from being overloaded.

stable circuit: A circuit which continuously alternates between its two unstable states. It can be synchronized by applying a repetitive input signal of slightly higher frequency.

stable-trigger circuit: An electronic circuit having two stable states, two input lines, and two corresponding output lines such that a signal exists on either one of the output lines if, and only if, the last pulse received by the flip-flop can store one binary digit (bit) of information.

stack: A portion of memory and several registers used for temporarily holding information. A stack often operates on the last-in-first-out principle. That is, the last item of information placed in the stack will be the first item of information used when information is required from the stack. Operators perform their operation on information at the top of the stack.

stacked graph: A graph with two or three x scales and the same number of y scales plotted in such a way that there are discrete plotting grids placed one above the other.

stacked job: See batched job.

stacked-job processing: A procedure of

automatic jobto-job transitions, with little or no operator intervention.

stack pointer: The address of a location at the top of the stack.

stagger tuning: A method used in television and radar receivers of broadening the intermediate-frequency (IF) band. The resonant circuits of the IF strip are tuned to various points in the IF band width.

staging: The moving of data from an offline or lowpriority device back to an online or higer-priority device, usually on demand of the system or on request of the user. Contrast with data migration.

stand-alone emulator: An emulator whose execution is not controlled by a control program; it does not share system resources with other programs and excludes all other jobs from the computing system while it is being executed.

stand-alone program: Any program that operates independently of system control; generally, it is either self-loading or loaded by another stand-alone program.

standard: 1. An accepted criterion or an established measure for performance, practice, design, terminology, size, etc. 2. A rule or test by which something is judged.

standard antenna earth station: A 97-foot dish-shaped antenna mounted atop a l6-foot high concrete pedestal. The antenna structure is mounted on wheels which can be rotated on a track 50 feet in diameter on top of the pedestal. The 10-story tall antenna structure can be rotated rapidly one degree per second and precisely track a satellite stationed at 22,300 miles altitude to within two one-hundredths (2/100ths) of a degree. Earth stations presently being added to the worldwide communications system incorporate the latest advances in space communications technology. All forms of long-haul commercial communications, set and received at the speed of light (186,000 miles per second), can be processed through the earth stations—

thousands of telephone calls, telegraph messages, high-speed data, facsimile, or television.

standard byte input/output (I/O) bus: Provides a path for transfer of data, control, and status between the processor and external peripheral devices. The direct memory access (DMA) channel option communicates directly with memory.

standard communication subsystem: Refers to a multiplexer that permits simplex communication circuits to share an input/output (I/O) channel and line terminal units.

standard distortion: A commercial speech transmission path with a bandwidth of 250 Hz to 3000 Hz.

standard error: The standard deviation when it is considered as a measurement of error.

standard form: A prescribed arrangement, format, layout usually a form of data presentation.

standard graph: A graph plotted with one x scale and one or two associated y scales forming a single plotting grid.

standard interface: The interface form (matching) previously designed or agreed upon so that two or more units, systems, programs, etc., may be joined or associated easily.

standardize: To adjust the exponent and mantissa of a floating-point result so that the mantissa lies in the prescribed normal range. See floating-point representation.

standard label processing: The use of the input/output label system to verify or create a standard label.

standard language symbols: Special graphic shapes used to represent special meanings or functions that can occur in any computer program.

standard subroutine: 1. A subroutine which is applicable to a class of problems. 2. See library subroutine.

standard symbols language: Prescribed graphical shapes used to represent special meanings or functions that can occur in any computer program.

standard test force power: One-milliwatt (0 dBm) at 1000 hertz.

standard test-tone power: One milliwatt at 1,000 cycles per second.

standby: 1. Condition of equipment which will permit complete resumption of stable operations within a short period of time. 2. A duplicate set of equipment to be used if the primary unit becomes unusable because of malfunction.

standby application: An application in which two or more computers are tied together as a part of a single over-all system and stand ready for immediate application.

standby block: Locations always set aside in storage for communication with buffers in order to make more efficient use of such buffers.

standby computer: An additional computer used to take over when the need arises (such as a system in air traffic control).

standby maintenance time: Time that a maintenance person is on duty but not actively involved in maintenance and repair of equipment.

standby register: A computer register containing information that may need to be available in case of an error in malfunction.

standby time: The elapsed time between inquiries when the equipment is operating on an inquiry application.

standby-unattended time: The time in which the machine is in an unknown condition and not in use working on problems.

This includes time in which the machine is known to be defective and work is not being done to restore it to operating condition. It also includes breakdowns which render it unavailable because of outside conditions such as power failures.

star configuration: A simple form of message-switching system employing a single central switching computer; has all its lines connected to the central message switch.

star network: A network in which each terminal and computer is linked to a central computer. Because of this structure, all communication between various computers and terminals takes place through the central computer.

start bit: A bit used in asynchronous transmission to precede the first bit of a character transmitted serially, signalling the start of the character.

start delay: The elapsed time from receipt of start command to start of tape motion.

start distance: Distance tape travels after receipt of a start command before velocity reaches and remains within a stated limit of fluctuation from the steady state tape speed (equals qualification time times nominal speed).

start element: The first element of a character in certain serial transmission, used to permit synchronization.

starting current: The electron-beam current at which oscillations are self-starting in a specific circuit. Such a circuit may be used deliberately as a regenerative amplifier with beam current kept below this value.

starting point: Found on a cathode-ray tube display device. Same as current beam position.

start key: A specific push button located on the control panel designed to initiate or resume the operations of the equipment after an automatic or programmed stop.

start-of-heading character: A single or set of characters communicated by a polled terminal, indicating to to other stations on the line that the data to follow specify the addresses of stations on the line which are to receive the answering message.

start of message (SOM): A Character or group of characters transmitted by the polled terminal and indicating to other stations on the line that what follows are addresses of stations to receive the answering message.

start-of-text (STX): A control character that terminates and separates a heading and marks the beginning of the actual text.

start pulse: Used in Baudot teletypewriter codes for a space pulse to be transmitted just ahead of the five bits representing each character as a start element.

start signal: In a start-stop system, a signal serving to prepare the receiving mechanism for the reception and registration of a character or for the control of a function.

start/stop multivibrator: A kind of multivibrator which has one stable state ond one unstable state and goes through a complete change cycle. The circuit provides a single signal of proper form and time from a varying shaped, randomly timed signal. Upon receipt of a trigger signal, it assumes another state for a specified length of time, at the end of which it returns, of its own accord, to its original state.

start-stop time: The time between the interpretation of instructions to read or write on tape, and the transfer of information to or from the tape into storage, or from storage into tape, as the case may be.

start-stop transmission: Asynchronous transmission in which each group of code elements corresponding to a character signal is preceded by a start signal which serves to prepare the receiving mechanism for the reception and registration of a character, and is followed by a stop signal which serves to bring the receiving mechan-

ism to rest in preparation for the reception of the next character.

start time: Elapsed time after receipt of a start command until velocity reaches and remains within a stated limit of fluctuation from the steady state tape speed.

state: 1. For a physical computer, the condition of all elements, e.g., the total bit configuration. 2. For tuning machines, an undefined concept.

statement: In computer programming, a meaningful expression or generalized instruction in a source language.

static: Having no particular orientation or directional characteristics. Also having no tendency to change position.

static circuitry: 1. Employs switching devices whose outputs are essentially d-c levels, and which can be switched from one state of the other at any arbitrary instant. The devices can be switched as seldom or as often as desired, up to a certain maximum speed. However, once they are switched to one state or the other, they are capable of remaining in that state indefinitely, and the output signal will be a d-c level. A typical example of a static circuit element is the flipflop or a stable multivibrator.

static dump: A dump that is performed at a particular point in time with respect to a machine run, frequently at the end of a run.

static errors: Specific errors independent of the time variable as contrasted with dynamic errors which depend on frequency, i.e., inadequacy of the dynamic response of a computing unit.

static gain: A particular ratio of an output to an input after steady-state has been reached.

static handling: Handling corresponding to translation which is done completely by the compiler program.

staticize: 1. To convert serial or time-dependent parallel data into static form. 2. Occasionally, to retrieve an instruction, and its operands from storage prior to its execution.

staticizer: 1. A storage device for converting time sequential information into static parallel information. 2. A type of buffer.

static magnetic cell: That specific binary storage cell in which two values of one binary digit are represented by different patterns of magnetization, and in which means of setting and sensing the contents are stationary with respect to the magnetic material.

static memory: A memory device containing neither mechanical moving parts nor fixed information.

static routine: A subroutine that involves no parameters other than the addresses of the operands.

static storage: The storage of data on a device or in a manner such that information is fixed in space and available at any time, e.g., flip-flop, electrostatic, or magnetic-core storage.

static subroutine: A subroutine which involves no parameters other than the addresses of the operands.

static vs. dynamic simulation: In a dynamic system the activity is time-dependent. This activity may be further classified as stable or unstable (under given conditions). One may choose to study steady-state or transient behavior of a dynamic system.

station: One of the input or output points on a communications system.

station address: See site address.

station arrangement: A device, like a data set, required on certain subvoice-grade leased channels to connect at terminal to a communications line.

station battery: The electric power source for signaling at a station.

station control: A switching network station directing operations such as polling, selecting, etc.

stationery continuous reader: A character reader that can only read certain forms such as cash register receipts.

station selection code: A computer code which indicates that access is required though a particular station.

station selector: The receiver device which chooses a particular carrier.

statisizer: A storage device which stores temporarily or converts information as received into parallel information, often considered a specific type of buffer.

statistic: A numerical property of a sample in contrast to a parameter, which is defined as a numerical property of a distribution, i.e., a population, or universe.

statistical-data recorder (SDR): Under disk-operating systems, a feature that records the cumulative error status of an input/output device on the system recorder file.

statistical error: Arises in measurements of average count rate for random events, as a result of statistical fluctuations in the rate.

statistical hypothesis: An assumption about the frequency distribution of observations whose numerical values depend upon chance.

statistical method: A technique used to obtain, analyze, and present numerical data. The elements of statistical technique include: (a) The collection and assembling of data; (b) Classification and condensation of data; (c) Presentation of data in a textular, tabular, and graphic form; and (d) Analysis of data.

statistical mistakes: Various types of mistakes to be avoided are: 1. Concealed change in the statistical unit—for example, the value of the dollar changes over time. 2. Misuse of percentages—for example, if 12 drops t

statistical multiplexer: Multiplexers which send two output characters for each input character: the terminal number and the data. This solves the problem of telling the receiver which character came from which input line. Also called asynchronous time division multiplexers (ATDM).

statistical sample: A small portion of the entire population. It is drawn so that every value in the population has an equal chance of being included. A sample must be representative of the population.

status maps: A status report of programs and input/output operations, usually in tabular form.

status word: Storage locations which are 64 bits in length that provide data to the program following a program or channel interrupt. Provides information necessary to resume processing following the servicing of an interrupt. See automatic interrupt.

steady state: A stabilized condition in which the output has lined, leveled out, or reached a constant rate of change for a constant input.

stencil bit: In a group of binary digits, a specific bit which is in the operation of the instruction word and usually designates a specific type of operation.

step: 1. One instruction in a computer routine. 2. To cause a computer to execute one instruction.

step-by-step switch: A switch that moves in synchronism with a pulse device such as a rotary telephone dial. Each digit dialed causes the movement of successive selector switches to carry the connection forward until the desired line is reached.

step-by-step system: A type of line-switching system which uses step-by-step switches.

step-down transformer: A component consisting of two coupled coils in which the output voltage is less than the input voltage.

step-index optic fiber: An optic fiber whose core material contains the same refraction index throughout. Step-index fibers pose a limit on the data transmission rate or bandwidth of the fiber because light that enters the fiber at an angle parallel to the axis (0 degrees) will traverse a shorter path than a light ray that enters the fiber at another angle. The greater the angle that a ray enters the fiber, the longer a path it will travel, and the greater the time spread between the moments that the axial rays and the large angle rays arrive at the far end. For example, a data pulse that consists of a short duration burst of light will not arrive at the fiber output at the same time, but will be spread out over a given time period. As the fibre length increases, this spreading also increases. When a second pulse of light is sent too close to the first, the fastest portion of the second pulse may reach the output before the slowest portion of the first pulse, resulting in an overlap of signals. This causes loss of discrete pulses and, consequently, places a limit on data transmission rates.

stepped-start-stop system: A start stop system in which the start signals come at regular intervals.

stepping motor: A motor in which rotation occurs in a series of discrete steps controlled electromagnetically by individual (digital) input signals.

stepping switch: A switching device or relay which has discrete conditions and advances from one condition to the next each time it receives an input pulse.

stepping switch: A switching relay which has discrete conditions and advances from one condition to the next each time it receives an input pulse.

step-response time: An element or system in which the time required for an output to make the change from an initial value to a large specified percentage of a steady-state either before or in the absence of overshoot, as a result of a step change to the input. This is usually stated for 90%, 95%, or 99% change.

step restart: A restart that begins at the beginning of a job step. The restart may be automatic or deferred, where deferral involves resubmitting the job.

step-up transformer: A component consisting of two coupled coils in which the output voltage is greater than the input voltage.

still video: A telecommunications system whereby a telephone is linked to a screen and calls are joined by fixed images of the caller or of information.

stochastic variable: A statistical variable which has a probability with which it may assume each of many possible values in a distinct set.

stop-and-wait: A protocol in which the sender transmits one frame and then waits for acknowledgment before continuing.

stop bit: The last element of a character designed for asynchronous serial transmission, used to insure recognition of the next start element.

stop code: A control character which, in the case of a teletype, turns off the paper tape reader.

stop distance: The distance tape travels after receipt of a stop command until taomes to a complete stop.

stop element: The last element of a character in certain serial transmissions, used to insure recognition of next start element.

stop instruction: A machine operation or routine which requires manual action other

than the use of the start key to continue processing.

stopper: The highest memory location in any given system.

stop signal: In a start-stop system, a signal serving to bring the receiving mechanism to rest in preparation for the reception of the next telegraph signal.

stop time: Elapsed time from receipt of a stop command until tape comes to a complete stop.

storage: 1. A device into which data can be entered, held, or retrieved. 2. Any device that can store data.

storage, location: A storage component that can represent any one of a finite set of data values.

storage address display lights: The many indicator lights on the control panel used to specify the bit pattern in a selected address.

storage allocation: 1. The assignment of blocks of data to specified blocks of storage. 2. See dynamic storage allocation.

storage block: A contiguous area of main storage consisting of 2048 bytes to which a storage key can be assigned.

storage capacity: The number of bits, characters, bytes, words, or other units of data that a particular storage device can contain.

storage cell: An elementary unit of storage, for example, a binary cell, a decimal cell.

storage circuit: A circuit that can be switched, or "triggered," into either of two stable states. One of these states can be defined as the 0 state and the other as the 1 state (zero and one). Input circuits are provided for triggering the storage circuit into either state. Because these circuits can be made to flip into one state or flop into the other, the name flip-flop has been applied to them. The input that triggers the flip-flop in the 1 state is frequently called the set input while the input that triggers it into the 0 state is called the reset input. There may be more than one kind of set and reset input, providing the logical designer with considerable flexibility. One important type of input is obtained by joining a set abd a reset input together in such a way that a signal applied to this T input will trigger the flip-flop to its opposite state.

storage cycle time: The time required in milliseconds, microseconds, nanoseconds, etc. for a storage cycle.

storage delay line: A delay line fed through a signal regeneration circuit. See delay line.

storage density: The amount of characters stored per unit length or area of storage medium (for example, number of characters per inch of magnetic tape).

storage device: A device into which data can be inserted, in which they can be retained, and from which they can be retrieved.

storage dump: A listing of the contents of a storage device, or selected parts of it.

storage dumping: A procedure or process designed to transfer data from one particular storage device to another or from one particular area to another.

storage fill: A set of instructions and data loaded into storage as a logical unit.

storage fragmentation: The inability to assign real storage locations to virtual addresses because the available spaces are smaller than the page size.

storage integrator: In an analog computer, an integrator used to store a voltage in the hold condition for future use, while the rest of the computer assumes another computer control state.

storage interference: In a system with shared storage, the referencing of the same block of storage by two or more processing units.

storage key: A special set of bits designed to be associated with every word or character in some block of storage, which allows tasks having a matching set of protection key bits to use that block of storage.

storage management: The problems in the time-shared management of storage—the protection of user files and the reduction of constraints on the size of user programs due to limited core space—which are common to all time-shared systems and have received considerable attention in software development.

storage mark: The name given to a point location which defines the character space immediately to the left of the most significant character in accumulator storage. An example would be A 7 4 6 7 4 8 9 in which the letter -A- would be the storage mark.

storage medium: Any device or recording medium into which data can be stored and held until some later time.

storage operation: A movement of data within storage from one location to another.

storage print program: A computer program used to print the contents of storage. See dump.

storage protection: A feature which includes a programmed protection key that prevents the read-in of data into a protected area of main memory and thus, prevents one program from destroying another.

storage-protection block: A block of 2048 contiguous bytes of storage, with a starting address that is a multiple of 2048, and which has associated with it a storage protection key (in some systems).

storage reconfiguration: A function that makes an area of defective storage unavailable and frees any system resources associated with it.

storage register: A device for holding a unit of information.

storage-search time: The time needed to locate a particular data field in storage.

storage subroutine: 1. A part of storage allocatd to receive and store the group of instructions to be executed. 2. The storage locations used to store the program.

storage switch: A manually operated switch or group of switches, most often on computer consoles to permit operators to read register contents.

storage tape: A tape or ribbon or any material impregnated or coated with magnetic material on which information may be placed in the form of magnetically polarized spots.

storage unit: Any unit capable of storing data.

storage volatility: The tendency of a storage device to lose data when the electric power is cut off. Storage media may be classed as volatile, e.g., electrostatic storage tubes.

store: 1. To transfer an element of information to a device from which the unaltered information can be obtained at a later time. 2. To retain data in a device from which it can be obtained at a later time.

store and forward: Applied to communications systems in which messages are received at intermediate routing points and recorded (stored). They are then retransmitted to a further routing point or to the ultimate recipient.

store-and-forward switching center: A messageswitching center in which the message accepted from the sender, whenever he offers it, is held in a physical store and forwarded to the receiver, whenever he is able to accept it.

store-cycle time: The least time required to retrieve an item of data from storage.

stored program: A data processing program stored internally within a data processing system. The program itself occupies storage in the same manner as the data used in the program and can be treated as if it were such data.

stored-program computer: A machine in which the instructions which specify the operations to be performed are stored in the form of coded information in main memory, along with the data currently being operated upon, making possible simple repetition of operations and the modification by the computer of its own instuctions.

stored-program numerical control: A control system possessing an internal memory structure. Once programmed, the internal memory can be altered by receiving new instructions or parameters. The physical configuration of the system is not altered or affected by virtue of reprogramming.

straight-line coding: A technique for achieving the repetition of sequence of instructions, with or without address modification, by explicitly writing the instructions for each repetition.

string: A set of records which is in ascending or descending sequence according to a key contained in the records.

string file: Tape, wire, or string used to arrange documents for convenient reference use.

stringing: The stage in which an input file is read completely.

string manipulation: A procedure designed for manipulating groups of contiguous characters.

string of bits: It is most common and conventional to add a string of bits at the end of a block, in magnetic tapes, to allow a parity check in the columns of the entire block or record.

strip chart recorder: A recorder in which one or more records are made simultaneously as a function of time.

strobe: The selection of a desired point or position in a recurring event or phenomenon, as in a wave, or in a device used to make the selection or identification of the selected point.

strobe pulse: A pulse to gate the output of a corememory sense amplifier into a trigger in a register. Also called sample pulse.

stroke: In character recognition, a straight line or arc used as a segment of a graphic character.

stroke analysis: A method used to identify characters by dissecting them into prescribed elements. The sequence, relative positions, and number of detected elements are then used to determine the specific character it represents.

stroke edge: In character recognition, the line of discontinuity between a side of a stroke and the background, obtained by averaging, over the length of the stroke, the irregularities resulting from the printing and detecting processes.

stroke edge irregularity: In optical character recognition, the deviation of any point on the edge of a character from its stroke edge.

stroke operation: Same as Sheffer-stroke operation, NOT-BOTH operation, NAND operation, non-conjunction. See NAND.

stroke width: In optical character recognition, the distance between the points of intersection of the stroke edges and a line drawn perpendicular to the stroke centerline.

structure: 1. The organization of data within a record or file. 2. A program-defined hierarchichal ordering of data for a record. Elements within a structure may be formatted differently from each other, whereas elements in an array must all have the same format.

structure (of a system): The nature of the chain of command, the origin and type of data collected, the form and destination of results, and the procedures used to control operations.

stunt box: A device designed to control the nonprinting functions of a teleprinter terminal. Control characters can be sent to it over the communications channel.

STX: See start of text.

SUB: See substitute character.

subaddress: A portion of an input/output device that is accessible through an order code. For disk storage units, the module number is the subaddress.

subalphabet: A subset of an alphabet.

sub-band: The frequency band from 6 megahertz (MHz) to 54 megahertz (MHz), which may be used for two-way data transmission.

subcarrier: A carrier used to modulate another carrier.

subcommand: A request for an operation that is within the scope of work requested by a previously-issued command.

subharmonic: Having a frequency which is a fraction of a fundamental. Subharmonics appear in some forms of nonlinear distortion.

submodular phase: Under disk-operating systems and tape-operating systems, a phase made up of selected control sections from one or more modules as compared with a phase that is made up of all control sections from one or more modules.

submodulator: Low-frequency amplifier which immediately precedes the modulator in a radio-telephony transmitter.

subparameter: One of the variable items of information that follows a keyword parameter and can be either positional or identified by a keyword.

subpool: All of the storage blocks allocated under a subpool number for a particular task.

subprogram: A part of a larger program which can be converted into machine language independently.

subroutine: A series of computer instructions to perform a task for many other routines.

subroutine, call: The subroutine, in object coding, that performs the call function.

subroutine calling sequence: A designed arrangement of instructions and data necessary to set up and call a given subroutine.

subroutine library: A set of standard and proven subroutines kept on file for use at any time.

subroutine-status table: The computer program routine used to maintain a list of subroutines in memory and to get subroutines from a file as needed.

subscriber: A customer of a common carrier.

subscriber CATV drop: This uses a flexible, selfsupporting cable which feeds a CATV subscriber from the tapping point or directional coupler on the CATV cable.

subscriber line: A telephone line between a central office and a telephone station, private branch exchange, or other end equipment.

subscriber's drop: The line from a telephone cable that "drops" to the subscriber's building.

subscriber's loop: 1. A channel that connects a subscriber to a central office exchange. 2. The service provided by the common carrier to connect a customer's location to a central office. This always includes the circuit and some circuit termination equipment, but may also include inptu/output equipment. Sometimes referred to as subscriber station.

subscript: 1. A letter or symbol in typography written below a set name to identify a particular element or elements of that set. 2. An indexing notation.

subscripted variable: A variable that is followed by one or more subscripts enclosed in parentheses; used to store and refer to a large number (array) of items by a single name and a number specifying the specific element within the array. e.g., "X(22)" refers to the twenty-second member of the array called "X".

subsequent counter: A specific type of instruction counter designed to step through or count microoperations; i.e., parts of larger operations.

subset: 1. A data set. 2. Any collection of objects or items contained within a larger set. 3. Contraction of subscriber's set, which is any device (but usually a telephone) installed on a subscriber's premises.

substitutable argument: A prototype card field in a macro-definition that is variable and is to be replaced with a parameter (quantity or symbol) when the macrooperation is used. It is also called a dummy argument.

substitute character (SUB): An accuracy control character intended to replace a character that is determined to be invalid, in error, or cannot be represented on a particular device.

substitute mode: A method of exchange buffering that allows for high-speed execution of input/output on computers which have good capability of modifying its hardware address. In substitute mode, segments of storage alternately function as program work area and buffer. The address of the program work area is interchanged with the address of the buffer segment, interchanging the roles of the two memory areas without moving any data.

substrate (of a microcircuit): The supporting material upon which or within which an integrated circuit is fabricated, or to which an integrated circuit is attached.

subsystem: A self-contained portion of a system that performs one of the major system functions usually with only minimal interaction with other portions of the system.

subtracter-adder: A logic element designed to act as an adder or a subtracter as ordered by the control signal applied to it.

subvoice channel: A channel with less bandwidth than a normal voice channel. Also called a narrowband channel.

subvoice-grade channel: A channel of bandwidth narrower than that of voice-grade channels.

suite (of programs): A number of interrelated programs which run one after the other as an operation job.

sum check: A specific check developed when groups of digits are summed, usually without regard for overflow, and that sum checked against a previously computed sum to verify that no digits have been changed since the last summation.

summary billing: The production of abbreviated (nonitemized) bills showing current charges; in hospital systems, typically performed weekly for patients having long stays.

sunspots: Electrical disturbances in the sun which affect the ionosphere and radio communication.

super band: The frequency band from 216 to 600 megahertz, used for fixed and mobile radios and additional television channels on a cable system.

superconductivity: The physical characteristic displayed by certain materials whose resistance to the flow of electric current becomes zero below a specified temperature i.e., a magnetic field can change threshold value of temperature at which superconductivity occurs and such phenomenon is used in cryogenic devices (Cryotron).

supergroup: A group of 60 voice-grade channels with a bandwidth of 240 Hertz.

superheterodyne: A receiver in which carrier frequencies at the forward end are reduced through heterodyning.

superimposed circuit: An additional channel from one or more circuits that does not cause interference if all are used at the same time.

superscript: A letter or symbol in typography written above a set name to denote a power or a derivative, or to identify a particular element of that set.

supervising system: 1. A program that controls loading and relocation of routines and in some cases makes use of instructions which are unknown to the general programmer. 2. A set of coded instructions that process a nd control other sets of coded instructions. 3. A set of coded instructions used in realizing automatic coding. 4. A master set of coded instructions.

supervisor: A routine that controls the proper sequencing and positioning of segments of computer programs in limited storage during their execution.

supervisor call instruction (SVC): An instruciton that interrupts the program being executed and passes control to the supervisor so that it can perform a specific service indicated by the instruction.

supervisor-call interrupts: Caused by the program issuing an instruction to turn over control to the supervisor (the operating system).

supervisor mode: A mode of operation under which certain operations, such as memory-protection modification instructuions, and input/output operations, are permitted.

supervisor state: A state during which the central processing unit can execute input/output and other privileged instructions.

supervisory: 1. Computers which handle functions such as optimizing and feed-forward computation, data logging and alarming, production scheduling, inventory control, etc. 2. When the computer performs process calculations but does not actuate the final element such as a valve.

supervisory control: A control system which furnishes intelligence, usually to a centralized location, to be used by an operator to supervise the control of a process or operation.

supervisory control signals: Characters or signals used to indicate the various operating states of circuit combinations, and which may actuate equipment or indicators automatically at a remote station.

supervisory instruction: Controls the operation of other routines or programs.

supervisory keyboard: Includes the operator's control panel, a keyboard and typeprinter, and a control unit for the keyboard and typeprinter. Optionally, a papertape reader and punch may be connected to the computer through the same control unit. Information transfer between the computer and any single device is performed and output channel assigned to the console auxiliaries. Two switches mounted on the control unit permit selection of the paper-tape reader or the keyboard, and the paper-tape punch or the type printer (in some computers).

supervisory printer: A small and relatively slow character-at-a-time printer (usually a typewriter) connected to the computer which prints out operational messages during a run.

supervisory program simulation: Imitates the supervisory program when the latter is unavailable.

supervisory signal: Signals used to indicate the various operating states of circuit combinations.

supplementary maintenance: Upkeep, inspection, or maintenance developed or performed outside of the normal periods of scheduled maintenance by prior plans and people. Various types of checklists are used during periods of regular idle or after-shift time to make checks, modifications, or to attempt to improve reliability or performance.

supply reference: A voltage source utilized in an electrical analog computer as a unit by which other voltages are measured.

support system: A programming system used to support the normal translating functions of machine oriented, procedural oriented, and/or problem oriented language processors.

suppressed-carrier transmission: Communication in which the carrier frequency is suppressed either partially or maximally. One or both of the sidebands may be transmitted.

suppression: See zero suppression.

suppression ratio: The ratio of a lower range-value to the span; i.e., of a suppressed zero range.

suppressor: The grid between screen and plate in the pentode.

suspense file: A file designed in such a way that specific matters are brought to the attention of particular persons at time sequences appropriate for the purposes designed e.g., loan expiration dates of bank customers, to forward due dates to them automatically, etc. Same as follow-up file and tickler file.

SVC: See supervisor call instruction.

SVC interruption: An interruption caused by the execution of an SVC, causing control to be passed to the supervisor.

SVC routine: A control program routine that performs or begins a control program service specified by an SVC.

swap: In systems with time sharing, to write the main storage image of a job to auxiliary storage and read the image of another job into main storage.

swapping: A design of memory multiplexing in which jobs are kept on a backing storage and periodically transferred entirely to an internal memory to be executed for a fixed time slice.

sweep circuit: The circuit in equipment that contains a wiring tube which guides the movement of the beam in the tube.

switch: 1. To establish a temporary interconnection between two or more stations over communications paths. 2. A short term for a line or message switcher.

switched line: A telephone line connected to the switched telephone network.

switched message network: A common carrier network service that provides selective calling of compatible terminals by one another. See exchange network.

switched network: The name associated with the common carrier provided telephone service.

switched service: A cable communications service in which each subscriber has a terminal and may communicate with any other subscriber.

switcher: A control which permits the selection of one image from any of several cameras to be fed into the television display or recording system.

switcher/fader: A device permitting gradual, overlapping transition from the image of one camera to another. Sometimes incorporated as part of a special effects generator.

switch hook: A switch on a telephone set, associated with the structure supporting the receiver or handset. It is operated by the removal or replacement of the receiver or handset on the support.

switching: Operations involved in interconnecting circuits in order to establish a temporary communication between two or more stations.

switching, torn-tape: 1. A center at which messages are produced in a physical form and then retransmitted to the proper destination. 2. A location where operators tear off incoming printed and punched paper tape and transfer it manually to the proper outgoing circuit.

switching algebra: Boolean algebra which is applied to switching circuits, digital systems, and some communications switching.

switching and processing center (SPC): A facility which performs the rapid communications required in point-oof-sale systems. An SPC links all of the retail terminals in a point-of-sale system to all of the banks in that system.

switching center: 1. An installation in a communications system in which switching equipment is used to interconnect communication circuits. 2. A messageswitching center is an installation in which incoming data from one circuit is tyransferred to the proper outgoing circuit.

switching center, automatic message: A location where an incoming message is automatically directed to one or more outgoing circuits according to intelligence contained in the message.

switching coefficient: A number that is the derivative of the magnetizing force related to the switching time.

switching distribution: A process performed by a switching stage in which the number of inlets is approximately the same as the number of outlets.

switching point: Point in the input span of a multiposition controller at which the output signal changes from one position to another.

switching processors: Enable a user to establish a connection with a particular computer by dialing a unique number to make that connection.

switching system, electronic (ESS): Any switching system whose major components utilize semiconductor devices.

switching time: 1. The time interval between the reference-time, or time at which the leading edge of switching or driving pulse occurs, and the last instant at which the instantaneous voltage response of a magnetic cell reaches a stated fraction of its peak value. 2. The time interval between the reference time and the first instant at which the instantaneous integrated voltage response reaches a stated fraction of its peak value.

switch matrix: An array of circuit elements interconnected specifically to perform a particular function as interconnected, i.e., the elements are usually transistors, diodes, and relay gates completing logic functions for encoding, transliteration

of characters, decoding number system transformation, word translation, etc., and most often input is taken along one dimension while output is taken along another.

switch message: One of the routing points in a store and forward switching system.

switch room: The part of a telephone central office building that houses switching mechanisms and associated apparatus.

switch-type function generator: A function generator using a multitap switch rotated in accordance with the input and having its taps connected to suitable voltage sources.

symbol: 1. A conventional representation of a concept or a representation of a concept upon which agreement has been reached. 2. A representation of something by reason of relationship, association, or convention.

symbol code: Letters or numbers used to identify equipment in a records inventory (equipment symbol code) or to identify periods of retention in schedule listings (retention symbol code). These are used to reduce time preparation requirements and to standardize on records programming terms.

symbol definition: The process of assigning a value to a symbol.

symbolic address: Arbitrary identification of a particular word, function, or other information without regard to the location of the information.

symbolic addressing: A fundamental procedure or method of addressing using an address (symbolic address) chosen for convenience in programming or of the programmer programmer in which translation of the symbolic addressinto an absolute address is required before it can be used in the computer.

symbolic assembly: The first level of language described for a class of processor programs.

symbolic code: A specific code designed to express programs in source language; i.e., by referring to storage locations and machine operations by symbolic names and addresses which are independent of their hardware-determined names and addresses.

symbolic-data set: In coding a program, the designation used to refer to a data set, the actual data set of whose data content is to be processed during a particular execution of the program is determined later. The later assignment may be an entire data set or a specific member of a directoried data set.

symbolic-editor tape: A program designed to edit symbolic programs. In some systems, the symbolic editor can be used to generate edit, correct, and update symbolic program tapes.

symbolic equivalent: A determination of a combination or pattern of meaningful coding, i.e. using punched holes, magnetic spots, etc.

symbolic input/output (I/O) assignment: A means by which problem programs can refer to an I/O device by a symbolic name. Before a program is executed, job control can be used to assign a specific I/O device to that symbolic name.

symbolic language: A programming language which expresses addresses and operation codes of instructions in symbols convenient to humans rather than in machine language.

symbolic logic: 1. The study of formal logic and mathematics by means of a special written language which seeks to avoid the ambiguity and inadequacy of ordinary language. 2. The mathematical concepts, techniques and languages as used in 1. whatever their particular application or context. Same as mathematical logic and related to logic.

symbolic manipulation: Because data are not usually numerical the formal use of a symbol manipulation has resulted in specific list-processing languages, the first real list processing language, information processing language (IPL), developed by Newell, Shaw and Simon in 1957.

symbolic-mathematical laboratory: An on-line system designed to complete formal algebraic manipulations based on use of display screens and light pens.

symbolic-units table: An area of main storage that holds the addresses of the unit control blocks (UCBS) and system control blocks (SCBS) for each symbolic unit.

symbolic name: A label used in programs written in a source language to reference data elements, peripheral units, instructions, etc.

symbolic parameter: In assembler programming, a variable symbol declared in the prototype statement of a macro definition. A symbolic parameter is usually assigned a value from the corresponding operand in the macro instruction that calls the macro definition. See also keyword parameter, positional parameter.

symbolic programming: The use of arbitrary symbols to represent addresses in order to facilitate programming.

symbolic unit: 1. A mnemonic in the symbolic units table which refers to an input/-output device. A symbolic unit may be assigned to an entire input/output device or to a portion of a device. 2. In coding a program, the designation used to refer to external storage, the actual storage to be used during a particular execution of the program is determined later.

symbol-manipulating language (LIST):   Particular languages developed for symbol manipulation and used primarily as research tools rather than for production programming (i.e., LISP). Most have proved valuable in construction of compilers and in simulation of human problem solving. Other uses have been generalization and verification of mathematical proofs, pattern recognition, information retrieval, algebraic manipulation, heuristic programming and exploration of new programming languages.

symbol point: A feature used in conjunction with a FORTRAN compiler to obtain a printout which lists the variables used and their memory locations. It also indicates the section of memory not used by the compiled data and program.

symbol rank: Same as digit place.

symbol string: A string consisting solely of symbols.

symbol table: A table of labels and their corresponding numeric values.

symmetric difference: A logical operation applied to two operands, which will produce an outcome depending on the bit patterns of the operands and on the rules for each bit position.

symmetric linear programming: A fast and efficient mathematical technique for solving distribution and allocation problems in manufacturing operations.

SYN: See synchronous idle character.

sync: See synchronization.

sync character: A character transmitted to establish character synchronization in synchronous communication. When the receiving station recognizes the sync character, the receiving station is said to be synchronized with the transmitting station, and communication can begin.

sync circuit: A circuit in radar and television which control the movements of the scope beam.

sync clipper: The stage in the cathode-ray tube (CRT) sync circuits which removes sync pulses from the video signal; same as sync sepaprator.

sync generator: A device used to supply a common or master sync signal to a system of several cameras. This ensures that their scanning pulses will be in phase. Scanning pulses out of phase produce distortion or rolling, sometimes called "sync loss."

sync pulse: An electrical pulse transmitted to a circuit by the master equipment to actuate the slave in synchronism with the master.

sync separator: The circuit in the television receiver which separtes the sync pulses from the video signal.

synchronizing signal: Can be generated by the transmitter or by a separate source that the transmitter uses for transmit timing. In either case the data must be transmitted and received sysnchronously with a common clock.

synchro: An induction machine or device which consists of stator and rotor elements each carrying one or more windings, the mutual inductance depending upon the angular position of the rotor with respect to the stator, i.e., it uses remote position indicators, controllers and components for analog computers which perform trignometric operations.

synchro generator: A shafted electronic component which emits a low frequency ac signal proportioned to the angle of rotation of its shaft.

synchrometer: A device which counts the number of cycles in a given time. If the time interval is unity, the device becomes a digital frequency meter.

synchronization: A process of coordinating or bringing into step the transmitted signal and the receiver's decoder used to unscramble or decode it. Usually synchronization implies a time function rather than frequency, but it can be both.

synchronization pulse: Pulses introduced to keep all components operating in order or step, i.e., into transmitters and receivers to keep order, or timing pulses to a master clock to keep all logic gates operating in order in synchronous computers.

synchronize: To lock one element of a system into step with another. The term usually refers to locking a receiver to a transmitter, but it can refer to locking the data terminal equipment bit rate to the data set transmitter.

synchronizer: A storage device used to compensate for a difference in a rate of flow of information or time of occurrence of events when transmitting information from one device to another.

synchronizing pilot: A reference pilot that either maintains the synchronization of the oscillators of a carrier system or compares the frequencies of the currents generated by these oscillators.

synchronous: Having a constant time interval between successive bits, characters, or events.

synchronous clock: 1. A computer in which each event, or the performance of each operation, is initially based on results of a signal generated by a clock. 2. Even in the case of static circuitry, a clock frequency is generally used to keep the various events in the computer in step and running at the proper rate. This action results in synchronous operation, as contrasted with asynchronous operation. In a synchronous system, the clock must be sufficiently slow to allow the slowest circuit sufficient time to switch. In an asynchronous system, the length of time for an operation is determined only by the operating speed of the circuits. Dynamic circuitry is inherently synchronous in operation.

synchronous communications satellite: Has an orbital period equal to the time of rotation of the earth on its axis. It is launched so that is remains directly above the same geographical point on the earths surface. This facilitates the Control of the aerial assembly of ground stations operating in counction with the satellite.

synchronous communications system: A system in which the sending and receiving instruments are operating at approximately the same frequency, and the phase is maintained by means of feedback.

synchronous computer: A computer in which all operations and events are controlled by equally spaced pulses from a clock. Contrasted with asynchronous computer and clarified by clock frequency.

synchronous converter: A rotary converter with synchronous windings which operates from a.c. supply at a controlled speed.

synchronous data link control (SDLC): An IBM computer networking protocol.

synchronous-data transmission: A system in which timing is derived through synchronizing characters at the beginning of each message.

synchronous idle character: A special control character designed to be transmitted in the absence of other traffic in order to maintain or achieve aynchronism between the apparatus at the various data terminals.

synchronous input: A terminal on a flip-flop, allowing data to be entered but only upon command of the clock.

synchronous line modems: Synchronous modulatordemodulators (modems) have permitted a higher modems over a voice grade facility. The nature of these transmission techniques has also resulted in higher efficiency by eliminating the need for synchronozing information with every character.

synchronous machine: A machine which has an operating speed related to a fixed frequency of a system to which it is a connected part, and is specifically timed, perhaps by a clock-pulse generator so that each event in t.

synchronous modem: Characters are sent in a continuous stream, thus requiring three levels of synchronization: bit, character, and message. Transmission is synchronized by a clock internal to the modem. This fixed rate transmission does not require start and stop bits.

synchronous operation: An operation in which each event or the performance of each operation starts as a result of a signal generated by a clock.

synchronous-serial transmission: In a serial-bit stream is sent over the line in the same manner asover the line and there are no start-stop bits with which to synchronize each character. In this technique, the entire block of data is synchronized with a unique code which, when recognized causes the receiver to lock in and set and to count the incoming bits and assemble a character. As in the asynchronous technique, the receiver must know the number of bits to a character.

synchronous time division multiplexers (STDM):   STDM's share a synchronous communication line by cyclically scanning incoming lines, peeling off bits or characters, and interleaving them into frames on a single high – speed data stream.

synchronous transmission: A mode for transmission using a precisely timed bit stream and character stream.

synchronous transmit/receive (STR):   A transmission mode in communications.

synchronous working: See synchronous computer transmit. The computer operation for the movement of data from one location to another, i.e., various forms of communication.

syndetic: 1. Having connections or interconnections. 2. Pertaining to a document or catalog with cross references.

synergetic: A tying together of every unit of a system, which when combined develop a total larger than their arithmetic sum (also called synergistic).

synonym: In an indirectly addressed file, a record whose key randomizes to the address of a home record.

syntactic errors: Considered the responsibility of the system and are further categorized as follows: (a) Composition—Typographical errors, violations of specified form, of statements and misuse of variable names (e.g., incorrect punctuation, mixed-mode expressions, undeclared arrays, etc.). (b) Consistency—Statements that are composed correctly but conflict with other statements (e.g. conflicting declarative, illegal statement ending a disk-operating range, failure to follow each transfer statement with a numbered statement, etc.). (c) Completeness—Programs that are incomplete (e.g., transfers to nonexistent statement numbers, improper disk-operating nesting, illegal transfer into the range of a disk-operating loop, etc.).

syntax: 1. (ISO) The relationship among characters or groups of characters, independent of their meanings or the manner of their interpretation and use. 2. The structure of expressions in a language. 3. The rules governing the structure of a language. 4. The relationships among symbols.

syntax checker: A program that tests source statements in a programming language for violations of the syntax of that language.

syntax-directed compiler: A compiler structured on the syntactal relationships of the character string.

syntax transducer: A subroutine designed to recognize the phase class in an artificial language, normally expressed in Backus normal from (formal language theory (BNF).

synthesis: The combining of parts in order to form a whole, e.g., to arrive at a circuit, computer, or program, starting from performance requirements.

synthesis, data capture, speech: A method of using speech as a direct form of input.

synthetic language: A pseudocode or symbolic language. A fabricated language.

synthetic relationship: A relation existing between concepts which pertains to empirical observation. Such relationships are involved, not in defining concepts or terms, but in reporting the results of observations.

SYSIN: A contraction of system input, and commonly used to refer to the principal input stream of an operating system. There can be only one SYSIN at a time, but many devices can be assigned SYSIN functions in succession.

sysout: An indicator used in data definition statements to signify that a data set is to be written on a system output unit.

system: 1. An assembly of components united by some form of regulated interaction to form an organized whole . 2. A collection of operations and procedures, by which a business is carried on. 3. A collection of parts united by some form of regulated interaction, an organized whole. 4. A collection of service routines which sequences programs through a computer.

system, addressing: The procedure used to label storage locations in a computer.

system analysis: The examination of an activity, procedure method, technique, or a business to find out what must be accomplished and how the necessary operations may best be accomplished.

systematic inaccuracies: Inaccuracies due to limitations in equipment design.

system availability: The time-lag required by the manufacturer to install and insure satisfactory operation of his system at the operational site of the customer.

system capacity: Quantitative system performance estimates relating to the expected efficiency and throughput of a given computer configuration.

system check: A check on the overall performance of the system, such as control totals, hash totals, and record counts. Usually not made by built-in computer check circuits.

system check module: A device that monitors system operability if power fails or deviations from desired computer operations develop. It initiates appropriate emergency actions by the computer.

system command: A typical executive program accepts and interprets a collection of system commands by a user allowing him to: log in and out; save and restore program and data files; compile and execute a program; interrupt and terminate a running program; edit, manipulate and list program and data files; request the status of system and user programs; and specify system subcomponents desired.

system-communications modems: Connect the communications multiplexor from the remote outlet to the interface device in the computer center. On the transmission end, the modulator converts the signals or pulses to the right codes and readies them for transmission over a communication line in alternating current. On the receiving end a demodulator reconverts the signals to direct current for communication to the computer via the computer interface device. The computer operates on direct current.

system components: A collection of hardware and software organized and designed to achieve the operational objective.

system control panel: The system control panel is divided into three major sections: operator control section, which contains only those controls required by the operator when the processor is operating under full supervisory control; operator intervention section, which contains additional controls required for the operator to intervene in normal programming operation; and the customer engineering section, which contains controls intended only for customer engineering use in diagnostics and maintenance. Manual control operations are held to a minimum by the system design and operating system. The result is fewer operator errors.

system debugging: The technique of detecting, diagnosing, and correcting errors (bugs) which may occur. Bugs can exist both in programs, e.g., failure to understand and describe a process, or in hardware, e.g., in the way a hardwired logic unit has been strapped.

system design: The specification of the working relations between all the parts of a system in terms of their characteristic actions.

system diagnostics: A program resembling the operational program rather than a systematic logical-pattern program which will detect overall system malfunctions rather than isolate or locate faulty components.

system engineering: A method of engineering which takes into consideration all of the elements in the control system, down to the smallest valve, and the process itself. It is believed to have the most promise as an intelligent approach leading toward fuller industrial automation.

system-improvement time: The machine down time needed for the installation and testing of new components and the machine down time necessary for modification of existing components. This includes all programmed tests following the above actions to prove the machine is operating properly.

system input unit (SYSIN): The unit used to input a job stream (to a computer system).

system-interface design: The engineering design of specialized input/output equipment for a computer system.

system log (SYSLOG): A data set in which job-related informtion, operational data, descriptions of unusual occurrences, commands, and messages to or from the operator may be stored.

system-management facilities (SMF): An optional control program feature that provides the means for gathering and recording information that can be used to evaluate system usage.

system monitor: The part of an operating system that contains routines and is needed for continuous system operation.

system noise: 1. Extra bits or words that must be ignored or removed from data when the data is used. 2. Errors introduced into data in a system, especially in communication channels. 3. Random variations of one or more characteristics of any entity such as voltage, current, and data. 4. Loosely, any disturbance tending to interfere with the normal operation of a device or system.

system programmed operators SYSPOP: A function making monitor mode service routines available to user mode programs without loss of system control or use of user memory space.

system programmer: A programmer who plans, generates, maintains, extends, and controls the use of an operating system with the aim of improving the wnerall productivty of an installation.

system reliability: The probability that a system will accurately perform its specified task under stated tactical and environmental conditions.

system-residence volume: The volume i.e., disk pack etc. that contains the operating system (software).

system resource: Any facility of the computing system that may be allocated to a task.

system restart: 1. A restart that allows reuse of previously-initialized input and output work queues. 2. A restart that allows reuse of a previously-initialized link pack area.

systems and procedures analyst: Investigates, analyzes, develops, and coordinates company operating policies and procedures.

systems analysis control: A definition or resolution of a control problem in the development of a solution to it.

systems analyst: A person who designs informationhandling procedures which incorporate computer processing. The systems analyst is usually highly skilled in defining problems and developing algorithms for their solution.

Systems and Procedures Association (SPA): A large and influential organization of top management personnel organized formally and informally to disseminate information, news, and education relating to their pursuits.

systems and support software: The wide variety of software including assemblers, compilers, subroutine libraries, operating systems, application programs, etc.

systems compatibility: Capability of two or more items or components of equipment or material to exist or function in the same system or environment without mutual interference. In data processing, two computers are compatible if programs can be run on both without modification. Sometimes this is not a two-way possibility; a computer is upward compatible with a second computer if a program written on and for the first can be run on the second, but not the reverse.

systems consultant: This individual supplies technical assistance and direction with specific emphasis on problem identification, organization analysis, conversion planning, forms control and analysis, and reports control.

systems engineering: The designed implementation of a hardware and software system which results from the analysis of a control problem.

system-service programs: Programs that perform portions of the functions of generating the initial basic operating system.

systems study: An examination of the mission, methods, and workloads to determine applicability.

systems timings: The determination of the time required by the computer equipment to perform a program step, i.e., the time is computed by adding the time required to perform each inter-dependent machine operation.

system subroutine: Input/output format control that provides for the various format statements used in the FORTRAN language. These subroutines are also available to other programs and may be called from the systems library tape.

system-support programs: Processing programs that contribute to the use and control of the system and production of results.

system task: A control program function performed under the control of a task control block.

system-transmission code: A character parity check as well as a block check to detect errors.

system unit: A symbolic unit that has a particular system use and a predefined relationship to a system data set.

system-utility device: Used for the temporary storage of intermediate data for a series of job steps.

system-utility programs: Problem state programs for use by a system programmer to perform programs such as changing or extending the indexing structure of the catalog.

system-variable symbol: In assembler programming, a variable symbol that does not have to be declared because the assembler assigns them read-only values.

T

2400 baud channel: A synchronous system, also accepting polar pulse input conforming to Electronic Industries Association (EIA) standards, and capable of delivering signals at the destination having the same characteristics. This channel permits transmission of punched cards at the rate of 100 per minute, or magnetic tape at the rate of 300 characters per second.

tab: A non-printing spacing action on a typewriter or tape preparation device whose code is used to separate words or groups of characters in the tab sequential format.

table lock-up: A method of controlling the location to which a jump or transfer is made. It is used especially when there are a large number of alternatives, as in function evaluation in scientific computations.

table look-at: Finding elements of a table by direct calculation rather than by a comparison search.

table look-up (TLU): A process or procedure for searching identifying labels in a table to find the location of a desired associated item. By extension, a digital computer instruction that directs the above operation be performed. The technique is used primarily to: (a) obtain a derived value for one variable given another where the relationship cannot be stated easily in a formula or algorithm; (b) to convert a discontinuous variable from one form to another (e.g., convert from one code to another), or (c) to provide conditional (logical) control functions (e.g., converting disk keys from symbolic to actual address or determining which of several discrete processes should be applied for a given state).

tabular data presentation: A statistical table is a systematic arrangement of data in columns and rows, according to clearly defined principles of classification. The title of the table should give the following information about the data: what, where, when, and in what units. The title should be comprehensive but concise.

tabular language: Composed of decision tables which become the problem-oriented language used in computation.

tabulate: 1. To form data into a table. 2. To print totals.

tabulating system: Any group of machines used for entering, converting, classifying, computing, and recording data.

tabulation: 1. A printed report produced on a punched card tabulator consisting of totals only. 2. The automatic movement of the the typewriter carriage or teleprinter through a series of specified positions in a succession of print lines.

tag: A unit of information whose composition differs from that of other members of the set so that it can be used as a marker or label, a sentinel.

tag converting unit: A machine that automatically reproduces information from perforated price tags to computer media.

tag file: A file containing only selected portions ("tags") from data file records, such as sort keys, file sequence keys, etc.

tag format: The design of a record used as a tag to locate an overflow bucket.

tag sort: A sort in which addresses of records (tags), and not the records themselves, are moved during the comparison procedure.

takedown: See tag sort.

take-up reel: The motor-driven reel in the tape recorder on which the tape winds.

tally register: A register that holds a tally count.

tandem switching exchange: A system used by long distance resellers and other common carriers. A compact, fully redundant system, it provides up to 8,000 non-blocking voice and data ports, and permits modular growth to meet increasing customer needs.

tank: 1. A container filled with memory and provided with a set of transducers for use as a delay-line channel or set of channels, each forming a separate recirculation path for the storage of data. 2. A circuit consisting of inductance and capacitance used that sustains electrical oscillations.

tap: A device installed in the feeder cable which connects the home television set to the cable network. Also called a drop.

tape: A ribbon of flexible material used as a storae medium, described by a qualifying adjective such as paper, magnetic, oiled, etc.

tape bootstrap routine: Serves to bring in the remainder of the resident and various other parts of the system. The bootstrap routines also provide a simple card load routine, a panic dump.

tape alteration: A selection, usually controlled automatically by a program, of first one tape unit and then another, normally during input or output operations, which permits successive reels of a file to be mounted and removed without interrupting the program.

tape bin: A magnetic tape storage device with moveable read/record heads or fixed heads for each loop. The heads and loops can move to particular or selected locations on tape thus providing more rapid access

time than on plain serial reels of tape which must be rewound.

tape cable: A cable containing flat metallic ribbon conductors, all lying side by side in the same plane and imbedded in a material which insulates and binds them together.

tape character check: Refers to the parity bit in a tape character code.

tape cluster: A set of magnetic tape decks which are built into a single cabinet. Each deck is capable of independent operation and occassionally arranged to share one or more interface channels for communication with a central processor.

tape-controlled carriage: That specific automatic carriage whose movements are controlled by the data as recorded on magnetic or paper tapes but exclusive of the normal character spacing.

tape control unit: A unit (including buffering) designed to control the operation of the magnetic tape transport.

tape-driver interrupt: In the interrupt routine, the driver determines whether a fail condition has occurred on the addressed unit. A fail condition is recognized when the unit is at the end of the tape, at a file mark, or if a parity fail has occurred. If no fail has occurred and the operation requested requires a series of commands, i.e., "special rewind," "ready to file," etc., the driver will give the next command and exit to the interrupt point.

tape dump: The transfer of complete contents of information recorded on tape to the computer of another storage medium.

tape editor: A program used to edit, correct, and update symbolic program tapes using the computer and the teletype unit. With the editor in the main memory, the user reads in portions of his symbolic tape, removes, changes, or adds instructions or operands, and gets back a corrected symbolic tape. The user can work through the program instruction by instruction, spotcheck it, or concentrate on new sections.

tape erasure: Removing the information on tape (the tape is then ready for re-recording).

tape group: One unit which has two or more tape decks.

tape input/output (I/O) swapping: A process most often controlled automatically by the program which causes one tape unit to be selected during I/O operations and then another during the mounting or removal of successive reels of a file without interrupting the program or the processing of data.

tape label: A record on magnetic tape used to identify the tape.

tape leader: The tape preceding or following the body of a program.

tape librarian: Classifies, catalogs and maintains a library of reels of magnetic or punched paper tape, decks of magnetic cards, or punchcards used for electronic data-processing purposes. (a) Classifies and catalogs material according to content, purpose of program, routine or subroutine, and date on which generated. (b) Assigns code conforming with standardized system. (c) Prepares index cards for file reference. (d) Stores materials and records according to classification and catalog number. (e) Issues materials and maintains charge-out records. (f) Inspects returned tapes or cards and notifies supervisor if worn or damaged. (g) May maintain files of program developmental records and operating instructions (run books). (h) May operate key-punch to replace defective punchcards and produce data cards to identify punchcard decks. (i) May work in computer room performing such tasks as loading and removing printout forms, reels of tape, and decks of cards from machines.

tape library: A collection of magnetic tapes in an installation.

tape light: Indicates an error during the read or write cycle.

tape-limited operation: Operation of a tape deck in a mode where the tape unit receives or transmits information at a rate slower than the computer is capable of supplying or accepting it. (Tape moves continuously without stopping in the inter-block gaps).

tape-load key: Causes the first tape unit to read and transfer data into internal storage until the interrecord gap is sensed, at which time the internal storage is read for the first instruction.

tape loadpoint: The position of magnetic tape where reading or writing can begin.

tape magnetic reader: A device capable of restoring information recorded on a magnetic tape to a train or sequence of electrical pulses, usually for the purpose of transferring the information to some other storage medium.

tape mark: A character written on tape to signify the physical end of recording.

tape memory: A serial, bulk-storage, off-line memory.

tape operating system (TOS):   Used for smaller systems without disk drives, this operating system has its component modules (i.e., compilers, linkage-editor, etc.) stored on a system tape. It uses tape libraries for storage of user program and data files. Contrast with disk operating system (DOS).

tape-processing unit: A unit capable of recording, transmitting, receiving, and converting data recorded in perforated paper tape.

tape pack: The form taken by the tape wound on to a reel. A good pack is one that has a uniform wind, has an acceptable E value and is free from spoking, cinching and layer-to-layer adhesion.

tape printing counter: Printing counter of a magnitic tape terminal that counts blocks transmitted or received.

tape reader: An input device that reads data from tape.

tape relay: A method used (using perforated tape as the intermediate storage) for relaying messages between the transmitting and receiving stations.

tape reservoir: A length of magnetic tape in the vacuum servo-mechanism used as a supply to take up or provide slack tape when the tape drives stop or change direction of movement.

tape-resident system: A system of operating routines.

tape-select switch: A control rotary switch which can select either a neutral mode during automatic operation or the use of one of the on-line tape units.

tape-serial number: An identification number, normally recorded on a tape header label, which is allotted to a new magnetic tape and remains the same through the life of the tape although all other identifying information may change.

tape skip: A machine instruction to space forward and erase a portion of tape when a defect on the tape surface causes a write error to persist.

tape-skip key: An operator control key which advances the tape until a tape skip restore character is sensed.

tape sort: A computer operation in which a file of data on magnetic tape is sorted into sequence according to a key contained in each record of the file.

tape speed: Steady running tape speed averaged over a period of 1 second or greater.

tape-speed variation: The difference between actual steady running tape speed, averaged over a period of 1 second or greater, and nominal tape speed, expressed as tolerance percentage on tape speed.

tape station: Same as tape unit.

tape swapping: A process which causes one tape unit to be selected during input/-output operations and then another during the mounting or removal of successive reels of a file without interrupting the program or the processing of data.

tape-switching center: The center where operators tear off punched paper tape as it comes in and manually transfer it to the proper outgoing circuit.

tape symbolic editor: A program designed to edit symbolic programs. In some systems, the symbolic editor can be used to generate, edit, correct and update symbolic program tapes.

tape-to-card converter: An off-line device that converts information from punched or magnetic tape to punched cards.

tape-to-printer program: A program designed to transfer data from magnetic tape to a printer.

tape transport: The mechanism which moves magnetic or paper tape past sensing and recording heads and is usually associated with data processing equipment.

tape unit: A device consisting of a tape transport, controls, a set of reels, and a length of tape which is capable of recording and reading information on and from the tape, at the request of the computer under the influence of a program.

tape-wound core: A magnetic core having a piece of ferromagnetic tape wrapped or coiled in spiral form on a spool or spindle.

target: The surface struck by the electron beam in a writing tube.

target computer: 1. The specific computer configuration needed for a particular program. 2. The computer which is not designed to use a particular program, but which must have another computer translate such a program for its ultimate use, is called a target or object computer.

target phase: The phase in which the target program is run.

target language: The language into which some other language is to be translated properly.

target screen: A fine screen near the image orthicon target which takes up secondary electrons emitted by the target.

tariff: The published rate for a specific unit of equipment, facility, or type of service provided by a communications common carrier.

task: A unit of work for the central processing unit; sometimes the basic multiprogramming unit under the control program.

task-control block: A unique control routine or function which selects from the task queue or lists the next task to be processed and gives it control of the central processor.

task dispatcher: A unique control routine or function which selects from the task queue or lists the next task to be processed and gives it control of the central processor.

task management: The set of functions of the control program or routine which controls the use of system resources other than the input/output devices by tasks.

task priority dispatching: The priority assigned to an active task in a multiprogramming or multitasking environment. An active task is non-real-time and nonforeground. The dispatch priority established precedence for the use of the central processing unit (CPU) when the operating system prepares to return control to the problem program.

task queue: The queue which contains all the task control blocks which are in the system at any one time.

TCAM: See telecommunications access method.

TCU: See transmission control unit.

teaching machine: A computer monitored or controlled with continuous and active response to each unit of information presented or queried. It provides immediate and recorded feedback from questions of the students' responses and an acknowledgment of correct or incorrect answers to the student with other alternative or remedial information and instructions. The teaching machine consists of both programs and hardware. The programs are either linear or branching types, or a mixture of both.

technique flow chart: Detailed flow charts showing data and information requirements and the specific method and calculations for processing the information.

teleautograph: A writing telegraph instrument in which movement of a pen in the transmitting apparatus varies the current in two circuits and causes corresponding movement of a pen at the remote receiving instrument.

telecommunications: Data transmission between a computing system and remotely located devices via a unit that performs the necessary format conversion and controls the rate of transmission.

telecommunications access method (TCAM): A communication subsystem designed to exchange messages between the communication network and a set of message queues, according to information contained in control blocks and message headers.

telecommunications circuit: A complete circuit with a specified bandwidth to enable instruments at each end to communicate one with the other.

telecommunications line: Telephone and other communication lines that are used to transmit messages from one location to another.

teleconferencing: The use of computer networks for personal communications among widely dispersed groups of people. Systems have been implemented to support multi-party conferences via computer.

telegraph: A system employing the interruption or change in polarity of direct current for the transmission of data signals.

telegraph-grade channel: 1. A communications path suitable for transmission of signals at speeds up to approximately 180 bauds, but not suitable for voice transmission due to restriction of bandwidth. 2. A narrowband channel.

telegraph signal: The set of conventional elements established by the code to enable the transmission of a written character (letter, figure, punctuation sign, arithmetical sign, etc.) or the control of a particular function (spacing, shift, line-feed, carriage return, phase correction, etc.); this set of elements is characterized by the variety, the duration, and the relative position of the component elements (or by some of these features).

telegraph word (conventional): A word comprising five letters together with one letter-space, used in computing telegraph speed in words/minute or traffic capacity.

telemeter: To transmit digital and/or analog measurement data by radio waves.

telemetry: Remote sensing of operating systems by an instrument that converts transmitted electric signals into units of data.

telephone: A telecommunications system designed for voice transmission, i.e., the basic transmittingreceiving equipment provided to a telephone company subscriber, including variations such as Touch-Tone systems.

telephone channel: See voice-grade channel.

telephone-circuit data: A circuit which allows the transmission of digital data.

telephone code: The standard five-channel teletypewriter code consisting of a start impulse and five character impulses, all of equal length, and a stop impulse whose length is 1.42 times all of the start impulses. The Baudot code has been used by the telegraph industry for about 100 years.

telephone-communication unit: The data sets used in communications systems providing half-duplex capability.

telephone company: Any common carrier providing public telephone system service. There are about 2400 telephone companies in the U.S.

telephone frequency: See voice frequency.

telephone line: 1. The conductor (including supporting or containing structures) extending between telephone stations and central offices. 2. The circuit appartus associated with a particular communication channel.

telephone secondary center: A particular switching telephone center selected from a group of local centers to which all local centers of a specific group are connected by trunk circuits.

telephone trunk: A telephone line between two central offices that is used to provide communications between subscribers.

telephone zone switching center: Telephonic trunk switching which serves as a switching hub for a group of primary centers, directly connected to every other zone center by trunk circuits.

telephony: The conversion of a sound signal into corresponding variations of electric current (or potential) which is then transmitted by wire or radio to a distant point where it is reconverted into sound.

teleprinter: A common alphanumeric input/output communications device, the teleprinter is essentially an electric typewriter with communications capability. The teletypewriter keyboard generates signals in serial form. At the microprocessor, these serial signals are converted into parallel words for processing. Parallel words in the microprocessor are converted into serial signals. The serial signals are sent to the teleprinter and are typed out.

teleprinter-exchange service: A service provided by communication common carriers to connect teleprinters. Similar to regular telephone service, customers dial calls from station to station but communicate using teleprinter equipment rather than telephone.

teleprocessing (IBM): 1. An IBM trademark referring to their equipment and services used in data communications. 2. A form of information handling in which a data processing system utilizes communications facilities.

teleprocessing network: A network in which data is transmitted from one point to another in the course of processing.

teleprocessing system: Data processing equipment used in combination with terminal equipment and communication facilities.

telereference: A process used to consult data at a remote location using closed circuit television.

teletype: Trade mark of the Teletype Corporation, usually used in reference to a series of different types of teleprinter equipment such as transmitters, tape punches, reperforators, page printers, etc., used for communications systems.

teletype input/output unit: An automatic send-receive (ASR) set (communications).

teletype network: A system of points interconnected by telegraph channels, which provides hardcopy and/or telegraphic coded (5-channel) punched-paper tape, as required, at both sending and receiving points.

teletype printer: A printer which presents type in a square block. The type square positions one character at a time from left to right. A hammer then strikes the character from behind, depressing it against the ink ribbon that faces the paper form.

teletype request-send: A teletype circuit that carries signals originating in terminal equipment. This circuit directs the signal converter to receive or transmit while terminal equipment designed for send only service will hold the send receive circuit at "on." Such a circuit is not necessary for full duplex service.

teletypewriter: 1. Teleprinter equipment. 2. The basic equipment made by Teletype Corporation.

teletypewriter automatic send/receive unit (ASR): Combines the other devices into one machine containing a keyboard, page printer, paper-tape transmitter, and paper-tape punch (reperforator or perforator).

teletypewriter-switching systems: Total message switching systems where the terminals are teletypewriter equipment.

teletypewriter transmitter/distributor (TD): Reads the punched paper-tape input and transmits the information as line signals.

television: Electric transmission of visual scenes and images by wire or radio, in such rapid succession as to produce, in the observer at the receiving end, illusion of being able to winess events as they occur at the transmitting end.

television cable: Transmits frequencies sufficiently high to accommodate television signals without undue attenuation or relative phase delay; usually coaxial, with as much air insulation as possible.

television channel: In television, a single path or section of the spectrum 6 MHz wide, which carries a television signal.

television demodulator: The circuitry of a television receiver which demodulates a received signal and produces a video signal and a sound signal.

television system: A complete assembly of units for the production, transmission (by radio or closed circuit), and reproduction of a television image and associated sound channel.

television typewriter (TVT): A terminal for displaying information on a television screen.

Telnet protocol: A network virtual terminal which permits all terminals on the network to provide a similar interface to processes in any host. This allows the use of any terminal supported by the network with any host system on the network even if that host could not support the particular terminal through its standard terminal controller.

telstar: The first international telecommunications satellite, sponsored by American Telephone and Telegraph Company, and designed by Bell Laboratories.

temperature cycling: An air-to-air temperature stress test usually performed at $-65°C$ for 10 minutes followed by $+150°C$ for 10 minutes for 10 cycles with a maximum transfer time of 5 minutes. This screen determines the reliability of a part that may be exposed to extreme high and low temperatures. Permanent changes in operating characteristics and physical damage result principally from variation in physical dimensions.

temporary-data set: A data set created and deleted in the same job.

temporary read/write error: An error that is eliminated by retrying a read/write operation.

temporary storage: An area of computer memory used for intermediate states of computation.

temporary storage location: A specific area of memory set aside for data in process of an intermediate state of computation, e.g., in the central processing unit (CPU), such storage often called, scratch pad memory.

tennis-match sort: A variety of bubble sort in which sort passes are made in alternating directions.

tera: A prefix denoting one billion (10^9) of a given unit.

teracycle: A mega megacycle per second—10^{12} cycles per sec.

terminal: 1. Any input/output device to receive or send source data in an environment associated with the job to be performed, capable of transmitting entries to and obtaining output from the system of which it is a part. 2. A point at which information can enter or leave a communication network.

terminal, display: Soft displays combine a method of generating characters and a viewing surface for displaying these characters. Under today's technology, the soft display for the system is likely to be a standard TV tube with 525 scan lines to the inch. Some of the key features of the display are: capacity, quality, highlighting.

terminal, printing: Concerns an impact or nonimpact device for providing the data desired in a hardcopy form.

terminal address: An identifying character (or group of characters) used to direct a message to a specific terminal within a group of terminals connected to a multi-drop of multi-point communication circuit.

terminal-based conformity: The specified value of nonconformity as determined after any translation or rotation of the actual curve is made to make it coincide with the specified curve at upper and lower range values.

terminal-based linearity: The particular value of non-linearity as determined after various translations or rotations of the actual curve are made to make it coincide with a straight line at upper and lower ranges.

terminal communication costs: The cost of the lines or the cost of purchasing time on a communication network.

terminal controller: Accepts input from a group of terminals, and funnels the output onto one line, and vice versa.

terminal converter: An add-on device that brings computing capability to an on-line terminal, making the terminal double as a microcomputer.

terminal data processing: Includes the preparation of a data input, manipulation and output typically using keypunches, teleprinter, cathode-ray tubes, and clustered systems.

terminal device: Equipment connected on either end of a communication line, channel, or link.

terminal equipment: The user-machine interface devices on the ends of a circuit, or the relays and components which terminate a circuit on a switch.

terminal-hardware cost: The cost to purchase, rent or lease a specific keyboard device and its peripherals.

terminal identification: A character or sequence of characters used to identify a transmitting or originating terminal.

terminal impedance: 1. The complex impedance as seen at the unloaded output or input terminals of a transmission equipment or line which is otherwise in normal operating condition. 2. Impedance of a specific device such as a cathode-ray tube, typewriter, transmission line or gate, amplifier, under no load conditions.

terminal I/0 wait: The condition of a task in which the task cannot continue processing until a message is received from a terminal.

terminal job: In systems with time sharing, the processing done on behalf of one terminal user from logon to logoff.

terminal-monitor program (TMP): Under time-sharing option, a program that accepts and interprets commands from the terminal, and causes the appropriate command to be scheduled and executed.

terminal name: The symbolic name for a terminal, as assigned by the user.

terminal repeater: A repeater for use at the end of a trunk line.

terminal room: A room, associated with a telephone central office, private branch exchange or private exchange, which contains distributing frames, relays, and similar apparatus.

terminal session: See session.

terminal symbol: A symbol on punched paper which indicates the end of a record or some other unit of information.

terminal system design costs: The cost to design and program the total system to effectively handle the terminal system for specific applications.

terminal table: An ordered collection of information consisting of a control field for the table and blocks of information on each terminal from which a message can originate, and each terminal, group of terminals, and processing program to which a message can be sent.

terminal teleprocessing: Includes the preparation, transmission, and receipt of messages typically using teleprinters.

terminal-text processing: Includes the data input and editing of text to be entered into a system for the photocomposition of newspapers, books, articles, etc. typically utilizing blind paper tape perforators, cathode-ray tubes, and clustered systems.

terminal-transmission card: The machine doing the transmitting reads data from punched cards and transmits it over telephone circuits to a receiving machine.

terminal transparency: The ability, in a network, to allow incompatible terminals to communicate by line control conversion and automatic code conversion.

terminal trunk: A trunk circuit connecting two or more terminals (telephone).

terminal unit: Equipment on a communication channel which may be used for either input or output.

terminal user: In systems with time sharing, anyone who is eligible to log on.

terminal-word processing: The preparation and dissemination of letters, memoranda, reports and articles using office typewriters and word processing systems.

terminated line: A transmission line with a resistance attached across its far end equal to the characteristic impedance of the line, so that there is no reflection and no standing waves when a signal is placed on it at the near end.

terminating symbol: A symbol on the tape indicating the end of a block of information.

termination rack: A type of equipment rack which contains field wiring terminals and associated signal conditioning equipment. It thus provides the termination interface between a computer control system and fieldmounted instrumentation.

ternary: A system of notation utilizing the base of 3.

ternary incremental representation: Incremental representation in which the value of an increment is rounded to one of three values, plus or minus one quantum or zero.

test: The process following debugging of a computer routine, to verify that the software and/or the hardware is functioning properly.

test board: Switchboard equipment with testing apparatus, arranged so that connections can be made from it to telephone lines or central office equipment for testing purposes.

test data: A set of data developed specifically to test the adequacy of a computer run or system. The data may be acutual data that have been taken from previous operations, or artificial data created for this purpose.

testing-program time: The time used to test the machine or system to insure that no faults exist or malfunctions are present by using special diagnostic routines for circuit testing or to discern status of conditions or components.

test instructions (debugging): Most good compiler systems are designed to automatically remove various temporary tracing (debugging) instructions after tests are automatically made to insure accuracy and precision. Such instructions are often combined with various switch settings.

test pack: A pack of punched cards which has both program and test data for a test run.

test pattern: A transmitted chart with lines and details to indicate particular characteristics of transmission system; used in television for general testing purposes.

test-program system: A checking system used before running any problem, in which a sample problem of the same type with a known answer is run.

test rate: A problem chosen to determine whether the computer or a program is operating correctly.

test result tape: A test of the application or operational program that is edited, formatted, and sorted by a post-edit program.

test routine: A checking routine or a diagnostic routine.

test rules for inventory management (TRIM): A simulation program of an inventory control system.

test subroutine: A routine designed to show whether a computer is functioning properly.

test systems: 1. The running of the whole system against test data. 2. A complete simulation of the actual running system for purposes of testing out the adequacy of the system. 3. A test of an entire interconnected set of components for the purpose of determining proper functioning and interconnection. 4. The running of the whole system of runs making up a data processing application against test data.

test tone: A tone used in identifying circuits for trouble location or for circuit adjustment.

tetrad: A group of four, i.e., four pulses, used to express a decimal digit.

tetrode: A four-electrode active device such as a four-electrode vacuum tube with a cathode, a plate or anode, a control grid, and a screen grid or various types of four-electrode transistors, etc.

tetrode transistor: A transistor in which an extra terminal is supplied to the base.

text: The part of a message which contains the substantive information to be conveyed.

text editor (QED): Allows the on-line user to create and modify symoblic text for any purpose. User capabilities include inserting, deleting, and changing lines of text; a line-edit feature; a symbolic search feature; automatic tabs, which the user can set; and ten string buffers (in some systems).

textural retrieval: The automatic recognition, selection, interpretation, and manipulation of words, phrases, sentences, or any data in any form, but particularly in a textural structure, and the relating of these data for conclusions and useful results.

T flip-flop: A flip-flop having only one input. A pulse appearing on the input will cause the flip-flop to change states. Used in ripple counters.

thermal display light: A display signal visible to machine operators and is on when internal equipment temperature is higher than a designed level.

thermal light: A display signal which is visible to a computer operator when the temperature in a piece of equipment is higher than it is supposed to be.

thermal shock: A wet-to-wet temperature stress test that usually takes 5 minutes at 100°C, followed by 5 minutes at 0°C for 15 cycles with a maximum transfer time of 10 seconds. The purpose of this test is to determine device resistance to sudden extreme changes in temperature.

thermistor: A specific resistor whose temperature coefficient of resistance is unusually high, it is also nonlinear and negative. It is often made by sintering mixtures of oxide powders of various metals and is thus a solid-state semiconducting material, in many types of shapes as, disks, flakes, rods, etc. to which contact wires are attached, the resistance of the unit varying with temperature changes, and thus a tester or sensor for temperature change.

thermocouple: A device used to measure temperature and current.

thick film: A method of manufacturing integrated circuits by depositing thin layers of materials on an insulated substrate (often ceramic) to perform electrical functions; usually only passive elements are made this way.

thin film: A layer which is (or approximates to) mono-molecular thickness and is laid down by vacuum deposition.

thin-film capacitor: Constructed by evaporation of two conducting layers and an intermediary dielectric film (e.g., silicon monoxide) on an insulating substrate.

thin-film circuit: A circuit whose elements are films a few molecules thick, formed on an insulating substrate.

thin-film magnetic modules: Made by the depositon of magnetic alloys, in a vacuum and under the influence of a high magnetic field.

thin-film memory: The use of an evaporated thin film of magnetic material on glass as an element of a computer memory, when a d.c. magnetic field is applied parallel to the surface. A large capacity memory will contain thousands of these elements which can be produced in one operation.

third generation computer: Computers which use microcircuits and miniaturization of components to replace vacuum tubes, reduce costs, work faster, and increase reliability. The third generation of computers began in about 1964 and helped to foster the growth of timesharing. There are "families" of third generation equipment, including IBM System 360, Honeywell's Series 200, NCR Century Series, GE's 400 and 600 lines, and RCA's Spectra 70. First generation computers used tubes (1954) and were made obsolete by second generation machines (1959–1960) which utilized transistors to increase speed and reliability and to decrease size and maintenance.

third-party transfers: The legal ability of a financial institution to provide one party with a legal document that can be transmitted to a third party and take the place of cash.

thrashing: An adverse condition which develops in time-sharing or multiprogramming systems that utilize dynamic relocation of program segments; if the area assigned to each program is too small relative to the size of the program and the distribution of references to other segments, the overhead (system resource consumption) involved in "roll-in" and "roll-out" of new and old program segments can become very high, especially if pages which have recently been rolled out to make room for new pages must be immediately rolled back in.

threaded file: To conserve searching time and space, some computer files are in chains. Each data item or key in a record in the chain has the address of another record with the same data or key. To retrive all data which contain the given key, only the first address need be found since the next address is adjacent to it, and that to another, etc. until all key records are found.

three-addressed machines: Specifies the address of the two operands and the address into which the result is stored automatically.

three-address instruction: An instruction consisting of an operation and 3 addresses.

three-input subtracter: Same as subtracter.

three-level subroutine: Uses two level subroutines.

three-plus-one address instruction: A four-address instruction, in which one of the addresses always specifies the location of the next instruction to be performed.

three-position controller: A multiple-position controller which has three discrete values of output.

three-row keyboard: The keyboard on Baudot-coded teletypewriter equipment.

threshold: 1. A logic operator having the property that if P is a statement, Q is a statement, R is a statement, ..., then the threshold of P, Q, R, ... is true if at least N statements are true, false if less than N statements are true, where N is a specified nonnegative integer called the threshold condition. 2. The threshold condition as in 1.

threshold element: A device that performs the logic threshold operation but in which the truth of each input statement contributes, to the output determination, a weight associated with that statement.

through path: The forward path from loop input to loop output in a feedback circuit.

throughput: The total useful information processed or communicated during a specified time period.

through-trunk supervision: The type of supervision used in a trunk-switching system in which one operator maintains a supervision of calls requiring trunk connection through all long-distance switching centers.

thyratron: A type of hot-cathode gas tube in which one or more electrodes control the start of a unidirectional flow of current, often a control device for printers.

thyristor: A thyratron-like semiconductor device for bistable switching between high conductivity and highfrequency modes.

tie line: A private line communication channel of the type provided by communications common carriers for linking two or more points together.

tie trunk: A telephone line or channel directly connecting two branch exchanges.

timber: The characteristic tone or quality of a sound, which arises from the presence of various harmonics or overtones of the fundamental frequency.

time-base generator: A device used to develop a time base for calculations and control, e.g., a digital clock.

time-comparator circuitry: The circuitry which compares the word time counter with the specified word time at the moment or coincident pulse. This is done in order to verify that the correct word is being read.

time classification: Refers to the classification of time, such as serviceable, effective, down, unused, etc., related to a computer or system.

time constant: The ratio of the inductance to the resistance in an electric circuit consisting of inductance and resistance; in circuits consisting of capacitance and resistance, the product of the capacitance and the resistance.

time discriminator: A circuit which gives an output proportional to the time difference between two pulses, its polarity reverses if the pulses are interchanged.

time division multiple access (TMDA): An advanced networking method used to communicate over satellites. It is a digital transmission technique. All signals are converted to digital bit streams. These bits are combined into a single stream for transmission, then separated at the receive station into separate bit streams and decoded to obtain the original message signals.

time-division multiplex carrier: The means of transmission of more than one voice channel over a wideband path by sampling the speech, coding the sample levels, and using digital techniques.

time-division multiplexer: A device which permits the simultaneous transmission of many independent channels of varying speeds into a single high speed data stream.

time-division multiplier unit: See mark-space multiplier unit.

time-division switching: A variation of packet switching in which each interface message processor (IMP) scans its input lines in strict rotation. Packets are immediately retransmitted on their respective output lines.

time factor: The comparison of the time between two events in a simulated computer run and actual real life time it would take for the same.

time out: A system action based upon the absence of an expected event during a prescribed time interval.

time proportioning controller: That specific controller whose output consists of periodic pulses, with durations varied to relate the time average of the output to the actuating error signal in some predesigned or prescribed manner.

time-pulse distributor: A device or circuit for allocating timing pulses or clock pulses to one or more conducting paths or control lines in specified sequence.

time-schedule controller: A specific controller in which the reference input signal (or the set point) adheres automatically to a predetermined time schedule.

time series: The discrete or continuous sequence of quantitative data assigned to specific moments in time, usually studied with respect to their distribution in time.

time-sharing: A method of operation in which a computer facility is shared by several users for different purposes at (apparently) the same time. Although the computer actually services each user in sequence, the high speed of the computer makes it appear that the users are all handled simultaneously.

time-sharing control (TSC) task: A system task that handles system initialization, allocation of timeshared regions, swapping, and general control of the time-sharing operation.

time-sharing conversational guidance: User/computer communications in a conversational or dialog mode, where the user takes some action and the system responds. The system then requests a specific category or input, or takes other action, and the user again responds. In this alternating stimulus-response mode, the system can and should provide guidance to the user on the form and content of the user response.

time-sharing driver: An addition to the dispatcher that determines which task is to execute next.

time-sharing dynamic allocator: An executive program that controls the activities of independent programs in a multiprogramming or time-shared system.

time-sharing education: Conversational visual terminals. Experiments are being conducted with all levels of students from first graders to advanced graduate students.

time-sharing HELP program: A special program designed to help the user operate the system.

time-sharing interface area: A control block used for communication between the time-sharing driver and the time sharing interface program.

time-sharing interface program: A program that handles all communication between the control program and the time sharing driver.

time-sharing mode: A mode in which users' program's are executed simultaneously.

time-sharing multiplexer channel: Provides the capability of polling and multiplexing devices.

time-sharing option (TSO): Provides conversational time-sharing from remote terminals.

time-sharing priority: A ranking within the group of tasks associated with a single use is used to determine their precedence in receiving system recources.

time-sharing scientific calculation engineering: Most time-shared systems provide conversational calculation facilities allowing research scientists, engineers and technicians to use the computer as a large slide-rule.

time slice: A designed interval of time during which a job can use a resource without being preempted.

time-switching multiplex: A sequential switching system that connects more than one piece of terminal equipment to a common channel by time slicing.

time warm-up: The time required after energizing a device, before its rated output characteristics begin to apply.

timing circuit: For many purposes it is desirable to produce a signal of a certain duration, starting with a triggering impulse. Signals of this type are frequently needed in connection with input/output devices, where signals occur more slowly than they do inside the computer. In the case of static circuitry, monostable circuits can produce pulses of any desired duration. In dynamic circuits, delay lines can produce time delays and pulse trains of a desired lenth.

timing considerations: The economics of designing a file or system in terms of machine time or the overall throughput speed for a run or a series of runs.

timing error: The program is not able to keep pace with the tape transfer rate or a new motion or select command is issued before the previous command was executed completely.

timing signals: Electrical pulses sent throughout the machine at regular intervals to ensure absolute synchronization.

TLU: See table look up.

TMG: A syntax-directed compiling language.

TMP: See terminal monitor program.

toggle: 1. A flip-flop. 2. Pertaining to a manually operated on-off switch, i.e., a two position switch. See toggle switch. 3. Pertaining to flip-flop, seesaw, or bistable action.

toggle switch: 1. A manually operated electric switch, with a small projecting knob or arm that may be placed in either of two states until changed. 2. An electronically operated circuit that holds either of two states until changed.

token: A distinguishable unit in a sequence of characters.

tolerance frequency: The maximum permissable deviation of the transmitted carrier frequency as related to assigned frequencies, and expressed as a percentage of assigned frequencies or hertz.

toll: A charge for making a connection beyond an exchange boundary.

toll center: Basic toll switching entity; a central office where channels and toll message circuits terminate. While this is usually one particular central office in a city, larger cities may have several control central offices where toll message circuits terminate.

toll-free number: A unique telephone exchange number that allows called party to be billed automatically for incoming calls.

tone: The audible result of a frequency within the audio range (approximately 20 to 20,000 Hz).

tone burst: A controlled burst of sine waves for test purposes.

tone-burst generator: Produces sound pulses of short duration, enabling direct audio sound to be separated from the reflected sound in acoustic measurements.

tone control: Control for altering characteristic response of audio-frequency amplifier in order to obtain more pleasing output quality.

tone-control circuit: A circuit network or element to vary the frequency response of an audio-frequency circuit, thus varying the quality of the sound reproduction.

tool function: A command identifying a tool and calling for its selection either automatically or manually. The actual changing of the tool may be initiated by a separate tool change command.

tool-length compensation (tool comp): A manual input which eliminates the need for pre-set tooling and allows the programmer to program all tools as if they were the same length.

tool offset: 1. A correction for tool position parallel to a controlled axis. 2. The ability to reset tool position manually to compensate for tool wear or for finish cuts.

top-down method: A compiling technique that uses a template-matching method; prototypes for a statement of unknown nature are assumed one-by-one, until one prototype is found which matches.

torn-tape switching center: A location where operators tear off incoming printed and punched paper tape and transfer it manually to the proper outgoing circuit.

total failure: Fault condition which has completely interrupted a service.

total-harmonic distortion: 1. Distortion, due to the nonlinear characteristics of a transmission, which results in the presence of harmonic frequencies in the response when a sinusoidal stimulus is applied. 2. The ratio of the power of all harmonics as summed measured at the output of the transmission system to the power of the fundamental frequency observed at the output of the system (because of its nonlinearity), when a single frequency signal of specified power is applied to the input of the system. The distortion is measured in decibels.

total-internal reflection: The reflection occurring within the fibre waveguide when the angle of incidence of light striking the surface is greater than the critical angle.

totals only: The printing of a report utilizing a punched card tabulator or a computer printer in a manner so that only totals are printed.

total-system concept: An equipment system providing pertinent information, at the right time and place, and in the right form, so that knowledgable decisions can be made.

touch-tone audio response telephone unit: A terminal device that makes remote systems easily accessible to many users. This type of input is coupled with audioresponse output. Magnetic tapes have words, syllables, or phonemes prerecorded. The computer puts together an aural response by stringing together sequences of these recorded elements.

touch-tone converter: A device which receives dualtone multi-frequency signals and converts them into dial pulses.

trace: An interpretive diagnostic technique which provides an analysis of each executed instruction and writes it on an output device as each instruction is executed.

tracing routine: A diagnostic routine used to provide a time history of one or more machine registers and controls during the execution of the object routine. A complete tracing routine would reveal the status of all registers and locations affected by each instruction each time the instruction is executed. Since such a trace is prohibitive in machine time, traces which provide information only following the execution of certain types of instructions are more frequently used. Furthermore, a tracing routine may be under control of the processor, or may be called in by means of a trapping feature.

track: The portion of a moving storage medium, such as a drum, tape, or disc, that is accessible to a given head position.

track address: Binary codes on magnetic tape or disc to locate data stored in other tracks by actual code patterns as indicated by the address, or by completing a count, or by simply noting their positions.

track bands: The portion of auxiliary storage which can be accessed without incurring seek time delays.

track hold: A facility that protects a track while it is being accessed. When data on a track is being modified by a task in one partition, that track cannot be accessed at the same time by a task or subtask in another partition.

traffic: The signals or information which pass through a communications system.

traffic analysis: The obtaining of information from a study of communications traffic. Includes statistical study of message headings, receipts, acknowledgments, routing, and so on, plus a tabulation of volumes and types of messages with respect to time.

traffic control: A method of optimizing the flow of work through a factory communication system or operation by means of a computer.

trailer label: See end-of-file trailer label and end-of-reel trailer label.

trailer record: A record which follows a group of records and contains pertinent data related to the group of records.

train: Sequence of pieces of apparatus joined together to forward or complete a call.

train-generator pulse: A circuitry system or device which with a signal stimulis, produces a fixed number of equally spaced pulses.

training mode: The training of terminal operators and the testing of a system in which normal operations are defined and carried on by the operator. The randomness and inventiveness of the inpur operator is used to check the formal test input and any inconsistancies.

training time: The machine time expended in training employees in the use of the equipment including such activities as mounting, console operation, converter operation, and printing operation.

trandir: A syntax-directed compiling language.

transaction codes: Numbers used in the on-us field of items to identify the nature or type of item. For example, the transaction code tells a machine that an item is a check and should be subtracted from the customer's balance, or that the item is a deposit ticket and should be added.

transaction file: A file containing current information related to a data processing activity and used to update a master file.

transaction record: One record in a file to be processed against a master file.

transceiver: A terminal device that can both transmit and receive signals.

transcribe: To copy, with or without translating, from one storage medium to another.

transcriber: The equipment associated with a computer for the purpose of transferring input (or output) data from a record of information in a given language to the medium and the language used by a digital computing machine, or from the language of a computing machine to a record of information.

transducer: An input or output device used to convert signals from one medium to another. For example, a microphone is a transducer which converts acoustic signals into electric signals.

transducer-translating device: Converts the error of the controlled member of a servomechanism into an electrical signal that can be used for correcting the error.the error.

transfer: 1. A mathematical expression frequently used by control engineers which expresses the relationship between the outgoing and the incoming signals of a process, or control element. The transfer function is useful in studies of control problems. 2. A mathematical expression or expressions which describe(s) the relationship between physical conditions at two different points in time or space in a given system, and perhaps, also describe(s) the role played by the intervening time or space.

transferability: As applied to software, the capability of a program to be operated on a computer other than the one on which the program was developed.

transfer algorithm: Used in a demand fetching system to determine the order in which segments demanded by concurrent processes are transferred from a backing store to an internal memory.

transfer buffering: A system of double buffering where data are read into or written from only one area in an object program, but are moved by the program to a second area for processing. This method is less effective than alternate buffering.

transfer check: A check which verifies that information is transferred correctly from one place to another. Usually, each character is compared with a copy of the same character transferred at a different time or by a different route.

transfer command: A particular order or instruction which changes control from one part of the program to another part by indicating a remote instruction.

transfer control: Same as transfer.

transfer-function comparison: Related to tabular, graphical or mathematical statements concerning the influence which systems or elements have no signals or actions compared at input and output terminals; i.e., the operation of the equivalent complex mathematical function.

transfer-function loop: Obtained in a closed loop by taking the ration of the Laplace Transform of its corresponding error signal.

transfer impedance: In any network or transducer, complex ratio of rms voltage applied at any pair of terminals to the rms current at some other pair.

transfer operation: An operation which moves information from one storage location or one storage medium to another, e.g., read, record, copy, transmit, or exchange.

transfer register: A back-lighted decimal display register, often located on the operator console and designed to permit the display and operator verification of data prior to acceptance.

transform: To derive a new body of data from a given one according to specific procedures, often leaving some feature invariant.

transformation signal: A generated signal

which meets very specific requirements relating to a specific computer system, and if such a signal is transformed or timed to conform to its original detail, as above, the signal is proved to have been regenerated or standardized.

transformer: A component made up of two or more coils wound around the same core.

transforming: The capability, procedure, or process of changing the form or media of the data but not the basic content.

transient: 1. A physical disturbance, intermediate to two steady-state conditions. 2. Pertaining to rapid change. 3. A build-up or breakdown in the intensity of a phenomenon until a steady state condition is reached. The time rate of change of energy is finite and some form of energy storage is usually involved.

transient area: A main storage area (within the supervisor area) used for temporary storage of transient routines.

transient error: An error which is eliminated by reprocessing the information a limited number of times.

transient overshoot: Excursions beyond the steadystate values of output resulting from step-input changes.

transient response: Output versus time in response to a step input.

transient   routines: Self-relocating routines that are stored permanently on the system-residence device and loaded (by the supervisor) into the transient area when needed for execution.

transient wave: Set up in transmission circuits or filters because of changes in the current amplitude and/or frequency, the effects dying out in local circuits but propagated along lines.

transistor: A tiny element in an electronic circuit; a basic component in computers.

transistor amplifier: Uses transistors as the source of current amplification. Depending on impedance considerations, there are three types, with base, emitter, or collector grounded.

transistor chip: A specific example is one in which the chips themselves are 28 thousandths-of-an-inch square. Some diodes can switch, or change their electronic state, in six nanoseconds (six billionths of a second). This is more than twice as fast as the fastest elements in previous computers. The reduced size and simplified design of the new transistors and diodes contribute to the increased speed and reliability of the circuits. Minute copper pellets, for example, replace whiskerlike wires more than one inch long that connect conventional transistors and diodes to circuit modules. The metal caps that protect conventional transistors are replaced by a glass film, 60 millionths-of-an-inch thick, that is deposited on more than a thousand chips at a time. Completed circuit modules are coated with plastic and mounted onto circuit cards. These, in turn, are plugged into larger cards and installed in various elements of the system equipment. Printed circuits on the larger cards eliminate much of the conventional wiring. (IBM).

transistor tetrode: A transistor in which an extra terminal is supplied to the base.

transistor-transistor logic (TTL): The most common form of integrated circuit logic. As a result, the relatively simple process used to produce TTL logic is a natural candidate for memory, since most memories are used with TTL logic. However, the TTL approach—even though the simplest bipolar process—is considerably more complicated and expensive than metal-oxide semiconductors.

transition: The switching from one state (e.g., positive voltage) to another (negative) in a serial transmission.

transition deviation: The difference between the theoretical encoder position reading and the actual encoder position reading.

translate: To transform information in a way which preserves meaning i.e., from one code to another, or form one language to another.

translating routine: Same as translator.

translation: The conversion of one code to a second code on a character-by-character basis.

translator: A device that converts information from one system of representation into equivalent information in another system of representation.

transliterate: To convert the characters of one alphabet to the corresponding characters of another alphabet.

transmission: 1. The sending of data to one or more locations or recipients. 2. The sending of data from one place for reception elsewhere. 3. In ASCII and communications, a series of characters including headings and texts.

transmission adapter: The transmission adapter (XA) provides for the connection of remote and local devices to the data adapter as well as the necessary controls to move data to or from the processing unit via the XIC (Transmission, Interface Converter). A number of data adapters are available to allow attachment of various remote devices through their communication facility as well as the attachment of various local devices.

transmission band: A section of a frequency spectrum over which minimum attenuation is desired, depending on the type and speed of transmission of desired signals.

transmission bridge: A device in telephony which separates a connection into incoming and outgoing sections for the purpose of signalling, at the same time allowing the through transmission of voice frequencies.

transmission code: A code for sending information over communications lines.

transmission-control character: Facilitates the routing of a message to its proper or correct destination in a telecommunications network.

transmission-control unit: A device that regulates the information flow between computers and communications terminals.

transmission density: The common logarithm of the transmittance of a processed photographic emulsion.

transmission facilities: Equipment which acts as a bearer of information signals.

transmission-frequency diversity: Methods for signal transmission or reception in which same information is transmitted simultaneously in two or more specific frequency bands to minimize the disturbances of selective frequency fading.

transmission interface converter: A device that controls transfer of information between a channel and adapter.

transmission interruption: The interruption of a transmission from a terminal by a higher priority transmission to the terminal.

transmission-level ratio: The expression in transmission units of the ratio P/Po, where P represents the power at the point in question and Po the power at the point chosen as the origin of the transmission system.

transmission line: The communication path for signals from point to point such as a coaxial cable, or highpower transmission lines, i.e., any of various lines used to carry electrical energy from source to destination.

transmission-line amplifier: An amplifier in which grids of valves are driven by appropriate pints on an artificial line, giving wideband amplification.

transmission-line control: Control of frequency of an oscillator by means of a resonant line in the form of a tapped quarter-wavelength stub.

transmission loss: A decrease in signal power in transmission from one point to another. Transmission loss is expressed in transmission units.

transmission modes: Field configurations by which electromagnetic or acoustic energy may be propagated by transmission lines, especially waveguides.

transmission pulses: Electrical impulses which can be transmitted and received through communication lines. Transmission pulses may be either voice or data communications in nature. In the latter case, computer interface equipment converts incoming pulses into the proper binary code and delivers the data to storage.

transmission speed: 1. The rate at which data is transferred. Usually measured in bits per second, characters per second, or words per minute. 2. The absolute time a signal requires to move between source and sink. This approaches the speed of light (about 186,000 miles per second) and is affected by distance, transmission medium, number of system components, etc.

transmission-suppressed carrier: This method of communication in which the carrier frequency is suppressed either partially or to the maximum degree possible. One or both of the sidebands may be transmitted.

transmission-system codes: Methods for a character parity check as well as a bit lock check to detect errors.

transmission tones: Standard telephone company data sets at each end of the telephone line convert signals from remote terminal units and central terminal units into tones for transmission over the line.

transmission-utilization ratio: The ratio of useful (acceptable) data output to the total data input.

transmit: To reproduce information in a new location replacing whatever was stored previously and clearing or erasing the source of the information.

transmit operation: The computer operation for the movement of data from one location to another, i.e., various forms of communication.

transmittable mode: A procedure by which the contents of an input/output buffer are made available to the program and by which a program makes records available for output.

transmittal mode: A communications procedure by which the contents of an input/output buffer are made available to the program and by which a program makes records available for output.

transmitter (transducer): A specific transducer designed to respond to a measured variable by using a sensing element. It converts it to a standardized transmission signal and this is a function of the measurement only.

transmitter-distributor (TD): The device in a teletypewriter terminal which makes and breaks the line in timed sequence.

transmitter start code: A Bell System term for a character sequence that is sent to an outlying teletypewriter terminal which automatically polls its tape transmitter or keyboard.

transparency: A data communication mode which enables the equipment to send and receive bit patterns of any form, without regard to their possible interpretation as control characters.

transparent mode: A means by which any bit pattern can be transmitted over the synchronous communications facility.

transponder: A form of transmitter-receiver which transmits signals automatically when the correct interrogation is received; e.g., a radar beacon mounted on a flight vehicle (or missile), which comprises a receiver tuned to the radar frequency and a transmitter which radiates the received signal at an intensity appreciably higher than that of the reflected signal. The radiated signal may be coded for identification.

transport: To convey as a whole from one storage device to another.

transverse interference: See normal mode interference.

transverse scanning: Scanning in which the read/write head moves along, but across, the recording tape. Used in some video tape recorders.

trap: An unprogrammed conditional jump to a known location, automatically activated by hardware, with the location from which the jump occurred.

trapped instruction: A special instruction which is executed by a software routine in cases where the necessary hardware is absent.

trapping: A feature of some computers whereby an unscheduled, i.e., nonprogrammed, jump is made to a predetermined location in response to a machine condition i.e., a tagged instruction.

trapping mode: A scheme used mainly in programdiagnostic procedures for certain computers. If the trapping mode flip-flop is set and the program includes any one of certain instructions, the instruction is not performed but the next instruction is taken from location O. Program-counter contents are saved in order to resume the program after executing the diagnostic procedure.

trap word: The core storage location used to store the instruction counter and trap identification data.

travel indicator: A designed length of the path or route described by the indicating means or the tip of the pointer moving from one end of the scale to the other, i.e., the path may be an arc or a straight line.

traveling-wave tube: An electron tube used to amplify ultra-high frequencies.

tree network: A network in which terminals and computers are linked to a main computer in a hierarchical manner. In a tree network each terminal or computer is linked6to one at a higher level.

tree structures: A switching or data file addressing structure designed to select an element by reduction cascading or all members of a set by expansion cascades. If used in chained data structures, the addresses associated with each item have multiple pointers to other items, i.e., to the next row member and the next column member.

triad: A group of three bits or three pulses, usually in sequence on one wire or simultaneously on three wires.

tributary station: A part of a switching network, i.e., one of the many stations subject to the direction of the control or master station.

tributary trunk: A trunk circuit connecting a local exchange with a toll center or other toll office through which access to the long-distance network is achieved.

trigger pair: A circuit which has two stable states and which, in each state, requires an appropriate excitation trigger to cause a transition to the other, i.e., an Eccles-Jordan circuit. The successive transitions may be caused by the appropriate excitation first of one and then of the other of two inputs or by the alternation of two different excitations of a single input, i.e., a bistable circuit.

trio: Neighboring red, blue, and green phosphor dots in the screen of the color cathode-ray tube.

triode: A three-electrode electronic device which is active, e.g., a vacuum tube or transistor and used frequently as an amplifier of electronic signals.

triple-length wording: The use of three machine words to represent a number to enhance precision.

triple precision: The retention of three times as many digits of a quantity as the computer normally handles.

tripler: A circuit which multiplies the frequency of an input signal by three.

trivial response: Under time-sharing option (TSO), a response from the system to a request for processing that should require only one time slice.

trouble location problem: A test problem whose incorrect solution supplies information on the location of faulty equipment. It is used after a check problem has shown that a fault exists.

trouble unit: A weighting figure applied to telephone circuit or circuits to indicate their expected performance in a given period of time.

true complement: Same as radix complement.

truncate: To terminate a computational process in accordance with some rule, i.e., to end the evaluation of a power series at a specified term.

truncation: The process of dropping one or more digits of a number, either at the left or the right, without altering any of the remaining digits..

truncation error: The error resulting from the use of only a finite number of terms of an infinite series, or from the approximation of operations in the infinitesimal calculus by operations in the calculus of finite differences.

trunk: A single circuit between two points, both of which are switching centers and/or individual distribution points.

trunk check: A set or group of parallel lines for transmission of data to a particular checking device or unit such as a check register, a parity checker, or a comparator.

trunk connector: Used in a step-by-step office to connect calls to subscribers who have a large number of exchange lines. The switch is able to step up to a level where there is an idle line, then around to the idle line.

trunk exchange: An exchange devoted mainly to interconnecting trunks.

trunk group: A set of trunk lines between two switching centers, distribution stations, or points, which employ the same terminal (multiplex) equipment.

trunk hunting: A designed procedure or arrangement in which an incoming communications call is switched to the next number in sequence if the original called number is busy.

trunk line: The major distribution cable used in community antenna television. It divides into feeder lines which are tapped for service to subscribers.

TSO: See time-sharing option.

T test: A comparison test of two units of quantitative data for the determination of their inequality, i. e., a determination of which quantity is the greater.

TTL (or T²L): See transistor-transistor logic.

TTY: See teletypewriter.

tune: To adjust for resonance or syntony, especially musical instruments or radio receivers.

tuned amplifier: Contains tuned circuits and is sharply responsive to particular frequencies.

tuned circuit: Comprises an inductance coil and a capacitor in series or in parallel, and offers a low or high impedance respectively to alternating current at the resonant frequency.

tuned relay: A relay which responds only at a resonant frequency.

tuner: A radio receiver without an audio amplifier; also the tuning system in a receiver.

tuning control: Mechanical means for tuning a resonant circuit; e.g., a knob or slider.

tunnel diode: A diode which has two stable conducting states or regions when in series with a resister and voltage source.

turnaround system: In character recognition, a system in which the inptut data to be read are printed by the computer with which the reader is associated.

turnaround time: The actual time required to reverse the direction of transmission from send to receive or vice versa on a half-duplex circuit.

turn-key system: A system, and its accompanying documentation, written in a way so that an untrained user can operate the system. The assumption is that the suer simply wants to have to "turn the key" and have his computer function for him.

turn-on time: The time required for an output to turn on (sink current to ground output, to go to 0-volts). It is the propagation time or time of an appropriate input signal to cause the output to go to 0 volts.

turnstile antenna: The antenna, consisting of crossed dipoles, of a television and frequency-modulated transmitter.

turntable: The rotating metal base disk of a phonograph.

tutorial: The instructing of basic fundamentals for a particular field of study or disciplene.

twin check: A continuous duplication check achieved by duplication of hardware and automatic comparison.

twisted-pair cable: A cable formed by twisting together two thin conductors which are separately insulated. This arrangement can reduce their intercapitance.

two-address: An instruction format containing two address parts.

two-address code: A specific instruction code containing two operand addresses.

two-address instruction format: Various instruction formats which contain one, two, ..., N address parts.

two-core-per bit storage: A storage unit in which each magnetic cell uses N cores and N stands for the appropriate figure, as one-core-per bit or two-core-per bit, etc.

two-dimensional storage: Direct access devices in which an area allocated to a specific file need not be a series of physically contiguous locations, but instead will be specified as a number of buckets drawn from one or more seek areas.

two-gap head: A magnetic tape piece of peripheral equipment which permits the reading of data at the time it is written to permit immediate error detection.

two-inch lines per frame display: The maximum number of two-inch lines which can be drawn flicker-free at the manufacturer's recomended refresher rate.

two-input adder: A logic element which performs addition by accepting two digital input signals (a digit of a number and an addend or a carry) and which provides two output signals (a carry digit and a digit for the sum).

two-input subtracter: A unit or device capable of representing the difference between two numbers, usually restricted to permitting the subtractend to have only one non-zero digit.

two-level subroutine: A subroutine which has another subroutine within its own structure.

two-phase modulation: A method of phase modulating in which the two significant conditions differ.

two-plus-one address: An instruction that contains two operand addresses and one control address.

two-position controller: A multiposition controller with two discrete values of output.

two-quadrant multiplier: Multiplier in which operation is restricted to a single sign of one input variable only.

two-scale: A number, usually consisting of more than one figure, representing a sum, in which the individual quantity represented by each figure is based on a radix of two. The figures used are 0 and 1.

two-tone keying: See frequency shift keying.

two-tone modulation: A telegraphic operation term relating to the method in which two different carrier frequencies are used for the two conditions of the code, i.e., the transition from one frequency to the other causes phase discontinuities.

two-valued variable: A variable which assumes values in a set containing exactly two elements, often symbolized as 0 and 1.

two-way circuit: A bidirectional channel, which operates stably in both directions; particularly used when sources at distances are contributing a montage to a program.

two-wire carrier system: A system using only a single pair of wires. Different frequency allocations permit transmissions in both directions.

two-wire channel: A channel for transmission in only one direction at a time.

two-wire circuit: 1. A special circuit formed by a source feeding a pair of metallic conductors which are insulated one from the other and which, in turn, feed a load. 2. A channel for transmission in only one direction at a time.

two-wire system: A system in which all communication transmitted or received is carried over a two-wire circuit or equivalent.

typebar: A linear type element containing all printable symbols.

type channel: A channel type refers to the way in which it is used: simplex, half-duplex, or full-duplex.

type face: In optical character recognition (OCR), a character style with given relative dimensions.

type fount: A type face of a given size.

type statements: A series of statements in FORTRAN used to override the normal mode of assigning variable names and also to reserve arrays.

typewriter control console: Enables the operator to centrally control and monitor all processing functions. An electric typewriter provides direct communication with the processor memory. Data can be entered into the memory through the typewriter keyboard. The processor can transmit data to the typewriter for output through the typewriter printer. Thus, through the console typewriter, the operator can interrogate the memory, input programs, and enter instructions to modify a program (some systems).

typewriter module: In some systems, typewriter control units store the computer output and translate it for distribution to the on-line typewriters.

typewriter-signal distortion: Distortion which is caused by the shifting of the transition points of the signal pulses from their proper positions relative to the beginning of the start pulse of start-stop teletypewriter signals.

typing reperforator: A reperforator which types on chadless tape about one half inch beyond where corresponding characters are punched.

U

u³ᴸ: A modified transistor-transistor logic (TTL) configuration in which a third transistor is added to the TTL output of a gate (logic switch) to boost drive capabilities and increase noise immunity.

uection: 1. To divide a program into self-contained parts. 2. In the COBOL system, a sequence of one or more paragraphs. Also, one of the portions of the progam defined as a section in the rules governing the format of a COBOL program, e.g., the file section and the constant section of the data division.

U format: A specific record format which the input/output control system treats as completely unknown and unpredictable.

ultra-high frequencies (UHF): The range of frequencies extending from 300 to 3,000 MHz; also, television channels 14 through 38.

ultrasonic cleaning: A cleaning method often used for telephone equipment, in which the items are immersed in a solvent that is agitated by a sound wave with a frequency above the human hearing range.

ultrasonic delay line: A delay line which utilizes the finite time for the propagation of sound in liquids or solids to produce variable time delays.

ultrasonic generator: One for the generation of ultrasonic waves; e.g., quartz crystal, ceramic transducer, supersonic air jet, magnetostrictive vibrator.

umbral: A distinct heading which is distinctly and totally relevant to the data being sought.

unallowable code check: A specific check, usually an automatic check, which tests for the occurrence of a non-permissible code expression. A self-checking code, or error-detecting code, uses code expressions such that one or more errors in a code expression produces a forbidden combination. Some of the various names that have been applied to this type of check are: forbidden-pulse combination, unused order, improper instruction, unallowable digits, improper command, false code, forbidden digit, non-existent code, and unused code.

unallowable digit instruction check: A character or combination of bits which is not accepted as a valid representation by the computer or the machine design or by a specific routine and suggests malfunctions.

unallowable instruction digit: A character or combination of bits which is not accepted as a valid representation by the machine design or by a specific routine. Instruction digits unallowable are detected and used as an indication of machine malfunction.

unary operation: An operation on one operand, i.e., negative.

unary operator: An arithmetic operator having only one term. The unary operators that can be used in absolute, relocatable, and arithmetic expressions are: positive (+) and negative (-).

unattended communications: Connections established through the common carrier's dial switching network for the purpose of data transmission are in many ways identical to similar connections for voice communication. A telephone number must be dialed and the called party must answer before any transmission or conversation can take place. When the transmission or the conversation is finished, both the calling and the called party must hang up before another call can be made or received. Some standard communication subsystems can be equipped automatically to dial remote locations using communication-line terminal (CLT)-dialing, and to hang up automatically upon the completion of a data transmission by using the unattended operation feature (which is a button) on many output CLTs.

unattended operation: The automatic features of a station's operation which permits the transmission and reception of messages on an unattended basis.

unbalanced: A condition of an indicated line, electrical transmission, or network in which the impedances measured from corresponding points on opposite sides are unequal.

unbalanced circuit: A circuit whose two sides are inherently unlike.

unbalanced error: Those errors or sets of error values in which the maximum and minimum are not opposite in sign and equal in magnitude, as contrasted to balanced errors, i.e., the average of all the error values is not zero.

unbalanced network: Arranged for insertion into an unbalanced circuit, the earth terminal of the input being directly connected to the earth terminal of the output.

unbalanced to ground: Cable pairs can be susceptible to noise and crosstalk and can cause crosstalk to other pairs.

uncommitted storage list: A list of blocks of storage that are not allocated for particular use at that moment.

unconditional branch (jump or transfer) instruction: Results in control being changed to another part of a program and is independent of any previous conditions of the program.

unconditional transfer: An instruction which switches the sequence of control to some specified location. Synonymous with

unconditional branch, unconditional jump and unconditional transfer of control.

uncontrolled lines: A line that contains terminals that may transmit to the central processor at any time they are ready to send. The central processor must be ready at all times to accept messages from this type of terminal.

undamped frequency: Second-order linear systems without damping; i.e., the frequency of free oscillation at radians or cycles per unit of time; i.e., in linear systems, the non-damping frequency is the phase of crossover frequency.

undefined record: A record that has an unspecified or unknown length.

under catalog: A compiled list of the holdings of two or more libraries.

underflow: The condition that arises when a machine computation a non-zero result that is smaller than the smallest non-zero quantity that the intended unit of storage is capable of storing.

undermodulation: 1. Modulation which is unnecessarily low in relation to the posssible level of modulation track. 2. The state of adjustment of radio-telephone transmitter at which the peaks of speech or music do not produce 100 percent modulation, so that carrier power is not used to full advantage.

undetected error rate: The ratio of the number of bits incorrectly received (but undetected or uncorrected by the equipment) to the total number of bits sent.

undistorted transmission: The transmission of any type of line for which the velocity of propagation and coefficient of attenuation are both independent of frequency.

undisturbed one output: The 1 output of a magnetic cell.

undisturbed output signal: An output signal from a core subjected to a full read pulse after it has been set to the one or zero condition (with no intervening partial drive pulses).

undisturbed response voltage: Output from storage, previously set to one or zero, when it is subjected to a full read pulse without intervening partial pulses.

undisturbed zero-output signal: Output from storage previously set to zero when subjected to a full read pulse.

unexpected halt: A stop in a program which is not due to an interrupt or halt instruction.

unidirectional antenna: An antenna in which the radiating or receiving properties are largely concentrated in one direction.

unidirectional current: A current which maintains the same direction in a circuit. It may fluctuate or go negative.

unidirectional pulse: Single-polarity pulses which rise in the same direction.

uniformly accessible storage: Reduces the effect of variation of access time for an arbitrary sequence of address.

uniform random number: Sets of digits constructed in a sequence so that each successive digit is just as likely to be any of n digits to the base of the number.

unilateral impedance: Any electrical or electromechanical device in which power can be transmitted in one direction only; i.e., a thermionic valve or carbon microphone.

unilateralization: The neutralization of feedback so that the transducer or circuit has unilateral response.

union: A logical operator having the property that if P is a statement and Q is a statement, then the OR of P, Q, is true if, and only if, at least one is true; false if all are false. P OR Q is often represented by P + Q.

unipolar: A type of electric signal in which both true and false inputs are represented by the same polarity.

unit address: The three-character address of a particular device, specified at the time a system is installed; for example, 196 or 293.

unit code element: The signal elements in which different arrangements of an equal-length multiunit telegraph code form an alphabet.

unit distance code: Any sequence of code words in which only one bit changes state between any two adjacent words and in which the respective values of the code words are prescribed by definition.

unit-equipment record: Noncomputer data processing hardware which uses punched cards as media.

uniterm: A word, symbol, or number used as a descriptor for retrieval of information from a collection.

uniterm indexing: A system of coordinate indexing which utilizes single terms, called uniterms, to define a document uniquely.

uniterming: The selection of words considered to be important and descriptive of the contents of a paper for later retrieval of the articles, reports, or other documents. The selected words are then included in a uniterm index.

uniterm system: A data-recording system used by libraries, based on classifying keywords in a coordinate indexing system.

unitized film: Microfilm mounted in some unit fashion; usually film mounted in a film jacket, aperture card, or film card—frames of microfilm instead of an entire roll.

unit record: A card containing one complete record, e.g., a punched card.

unit separator: A character developed to demarcate a logical boundary between items of data that are referred to as separate and distinct units.

unit synchronizer: A routine that coordinates completion of input and output operations on a given unit with the calling program according to the specifications of the programmer.

universal-character set (UCS):   A printer feature that permits the use of a variety of character arrays.

universal decimal classification: Refers to an expansion of the Dewey decimal system.

universal interconnecting device: A unit that can be used with multiple systems to switch units from one system to another.

universal set: The all-inclusive set of things having a certain characteristic or property.

universal Turing machine: A Turing machine that can be used to simulate any other Turing machine.

uni-vibrator: A circuit which holds information for a fixed time which is determined by the type of the circuit elements.

unpack: To decompose packed information into a sequence of separate words or elements. See pack.

unrecoverable error: An error that results in abnormal termination of a program.

unscheduled-maintenance   time: The elapsed time during scheduled working hours between the determination of a machine failure and placement of the equipment back into operation.

unshift on space: A feature on 3-row teletypewriter (Baudot code) page-printing devices that unshifts the carriage (upper- to lowercase) upon receipt of a space character, in addition to the receipt of a LTRS (letters) character.

unused command: A character or combination of bits which is not accepted as a valid representation by the machine design or by a specific routine. Illegal characters are commonly detected and used as an indication of machine malfunction.

unwind: To code explicitly, at length and in full, all the operations of a cycle to eliminate all red tape operations in the final problem coding.

update: 1. To put into a master file changes required by current information or transactions. 2. To modify an instruction so that the address numbers it contains are increased by a stated amount each time the instruction is performed.

updating   and   file   maintenance: Procedures to maintain information by adding, deleting, or correcting data or information to properly reflect the current and real situation.

uplink: The earth station or terminal, and its transmissions, to a communications satellite.

upper curtate: The top six rows on a punched card, containing the top 3 rows of holes.

upstream: Signals traveling from subscribers to the headend.

uptime: The time a computer is operating free of component failure, plus the time the computer is capable of such operation.

upward reference: In overlay, a reference made from a segment to another segment higher in the same path; that is, closer to the root segment.

use, joint: The simultaneous use of a pole, line, or plant facility by two or more kinds of utilities.

user attribute data set (UADS):   Under time-sharing option (TSO), a partitioned data set with a member for each authorized user.

user exit: A point in a program at which a user exit routine may be given control.

user group: A group of users of a specific manufacturer's equipment of software. The group meets to discuss common problems, share information and programs, etc.

USERID: See user identification.

user identification (USERID):   A one-to-eight-character symbol identifying a system user.

user main storage map: A map of the allocated storage in a user's region, built by the region control task, and used to determine how much of the region needs to be swapped.

user oriented time sharing languages: Languages typically easier to use than others; more English language-related.

user-profile table: In systems with time sharing, a table of user attributes kept for each active user, built from information gathered during logon.

user programs: A group of specific programs, subprograms or subroutines that have been written by the user.

user set: Apparatus located on the premises of a user of a communication or signaling service and designed to function with other parts of a system.

user terminal: An input/output unit by which a user communicates with an automatic data processing system.

utility control sonsole: A console used primarily to control utility and maintenance programs.

utility routine: A standard routine used to assist in the operation of the computer, e.g., a conversion routine, a sorting routine, a printout routine, or a tracing routine.

utility unit: A unit that is available for use by the system or by the programmer for any purpose.

utilization factor: The ratio of the arrival rate to the service rate.

utilization ratio: The ratio of effective time to serviceable time.

V

validation-cross: The verification of results by replicating an experiment under independent conditions.

valid-exclusive reference: In overlay, an exclusive reference in which a common segment contains a reference to the symbol used in the exclusive reference.

validity: The correctness, especially the degree of the closeness, by which iterated results approach the correct result.

validity check: A check based upon known limits or upon given information or computer results, e.g., a calendar month will not be numbered greater than 12, and a week does not have more than 168 hours.

validity checking: 1. A procedure for detecting invalid or distinctly unreasonable results; i.e., illogical bit combinations, highly improbable numeric codes, storage addresses, etc. 2. A data screening procedure wherein data input records are checked for range, valid coding, valid representation, (e.g., calendar data, etc. related to input editing).

value: In the COBOL system, the information represented by a data item, arithmetic expression, or conditional expression.

value-added network: Utilizes the existing common carrier networkd for transmission while providing added data service features with separate equipment.

valve: Simple vacuum device for amplification by an electron stream, covering diode, hexode, pentode, screened-grid, triode.

valve nomenclature: Description of valves in terms of the number of electrodes therein; i.e., diode, triode, tetrode, pentode, hexode, heptode, octode, etc.

valve output module: A device designed to translate the computers output data into analog signals suitable to position and control valves of other devices (some systems).

Van Allen belts: Electron belts at 1500-20,000 miles above the surface of the earth, the electrons traveling great distances along the lines of the earth's magnetic field.

V-answerback: The response to a transmitter start code (TSC) of a polled station in a teletypewriter switched network if the station has no traffic to send, or the response to a call-directing code (CDC) of a station that is prepared to receive traffic.

variable: A quantity that can assume any of a given set of values.

variable-block format: A format which allows the number of words in successive blocks to vary.

variable capacitors: Can alternate the capacitance or storage ability.

variable connector: 1. A flow chart symbol representing a sequence connection which is not fixed, but which can be varied by the flow-charted procedure itself. 2. The device which inserts instructions in a program corresponding to selection of paths appearing in a flow chart. 3. The computer instructions which cause a logical chain to take one of several alternative paths. Same as n-way switch and programmed switch.

variable-cycle operation: A computer action in which any cycle of action or operation may be of a different time length.

Such action is characteristic of an asynchronous computer.

variable field: A field whose length may vary within certain prescribed limits according to needs of data.

variable-field storage: An indefinite limit of length for the storage field.

variable-format messages: Messages in which line control characters are not to be deleted upon arrival nor inserted upon departure; variable-format messages are intended for terminals with similar characteristics.

variable-function generator: A function generator which operates with reference to a set of values of the function which are preset within the device with or without interpolation between these values.

variable-length instructions: A feature which increases main memory efficiency by using only the amount necessary for the application and increases speed because the machine interprets only the fields relevant to the application. Halfword (2 byte), two-halfword (4 bytes), or three-halfword (6 bytes) instructions are used (in some systems.)

variable-length records sorting: Sorting records in which the number of words, characters, bits, fields, etc., vary in length.

variable-length record system: A file containing a set of records that vary in length.

variable-length system file record: A file containing a set of records that vary in length.

variable logic: The internal logic design which is alterable in accordance with a precompleted program which controls the various electronic interconnections of the gating elements, i.e., the instruction repertoire can be electronically changed, or the machine capability can be matched to the problem requirement. A type of variable logic.

variable multiplier: A device causing the generation of a continuously varying analog representation of a product of two continuously varying analog input signals, as particular independent variables, e.g., time or distance, change.

variable-point representation: A positional representation in which the position of the radix point is explicitly indicated by a special character at that position.

variable-precision coding compaction: A data compaction procedure which is accomplished using precision which is reduced in relation to the magnitude of the function, the time, the independent variable, or some other parameter.

variable problem: 1. A multiplier used by the programmer converting quantities occurring in a problem into a desired range. 2. A method of modifying the location of a decimal or binary point.

variable-resistance pickup: A transducer whose operation depends upon variation of resistance; e.g., a thermistor or strain-gauge element.

variables data: Read and recorded data from parametric (usually electrical) tests; may be required for pre and post burn-in electrical tests.

variable symbol: In assembler programming, a symbol used in macro and conditional assembly processing that can assume any of a given set of values.

variable-tolerance-band compaction: A data compaction procedure which is accomplished by using multiple discrete bands when specifying the operational limits of a quantity or parameter.

variable word: A computer feature in which the number of characters handled by the unit is not constant.

variance: The measure of dispersion about the mean; i.e., the average of the squared deviations between observations and the mean. The square of the standard deviation.

variance analysis: The estimate of probability relatedness by comparison of between-columns variance with within-columns variance.

varigroove: An arrangement of variable groove spacing on microgroove records, which allows more recording time per radial inch of record to be accommodated.

vector: 1. A quantity having magnitude and direction, as contrasted with a scalar which has quantity only. 2. A 1-dimensional array.

vector quantity: A quantity which has both magnitude and direction such as field intensity, momentum etc. as contrasted with scalar quantities.

vector-transfer table: A table that contains a list of transfer instructions of all the programs that are in main memory which enables transfer of control to be made from one program to another program.

Veitch diagram: A table or chart showing information contained in a truth table.

velocity: In a wave, the distance travelled by a given phase of a wave divided by the time taken.

velocity limit: A limit concerning the rate of change of a specified variable which cannot be exceeded.

verification mode: In systems with time sharing, a mode of operation under the EDIT command in which all subcommands are acknowledged and any textual changes are displayed as they are made.

verify: 1. To determine whether a transcription of data or other operation has been accomplished accurately. 2. To check the results of keypunching.

vertical blanking: The elimination of the vertical trace on a cathode-ray tube during frame flyback.

vertical deflecting coils: The deflecting coils of a writing tube which exert an up and down force on the writing beam.

vertical deflecting plates: The deflecting plates in a writing tube which exert an up and down force on the writing beam.

vertical display: The height, in inches, of the display area of the cathode-ray tube.

vertical-hold control: The control in a television receiver which varies the free-running period of the oscillator providing the vertical deflection.

vertical oscillator: A relaxation oscillator in the vertical sync circuit of the cathode-ray tube.

vertical-output stage: The power amplifier stage in the cathode-ray tube vertical sync circuit.

vertical parity: A technique of error checking which utilizes a check or parity bit with each character.

vertical-raster count: The number of coordinate positions addressable across the height of the cathode-ray tube.

vertical-redundancy check (VRC): An odd parity check performed on each character of a transmitted block of ASCII-coded data as the block is received.

vertical sync pulses: The series of pulses which controls the cathode ray tube receiver's vertical and horizontal oscillators.

vertical-sync signal: The signal which instructs the television set to return its beam to the top of the screen and begin a new field.

vertical tabulation character: A control character developed to cause the printing or display position to be moved a measured number of lines at right angles to the line of printing.

very-high frequency (VHF): The range of frequencies between 30 and 300 MHz and the television channels 2 through 13.

very-low frequency (VLF): Frequencies below 30,000 Hz.

vestigal sideband: Reduction of total bandwidth associated with normal amplitude modulation by markedly reducing one sideband, especially for television transmission.

vestigal-sideband filter: The transmission of a modulated carrier wave in which the frequencies of one sideband, the carrier, and only a part of the other sidebnd are transmitted.

vestigal-sideband transmission: A method of communication in which frequencies of one sideband and only a portion of the other sideband are transmitted.

V format: A data record format designed so that the logical records are of variable length and each record begins with a record length indication.

VHF: See very-high frequency.

vibrating-sample magnetometer (VSM): A device used to determine the magnetic properties of magnetic material.

video: The bandwidth (-megahertz) and spectrum position of the signal arising from television scanning.

video amplifier: A wideband amplifier which, in a television system, passes the picture signal. Bandwidth extends from zero frequency to one which maintains the required definition.

video carrier: Same as picture carrier.

video circuit: A circuit capable of handling nonsinusoidal waveforms involving frequencies of the order of megahertz.

video data interrogator: A terminal unit that is comprised of a keyboard and separable associated display, providing a terminal facility for conventional communications lines.

video integration: In facsimile reception, the integration and averaging of successive video signals to improve the overall signal/-noise ratio.

videoscan: A technique for machine recognition of characters by their images.

videoscan optical character reader: A unit that combines an optical character reader with mark sensing and card reading.

video signal: The part of a television signal which conveys all the information (intensity, color, and synchronization) required for establishing the visual image in monochrome or color television.

videotape recording: Registering television signals on a high-speed magnetic tape (transverse or longitudinal) for subsequent transmission.

video terminal: A computer terminal that incorporates a cathode-ray tube (CRT) for displaying information on a screen. Some terminals are designed for data entry as well as display, and feature built-in minicomputers so that they can both edit and format input and operate as stand-alone data processing systems.

videotex: Electronic systems that makes computer-based information accessible via visual display units, or adapted TVs, to a large and dispersed audience.

video transmitting power: The power radiated in the video band by a television transmitter.

video unit files: A completely automated microfiling system, stores documents as recordings on magnetic video tape and provides fast, automatic access and unusual flexibility in file organization. Files are presented to the user either as pictures on a television screen or as printed copies.

violations of subroutines: Violation occurs when the input to the subroutine doesn't match the input as specified.

virtual: Conceptual or appearing to be, rather than actually being.

virtual address: The immediate address or real-time address.

virtual circuits: Established in the tables of the switching computers logically connecting an input port to an output port for the duration of interaction between processes.

virtual computing system: Same as virtual machine.

virtual cut through: A hybrid form of packet and circuit switching in which the packet header is analyzed upon its arrival, to determine the appropriate outgoing line. If that line is available, retransmission is immediate, without waiting for the entire packet. If the line is busy, the packet is stored and forwarded as in the message switching method.

virtual earth: Live input terminal of a high-gain directly-coupled amplifier which remains approximately at earth potential although not connected to earth.

virtual link packet switching: A packet switching method where a network path is pre-established for each packet.

virtual machine: A computer designed to be a partly simulated program.

virtual memory pointer: Pointers or lists used to keep track of program segments in virtual memory.

virtual storage: A conceptual form of main storage which does not really exist, but is made to appear as if it exists through the use of hardware and programming.

visual inquiry station: An input/output unit which permits the interrogation of an automatic data processing system by the immediate processing of data from a human or terminal (automatic) source together with the display of the results of the processing, uaually on a cathode-ray tube (CRT).

visual range: 1. The optical range of transmitter. 2. The observable range of ionizing particle in bubble chamber, cloud chamber, or photographicemulsion.

visual scanner: 1. A device that scans optically and usually generates an analog or digital signal. 2. A device that optically scans printed or written data and generates their representation.

visual-supervisory control: The processor-controller (P-C) communicates messages and commands to the operator and, if desired, directly to the process equipment and instrumentation. The sensors that measure process conditions are continuously monitored by the P-C. The P-C program analyzes this information and then generates the required output information. Messages from the P-C to the operator may be displayed by several methods in the operator's working area. These messages guide the operator in adjusting the status of instruments located at the point of control. Data messages based upon visual obsevation of the process and its instrumentation are sent back to the P-C or the process operator.

vital records master list/schedule: A brief outline of protection procedures, usually attached to retention schedules, to indicate department responsibility.

voice answerback (VAB): This refers to an audio response unit which can link a computer system to a telephone network to provide voice responses to inquiries made from telephone-type terminals. The audio response is composed from a vocabulary prerecorded in a digital-coded voice or a disk-storage device.

voice frequency: Any frequency within that part of the audio-frequency range essential for the transmission of highly intelligible speech. Voice frequencies used for telephone transmission of speech usually lie within the range of 200 to 3,400 Hz, although the extreme ends of this range may not be transmitted at an optimum level.

voice-frequency carrier telegraphy: A form of carrier telegraphy in which the carrier currents have frequencies such that the modulated currents may be transmitted over a voice-frequency telephone channel.

voice-grade channel: A channel suitable for transmission of speech, digital or analog data, or facsimile, generally with a frequency range of about 300 to 3000 Hz.

voice-grade circuit: A circuit suitable for the transmission of speech, digital or analog data, or facsimile, generally with a frequency range of about 300 to 3000 Hz.

voice-grade line: The common communications line used in normal telephone communications. It is an essential part of most communications systems involving computers and data transmission. The voice-grade line has a band width of 0-3000 Hz. There is also a narrow band line which opertes on a lower frequency than voice-grade and a broad band which operatesat a higher frequency.

voice-grade service: A service utilizing lines capable of carrying voice transmission.

voice-operated device: A device used on a telephone circuit to permit the presence of telephone currents to effect a desired control.

voice-operated gain-adjusting unit: A device related to telephone systems which affects a compressor, since it is used to reduce the fluctuations in levels which are common in speech.

voice unit (VU): A measure of the gross amplitude or volume of an electrical speech or program wave.

void: In character recognition, the inadvertent absence of ink within a character outline.

volatile display: The nonpermanent image appearing on the screen of a visual display terminal.

volatile storage: A storage medium in which information cannot be retained without continuous power dissipation.

volatile-dynamic storage: A specific storage unit which depends only on the external supply of power for maintenance of stored information.

volatility: The percentage of records on a file that are added or deleted in a run.

voltage drop: 1. Diminution of potential along a conductor, or over an apparatus, through which a current is passing. 2. Possible dimution of voltage between two terminals when current is taken from them.

voltage feed: Connection of an antenna feed to the antenna at the point of maximum potential variation.

voltage gain: Ratio of output to input voltages for amplifier, attenuator, etc.

voltage generator: Concept of total signal source, often with no internal impedance.

voltage jump: An abrupt discontinuity in voltage drop across a discharge tube, normally associated with a marked change in the geometry of the discharge.

voltage multiplier: A circuit for obtaining high dc potential from low voltage ac supply, effective only when load current is small.

voltage regulation: A measure of the degree to which an electrical power source maintains its output voltage stability under varying load conditions, with regulation given in percents.

voltage-supply drains: The current drain shown in the specifications for each module type that is consumed by the circuit in its worst-case state. The supply voltage component or module will not use the maximum current from all voltage sources simultaneously.

volt-amperes: The product of actual voltage (in volts) and actual current (in ams) in a circuit.

voltmeter: An instrument for measuring electric potential differences.

volume-serial number: A number in a volume label that is assigned when a volume is prepared for use in the system.

volume table of contents (VTOC): An index record near the beginning of each volume (i.e., a disk pack), which records the name, location, and extent of every file or data set residing on that particular volume.

volume test: The processing of a volume of actual data to check for program malfunctions.

volume unit (VU): The unit of measurement for electrical speech power in communication work as measure by a VU meter in the prescribed manner. The VU meter is a volume indicator.

voluntary interrupt: An interrupt to the processor or operating system caused by an object program's deliberate use of a function known to cause an interrupt, and hence under program control.

Von Neumann, John (1903-1957): A great pioneer of the modern computer. In 1947 he devised a procedure for converting the ENIAC externally programmed computer to a stored-program computer. He used numerals as instruction codes which could be stored electronically just as data numerals were stored, to thus eliminate instruction wiring. His projects toward developing computers capable of reproducing themselves is yet unfinished. He is most often recognized as the true father of modern computing.

VS: See virtual storage.

V-type address constant: In the assembler language, an address constant used for branching to another module. See also A-type address constant.

VU: See voice unit.

W

wait before transmit positive acknowledgment (WACK): A positive acknowledgement to the received data block or to selection.

waiting list: A procedure for organizing and controlling the data of unprocessed operational programs. These lines are maintained by the control program. Same as queue.

waiting-queue channel: The group of items in the system needing the attention of the channel scheduler program which executes the items in queue in a desirable sequence.

waiting state: The state of an interrupt level that is armed and has received an interrupt trigger signal, but is not yet allowed to become active.

walkie-talkie: A sender and receiver radio communication set which is carried by a single person, and may be operated while moving.

warm start: See system restart.

warm-up period: The time which is required after energizing a device, before its rated output characteristics begin to apply.

warning message: An indication that a possible error has been detected.

wave: 1. A propagated disturbance, usually periodic, such as a radio wave, sound wave, or a carrier wave used for transmitting data signals. 2. A single cycle of a periodic propagated disturbance.

wave analyzer: Separates frequency components in a continuously repeated waveform, usually by a quartzcrystal filter or gate.

wave antenna: A directional receiving antenna composed of a long wire running horizontally in the direction of arrival of the incoming waves, at a small distance above the ground. The receiver is connected to one end, and the other end is connected to earth through a terminating resistance. The induced voltage depends on the forward tilt of the ground wave.

waveband: The range of wavelengths occupied by transmissions of a particular type; e.g., the medium waveband (from 200 to 550 meters) used for broadcasting.

waveform generator: A circuit driven by pulses from the master clock; it operates in conjunction with the operation decoder to generate timed pulses needed by other machine circuits to perform the various operations.

waveguide: A hollow metal conductor within which very-high frequency energy can be transmitted efficiently in one of a number of modes of electromagnetic oscillation.

waveguide attenuator: Conducting film placed transversely to the axis of the guide.

waveguide bend: A bend in a length of rigid or flexible waveguide.

waveguide filter: A filter which has distributed properties that give frequency discrimination in a waveguide where it is inserted.

waveguide junction: A unit that joins three or more waveguide branches; e.g., hybrid junction.

waveguide lens: An array of short lengths of waveguide which convert and incident plane wavefront into an approximately spherical one by refraction.

waveguide stub: Consists of a piston (waveguide plunger) which moves in a short length of pipe connected to the waveguide; used for tuning or detuning the guide.

waveguide tee: A t-shaped junction for connecting a branch section of a waveguide in parallel or series with the main waveguide transmission line.

waveguide transformer: A unit placed between waveguide sections of different dimensions for impedance matching.

wave interference: Stationary patterns of amplitude variation over a region in which waves from the same source (or two different coherent sources) arrive by different paths of propagation.

wave length: The distance (usually given in meters or centimeters) between the peaks of two consecutive waves in a wave train.

wave trap: A circuit tuned to parallel resonance connected in series with the signal source to reject an unwanted signal; e.g., between a radio receiver and the serial.

way station: A telegraph term for one of the stations of a multipoint circuit.

weak external reference (WXTRN): An external reference that does not have to be resolved during linkage editing. If it is not resolved, it appears as though its value was resolved to zero.

weighted-area masks: In character recognition, a set of characters (each character residing in the character reader in the form of weighted points) which theoretically render all input specimens unique, regardless of the size or style.

weighted average: An average performed on data in which some of the values are more heavily valued than others.

weighted value: The numerical value assigned to any single bit as a function of its position in the code word.

Wheatstone bridge: An apparatus for measuring electrical resistance by the null method, comprising two parallel resistance branches, each branch consisting of two resistances in series. Prototype of most other bridge circuits.

wheel printer: A printer where each print position is on a wheel on the face of which is engraved a type font.

whirley bird: The slang reference or expression to designate disk-pack equipment.

white noise: Noise which has equal energy at all frequencies. White noise has equal energies within a specified band and zero energy elsewhere if it is band-limited.

white space skid: On some facsimile transmission machines, transmission is accelerated by the scanner "skidding" over the blank spaces on the transmitted document.

who-are-you (WRU): A transmission control character used for switching on an answerback unit in the station with which the connection has been set up, or for initiating a response including station identification and, in some applications, the type of equipment in service and the status of the station.

wide area telephone service (WATS): A service provided by telephone companies which permits a customer, by use of an access line, to make calls to telephones in a specific zone on a dial basis for a flat monthly charge.

wideband antenna: A dipole antenna with large diameter effective radiating elements, usually made up of spaced groups of wires or rods.

wideband channel: A channel wider in bandwidth than a voice-grade channel.

wideband data set: Data sets that permit rates of 72,000 bits per second.

width, band: The contrast between the highest and lowest frequency in a band.

width control: The cathode-tube ray receiver hand control which varies the width of the picture.

willful intercept: The act of intercepting messages intended for stations having equipment or line trouble.

Winchester disk: A specific disk memory in which the disks and magnetic head assemblies are contained within an enclosure sealed against dust or other contamination.

wire board: An electrical panel which can be changed with the addition or deletion of external wiring. Same as a plugboard, panel, or board.

wired-in: Components that are connected in circuits, particularly subminiature valves and semiconductor devices, which are too small to be plugged safely into a holder.

wired-program computer: The operations of such a computer are performed or their sequence is controlled by the placement and interconnection of wires, as on a plugboard.

wireless terminal: A portable terminal that communicates with a computer by radio.

wire printer: A high-speed printer that prints character-like configurations of dots through the proper selection of wire-ends from a matrix of wire-ends, rather than conventional characters through the selection of type faces. Same as matrix printer.

wire sense: A wire used to determine or interrogate storage locations in core devices by sending a predetermined pulse down the sense winding.

wire storage: A wire made of or coated with a magnetic material and used for magnetic recording.

wire wrap: A method of making an electrical connection in an electrical circuit by wrapping wires around specially designed terminals.

wiring diagram: A circuit diagram that indicates the physical layout of the connections.

word (communications):   A set of bits comprising the smallest address able unit of information in a programmable memory.

word address format: The order of appearance of character information within a word.

word-comparator time: The circuitry which compares the word time counter with the specified word time at the moment or coincident pulse. This is done in order to verify that the correct word is being read.

word control (sorting):   A continuous group of characters within a record designed to form all or part of the control word.

word count: The first word of a record in a backing store file which indicates the length of the record to the housekeeping software and enables the software to unpack logical records from physical blocks or buckets.

word length: The number of bits in a word.

word-mark: An indicator that signals the beginning or end of a word.

word memory: A limited characteristic of some equipment, whereby the words are available from the storage and not from individual characters.

word-organized storage: A type of storage composed of magnetic cells in which each word of the storage has a separate winding common to all the magnetic cells of the word.

words per minute (WPM): A common measure of speed in telegraph systems, measure of speed.

word time: 1. The amount of time required to move one word past a given point. 2. The time required to transport one word from one storage device to another.

word-time comparator: The circuitry used to compare the word-time counter to a specified word time.

word-time rate: The data translate rate, in words per minute, between a device and the computer.

work tape (sorting): Tape(s) used to store intermediate-pass data during a run.

work area: A portion of storage in which a data item may be processed or temporarily stored.

work assembly: A clerical function that is concerned with the assembly of data file and materials required to run a program or set of programs.

work distribution chart: 1. A listing or inventory of the duties, responsibilities, and sequence of the personnel in the job or task force under study. 2. The establishment of each duty relationship performed by the individual in relation to the specific task or function, which includes brief volumes-of-occurrence indicators, and the estimated and projected times to perform each item of work.

work file: In sorting, an intermediate file used for the temporary storage of data between phases.

workflow, serial: A system of operation in which each operation is performed singly and not at the same time that other tasks are being completed, i.e., the work moves along a single line or channel where one type of operation is performed in succession. No tasks are performed simultaneously with other tasks.

working files: Aggregation of data sets for definite usage. The file may contain one or more different data sets. A working data file is a temporary accumulation of data sets which is destroyed after the data has been transferred to another form. Compare files, permanent.

work-process schedule: A schedule of an electronic data processing activity.

work volume: A volume made available to the system to provide storage space for temporary files or data sets at peak loads.

worst case: The circumstance or case in which the maximum stress is placed on a system.

worst-case design: A design in which the circuit is designed to function normally even though all component values have simultaneously assumed the worst possible conditions. Worst-case techniques are applied to obtain conservative derating of transient and speed specifications.

worst-case noise pattern: Sometimes called a checkerboard or double-checkerboard pattern. Maximum noise appearing when half of the half-selected cores are in a 1 state and the other half are not.

wow and flutter: See flutter and wow.

wrap: One turn of the metallic magnetic tape in tapewound magnetic cores. The tape is usally wrapped around a bobbin with the coils of wire passing through the bobbin. The cores are often used as switching cores in digital computers.

wrap-around: 1. The continuation of an operation from the maximum addressable location in storage to the first addressable location. 2. The continuation of register addresses from the highest register address to the lowest. 3. In a cathode-ray tube device, the continuation of an operation from the last character position in the display buffer to the first position in the display buffer.

wrap-around memory: See wrap-around storage.

wrap-around storage: An arrangement of core storage in which the lowest numbered storage location is the successor of the highest numbered one.

write: To make a permanent or transient recording of data in a storage device or on a data medium.

write-field key: The part of the program status double word that contains the write key.

write half-pulse: A pulse of a magnitude which by itself cannot switch a magnetic core, and thus can not store a digit by itself, but when combined with a second pulse in the same direction, can switch the core to a prescribed state and can thus store or write a binary digit according to convention, i.e., one write pulse will drive a row of cores in an array, another a column.

write-interval time: The interval during machine operation when output data is available for an output operation.

write pulse: The drive pulse (or the sum of several simultaneous drive pulses) which can write into a magnetic cell or set a cell to a one condition.

write rate: The quickest rate at which the phosphor dot on the terminal screen can produce a distinct image.

write time: The amount of time it takes to record information.

writing head: A magnetic head designed and used to write.

writing machine: Typewriters capable of writing a document automatically from tapes or cards. They can also produce a selectively punched tape containing part or all information written on the document.

writing speed: 1. The speed of deflection of trace on phosphor. 2. The rate of registering signals on a storage device.

writing tube: A tube in which an electron beam automatically writes or scans information.

WRU: See who-are-you.

WXTRN: See weak external reference.

X

xerographic printer: A device for printing an optical image on paper in which dark and light areas of the original are represented by electro-statically charged and uncharged areas on the paper. The paper is dusted with particles of finely powdered dry ink and the particles adhere only to the electrically charged areas. The paper with ink particles is then heated, causing the ink to melt and become permanently fixed to the paper.

xmas-tree sorting: A method utilized in the internal portion of a sort program. The results of the comparisons between groups of records are stored for later use.

X-Y coordinates CRT display: A typical CRT display is a 16-inch random-position, point-plotting cathoderay tube which permits rapid conversion of digital computer data into graphic and tabular form. A self-contained unit with built-in control and power supplies, the CRT requires only logic level inputs for operation and thus may be easily connected to any digital system. Location of any desired point may be specified by any of the 1024 X and 1024 Y coordinate addresses contained in a $9\frac{3}{8}$ inch square on the tube face. X and Y coordinate information in two ten-bit words is received from the computer, and, on command, displayed as a spot of light on the tube face. Discrete points may be plotted in any sequence at a 20-kilocycle rate (one point every 50 microseconds). Magnetic deflection and focusing techniques result in uniform resolution.

XY plotter: Device used with a computer to plot graphs.

XY recorder: A device which is designed to trace the relation between a pair of variables onto a set of plane rectangular coordinates.

Y

yagi antenna (or array): A system of end-fire radiators or receivers, characterized by directors in front of the normal dipole rediator and rear reflector.

yoke: 1. In cathode ray tubes, the yoke is the set of wire coils that is wrapped around the end of the electron gun. When a voltage is applied to the coils, an electromagnetic field is produced which deflects the electron beam along a specific axis, to a position on the screen. Typically, a cathode-ray tube contains two yokes, one for deflection along the y-axis. The combination of these two yokes enables the electron beam to be deflected to any point on the CRT screen. 2. In magnetic recording, the yoke is a group of read/write heads that are mounted and moved as a unit for reading and writing on media which consists of two or more tracks such as disks and magnetic tape.

yoop update: The process of supplying current parameters associated with a particular loop for use by that loop's control algorithm in calculating a new control output.

Z

zener: A semiconductor diode which, under reverse bias, is capable of conducting heavy currents.

zenith: The point on the celestial sphere which is directly overhead.

zero-access storage: Storage for which the latency (waiting time) is negligible at all times.

zero address format: Contains no address partly because it is used either when no address is required or when it is implicitly shown in some way.

zero-address instruction: An instruction specifying an operation in which the locations of the operands are defined by the computer code, so that no address need be given explicitly.

zero adjust: A control for setting the reading of a device to the zero mark in the absence of any signal.

zero balance: The outcome of a method of balancing if details and totals are both correct.

zero-based conformity: A specific value of nonconformity which is determined after various translations and/or rotations of the actual curves are made to thereby make it coincide with zero on the specified curve which minimizes the maximum deviation.

zero center: A particular telephone trunk switching center which serves as a switching hub for a group of primary centers and which is connected directly to all other zone conters by trunk circuits.

zero compression: A technique used to eliminate the storing of nonsignificant leading zeros.

zero energy entropy: Energy which is completely predictable in nature and furnishes no information.

zero-entropy source: A source of energy which is completely predictable in nature and furnishes no information.

zero error: 1. Residual time delay which has to be compensated in determining readings of range. 2. Error of any instrument when indicating zero, either by pointer, angle, or display.

zero error multiplier: The particular error voltage at the output of an analog multiplier unit when one of the input voltages is zero and the other is arbitrarily selected, i.e., when it has its maximum value.

zero-error reference: A constant ratio of incremental cause and effect. Proportionality is a special case of linearity in which the straight line passes through the origin.

zero fill: A procedure to fill in characters with the representation of zeros, but which does not change meaning or content.

zero frequency: Indicates that a complex signal, such as video, has a reference value which must be transmitted without drift.

zerography: A dry copying process involving the photo-electric discharge of an electrostatically charged plate. The copy is made by tumbling a resinous powder over the plate. The remaining electrostatic charge is discharged, and the resin is transferred to paper or an offset printing master.

zero gravity: The condition, as in an orbiting satellite, when centrifugal force exactly counterbalances gravitational attraction.

zero level: Any voltage, current, or power reference when other levels are expressed in decibels (dB) relative to this.

zero-level address: An instruction address in which the address part of the instruction is the operand. Same as immediate address.

zero-level transmission reference point: An arbitrary chosen point in a circuit to which all relative transmission levels are referred. The transmission level at the transmitting switchboard is taken as the zero transmission-level reference point.

zero offset: The manual insertion of dimensional data into the control unit, or feedback unit, which will add to, or subtract from, the machine position, thus altering the programmed cutter path.

zero output: The output from a magnetic cell in the zero condition.

zero output signal: The output given by a magnetic cell in the zero condition when a read pulse is applied.

zero potential: The potential of a point at an infinite distance; used to define capacitance.

zero shift: Any parallel shift of the input/output curve.

zero-suppression: The elimination of non-significant zeros to the left of significant digits usually before printing.

zero-transmission level reference point: An arbitrarily chosen point in a circuit to which all relative transmission levels are referred. The transmission level at the transmitting switchboard is frequently taken as the zero transmission level reference point.

zone: 1. A portion of internal storage allocated for a particular function or purpose. 2. The three top positions of 12, 11 and 0 on certain punch cards. In these positions, a second punch can be inserted so that with punches in the remaining positions of 1 to 9, alphabetic characters may be represented.

zone bit: 1. One of the two left most bits in a commonly used system in which six bits are used for each character. Related to over-punch. 2. Any bit in a group of bit positions that are used to indicate a specific class of items; e.g., numbers, letters, special signs, and commands.

zone digit: The numerical key to a section of a code. Zone digits may be used independently of other punchings for control significance, etc.

zone leveling: An analogous process to zone refining, carried out during processing of semiconductors in order to distribute impurities evenly through the sample.

zone switching center: Telephonic trunk switching which serves as a switching hub for a group of primary centers directly connected to every other zone center by trunk circuits. See zero center.

zoom: The process of rapidly enlarging, by optical or electronic means, a part of a television picture at the transmitter or at the controls of some visual-display units.